CADOGAN

W9-DCH-820

g

Syria
& Lebanon

Introduction	viii
Travel	1
Practical A–Z	9
History of Syria and Lebanon	23
Topics	39

Syria

Damascus	45
The Hauran and the Jebel al-Arab	99
The Anti-Lebanon	121
The Orontes and the Central Plain	131
The Mediterranean and the Jebel al-Sariya	159
Aleppo	201
The Northern Highlands	223
The Euphrates and the Gezira	237
Palmyra and the Syrian Desert	261

Lebanon

Beirut	289
The North	303
The South	329
The Chouf Mountains and the Bekaa Valley	341
Glossary, Chronology, Language, Reading, Index	358

Cadogan Books plc
West End House, Hills Place, London W1R 1AH, UK

Distributed in North America by
The Globe Pequot Press
6 Business Park Road, PO Box 833, Old Saybrook,
Connecticut 06475–0833

Copyright © Michael Haag 1995, 1999
Updated December 1999
Illustrations © Matthew Higgins 1995

Book and cover design by Animage
Cover photographs by Christopher Portway/Eye Ubiquitous (*front*)
and James Davis Travel Photography (*back*)
Maps © Cadogan Guides, drawn by Map Creation Ltd

Editorial Director: Vicki Ingle
Series Editor: Linda McQueen

Editor: Dominique Shead
Indexing: Caroline Wilding
Production: Rupert Wheeler Book Production Services

A catalogue record for this book is available
from the British Library

ISBN 0–86011–925–5

Printed and bound in the UK by Cambridge University Press.

Please Note

The author and publishers have made every effort to ensure the
accuracy of the information in the book at the time of going to press.
However, they cannot accept any responsibility for any loss, injury
or inconvenience resulting from the use of information contained in
this guide.

To Philipp

About the Author

Michael Haag has been travelling to Syria since the mid-1980s and is glad to have got there before the rest of you, while his first visit to Lebanon was just before the civil war. His knowledge of these countries is grounded in a wider knowledge of the Mediterranean and the Middle East, about which he has written in books and articles and has broadcast for the BBC. He is also the author of the *Cadogan Guide to Egypt*. Michael Haag lives in London though spends part of each year in Alexandria, Egypt.

Contents

Introduction   viii   Geography and Highlights   ix

Travel   1–8

Syria

Getting There   2

Entry Formalities   2

Getting Around   3

Lebanon

Getting There   5

Entry Formalities   6

Getting Around   7

Tour Operators   7

Practical A–Z   9–22

Business Facilities   10

Children   10

Climate and When to Visit   10

Communications   11

Crime and Security   11

Disabled Travellers   12

Electricity   12

Embassies   12

Entertainment   13

Food and Drink   13

Health and Insurance   14

Maps, Media, Money   15

National and Religious Holidays   17

Opening Times   18

Packing   19

Photography   20

Shopping, Sports and Activities   20

Students   20

Time, Tipping, Toilets   21

Tourist Information   21

Where to Stay   21

Women   22

History of Syria and Lebanon   23–38

Historical Syria   24

c. 9000–3000 BC: The Neolithic and Chalcolithic Ages   25

c. 3000–2000 BC: The Early Bronze Age   25

c. 2000–1600 BC: The Middle Bronze Age   25

c. 1600–1200 BC: The Late Bronze Age   26

c. 1200–539 BC: The Iron Age   26

539–333 BC: The Persian Period   27

333–64 BC: Hellenistic Period   27

64 BC–AD 395: Roman Period   28

AD 395–632: Byzantine Period   29

632–61: The Arab Conquest   30

661–750: The Umayyads   30

750–1199: The Abbasids   31

From 1098: The Crusades   32

1144–1250: Zengids & Ayyubids   33

1250–1516: The Mamelukes   33

1516–1918: The Ottomans   34

The French Mandate   36

1945–Present: Independence   37

Topics 39–44

Agatha Christie	40	Lebanon: The Cost of War	43
The Genesis of Lawrence of Arabia	40	T-shirts of the Party of God	43
		Water, War and Peace	44

Syria

Damascus 45–98

Getting There and Around	48	Around the Umayyad Mosque	73
Tourist Information	52	Souks, Khans and the Azem Palace	79
Along the Barada	56	Straight Street and the City Walls	82
The National Museum	57	Salihiye	90
The Tekkiye Mosque Complex	60	Mount Kassioun	91
Along the Souk al-Hamidiye to the Great Mosque	63	Where to Stay	93
The Umayyad Mosque	67	Eating Out	95

The Hauran and the Jebel al-Arab 99–120

Getting Around	102	Bosra	110
Shahba	103	Deraa	117
Qanawat	107	Ezraa	119

The Anti-Lebanon 121–30

Getting Around	124	Barada and Burqush	126
Up & Around the Barada Valley	125	Along the Flanks of the Anti-Lebanon	127
Zabadani and Bludan	125	Maalula	129
Ancient Sites at Suq Wadi			

The Orontes and the Central Plain 131–58

Getting Around	133	Shaizar (Qalaat Shaizar)	150
Kadesh (Tell Nebi Mend)	134	Apamea (Qalaat Mudiq)	150
Homs	138	The Steppe Eastwards of Hama	154
Hama	142	Hama to Aleppo	156
Along the Orontes Valley to Jisr al-Shugur	149		

The Mediterranean and the Jebel al-Sariya — 159–200

Getting Around	162	Arwad	181
Krak des Chevaliers	163	Amrit	182
Safita	172	Margat (Qalaat Marqab)	184
Husn Suleiman	173	Saône (Qalaat Saladin)	190
Masyaf	174	Latakia	193
Tartus	176	Ugarit (Ras Shamra)	197

Aleppo — 201–22

Getting There and Around	205	The Citadel	214
Tourist Information	207	The Jdeide Quarter	217
The Aleppo Museum	209	Where to Stay	219
The Great Mosque	212	Eating Out	222

The Northern Highlands — 223–36

Cyrrhus and Ain Dara	227	Qalaat Samaan (Saint Simeon)	229
The Jebel Samaan	228	The Jebel al-Ala	234
Deir Samaan	228	The Jebel Riha	235

The Euphrates and the Gezira — 237–60

Getting Around	241	Deir ez Zor	253
Resafa	244	Dura Europos (Salihiye)	255
Raqqa	248	Mari (Tell Hariri)	258
Halabiye	251	Into the Gezira	260

Palmyra and the Syrian Desert — 261–80

Getting Around	263	Palmyra (Tadmor)	265
Approaches to Palmyra from the West	263	The Desert East of Palmyra	288

Lebanon

Beirut — 289–302

Getting There	292	East Beirut	299
Tourist Information	294	Where to Stay	300
Around Martyrs' Square	296	Eating Out	301
West Beirut	298		

The North 303–28

Getting Around	304	Byblos (Jbail)	310
The Dog River (Nahr al-Kelb)	304	From Byblos to Tripoli	318
Jounieh	306	Tripoli (Trablus)	320
Afqa	308	To the Cedars of Lebanon	326

The South 329–40

From Beirut to Sidon	330	Sidon to Tyre	336
Sidon	333	Tyre (Sour)	337

The Chouf Mountains and Bekaa Valley 341–57

Getting Around	342	Into the Bekaa Valley	347
Into the Chouf	342	Baalbek	348
Beit Eddine	344	Anjar (Haouch Mousa)	356

Glossary, Chronology, Language, Further Reading, Index 358–74

Maps and Plans

Syria and Lebanon	inside front cover	Tartus	178
		Saône	191
Damascus: Old City	inside back cover	Latakia	195
		Ugarit	199
Damascus	54–5	Aleppo	208
The Umayyad Mosque	68	The Northern Highlands	224
The Hauran	100	The Euphrates and Gezira	238–9
Qanawat Serai	109	Resafa	247
Bosra	111	Raqqa	249
The Anti-Lebanon	122	Deir ez Zor	254
The Orontes and the Central Plain	132	Dura Europos	257
Homs	141	Palmyra and the Syrian Desert	262
Hama	144	Palmyra	273
Apamea	152	Beirut	296–7
The Mediterranean and the Jebel al-Sariya	160	Lebanon	302
		Ancient Byblos	315
Krak des Chevaliers	165	Tripoli	321
		Baalbek	351

Introduction

The fascination and delight of Syria and Lebanon are their remarkable sudden shifts of landscape and their unending play of historical variety. Imagine the Mediterranean on one side, the desert and the Euphrates on the other, each impressing itself on the lands between, while mountains rise like islands above the contesting currents that have flowed across the coasts and plains. Often called the meeting place of East and West, Syria and Lebanon have also been frontiers and battlegrounds, and have often been swept by migrations, a perennial jigsaw puzzle taken apart and reassembled, Crusader castles standing on Phoenician stones, Mameluke mosques built of Byzantine churches, Bedouin tents pitched amid Palmyrene tombs, Druze inhabiting Roman remains, the most prodigious monuments telling a story of flux and impermanence to an unchanging backdrop of sea, desert and snow-capped mountains.

It can be a strange and often contradictory story to follow, but you are helped by the remarkable qualities of the Syrian and Lebanese people. In Lebanon the impression is of a young country, as though the war has given its people a new sense of common interest, so that with their characteristic verve they go about reconstructing not only the fabric of their country but its spirit, only worrying that you will find things not yet up to scratch. If the spirit of Lebanon is mercantile and indeed at times frankly mercenary, Syria is an altogether more traditional country, where you encounter a warm but dignified courtesy. You will often be invited into houses and be offered coffee and told 'welcome to your home—you are our guest and must treat our home as your home'. This may be convention, but underlying it are a kindliness and a curiosity that are genuine, and you soon relax into the charm of its mood. Encouraged by the welcome in both countries, you happily set about exploring, best of all enjoying having such riches so much to yourself. Not for long, but for a little while longer yet.

How This Guide is Organised

The guide starts with Travel and Practical A-Z chapters for both countries, which contain everything you need to know in order to plan your visit to Syria and Lebanon. This is followed by History and Topics, including observations on the Middle East water crisis, Agatha Christie, T. E. Lawrence and the Lebanese civil war. Then the sights of Syria and Lebanon are described in turn. At the back of the guide there is a Chronology, a Glossary, a short chapter on Language, a Further Reading list and a general index.

Geography and Highlights

Both Syria and Lebanon have a Mediterranean coastline backed by mountains, with two parallel ranges running the length of Lebanon, cradling between them the high Bekaa valley. In the case of Syria there is a deep hinterland that includes the Orontes valley, the northern highlands, the central plains and steppe, as well as the Euphrates with the developing agricultural region of the Gezira to the northeast of it and the Syrian desert to the south.

The guide describes Syria first, starting with Damascus, an urban oasis between the Anti-Lebanon mountains and the desert, one of the great caravan cities and religious centres in the Middle East, its walled Old City filled with souks and khans, with madrasas, maristans and hamams, with Saladin's tomb and the Azem Palace of its Ottoman governor, traversed by the biblical Straight Street and at the heart of the city the magnificent Umayyad Mosque, in part built on the remains of a Christian cathedral that in turn stood on the site of a pagan temple.

The guide then heads southwards into the Hauran and the Druze country of the Jebel al-Arab with their Roman and Byzantine remains that seem like photographic negatives, not marble white but built with the local black basalt. The eastern flank of the Anti-Lebanon range is described next with its mountain resorts and several Christian villages, where in at least one of which Aramaic, the language spoken by Jesus, is spoken still.

North of Damascus and clear up to Aleppo is the central plain, well cultivated in parts, steppeland in others, a region dominated nearly 5000 years ago by the only recently discovered city of Ebla, and where you begin to see beehive houses. To the west of this is the valley of the Orontes river spilling down out of Lebanon past Kadesh, where Ramses II fought the Hittites, past Homs and through Hama with its creaking waterwheels, and on beneath the headland of Apamea, known to Mark Antony and Cleopatra.

Rising to the west of the Orontes valley is the Jebel al-Sariya, the refuge of sects escaping the conformities of the lowlands, including the Alawis, the Ismaelis and the Assassins. Here overlooking the passes the Crusaders built their greatest castles: Krak des Chevaliers, Saône and, overlooking both mountains and sea, Margat. Along the Mediterranean coastline is the Templar town of Tartus, the modern port of Latakia and the pre-Phoenician city of Ugarit from where the alphabet was exported westwards to the Greek world.

Aleppo sits in a bowl surrounded by the northern plains, once far wealthier than Damascus as a caravan city and still possessing the largest covered bazaar in the Middle East. From here you can make an excursion to the northern highlands, a bleak and rock-churned plateau, yet rich on wine and olives in the past and scattered with Byzantine dead cities and churches, most famously Qalaat Samaan built round the pillar atop which St Simeon lived and prayed for most of his life. Off eastwards from Aleppo flows the Euphrates, tamed now by the great dam at Al-Thawra, sometime frontier and avenue of trade, where Abbasids, Byzantines, Romans, Seleucids and people long before them built Resafa, Raqqa, Halabiye, Dura Europos and Mari. Between the Euphrates and the Tigris is the Gezira marked by ancient *tells*.

Finally the guide describes the Syrian desert stretching away eastwards from Damascus to the Euphrates, with its Umayyad palaces and most spectacularly the sand-swept ruins of Palmyra, centre of Queen Zenobia's brief challenge to the Roman Empire.

Lebanon then follows, starting with Beirut, ambitiously rebuilding with the intention of again becoming the financial centre of the Middle East. Next the north of the country is described, including Byblos with its charming fishing harbour, which already 5000 years ago was on its way to becoming a great cosmopolitan port, its Phoenician and Roman remains laid bare beneath the gaze of a Crusader fortress. Farther north is Tripoli with its Castle of Saint-Gilles and its Mameluke monuments. In the mountains is the grotto of Adonis, the lover of Venus, and towards the highest ridges what remain of the Cedars of Lebanon that once covered the slopes of the entire country.

South of Beirut are the Phoenician cities of Sidon and Tyre, though their remains are almost entirely of the medieval and Roman periods.

Inland are the Chouf mountains and the palace of Lebanon's 19th-century overlord at Beit Eddine. Climbing a pass over the Lebanon range you come into the Bekaa valley with its gigantic Roman temples at Baalbek and the elegant Umayyad remains at Anjar.

Syria
  Getting There 2
    By Air 2
    By Sea 2
    By Train, Bus and Service Taxi 2
  Entry Formalities 2
  Getting Around 3
    By Air 3

Travel

    By Rail 3
    By Bus and Microbus 4
    By Car with Driver 4
    Car Hire 4
    By Bicycle 5
    By Thumb 5

Lebanon
  Getting There 5
    By Air 5
    By Sea 6
    By Bus and Service Taxi 6
  Entry Formalities 6
  Getting Around 7
    By Car 7
    By Taxi and Service Taxi 7
    By Bus 7

Tour Operators
  to Syria and Lebanon 7

Syria: Getting There

Almost all flights arrive at Damascus International Airport. Aleppo is served by a few flights, mostly from the Middle East and Turkey. Direct scheduled flights from Britain are operated by British Airways, ✆ 0345 222111, and Syrian Arab Airlines (Syrianair), ✆ (020) 7493 2851. The one advantage Syrian Arab Airlines has over British Airways and other Western European airlines is that their flights arrive in Syria at a reasonable hour (usually early evening), whereas the others tend to arrive very late at night. Otherwise Syrian Arab Airlines comes off very badly: inflight service is basic, passenger handling is disorganised, flight timings are unreliable, administration is chaotic, and overall you get the impression that the airline is run by chimpanzees. Many other European national carriers fly to Syria, e.g. Air France and Lufthansa. From North America the most convenient services to Syria are operated by British Airways, either on its own or in cooperation with a North American carrier, e.g. United Airlines.

From whatever your country of departure, you can save a great deal on the normal fare by purchasing an Advance Purchase Excursion (Apex) or other discounted fare ticket. Otherwise you can go to a specialised agent or consolidator who can usually offer you a seat at half price or better. One of the best outfits in Britain for discounted fares is Trailfinders, 194 Kensington High Street, London W8 7RG, ✆ (020) 7938 3939.

You should also compare the cost of a flight to what the tour operators (*see* p.7) have to offer; even for independent travellers who do not want a full-blown tour or any tour at all, they can sometimes offer some attractive deals. Also consider flying in to Beirut (*see* p.5), from where it is about 110km by road to Damascus.

There is a LS200 airport departure tax.

By Sea

Latakia is Syria's port of entry by sea. Depending on the season and whether the shipping companies think it is worth their while, there may be services from Greece, Turkey, Cyprus and Egypt. Cruise ships sometimes put in at Tartus.

By Train, Bus and Service Taxi

Buses and service taxis operate between Beirut in Lebanon and Damascus and Tartus in Syria. The journey by bus will cost about $6, by service taxi about $12 (*see* 'Getting There', **Beirut**, p.292). Travelling between Amman in Jordan and Damascus via Deraa will cost about $6 by bus, $9 by service taxi. There is also a new daily rail service between Amman and Damascus. There are several buses a day from Istanbul and other points in Turkey to Aleppo and Damascus (*see* pp.206 and 50). This journey can also be done by rail: there is a weekly service from Istanbul to Aleppo, taking about 36hrs (*see* p.205).

Entry Formalities

Passports and Visas

All visitors require a visa, which should be obtained from a Syrian embassy or consulate in your own country (it can be difficult obtaining one abroad, and there is no Syrian embassy in

Lebanon). You will need to fill in a form, provide two photographs and a letter from your employer saying you have a job to return to, and you will have to pay a stiff fee. Visas take three days to issue if you apply in person. You can also apply by post, first sending in a stamped addressed envelope for the application form, then allowing at least two weeks for the visa to be issued. Visas can be obtained for single or multiple entry; each allows you to stay in Syria for 15 days in the first instance. A single-entry visa must be used within three months, a multiple-entry visa within six months. If you are intending to visit Lebanon from Syria and then return to Syria, you are strongly advised to obtain a multiple-entry visa, otherwise you will have to obtain a re-entry visa in Syria; also visas can easily be extended beyond 15 days once you have arrived in Syria (*see* p.56).

Your passport must be valid for at least six months after your visit to Syria. You will be refused entry if your passport contains an Israeli stamp or an Egyptian or Jordanian land border stamp indicating that you have crossed into Israel (though this could change if the peace process in the Middle East develops favourably).

Tour companies will often include you on a group visa.

Customs

In addition to the usual run of personal effects both old and new, you may bring in, duty free, 200 cigarettes and a litre of spirits. Possession of drugs will mean a massive fine and a long prison sentence, while trafficking in drugs can be punishable by death.

The export of objects more than 35 years old and of hand-woven carpets (except, usually, a small one for your personal use) is restricted. A reputable dealer can advise you on the need to obtain a permit.

Currency

You do not have to declare currency imports of up to US$5000 and currency exports of up to US$2000. It is no longer necessary to exchange US$100 or its equivalent at the airport on arrival. Try to spend all local currency in Syria, as it has virtually no value outside the country. The local currency is the Syrian pound (LS).

Getting Around

You should carry your passport at all times, though in practice, except when checking into hotels or at checkpoints on roads leading towards the Iraqi border, it is almost never asked for.

By Air

Syrian Arab Airlines (Syrianair) operates domestic flights between Damascus and Aleppo, Latakia, Deir ez Zor and Qamishli. Flights are inexpensive. For Damascus offices, *see* p.49.

By Rail

From Damascus there are trains south to Deraa, close to the Jordanian border, and north to Homs, Tartus (via Homs), Hama, Aleppo and (via Aleppo) Latakia, Deir ez Zor and Qamishli. There is a sleeper service between Damascus and Qamishli. There is also a narrow-gauge line between Damascus and Zabadani in the Anti-Lebanon. Trains are cheap and comfortable, and first-class carriages have air conditioning. But though trains tend to leave Damascus and

Aleppo on time, they arrive at and depart from almost everywhere else often hours late. Also services are infrequent, timings inconvenient and stations are often located some distance from the centre of towns. Buses are more frequent, faster, generally arrive in town centres and are a bit cheaper. There is one journey that is worth making by train, however: that between Aleppo and Latakia for the dramatic beauty of the scenery en route, largely missed if travelling by road.

By Bus and Microbus

Until a few years ago almost all long-distance bus travel was in the hands of the state-owned Karnak company, but deregulation has seen Karnak's services reduced to major destinations while a large number of private companies now compete over routes throughout the country. When referring to long-distance services in this guide a distinction is made between **Karnak** (which will sometimes have its own terminal) and the **'luxury'** or **'Pullman'** private services. These latter generally have newer equipment and their fares are a bit higher, though inexpensive nonetheless, e.g. about $3 between Damascus and Aleppo. Long-distance bus travel is air-conditioned, comfortable, fast and frequent, and between major cities like Damascus, Homs, Hama and Aleppo you can usually rely on showing up at the station to get a seat (though better to try in the morning); otherwise you should book a day in advance. Normally neither Karnak nor the private companies will drop you off en route, and if they do they will make you pay the full fare to the next destination; and they will never stop to pick you up en route.

Then there are **ordinary or local buses**, older and less comfortable, also cheaper, which may or may not travel far but in any case make numerous stops on the way. They also stop on demand en route to drop off or pick up passengers, hence their popular name, Hob-Hob buses, meaning Stop-Stop.

Microbuses (*meecro*) run parallel to bus routes over both short and long distances, also going to places the buses never reach. These operate to no schedule but depart when full up; they cost more than buses and are less comfortable, but they are often faster and they will stop en route to let you off or pick you up. Microbuses are also an important part of the transport system within major cities like Damascus.

Intercity **service taxis** (*serveece*) carry five passengers and depart when full. They cost nearly twice as much as long-distance buses but are faster and more frequent. Mostly they run between Damascus and Beirut in Lebanon and Amman in Jordan.

Car Hire

The principal car hire company in Syria is Europcar, with offices in Damascus (both in town and at the airport), Homs, Latakia, Aleppo and Deir ez Zor. Credit cards are accepted. It is best to reserve a day in advance. Prices begin at about $30 per day including unlimited mileage and full insurance. A full current driving licence must have been held for a minimum of one year, and you must be at least 21 years of age. There are also Avis, Budget and various local companies but either they are more expensive or adequate insurance is not included. See car hire under Damascus, p.52, for further details. Some companies offer car with driver, which you might prefer after reading about driving in Syria (*see* below).

Having a car, with or without a driver, is a tremendous advantage and allows you to reach many places you will otherwise find difficult to get to. But Syrians often drive fast and carelessly, and so you should drive with caution and an alertness to the unexpected.

In the event of an **accident** in which someone is injured, immediately inform and stay with the police, as there is the possibility that things can turn ugly. In a town you can assist the injured party; in villages and out-of-the-way places, drive off to find the police or insist on being taken to them. In the event of the serious injury or death of another party, you will be arrested immediately. A government doctor should examine the injured party and state to what degree they are injured. In serious cases you will be kept in jail until the judge or the injured party releases you, or until you have come to a financial arrangement with the family of the dead person. You should contact your embassy at the earliest moment.

Some **driving tips**: avoid driving at night except in well-lit urban areas; fill your petrol tank whenever possible as you can travel long distances before seeing another petrol station; have another person with you; carry lots of cash; even on divided highways, do not assume there will not be someone coming in your direction, or reversing or stopping; watch out for children, Bedouin and animals wandering onto roads; and never drink and drive. Driving is on the right in Syria.

Important historical sites are often marked by yellow signs, usually first in Arabic, the next a few hundred metres on in English—but even if you see a sign in Arabic you will know you have arrived at the turning you have been looking for.

By Bicycle

Short of having a car, a bicycle is the best way of seeing Syria, especially if you want to thoroughly explore areas like the Jebel al-Sariya or the Northern Highlands where there are many interesting and out-of-the-way places to visit. You cannot hire bicycles in Syria, but you could transport your own (some airlines carry them free), in which case you should also bring a full tool kit and a supply of spare parts too, as you may not find what you need when you get there. Or buy a bike in Syria, knowing that the spare parts for it will be available locally. Luxury buses in Syria can carry your bicycle in their luggage hold, while ordinary buses can fix it to the roof rack.

By Thumb

In practice, this will usually mean offering someone money in exchange for a ride; hitchhiking for free is uncommon.

Lebanon: Getting There

By Air

Beirut's international airport is served by numerous European and Middle Eastern airlines. Non-stop scheduled flights from Britain are operated by British Airways, ✆ 0345 222111, and MEA (Middle East Airlines), ✆ (020) 7493 5681, the Lebanese carrier, though the standard of its inflight service is poor. Otherwise everything said about flying to Syria (*see* p.2), whether from Britain, continental Europe, North America or elsewhere, can be applied to Lebanon as well.

There is an airport departure tax of $35 economy class, $70 business class.

By Sea

There is a passenger ferry service between Larnaca in Cyprus and Jounieh, north of Beirut. There is a sailing a week in each direction, and the voyage takes 4hrs. Cruise ships occasionally put in at Beirut and Tripoli.

By Bus and Service Taxi

There are about 6 buses a day to Beirut from Damascus and Tartus in Syria, costing about $5; service taxis between Beirut and Damascus cost about $9 (*see* 'Getting There', **Beirut**, p.293). There are bus services from Turkey and Jordan via Syria.

Entry Formalities

Passports and Visas

You can either obtain a visa from a Lebanese consulate abroad or, if you are a national of one of the following countries, you can obtain one on arrival: Australia, Austria, Belgium, Canada, Denmark, Finland, France, Germany, Greece, Holland, Ireland, Italy, Japan, Luxembourg, Malaysia, New Zealand, Norway, Portugal, South Korea, Spain, Sweden, Switzerland, the United Kingdom, the United States of America.

If you apply for a visa abroad, this can be done in person and will take 48hrs. You will need two application forms, two photographs, and you will have to pay a fee and present your passport, which must be valid for at least six months beyond your stay in the country. At present, if it contains an Israeli stamp you will not be permitted to enter the country. (*See also* visa requirements for Syria.) Additionally, you must undertake not to accept employment in Lebanon, for example by presenting a letter from your employer saying you have a job to return to. You can also apply by post, but allow at least two weeks. Both single- and multiple-entry visas permit you to remain in Lebanon for three months, and both must be used within three months of issue. Tour companies will often include you on a group visa.

If obtaining a visa on arrival, your options are a 48hr transit visa (free), a 15 days single-entry visa, a three months single-entry visa and a three months multiple-entry visa. Visas obtained on arrival cost somewhat more than those obtained abroad; you must hold a return ticket (though this is usually ignored if you are arriving overland from Syria); your passport must be valid for at least six months, and it must not contain an Israeli stamp.

Note that to enter Syria you must obtain a Syrian visa abroad; there is no Syrian consulate in Lebanon. Also, if travelling from Syria to Lebanon and back again, you should get a multiple-entry visa for Syria, or failing that and at some inconvenience to yourself you will have to obtain a re-entry visa before leaving Syria. Visas to Syria are not issued at the border.

You must carry your passport on your person for the entire period of your stay in Lebanon as there are frequent police and army checkpoints.

You may bring into Lebanon anything required for personal use, also 200 cigarettes and 2 litres of spirits or 400 cigarettes and 1 litre of spirits.

Money may be taken in and out of the country in any amount. The local currency is the Lebanese pound (LL).

Getting Around

Carry your passport with you at all times as there are frequent roadblocks manned by the Lebanese police and army and by the Syrian army.

Lebanon is too small a country to have domestic flights, while its small railway system and most of its public buses were destroyed in the war. Hitchhiking is not advisable for security reasons.

By Car

To hire a car you will need a valid driving licence (held for at least two years) and depending on the company will need to be at least 21 to 25 years of age. Third party and public liability insurance is included in the cost of hiring, but you have to pay extra for collision damage waiver and personal insurance. Make sure that you are well insured; if anything the Lebanese are worse drivers than the Syrians. For further details, *see* **Beirut**, p.294.

By Taxi and Service Taxi

Service taxis follow regular routes, for example from Beirut to Tripoli. You go to the depot or flag one down, jump in and pay for your seat. It is a fast, convenient and inexpensive way to travel. You can also have the taxi for your own use, paying for all the seats and the driver's time, and so go where you want to go. It comes down to agreeing a price. This can be fairly reasonable if there are several of you. For further details, *see* **Beirut**, p.294.

When hailing a taxi or service taxi, note that they are usually Mercedes and have white on red number plates, while private cars have white or silver on black number plates.

By Bus

There are limited bus services in Lebanon. *See* 'Getting Around', **Beirut**, p.294, for further information.

Tour Operators to Syria and Lebanon

Tours within Syria, both off-the-peg and self-invented, can be arranged through companies in Damascus (*see* p.52) and elsewhere.

from the UK

British Museum Tours, 46 Bloomsbury Street, London WC1B 3QQ, ✆ (020) 7323 8895, ✉ (020) 7580 8677: expert tours to both countries, accompanied by local guides qualified in archaeology as well as by guest lecturers from the British Museum.

Bales Tours, Junction Road, Dorking, Surrey RH4 3HB, ✆ (01306) 885991, ✉ (01306) 740048: tours to both countries, usually accompanied by expert lecturers as well as local guides.

Cox and King's, Gordon House, 10 Greencoat Place, London SW1P 1PH, ✆ (020) 7873 5000, ✉ (020) 7630 6038: runs a number of expert-led tours to Syria, both long and short.

Jasmin Tours, 53 Balham Hill, London SW12, ✆ (020) 8675 8886: tours of Syria, some also combined with Lebanon, accompanied by a local guide.

Swan Hellenic Tours, 77 New Oxford Street, London WC1A 1DS, ✆ (020) 7800 2300, ✉ (020) 7831 1280: tours of both countries with expert lecturers and local guides.

Swan Hellenic Cruises, 77 New Oxford Street, London WC1A 1DS, ✆ (020) 7800 2200, ✉ (020) 7831 1280: some cruises include Syria or Lebanon.

Voyages Jules Verne, 21 Dorset Square, London NW1 6QG, ✆ (020) 7616 1000, ✉ (020) 7723 8629: escorted tours to both countries, with guest lecturers.

from the USA

Far Horizons Archaeological and Cultural Trips, PO Box 91900, Albuquerque, NM 87199, ✆ (505) 343 9400, ✉ (505) 343 8076, *www.farhorizon.com*: exellent though expensive tours of Syria and Lebanon accompanied by an experienced archaeologist or similar authority.

Business Facilities   10
Children   10
Climate and When to Visit   10
Communications   11
Crime and Security   11
Disabled Travellers   12
Electricity   12

Practical A–Z

Embassies   12
Entertainment   13
Food and Drink   13
Health and Insurance   14
Maps   15
Media   15
Money   15
National and Religious Holidays   17
Opening Times   18
Packing   19
Photography   20
Shopping   20
Sports and Activities   20
Students   21
Time   21
Tipping   21
Toilets   21
Tourist Information   21
Where to Stay   21
Women   22

9

Business Facilities

In **Syria**, five-star hotels in Damascus, Aleppo and often elsewhere have business centres for use by both guests and non-guests, providing secretarial, translation and other services. But they will not at this moment handle e-mail. The government likes to eavesdrop on communications and finds it hard to do so with e-mail transmissions; therefore to send or receive e-mail you must know someone with legal e-mail facilities (some foreign companies) or illegal e-mail (many Syrians are registered in Lebanon). The situation is likely to change soon, however, and meanwhile most hotels in all but the lowest categories will have faxes (themselves illegal until a few years ago).

In **Lebanon**, several of the better Beirut hotels have either business centres or can make facilities, including fax and e-mail, available to businessmen. Most hotels in whatever category will have fax lines, some will have e-mail, and there are other places where e-mail can be sent and received (*see* 'communications', p.295).

Children

You are struck, particularly in Syria, by how very happy the children always seem to be. Syrians are warm and indulgent towards children, and if you bring your own you will find that they are welcome everywhere. But this lack of restrictiveness towards them can also expose the unwary to dangers: be careful about traffic, and beware at archaeological sites, where for example there can be some very deep holes they (or you) can fall into.

Be sure that your children observe careful hygiene, and protect them against the sun with lotions, sunglasses, hats and adequate clothing. The better hotels can recommend a doctor if necessary, and some may be able to arrange childminders for a few hours.

Children will often more readily take to the strangeness of their environment than you do. Museums and monuments will probably seem not half so much fun to them as the dress, the scent and the bustle of the bazaar, while something as simple as dining outdoors can be novel.

Climate and When to Visit

In **Syria** summers can be very hot and dry in Damascus and Aleppo and generally on the plains and in the desert, though desert nights can get quite cool, while on the coast and in the Orontes valley it gets humid. From November to March it can be cool and wet, the more so the farther north you go, and can even become very cold in the mountains and at night in the desert. Variations in topography and altitude make a difference at any time of year. In the evenings there is often a strong fresh breeze on the coast and in the desert, also in Damascus, which is on the desert's edge. Also in Damascus it gets dark early owing to the Anti-Lebanon rising immediately to the west. Spring and autumn are the best times to visit, especially as hotel prices tend to be higher in summer which perversely is the high season.

Lebanon enjoys a Mediterranean climate, shifting between mild winters and warm summers. Spring and autumn hardly exist. Winds, the sea and altitude are important factors. On the coast humidity can be high in summer, and from November to April there are heavy rainfalls. In March and April there can be considerable meteorological alterations; this is the time of the *khamsin* (meaning 50, as it is said to last for 50 days), a dry, stifling and sand-laden wind that blows in from Saharan Africa. In the mountains there is much rain in winter and considerable falls of snow, while summers are warm and humidity is almost nil. The Bekaa is cool and rainy in winter and warm and dry in summer. It follows that the most comfortable time to visit Lebanon is from April to the end of October.

Communications

Postal Services

The post between **Syria** and Europe takes about four to five days, to North America up to 15 days. For greatest efficiency, you will do best to use a letter box at a post office or at a hotel. As well as post offices, most hotels can provide you with stamps for postcards and letters. Letters are sometimes opened by the authorities, and certainly anything that is not a simple letter or postcard will attract their attention and might therefore take much longer. There are procedures to follow for sending packages; see under the postal services for Damascus, p.53.

The postal service between **Lebanon** and abroad works perfectly well. Hotels will usually sell stamps and post your letters and cards for you, but often at an outrageous premium. It is always cheaper and more reliable to buy stamps and do your mailing at a post office.

Telephone, Fax, E-mail and Courier Services

Phone calls made from hotels in **Syria** are charged at exorbitant rates. International calls are best made from the telecommunications buildings in Damascus, Aleppo and other major cities. Most hotels of all but the lowest categories also have fax machines, but if you are keen to save money go to the telecommunications buildings in major cities. E-mail is *verboten* in Syria as it is all but impossible for the government to eavesdrop, but some people, who register themselves in Lebanon, are hooked up to the Internet illegally—ask and you may well find. Faxes were also initially banned in Syria but are now common; e-mail is likely to follow suit soon. Courier services like DHL have offices in Damascus and Aleppo; see pp.53 and 207.

In **Lebanon** most hotels in all but the lowest categories will have both telephones and fax machines that you can use for national and international communications, though you will save money if you go to the telecommunications building ('Centrale') in the major towns. Business centres at the top hotels also offer e-mail services, as do various other places; see p.295 for details on these and also courier services.

Crime and Security

Syria is a very safe country so far as both crime and security are concerned, and you need have no qualms about moving about anywhere in the cities or round the country at any time of day or night. People are friendly without being intrusive, and when assistance is needed they can be remarkably kind and helpful. There are occasional checkpoints, especially on the desert road to Palmyra. You should always carry your passport with you. In **emergencies**: ambulance, ✆ 110; police, ✆ 112; fire, ✆ 113; traffic police, ✆ 115.

In terms of everyday crime, **Lebanon** is a safer place than Europe or North America. As for security, all the former militia groups have been disarmed with the exception of Hezbollah, which as a military force exists on Syrian sufferance, and the South Lebanese Army (SLA) which is a creature of Israel. The aim of Hezbollah has been to destroy Israel and turn Lebanon into an Islamic theocratic state. It stands no chance of accomplishing either. In the south it continues to operate against Israel and the SLA but in return it is on the receiving end of Israeli air strikes. Elsewhere in the country Hezbollah's activities are contained and it has begun participating in the more normal processes of the state machinery, including elections.

The Lebanese army has been reconstituted and is backed, often quite literally as you will see at checkposts, by the Syrians, who have around 40,000 troops in the country. Travel is safe throughout the north, in the south as far as Tyre, and also in the Bekaa Valley along and north of the Beirut–Damascus highway. South of Tyre and in the southern Bekaa Valley it is Israeli air strikes that you have to watch out for.

Disabled Travellers

Syria is not geared up for disabled travellers, but you could come to an arrangement with a local tour company or car-with-driver outfit.

Do not expect any facilities for the disabled traveller in **Lebanon**. The country can barely cope with its own problems: a quarter of a million Lebanese were wounded, many disabled, during the war.

Electricity

The electricity supply in both countries is 220 volts, 50 AC. Sockets take the standard continental European round two-pronged plug. Plug adaptors and current converters, as well as dual voltage appliances, can be bought at home.

Most of **Syria**'s electricity comes from the generators at Al-Thawra where the Euphrates has been dammed to create Lake Assad. But the Turks have built their massive Atatürk Dam higher upstream, so that the flow of the Euphrates is often much reduced by the time it enters Syria. In consequence there are frequent electricity shortages, with moments and even hours in the day when the lights go out in the cities and across large areas of the country. Many hotels and other places have their own generators, though candles seem to be equally popular.

The electricity grid in **Lebanon** was badly damaged during the war and has been undergoing renovation. The electricity supply in Beirut is now reliable, but elsewhere there is often no more than four hours of electricity a day. Many homes and almost all hotels have generators, however, so the lack of electricity is hardly noticed by the visitor.

Embassies

Syria: there is a list of foreign embassies in the Damascus chapter, *see* p.53. There is no Lebanese embassy in Syria. The Syrian Embassy in Britain is at 8 Belgrave Square, London SW1, ✆ (020) 7245 9012, and its embassy in the USA is at 2215 North Wyoming Avenue NW, Washington DC 20008, ✆ (202) 232 6313.

Lebanon: there is a list of foreign embassies in the Beirut chapter, *see* p.295. There is no Syrian embassy in Lebanon. In Britain the Lebanese embassy consular section (for visas) is at 15 Palace Garden Mews, London W8, ✆ (020) 7727 6696, and its embassy in the USA is at 2560 28th Street NW, Washington DC 20008, ✆ (202) 939 6300, ✆ (202) 939 6324, e-mail emblebanon@aol.com.

Entertainment

In **Syria**, entertainment at the big hotels amounts to a bellydancer, crooner and folkloric dance troupe; otherwise there are sleazy nightclubs and cinemas showing trashy films to all-male crowds. The best thing to do is to hang out at a café, stoke up a *narghileh*, and watch the passing parade.

In **Lebanon** the once-legendary entertainment scene succumbed to the civil war, the girls at the fabulous Casino du Liban among the last to give up the struggle. But they are back, and here and there in Beirut the good-time people are launching offensives amidst minefields of Islamic disapproval. For the full Monty, however, and provided you have a very full wallet, you need to go to the truly lavishly vulgar nightspots of Jounieh, a Christian city north of the capital.

Food and Drink

Syria

Most hotel restaurants and pricier restaurants generally offer both international and Middle East cuisines. Syrian cuisine has similarities with that of Lebanon but is generally not as good, nor has it the variety. There are numerous simple restaurants and snack stands providing the inevitable falafel, which is deep-fried balls of spiced chickpea paste served in a piece of unleavened bread (*khubz*) together with tomato, pickled vegetables and perhaps yoghurt; *hummus*, which is a purée of chickpeas, *tahina* (sesame) and olive oil; *tabouleh*, a finely chopped salad of parsley, onion, tomato and wheat; *moutabal*, a purée of eggplant, *tahina* and olive oil; and *shawarma*, which is finely sliced pieces of compounded lamb on a spit.

Fish is commonly available along the coast, and there is a wide variety of fruit throughout the country, including citrus fruits, pears, apricots, figs, olives, plums, grapes and watermelons.

Syrian vineyards around Aleppo, Homs, in the Anti-Lebanon and in the Jebel al-Arab produce red, white and rosé wines, drinkable but not nearly as good as Lebanese wines, and also from the grape comes *arak*, a clear strong drink like ouzo. The country also makes its own lager beer.

Syrian coffee is thick and black, and will usually come sweet (*ziyada*) unless you specify otherwise: medium (*mazboota*) or plain (*saada*). Unlike Greek and Turkish coffee, it is usually flavoured with cardamom.

To be on the safe side, you should sterilise tap water or drink bottled mineral water.

Lebanon

Most hotel restaurants offer both international (i.e. bland with perhaps a French touch) and Lebanese cuisines. Lebanese cuisine is widely regarded as the best in the Middle East.

The most characteristic Lebanese dishes are: *kebbeh*, which consists of mincemeat or fish, ground wheat, onions and spices, usually served up as a flat cake cooked in the oven. *Kebbeh* is often accompanied by *labneh*, a white creamy cheese made with ewe's milk, or by by *leben*, a curdled milk. *Yabrak* is meatballs made with minced mutton and mixed with rice and fresh vegetables, and rolled and cooked in vine leaves. *Yakhneh*, a meat and vegetable stew, is usually served with rice. *Assafir* is a dish prepared with small roast birds. *Lahm meshwi* is roast mutton stuffed with vegetables, rice and seasoning. *Shishlik* is small pieces of mutton roasted on a skewer; *shawarma*, finely sliced pieces of compounded lamb on a spit; *shish kebab*, fillets of mutton roasted on a skewer; *nkhaa mekli*, fried brains, sometimes put in an omelette; *fattush* a salad of cucumber, mint, purslane, etc., sprinkled with *sumac* juice. Meze, an hors d'oeuvre or meal on its own, consisting of a wide variety of morsels including *hummus*, a chickpea and sesame purée, and perhaps sparrow kebabs and sheep's testicles. The meze is eaten with the fingers and *khubz arabi*, a flat round bread, and is accompanied by *arak*, a clear aniseed-flavoured spirit made from grapes, similar to the Greek ouzo.

Desserts are sweet and filling, for example *halwa* (*halva*), ground sesame seeds with nuts and honey, and *baklawa* (*baklava*), a filo pastry filled with nuts and honey.

Lebanon brews its own lager beers; for example Almaza and Amstel are brewed under one roof in Beirut. Lebanese wine is reasonably good. The best of the commonly available wines are Kefraya and Ksara, both offering dry reds and dry to medium-dry whites. A better wine is Château Musar, red, rosé and white, but this seems to be sold only for export at the moment and at the Beirut airport duty-free shop. Lebanese vineyards are in the Bekaa Valley.

Lebanese coffee is thick and black, served sweet (*ziyada*), medium (*mazboota*) or plain (*saada*). Often it is flavoured with cardamom.

To be on the safe side, you should sterilise tap water or drink bottled mineral water.

Health and Insurance

If you are unwell in Syria or Lebanon, you can first seek advice from your hotel, which can refer you to a pharmacist, doctor, dentist or hospital. Doctors are well-trained, mainly in the West. Your embassy will also be able to recommend medical assistance.

No shots are required for entering Syria or Lebanon, but you should check with your doctor to see what he might recommend for your own benefit—possibly protection against hepatitis A, polio, tetanus and typhoid. The cholera vaccine is no longer considered to provide protection of any value, and malaria tablets are not necessary except perhaps if you are travelling down the Euphrates (Syria) in high summer. There is no real rabies danger in the cities but there could be in the Syrian desert.

Some foreign pharmaceutical drugs can be bought, but there might be difficulty in quickly getting something you specifically want. Any special prescriptions and medication should be brought with you.

Some people prefer to plunge into local eating habits, fruits, salads and all; an upset stomach is most likely a reaction to a change of diet and will pass after a few days. For the more fussy, who will probably get ill no matter what they do, avoid green salads, unpeelable fruit, fruit juices and ice cream. In the bigger hotels the water is safe, though highly chlorinated. Elsewhere it is safer to sterilise tap water or to drink bottled mineral water and to avoid ice cubes. Standard preparations for digestive upsets are available at pharmacies. *Arak* is also a specific against an upset stomach.

The air can be extremely drying, so if you wear contact lenses, carry sufficient lens-wetting solution (available locally), and against both dryness and sun use high-block sunscreens, moisturising cream and in summer drink at least three litres of water a day. Rehydration salts for the treatment of diarrhoea are available, but they are unflavoured; if its flavour you want, bring your own.

Be insured, but before signing up for a policy read it carefully: many of them offer inadequate cover, some are not worth the paper they are written on, and most of them are foisted on travellers by travel agents as a way of looking after their pockets, without much regard for their benefit to you. If going to Lebanon, make sure that your policy covers you there—not all of them do.

In Syria there are excellent hospitals in Damascus and Aleppo and fairly good medical facilities in most larger towns. In Lebanon there are numerous excellent hospitals in Beirut, and the standard of medical facilities thoughout the rest of the country is high. Private hospitals, however, may not (in Syria) or will not (in Lebanon) accept even emergency cases without seeing the colour of your money—be prepared to pay cash, as your medical insurance might not be accepted on the spot, though you can reclaim later. Make sure, therefore, that you are adequately insured.

Maps

The best map of **Syria** is published by Freytag and Berndt. It includes good city maps of Damascus and Aleppo and a sketch map of Palmyra.

The best map of **Lebanon** (plus map of Beirut on the reverse) is published by Geoprojects, Beirut, who are also in Britain: 9–10 Southern Court, South Street, Reading, Berkshire RG1 4QS, ✆ (01734) 393567, ✉ (01734) 598283.

Media

The BBC World Service broadcasts to Syria and Lebanon on 1323KHz medium wave, and it can also be picked up in Lebanon on 720KHz medium wave.

Foreign newspapers and magazines in **Syria** such as *The International Herald Tribune*, *Le Monde*, *The Middle East*, *Der Spiegel* and *Newsweek* are available three days late at the kiosks of the better hotels; anything in them about Syria is likely to be cut out. The daily government-run English-language *Syria Times* is a fairly useless piece of censored and propagandistic rubbish but sometimes contains bits of helpful information such as emergency telephone numbers, exchange rates, and the times for the foreign-language broadcasts of Syrian television. Damascus is the only place in the country with a few halfway decent bookshops.

Foreign newspapers and magazines in **Lebanon** are sold a day or so late at the kiosks of the better hotels. Also hotels often receive CNN and other foreign news broadcasts. There is almost none of the censorship that is so common in Syria, and Lebanon is burgeoning with its own home-grown newspapers, magazines, radio and television. There are two English-language dailies, the *Daily Star* and the *Beirut Times*, and a weekly magazine, *Mon Morning*, packed with interesting features on national and social issues, also the latest high society hot gossip. These provide information too on the English- and other foreign-language broadcasts of Lebanese TV and radio.

Money

Syria

The unit of currency is the Syrian pound (LS, from Livre Syrienne), and there are 100 piastres (*qirsh*) to the pound, though in practice you are unlikely to ever meet a piastre. Notes are in English on one side, Arabic on the other.

Officially, all foreign exchange transactions (both cash and travellers' cheques) must take place at branches of the government-run Commercial Bank of Syria. Cash and travellers' cheques are exchanged at very close to the same rate (in fact US dollars and travellers' cheques attract exactly the same rate, as do British pounds and travellers' cheques), but exchanging cash attracts no commission, whereas there is a small charge of SL25 for each transaction in travellers' cheques. The official rate of exchange is about SL44 to the dollar and SL72 to the pound (in each case whether cash or travellers' cheque).

There is also a flourishing blackmarket offering up to SL50 for the American dollar and up to SL80 for the British pound. Blackmarket dealing, though illegal (and punishable by 15 years' imprisonment), is in fact tolerated—you are likely to be approached in the souks of Damascus and Aleppo, quite possibly at your hotel, but if not, no one will blanch if you discreetly ask at a shop or across the reception counter.

The US dollar is the most convenient currency to take into Syria (though in the case of the $100 bill, take in only those issued in 1996 or later as earlier issues were often forged and you are likely to meet resistance when trying to exchange them). Indeed all but the cheapest hotels require payment in US dollars.

Major credit cards, e.g. Visa, Mastercard, American Express and Diners Club, are accepted at hotels from the very expensive down to the moderate, and sometimes at less expensive places too; also at the larger tourist-orientated shops in Damascus, Aleppo, Palmyra and sometimes elsewhere; and to pay for airline tickets and often car hire. But you cannot obtain cash advances against credit cards, nor are there any cash machines (ATMs) in Syria.

Lebanon

The unit of currency is the Lebanese pound (LL, from Livre Libanaise). Notes are in Arabic on one side, in French on the other.

At the time of going to press the approximate rate of exchange is LL1500 to the US dollar and LL2500 to the pound.

The American dollar serves as a parallel currency. It is much better to bring dollars to Lebanon than any other currency. You will often see prices quoted in dollars, and you can spend them anywhere, from the top hotels down to the humblest street market. As a huge quantity of American dollars in worldwide circulation is reckoned to be counterfeit, and as rumour has it that the Lebanese may have contributed to the glut, it might be best to follow the adage, so far as the dollar is concerned anyway, that it is better to give than to receive. At any rate, do not bring $100 bills issued before 1996 into the country, as it was these that were most often forged, and the knowing Lebanese will probably refuse them.

Foreign currency can be freely exchanged anywhere, at banks, hotels, shops, etc. The use of credit cards is nearly as universal as in Western Europe and North America. All major cards are accepted, cash advances are given, and you can withdraw money from cash machines (ATMs).

Travellers' cheques are the one fly in the ointment. Owing to a history of forgeries, the Lebanese are extremely reluctant to accept them. American Express travellers' cheques can only be changed at their Beirut office. The British Bank of the Middle East will change most major currency travellers' cheques, but not those of American Express. Moneychangers will change anything, travellers' cheques, your grandmother, etc., but at an extortionate rate. Needless to say, there is no blackmarket.

Syria

Syria officially uses the Western calendar. Friday is closing day for government offices, banks and post offices, and also for Muslim-run businesses. Christian-run shops close on Saturday afternoons and Sundays. Jewish-run shops close on Saturdays.

The following are fixed holidays when government offices, banks, post offices and big companies are likely to be closed, though small shops may stay open:

New Year (1 January), Revolution Day (8 March), Independence Day (17 April), Labour Day (1 May), Victory Day (6 October), Christmas Day (25 December).

The following Muslim and Christian holidays are moveable. All Muslim holidays are moveable because they follow the Islamic calendar which is lunar (see below), while the date for Easter is set according to the number of full moons after Epiphany, though the various Christian Churches use different calculations. On all these holidays almost everything is closed.

New Year's Day (Ras al-Sana al-Hegira, on the first day of Moharram), the Birth of the Prophet (Moulid al-Nabi, on the 12th day of Rabei al-Awal), the Breaking of the Fast (Eid, for three days at the end of Ramadan) and the Feast of the Sacrifice (Qurban Bairam, 10–13 Zoul Hagga); also Easter Sunday (Western Churches) and Easter Sunday (Orthodox Churches).

The month of **Ramadan** in the Islamic calendar is a time of fast from sunrise to sundown, when nothing may pass the lips—neither food nor drink—nor may one smoke or have sexual intercourse. Between sundown and sunrise, however, Ramadan takes on something of the character of a festival, when people visit one another to share a meal and a great deal of socialising goes on. As Ramadan proceeds, people get more worn out from fasting and lack of sleep, and so everything tends to slow down. In 2000, Ramadan begins late in November.

Lebanon

Lebanon officially uses the Western calendar, with Sunday as the day of rest. Independence Day, 22 November, is a national holiday.

The following are the Christian festivals observed in Lebanon (where no date is given, the holiday depends on Easter, which is moveable): New Year's Day (1 January), St Maron's Day (9 February), Shrove Tuesday, Mid-Lent, Good Friday, Easter Monday, the Ascension, Corpus Christi, the Assumption (15 August), All Saints' (1 November), All Souls' (2 November) and Christmas Day (25 December).

The Muslim festivals (all according to the Muslim calendar, *see* below) are: New Year's Day (Ras al-Sana al-Hegira, on the first day of Moharram), the Birth of the Prophet (Moulid al-Nabi, on the 12th day of Rabei al-Awal), the Breaking of the Fast (Eid, at the end of Ramadan) and the Feast of the Sacrifice (Qurban Bairam, 10–13 Zoul Hagga).

The Islamic Calendar

Month		No. of days	Month		No. of days
1st	Moharram	30	7th	Ragab	30
2nd	Safar	29	8th	Shaaban	29
3rd	Rabei al-Awal	30	9th	Ramadan	30

4th	Rabei al-Tani	29	10th	Shawal	29
5th	Gamad al-Awal	30	11th	Zoul Qidah	30
6th	Gamad al-Tani	29	12th	Zoul Hagga	29 (30 in leap years)

The Islamic calendar dates from the flight of Mohammed from Mecca in AD 622 and is based on 12 lunar months. This means that it rotates in relation to the Western solar calendar, each Islamic year beginning 11 days sooner than the last.

If you want to know the equivalent Western date for an Islamic (AH, *anno Hegirae*) year, you should use this simple formula:

1. Divide the Islamic year by 33 (the Islamic year is 11 days, or one thirty-third, shorter than a Western year).

2. Subtract the result of (1) from the Islamic year.

3. Add 622 to the result of (2) and this will give you the Western year.

For example:

1. AH 1421 divided by 33 = 43.

2. 1421 less 43 = 1378.

3. 1378 plus 622 = AD 2000.

In fact, AH 1421 begins in early April 2000 and ends in late March 2001.

Note that a day in the Islamic calendar begins at sundown, so that festivals begin on the evening before you would expect if going by the Western calendar, that evening assuming as sacred a character as the following waking daylight period (compare Christmas Eve and Christmas Day in Christian usage).

Opening Times

Syria

Many museums, castles, archaeological sites, etc., are closed on Tuesdays. Otherwise they are open daily, usually from 8 or 9am. Closing times can differ greatly, often at about 6pm in summer, 4pm in winter, but smaller, less visited places may close as early as 2pm year round. On Fridays and at Ramadan places may close early or close at lunchtime and re-open in the afternoon; while at Palmyra, for example, temples, tombs and museums close during the hottest hours of the day. Entrance to almost all Syria's museums and sites is LS300 (about $6), but students with an ISIC card pay a fraction of that, as do Syrians themselves.

Government offices are open daily except Fridays from 8am to 2pm. There is considerable variety in post office opening times. It is usually safe to assume that smaller post offices round the country will be open from 8am to 2pm Saturday to Thursday. In Damascus the central post office is open from 8am to 7pm, Saturday to Thursday, and 8am to 1pm on Friday; in Aleppo it is open daily from 8am to 5pm. Banks are generally open from 8am to 12.30pm or sometimes to 1.30pm, Saturday to Thursday, closed Friday, while in some of the luxury hotels there will be exchange offices that keep much longer hours and are open on Fridays.

Airline offices, travel agencies and shops are generally open from 8.30am to 1.30pm and from 2pm or 2.30pm to 6 or 8pm. The siesta is more likely to be observed during summer. The great majority of businesses and shops close on Friday; Christian shops and the gold souks close mid-day Saturday and on Sunday; Jewish shops close on Saturday. The souks in Damascus and Aleppo are open from 8am to 8pm and sometimes to 10pm in summer, but they are dead on Fridays.

Lebanon

Sites are generally open seven days a week, usually from 8am to about 4 or 5pm in winter, to 6pm or later in summer, while museums are usually closed on Sundays.

Banks, post offices, government offices, businesses and shops are closed on Sundays. Banks are open from 8.30am to 12.30pm, Monday to Friday, and to noon Saturday. Post offices and government offices are open from 8am to 2pm Monday to Thursday, to 11am on Friday, and are closed on Saturday and Sunday. Shops and businesses are usually open from 9am to 6.30pm Monday to Saturday, though at the height of summer some may close as early as 3pm. Muslim shops and businesses close in the afternoon during Ramadan but many re-open after sunset.

Packing

Pack long-sleeved shirts, long trousers, long skirts, a sun hat, comfortable walking shoes and swimwear. Other recommended items are ultra-violet filter sunglasses (preferably with polarised lenses); flashlight with batteries and also a pair of binoculars for exploring sites; a Swiss Army knife, a water bottle, a travel plug-adaptor, film and camera batteries (*see* 'Photography').

Syria

No matter what time of year you go, bear in mind the great diversity of Syria's topography, ranging from desert (hot and dry, but cool at night), through the humid Orontes valley and the cooler mountains. In winter it can be wet and cold, so provide for the variety. On the whole, it is best to cover up, both in summer and winter. This also fits in well with local sensibilities which, though varying between those of Muslims, Christians and others, and from city to village to desert, are generally conservative. Shorts on both men and women, and short skirts and too-revealing blouses should be avoided.

A number of familiar-looking products sold in Syria may not be the same as those you are used to at home. For example the Syrian version of brand detergents and toiletries are often harsher. The following items are either unavailable in Syria or hard to find: sanitary towels, high protection factor sun creams, sun hats, shampoos without strong chemicals, well-known brands of moisturisers and make-up, contraceptives, diabetic foods, camera batteries, insect repellant, detailed or accurate maps, good walking shoes and sandals, soft detergents for washing baby clothes, disposable baby's nappies (diapers) and phonetically-translated English to Arabic dictionaries.

Additionally consider if you have any special requirements which you would not want to find yourself without; to be safe, bring them.

Lebanon

No matter what time of year you go, remember that temperatures are cooler at higher altitudes, and so even in summer you should pack a sweater and in winter pack a set of warm clothing. In general the Lebanese are tolerant of foreigners' ways and dress, but outside the cities and larger towns people are more traditional. In Muslim areas especially, such as the south and in Tripoli, you should dress conservatively. This is especially the case for women, who when visiting mosques should wear clothing that covers their shoulders and arms (a scarf is a good idea) and their legs. Neither men nor women should wear shorts in mosques nor in Muslim areas generally. You can dress in a much more relaxed style in Christian areas on the coast.

A good range of toiletry items is available, but if you have any particular requirements which you would not want to find yourself without, bring them, for example contraceptives, high-screen suntan lotion, a special contact lens solution, a certain size battery for your camera.

Photography

Colour negative (print) film is widely available in Syria and Lebanon, though in Syria especially the choice of film speed (i.e. other than 100 ASA) might be limited and you should check expiry dates. Colour transparency (slide) film is readily available in Damascus, Aleppo and Beirut but can be difficult to get elsewhere, while black and white film is yet less available everywhere. The shops at the luxury hotels in Syria, especially at Damascus and Aleppo, are the best places to find what you need, and in Beirut there are plenty of shops, including 24hr processing places, especially along Hamra Street. While a standard range of camera batteries is available in such places, it is a good idea to bring spare batteries and also any special film that you require.

You are unlikely to experience any objection to taking photos in mosques or other Islamic monuments, nor in churches and monasteries, though you should be courteous and unobtrusive. Do not photograph military installations or anything else that might be deemed sensitive. You will not usually be permitted to take photographs in museums—which becomes ridiculous, indeed outrageous, in the case of the so-called Tartus 'Museum', which you visit not for its sparse collection of antique junk but because it was built as a cathedral and is one of the finest Crusader religious buildings anywhere in the Middle East.

Shopping

The souks of Damascus and Aleppo in **Syria** are wonderful places for shopping. Their wares—such as brass, carpets, inlay work, jewellery and brocades—are described in detail, and other shopping opportunities are mentioned, in the relevant chapters. Except where fixed prices are marked (and often even then), bargaining is customary.

In **Lebanon**, there is very little of local or traditional interest available. See under Beirut, p.300, and at the souk in Byblos, p.313.

Sports and Activities

Sport and related activities in **Syria** are limited and are offered mostly at the top hotels. The Hash House Harriers, based in Damascus, go running round the city, go running up to Krak des Chevaliers, go running just about anywhere they can think of (*see* **Damascus**, p.91). The foreign cultural centres such as the Goethe Institut, the French Cultural Centre and the British Council put on films and various events and offer Arabic language courses (*see also* **Damascus**, p.98).

In **Lebanon**, there are watersports at hotels along the coast and skiing in the mountains, for example above Bcharré.

Students

Anyone in full-time education is entitled to an International Student Identity Card (ISIC); it can be issued by student travel offices worldwide. In Syria an ISIC is a great boon: instead of paying the usual LS300 ($6) entry fee to sites and museums, you will be charged LS30, maybe less. In Lebanon, however, an ISIC entitles you at best to a kick in the teeth.

Time

Syria and Lebanon are two hours ahead of GMT in winter (October to March) and three hours ahead of GMT in summer. So in winter when it is noon GMT it is 2pm in Syria and Lebanon; and in summer when it is noon GMT it is 3pm in Syria and Lebanon.

Tipping

Tipping is usually expected as a reward for services, and is essential for supplementing incomes. Most restaurants include a service charge in the bill, but it is customary to leave an extra tip of 5 to 10 per cent of the total in both countries.

Toilets

In the best tradition of distant lands, many of the toilets you are likely to encounter in public places are of the squat-over-a-hole variety and are generally disgusting. A bucket of water or a pipe for squirting water may or may not be provided. The left hand is used, though oddly the bucket or spigot always seems to be on the right. It is a good idea to travel with a roll of toilet paper—or a bucket of water.

Tourist Information

There are no **Syrian** tourist offices abroad and those working at Syria's embassies and consulates give the impression of never having been there. The tourist offices in Syria are marginally more helpful.

There are **Lebanese** tourist offices in London, Paris, Cairo, Jeddah and Frankfurt. In Britain: Lebanon Tourist and Information Office, 90 Piccadilly, London W1, ✆ (020) 7409 2031, @ (020) 7493 4929. The Ministry of Tourism headquarters is at 550 Banque du Liban Street, Beirut, ✆ (01) 343073. Additionally, Lebanese embassies and consulates, and also offices of the national airline MEA (in English Middle East Airlines, in French Air Liban), may be able to provide basic information.

Where to Stay

Syria

Hotels in Syria are officially rated from five-star (luxury) to one-star. As a rule of thumb, any three-star hotel will do; below that, you should have a look for yourself. In this guide, hotels have been ordered according to price. But neither star system nor price can give a true indication of quality, ambience or location. All hotels except those in the lowest categories will quote their room rates in US dollars and will expect payment in same.

Hotels in the very expensive and the expensive categories are those usually used by tour operators who of course get rooms at a far lower rate than that paid by the punter coming in off the street. The freelance traveller is more likely to stay at the more affordable lower category hotels. But whatever the category, addresses and phone and fax numbers have been provided wherever possible so that you can make your own arrangements.

Note that there are few provisions for camping in Syria. There are hotels at Krak des Chevaliers and Palmyra that permit it on their grounds, and elsewhere, if you ask, you might be allowed. But you should not sleep out any old where.

Lebanon

The hotel star rating system in Lebanon is a bit slap-happy and should be treated with particular caution; places are being built or rebuilt or refurbished, or they are languishing, falling down or are being replaced, so that what was true yesterday is quite likely not to be true tomorrow—though as a general rule places are improving, and they are becoming more expensive. As a rule of thumb, any three-star hotel will do; below that, you should have a look for yourself. In any case, neither star system nor price can give a true indication of quality, ambience or location.

At the moment, capacity probably still exceeds demand. Nevertheless, it is a good idea to make reservations, especially during summer. Addresses, telephone numbers and fax numbers of hotels have been provided wherever possible.

Note that there is little really cheap accommodation in Lebanon.

You should not go freelance camping anywhere in Lebanon—it is not safe. At the moment there is only one organised campsite in the country, at Amshit, north of Byblos.

Price categories for Syria and Lebanon

The price categories given below are the same for Syria and Lebanon; they are indicative only and are for double rooms. As almost all hotels quote in US dollars, that is how room rates are given here.

very expensive:	over $180
expensive:	$100–$180
moderate:	$50–$100
inexpensive:	$20–$50
cheap	up to $20

Women

Women are unlikely to experience any difficulties in either country, but they should take extra care to behave and dress on the conservative side. Shorts should not be worn. Wearing a wedding ring can be helpful. Look confident and keep cool. It would be utterly unacceptable for a local woman to be pestered, so there is no reason for you to put up with it. If pressed to it, you can first say '*sibnee le waadee!*', which means 'leave me alone'. If something stronger is called for, shout '*imshee!*', which means 'get lost!' By this time, people should be coming to your assistance, and the man will be thoroughly ashamed and probably on the run.

Historical Syria   24

c. 9000–3000 BC: The Proto-Neolithic, Neolithic
   and Chalcolithic Ages   25

c. 3000–2000 BC: The Early Bronze Age   25

c. 2000–1600 BC: The Middle Bronze Age   25

c. 1600–1200 BC: The Late Bronze Age   26

c. 1200–539 BC: The Iron Age   26

539–333 BC: The Persian Period   27

333–64 BC: The Hellenistic Period   27

History of Syria and Lebanon

64 BC–AD 395: The Roman Period   28

AD 395–632: The Byzantine Period   29

632–61: The Arab Conquest   30

661–750: The Umayyads   30

750–1199: The Abbasids   31

From 1098: The Crusades   32

1144–1250: The Zengids and Ayyubids   33

1250–1516: The Mamelukes   33

1516–1918: The Ottomans   34

The French Mandate   36

1945–Present: Independence   37

*Statue of goddess of water,
Mari, 1800 BC*

Historical Syria

The present-day states of Syria and Lebanon form the northern part of that area historically termed Syria. 'Syria borders on Egypt, and the Phoenicians, to whom Sidon belongs, live in Syria.' So wrote the 5th-century BC Greek historian Herodotus, who described Syria as being 'the Mediterranean coast of Arabia' and added that 'from Phoenicia to the boundaries of Gaza the country belongs to the Syrians known as 'Palestinian'. But that was not the whole of it, for throughout most of history the term Syria has included all that area from the Taurus Mountains in what is now Turkey to the north down to the borders of Egyptian Sinai in the south, and from the Mediterranean in the west into the desert which reaches eastwards to the Euphrates. The present-day states of Syria and Lebanon, as well as Israel, Jordan and that part of Turkey known as the Hatay, and which includes Antakya (ancient Antioch), were all part of the expression 'Syria'.

Nor was this only an ancient definition: Baedeker followed it almost exactly in the 1912 edition of his guide. For the traveller's convenience he subdivided Syria into North Syria (from Homs to the Hatay), Phoenicia (corresponding to present-day Lebanon, but including also Damascus, presumably because it was easy to reach from Beirut), Palestine (corresponding to Israel and the west bank of the Jordan River), and the area east of the Jordan and south to Petra (corresponding to present-day Jordan). Baedeker gave special attention to Palestine on account of its biblical interest (hence his title, *Palestine and Syria*), but said that 'with regard to scenery the two north sections'—what today are Syria and Lebanon—'were far superior to the two to the south'. He might also have said they were richer and more varied in their historical monuments, but parts of present-day Syria were extremely difficult to reach in the early 20th century, and many ancient sites still lay undiscovered or had been only partly excavated and restored.

In many ways this historical Syria formed a single geographical unit, and yet its natural boundaries did little to ensure its security. The Euphrates was as much a highway for invasion from Mesopotamia as an obstacle, while the desert has always been open to incursions from Arabia, the Muslim conquest putting the seal on a long history of migration from that quarter. Egypt's pharaohs repeatedly marched in from the south, and from Egypt too came the Mamelukes and Ibrahim Pasha, and though the mountains to the northwest, setting off Syria from Asia Minor, offered a better frontier, they did not stop the Hittites or Alexander or the Crusaders, to name a few, from seizing the passes and finding the plains of northern Syria open before them. Though historical Syria had geographic coherence, its borders have been permeable, and through them have passed successive waves of migration and conquest from every direction.

No single sovereign state has ever coincided with these borders. More often than not this wider geographical Syria has been the province of some greater empire or has been shared between two or more outside powers. When this has been the case, and when stability has been imposed throughout the region, trade has flourished, goods passing between China and India on the one hand and the Mediterranean world on the other. A certain political suppleness has been the consequence, and an ability to assimilate new cultures while preserving elements of the old. 'Bow down to every nation which passes over you, but remember me in your hearts,' said a founder of the Druze sect, though it was a lesson learnt not only by the Druze. Another consequence has been a genius for commerce, though trade has not only been in material things: the alphabet must count as the greatest export to have travelled westwards from these shores and eastwards along the caravan routes to Arabia, Persia and India. This has also been fertile ground for the development of religious beliefs. Here the gods of Egypt, Greece and Rome syncretised with Semitic deities and tended increasingly towards a universalism; the monotheistic faiths of Judaism and Christianity have their origins here and prompted the rise of Islam.

Taken together, this traffic in empires and trade, cultures and religions, has left its mark in an astonishing and romantic array of monuments, on the coasts and in the mountains, in the valleys, highlands, plains and deserts. This is especially so in the northern part of that old historical region, now the states of Lebanon and Syria, always famous for its many harbours, for its great merchant cities and the dense crisscross of its caravan routes, and incomparable today for the layered variety of human endeavour over thousands of years of recorded time.

c. 9000–3000 BC: The Proto-Neolithic, Neolithic and Chalcolithic Ages

Agriculture was developed in the Middle East from about 9000 BC. Agriculture's advantage over hunting and gathering was a degree of predictability and the possibility of a surplus in food production, and as stone implements were gradually replaced by those of copper and then bronze, agriculture became still more productive. Agriculture meant settled communities; surpluses meant that not everyone had to be engaged in food production. In consequence, the period from about 9000 BC to 3000 BC saw the development of the first urban communities, where the economic activities of the population were differentiated, permitting some to engage in large-scale trade. The excavations at Byblos clearly record these stages of development.

c. 3000–2000 BC: The Early Bronze Age

The age sees the rise of wealthy trading cities such as Byblos on the coast, Ebla in the central plain and Mari on the Euphrates. The invention of writing (in Mari and Ebla cuneiform, a form of syllabic writing using wedge-shaped strokes, while in Byblos a kind of hieroglyphics) furthered the complexity of trade and law, whose effective administration, along with the control of irrigation along the Euphrates, was the basis of royal power. Both Mari and Ebla were sacked by the Akkadians, a people whose empire was based in Mesopotamia, in about 2250 BC. Meanwhile Byblos had enjoyed a close trading relationship with Old Kingdom Egypt, exporting timber from the slopes of Mount Lebanon that was used by the pharaohs for boat building, their palace furnishings and to assist construction of the Pyramids.

Towards the end of this period Syria and Lebanon were overrun from the east by the Amorites, who like the Akkadians were a people belonging to that language group called Semitic, to which the later Phoenician, Aramaic, Hebrew and Arabic languages have all belonged. The Amorite success in Lebanon was probably made easier by the collapse of the Old Kingdom in about 2100 BC.

c. 2000–1600 BC: The Middle Bronze Age

Once the Amorites had become settled in the fertile lands of Syria and Lebanon, trade and urban life, which had been disrupted by their arrival, gradually recovered, though in new patterns. Now the Amorite kingdom of Yamkhad centred on Aleppo exercised hegemony over Ebla and trade again flourished throughout northern Syria. But Mari, after a brief florescence under its own Amorite dynasty, was destroyed by Hammurabi, ruler of the Amorite kingdom of Babylon, in the mid-18th century BC.

The restoration of authority in Egypt during that period known as the Middle Kingdom (2040–1648 BC) led to renewed contacts with Byblos, whose ways became significantly Egyptianised, its goddess Baal-lat becoming identified with Hathor, the goddess of Egypt's foreign interests.

c. 1600–1200 BC: The Late Bronze Age

During this period, Syria was the battleground between two great powers, the Hittite Empire, whose capital was in central Anatolia, and New Kingdom Egypt (1540–1069 BC).

Advancing southwards, the Hittites put an end to the Babylonian Empire early in the 16th century BC and by the late 14th century BC had absorbed the Mitanni, who were centred on the Khabur River in northeast Syria.

Meanwhile, under such warrior pharaohs as Tuthmosis III (1479–1425 BC), Egyptian armies advanced as far north as the Euphrates, and its earlier mercantile relations with the coast were often reinforced by military garrisons. From about 1500 BC the Mycenaeans were following in the earlier wake of the Minoans, calling at Ugarit and Byblos, which over the course of the next several hundred years developed the alphabet and exported it westwards to Greece.

Egypt's attention to affairs in Syria and Lebanon was distracted, however, by the religious turmoil at home during the reign of Akhenaton (1353–1337 BC). Faced with having to align their loyalties with one or other of the great powers, Byblos, Tripoli, Sidon and Tyre wrote cuneiform letters to the Egyptian foreign office, seeking support (these are among the famous Amarna Letters found at Amarna, Akhenaton's capital, in the late 19th century AD).

The Hittites and the Egyptians, led personally by Ramses II (1279–1213 BC), finally met at Kadesh, a battle celebrated by Ramses as a victory but in fact confirmation that the Hittite sphere of influence had extended farther south. The Hittites had already taken Damascus, and now by treaty they controlled the ports of Ugarit and Tripoli. The 3000-year habit of carving inscriptions at the Dog River was begun by Ramses during his Kadesh campaign.

The Exodus probably dates to the reign of Ramses or his son Merneptah, Moses leading the Israelites out of Egypt to settle eventually in the hill country around Jerusalem and the fertile plains to the north.

c. 1200–539 BC: The Iron Age

One likely reason for the Hittites' success in Syria was their superior iron weaponry as opposed to the Egyptian bronze. Iron came from Anatolia but was entirely lacking in Egypt. But that did not preserve the Hittites against the massive and aggressive migration of the Sea Peoples, a barbarian coalition that emerged from the lands around the Aegean and both overland and by sea overwhelmed the Mycenaean and Hittite worlds and was stopped only at the land approaches and delta estuaries of Egypt in the reign of Ramses III (1184–1153 BC). The identity of the Sea Peoples is the subject of speculation; some are thought to have been the Lycians of southwest Anatolia, others Etruscans and Sardinians (though as yet on their way to their eventual homelands), others the Pelesets who would give their name to Palestine. The coastal lands of the eastern Mediterranean were overrun by the Sea Peoples, and at Ugarit a last message for help at their approach was found in the ruins of the city they destroyed. Other coastal cities, whose culture can henceforth be called Phoenician, revived and resumed their role in the trade of goods and ideas between Asia, Egypt and Greece. In the 10th century BC,

Tyre, under the rule of Hiram, became the pre-eminent Phoenician city and had close relations with King Solomon to the south, supplying timber for the Temple at Jerusalem. The Phoenicians established colonies throughout the Mediterranean, most famously Carthage, which was founded from Tyre in the 9th century BC.

Meanwhile the Arameans, a Semitic Bedouin people, moved into central and northern Syria, from Hama up to Tell Halaf and Tell Brak, and adopted the outward forms of the old Hittite culture; these are called the Neo-Hittites. Ultimately their language, Aramaic, became the *lingua franca* over much of present-day Syria, Lebanon, Israel and Jordan, and 1000 years later was spoken by Jesus, and still survives at Maalula today.

In northern Mesopotamia a new empire arose, the Assyrian, and from the 9th century to the 7th century BC it imposed its administration on almost the whole of Syria and Lebanon, but in 612 BC its capital at Nineveh fell to the Babylonians, who took over their possessions in the west. This was the period of the famous hanging gardens, and of the Babylonian Captivity of the Jews.

539–333 BC: The Persian Period

The Persians captured Babylon in 539 BC and within two decades had established their authority across the whole of the Middle East, Egypt and Asia Minor. Their provinces were well-governed and their empire was linked by an excellent system of roads that did much to encourage trade and cultural exchange. But on the Aegean coast of Asia Minor the Greek population rose in revolt, abetted by Greece itself. To deal with this irritant, the Persians, with the help of Phoenician ships, twice invaded Greece but were defeated at Marathon in 490 BC, and at Salamis in 480 BC and Plataea in 479 BC. Though it may not have seemed that way to the Persians at the time, the Greeks took the view, as expressed by the mid-century historian Herodotus, that these events were a titanic clash between Asia and Europe, between East and West. In the event, before the end of the following century the Middle East would come under Western rule, which would last for 1000 years.

333–64 BC: The Hellenistic Period

In the spirit of a pan-Greek crusade against Persia, Alexander of Macedon led his troops across Asia Minor, in 333 BC inflicting a crushing defeat on Darius' far larger army at Issus, north of present-day Iskenderun in Turkey. But Alexander did not immediately pursue Darius eastwards, as the greatest threat to the Greeks' lines of communication were the Phoenician ships in the service of the Persians. Therefore Alexander marched south along the coasts of Syria and Lebanon, taking by surrender or by force one port city after another and building a great port city of his own at Alexandria in Egypt. He was only 33 when he died at Babylon in 323 BC, but had created an empire even greater than the Persian, a Hellenistic empire compounded of Eastern and Western cultures, with Greek culture predominant.

Asked on his deathbed to whom he would leave his empire, Alexander answered, 'To the strongest'. His two most able generals were Ptolemy, who took Egypt and also southern Lebanon and Syria, including Damascus, and Seleucus, who made himself master of Mesopotamia, northern Syria and Asia Minor. During the 2nd century BC, the Seleucids confined the Ptolemies to Egypt, but they lost Asia Minor to the Romans and Mesopotamia to the Parthians, the successors to the old Persian Empire.

The Seleucids founded Antioch as their capital and Apamea as a military headquarters, refounding Latakia as its port, while on the Euphrates they built the fortress city of Dura Europos. To these cities and older ones, including Aleppo and Damascus, the Seleucids gave the characteristic Hellenistic grid plan that remains evident today. The Greek numbers were always small, however, and mostly confined to the cities rather than settled on the land; their culture was adopted in form but not in spirit, and in the end they lacked the muscle to hold on. From the south came the Nabateans, an Arab people, who in the 1st century BC took Bosra and Damascus, while from Asia Minor the Romans became increasingly involved in Syrian affairs.

64 BC–AD 395: The Roman Period

In 64 BC the Roman general Pompey abolished what remained of the Seleucid Empire and turned Syria into a Roman province with its capital at Antioch, though some parts of the country, chiefly in the south (including Damascus), were allowed to remain autonomous or under Nabatean control for a century longer. Earlier, by 30 BC, the Romans had brought the entire coast of Lebanon under their control.

Under the settled conditions of the 250-year Pax Romana that began with the reign of the first emperor, Augustus (27 BC–AD 14), trade and agriculture reached new heights of prosperity. The Bekaa was more intensively cultivated than it is today, the Hauran was developed and became a breadbasket of the empire and even the marginal northern highlands west of Aleppo became productive, flourishing on the export of olives. An improved and extended road system promoted long-distance trade, and it was now that Palmyra rose to prominence. Cities were embellished, streets broadened and arcaded, as for example Straight Street in Damascus (visited by St Paul c. AD 37 after his vision), while there and at Baalbek and elsewhere sacred precincts assumed monumental proportions. Significant remains of the Roman presence survive also at the port cities of Byblos and Tyre. Though governed from Rome, the East, certainly its upper classes, remained Greek in culture and language.

In AD 106 the Nabatean kingdom based on Petra in present-day Jordan was absorbed into the Roman province of Arabia, with its capital at Bosra. This occurred during the reign of the Emperor Trajan (AD 98–117), whose aggressive Eastern policy against the Parthians took him to the shores of the Persian Gulf, though afterwards Hadrian (AD 117–38) established a more defensible imperial boundary along the Euphrates. Under Augustus, only four legions (about 20,000 men) had been assigned to Syria (Germany had eight), but by the end of the 2nd century AD seven legions were needed to oppose the mounting Parthian threat, replaced from AD 224 by a new Persian dynasty, the Sassanians. Necessity was overtaking aggrandisement in shifting the balance of imperial preoccupation from West to East. The end of Italian supremacy over the provinces was marked by the accession of Septimius Severus (AD 193–211), who had married the daughter of the high priest of Homs and was acclaimed emperor by his Syrian legions, while later Philip the Arab (AD 244–49), himself a Syrian, was raised to the imperial throne. One of Severus' acts was to create in AD 194 the new province of Coele Syria, 'hollow Syria', centred on the Bekaa Valley.

But in AD 256 the Sassanians took Dura Europos and four years later captured the Emperor Valerian, though he commanded a force of 70,000 men. These events made Palmyra an indispensable bastion of empire, and its ruler, Odainat, was made the semi-independent commander of Rome's entire defensive system in the East. After his murder in AD 266, however, his widow Zenobia threw off the mantle of imperial ally, conquering Egypt and most of Asia Minor and declaring herself Roman empress. Her rebellion was short-lived, and in AD 272 her armies were defeated, Palmyra taken and Zenobia captured by the Emperor Aurelian.

To remedy the perilous strategic situation, the Emperor Diocletian (AD 284–305) divided the Roman Empire into eastern and western administrations, each with its own emperor, each half further divided in two under the rule of caesars, with Diocletian himself in overall command from his new capital at Nicomedia (present-day Izmit in Turkey). Without Diocletian's dominating personality to steer it, however, the arrangement quickly broke down, his successors fighting for supreme power, the struggle won by Constantine the Great (AD 306–37), who became sole emperor in AD 324 and then, confirming the strategic shift eastwards, founded Constantinople as his new capital in AD 330.

Meanwhile, despite sporadic and sometimes ferocious persecutions, Christianity had spread throughout the empire, and though Christians numbered only about one-seventh of the population, their influence went far wider. The Christian doctrine of equality of the individual soul gave it a universal appeal, it was well organised, and it was attracting some of the best minds of the time, who in rooting its theology in Greek philosophy made it intellectually acceptable. By promulgating the Edict of Milan in AD 313, which tolerated Christianity and gave it rights in law, Constantine won the support of the strongest single group in the Roman world. Constantine's conversion had already occurred in AD 312 when his vision of the Cross accompanied by the words *In hoc signo vinces*—in this sign you will conquer—preceded his victory against a rival emperor at the Battle of the Milvian Bridge outside Rome, though he was baptised only on his deathbed. During his lifetime, however, and in the reigns of his successors, Christianity flourished under imperial patronage and by the end of the 4th century dominated the empire. In AD 392 the Emperor Theodosius I (AD 379–95) declared Christianity the official religion of the Roman Empire: henceforth paganism was proscribed. During his reign the temples of Jupiter at Baalbek and Hadad at Damascus were in whole or in part destroyed and churches built, that of St John the Baptist at Damascus in turn superseded by the Umayyad Mosque.

AD 395–632: The Byzantine Period

On the death of Theodosius in 395 the Roman Empire was officially divided between East and West, the date most often taken to mark the beginning of what historians call the Byzantine Empire, that amalgam of Roman institutions, Christian faith and Greek culture, with its capital at Constantinople. The Roman Empire in the West fell to Germanic invaders in 476, but in the East the Byzantines went on calling themselves Romans right down to the final fall of Constantinople to the Ottomans in 1453.

At first the prosperity of Syria and Lebanon continued as before and is reflected especially in the profusion of religious buildings in the Hauran and the northern highlands, rich in variety and innovation, drawing on both metropolitan and local architectural styles. Grandest of these was Qalaat Samaan, built round the pillar upon which St Simeon the Stylite (389–459) had stood and prayed for 38 years. The relationship between God and man was not always satisfied by resort to a pillar, however, and these were times when the imperial orthodoxy was challenged by monophysitism and monothelitism, the Maronites, found principally today in Lebanon, being a product of the latter. The disputes could be bitter and took on a nationalist colouring that undermined Byzantine rule.

The empire reached its apogee during the reign of the Emperor Justinian (527–65), who won back much that had been lost in the West, so that he ruled over an area that all but encompassed the Mediterranean and extended east to the Euphrates. Except for France, central and northern Spain, Britain and the Germanic areas north of the Alps, Justinian's empire included almost all the Roman world of Diocletian.

But, as well as religious divisions within the empire, the Byzantines faced the relentless Sassanian threat from the East, which they met, especially under Justinian, by bolstering their defences along the Euphrates frontier, as at Resafa and Halabiye. In the late 6th and early 7th centuries, however, the standoff between the two powers gave way to a titanic struggle marked by extremes of fortune that was to prove ruinous to both. In 611, after earlier raids that reached Apamea and Antioch, the Sassanians invaded and occupied Syria. In 622 the Emperor Heraclius (610–41) counterattacked and in the course of a six-year campaign reached deep down the Euphrates and Tigris rivers and regained control of Syria. But having fought one another to exhaustion, neither the Byzantines nor the Persian Sassanids were capable of resisting the Arabs, afire with the faith of Islam.

632–61: The Arab Conquest

Mohammed, the founder of Islam, died in Mecca in 632, having united the Arabian tribes by a combination of warfare and faith. His successors, known as caliphs (from Khalifat rasul-Allah, Successor to the Apostle of God), extended Arab energies northwards. Under the first caliph, Abu Bakr (632–34), the Muslim armies pushed up into the Syrian desert and to the lower reaches of the Euphrates; under Omar (634–44) they conquered all of the Byzantine Middle East, including present-day Syria, Lebanon, Jordan, Israel and Egypt, and won an important victory over the Persians. Several centuries passed, however, before the majority of the population in the region became Muslim.

The decisive battle for the conquest of Syria was fought in 636 against a Byzantine army at the Yarmuk River, which flows out of Syria into the Jordan. Damascus fell twice, in 635 and again in the following year after the Arabs had abandoned it to face the approaching Byzantines.

Under Othman (644–56), the third caliph, the whole of Persia was conquered. During all this time the Arab conquests were ruled from Medina, but under Ali (656–61), the fourth caliph, the capital was transferred to southern Iraq, and his authority did not run to Syria. His accession was tainted as it was owed to the assassination of his predecessor, and though he was not himself guilty of it, it helped crystallise opposition to him in some quarters, especially when he dismissed many of those whom Othman had appointed. Among these was Muawiya, Othman's nephew and governor of Syria, who demanded vengeance for his uncle's murder. In 656, Ali and Muawiya met in battle at Saffin near Qalaat Jaber on the Euphrates, which ended in negotiations that weakened Ali's position and ultimately led to his assassination by a disaffected follower in 661. Muawiya, founder of the Umayyad dynasty, was acclaimed caliph (661–80) and made Damascus his capital.

661–750: The Umayyads

Under the Umayyads Damascus became the capital of the Arab Empire at its greatest extent, reaching from the Indus to Spain, its caliphs aspiring to be the cosmopolitan successors to the Roman and Byzantine empires from whose cultures they readily borrowed—unmistakable in the architecture and decorations of Anjar in Lebanon, the Umayyad Mosque in Damascus (the latter and probably the former the works of the Caliph Walid I, 705–15) and even in the desert palaces of Qasr al-Heir East and West (built by the Caliph Hisham, 724–43).

Though hardly a secular state, religion played a secondary role in the empire of the Umayyads, who placed primary emphasis on the political and economic aspects of government, their authority based on the Arabs' traditional pre-Islamic loyalty to their leaders, which involved consultation and persuasion more than force. The Umayyads showed tolerance towards their subjects and administered through them (Muawiya's chief secretary was a Syrian Christian), co-opting rather than destroying the institutions bequeathed them by the Byzantines. Indeed 50 years passed after the Arab conquest before Arabic replaced Greek in the state registers.

Against the tolerance and scepticism, the intellectual curiosity and lively aesthetic sense of the Umayyads, and their taste for poetry, music, dance and wine, were opposed more tight-laced and theocratic versions of Islam, both in Arabia and to the east. Weakened by dissension and propaganda, and perhaps themselves too relaxed and idiosyncratic a breed to suppress their enemies ruthlessly, the last Umayyad caliphs retreated into self-indulgence and debauchery. The final attack came from Iraq and was led by Abu al-Abbas, who in 750 took Damascus and exterminated the Umayyad leadership, only Abd al-Rahman, a grandson of the last caliph, escaping to establish an Umayyad dynasty in Spain.

750–1199: The Abbasids

The replacement of the Umayyads by the Abbasids was far more than a change of dynasty. The free-wheeling spirit of the desert was replaced by an autocratic system that owed much to Persian pomposity, the habit of Abbasid caliphs to grant audiences from behind a curtain prompting one ambassador to ask if he were being shown God. By moving the capital from Damascus to Baghdad on the Tigris, the new masters of the Islamic world were renouncing any notion of being successors to a Mediterranean-based civilisation and instead rooting their empire in the cultures of Mesopotamia and Persia. Divine right, military force and an elaborate bureaucracy, in all of which the Arabs played a diminishing role, were the means used by the Abbasid caliphate to assert its power. Its apogee was reached during the reign of Haroun al-Rashid (786–809), a time famously recounted in *The Thousand and One Nights*, though the setting is a blind, for the tales were composed centuries later and are a thinly veiled description of Mameluke Cairo.

For Syria the change of dynasty was a disaster, the lack of Abbasid architecture in Damascus indicative of the utter neglect with which they treated the country as a whole, their only significant remains being at Raqqa on the Euphrates, a sort of long-distance suburb of Mesopotamian Baghdad. More generally it was a disaster for the Arabs, as soon after Harun al-Rashid's reign the caliphate was infiltrated and eventually became the creature of Turkish nomads advancing from farther east.

The empire fragmented, and Syria in particular was made a chaotic battleground. Egypt became independent under a Turkish dynasty, the Ikhshidids, from 939 to 969, when they were supplanted by the Fatimids, a Shia dynasty that had proclaimed their own caliphate in North Africa in 909, transferring it to Cairo, which they founded and made their new capital. In 978 the Fatimids took possession of southern Syria, while from 969 the Byzantines had begun re-establishing control over parts of the north, where in the 10th and 11th centuries Aleppo was successively ruled by the Hamdanids, Arab refugees from Iraq, and by the Bedouin

Mirdasids. In 1037 the Abbasid caliph was reduced to a puppet of the Seljuk Turks who made themselves masters in Baghdad; in 1071 they defeated the Byzantine army at Manzikert in eastern Anatolia, having captured Aleppo the year before; and by 1075 the Seljuks had taken most of Syria, including Damascus.

Exposed to the conflicting claims of the various contestants, the population of Syria and Lebanon became similarly fragmented and often fearful, many sects taking to the mountains, among them the Druze, for whom the Fatimid Caliph Hakim (996–1021) was a kind of messiah, and the Maronites.

Various events, including Hakim's widespread destruction of churches in the Holy Land, the harassment of pilgrims, and the Byzantines' appeal for help against the Seljuks, prompted Pope Urban II at Clermont-Ferrand on 27 November 1195 to call for a crusade to restore Christian authority in the East and most particularly to reclaim Jerusalem.

From 1098: The Crusades

After marching across Europe the Crusader armies arrived in the spring of 1097 at Constantinople, their numbers between 60,000 and 100,000, almost all French and including a large proportion of rabble and non-combatants. Fighting their way across Turkish-occupied Asia Minor, they came to Antioch that autumn. The Byzantines had recaptured Antioch in the 10th century and had lost it to the Turks only in 1085. Now it was in the hands of a Seljuk vassal. Laying siege to the city, the Crusaders finally took it in June 1098, by which time fighting, disease, famine and defections had greatly reduced their numbers. Desperate for food and eager to protect their eastern flank, Bohemond and Raymond de Saint-Gilles, Count of Toulouse, marched up the lower Orontes valley and then turned inland for Maarat al-Numan, in December storming the town and massacring its male population.

Thereafter Antioch was left in the possession of Bohemond, and in January 1099 the remainder of the army set out for Jerusalem under Raymond's command. His route was via the upper Orontes valley, passing between Shaizar and Hama to Masyaf and then through the Homs Gap, where the Crusaders briefly occupied the site that was to become the great castle of Krak des Chevaliers, and so down the coast via Tripoli, Beirut, Sidon and Tyre to near Jaffa, from where they wound up through the Judaean hills, arriving before the walls of Fatimid-held Jerusalem on 7 June 1099. The Crusaders' numbers now were about 12,000 foot soldiers and 1200 or so mounted knights, in addition to numerous camp followers. On 15 July Jerusalem fell in a fury of bloodlust, its Muslim and Jewish inhabitants slain (the latter because they were thought to have helped the former), an event that shocked the world and forever poisoned relations between Christians and Muslims in the Holy Land.

The First Crusade created three Latin enclaves in the East, the County of Edessa (present-day Urfa in Turkey), the Principality of Antioch and the Kingdom of Jerusalem, none adjoining another. These were augmented and also added to by the creation of the County of Tripoli, so that by 1144 there was a continuous belt of Crusader states running from Cilicia and Edessa down to Eilat on the Gulf of Aqaba. But in 1144 Edessa fell to the Muslims under Zengi, prompting the Second Crusade of French and Germans. Some came by sea, but those passing through Asia Minor suffered heavy losses; the attempt to recapture Edessa was abandoned; and an attack on Damascus in 1148 proved a failure. These setbacks dampened enthusiasm in the West, and the defence of the Latin states was now left primarily in their own hands. Their numbers being few, they relied increasingly on formidable castles, such as Margat, Saône and Krak des Chevaliers, usually manned by autonomous orders of knights, the Templars and Hospitallers.

1144–1250: The Zengids and Ayyubids

The decisive moment in Muslim resistance to the Crusaders came with Zengi's capture of Edessa on Christmas Eve, 1144. Twenty years earlier the Crusaders had laid siege to Aleppo but it was saved by a Seljuk force representing the moribund Abbasid Caliphate in Baghdad. Among them was Zengi, who became the local ruler (1128–46) and was succeeded by his son Nur al-Din (1146–74), who extended his authority over Damascus. As part of their resistance to the Crusaders, the Zengids imposed orthodox Sunni Islam on the population, building madrasas that survive still in Aleppo and Damascus, and driving Shia sects, including the Ismaelis and that branch of the Ismaelis known as the Assassins, into the coastal mountains.

Against the Shia Fatimids in Egypt Nur al-Din sent Saladin, a Kurd from Iraq. In Cairo in 1171 Saladin abolished the Fatimid Caliphate and restored Egypt to Sunni Islam and to notional Abbasid authority. In 1176, two years after Nur al-Din's death, Saladin took up the succession in Syria and by 1186, for the first time since the overthrow of the Umayyads, had united all the Muslim lands from Cairo to Baghdad, founding a dynasty named after his father Ayyub, whose house, reworked into a Sunni madrasa, stands near the tomb of his famous son in Damascus.

Free to turn his attentions against the Latins, in 1187 Saladin crushed a Crusader army at Hattin in Galilee and reconquered Jerusalem, gaining also Acre, Sidon, Beirut and Byblos. In the following year in the course of a four-month campaign he sacked Tartus and Latakia and captured Saône. The loss of Jerusalem and the perilous situation along the coast provoked a massive reaction in the West, the pan-European Third Crusade advancing by land and sea for Acre (in northern Israel), which was recaptured in 1191. Richard I, the Lionheart, king of England, twice came within sight of Jerusalem but failed to take it, settling for an agreement that granted pilgrims the freedom to visit the Holy Sepulchre. By 1197 the Crusaders had recovered most of the coast (Jerusalem was even re-acquired by treaty from 1229 to 1244) and were to hold it for another half century and more until the coming of a more ruthless adversary, the Mamelukes.

1250–1516: The Mamelukes

Saladin's Ayyubid successors continued to rule from their seat in Cairo but came increasingly to rely on highly trained and disciplined slave troops, mostly Kipchak Turks from the steppes north of the Black Sea. These Mamelukes (from *mamluk*, meaning owned) showed their mettle in 1249 when they defeated and captured St Louis, the French king, who had landed at Damietta in Egypt at the head of the Seventh Crusade. The sultan, al-Salih Ayyub, lay dying, and the battle was directed by his wife Shagarat al-Durr, who in 1250 attempted to rule in her own right but was soon obliged to marry the chief Mameluke, who became sultan.

The gravest danger the Islamic world was ever to face came in the form of the Mongols. In 1258 they destroyed Baghdad and then invaded Syria. Nothing, it seemed, could stop them, but in 1260 at the battle of Ain Jalud in Palestine the Mongols were defeated by the Mamelukes. Among the outstanding commanders both there and at Damietta was Baybars (1260–77) who on the way back to Cairo murdered the Mameluke sultan and became sultan in his stead.

Though the Mongols were to continue to cause havoc over the next 40 years or so, the Middle East was sufficiently secure for the Mamelukes to turn their attentions towards the Crusader states. Antioch fell to Baybars in 1268, and Krak and Safita in 1271, followed by the campaigns of Sultan Qalaun (1280–90), who took Margat in 1285, Latakia in 1287 and Tripoli in 1289, leaving the coup de grâce to his successor Sultan Khalil, who took Acre and Tartus in 1291. Except for a garrison which clung to the island of Arwad, opposite Tartus, until 1302, the Crusader venture in the Middle East was finished.

A new phase began in 1382, when the earlier Bahri Mamelukes (named after their Cairo barracks on Roda Island in the Nile—*bahr* means river) were replaced by the Burgi Mamelukes (named after their barracks in the Cairo Citadel, *burg* meaning tower), also Turkish but who came mostly from the Caucasus. The decades of transition between the late Bahri and early Burgi periods were marked by vicious rivalries that distracted the Mamelukes from the business of defence and left Damascus unprotected at the advance of Tamerlane (Timur) who devasted the city and much of Syria in 1400. The financial and human cost and the blow to morale was never really overcome, and Portugal's opening up of a sea route round Africa during the 15th century also undermined the flow of trade. To their credit, however, and in addition to their fierce warrior qualities, both the Bahri and Burgi Mamelukes were tasteful and magnificent builders, who filled Tripoli, Aleppo and Damascus with many of their finest surviving monuments.

In the 14th century a new Turkish power, the Ottomans, had arisen in Asia Minor, and though their army had been crushed by Tamerlane at Ankara in 1402, their dynastic vigour remained unbroken and their revival had been swift. In 1453 they conquered Constantinople, finally extinguishing after more than 1000 years what remained of the Byzantine Empire. In the backstabbing Mameluke system, in which rulers rarely died a natural death, the reign of Sultan Qayt Bey (1468–95), who is commemorated by his great minaret at the Umayyad Mosque in Damascus, was exceptionally long and one of comparative stability. But it was a presage of things to come when in 1486 he clashed with the Ottomans for possession of Adana and Tarsus in Cilicia.

1516–1918: The Ottomans

In 1516 the Ottoman Sultan Selim I (1512–20) marched into Syria, defeated the Mamelukes north of Aleppo and occupied Damascus. Advancing south via Jerusalem, Selim took Cairo early the following year, where the last Mameluke sultan was captured and hanged. The Muslim holy cities of Medina and Mecca also fell to the Ottomans, who from their capital at Constantinople (officially renamed Istanbul only in 1930) ruled an empire stretching from the Red Sea to the Crimea and from the Caucasus to Bosnia. Its territories were further enlarged by Suleyman the Magnificent (1520–66), who added Serbia, Hungary, Rhodes, Mesopotamia and all of North Africa except Morocco. During his reign Damascus was graced by the Tekkiye Mosque, built by Sinan, the greatest of all Ottoman architects, who in Constantinople built the Suleymaniye Mosque. Selim II (1566–74) conquered Cyprus but in 1571 his fleet was defeated by an alliance of Western powers under Don John of Austria at Lepanto off the west coast of Greece, though Ottoman expansion was only finally checked when its army was forced to abandon the siege of Vienna in 1683.

When the Mongols destroyed Baghdad in 1258, a man claiming to be a relative of the last caliph fled to Cairo where he was proclaimed caliph in turn, though as a puppet of the

Mamelukes. On taking Cairo in 1517 Selim I went one better, and assumed the caliphate himself, which helped to legitimise Ottoman rule over those conquered Muslim territories that shared their Sunni orthodoxy. In furtherance of their caliphal role the Ottomans were assiduous in organising and provisioning the annual pilgrimage, in which Damascus played a special part, for it was said to mark the midway point between Constantinople and Mecca (identified, to be exact, as the ablutions fountain in the courtyard of the Umayyad Mosque), and was the pilgrims' last staging point before they embarked on the arduous desert crossing. The economic benefit to Damascus was considerable, as evidenced by its great khans and souks, yet even these were exceeded by those of Aleppo, which in the first century of Ottoman rule was opened up to European merchants and became the leading city for East-West trade in the Levant.

Ottoman policy towards those they conquered, especially non-Muslims, was of a shepherd to a human flock that was to be milked and fleeced but otherwise left alone provided it caused no trouble. Normally the task was delegated to a governor, the most outstanding being Assad Pasha, who in the mid-18th century built handsome khans and palaces at Hama and Damascus, and baths at Tripoli. In the mountains of Lebanon the feudal factions of Maronites and Druze were left to govern themselves as they saw fit as long as they paid tribute. Twice, under Fakhr al-Din II (1585–1635) and the Emir Bechir (1789–1840), whose palace is at Beit Eddine, Lebanon became virtually an independent state. Both cultivated commercial and cultural relations with the West, but ultimately both were removed for the threat they presented to Ottoman authority, Fakhr al-Din by the still-powerful Ottomans themselves, Bechir handed over by the British to the by then enfeebled Ottomans .

This followed Britain's alarm at the remarkable campaign of Ibrahim Pasha, son of Mohammed Ali, an Albanian adventurer who ruled Egypt from 1805 to his death in 1849 and won its independence from the sultan in Constantinople. Ibrahim, a brilliant general and enlightened administrator, captured Damascus in 1832 and for the first time in centuries gave Syria a centralised government. It was the beginning of the modern era: he rationalised the system of taxation, reformed the judiciary, encouraged agriculture and commerce, founded schools, and placed Jews and Christians on an equal footing with Muslims and for the first time allowed foreigners to enter the city in European dress. It was then also that the first British consul took up residence in Damascus, a position held nearly 40 years later by Sir Richard Burton, who translated there *The Thousand and One Nights*. By 1839, Ibrahim had penetrated deep into Asia Minor and was poised to overthrow the Ottoman dynasty itself, but the British intervened, preferring the 'Sick Man of Europe' to a vigorous and modernising power in the region. To reassert their authority in Lebanon, the Ottomans connived at setting Druze against Maronite, which in 1860 culminated in the Druze massacre of 10,000 Christians in the mountains and led to the massacre of thousands more in Damascus at the hands of the Muslims, provoking the landing of French forces on the Lebanese coast. From this time Beirut, to which many Christians had fled, began its prosperous career as a window on the West.

In 1909 the Ottoman sultan was deposed and a puppet put in his place, power passing to a junta, the Young Turks. An intolerant nationalism had been developing among Turks for some decades, and the 1890s had already seen widespread massacres of Armenians in Asia Minor. During the First World War, genocide became Turkish policy, with Deir ez Zor a Turkish-run Belsen. There and elsewhere the Turks murdered between one and a half to two million Armenians. On 15 September 1915 the Minister of the Interior in Constantinople cabled the

Turkish governor in Aleppo: 'The government has decided to exterminate entirely all the Armenians living in Turkey. No one opposed to this order can any longer hold an administrative position. Without pity for women, children and invalids, however tragic the methods of extermination may be, without heeding any scruples of conscience, their existence must be terminated.' In the event, those Armenians who fled or were already living in Aleppo were protected by the Syrians themselves and by the inconvenient presence of too many Western eyes, while others found protection in Lebanon. Meanwhile, Damascus was the headquarters for the Ottoman command in the Middle East, together with that of their allies the Germans.

The Arab Revolt against the Turks, in which T. E. Lawrence played a part, began in 1916 and was answered in Damascus and Beirut by the hanging of 21 Arab nationalists, both Muslim and Christian, on 6 May, still commemorated as Martyrs' Day in both Syria and Lebanon, the sites of execution in each city called Martyrs' Square. The revolt culminated with the entry of British troops under General Allenby and Arab forces led by the Emir Feisal, son of Hussein, the Sherif of Mecca, into Damascus on 1 October 1918.

The French Mandate

In the Ottoman system of provincial government, a *vilayet* or province, ruled by a governor, was subdivided into *sanjaks* or departments, though sometimes a *sanjak* could be independent of any *vilayet*. Both *vilayets* and independent *sanjaks* were directly responsible to Constantinople. The Vilayet of Aleppo included much of northern Syria; Deir ez Zor was an independent *sanjak*; the Vilayet of Syria, with its capital at Damascus, stretched from Hama to Medina and Mecca in the Hejaz; the Vilayet of Beirut included the entire coast from Latakia to just north of Jaffa (now part of Tel Aviv), as well as the Jebel al-Sariya and all that country between Sidon and the Jordan River; the independent Sanjak of Lebanon included Mount Lebanon from south of Tripoli to north of Sidon; while Jerusalem was an independent *sanjak*.

Not surprisingly, in 1907 Gertrude Bell wrote that 'there is little or no sense of territorial nationality. . . Syria [loosely meaning the areas described above] is merely a geographical term corresponding to no national sentiment in the breasts of the inhabitants'.

Even so, the Arab Revolt engendered a new-found sense of identity, and in the course of it the Arabs understood from their British allies that when the Ottomans were defeated the region would become self-governing. In 1918 a parliamentary government was formed at Damascus which in 1920 declared Feisal, son of the Sherif of Mecca, king of Syria 'in its natural boundaries, from the Taurus [the mountains north of Cilicia in present-day Turkey] to Sinai'. But in 1916 the French and British had made the secret Sykes-Picot agreement to divide the Middle East between themselves, and in 1920 the European powers meeting at San Remo in Italy partitioned the Ottoman Empire, in the Middle East giving Britain mandates over Palestine and Trans-Jordan, and France mandates over Lebanon and Syria. In the same year the French imposed their mandatory powers over Lebanon and Syria by force of arms. In compensation for the loss of his throne at Damascus, the British made Feisal king of Iraq, while his brother Abdullah became ruler and ultimately king (1946) of Trans-Jordan, with Amman as his capital.

Meanwhile, in 1917, Lord Balfour made his famous declaration that the British Government 'views with favour the establishment of a national home in Palestine for the Jewish people', though exactly what that meant was far from clear. Certainly it did nothing to discourage Jewish immigration into Palestine, which, despite being forbidden, had begun under Ottoman rule from 1878, so that already in the years immediately before the First World War there was at least one Jew for every five Muslims in the Sanjak of Jerusalem, while in the city of Jerusalem itself the Jewish population amounted to over two-thirds of the whole, the rest divided among Christians and Muslims, the last forming the smallest group.

The French Mandate territories comprised the State of Greater Lebanon (now the Republic of Lebanon) and also an area corresponding to the present-day Syrian Arab Republic, but also including what is today Turkey's Hatay province around Antakya and Iskenderun. But to discourage the growth of nationalist sentiment, the French at first divided Syria into so-called states centred on Damascus, Aleppo, the Hauran with its large Druze population and Latakia with its numerous Alawi population in the northern Jebel al-Sariya. At the beginning of 1925 Aleppo was brought into the State of Syria with its capital at Damascus, which included also the partly autonomous Sanjak of Alexandretta (the Hatay).

But French rule never sat easily, and in 1925 a revolt broke out among the Druze in the Hauran and the Jebel al-Arab (known until recently as the Jebel Druze) which spread to Damascus, to which the French responded by bombarding the city. In 1939, by way of gaining Turkish neutrality before the Second World War, the French ceded the Sanjak of Alexandretta (the Hatay) to Turkey, a cession the Syrians have never accepted, their maps still showing it as part of Syria. In 1942 the states of Hauran and Latakia were incorporated into the State of Syria.

With the fall of France to the Germans in 1940, the French forces in Syria and Lebanon remained loyal to the collaborationist Vichy government, but in the following year an invasion by British and Free French forces placed the Mandate territories under Free French control. Syria and Lebanon became independent in 1945, though French forces evacuated only in 1946.

1945–Present: Independence

Independence resurrected the dream of pan-Arab unity, and various schemes were advanced for joining Syria and Lebanon, which already shared in a customs union, and also Iraq, Jordan and Palestine, though none of the permutations satisfied all the parties. The end of Britain's mandate over Palestine and the United Nations' plan for its partition between Jews and Arabs led to the outbreak of guerrilla fighting between the two. In 1948, with the declaration of the state of Israel, the surrounding Arab countries attacked, were defeated, and in 1949 signed an armistice.

Syrian energies were entirely consumed by political and military matters to the detriment of other aspects of life. Changes of government, both civilian and military, were frequent. In contrast, Lebanon enjoyed a stable parliamentary government which preferred to pursue policies of free trade and an open market. In 1950 the customs union between Syria and Lebanon was ruptured, Syria embarking on a protective tariff policy, Lebanon closing its frontier to Syrian exports and giving asylum to Syrian political refugees. In 1958, however, Syria merged with Egypt to form the United Arab Republic under the leadership of the Egyptian president, Gamal Abdel Nasser, though the venture was dissolved in 1962. In 1963 the Baathist party came to power in Syria (*baath* means renaissance; in practice the Baathists have espoused Arab regeneration through a vaguely defined self-help socialism).

Syria was involved, but Lebanon was not, in the 1956, 1967 and 1973 Arab-Israeli wars. The 1967 war cost Syria the Golan Heights, which were occupied by Israel. In 1970 General Hafez Assad ousted the civilian government and in the following year became president of the Syrian Arab Republic. The Baathists had originally been broadly based; under Assad it became dominated by his fellow Alawi. This had its advantages, as the Alawi are a minority group, part of that 40 per cent of the population who are Christian, Druze or non-Sunni Muslim, who otherwise might have been more completely dominated by the Sunni Muslims, among whom runs a strong fundamentalist streak. In the event all groups, both minority and majority, have had to be taken into account.

Lebanon's population is also mixed, and this has been such a potential source of disunity and conflict that no census has been carried out in the country since 1932. It was assumed, however, that the Christians were in a slight majority, and that among the Muslims the Sunni were in a majority over the Shia, with the Druze forming a small and distinct minority. Political representation and the appointment to ministerial offices was based on these assumptions. Lebanon's orientation towards East and West has also been a factor in its politics. These tensions led to civil war in 1958, which was ended when the United States landed troops to support the Western-inclined government.

But the growing numbers of Palestinian refugees in Lebanon, at one point perhaps reaching a million, continued to unsettle the balance; and also the old assumptions were changing, the Muslims thought to be in the majority over the Christians, and among the Muslims the Shia to be in the majority over the Sunnis. In 1975 a second civil war broke out between the Maronite-led Lebanese Forces and the National Movement backed by the Palestinian Liberation Organisation, leading to Syrian occupation of all but the south of the country in 1976. In 1978, following Palestinian attacks on its borders from Lebanon, Israel occupied the south of the country, then in 1982 marched up as far as Beirut and put the city under siege for three months, forcing the PLO to evacuate. Under Israeli cover, Christians massacred Palestinian civilians in Beirut's Sabra and Shatila refugee camps. Israel then agreed to withdraw from Lebanon if Syria would also, but Syria refused, though in 1985 the Israelis withdrew to a buffer zone in the extreme south, where they continued to fend off the Iranian-backed Hezbollah, a Shia militia group. Hostage-taking, practised by all sides, also began in 1985.

The Lebanese parties in the conflict finally negotiated a peace in 1989 that reasserted the belief in a state where the different religions (confessions) would coexist, and gave increased powers to the prime minister (traditionally a Muslim) while reducing those of the president (traditionally a Christian). The collapse of the Soviet Union, which had long offered Syria its support, altered the international situation, as did the 1990–91 Gulf War in which Syria, unfriendly towards Iraq, contributed forces to the Allies and began a rapprochement with the United States. Subsequently the militias, excepting Hezbollah, were disarmed, and the Green Line dividing Muslim West from Christian East Beirut was dismantled.

The cost of the civil war to Lebanon was 125,000 dead, 250,000 wounded, 17,500 missing and the complete destruction of 180,000 homes with many more seriously damaged.

Now, under an elected government in which the Shia have gained additional seats, and with the authority of the Lebanese army restored and backed by the Syrian army throughout the country, the country is secure and has begun rebuilding its fortunes.

Most recently, the Israelis have announced their intention to withdraw from the buffer zone they have occupied in southern Lebanon, and the Syrians and Israelis have been holding negotiations over the return of the Golan Heights and a possible peace treaty. Improved relations in the region and between Syria and the West, also the gradual liberalisation of the Syrian economy, have stimulated investment in the country, are encouraging tourism, and are promoting a marked rise in prosperity.

Agatha Christie   40

The Genesis of Lawrence of Arabia   40

Lebanon: The Cost of War   43

T-Shirts of the Party of God   43

Water, War and Peace   44

Topics

Agatha Christie

Agatha Christie (1891–1976), author of the famous detective novels, married the archaeologist Max Mallowan (1904–78) in 1930. By then she was already famous, having written her first book, *The Mysterious Affair at Stiles*, in 1920, which also marked the debut of Hercule Poirot. Mallowan had first excavated at Tell Brak in northeast Syria, his wife accompanying him on his digs, and Poirot too, it seems.

Agatha and Max would arrive by sea at Beirut and continue on to Homs, Palmyra and Deir ez Zor, or they would travel aboard the Orient Express to Istanbul and then take the Baghdad railway along the Euphrates via Aleppo. On one occasion, when Agatha was immersed in writing a book during her stay at Aleppo's Baron Hotel, the proprietor, Coco Mazloumian, asked her what she was up to; *Murder on the Orient Express*, she replied.

The archaeologist's life fascinated Agatha, not surprisingly, as it is very much another sort of detective work. *Come, Tell Us How You Live*, published in 1946, is her amusing account of those years with Max in Syria, its title referring as much to the archaeologist's probing into the past, his wanting to discover how people lived then, as about her own adventures with Max. It might have been the age difference between them that made her think of the veil in a kindly way: 'I reflect enviously that it must be nice to have your face veiled. It must make you feel very private, very secret... Only your eyes look out on the world—you see it, but it does not see you... I take out the glass from my handbag and open my powder compact. "Yes," I think, "it would be very nice to veil *your* face!"'. But also Agatha developed a deep sympathy with Syrian ways and with its people, and concluded her book with this fond testament: 'I love that gentle fertile country and its simple people, who know how to laugh and how to enjoy life; who are idle and gay, and who have dignity, good manners, and a great sense of humour, and to whom death is not terrible.'

The Genesis of Lawrence of Arabia

In October 1918 Lawrence of Arabia entered Damascus at the triumph of the Arab Revolt. He walked to the tomb of Saladin and stood there alone and in reflection. It is a strange scene, the Englishman who had led an Arab crusade paying homage to the man who had driven the Crusaders from Jerusalem 750 years before.

Lawrence's crusade had been taking shape in his imagination for 20 years. At Witney Church near Oxford lies the body of a knight, and there Lawrence, nine years old, rubbed his first brass. 'As the years passed,' his mother later wrote, 'he visited every church in England that had old brasses of knights. The rubbings were pasted by his own hands on the walls of his bedroom and formed a marvellous wall decoration.' She added that 'being always very strong physically he was full of enthusiasm for every subject in which he was interested. He had a most loving and unselfish nature and no boy or man ever did more thoroughly whatever his hand found to do'. Lawrence's enthusiasm was attested by a friend who confessed how some of the brass rubbings were obtained: 'In Waterperry Church there were brasses inaccessible behind some pews. Lawrence, already ruthless, made short work of the obstruction, and I still hear the splintering woodwork and his short laugh, almost sinister to my timorous ears.'

Like some Gordian knot the pews were cut. 'I had dreamed, at the City School in Oxford,'— these are the last lines of *Seven Pillars of Wisdom*—'of hustling into form, while I lived, the new Asia which time was inexorably bringing upon us. Mecca was to lead to Damascus; Damascus to Anatolia, and afterwards to Baghdad; and then there was Yemen. Fantasies, these will seem, to such as are able to call my beginning an ordinary effort.' The boy dreamed a thousand years out of time of being a crusader, and he would create a crusade so that he could join it. Also from *Seven Pillars*: 'All men dream: but not equally. Those who dream by night in the dusty recesses of their minds wake in the day to find that it was vanity: but the dreamers of the day are dangerous men, for they may act their dream with open eyes, to make it possible. This I did.'

T. E. Lawrence was born on 16 August 1888. His childhood interest in brasses extended to church architecture and then to medieval castles. On his bicycle, often alone, he travelled through the Middle Ages, covering sometimes nearly 300km in a day. He prided himself on his austerity, living on bread, milk and fruit, carrying no more than a change of clothes, a waterproof cape, a sketchbook and sometimes a camera. By the spring of 1907 he had visited nearly every medieval church and castle in England and Wales, and beginning with the summer of his 17th birthday in 1906, he made three lengthy summer tours of France.

In a letter home from Aigues-Mortes, 2 August 1908, he records an intense emotional experience, when the jigsaw pieces of his historical sensibility come together in a powerful vision. First, from Les Baux, he is watching the muted colours change on the distant horizon when the sun leaps out from behind a cloud and surprises Lawrence with his first silver glimpse of the Mediterranean. '*Thálassa, thálassa*' ('The sea, the sea!'), he cries out, echoing the shout of Xenophon's men after their long mapless march from Mesopotamia through the snows and hostile tribes of the Armenian mountains to the familiar shore—Xenophon, the young, educated gentleman-soldier who had talked with Socrates. Then Lawrence descends to Aigues-Mortes where, he remembers, St Louis embarked on the Seventh Crusade, and bathes in the sea: 'I felt that at last I had reached the way to the South and all the glorious East; Greece, Carthage, Egypt, Tyre, Syria, Italy, Spain, Sicily, Crete . . . they were all there, all within reach . . . of me . . . Really this getting to the sea has almost overturned my mental balance.' It is a not so untypical reaction; but what is odd is the connection Lawrence makes between the waves and the rippled sand: quoting from Shelley's *Julian and Maddalo* ('I love all waste/And solitary places'), it is the level plain that most originally excites him, the rapture of the steppe that he was to know again in Arabia.

Lawrence's family had lived in Oxford since 1900; with traditions reaching back to the Middle Ages, the city was a base for his nostalgia for the past. He matriculated at Jesus College in October 1907 and during this freshman year argued that with the arrival of gunpowder and printing the real world had been destroyed. 'At about the age of fifteen,' his mother recalled, 'his interest was aroused in medieval pottery when some was turned up in excavations for a public-house in Cornmarket Street. From that time he made a habit of going to see all the deep foundations, paying the workmen to keep all the little pieces that they found.' In this way Lawrence was able to make a number of important donations of medieval artefacts to the Ashmolean Museum, where also he established friendly relations with its Junior Assistant Keeper, Leonard Woolley, and a father-son relationship with the Keeper, David Hogarth.

E. M. Forster, who also possessed a romantic passion for the East (evoked, he said, 'with almost intolerable violence' when he read *Seven Pillars*), wrote this portrait of Lawrence after his death:

'If when the schoolboy grows up he takes to archaeology seriously, he seldom loses this primitive excitement, this thrill of adventure, reinforcing the thrill of research. The trespassing-spirit persists, the angry farmer becomes an Arab with a gun, the clergyman and the policeman coalesce into a foreign government, which it is a pleasure to fool and a duty to spy on. It is not surprising that so many archaeologists take to secret service and do well in it. Their mentality as well as their opportunities qualifies them.

'. . . . Those who get the best out of orientals usually despise the East, but he was always able to respect while he controlled them; it was one of his great virtues. And at Carchemish the idea of a crusade, vaguely conceived amongst medieval oddments, takes a bold habitation and a non-Christian character: he will free the Arabs.

'. . . . The notion of a crusade, of a body of men leaving one country to do noble deeds in another, now possessed him, and I think it never left him, though the locality of the other country varied: at one time it was Arabia, later on it was the air. Had he been a Christian, his medieval equipment would have been complete and thought-proof: he would have possessed a positive faith and been happier: he would have been the 'parfit gentil knight", the defender of orthodoxy, instead of the troubled and troublous genius who fascinated his generation and failed to fit into it. He would have been much smaller.'

From the beginning of 1911 to the First World War Lawrence worked under Hogarth and later Woolley excavating the mound of Carchemish, a Neo-Hittite city. Hogarth had dug at Ephesus and with Arthur Evans at Knossos, sites from which he kept one eye on the political events within the Ottoman Empire. It was Hogarth who had suggested to Lawrence that he could ensure a good degree by writing a thesis on medieval architecture in the Middle East; who had obtained the *iradés* or letters of safe conduct that made Lawrence's walk through Ottoman Palestine and Syria possible; and who had now obtained for Lawrence the post of assistant archaeologist at Carchemish which apart from its antique interest had the virtue, from the British point of view, of being along the route of the projected Berlin to Baghdad railway. Hogarth was in British Intelligence and Lawrence was his recruit. From this mound near what is now the Turkish-Syrian border and at the northern extent of the Arabic-speaking world, Lawrence could photograph the Germans building their railway, assess the local mood towards Constantinople, and build on the Arabic he had begun learning while visiting Crusader castles. Carchemish was the practical or career link between Lawrence's Oxford student days and his Arabian wartime adventure.

Whether it was at Carchemish or, as Lawrence himself maintained, earlier that the ambition was conceived for a specifically Arab crusade, it was during the summer months of 1909, the summer of Lawrence's 21st birthday, that he was able to test his dreams from Witney Church and Aigues-Mortes against the reality of his first encounter with the East. C. M. Doughty, author of *Arabia Deserta*, had warned Lawrence before his departure that 'long daily marches on foot a prudent man who knows the country would I think consider out of the question. The populations only know their own wretched life and look upon any European wandering in their country with at best a veiled ill will. . . I should dissuade a friend from such a voyage, which is too likely to be most wearisome, hazardous to health and even disappointing'.

Undeterred, Lawrence walked 1800km during the three hottest months of the year through Palestine and Syria. From 9 July to 31 July he walked from Beirut to Galilee, then west to Mt

Carmel and the Mediterranean, and north along the coast through Tyre and Sidon to Beirut. From 6 August to 6 September he walked north from Beirut to Tripoli, then zigzagged between the coastal and mountain castles of northern Syria, after Latakia heading east to follow the Orontes north to within sight of Antioch and passing through desolate highlands where 'I seem to have been the first European visitor', then east again to Aleppo. From sometime after 7 September to sometime before 22 September he travelled by carriage to Edessa (Turkish Urfa) and back to Aleppo. Of the 50-odd castles in the region, Lawrence had devised a route that would take him to 37 of them, all but one of which he finally managed to see. When it was over, he wrote casually to Doughty: 'You may remember my writing to you in the beginning of the year, to ask your opinion on a walking tour in Northern Syria. That has ended happily and the Crusading Fortresses I found are so intensely interesting that I hope to return to the East for some little time.' To the Principal of Jesus College Lawrence wrote on 24 September from the Baron Hotel, Aleppo: 'I have had a most delightful tour . . . on foot and alone all the time, so that I have perhaps, living as an Arab with the Arabs, got a better insight into the daily life of the people than those who travel with caravan and dragomen.' And to his mother, on 29 August from Latakia, he wrote: 'I will have such difficulty in becoming English again: here I am Arab in habits.'

Back at Oxford Lawrence got a First, his thesis singled out for being 'very remarkable'. But what most impressed was the adventure itself through Palestine and Syria: 'He had climbed the old walls barefoot,' so a don remembered later, 'he had had his troubles with Bedouin, and once (I think he told me) been assaulted and left unconscious.' The legend of Lawrence in the East had been planted, and Lawrence himself was discovering that he could dream with open eyes and make his dreams possible.

Lebanon: The Cost of War

At least 360,000 people, 14 per cent of the population, had at least one member of their family killed, wounded or kidnapped during the war. More than half the population became internal refugees and nearly a quarter went abroad at some point, mostly professionals and skilled workers.

Income per head of the population fell from $1869 in 1974 to $979 in 1985.

There was not a single year during the war in which most schools did not have to close due to fighting. Many acted as refugee centres for long periods. In consequence, 20 per cent of Lebanese over 20 years of age are illiterate.

The water table and most of the natural springs have been polluted. Solid and toxic waste has been dumped into the sea. Air pollution in Beirut is among the highest in the world. Deforestation, including the mountain cedars which are Lebanon's national emblem, has left only three per cent of the country forested, compared with 18 per cent in the 1950s.

T-Shirts of the Party of God

Recently a Beirut company specialising in the import of Scotch whisky and American sportswear received an order from the Shia militia group Hezbollah, the Party of God, for 200,000 black T-shirts. The goods were air-freighted directly from the United States and the account was immediately settled in dollars. Five days later the shirts were on the backs of their new owners who were marching through West Beirut demanding the overthrow of American imperialism.

Water, War and Peace

You might discover it one late morning in Damascus when you ask for coffee or tea and are answered with a shruf and are told 'later'. Or it might be in your hotel room in Aleppo when you try to run your bath and nothing more than a dry gasp issues from the tap. Or in Hama as you sit at a restaurant by the Four Norias of Bechiriyat, and you notice that the waterwheels stand motionless, that there are no boys leaping from them into the Orontes, because of the waters of the river are too low to set the norias turning, and there is hardly an Orontes to leap into.

What you are witnessing in an incidental way is the most serious problem confronting not just Syria but the entire Middle East today, a matter of life and death, or peace or war: the rapidly accelerating shortage of water.

Damascus is fed by the waters of the Barada, much of Syria's central plain by the waters of the Orontes, both rivers rising in the mountains of Lebanon where rainfall is higher than anywhere else in the region. But in recent years rainfall throughout the Middle East has been well below average, and in Lebanon it has been thirty years since anyone can remember such a scarcity of rain and snow.

But the drought has merely highlighted a long-term problem, for projections by the United Nations and other international bodies show that within a few years Syria will be suffering from a chronic scarcity of water as its demands increase to meet the needs of population growth, of irrigation, of industralisation and urbanisation.

It is a problem that Syria shares with its bordering countries of Iraq, Jordan and Israel, which like Syria itself all lie downstream of the river sources on which their very existence depends. Just as the Barada and Orontes rise in Lebanon, so the Tigris and Euphrates rise in Turkey before flowing into Syria and Iraq, while a quarter of the catchment area of the River Jordan on which Jordan itself feeds, as do Israel and the nascent Palestinian state, lies in Syria. Israel's occupation of Syria's Golan Heights and of southern Lebanon up to the Litani River, not to mention its occupation of the West Bank of the Jordan itself, has much to do with its concern for its water supplies; as does Syria's presence in Lebanon, and the tension betwen Syria and Turkey, whose vast Atatürk Dam project in the Kurdish southeast of Anatolia is set to reduce Syria's supply of water from the Euphrates by half, making its own dam at Al-Thawra largely redundant.

Indeed the single most likely cause of war in the Middle East today is not territorial claims nor the clash of religions but the rising demand for water and control over its sources, while the prospects for peace depend on whether the parties can find a fair and just solution—a point to consider next time you take a shower.

Damascus

Getting There and Getting Around 48

Tourist Information 52

Along the Barada 56

The National Museum 57

The Tekkiye Mosque Complex 60

Along the Souk al-Hamidiye to the
  Great Mosque of the Umayyads 63

The Umayyad Mosque or Great Mosque 67

Around the Umayyad Mosque 73

Souks, Khans and the Azem Palace 79

Straight Street and the City Walls 82

Salihiye 90

Mount Kassioun 91

Shopping 92

Where to Stay 93

Eating Out 95

This 'Holy' Damascus, this 'earthly paradise' of the Prophet, so fair to the eyes, that he dared not trust himself to tarry in her blissful shades, she is a city of hidden palaces, of copses, and gardens, and fountains, and bubbling streams. The juice of her life is the gushing, and ice-cold torrent that tumbles from the snowy sides of Anti-Lebanon. Close along on the river's edge through seven sweet miles of rustling boughs, the deepest shade, the city spreads out her whole length; as a man falls flat, face forward on the brook, that he may drink, and drink again, so Damascus, thirsting for ever, lies down with her lips to the stream, and clings to its rushing waters.

Alexander Kinglake, *Eothen*, 1844

The reference to the Prophet recalls the occasion when Mohammed, still then working the caravan route between Syria and Mecca, overlooked the delightful city from Mount Kassioun but would not tempt his frailty by entering into it, remarking that there was but one paradise for man and for his part he was resolved not to take his in this world.

Pressing through the busy shadows of the Souk al-Hamidiye, you emerge into a splash of sunlight beneath a Roman arch and a high Corinthian colonnade at the heart of the Old City of Damascus. Before you the temple of Jupiter Damascenus once stood, and earlier still an altar to Hadad, god of storm, rain and fertility. The Byzantines converted Jupiter's temple into the Church of St John, but now the call to prayer floats out from the 8th-century Great Mosque of the Umayyads. For thousands of years this has been the holiest place in what claims to be the world's oldest continuously inhabited city, venerable for its Muslim, Christian and pagan stones.

When T. E. Lawrence approached Damascus at the triumph of the Arab Revolt, he described 'the silent gardens blurred green with river mist, in whose setting shimmered the city, beautiful as ever, like a pearl in the morning sun'. It is an old vision, preserved within the courtyard of the mosque by the mosaics of trees and streams in green and gold which ripple with the changing angle of the sun. And it is a vision lost to the present-day traveller, for outside the walls of the Old City the new has built upon the river meadows and climbs the half-encircling mountains. Modern Damascus is not a catastrophe; merely, like other cities that discovered the 20th century, it is pedestrian. But if Westernised Damascus is charmless, there is no obvious poverty or filth or overcrowding or chronic disorder. Things work and get done. Even the Old City is clean, and there is a tremendous amount of restoration work going on, neglected edifices being realised for their historic and cultural—and their touristic—value.

Damascus (al-Shams, Dimashq) is not a fleshpot capital, not a place where Arabs and others come for a good and a low, even a high, time—rather a relief from the flat and the hot and the dry, something of a holy place, a place of pilgrimage for some. Mountains wall it off from the Mediterranean; Damascus looks out upon a desert sea towards Mecca. You are conscious that its visitors are people of the plains and steppes and desert, and with them the Damascenes share a quietness, a reserve, sometimes a severity. Even in the souks they hardly importune and elsewhere never. They are a proud people, but also courteous and pleasant. The food is excellent. The Old City is absorbing. There is the enjoyment of seeking things out that are both wonderful and as yet not well-known.

History

For a city that claims a history of continuous inhabitation older than any other (a claim disputed by Aleppo), Damascus has little to show for even its classical past, its most ancient monument the 3rd century AD Roman Gate of the Sun, now called Bab Sharqi, the Eastern Gate. Yet the oasis formed by the Barada dribbling into the desert has been inhabited by a settled community since about 4000 BC, and by about 2500 BC the name Dimashq was appearing in the archives at Mari. Five hundred years later, the Amorites, a Semitic people, established themselves in the city. During the 15th and 14th centuries BC, Syria was contested by the superpowers of the day, the Hittites of Anatolia (present-day Turkey) and New Kingdom Egypt, Damascus falling within the Egyptian sphere after Tuthmosis III's victory at Armageddon but slipping away again after Ramses II's narrow escape at Kadesh (see p.135).

The Hittite Empire collapsed and Egypt's New Kingdom ambitions in Syria were destroyed with the invasion of the Sea Peoples around 1200 BC, and Damascus again fell into the hands of a Semitic people, the Arameans, who on the spot now occupied by the Umayyad Mosque built their temple to Hadad, while abroad they warred against the biblical kingdoms of Israel and Judaea. In a new age of empire, Damascus fell to the Assyrians in 732 BC, to the Babylonian King Nebuchadnezzar in 572 BC and to the Persians in 539 BC.

Following Alexander the Great's victory over the Persians at the battle of Issus (north of present-day Iskenderun in the Turkish Hatay) in 332 BC, he sent his general Parmenion to seize Damascus while he continued southwards along the Phoenician coast. At Alexander's death in 323 BC, his vast Asian empire was divided up among his generals, Seleucus establishing control over Syria and introducing Hellenistic town planning to Damascus. Though the Romans conquered Syria in 64 BC, they allowed the Nabateans, an Arab people, to exercise local control over Damascus to AD 54.

Under Roman rule Damascus became an increasingly important trading hub, especially for its cross-desert link with Palmyra. The city was ringed by walls and gates, and the worship of Hadad was absorbed in that of Jupiter in a vast new temple. A large Jewish population, some influenced by the teachings of Jesus, occasioned Paul's journey along the road to Damascus, his intention to punish the offenders, but resulting in his conversion. The city continued to be embellished by the Romans, and later, with the adoption of Christianity throughout the empire, by their successors in the East, the Byzantines, who made the Temple of Jupiter into the Church of St John.

In 635, only three years after the death of Mohammed, Damascus fell to a Muslim Arab army, which abandoned it again to defeat the Byzantines at the battle of Yarmuk, retaking the city in 636 and so ending nearly a thousand years of Western rule. In 661 Muawiya, the fifth caliph, made Damascus the capital of the Arab Empire, and by 715, with the completion of the Great Mosque on the site of the Church of St John, his Umayyad dynasty ruled over a Muslim world that stretched from the Indus to the Pyrenees.

But after only 90 years the Umayyads were overthrown by the Abbasids, who built Baghdad as the new capital of the Arab Empire. Damascus was sacked and so far as present remains are concerned, the next four hundred years are an architectural blank. In 878 Damascus fell to Ibn Tulun, governor of Egypt, who had made himself independent of the Abbasids; in 968 it fell to the Cairo-based Fatimids, a Shia dynasty of North African origin. Meanwhile, trade, political stability and population all declined, and the inhabitants of Damascus sought what security they could within their own religious and ethnic communities, so making a defensive maze out of the once open Graeco-Roman street grid of the city.

The First Crusade captured Jerusalem in 1099 and over the next forty years the Franks directed several attacks against Damascus. The consequence was a Muslim revival led from Aleppo by Nur al-Din who in 1154 entered Damascus and set about rebuilding its walls. His successor was Saladin (1176–93), who united Egypt and Syria under his rule and once more raised Damascus to importance. The city underwent a great rebuilding programme, not least in the establishment of Sunni madrasas to counter the Shia influence of the departed Fatimids. Saladin's Ayyubid dynasty gave way to the Egyptian-based Mamelukes who defeated the Mongols in 1260 and under Baybars especially (1260-77) drove the Crusaders from the East, but failed to save Damascus from the ravages of Timur (Tamerlane) in 1400.

In 1516 the Ottoman Sultan Selim entered Damascus. The city underpinned the Ottomans' claim to the caliphate which rested on their control of Mecca and the annual pilgrimage, for which Damascus became the last staging post between Turkey and the arduous three-week desert crossing. But the Ottoman governors of the city, with occasional exceptions such as that of Assad Pasha, were short-serving, short-sighted and exploitative in their office. In the 1830s the Damascenes eagerly supported Ibrahim Pasha, the son of Egypt's Mohammed Ali, in his campaign to wrest Syria from the Ottoman Empire. In 1860 a massacre of Christians in Damascus was touched off by the conflict between Druze and Maronites in Lebanon, where the French made a show of force. The triumph of the Arab Revolt was crowned by the seizing of Damascus in 1918, but instead of the independence they expected, the Syrians found themselves subject to the French Mandate. A Druze-led revolt that began in the Hauran and spread to Damascus was met by a French bombardment of the city in 1925. Not until 1945 did Damascus become the capital of an independent Syria.

Getting There and Away

By air: Damascus Airport is 30km southeast of the city. Getting through passport control can take quite some time, so do your best to get off the plane quickly and be at the front of the passport control queue. Make sure you are in the correct queue for foreigners.

When leaving Syria by air, there is a LS200 airport departure tax. You must buy a stamp at the small booth as you leave the checking-in area.

In the arrivals hall there is a bank for changing cash and travellers' cheques, also a post and telephone office, all open 24 hours. There is also a tourist information counter and bus, taxi, car hire and hotel counters. It may prove helpful to ask at the information counter for a second (though not necessarily reliable) opinion on bus and taxi prices.

Airline Offices

Most airline offices and travel agencies are in the vicinity of Yousef al-Azmeh Square (just east of the Cham Palace Hotel) or a short walk from it.

Air France: Al-Jabri Street, inside the Semiramis Hotel, ✆ (011) 2218580.

Air Malta: Port Said Street, ✆ (011) 2311700.

Alitalia: Fardoos Street, ✆ (011) 2222662.

Austrian Airlines: Maisaloun Street, opposite the Cham Palace, ✆ (011) 2236001.

British Airways (representing also **Qantas**): Argentina Street, near the Assad Bridge, ✆ (011) 3310000.

Cyprus Airways: Alani Avenue, just off 29 May Street, ✆ (011) 2225630.

Egyptair: Hejaz Square, by the railway station, ✆ (011) 2223992.

Gulf Air: Maisaloun Street, opposite the Cham Palace, ✆ (011) 2221209.

KLM: Fardoos Street, ✆ (011) 2211165.

LOT (Polish Airlines): Yousef al-Azmeh Square, ✆ (011) 2213441.

Lufthansa: Maisaloun Street, opposite the Cham Palace, ✆ (011) 2211165.

Malev: Fardoos Street, ✆ (011) 2226188.

MEA: 88–90 Barada Street, near Martyrs' Square, ✆ (011) 2224993.

Olympic Airways: Maisaloun Street, opposite the Cham Palace, ✆ (011) 2217720.

Royal Jordanian Airlines: 29 May Street, ✆ (011) 2211267.

Syrian Arab Airlines: Hejaz Square by the railway station for international flights, and on the roundabout (near the Central Bank of Syria) at the north end of 29 May Street for domestic flights; for both call ✆ (011) 2232154.

Turkish Airlines: Maisaloun Street, opposite the Cham Palace, ✆ (011) 2239770.

Nahas Travel and Tourism, Fardoos Street, ✆ (011) 2232000, represents a number of airlines, including several that do not fly into Damascus.

The airport bus runs half-hourly from 5.30am to midnight, dropping you a block north of Martyrs' Square at Al-Ittihad Street just east of Port Said Street in the downtown area. The journey takes 45 minutes and costs LS10.

Taxi companies at the airport charge $20 for the journey into central Damascus, though with some bargaining you can get this down to $10 or SL500, paying in either currency. If coming from town to the airport by yellow taxi, the standard fare is SL500.

By train: trains to and from Aleppo, Qamishli, Deir ez Zor, Latakia, Tartus, Hama, Homs and other destinations north of Damascus use the Kadam railway station in the Meidan suburb 3km south of downtown Damascus.

The Hejaz railway station, a beautiful turn-of-the-century Ottoman structure worth visiting in its own right, is a few blocks west of Martyrs' Square in downtown Damascus. It is served by trains to and from the Anti-Lebanon resort of Zabadani, Deraa and Bosra in the south of the country, and Amman in Jordan.

Long-distance Bus and Microbus Stations

Pullman bus station (Garagat al-Pullman al-Jadide) is about 3km east of Abbasid (Abbassayeen) Square (and about 5km east of Martyrs' Square in central Damascus). Luxury coaches operated by both private companies and state-owned Karnak run from here to destinations north and northeast of Damascus (e.g. Homs, Tartus, Latakia, Hama, Aleppo, Palmyra, Deir ez Zor, Qamishli). Departures are frequent, so it should not be necessary to book in advance, but if you want to make sure or wish to make enquiries, then several of these companies have offices near the centre of town, e.g. Zeitouni, by the Kairawan Hotel on Al-Ittahad Street near the corner of Yousef al-Azmeh Street (they also run a shuttle to the bus station); Damas Tour, under Assad Bridge; Kadmous, under Assad Bridge; Al Ahliah, Palestine Street, south of the National Museum.

Abbassayeen bus station (Garagat Abbassayeen), just under 1km east of Abbasid (Abbassayeen) Square, has ordinary buses departing for all and more of the destinations covered by the luxury coaches from the Pullman station.

Maalula bus station (Garagat Maaloula), a bit farther east of the Pullman station, has microbuses to Seidnaya and Maalula.

Baramkeh bus station (Garagat Baramkeh) is on Palestine Street south of the National Museum and near Damascus University. Ordinary buses and microbuses depart from here to destinations to the south of Damascus, e.g. Deraa, Bosra, Suweida; to the west, e.g. Zabadani; and a few to the northeast. This is also the station for international luxury coaches, with Karnak running services to Beirut and (along with JETT, the Jordanian state-owned company) to Amman. Note that tickets for Amman must be paid for in Jordanian dinars or US dollars. Other companies run services to Turkey, Saudi Arabia, Kuwait, Egypt and Libya.

Deraa bus station (Garagat Deraa), south of central Damascus and just south of Yarmuk Square, has bus and microbus services to Ezraa, Deraa, Shahba and Suweida.

By long-distance bus and microbus: there are several bus stations in Damascus serving different parts of the country and different types of vehicle (*see* box above), i.e. luxury coach, ordinary bus or microbus (for general information about buses, *see* p.4).

By long-distance service taxi: the long-distance and international service taxi depot is next door to the Baramkeh bus station (Garagat Baramkeh) on Palestine Street, south of the National Museum. Homs, Hama and Aleppo are common destinations, as are Beirut (and elsewhere in Lebanon) and Amman (and elsewhere in northern Jordan). There are also service taxis to towns in southern Syria from Bab Moussala at Yarmuk Square, about 1.2km south of central Damascus.

By hire car: for general information, *see* p.4 and pay particular attention to the notes concerning insurance and driving in Syria.

Among the numerous car hire firms, both international and local, that are now springing up in Damascus and elsewhere in Syria, the best remains Europcar with branches at the Sheraton (✆ (011) 2229300), Meridien (✆ (011) 2229200, Omayad (✆ (011) 2217700) and Semiramis (✆ (011) 2213813) hotels, and at the airport (✆ (011) 5431536).

By car with driver: as an alternative to hiring a car and driving it yourself, you can hire a car with driver. Several firms offer this, and also your hotel might be able to arrange it.

An excellent English-speaking driver with his own yellow Damascus taxi who can be recommended for taking you both round the country and the city is Abd el Nasser al-Shati, ☎ (011) 5411486/4419697, 📠 (011) 5225446.

Orientation

Damascus, including the Old City, is approximately orientated west–east, though with a somewhat northwest–southeast inclination. Therefore when a direction is described here as west, it may be more truly west-northwest, while east may more truly be east-southeast, and so on.

The Old City, that is the ancient walled city of Damascus, is the chief area of interest, and this together with the newer Ottoman extension immediately to its west is best covered on foot.

Modern downtown Damascus, where most of the hotels are, centres on this western area, mostly north of the Barada River which flows into Damascus from the Anti-Lebanon.

Getting Around

On foot: the Old City and the downtown area to its west and northwest are sufficiently compact to make walking practicable and indeed the best way of getting around. Reaching Salihiye on the slopes of Mount Kassioun to the north and Meidan to the south of the Old City involve sufficient distances that taking a taxi might be worthwhile, while getting to the summit of Mount Kassioun definitely requires a taxi.

By bus and minibus: the blue and white city buses have been almost entirely phased out in favour of the white microbuses (*meecro*). But using either is difficult as they display their route numbers and destinations in Arabic only, no route maps are available, and no information is posted at stops along the way. Damascenes seem to be born with the system imprinted into their minds; mere tourists are better off sticking to taxis.

However, if you want to give buses and microbuses a try, go to the central depot under Assad Bridge just west of the National Museum. By persistent asking you ought to be able to get to where you want to go. From here there are services to the Abbassayeen bus station (Garagat Abbassayeen), from where you can catch a microbus to the Pullman bus station (Garagat al-Pullman al-Jadide). To reach the Deraa bus station (Garagat Deraa), take a bus from Fakhri al-Baroudi Street south of Martyrs' Square.

Microbuses, unlike buses, can be flagged down en route. Both will cost no more than LS10.

Street water-seller

By taxi: Damascus' yellow taxis are a cheap alternative to a long walk or to grappling with the city bus and microbus system. Some taxis will have working meters, and you pay accordingly. Otherwise you should agree the fare beforehand: about LS30 for shorter journeys, LS60 to the outskirts of the city—these being close to double the fares that would be clocked up on a working meter. Their most welcome value is as a ride back to your hotel at the end of a day's exploration. Get your hotel to give you one of their cards in Arabic, or to write down their name and address in Arabic, so that you can show it to the taxi driver in case he does not speak English or know where your hotel is (though this will not help if your driver turns out to be illiterate). You can also ask someone at the hotel to repeat its name and address slowly while you write it down phonetically so that you can repeat it later.

The one place to which you will need to take a taxi if you do not have your own car is the summit of Kassioun. You can strike a reasonable deal with the driver to take you up, wait an hour, and then bring you back into town. If you take a taxi up to Kassioun and discharge it, do not count on being able to find another to take you back down.

By private taxi or hire car with driver: you can also hire a taxi by the day, or for several days, combining for example a half-day round Damascus with a half-day excursion to Seidnaya and Maalula, or for a day's excursion to Shahba, Suweida, Qanawat, Bosra and Ezraa. Abd el Nasser al-Shati, who is English-speaking and has his own yellow taxi, is recommended (*see* p.51). Several car hire firms also offer this service. Also some hotels will make arrangements for you.

Car hire: for travelling round within Damascus you are probably much better off hiring taxis as you need them or a car with driver by the day. *See* above and also pp.4 and 50 for further information.

Tours: the usual tour on offer is to the Souk al-Hamidiye, the Umayyad Mosque, the Azem Palace, and along Straight Street to Bab Sharqi with visits to St Paul's Window and the House of Ananias. Saladin's Tomb, the Epigraphy Museum (Madrasa Djaqmaqiya), the Tekkiye Mosque and the National Museum might also be included. Tours include guide, entrance fees and transport by car or minibus. There are also tours to Seidnaya and Maalula and to Palmyra.

Among the better known tour companies offering tours of Damascus and beyond are American Express, Sudan Airways Building, 1st Floor, Balkis Street (between Fardoos and Montanabi streets), ✆ (011) 2217813; Adonis, 34–6 Montanabi Street, ✆ (011) 2236272; and Mimoza, Halbouni Street, behind the Hejaz railway station, ✆ (011) 2235707.

Tourist Information

There is a tourist information counter in the arrivals hall at the airport, which is meant to be open 24hrs daily, closed Fridays. As with the other tourist offices mentioned below, opening times should be taken with a handful of salt.

In town, the main Tourist Office is on the west side of 29 May Street, just north of the Peasants' Monument in Yousef al-Azmeh Square. It is open 23hrs daily (*closed 8–9am*). There is a smaller office at the Ministry of Tourism building, which is by the east entrance to the craftsmen's souk which runs in front of the Selimiye Madrasa adjacent to the Tekkiye Mosque (*open 24hrs daily, closed Fri*).The staff speak English and try to be helpful. With any luck they will have a supply of their free map of Syria, which has plans of Damascus, Aleppo and Palmyra on the reverse, and they can provide brochures and maps to other parts of the country, as well as hotel and travel information.

communications

The **central post office** is at the north end of Said al-Jabri Street (which runs from the Hejaz railway station to Al-Quwatli Street). It is open Sat–Thurs 8–7, also on Fri and holidays 8–1 (but for stamps only). You can have letters sent to you here and you will need your passport to collect them (Sat–Thurs, 8–5). You should be addressed as follows: Your name, Syria, Damascus, Poste Restante. There are also post offices in every district of Damascus and, given sharp eyes, you might also spot the occasional red letter box.

To mail a parcel, go to the parcel office behind the central post office. Take your parcel unwrapped and a customs official will examine it. You cannot send any item that has been imported into Syria, nor antiques, carpets (except prayer rugs), medicines or cigarettes. Next you will be asked to fill in four forms per parcel and if it exceeds 20kg you must fill in another four. You can then wrap the parcel yourself, either using the box you have brought with you or purchasing one on the spot (many people like to first slip their goods into a plastic bag). There are numerous men hanging about who will undertake the entire process for you, from customs to packing, charging about LS400.

A **courier service** is operated by DHL next to the Madina Hotel on Omar bin Abi Rabea Street, which curves west off Al-Jabri Street towards the Tekkiye Mosque, ✆ (011) 2227692.

Telephone calls can be made 24 hours a day from the Telecommunications Building in Al-Nasr Street just east of the Hejaz railway station. Costs are very much less than those charged by the major hotels. Be sure to take your passport. To make an international phone call, go to the small office on your right to hand over your passport. Give the phone number and wait until you are told which phone box to go into. When it rings, pick up the hand set. Afterwards go back to the office to pay and collect your passport. There is a 3min minimum. Phone cards are also sold here which can then be used in the card-phones outside, though these are often very busy and you may have to wait up to 30mins. Local phone calls can be made at the pay phones in the Telecommunications Building or from the red phone booths here and there about the city.

Faxes and **telegrams** can also be sent from the Telecommunications Building between 8am and 10pm. You must enter your passport number on the message form.

embassies

Australia: 128A Farabi Street, Al Mezzeh, ✆ (011) 6132424.
Canada: Autostrade, Al Mezzeh, ✆ (011) 6116692.
Jordan: Al Jalaa Street, Abu Rumaneh, ✆ (011) 3334642/3339313.
Turkey: Hejaz Street, Abu Rumaneh, ✆ (011) 3331411/2.
UK (representing also Ireland and New Zealand): Kotob Building, 11 Mohammed Kurd Ali Street, Malki, ✆ (011) 3712561/2/3.
USA: 2 Al Mansour Street, Abu Rumaneh, POB 29, ✆ (011) 3718678.

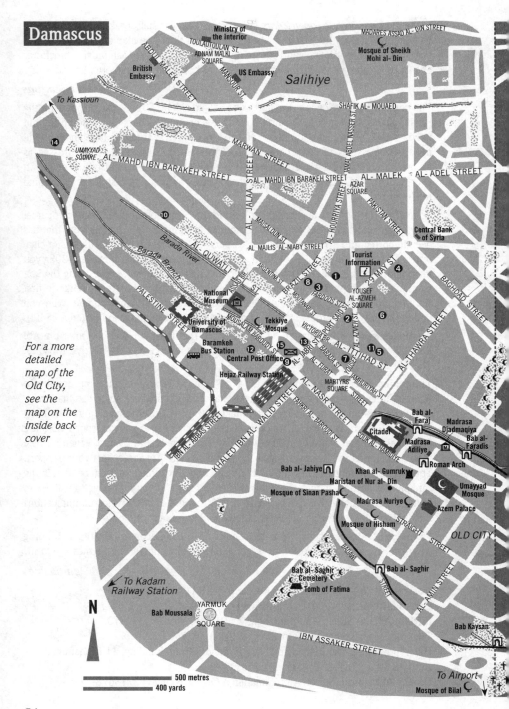

Damascus

Salihiye

Ministry of the Interior

British Embassy

US Embassy

MADARES ASSAD AL-DIN STREET

Mosque of Sheikh Mohi al-Din

TOULAUTOULAN ST.

ADNAM MALKI SQUARE

MANSOUR ST.

ABDUL MALEK STREET

To Kassioun

UMAYYAD SQUARE

14

AL-MAHDI IBN BARAKEH STREET

MARWAN STREET

SHAFIK AL-MOUAED

AL-MAHDI IBN BARAKEH STREET

AL-MALEK

AL-ADEL STREET

AZAR SQUARE

JAMAL ABDEL NASSER STR.

AL-HOURRIYA STREET

AL-JALAA STREET

PAKISTAN STREET

BAGHDAD STREET

Central Bank of Syria

10

MAISALOUN ST.

AL-QUWATLI

Barada River

Barada Branch

AL-MAJLIS AL-NIABY STREET

ARGENTINA ST.

AL-ASFER ST.

BRAZIL STREET

MOUSALAM BAROUDY ST.

FARDOOS ST.

PORT SAID ST.

YOUSEF AL-AZMEH SQUARE

Tourist Information

i

29 MAY ST.

4

1

8

3

2

6

PALESTINE STREET

National Museum

University of Damascus

Tekkiye Mosque

Baramkeh Bus Station

Central Post Office

12

15

13

9

AL-JABRI ST.

VICTORIA BR.

AL-AZMEH ST.

AL-ITTIHAD ST.

AL-FURAT ST.

BARADA ST.

AL-JAMHURIYAH ST.

11

5

7

AL-THAWRA STREET

Hejaz Railway Station

FAHRI AL-BAROUDI ST.

AL-NASR STREET

MARTYRS SQUARE

STREET

IBN AL-ABBAS STREET

KHALED IBN AL-WALID STREET

For a more detailed map of the Old City, see the map on the inside back cover

Citadel

SOUK AL-HAMIDIYE

Bab al-Faraj

Madrasa Djadmaqiya

Madrasa Adiliye

Bab al-Faradis

M

Roman Arch

Bab al-Jabiye

Khan al-Gumruk

Maristan of Nur al-Din

Mosque of Sinan Pasha

Madrasa Nuriye

Umayyad Mosque

Azem Palace

Mosque of Hisham

STRAIGHT STREET

OLD CITY

AL-AMIN STREET

To Kadam Railway Station

BADAWI

Bab al-Saghir Cemetery

Tomb of Fatima

Bab al-Saghir

N

Bab Moussala

YARMUK SQUARE

Bab Kaysan

IBN ASSAKER STREET

To Airport

500 metres

400 yards

Mosque of Bilal

Hotels

1. Cham Palace
2. Damascus Int'l
3. Fardoos Tower
4. French Tower
5. Al Haramain
6. Al Majed
7. Omar Khayam
8. Omayad
9. Orient Palace
10. Meridien
11. Al Rabie
12. Salam
13. Semiramis
14. Sheraton
15. Sultan

health and emergencies

Your embassy or hotel can put you in touch with a local doctor or hospital if necessary, though for minor ailments a pharmacist can often help, both diagnosing your trouble and prescribing an appropriate medicine. The best pharmacy in Damascus is the Kanawati Principale on Yousef al-Azmeh Square. For general information on health, *see* pp.14–15.

Ambulance (government), ✆ 110; **ambulance** (Red Crescent), 8am–2pm, ✆ (011) 3331441; 2pm–8pm, ✆ (011) 4443109 (office numbers). **Police**, ✆ 112; **traffic police**: ✆ 115; **fire**, ✆ 113.

maps and publications

The best map of Syria, which also includes detailed maps of Damascus and Aleppo and a plan of Palmyra, is published by Freytag and Berndt.

The Tourist Information Offices provide a good free map of Syria, including Damascus, Aleppo and Palmyra.

The three best bookshops in Damascus are **Librairie Universelle**, on the corner of Port Said and Bahsa streets, just south of Yousef al-Azmeh Square, with also a small shop in the Cham Palace Hotel; **Librairie Avicenne**, Tahjiz Street, near the Omayed Hotel, with branches at the Meridien and the Sheraton; and the **Family Bookshop**, Al Majlis al-Niaby Street, just east of its intersection with Maisaloun Street. All sell English-language books, newspapers and magazines.

money

You can change cash and travellers' cheques at branches of the Commercial Bank of Syria. There are branches at Yousef al-Azmeh Square and at the Meridien and Sheraton hotels, and exchange kiosks in Martyrs' Square and in the Hejaz railway station. There is also a 24hr bank at the airport.

needs and services

Repairs of all kinds (shoes, clothing, zips) are undertaken on the spot by the ranks of sewing machine men on Al-Thawra Street just north of the Citadel.

There are studios for **instant photographs** (for visas, etc.) on Maisaloun Street near the Cham Palace Hotel and near the Immigration Office on Palestine Street, just west of the Baramkeh bus station.

For a cheap shave and haircut with atmosphere there is a **barber** opposite the Nawfarah Café at the bottom of the steps on the east side of the Umayyad Mosque.

For a **Turkish bath** and massage (men only), try the 12th-century Hamam Nur al-Din (*see* p.81), just north of Khan Assad Pasha. Women can go to the Bakri Baths near Bab Touma (*see* p.89).

If you get caught short in the Old City, there is a **men's toilet** next to the Nawfarah Café on the east side of the Umayyad Mosque and **men's and women's toilets** across the street from the southwest corner of the mosque.

visas

Visa extentions. To extend your visa, go to the Immigration and Passport Department (written in English and Arabic) on Palestine (Filastin) Street, one block west of the Baramkeh bus station. You will need three photographs, which can be obtained near by (apart from an instant photo studio there is also a fellow with an old wooden box camera on a tripod). Go to the third floor, fill in three forms, and hand over your three photographs together with your passport. There is no fee. Ask for at least a two-week extension, longer if you need it. No questions are asked; the procedure is quite efficient. They close at 2pm, so get there by 1pm and you can collect your visa at 1pm the following day.

Re-entry visa. If you do not have a multiple-entry visa for Syria and you want to visit Lebanon and return, go to the Passport and Immigration office on Furat Street between Al-Jabri Street and Martyrs' Square. They fax your details to the border post (you will have to specify where you are re-entering), where they will issue you with and charge you for your re-entry visa.

Qunaitra (Golan) permits. Qunaitra (*see* p.122), in the demilitarised zone of the Golan Heights, requires a permit: take your passport to the Ministry of the Interior (*open daily, 8–2, closed Fri*) on Toulaitoulah Street next to the Kuwaiti Embassy (and not far from the British and US embassies) in the northwest of the city. The permit is quickly issued on the spot and must be used on the day you specify, which they may insist should be the following day.

Along the Barada

The Barada flows down from the Anti-Lebanon and until early in the 20th century passed through a great meadow to the west of the Old City. Here 500 years ago and more the Mamelukes paraded their troops, and in the late 17th century Henry Maundrell found cool shaded coffee houses along the stream banks and observed Turks 'regaling themselves in this pleasant place; there being nothing which they behold with so much delight as greens and water: to which if a beautiful face be added, they have a proverb, that all three together make a perfect antidote against melancholy'. The Barada continued, as it does today, along the north walls of the Old City, its waters feeding all the cisterns and fountains of Damascus.

But now the meadows have been built over and the Barada is a stagnant open sewer, full of vegetation, scum, plastic bottles, rubber tyres and general waste. Farther upstream, beyond the Sheraton, the river is less stomach-turning and there are still a few open-air eating places by its banks. You follow its course towards the Old City, however, only because it is convenient to do so—Al-Quwatli Street, the principal western approach to the city, parallels the river—and because the National Museum, the Tekkiye Mosque and a few other points of interest are along the way.

The National Museum

Open daily 9–6, closed 12.30pm–2pm Fri and all day Tues; adm.

The National Museum, containing a world-class archaeological and historical collection, is immediately south of Al-Quwatli Street and the Barada and a block west of the Tekkiye Mosque. It is about 1.5km west of the Old City.

The posted opening times should be double-checked by personal enquiry, as variations may occur between summer and winter and at Ramadan, and also because 'anything can happen in this country', as the man at the ticket kiosk says. Cameras must be left at the entrance (checked free), where also postcards, books and an excellent guide to the museum are for sale. Most exhibits are labelled, though usually in French and Arabic or Arabic only.

The collection requires a half-day's visit to see the highlights. After a general survey of the collection, it is worthwhile returning to particular exhibits either before or especially after visiting sites around the country.

You enter from the north and there are two wings: the new **west wing** to your right, built in 1953 and since enlarged, which contains the **pre-classical and Arab-Islamic collections**, and the old **east wing** to your left, built in 1936, which contains the **classical and Byzantine collections**.

Therefore to see things chronologically you would have first to visit the pre-classical collection in the west wing, then go to the east wing for the classical and Byzantine collections, and finally return to the west wing for the Arab-Islamic collection. Even then, matters are not entirely straightforward, for the contents of cases change, exhibits are moved, and sometimes what is supposed to be in one room turns out to be in another, if you can find it at all. Your exploration of the museum, therefore, should be undertaken with a certain sense of adventure.

So far as this description is concerned, first the west wing and then the east wing will be covered and then only the highlights mentioned.

Entering the Museum

Entering the museum precincts from the north, you pass through a **garden** well-planted with trees, shrubs and classical statuary and architectural elements. There is also a very pleasant outdoor café here (with clean toilets adjacent). You then come to the north façade of the museum created from the shattered stucco fragments of the twin-towered **gateway of Qasr al-Heir al-Gharbi** (*see* p.264), the 8th-century Umayyad desert palace whose remains you can visit on the way to Palmyra. Notice on the towers the relief busts of bare-breasted dancing girls, an indication of how the Umayyads, the first Islamic dynasts of Syria, were anything but puritanical. More decorative and architectural details from the palace, such as fine latticed windows, are on display inside the entrance vestibule, along with two scale models, one of the palace as found, the other as it was originally, a central square enclosed by two-storeyed arcades of Corinthian columns off which were the palace apartments.

The West Wing

Turning right into the west wing, you come to two rooms devoted to finds from **Ras Shamra (Ugarit)** (*see* p.197), the Bronze Age site on the Mediterranean coast north of Latakia.

In the first room, in Case 4, note item 12-63, the small finger-shaped clay tablet bearing the thirty characters of **Ugaritic alphabet** of the 14th century BC. It is not the world's oldest alphabet, as the Syrians claim (that honour belongs to an alphabet derived from Egyptian hieroglyphs and found in Sinai), but it is nearly so and it would have been from ports like Ugarit that the alphabet was transmitted to the wider Mediterranean world. Also in this first room, Case 10 contains some intricately carved **ivories**, while in Case 12 is the finely-formed **ivory head**, perhaps of a prince, found in the royal palace.

In the second Ras Shamra room, Case 14 contains a fascinating collection of **cylinder seals**. They are finely carved with religious and social scenes which you can barely make sense of on the cylinders themselves, but when they are rolled across soft clay they leave a wonderfully detailed impression, as examples here show—like comic strips. Ugaritic craftsmanship is always of a high standard, the work of a sophisticated court culture, which can seem at times too formalised, and so it comes as something of a relief to encounter, as in Case 17, the seemingly naive **Mycenaean pottery** imported from Greece. Dashed off with painted figures of dolphins and octopi and galloping chariots, they delight in the curving line, in movement and character.

Beyond the Ras Shamra rooms is a long gallery devoted to other Bronze Age sites of both the coast and the interior. Turning right and doubling back, you pass through rooms devoted to **Mari** (*see* p.258), the Bronze Age site on the Euphrates, where in Case 6, displaying the mid-3rd millennium BC **Treasure of King Cansud**, there is a marvellous gold and lapis lazuli **eagle**. In this showcase and elsewhere you are often struck by a variety of human figures with characteristic large eyes and arched eyebrows, always a look of surprise on their faces as though happily brain-damaged.

(*If you want to continue with an attempt at a chronological tour of the museum, you should now go to the east wing (see below) and then return to the west wing to finish off with the Islamic period described here.*)

Following the Mari rooms you leap forward several thousand years to the hall containing finds from **Raqqa** (*see* p.248), the great Abbasid city on the Euphrates, where the outstanding piece, in Case 8, is the 12th-century polychrome ceramic **mounted horseman**, the figure Chinese and probably imported from Turkestan.

From here, turning left, you again double back, passing along the first and second galleries containing **coins, jewellery and armour**, mostly Islamic, off which are rooms devoted to **Islamic ceramics and glass**, the most exquisite objects in the museum. The glass especially is immensely appealing—for its beauty and also for its fragility which is a part of that beauty, and because you marvel that in spite of its fragility it has survived.

Beyond this, at the northwest corner of the west wing, is the **Damascus Salon**, a wood- and marble-panelled hall from an 18th-century palace of the Old City, though the decorative motifs are 19th-century. Here you should ask the keeper to turn on the fountains.

The East Wing

Again beginning at the entrance vestibule, turn left into the east wing and enter what is called the second gallery (running northwards) containing **pottery, glassware and sculpture** from the Phoenician to the classical periods. Cases 12, 14, 15 and 16 all contain lovely pieces of earthenware, ceramic and glass. In Case 13 are green enamelled ceramics of the type called Alexandrian because originally manufactured there, though the technique was soon imitated in Syria. The finest example is item C7619, found in the neighbourhood of Homs, depicting **Kore**, daughter of Demeter.

Off this gallery, to the left, are the **Hauran and Jebel al-Arab** rooms (*see* p.99). Black basalt was the locally available material for buildings and sculpture, a hard rock and difficult to work, which you immediately appreciate from the crudeness of the sculpture here, though you also wonder if the conception and technique were in any case poor, as though the hopeless task was left to hacks. From the Hauran come the black stone blocks used in the characteristic black and white *ablaq* of Damascene Islamic architecture. Of white marble is a 2nd-century AD **Roman sarcophagus** carved in high relief with deep undercutting, depicting a battle on sea and land. And having nothing to do with the region is the **mosaic pavement representing the Orontes** (*see* p.148), found near Latakia.

Now return to the entrance vestibule and enter the corridor running eastwards, called the first gallery, containing **classical statues** of ivory, bronze and marble found at Palmyra, Apamea and Latakia. Most notable are the marble **statue of Aspasia**, Pericles' mistress, found at Hama, item 2711 in Case 1, and the bronze **bust of a woman**, possibly a princess, item C16967 in Case 6.

In contrast to the magnificence of the Palmyra site is the tedious tomb sculpture of its inhabitants, as you discover in the **Palmyra** room to the right off the first gallery. You feel that, once bereft of their merchant activities, they had nothing to say, certainly nothing about human character or matters of the spirit. With no more deals to do, their sculptured features are heavy and blank. Palmyrene taste improves, however, when the subject is not death: on the south wall, and discovered in a Palmyrene house, is a 3rd-century **mosaic of Cassiope** who reveals her nude beauty to the Nereids.

(*To continue with Palmyra, you could now visit the hypogeum of Yarhai, which otherwise you come to after the Dura Europos room and synagogue.*)

Adjacent is the **Dura Europos** room displaying finds from the Hellenistic and Roman site on the Euphrates (*see* p.255). The **frescoes** on the east and west walls, both from the temple of the Palmyrene gods, are interesting for the glimpse they give you of Palmyrenes in a medium other than stone sculpture. Note especially on the east wall fresco the colouring of the jewels and the extraordinary headdress of Konon's daughter. The lightness of line and washed out pastels give it the feeling of something between a Japanese print and a Mondrian.

The prize of the museum, also from Dura Europos, is the mid-2nd-century AD **synagogue**, reconstructed beyond the east end of the first gallery, across the courtyard. Against Talmudic injunctions, its walls are covered with paintings of human figures representing scenes from the Scriptures, the style both Parthian and rustically local, the colours bold, each panel like a comic book frame, the Judgement of Solomon in one, in several the hand of God reaching down from the sky, in another winged angels fluttering over a carnage of disembodied heads and limbs, while on the beamed ceiling the panels are painted with faces, fish, flowers, fruit, centaurs, eyes and pine cones. They are entirely entertaining, but their point is messianic. The experience of such catastrophes as Nebuchadnezzar's destruction of Jerusalem early in the 6th century BC and with it the Temple of Solomon, and again Titus' siege of Jerusalem in AD 70 and his destruction of the Temple built by Herod, promoted a messianic outlook among many Jews that was given focus on the walls of *his* temple by the rabbi at Dura Europos. The walls have three registers, each depicting a cycle: Salvation below, the Witness of Salvation above, and between them the cycle of Trials. The messianic temple is itself depicted on the east wall, where the prayer niche, surmounted by a sea shell cupola, prefigures the apse and mihrab of later churches and mosques.

Stairs between the first gallery and the synagogue lead down to the early 2nd-century underground tomb or **hypogeum of Yarhai**, removed here from the Valley of the Tombs in Palmyra. Here in that same coolness that you experience in the actual tombs, you see how up to about fifty bodies of the family could be slotted into shelves around the walls like so much left-luggage, with a bust of the deceased slapped onto each door panel—in this case, two hundred years' worth of Yarhais. Death is conventionally represented by the veil partly drawn across the faces of the women or a shawl over the right shoulder of the men. At the far end of the main vault to the right is the triclinium, site of the funeral banquet. Emerging from the hypogeum into the vestibule called the Hall of the Museum, you see a number of statues from Shahba (*see* p.103) and elsewhere, the finest for sheer beauty and sensuality being item C4857 found at Latakia, **Aphrodite** draped in a wet form-clinging robe.

You can now return to the museum entrance through the **Byzantine** rooms where in Case 1 are the handsome 12th-century finds made at Resafa (*see* p.244) in 1982.

The Tekkiye Mosque Complex

The Tekkiye Mosque is immediately east of the National Museum and on the south side of the Barada just over a kilometre west of the Old City. Built at the command of Suleiman the Magnificent, the mosque, still a place of worship, is a modestly proportioned masterpiece and the finest Ottoman monument in the city. Its architect was Sinan, who was given the commission in 1554 and drew up the plans in Istanbul, his work executed in six years by Christian converts to Islam. Sinan also designed the arcaded buildings that surround the mosque's courtyard on its north, east and west sides, originally to accommodate Whirling Dervishes (a tekke is a monastery for dervishes), though later it served as a khan to house pilgrims bound for Mecca. Incongruously, the former kitchens and refectory of the khan now house a shoddy military museum. To the east, and adjacent to the mosque and khan, is the Selimiye Madrasa, a koranic school, built during the reign of Suleiman's successor, Sultan Selim II (1566-74), and not the work of Sinan. The prayer room of the madrasa still serves as a school, while the buildings round its court have been given over to craftsmen.

Entering the **courtyard** of the Tekkiye Mosque from the east, perhaps the best thing to do is to get the **Military Museum** (small entry fee) out of the way first. For the most part a collection of clapped-out modern weaponry, it spills into the courtyard garden where howitzers, armoured vehicles, a Russian space capsule and the remains of shot-down Israeli jets blight your initial appreciation of Sinan's mosque, though at least families of ducks delight in the shade of the Syrian Air Force MiG standing amid the shrubbery. There is more of this sort of thing inside what used to be the refectory and kitchens in the north wing of the khan. The one worthwhile room is mysteriously identified as containing 'The White Wlapons', full of swords, daggers, helmets and mail, as well as models of siege engines, most of these items 13th-century and so contemporary with the collapse of the Crusader states and with the Mongol invasion. Many of the swords are finely damascened in silver or gold.

Now, trying to put the intrusive museum behind you, you can begin enjoying the masterly beauty of Sinan's architecture. Round three sides of the courtyard with its pool and splashing fountain are the wings of what were originally quarters for the Whirling Dervishes, a Turkish Sufi sect founded in 13th-century Konya by the poet, philosopher and mystic Celaleddin Rumi (Jalal ud-Din Rumi). This helps explain the monastic tranquillity of the place, which later became a **khan** for Mecca pilgrims, its interplay of arches, chimneys and smaller and larger domes combining in harmonious rhythm.

On the south side of the court is the **mosque** itself, with two slender minarets rising on either side of a low dome. Though best known for his great imperial mosques such as the Suleimaniye in Istanbul and the Selimiye in Edirne, you recognise Sinan's touch at its most delicate here in the elegant proportions of the seven-arched, slope-roofed double porch, reminiscent of the Sokollu Mehmet Pasha Camii, the most beautiful of his smaller mosques in Istanbul. The arches of black and white *ablaq* (a Syrian gesture) are lifted by smooth mono-lithic columns of grey and pink marble surmounted by lozenge capitals.

If the mosque is locked, a look of persistent curiosity will eventually attract the keeper with the key. Inside it is adorned with fine tiles with clear colours and that special deep tomato red of impenetrable opacity that distinguishes Iznik work of the highest period. The dome rests on an inclined drum pierced by Romanesque windows filled with coloured glass and is supported by four arches springing from the walls, the absence of interior columns enhancing the sense of space.

Leaving the courtyard through its east gate you enter the smaller but charming vine-trellised court of the **Selimiye Madrasa**, surrounded by artisans' workshops and with a modest craftsmen's souk filling the lane running alongside, selling copper, carpets, jewellery, leaded glass, inlaid boxes and so on. The place is agreeable for its isolation and stillness and does not suffer from MiG fighters and other military junk standing about and so makes a delightful first impression. The prayer hall to the south, however, the work of a Persian architect, stands no comparison with Sinan's mosque next door, the high dome and narrow triple-arched porch having a squat feeling. On the other hand, the porch and façade are nicely decorated with jiggled black, white and red (only painted) *ablaq*, while some bands are ornamented with tile and terracotta.

Around Martyrs' Square

The Barada soon disappears beneath streets and buildings as you walk eastwards along Al-Quwatli Street towards the Old City. At Al-Jabri Street (with the Semiramis Hotel on the corner) turn right (south) for the short walk past the Central Post Office to the **Hejaz railway station**, one of the last Ottoman buildings in the city, built in 1913 in a delightful fusion of Syrian and Turkish styles and with a magnificent ceiling. Trains depart from here for Zabadani (*see* p.125) in the Anti-Lebanon, Deraa (*see* p.117) in the Hauran, and Amman in Jordan. An open-air restaurant is situated along one of the platforms where there is an antique train, the locomotive Swiss-made in 1894, the carriages with sleeping rooms and salons German-made in 1913. If you now walk eastwards again from the station along Al-Nasr Street you come to the Old City, the entrance to the Souk al-Hamidiye almost directly in front of you, the Citadel to the left (north).

Or if you work your way northwards off Al-Nasr Street you come in a couple of blocks to **Martyrs' Square** (Place Merjeh) with its curious column wound with telegraph wires and poles and surmounted by the bronze model of a mosque. Damascus was the operational centre for the Ottoman and German forces in the Middle East during the First World War and was governed with an increasingly iron hand as the Arab Revolt, in which T. E. Lawrence played an important part, spread northwards. The square owes its name to the Syrian patriots who were hanged here by the Ottomans during the war. The **Telegraph Column** is explained as commemorating the completion of the first telegraph line to Mecca, among other things permitting the Damascenes to obtain instant notice of the sighting of the new moon which inaugurates Ramadan, the month of fasting. The area north of the square has been undergoing considerable redevelopment. Formerly the square itself marked the centre of modern Damascus, but that has drifted northwards. Heading east from the square brings you to the Citadel.

The Old City

As you explore the Old City you should refer to the detailed colour map on the inside back cover.

The Old City is described in five sections: the Souk al-Hamidiye to the Umayyad Mosque; the interior of the mosque; places of interest around the mosque; an exploration of souks, khans and the Azem Palace, all to the south of the Umayyad Mosque; and finally a walk along Straight Street and excursions following the southern and northern walls. The first section begins after pausing at the Citadel, while the last section ends at the Citadel.

The **Citadel**, which stands at the northwest corner of the Old City, is not to be compared for impressiveness to that of Aleppo. For one thing it stands on level ground and is largely hemmed in by more recent buildings. For another it was allowed to fall to ruin during the four hundred years of Ottoman rule, and indeed Baedeker recorded in 1912 that it was 'shortly to be demolished'. As it happens, the Ottomans were demolished first and over recent years the Citadel has been undergoing heavy restoration with the intention of using it as a technical or crafts college. Until 1985 it was a prison.

The Roman castrum or military camp was here, and probably the site was a stronghold long before that. What stands today dates largely from the Ayyubid and Mameluke periods and helped preserve Damascus from three Crusader attacks in the 13th century, though both the Mongols in 1260 and Tamerlane in 1400 did it considerable damage, which later the Turks hardly bothered to repair. Even so, John Green could describe the Citadel in 1736 as being 'like a little town, having its own streets and houses'. Nearly fifty years earlier Maundrell managed to get just within the gate, 'where we saw store of ancient arms and armour, the spoils of the Christians in former times. Among the artillery was an old Roman balista. At the east end of the castle there hangs down in the middle of the wall a short chain cut in stone; of what use I know not, unless to boast the skill of the artificer'.

Outside the Citadel and charging into the traffic is an impressive equestrian statue of Saladin.

Along the Souk al-Hamidiye to the Great Mosque of the Umayyads

Except on its west side between the Citadel and Straight Street, the **Old City** is still encompassed by its **walls**, originally over 5km in circumference. The walls preserve the ancient plan of Damascus (longer from east to west than from north to south, though in Roman times it was more rectangular, the Arabs having rounded its corners to create its present oval form), and indeed it is easy to distinguish the large and well-hewn Roman masonry of the lower courses from the progressively inferior Arab and Ottoman upper courses. Entrance to the walled city of Damascus in Roman times was by one of eight gates to which the Ayyubids added a ninth. All survive except the Roman gate called by the Arabs Bab al-Nasr, the Gate of Victory, pulled down in 1863. Its site in the now missing western walls of the Old City corresponds to the entrance to the Souk al-Hamidiye.

The **Souk al-Hamidiye** is the principal bazaar street of the Old City and runs 500m from west to east, ending at the Roman arch that stands before the square in front of the Umayyad Mosque. This was not the decumanus maximus, the major east–west street of Roman cities (Straight Street was that); instead it follows the line of the western approach to the Temple of Jupiter, whose site is now occupied by the mosque. Nor was it always the broad and direct thoroughfare that it is today. Over the centuries the approach became constricted and in places built over, so that in the Reverend J. L. Porter's *Five Years in Damascus*, published in 1855, his map shows a street working its way round the southern and eastern walls of the Citadel, and from there a series of streets wiggling southeastwards to the Roman arch. In fact the clearance operation that resulted in the Souk al-Hamidiye began only in 1873 and was completed, corrugated roofing and all, during the reign of the Ottoman Sultan Abdel Hamid II (1876–1909), after whom it is named. It therefore lacks the oriental atmosphere of many of the older souks in Damascus, not to mention those in Aleppo, and is more like walking through an extremely long Victorian railway station without the power and delicacy of Brunel's arches at Paddington. The Souk al-Hamidiye is more a transitional passage from the modern outer world to the ancient inner one of Old Damascus.

The Hamidiye and the other souks are dead on Fridays but are otherwise lively places, especially in the evenings up until about seven-thirty or eight o'clock, corresponding in summer with the last call to prayer. Then under the supervision of the police, the shutters are drawn down, as they are all day Friday when kids zoom through the deserted souks on their bicycles, only a couple of pudding shops open as groups of worshippers walk along the Hamidiye to the Umayyad Mosque.

For much of its distance the souk is arched over with high iron ribs sheeted with corrugated metal. You notice a great number of holes in the roof, bright buttons of light, some evidently where rivets have worked loose, others in lines and clusters caused by French bombardments and aircraft fire during the Druze-led rebellion of 1925. It is also said that the Bedouin would sometimes celebrate their shopping trips to Damascus with the occasional shotgun blast.

The Hamidiye is a souk for general goods and tourist tat, including shoes, sandals, men's and women's clothing from *galabiyyas* to gold lamé toreador pants, English worsted, carpets, *narghilehs*, jewellery, chessboards and boxes inlaid with coloured woods and mother of pearl, plaques inlaid with Koranic verses or in English with 'In God We Trust', brassware of all kinds from lamps to charcoal burners to pilgrims on horseback, Dior cosmetics, American deodorants, keychains with miniature $100 bills, musical instruments (*ouds, rababs, nais, riqs, dufs, tablas, kanoons*), watches, swords, daggers, mosquito curtains and inflatable plastic Santa Clauses. Best of all are the stalls selling cold yoghurt drinks and a sticky ice cream (*kaimak*) sprinkled with crushed pistachios. And then there are the itinerant musicians and that most popular of street cries, 'Marlboro, Marlboro', with such occasional variations as 'Boll Moll' (Pall Mall) and 'Lucky Lucky Lucky Lucky Lucky'. Back in Martyrs' Square it is the same—big distributors breaking open cartons of cigarettes, passing on handfuls of packs to the street boys. This is the regular arrival of new shipments from Lebanon. It is remarkable how good the distribution system is: earlier in the afternoon nothing, but by late afternoon the shipment is all over the city, and at the same fixed price everywhere.

The Giving-Up-Smoking-Man

It is then that the Giving-Up-Smoking-Man does a roaring trade. The police occasionally take away hawkers who have illegally spread out their wares in the middle of the thoroughfare and who have been too slow to run for it— though in fact they generally have a good early warning system and can be seen from a distance gathering up their gewgaws into shawls or boxes, this motion repeated like a rolling wave all along the souk as the police approach and losing itself in the sea of people. Moments later, when the coast is clear, you see them back again where they were, for all the world like immovable barnacles. The whole thing seems silly, a game, and you would think it would make everyone, hawkers and police and crowds alike, smile. But the hawkers are genuinely nervous about being caught.

Only the Giving-Up-Smoking-Man does not give a damn. He stands at the mouth of the Hamidiye delivering a wonderful spiel, a fascinated crowd around him. His hands are filled with cigarettes which to onlookers' gasps he snaps one by one in his fingers, and then produces his magical giving-up-smoking-pills which go like hot cakes. A policeman comes up behind him, and the Giving-Up-Smoking-Man reaches his hand behind his back to give him a confiding shake, and the policeman joins in with the crowd, for this is not selling, it seems, especially as no Syrian in his right mind would consider giving up smoking, rather more an ancient entertainment and popular mystery.

By making a short diversion off the Souk al-Hamidiye you can visit one of the most beautiful and fascinating places in Damascus, the hospital or **Maristan of Nur al-Din**, Saladin's predecessor (*open 8–2 daily, closed Fri; adm*). When built in 1154 it was the most advanced medical institution in the world. It continued in use as a hospital until the 19th century and since 1978 has been a museum of Arab science and medicine. To find it, walk east along the Souk al-Hamidiye to a point where the roof gives way to sky (beyond this, where the souk angles slightly to the left, the roofing resumes). If you have been counting, this is at the fifth intersecting street. Here you turn right and can immediately see about 50m distant the red stalactite dome of the maristan on the left.

A stalactite portal over a classical pediment marks the entrance to the maristan. The street bustle falls away as you step into a verdant courtyard of remarkable tranquillity, a fountain splashing in a rippling pool, on four sides the silence of towering liwans, and towards the corners the delicate repeated patterns of interwoven geometric and floral stucco grilles over chamber doors.

These chambers contain the museum exhibits, including stuffed animals, herbal pharmaceuticals, medical and pharmaceutical glassware of the medieval period (including beautifully blown distilling apparatus), as well as Roman, Byzantine and Arab dental and surgical instruments (among them circumcision pincers) and Arab anatomical drawings of the eye. The collection is slight but often fine.

Consultations were held in the east liwan, opposite the entrance, where there is a modern bust, unfortunately insipid, of Ibn Sina, better known in the West as Avicenna (980–1037), who among others put Arab medical theory and practice far ahead of anything known to Europe at that time. The south liwan, containing the mihrab, is richly decorated with marble friezes and odd fragments and slabs stuck into the walls, including the remains of two Byzantine or Crusader altars.

The shock of the Crusades helped revive Damascus, which the Abbasids, ruling from far-off Baghdad, had neglected. The threat from the West made Damascus a frontline city and in 1154 Nur al-Din, the emir of Aleppo, brought it under his control, creating that axis, extended by Saladin to Cairo and stiffened by the Mamelukes, that would contain and ultimately repel the Franks. So little did the Abbasids contribute to Damascus that nothing of their period survives, and the 450 years from the completion of the Umayyad Mosque to the foundation of Nur al-Din's hospital is an architectural blank. The maristan was lucky to survive the French bombardments of 1925 which badly damaged the quarter south of the Souk al-Hamidiye.

Much of the area between the Citadel and Straight Street then suffered 'redevelopment' as recently as the 1940s and 1950s, many surviving old buildings destroyed and winding lines replaced by a ruthless grid.

Returning to the Souk al-Hamidiye and continuing eastwards, you come to the light at the end of the tunnel, the clean white marble of a classical order rising through a blaze of sunlight above the shadowy hubbub of the bazaar. Once this Roman **triumphal arch** would have announced your arrival at the western outer precincts of the Temple of Jupiter (though its principal approach was from the east, see p.75); now as dramatically it opens upon your first view of the Umayyad Mosque. The form is a semi-circular arch set within a triangular pediment originally 21m high and raised on 12m Corinthian columns. Beyond this is a Byzantine **colonnade** with Corinthian capitals surmounted by wedge-shaped abacuses, not unlike the columns round the courtyard of the mosque. This colonnade was part of a 4th-century shopping precinct which in recent centuries became known as the Booksellers' Bazaar, though now only a few sellers of Korans remain.

The best view of the arch and colonnade is from the roof terrace of a house, now a shop called **Kahwaji Bazaar**, immediately to the south, which has a good selection of antique traditional costumes and textiles, plus small antiquities including coins, lamps, Byzantine glass and Bedouin jewellery and tent decorations.

The square before the mosque has recently been cleared of numerous souk stalls that had huddled about the colonnade and had clung to the mosque walls, and a fountain has been set into the paving. The local property-owners who have had their shops and houses demolished are suing the government for millions of dollars in compensation. The square resonates with the call to prayer, an especially exquisite call, the voice high and pure, the *muezzin* an Egyptian they will tell you, famous for the sweet clarity of his song.

> *God alone is great. There is no god but Allah, and Mohammed is his Prophet. Come to prayer. Come to salvation. God alone is great. There is no god but God.*

It is beautiful to be here for that, and also to watch the troupes of women, covered from head to foot in their black *izzars* and faceless behind their veils, following their husbands into the mosque. As these women stoop to remove their shoes, elegant high-heeled Italian numbers sometimes, they occasionally reveal black lace stockings studded with pearls running up the side of their calves. And then you recall among the brassware and deodorants and plastic Santa Clauses of the souks the prominent display of dark stockings variously patterned and brief under-wear and revealing bras. The premium is on the sexually alluring—beneath those black robes.

The Mecca Pilgrimage

The Umayyad Mosque was the official starting point for the annual pilgrimage to Mecca, which in 1697 coincided with Henry Maundrell's Easter pilgrimage to Jerusalem:

'In this famous cavalcade there came first forty-six dellees, that is religious madmen, carrying each a silk streamer, mixed either of red and green or of yellow and green; after these came three troops of segmen, an order of soldiers among the Turks; and next to them some troops of spahees, another order of soldiery. These were followed by eight companies of Maghrebines [North Africans] on foot: these were fellows of a very formidable aspect and were designed to be left in a garrison, main-tained by the Turks somewhere in the desert of Arabia and relieved every year with fresh men. In the midst of the Maghrebines there paced six small pieces of ordnance. In the next place came on foot the soldiers of the castle of Damascus, fantastically armed with coats of mail, gauntlets and other pieces of old armour. These were followed by troops of janisseries, and their aga, all mounted. Next were brought the pasha's two horse tails, ushered by his aga of the court; and next after the tails followed six led horses, all of excellent shape, and nobly furnished. Over the saddle there was a girt upon each led horse and a large silver target gilded with gold.

After these horses came the *mahmal*. This is a large pavilion of black silk, pitched upon the back of a very great camel, and spreading its curtains all round about the beast down to the ground. The pavilion is adorned at top with a gold ball and with gold fringes round about. The camel that carries it wants not also his ornaments of large ropes of beads, fish shells, foxtails and other such fantastical finery hanged upon his head, neck and legs. All this is designed for the state of the Koran, which is placed with great reverence under the pavilion, where it rides in state both to and from Mecca. The Koran is accompanied with a rich new carpet which the grand signieur sends every year for the covering of Mohammed's tomb, having the old one brought back in return for it, which is esteemed of an inestimable value, after having been so long next neighbour to the Prophet's rotten bones. The beast which carries this sacred load has the privilege to be exempted from all other burdens ever after.

After the *mahmal* came another troop, and with them the pasha himself; and last of all, twenty loaded camels with which the train ended, having been three quarters of an hour in passing.'

The Umayyad Mosque or Great Mosque

Open 9–5 daily; closed to visitors during Friday prayers 12.30–2pm; adm fee includes entry to Saladin's tomb.

After Mecca, Medina and the Dome of the Rock in Jerusalem, the Great Mosque at Damascus is for Muslims the holiest place on earth. For anybody, it is a place of remarkable beauty and calm, a transcendent aesthetic experience. The mosque is at the east end of the Souk al-Hamidiye.

As you approach you should survey the enormous 150m-long **west wall** of the mosque that rises 100m high before you. The lower courses of large, well-cut and precisely-fitted blocks are Roman, while the patchy upper courses are Arab work. The rectangular holes in the wall which you can sometimes make out (recently they have been filled in) received the beams that supported the upper storeys and roofs of recently cleared-away houses and shops built up against the mosque. (For a tour of the exterior of the mosque and nearby monuments, *see* p.73.)

The faithful enter through the main gate in the west wall, the **Bab al-Barid** (Post Gate), while the **visitors' entrance** is through the gate on the north side, east of Saladin's tomb. In a narrow street along the north side of the mosque is the ticket office. Here women (also men in shorts) must don a black robe; shoes have to be removed only in the prayer hall of the mosque itself, not in its courtyard.

History of the Great Mosque

Three thousand years ago on this spot stood a temple to Hadad, the Aramean god of the sun and thunder. His consort was Atargatis, whose priests were eunuchs and who spoke in prophecies and broke into delirious dances as the temple girls played flutes and cymbals round the altar of the goddess. The worship of Hadad and his consort continued here even after the Greeks and Romans came to Syria, but then as at Baalbek the qualities of Hadad were syncretised with those of Jupiter and in the first century AD a new temple to Jupiter Damascenus was

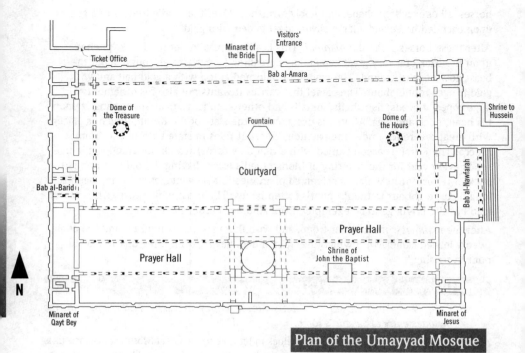

Plan of the Umayyad Mosque

erected on an imperial scale. Its temenos more or less corresponded to the walls enclosing the present mosque and courtyard, while the outermost walls of the precinct extended much farther, as indicated by the Roman arch at the mosque end of the Souk al-Hamidiye and a triple arch to the east. During the reign of Septimius Severus (193–211), who adorned the streets of Damascus with colonnades, the temple was further embellished.

The transfer of the imperial capital from Rome to Constantinople in 330 was followed over the next fifty years by the increasing Christianisation of the empire. In 379 the Emperor Theodosius ordered a stop to pagan worship at the temple, which was made the cathedral of the city and dedicated to John the Baptist, its bishops second in Syria only to those of Antioch (now Turkish Antakya).

Even after the Arab conquest of Damascus in 636 the church remained in Christian hands, though for their own prayers towards Mecca the Muslims built a mud brick structure against the south wall of the church courtyard. But over the next seventy years the Muslim influx grew to outnumber the original Christian and Jewish populations, who were gradually pushed into the eastern quarters of the city. The story later grew up that at the conquest the church had been partitioned between Muslims and Christians, as half the city had been taken by force and half had surrendered, but in the opinion of scholars the tale was invented to put a better face on the expropriation of the church by the Umayyad Caliph Walid I in 708. 'O Commander of the Faithful,' the bishop warned him, 'we find in our books that whosoever shall demolish this church will go mad.'

As though to fulfill the prophecy, Walid and his emirs hacked at every evidence of Christian worship within, until only the rectangle of the Roman walls remained, and then spent wildly on its reconstruction as a mosque, which is said to have eaten up the whole of the state's revenue over the next seven years. When the accounts were brought to Walid on the backs of eighteen camels, he refused to look at them, saying, 'Truly we have spent this for Allah and we will make no account of it.' The mosque was designed by Byzantine architects, and thousands of craftsmen came from Constantinople, as well as Egypt and Damascus. The prayer hall was hung with 600 lanterns of gold and its capitals sheathed in more of the same. The courtyard, repaved in white marble in the 19th century, was originally covered in mosaics, while millions of brilliantly coloured tesserae were set into the surfaces of the arcades and the transept façade. With the exception of the 12th-century Cathedral of Monreale in Palermo, it is the greatest mosaic composition ever attempted, though much of it is now lost.

In 1069, during fighting between the Damascenes and Fatimid soldiers, the prayer hall was gutted by fire, and in 1400 sections of the arcades suffered burning when Tamerlane set up mangonels in the courtyard to bombard the Citadel. Again in 1893 conflagration collapsed the prayer hall. And yet the Great Mosque survives, patched up and restored, its magnificence owed to its eccentric conception, combining elements from Roman to Arab, and to the strange harmony of battered age.

The Umayyads

The Umayyads were Meccans but with strong Bedouin ties, and like many desert peoples they wore their faith lightly. Taking advantage of dissension among the Prophet's successors, they seized the caliphate in 661 and promptly removed themselves from the constricting atmosphere of Mecca and Medina. Muawiya, their first caliph, was invested in Jerusalem and made Syria the basis of his power. Here on the rim of the Mediterranean world the cultural influence was Byzantine; what Greece had been to Rome, so Syria was to the Arabs, and for a time under the Umayyads, Damascus, capital of the Islamic empire, enjoyed a mood of liberal scepticism in matters of dogma, a sense of fancy and poetry and a taste for earthly pleasures. To the modern Westerner it is attractive; to many Muslims the Umayyad period is an abhorrence. Within a century the Umayyad dynasty was overthrown by the Abbasids. Marwan II, the last Umayyad caliph, was beheaded, over seventy members of the royal family were murdered, and even the bones of his predecessor, Hisham, were exhumed and flogged. Almost the only member of the Umayyad dynasty to survive the devastation and carnage was Abd al-Rahman, who founded the Umayyad dynasty at Córdoba, bringing with him from Syria the first palm tree to be planted in Spain. The Abbasids meanwhile assumed the caliphate and made Baghdad their capital. Islam's geographical and cultural links with the West were ruptured, Syria was neglected and Damascus declined.

The Courtyard

In fact it is the courtyard that impresses, far more than the prayer hall interior. You immediately think of the Piazza San Marco in Venice, not for its size (it is not nearly so large), but for its arcades and mosaics, and for its grandness. As you linger you become aware of a great sense of restfulness and peace that inhabits the place, untranslatable into photographs. At no one point, in no few details, can you find it all expressed, rather it has something to do with the irregularity of its parts which combine in an organic wholeness—the arches round the arcade for example vary in breadth, the upper-storey double windows do not quite exactly sit over the arches below, the patterns on no two columns are the same—but overall, in the assembly, there is a genius of harmony. Very little fills the court: a fountain, two domed structures, all the rest an enclosed yet vast open space. It is tempting to think that its magic rises from the long-hallowed ground, but that is an excuse. The more you return to this courtyard the more you love it: the play of people across the stones, the flights of birds, the glow of the columns and mosaics and marble paving in the softening light of evening. It is a place that is full of movement but is still; contemplative, absorbing, full of wonder and delight; exquisitely, enchantingly beautiful.

The **courtyard** measures 50 by 122m, its present marble paving laid in the 19th century to replace 11th-century stone and tiles, which in turn had replaced the original mosaic paving. The prayer hall is on the right (south) side of the courtyard as you enter. Arcades run round the other three sides, their pattern originally two columns alternating with a pier (as at the Haghia Sophia and perhaps also early Byzantine palaces in Constantinople), but over time the columns on the north side were entirely replaced by piers.

Only three features interrupt the expanse of paving. At the centre of the courtyard is a modern **ablutions fountain**, replacing an earlier though not original domed fountain, said to mark the midway point between Istanbul and Mecca, and to the east is the Kubbet al-Saa or **Dome of the Hours**, an 18th-century pavilion employing Byzantine columns which derived its name from the collection of clocks once stored here.

Plant-motif **mosaics** of gold and green cover each panel of the late 8th-century Kubbet al-Khazneh or **Dome of the Treasure** in the western part of the courtyard, an octagonal structure that contained the mosque's treasury and was raised on eight ancient columns for security. Repeated on three of the panels is a tree of life motif in the form of a date palm standing by a pool. All these Treasury mosaics are 13th-century restorations of the original Abbasid work.

Almost every surface round the courtyard was once covered by **mosaics**, but much has been lost or damaged or restored and then not always very successfully. You can now review these in turn. The largest expanse of mosaic is on the **transept façade** of the mosque where a landscape of villas and trees is depicted, though in accordance with Muslim prohibition no human figures are represented. All but the darker areas here were restored in the 1960s. The landscape theme is enlarged upon in colour range and subject along the **west arcade**. On the exterior façade it is damaged, but on both sides within the arcade and on the soffits of the arches it has been well restored. A scene within the arcade is an especially delicious celebration of water and greenery. Along the banks of a flowing stream are kiosks, villas and palaces among tall trees, a picture of beauty and delight especially for people of the desert.

> *This is the Paradise which the righteous have been promised: it is watered by running streams: eternal are its fruits, and eternal are its shades.*

> *The Koran, Sura 13:35.*

Yet the stream could also be the Barada, the scene answering to Maundrell's description of the environs of Damascus at the end of the 17th century.

> *The gardens are thick set with fruit trees of all kinds, kept fresh and verdant by the waters of Barrady. You discover in them many turrets, and steeples, and summer houses, frequently peeping out from among the green boughs, which may be conceived to add no small advantage and beauty to the prospect.*

And then you remember that Mohammed would not tempt his human frailty by entering Damascus, so much like Paradise did it seem.

While at the west arcade, have a look at the vestibule within the main entrance gate, the **Bab al-Barid**, with its patches of 8th-century mosaic executed for the Umayyads by Byzantine craftsmen, and its patterned and painted wooden roof and great bronze-panelled doors, both 15th-century. Also here and along the **east arcade**, notice the elegance of the columns, their acanthus capitals surmounted by a wedge-shaped abacus upon which the arches rest. All the arches round the court except the three marking the north gate have a slight return, a feature occasionally found in Byzantine architecture at the time but which did not continue in Islamic architecture beyond the Umayyad period.

In a room of Roman date off the east arcade is a **shrine to Hussein**, who fell at the hands of the Umayyads at the battle of Kerbala in present-day Iraq (*see* p.243). After the battle, Hussein's head was briefly placed in a recess here, now bordered with silver and marble, a place of pilgrimage for Shia, many of them stubble-chinned garrulous Iranians leading flocks of black-robed women, who stick their heads into the niche and kiss the tiles. Now, according to competing traditions, the head is in the room beyond, in a casket draped in green, or it is at the mosque of Sayyidna al-Hussein in Cairo, or it is back with its body, which is buried at Kerbala. A neighbouring casket draped in blue silk is said to contain a hair from Mohammed's beard.

From different vantage points in the courtyard you can look up at the mosque's three **minarets**. The **Minaret of the Bride**, rising above the centre of the north arcade, is a 9th-century structure to which the upper storey was added in the 12th century. Legend attributes the minaret's name to a caliph's bride, the daughter of a merchant who donated the lead covering the roof of the lower storey.

The two minarets rising from the outer corners of the prayer hall may stand on the remains of Roman towers. At the southwest corner is the **Minaret of Qayt Bey**, built by that Mameluke sultan in 1488. The square base, octagonal shaft and round upper storey is typical of medieval architecture in Cairo, which was the Mameluke capital. The minaret became famous for the ascetics and holy men who came to inhabit it and who in a lifetime of aerial seclusion were reduced to a tenuous physicality, their hair long and matted on bodies of skin and bone.

The **Minaret of Jesus** at the southeast corner is at nearly 60m the tallest of the three. An Ayyubid work of 1247, it replaced an earlier Umayyad structure, though the pencil-like upper storey is Ottoman. No one seems to know how the minaret first got its name, but the association is not surprising, given that this was once the site of a great cathedral and that Islam has adopted Jesus as one of the prophets. Indeed he is singularly exalted, the Koran saying that he was born of a virgin, crediting him with miracles and describing him as a 'Spirit from God' and as the 'Word of God'. But Jesus did not die upon the cross; instead a substitute was put in his place, and Jesus was taken directly up to God where he lives outside the world and time. This preserves, in the Muslim view, the absoluteness of God, while the religion founded in Jesus' name and that has as its basis his divinity is dismissed as a grievous historical error. According to certain Muslim traditions (*hadiths*), Jesus will return to earth before the Day of Judgement to destroy the Anti-Christ who has led mankind into its final and fatal delusion. According to Damascene tradition, it is via this minaret that Jesus will descend from heaven for that last combat.

The Prayer Hall

The prayer hall follows the alignment of the destroyed Byzantine Cathedral of St John, that is it is a basilica orientated east–west. In Syrian churches the altar was always at the east end, the mystery enacted there the focus of the congregation's attention. On the other hand, Muslim observances involve no enactment of a mystery, rather prayerful acknowledgement of the absoluteness of God, which is done in the direction of Mecca to the south of Damascus. Therefore, as basilical churches were converted to mosques, what had been a nave became wings, and this habit seems to have been carried forward into the construction of the prayer hall here, explaining its shallow depth but great width.

To direct focus towards Mecca, however, two features were added—a prayer niche or mihrab in the centre of the south wall (its first recorded use in a mosque), and a north–south transept midway across the basilica (a variation on the narthex at the west end of a Christian basilica). Something like this arrangement existed at the praetorium in Palmyra (*see* p.281), seat of the commander of the Roman legion based there and dating from Diocletian's reign, and it was repeated at Diocletian's retirement palace at Split, where the audience hall (corresponding to the transept) was surmounted by a dome. Here at the prayer hall a dome is also mounted upon the transept, emphasising its centrality. In this and other ways (including the outer façade of the transept with its triple portal which is thought to bear strong resemblances to the vanished 6th-century Chalki Gate of the imperial palace at Constantinople and the façade of Theodoric's palace at Ravenna) the Greek architects of the prayer hall of the Umayyad Mosque looked for their inspiration to classical and Byzantine models.

The original wooden dome burned down in 1069 and was replaced by one of stone. This dome too and much else of the prayer hall suffered destruction in the fire of 1893 and had to be rebuilt (the columns, for instance, are neoclassical), resulting in a structure which, though following its original plan, has a 19th-century Turko-European style about it that largely fails to impress. A few early details remain: the wood panelling of the transept ceiling towards the courtyard end; small areas of mosaic, probably 11th-century, on the north wall; and the 8th-century geometrically interlaced marble grilles of the windows at both ends of the transept (there are similar survivals in the rooms off the east and west arcades), the oldest examples of their use in Islam, though such hexagonal and octagonal patterns were well known in the classical world.

The mosque is said to have contained the first Koran, handwritten by the Caliph Uthman, and claims to have possessed a curtained sanctuary where Aisha, Mohammed's favourite wife, lived and recounted the sayings of the Prophet. The surviving attraction is the **shrine of John the Baptist's head** in the east wing of the prayer hall. A late-Ottoman marble monument with a crescent-topped green dome stands upon the supposed site of its burial (though Aleppo, Venice and other cities have also claimed the honour). There are several stories connected with this disconnected head. One is that Herod sent it to the Romans at Damascus so that they could bear witness to the execution; another is that when Damascus fell to the Arabs, the Baptist's blood angrily bubbled up and spread throughout the church; and also that when the church was demolished, the head was found in a casket beneath it, still covered with skin and hair, at which Walid ordered that a shrine be made for it. Women especially come to pray here beneath the twirling fans, in expiation, you wonder, or in dimly remembered satisfaction perhaps, at Salome's request that for the pleasure of her dance Herod should grant her on a platter the head of John the Baptist.

Around the Umayyad Mosque

There is more to discover about the Roman, Byzantine and Arab history of this holy site by walking round the outer walls of the mosque. Along the way, there is also a charming café to lounge at, and to the north of the mosque there are the tombs of Saladin and Baybars, the two men most responsible for beating back the Crusades.

The South and East Sides of the Mosque

This walk around the mosque is undertaken in a counter-clockwise direction, so that as you emerge from it you should turn left towards its southwest corner and left again into a street filled with furniture-makers and picture-framers running along the south side of the mosque. (Here in this street, opposite the southwest corner of the mosque, are the **public toilets**.) The south entrance to the mosque, the **Bab al-Ziyadeh**, is 30m east along this street. (Opposite the Bab al-Ziyadeh and running south is the Suq al-Silah, filled mostly with goldsmiths and leading to the Azem Palace—*see* p.79.)

Two-thirds of the way from the southwest corner of the mosque to the Bab al-Ziyadeh, its southern entrance, look up at the wall: six courses or about four metres up there is a projecting **Roman bust**, the toga draped from the left shoulder, the hair evident round the battered head, but the face entirely hacked away, a relic of the Temple of Jupiter. These lower courses belonged to its inner temenos wall, explaining why the windows of the prayer hall are placed so high, for the Roman wall and its cornice was retained and the Umayyad wall, into which the windows were set, was built upon it.

Midway along this south wall you come to a **triple portal**, the original south entrance to the temple's compound, serving later as an entrance to the church precincts but blocked up when the mosque's prayer hall was built. An electricity substation, thick cables writhing from it, has been slapped up against the left-hand portal. There is a badly damaged Greek inscription over the right-hand portal. But the **inscription over the central portal** and dating from the reign of Theodosius can be readily made out:

$$BACIΛIA \quad COY \quad X(PIΣTOΣ) E(ΣTI) BACIΛA \quad ΠANTΩ$$
$$NAIΩNΩN \quad KAH \quad ΔECΠOTIA \quad COY \quad EN \quad ΠACH \quad ΓENEAKAIΣ$$

This translates literally as 'Your kingdom, Christ, is the kingdom of all eons and your rule [is] in all generations'. The words are from Psalms 145:13, though 'Christ' is an interpolation. In the King James version of the Bible the line is rendered as: 'Thy kingdom is an everlasting kingdom, and Thy dominion endureth throughout all generations.'

Now continue along the south wall to the southeast corner and turn left (north) down steps past a café to the east gate of the mosque, called the **Bab al-Nawfarah**, or Fountain Gate, named after the renovated but originally early-11th-century fountain 10m from the bottom of the broad flight of stairs running east. In 1150 a mechanical clock was installed in the vestibule of this east gate, and every hour one of two brass falcons would drop a weight from its beak into a vase, while at night a lantern inside the clock would be turned round by a water device and would shed its light through a circlet of red glass. This gate, a triple portal, was the principal entrance to the inner temenos of the Roman temple, so that you approached from the east along a colonnaded sacred way and ascended the broad flight of stairs to a columned porch that projected from the triple portal. On the north flank of the gate you can see capitals and a section of architrave, survivals of the colonnades.

At the bottom of these eastward-descending steps is the **Nawfarah café** on the south side of the street. Men gather here at sundown, playing cards inside or listening raptly to a berobed and turbaned story-teller, while beneath a vine trellis out front they sit at marble tables and smoke *narghilehs*, sip heavily sugared tea and chat to one another, or just suck and bubble quietly to themselves. It is good to sit at this delightful place below the great wooden doors of the mosque, beneath the vines and evening lights and amid the sing-song conversation, letting

moments elide. For 2000 years the street before you, **Badreddin al-Hassan Street**, the ancient avenue into the holy heart of the city, has been animated by this same passage of people ascending and descending the Roman stairs.

After having a tea or coffee, you should follow this street as it runs off to the east, leading in 120m to a triple **gateway**, marking the eastern entrance to the outer compound of the temple. Now you can appreciate the vast scale of the temple precinct, which extended east to west from here to the Roman arch you passed through when you first glimpsed the mosque after emerging from the Souk al-Hamidiye. The gateway has become half-buried beneath the rising ground level so that, but for the excavations round it, the portals to left and right would only barely be visible. How much deeper the gateway goes is not clear, but obviously it was of monumental proportions. Windows are set above these side portals, though the lintel of that on the south as well as the entire arch across the top of the high central portal have fallen. Huge monolithic Corinthian columns frame the gateway to north and south.

Looking at the gateway from the east, you can make out Greek **inscriptions** between the portals and the windows as well as a Greek inscription on the lintel of the left portal and an Arabic inscription (presumably replacing an earlier Greek one) on the lintel of the right portal. Their condition and the dust attached to them make them difficult to read, but the Greek inscription between the lintel and the window over the left portal contains a date (expressed in the letters HKT or HNT, bottom line right, in which system H=8, K=20, N=50, T=300), the year 328 or 358, most likely as computed according to the Seleucid calendar and corresponding to either AD 16/17 or AD 46/47. If either reading of the date is correct, that places the inscription and perhaps construction of the gateway itself during the period when the Nabateans were allowed by the Romans to exercise control in Damascus, though it would seem that either Greeks or Romans administered and embellished the temple.

Some column drums and capitals lie about, perhaps from the once broad, straight, colonnaded sacred way that continued eastwards from here. In 250m it led to the agora, at that time the commercial heart of the city. Nowadays Badreddin al-Hassan Street crooks near the gateway and if you continue to follow it eastwards you enter narrow and twisting streets where once the Greeks and Romans had imposed their grid. So much has this been overgrown by a maze that you suspect it has been deliberate. The different religious and ethnic communities in Damascus have not always lived harmoniously with one another, and this tangle of streets could offer each some protection against the others, as well as against an external enemy, while the final defence has been the houses themselves, blank walls on the ground floors, windows only on the first usually and these often screened, and a single door leading into the courtyard filled with flowers and the sound of splashing water. In fact heading east from the gateway you pass through the **Christian quarter** that extends from Bab Touma in the north walls down to Straight Street. This and the **Shia quarter** of Amara to the northeast of the Umayyad Mosque are the most picturesque of Damascus.

Along the North Side of the Mosque

Continuing your counter-clockwise perambulation round the mosque you now thread your way round its northeast corner through that Amara quarter. Soon you come to the handsome façade of the **Madrasa Jaqmaqiya** on a corner, built by Emir Jaqmaq, governor of Damascus, in 1421, and housing the **Epigraphy Museum** (*open 9–2, closed Tues; adm*) with a collection of Arabic inscriptions. By turning left (south) at this corner you arrive at the north gate of the mosque, **Bab al-Amara**, through which, you will notice, many Iranians, being Shia, choose to enter to visit the shrine of Hussein. The substantial remains of a Byzantine **colonnade** stand to the north of this gate.

Saladin's Tomb (*open daily 10–5; adm included in Umayyad Mosque ticket but in fact nobody asks*) is the dome seen when looking west through this colonnade. You reach it by returning to the Madrasa Jaqmaqiya and turning left (west); it is about 50m along, set back in a garden of myrtles, lemon trees, bougainvillaea and with trellised vines suspended over a pool on the left (south) side of the street. (Alternatively, it is about 50m east from the northwest corner of the Umayyad Mosque.) Originally the complex included a madrasa, but only a great arch of this remains. Beside it is the modest domed tomb chamber completed in 1196 after Saladin's death at Damascus three years before.

The tomb chamber is hardly imposing for so considerable a historical figure. A fine faience inscription gives him thanks for liberating Jerusalem from the unbelievers. Otherwise there is the austerity of the basalt and limestone walls and above these a ribbed dome resting on an eight-sided drum supported by arches springing from corner piers, these faced with 17th-century tiles of little distinction. The place was left to deteriorate over the centuries and was restored only in 1898 by Kaiser Wilhelm II of Germany, who was promoting the alliance with the Ottoman Empire that would bring them both defeat in the First World War. Twenty years earlier Sultan Hamid provided the ornate white marble tomb you see at the centre of the chamber (the silver lamp above it bears his monogram and the Kaiser's); next to it is the original sarcophagus of walnut wood, delicately carved but rotted, the inscription on it reading, 'O Allah, receive this soul and open to him the gates of Paradise, the last conquest for which he hoped'.

Saladin

Saladin's achievement was to unite the Muslim world against the Crusader states, and this he did with a sure sense of strategy. For all the emotive significance of Jerusalem, the real need for either side was to bring into combination with Damascus and Aleppo the great resources of wealth and manpower of Egypt. The Crusaders failed to awake to this strategic necessity until it was too late, nor perhaps did they ever have sufficient means to succeed in the attempt.

From North Africa the Fatimids, a Shia dynasty, invaded Egypt in 961 and soon afterwards contested Syria with the Sunni Abbasid Caliphate in Baghdad. Simply put, this was the split in the Muslim world that gave the Crusaders their chance to establish a foothold in the East. Saladin, a Kurd owing nominal allegiance to Baghdad, reconquered Egypt for Sunni orthodoxy in 1171, and using Damascus as his forward base set about uniting the whole of Syria, taking control of Aleppo in 1183. Now with the advantage of ample resources, strategic depth and interior lines of communication, he made war against the Crusader states. Jerusalem fell to him in 1187 after he destroyed a Crusader army at the battle of Hattin in Galilee, and in the following year he launched his lightning campaign along the Syrian coast, sacking Tortosa (Tartus) and Latakia, storming the great castle of Saône in the Jebel al-Sariya and taking Qalaat Burzey overlooking the Orontes.

Saladin could be ruthless, and in the interests of policy he did not shrink from bloodshed. He was a devout Muslim who abhorred free-thinkers, and though he made many friends among the Christians, he never doubted that their souls were doomed to damnation. Yet as men the Franks had his respect, and he treated them as equals, and unlike the Crusaders who allowed differences in religion to excuse them from fair dealing, Saladin never broke his word to any man. His genius in war, his strict sense of justice and honour, and his many gestures of kindness and gallantry, won him the admiration of his adversaries. Dante, writing early in the 14th century, consigned Mohammed, as a Sower of Discord, to the Eighth Circle of Hell (there are nine circles, so it could have been worse), but Saladin he honoured, his one lapse having not been baptised, by placing him in Limbo among such Virtuous Pagans as Homer, Socrates, Plato, Hippocrates, and Averroës the philosopher and Avicenna the physician, both Muslims.

Saladin's power reached beyond the Tigris and the Nile, yet ostentation repelled him and his tastes remained simple. There is a story that seeing the threadbare clothing of a poor man at the baths, Saladin went off in them, leaving his own fine garments in their place. He was without personal wealth, and a Christian chronicler records that as Saladin lay dying he summoned his standard-bearer, telling him, 'You who have carried my banner in battle will now go round Damascus with a rag from my shroud on your lance, calling out that the monarch of all the East has taken nothing with him to the tomb but this cloth.'

Saladin died at the age of 54, exhausted by his many years of battle. He had reclaimed from the Crusaders everything but Antioch and a little land around, Tortosa, Krak des Chevaliers, Tripoli and a narrow strip of coastland between Tyre and Jaffa. He might have driven them from the East altogether but for the Third Crusade and Richard the Lionheart in particular. Saladin established a dynasty, the Ayyubids, which ruled capably but without his energy and genius, and the Crusaders hung on for a century yet.

For the very reasons that Saladin has been honoured in the West, so he has been exalted less in the East where the sentiment is that instead of being chivalrous, he should not have missed a chance to put the boot in. The man who did that was Baybars, whose tomb is near by.

West along the street of Saladin's tomb and first right brings you, on the left (west) to the **Madrasa Adiliye**, theological school and burial place of Sultan al-Adil, brother of Saladin, who died in 1218, with a high stalactite portal. It is not nearly as effective, however, as the doorway of the building opposite, the Madrasa Zahiriye, better known as the **Mausoleum of Baybars**, the great Mameluke sultan whose victories put the final term on the Crusaders' presence in the East. He died in Damascus in 1277; the last Crusaders abandoned the mainland in 1291.

The deeply recessed portal, inset with three marble bands of finely-worked inscriptions (relating to the madrasa's endowments) is carved with cascading stalactites and is surmounted by a scallop-shell cupola. This and the domed tomb chamber on the right of the courtyard within were additions to what was originally the house of Saladin's father, that Ayyub who gave his name to the Ayyubid dynasty. The chamber is adorned with marble-panelled walls and a splendid mosaic frieze similar in its golds and greens, its garlands and fruit trees, its villas and bulbous-domed palaces or mosques, to those at the Umayyad Mosque, if not so fine.

At the centre of the floor on a raised marble platform are two parallel triangular ridges, the graves of Baybars and one of his sons. You can see the originals of such graves at the al-Saghir cemetery (*see* p.83) just south of the walls of the Old City, filled with hundreds of tapering heaps of earth mixed with straw and covered over with clay or plaster to hold them firm.

The madrasa serves also as an extension of the National Library, the tomb chamber itself until recently used to house Arabic manuscripts, though these now are distributed in other rooms round the courtyard.

Baybars

Towards the end of Saladin's dynasty, the Ayyubid sultans in Cairo relied increasingly on highly-trained slave warriors, known as Mamelukes, mostly Kipchak Turks from the steppes north of the Black Sea. In 1249, as Sultan al-Salih Ayyub lay dying, St Louis, the king of France, was landing at the head of the Sixth Crusade at Damietta on the eastern mouth of the Nile Delta. To save the situation, al-Salih's wife, Shagarat al-Durr (her name means Tree of Pearls), kept his death a secret, issuing orders to her Mameluke commanders in his name. The Crusade was beaten and St Louis was made to pay a huge indemnity before being allowed to sail for France. The victory was owed to Shagarat al-Durr's resolution and to the fierce fighting qualities of the Mamelukes, the ablest of whom was the young Baybars, who owing to an imperfection in one eye had been purchased for a bargain price at the Damascus slave market. Al-Salih's son, who had been posted to the Gezira as viceroy, returned to Cairo to claim his throne, but unwisely he attempted to brush aside both Shagarat al-Durr and her Mamelukes. Baybars hacked him to death with his sword.

The Mamelukes became the effective rulers of Egypt and Syria, though at first for the sake of legitimacy they ruled through Shagarat al-Durr. After her death in 1257 the Mamelukes ruled in their own right, as sultans. Almost immediately their mettle was tested when the Mongols invaded Syria in 1260. In a battle that saved the fortunes of Islam, the Mamelukes led by their Sultan Qutuz defeated the Mongols at Ain Jalud in Palestine. Again Baybars was outstanding, but he felt slighted when Qutuz refused him the governorship of Aleppo. So as Qutuz was returning to Cairo in triumph, Baybars stabbed him in the back, himself entering Cairo as sultan.

Over the next seventeen years Baybars directed the same ruthlessness and treachery towards the Crusaders. Saladin took one look at Krak des Chevaliers and marched away again; Baybars, after first taking nearby Safita, bullied and tricked the knights of Krak into surrender. Castle after castle, town after town fell to Baybars, until the Crusaders were left with only a discontinuous series of toeholds along the coast. Meanwhile he rebuilt his fortresses (the towers of the Damascus Citadel are his), made harbours and dug canals, and built a fast road between his two capitals so that on Saturday he could play polo at Cairo and on the following Friday lead prayers in the Umayyad Mosque at Damascus. Rough in manner, disloyal and cruel, he had none of those personal qualities that won Saladin the respect of even his enemies. But he was an energetic administrator and a brilliant general, and to this day he is the symbol of the victorious struggle against the Crusaders.

Sold in Damascus as a slave, he was buried here forty years later as the most powerful man in the Muslim world. Not surprisingly, he died by poison, one version being that after offering the fatal cup to his victim, he refilled it and incautiously drank from it himself. In this slip, at least, he made himself endearing.

Souks, Khans and the Azem Palace

In Hellenistic and Roman times the agora lay east of the Temple of Jupiter, which itself faced in that direction, but over the centuries the commercial centre of the Old City has shifted westwards. During the Arab period commerce was concentrated along the central stretch of Straight Street. It swung farther round to the area southwest of the Umayyad Mosque when the Mamelukes and Ottomans built their khans there, and finally the 19th-century Souk al-Hamidiye brought the commercial focus of Damascus right round to the west of the mosque, reversing the Graeco-Roman orientation of the city.

Though you need to go to Aleppo for the best covered bazaar in the Middle East, the area south from the Umayyad Mosque to Straight Street has the most atmospheric souks in Damascus and a number of interesting Ottoman khans to visit along the way, as well as the Azem Palace, built by an 18th-century Ottoman governor of the city. The khans served both as inns and warehouses, trade goods stored and animals stabled off the central open courtyard, while travelling merchants were accommodated in upper-storey rooms. In later khans, the central court was covered over by domes, as at the Khan of Assad Pasha, the finest in the city. Most of the surviving khans are still hives of commercial or artisan activity and are fascinating places to explore.

Along the Souk al-Haiyatin

Get your bearings at the **triumphal arch** at the east end of the Souk al-Hamidiye, the Ummayad Mosque before you. Now turn right (south) into the long narrow **Souk al-Haiyatin**, the Souk of the Tailors, more generally a cloth bazaar selling everything from bright spools of thread to English worsted and, where it runs into Straight Street (*see* p.84) 300m down, Arab headgear (the *kefieh*). At 50m on your right (west) you come to the *ablaq* doorway to the **Khan al-Gumruk** built in 1609, its L-shaped hall surmounted by a series of six domes. This was the customs house (*gumruk* is derived from the Greek *emporikós*, meaning commercial: *see* the Khan al-Gumruk in Aleppo, p.211) where duties were imposed.

Opposite (east) was the slave market, and a few metres farther along on this same (east) side is the 16th-century **Hamam al-Qishani**, the Tiled Bath (though it is now a souk), taking its name from the blue faience within its doorway and (now replaced by modern painted decoration) on the pendentives of its dome. Continuing 50m south, you come on your left (east) to the street leading to the Azem Palace (*see* below). But for the moment carry on a farther 25m to the **Madrasa Nuriye** on a corner to your right (west). Here beneath a stalactite dome lies Nur al-Din, who with his father Zengi made Aleppo a bastion against the Crusaders and later brought Damascus under his control, so preparing the ground for Saladin's great counterthrust.

The Azem Palace

Open daily 9–5.30, closed 12–2pm Fri and all day Tues; adm.

Osman Aidi Street, carrying motorised traffic, is 50m south of the Hamam al-Qishani and 25m north of the Madrasa Nuriye. Turn east into this street and you come in 120m to a square (on which is the celebrated antique shop, **George Dabdoub's Azem Palace Bazaar**, closed on Saturdays as they are a Jewish family). The square leads on to the Azem Palace.

Another approach to the palace is from the southwest corner of the Umayyad Mosque. Walk east along its wall to the mosque's south entrance (the Bab al-Ziyadeh), opposite which, running south, is the Souk al-Silah, formerly a weapons bazaar but now filled mostly with goldsmiths. This too brings you to the square in front of the Azem Palace.

> In the inside, the houses discover a very different face from what you see without. Here you find generally a large square court, beautified with variety of fragrant trees, and marble fountains, and compassed round with splendid apartments and divans. The divans are floored and adorned on the sides, with variety of marble, mixed in mosaic knots and mazes. The ceilings and architraves are, after the Turkish manner, richly painted and gilded. They have generally artificial fountains springing up before them in marble basins; and, as for carpets and cushions, are furnished out to the height of luxury. Of these divans they have generally several on all sides of the court, being placed at such different points, that at one or other of them you may always have either the shade or the sun, which you please.
>
> Henry Maundrell, *A Journey from Aleppo to Jerusalem at Easter* AD *1697.*

Assad Pasha al-Azem, Ottoman governor of Damascus in the mid-18th century, was an exception to the rule: at a time when governors rarely survived in office for longer than a year, he remained governor of the city for fourteen. He had earlier been governor at Hama and built himself a palatial residence there (*see* p.147); now in 1749 he built on an even grander scale in Damascus. As he diverted the waters of the Barada to his gardens, so he diverted every carpenter and mason in the city to his project, and commanded that Roman columns from Bosra and ancient paving from Baniyas be hauled to his building site in the heart of the city.

Istanbul looked upon these activities with suspicion. A governor's job was simply to extort the maximum in taxes from the local population. He was not to settle in nor demonstrate any ability, and he was certainly not to care about his subjects' welfare. Yet Assad Pasha won the approbation of the Damascenes, checking the insurrectionary tendencies of the Druze, easing communal dissensions, building the magnificent khan that bears his name (*see* p.81) and curbing the cartels of wealthy merchants, thereby relieving scarcities and high prices by ensuring the free flow of goods. When he was removed from office in 1756, the city erupted, rival contingents of Druze, Turcomans, Kurds, Moors, Janissaries and others fighting one another in the streets. The Mecca caravan, which Assad Pasha had led for fourteen years running, was plundered by Bedouin and 20,000 pilgrims were left to die in the desert. Accused of bitter complicity in this event, in 1758 he was followed to the baths of Ankara by an agent of the Sultan and strangled.

Though the Azem Palace meets Maundrell's description of a great Damascene house, a yet grander scale and imposing formality deny it that intimacy which charms.

There were separate quarters, each arranged around a court, one for the kitchens and other services; another, the *haremlek*, the family's private apartments; the third, the *selamlek*, where the males of the family received guests. The *selamlek* is arranged around the largest court. On its south side there is a liwan (called a divan by Maundrell) of such depth that it would be free from the sun throughout the day. Next to this liwan is a high reception room with a fountain at the centre of its marble floor, the walls panelled also with marble, often beautifully cut and patterned. Male mannequins sit about here drinking coffee, for the *selamlek* provides also the principal rooms of the **Museum of Popular Arts and Tradition**.

Arrows lead you round the palace from room to room, panelled in dark wood and richly carved and decorated. One room shows a woman preparing for a marriage; another displays Damascene inlaid furniture; yet another shows the preparations made for a pilgrimage to Mecca, with mannequins dressed for the journey, a *mahmal* (*see* p.67) covered in green velvet and embroidered with silver, and some photographs of the pilgrimage setting out from Damascus in the 19th century. Round the smaller court to the south are rooms exhibiting various crafts and domestic activities such as baking, weaving, printing on cloth and leatherwork, while there is a room devoted to traditional women's costumes. Downstairs there is a hamam.

The most pleasing aspect of the palace is the great court with a large pond shaded by citrus trees, so remarkably quiet that you hear only birdsong and would not guess that you are at the heart of the city amid traffic-filled streets and the clamour of its souks.

Along the Souk al-Bazuriye

Leaving the Azem Palace, turn left (south) into the broad Souk al-Bazuriye of spices, nuts and sweetmeats. In 200m this brings you to Straight Street (*see* p.84) after passing one of the oldest public baths in Damascus and the city's outstanding khan.

The **Hamam Nur al-Din** (*open daily 8am–midnight, men only, © (011) 2229513; LS290, includes sauna, oriental bath, scrub, massage and drinks*) dates from the 12th century, its proceeds intended for the upkeep of the Nuriye madrasa containing Nur al-Din's tomb (*see* p.79). The dome is an Ottoman restoration, but it remains a good example of a public bath of the Arab period, and indeed is in full operation as such today. (For a hamam open to women, *see* p.89.) It is somehow amazing that anyone can own one of these ancient places; that all the Old City is not a museum.

Immediately adjacent to the south is the monumental **Khan of Assad Pasha**, the largest and most architecturally satisfying in Damascus. Built in 1749 by that same Assad Pasha of the

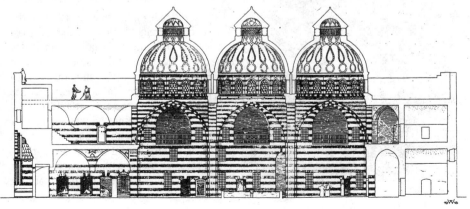

The Khan of Assad Pasha, after Wulzinger

Azem Palace, it continued in use through the early part of the 20th century, but then the great central dome collapsed. Since the late 1980s the khan has been undergoing extensive renovation (it is soon to become a hotel). If you are able to get into it, you should climb to the top for marvellous views along the caterpillar humps of the covered souks. A stalactite-vaulted portal leads into a voluminous court round a central fountain. Eight lesser domes (some of which fell and were imperfectly restored in the 18th century) encircled the great dome where now the sky pours through, the pendentives and drums of each repeating in curves of bold *ablaq* the striking grey and white stonework of the walls.

Straight Street and the City Walls

This description begins at the southwest walls and then follows Straight Street from west to east along its 1300m length to Bab Sharqi, the East Gate. Including diversions en route, this walk is 3km in all. The Christian and Jewish quarters are in this eastern end of the Old City. Then from Bab Sharqi a return route is described, following the curve of walls northwards and then westwards round to the Citadel, which again with diversions is a 3km walk. You might prefer to make two or more excursions out of all this or combine parts of it with other walks already described.

The Southwest Walls

The west entrance to Straight Street is about 250m south of the west entrance to the Souk al-Hamidiye. The city walls have been razed along this stretch. About a third of the way along, on the west side of this street is the striped façade of the **Mosque of Darwish Pasha**, Ottoman

governor of Damascus in the early 1570s, whose tomb is in the small building adjacent to the south. The mosque doorway leads into a court with the domed prayer hall to your left, its portico decorated with Damascene tiles. On the same side of the street, 60m farther south, is the **Madrasa Sibaiye**, completed in 1515, a year before the Ottoman conquest, and commemorating one of the last Mameluke governors of the city.

On the east side of the street, in 100m, is the entrance to Straight Street, but continue past it to the **Mosque of Sinan Pasha** a few metres to the south with its striped black and white *ablaq* façade and its minaret of green and turquoise glazed brick. This Sinan has nothing to do with the great architect of the Tekkiye Mosque, rather he was yet another Ottoman governor of Damascus, but his mosque, dating from 1590, is a delight. A high recessed portal with a stalactite cupola leads into a small irregular court, a charming oasis of vines, flowers and trees. For those who come to pray here several times a day it offers a welcome retreat from the heat, noise, grime and distraction of the streets and souks, a release from labour. There is the fountain, the drinking, the washing of feet, perhaps the splashing of one's head with water, and then the privacy and quiet of one's prayers.

The striped *ablaq* of the exterior is carried on round three sides of the court and on the paving, while more complicated patterns and colours adorn the façade of the prayer hall. Its porch is supported by six columns bearing lozenge capitals, the two at the centre black with spiral fluting, the remaining four smooth and of paler stone with some black streaking. A nice touch is the tiling filling the arches above the doors and windows of the prayer hall, a deep blue predominantly, but also green and black with floral motifs. These tiles are Damascene, usually inferior to the Iznik tiles of Turkey, but in this case very delicate in both line and colour. The entire effect of courtyard and porch is highly pleasing for its variety and intimacy. Unfortunately the decoration within the domed prayer hall is cluttered and vulgar. From the court you should look again at the glazing on the minaret, in much better condition on this side than when viewed from the street, where many of the bricks have lost their colour and lustre.

Just south of the Sinan Pasha Mosque there is a fork, one branch curving eastwards and following the outer perimeter of the walls. This is the covered **Souk Sinaniye**, selling sheepskins, and leads through a broken-down but lively quarter of Damascus, with glimpses of the **walls** to your left, sometimes standing free, sometimes a round tower serving as the foundation for a house. Always continuing left you come into Badawi Street which passes below **Bab al-Saghir**, meaning the Small Gate, an Arab replacement of the Roman Gate of Mars, and along the north side of **Bab al-Saghir cemetery**, a Muslim burial ground since the Arab conquest of Damascus and containing many venerable tombs. Among these, towards the centre and beneath a silver dome, is the supposed **tomb of Fatima**, daughter of Mohammed and wife of Ali, which attracts Shia pilgrims, especially from Iran.

Back at the fork near the Mosque of Sinan Pasha, the other branch heads south to **Meidan**, a straggling suburb of the Old City that grew up in the Mameluke and Ottoman periods. It was literally a strip, 3km long, lined with markets, hamams and mosques catering to the overflow of pilgrims who gathered here to join the caravan, its official starting point the Umayyad Mosque, as it issued from Damascus bound for Mecca. Nowadays the area has fattened out, the old buildings hemmed in by modern shops and apartment blocks. The Kadam railway station is here, the departure point for all train journeys in Syria except those to Zabadani and Deraa, which leave from the Hejaz station in town, as do those to Amman in Jordan.

Along the Western Section of Straight Street

The Roman Via Recta, or **Straight Street**, was the principal east–west thoroughfare of Damascus, its decumanus maximus lined with colonnades. Today known in Arabic as Souk al-Tawil, the long souk, it remains the most obvious survival of the city's Hippodamian street plan. After the conquests of Alexander the Great in the late 4th century BC, cities throughout the Hellenistic world were planned in accordance with the ideas of Hippodamus of Miletus, who during the time of Pericles in the 5th century had introduced at Piraeus, the port of Athens, his rectilinear grid pattern of intersecting streets. In the East the Romans followed the Greeks in this, and in many cities of Syria, among them Aleppo and Damascus, this Hippodamian pattern can still be traced despite the haphazard overlays of later times.

The street is famous for its association with St Paul after his blinding vision on the road to Damascus, though interestingly Acts 9:11 describes it as 'the street which is *called* Straight', suggesting that then as now it did not quite live up to its name. The reason is discovered when you walk about in that area between the east of the Umayyad Mosque, originally the site of the temple of Hadad, and Straight Street, where you become aware of a couple of low rises upon which the earliest settlement was founded. The pre-classical street skirted these rises and its course was followed by the Greeks and Romans, who had to make allowances too for existing buildings. Since then the margins of the street have been encroached upon, so that it is only a quarter of the 26m width it enjoyed in Roman times.

Instead of immediately starting at the west entrance to Straight Street, walk a few metres south to the Mosque of Sinan Pasha and then pass through the Arab Gate of the Water Trough, **Bab al-Jabiye**, just behind it. The Roman Gate of Jupiter stood here. This brings you into **Souk al-Kumeile**, literally louse market, selling second-hand clothing, cheap suits and the like, which for about 300m parallels Straight Street (Souk al-Tawil) and then converges with it. Taken together, both Souk al-Kumeile and Souk al-Tawil occupy the original 26m width of the Via Recta. On the right side of Souk al-Kumeile, near its convergence with Straight Street, is the Mameluke **Mosque of Hisham**, built in 1427, with fine stalactite decoration. Somewhere just south of here is thought to have been the **theatre** built by Herod the Great in the 1st century BC. No trace of it survives, but curving passages in the vicinity perhaps record its outline.

Now cut through to the **covered section of Straight Street** which runs eastwards from its entrance north of the Sinan Pasha mosque, its shops selling cloth, traditional dress and a wide variety of household goods. (To confuse things, this covered section, which ends at about the intersection with Souk al-Bazuriye, is also known as Souk Midhat Pasha.) On the north side of the street just west of Souk al-Haiyatin (which runs north to the triumphal arch in front of the Umayyad Mosque) are two khans, that nearest the corner the **Khan Djaqmaq**, a Mameluke edifice built in 1420 and now in a bad state. About 50m west of it is the late 16th-century **Khan al-Zait**, originally a caravanserai for olive oil. You enter a large airy court surrounded by vaulted arcades, a tree to one corner offering its leaves like an awning against the sun. 'All this is small factories', you are told as you climb up to the gallery, within each arch a workshop, these combining in a complete minor industry specialising in the various phases of making the black headbands that hold the Arab headdress, the *kefieh*, in place. The khan is filled with air and light and has water in the courtyard, a shade tree and little potted plants, while someone produces endless glasses of tea. The work is repetitive but is performed in the most pleasant environment, so much more agreeable than the workplaces of early industrial Europe, and also efficiently and cooperatively organised, yet each man here is his own, subject only to the market, not a boss-driven drudge.

Just east of Souk al-Haiyatin and on the south side of Straight Street is the striped *ablaq* entrance to the **Khan Suleiman Pasha**, built on an ambitious scale in 1732, but the twin domes that once covered its central courtyard have collapsed and the place is in a poor state. Its trade was once in silks and Persian carpets; now coffee is roasted here, and there are shops selling cottons of crude design, plastic hoses and big rolls of cellophane wrappers for McVitie's Rich Tea, Sainsbury's Wheat Crackers, KP Salted Nuts and Cadbury's Fudge.

Along the Eastern Section of Straight Street

Up to this point, Straight Street has been covered and diverting. Now eastwards to Bab Sharqi it is dull, with much concrete intrusion among the few older buildings. Concrete is a disaster. In the past, anything really solid was built of stone and if it was rearranged or even torn down, some of its stones remained to serve as foundations or walls or could be recycled as building blocks—and they would be spared for that reason: their usefulness. To build in stone meant following certain principles: the result might not be delightful but it was very rarely ugly. Any idiot can build in concrete, throwing everything away that has been before, not only stones but all sense of form. And he will leave behind him chunks amorphous and indestructible that will have to be carried away to some pit or used to fill in some bog before starting again—as ugly as before. So this is what Straight Street brings to mind as you walk eastwards past the Roman arch into the Christian quarter, first announced by the steeple of al-Mariam, the Greek Orthodox Patriarchate.

Since Graeco-Roman times the ground level of Damascus has risen by about 5m, in some places more, through the accumulation of debris. The **Roman arch**, which is about two-thirds of the way along Straight Street, had been entirely buried and forgotten in this way until it was found during the French Mandate by workmen who were demolishing houses near by. Originally it spanned the northern colonnade and may have been part of a 3rd-century AD tetrapylon marking the intersection of the decumanus maximus (the Via Recta) with the principal north–south street, the cardo maximus. Now flanked by fluted columns, it has been reconstructed with some use of new stone at the present ground level.

As far back as Byzantine times a church has stood on the site of the present **Greek Orthodox Patriarchal Church of the Virgin Mary** (al-Mariam), immediately north of the arch. The previous church was burnt to the ground in 1860 during the Muslims' wholesale massacre of the city's Christians. Six thousand died in all, including three hundred who had sought the Virgin's protection and were burnt alive inside the church. East and north of here is the **Christian quarter** of Damascus, for at the Arab conquest in 636 the Christians were guaranteed the right to their churches here.

To the south is the Haret al-Yehud, the traditional **Jewish quarter**, though no more than two or three streets are actually inhabited by Jews, who in the whole of Syria number only 3000–4000. Instead the area has become almost totally Christian. You can walk through its narrow twisting lanes, many of them blind, lined with white-painted overhanging houses, to reach **Bab Kaysan** in the southeast stretch of the city walls, but you will probably lose your way; instead go first to Bab Sharqi and follow the walls back. Named after the personage who built it, Bab Kaysan occupies the site of the Roman Gate of Saturn. To this place attaches the story of Paul escaping from the city in a basket let down the walls. He had come to Damascus to persecute Christians but owing to his vision preached Christ in the synagogues instead. He was condemned to death by the Jews for heresy (Acts 9:20-25), and the governor attempted to apprehend him, so that, as Paul writes in II Corinthians 12:33, 'Through a window in a basket was I let down by the wall, and escaped his hands.' The lower courses along this section of the wall might well have been those that Paul was let down like a cat, as they are Roman, but the upper courses are of Nur al-Din's time and into these was built a Mameluke gate, around which has been constructed in the 20th century **St Paul's Chapel**, its outer walls emblazoned with the Chi-Rho symbol, where you will be shown the very window from which Paul anachronistically made his escape. There is no reason to doubt that Paul did indeed flee the city in this way but the Scriptures fail to identify the spot, which subsequently was localised here perhaps because of the **Christian cemetery** stretching away southwards before you along the east side of the airport road. Still later, the vicinity laid claim to the site of **Paul's vision on the road to Damascus**. In the Middle Ages Christian tradition had agreed that the vision occurred at the village of Kokab, 15km to the southwest, but then in the 18th century the event was shifted conveniently closer, to a point just beyond the Christian cemetery. Maundrell walked out to have a look: 'It is close by the wayside, and has no building to distinguish it, nor do I believe it ever had: only there is a small rock or heap of gravel which serves to point out the place.' The Franciscans have recently remedied the oversight and have built a chapel on the spot.

As though not to be outdone, on the west side of the airport road and conspicuous to airline passengers coming in to town is the towering minaret of the modern **Mosque of Bilal**, Mohammed's *muezzin* and the first man to call the faithful to prayer, which he did from the top of the Kaaba in Mecca. According to some accounts, Bilal is also buried here. A black slave from Abyssinia, Bilal was ransomed by Abu Bakr, a wealthy Meccan merchant who, second only to Khadijah, Mohammed's wife, became the first convert to the Prophet's message and, after his death, the first caliph. Though Bilal's pronunciation of Arabic was imperfect, Mohammed chose him for his fine voice, which is now echoed, sonorously or otherwise, in the ears of over 700 million Muslims from the Atlantic to the Pacific: *Allahu Akbar. Ashadu an la ilaha illa-Llah. Ashadu anna Muhammadan rasulu-Llah. Hayya ala-s-salah. Hayya ala-l-falah. Allahu Akbar. La ilaha illa-Llah* (*see* p.66).

The cemetery and, at the end of Straight Street on its south side, the **Armenian and Greek Catholic Patriarchates**, explain the lively trade in death—vans loaded with floral crosses and an abundance of black-bordered death notices—in the vicinity of **Bab Sharqi**, the East Gate. This is the Roman Gate of the Sun, built in the early 3rd century AD and the oldest extant monument in Damascus. The central arch was for traffic (and still is), while the smaller portals on either side were for the passage of pedestrians along the arcaded pavements. A **minaret** over the north portal marks a mosque built at the time of Nur al-Din's rebuilding of the city walls. Outside the gate is **Nassan's Palace**, an old shop specialising in oriental brocade and furniture, the silk spinners working in the courtyard behind. Remains of the **kilns** where the famous Damascus tiles were fired have been found outside the gate. At their best, for example in the Mosque of Sinan Pasha, they ran a close second to the more celebrated tiles of Iznik.

Now inside the gate and facing west down Straight Street, take the first turning right (north) into Hanania Street where you can stop in at number 5, which is the shop of **Giovanni Haddad**, specialising in antiques, lamps, carpets, glassware and furniture. It is also a good place to buy brocade. A long, narrow shop immediately adjacent to Giovanni's is interesting— it is where very old, traditional Damascene furniture, including ornate painted panels and huge doors, is being restored. Continue north 150m along this street to the point where you can go no farther in a straight line and you are at the **House of Ananias** (*closed Sun*), who in Acts 9:17 restored Paul's sight. Unlike St Paul's Chapel at Bab Kaysan, there is no anachronism here, as archaeologists have dated parts of what is now a chapel, reached by steps descending five metres below the modern street level, to the 1st century BC. Whether this was indeed the house of Ananias is another matter, for as we have seen (p.84) these venerated spots have a way of moving around.

Paul's Vision on the Road to Damascus

Paul (or Saul as he was first known) was a Jew of Tarsus, in present-day Turkey, and descended of a family of Pharisees. He spoke Aramaic and Hebrew, but also Greek, for the inhabitants of Tarsus were thoroughly Hellenised, and Paul would have been familiar with Stoic philosophy, of which the city was a great centre, the 'Athens of Asia Minor'. Additionally, Paul came from a wealthy family that had been granted Roman citizenship. By background, therefore, he was a man of several worlds.

Yet at first Paul chose to be narrowly sectarian. Jesus had already been crucified when Paul came to Jerusalem to study at the rabbinical school, though a small circle of his followers endeavoured to keep his teachings alive. Their beliefs and their organisation have been debated by scholars, and on one view it can be said that they were no more than a Jewish sect without rituals or holy places or a priesthood of their own. With the death of their teacher, there was every chance that in time they would be reabsorbed back into the mainstream of Judaism. If they asserted the divinity of Jesus, then that was heresy and there was no going back. But for the followers of Jesus there was no going forward unless they could succeed where Jesus himself had already failed—to reform or transcend Judaism by finding salvation beyond the fulfillment of the law, those 613 conflicting injunctions and prohibitions that no man could hope completely to honour, and so casting all men as sinners. Yet legalism was the stock and trade of the Pharisees, and by background Paul was one of their number.

Stephen became the first Christian martyr in about AD 35 by asserting the divinity of Jesus, and Paul was an approving witness of his stoning. Nor was the role of complicit bystander enough for Paul, who now 'made havoc of the church, entering into every house, and haling men and women committed them to prison' (Acts 8:3). Yet the way the story is told you get the impression of a man driving himself towards fanaticism lest something within himself gives way: Paul 'breathing out threatenings and slaughter against the disciples of the Lord, went unto the high priest, and desired of him letters to Damascus to the synagogues, that if he found any of this way, whether they were men or women, he might bring them bound unto Jerusalem' (this and the following from Acts 9:1-25).

'And as he journeyed, he came near Damascus: and suddenly there shined round about him a light from heaven: and he fell to the earth, and heard a voice saying unto him, Saul, Saul, why persecutest thou me? And he said, Who art thou, Lord? And the Lord said, I am Jesus whom though persecutest.' Paul rose from the ground blinded by the vision and had to be led into town, to the house of one called Judas in Straight Street, where for three days he neither saw nor ate nor drank. On the third day, responding to a vision, Ananias went to Paul and put his hands upon him: 'And immediately there fell from his eyes as it had been scales: and he received sight forthwith, and arose, and was baptised.' At once Paul rushed round the synagogues preaching the very heresy that Jesus' followers in Jerusalem had hesitated to embrace, that Jesus was the divine Son of God. Not surprisingly the Jews were 'amazed' and 'they watched the gates day and night to kill him', so necessitating Paul's night-time escape, at Bab Kaysan or elsewhere (*see* p.85), in a basket.

By the instantaneousness of Paul's conversion, he dispensed with the doubts, the hesitations, the halfway houses that accompany argument and reflection, and became free to find radical solutions to the predicament of the Jesus cult. The very divinity of Jesus, the idea that a man could be a god, while utterly alien to Judaism, was in keeping with Hellenistic culture. To that culture, to the gentiles and to the Jews of the diaspora, he directed his mission, bypassing the Jerusalem brethren. They had known Jesus in his lifetime, as a Galilean, as a Jew, as a teacher who had tried to work within the particularity of his environment. But Paul's authority was to have known Jesus through that vision on the road to Damascus, to have known him as divine, as boundless and universal. Abandoning such Jewish shibboleths as circumcision, objectionable to the gentiles, while presenting his doctrines in the concepts and terms of Greek language and thought he had known at Tarsus, Paul embarked on a series of proselytising journeys that took him from the Middle East to Asia Minor, Cyprus, Greece and ultimately to Rome itself, where he is thought to have been martyred in about AD 65.

Following the Walls from Bab Sharqi to the Citadel

From Bab Sharqi you can walk north along the outer perimeter of the walls towards Bab Touma, which can also be reached by threading your way through the Christian quarter from the House of Ananias, which is just inside the east walls.

At the northeast corner of the Old City walls (400m north of Bab Sharqi or 250m east of Bab Touma) is the **Tower of al-Salih Ayyub**. This dates from the last years of Saladin's dynasty, the Ayyubids, for just as Egypt was being threatened by St Louis at the head of the Seventh Crusade, al-Salih died, and though his widow, Shagarat al-Durr, boldly saved the day, it was at the cost of issuing in Mameluke rule over both Egypt and Syria (*see* Baybars, p.78).

Opposite this place in 635 the Muslim army fell to its knees and prayed before laying siege to Christian Damascus. Twice the armies sent by Heraclius, the Byzantine emperor, to relieve the city were routed. The emperor's son-in-law, Thomas, commanded the garrison within and, as the months passed in growing desperation, he decided to launch a counter-attack through the gate now called **Bab Touma**. Before leading his men out to battle, Thomas placed his hand on the Bible and called to God, 'If our faith be true, aid us, and deliver us not into the hands of its enemies.' The Muslim chroniclers, to whom this account is owed, recorded great feats of heroism on both sides. Many Muslim commanders were killed, but Thomas was shot through the eye with an arrow and the Christians were forced back within the walls. When finally Damascus fell, those Christians who wanted to leave the city were given three days' safe passage, and among these were Thomas and his wife, the emperor's daughter. They made for the mountains of Lebanon but after the third day they were hunted down, and Thomas, his wife and the others were slaughtered in the meadows, only one Christian escaping to carry the news of the disaster to Constantinople. After this Thomas is Bab Touma, the Gate of Thomas, named. The present gate, standing apart in a park and surrounded by traffic, is a 13th-century Ayyubid reconstruction of the original Roman Gate of Venus. Bab Touma has given its name to the northeastern quarter of the Old City. Here women go about without robes and veils, though the churches are mute, and what fills the air are the cries of neighbouring *muezzins*.

(For a good hamam that takes women, provided they come as a group and book the entire place, walk into the Old City through Bab Touma and take the first right. At the end of this street are the **Bakri Baths,** ✆ (011) 5426066, open daily 8am–midnight. Normally reserved for men, up to 12 women can book the whole baths, paying LS780 for the entire group for an hour.)

Walking west from Bab Touma along the outside of the walls, you notice their lower courses of great Roman and Byzantine blocks precisely cut and above these the smaller, neatly laid Arab stones, while uppermost is the patchwork of Ottoman times. Houses are built onto or even into the wall. On the other (north) side of the street flows the **Barada**, the Cold River (*see* p.125). After being covered over near the Tekkiye Mosque it has resurfaced at the Citadel and you feel its coolness immediately, its stream here overhung with branches and crossed by footbridges leading to houses on a leaf-shaped island—if only the Barada did not stink so much and its waters were not fouled with debris you could more easily imagine how pleasant a scene this used to be.

Here the river meandered through delightful gardens and fragrant orchards, wrote the Reverend J. L. Porter (*Five Years in Damascus*, 1855):

> *During the spring and autumn months these gardens form the most delicious retreats around the city. In the evenings groups of the citizens here squat along the banks of the gently flowing river, and, as they lazily inhale the smoke of their perfumed nargilies, and silently gaze on the transparent waters, realise the acme of Eastern felicity. Music and dancing-girls sometimes enliven the scene; but the thorough Oriental is too listless and apathetic to derive much pleasure from these.*

At 300m west from Bab Touma you come to the most impressive of the gates of Damascus, **Bab al-Salaam**, the Gate of Peace, so called because the strength of the walls here and the depth of the river discouraged the Arabs from attacking at this point. Originally this was the Roman Gate of the Moon. It was reconstructed by Nur al-Din in 1171 and further reworked by al-Salih Ayyub in 1243 at the same time as he built his tower farther east.

You should continue west along Bein al-Sorain Street, which passes between the inner and outer walls and in 250m reaches **Bab al-Faradis**, the Gate of the Orchards. Dating from 1241, this too was built by al-Salih Ayyub. Facing the gate from the south, go down the steps to your right (east) and turn left. This brings you to two short Corinthian **columns**, survivals of the original Roman Gate of Mercury atop which and a bit to the west the Arab Bab al-Faradis was built. A metal door to the immediate left of the columns lets into a guard room, now a unisex public toilet, with an arrow-slit over the Barada. The Shia quarter lies between here and the Umayyad Mosque to the south.

Just back from the Bab al-Faradis, that is within the Old City, is a new **Shia mosque**, typically flashy, recognisable by its bulbous Iranian-style dome. The mosque houses the shrine and body of Lady Roqaiya, who died in AD 680, the daughter of Hussein (see p.71) and therefore the granddaughter of Fatima and Ali and the great granddaughter of the Prophet (see p.243). The courtyard is decorated with a frieze of blue, green and gold tiles which also fill the liwans. Going inside the mosque you are startled by a blaze of refracted light: thousands upon thousands of small mirrors are set at angles in the ceiling from which are suspended huge chandeliers like gargantuan artichokes and swathes of gold tiles cover the walls—the gaudy dazzling glitter far surpassing the most retina-damaging London or Manhattan disco. But here the sound is of the Koran mumbled repeatedly and of children tearing about, laughing and shouting as they slide across the marble floor. The children are here because the shrine of the Lady Roqaiya attracts women especially. The shrine is green and pulsates with light, and the women press their faces against it. And afterwards they go out into the courtyard, light up a cigarette, and have a good chatter and smoke.

Bein al-Sorain Street continues west, often vaulted, and in 250m comes to **Bab al-Faraj**, the Gate of Deliverance, again part of al-Salih Ayyub's refortification work. This is the one case where there had been no earlier Roman gate, Nur al-Din first opening up the walls here. You are now close by the northeast corner of the **Citadel** (*see* p.62) and have completed your tour of the Old City—though it repays revisiting again and again, best of all when you wander aimlessly.

Salihiye

On the lower slopes of Mount Kassioun is Salihiye, once a distinct village two kilometres north of the Old City but now washed by the outflow of modern Damascus. Yet the original settlement keeps much of its character, especially along the east–west **Madares Assad al-Din Street** (or Al-Madares Avenue, meaning the street between the madrasas) lined with numerous mosques, tombs and madrasas, mostly of the 13th and 14th centuries. Salihiye was settled by refugees from Crusader-occupied Jerusalem in the 12th century, and in the 19th century attracted numerous non-Arab refugees, especially Kurds, who established themselves towards its eastern end, and after 1896 Muslims forced out of Crete, who settled towards the west.

The climate of Salihiye and its views appealed to Sir Richard Burton, who while British Consul at Damascus from 1868 to 1871 lived in its Kurdish quarter. He had already made a pilgrimage to Mecca, disguised as a Pathan, and had travelled in search of the source of the Nile, and now at Salihiye, where he would join in the *muezzin*'s cry from the minaret outside his window, he began his translation of *The Thousand and One Nights*. A neighbour was the famous beauty Jane Digby al-Azrab, who between her maiden and final names had been the wife of Lord Ellenborough and mistress to among others King Ludwig I of Bavaria, King Otho I of Greece and Honoré de Balzac, finally marrying a sheikh of Palmyra. Together with Abd al-Kader, the exiled leader of Algerian resistance to France, author of a book of erotic poetry to a lady of Mecca and the saviour of many thousands of Christians during the 1860 massacre in Damascus, they would spend the summer evenings on Burton's rooftop talking of everything from mysticism to harem intimacies.

Midway along Madares Assad al-Din Street and just west of the covered vegetable and household goods market is the **Mosque and Mausoleum of Sheikh Mohi al-Din** (also called Jami al-Selimi). Mohi al-Din Ibn al-Arabi was a Sufi mystic who in 1202 left his native Andalusia for what was then the freer intellectual atmosphere of Damascus. He was buried here in 1240, and the mosque was built over his tomb by Sultan Selim, the Ottoman conqueror of Damascus, in 1518. Al-Arabi has been described by the historian Philip Hitti as 'a pantheistic philosopher' and 'the greatest speculative genius of Islamic mysticism. He recognised the inner light as the one true guide', and influenced Dante's conception of the *Inferno*. Al-Arabi's tomb is in a chamber at the far left corner of the mosque's courtyard and, like the head of John the Baptist in the Umayyad Mosque, especially attracts women, who kneel before it reading their Korans. But their kisses polish the grille of the adjacent tomb, surprisingly that of Abd al-Kader. His body, however, was returned to Algeria following its independence, where now he must be turning over in his grave.

Mount Kassioun

Rising above Salihiye and overlooking Damascus from the north is 1200m-high Mount Kassioun, its ridge twinkling with lights late into the night. The only way to get here is by car, and if you take a taxi, then arrange for it to wait for you. As you drive up you pass the **Tomb of the Unknown Soldier**, looking like an enormous breakfast boiled egg; also the **Tishreen Palace** for visitings VIPs (Bill Clinton stayed here); and behind it the **Presidential Palace**.

The ridge turns out to be a Mulholland Drive for lovers, a carnival for families, a string of cafés and food stalls where you can sit out on the edge of the sky and have coffee or tea, falafel or a boiled ear of corn, and be ghetto-blasted with Arab music. There is a funfair at one end with dodgems, a train ride and a drag car track where Damascenes pay for doing what they do all day anyway—drive wildly, though here they are free to crash. Here appropriately Cain slew Abel.

Also here Mohammed halted, saw the beautiful city amid streams and orchards, and turned away from earthly paradise. The view is superb, and the air has that special coolness and freshness of altitude. Sundown is magnificent, but also night when Damascus shines like a galaxy on the black horizon of illimitable desert.

Sports and Activities

All the top hotels have swimming pools, of which the Sheraton's is by far the best—at a price. The rich kids of Damascus lounge there and around its three tennis courts. There is a running track and tennis at Al-Jalaa stadium, just off the autoroute to Mezzeh. The Tishreen stadium has a public swimming pool and tennis courts. Just off the airport road is the Andalous swimming pool. Farther out at the Ebla Cham are tennis courts, riding facilities and a golf course.

Every week—on Tuesday evenings in summer, Friday afternoons in winter—the Damascus Hash House Harriers meet for a hare and hound run at any one of 70 sites within about an hour's drive of Damascus. First established in Kuala Lumpur in 1938 by a group of British colonials who considered themselves drinking too much and in need of exercise, the HHH now have around 500 branches in 70 countries. The idea is that 'hares' set a trail of washable paint markers a few hours in advance of the start, as well as false trails; later, the good runners spend time scouting for the correct trail while the slower harriers catch up. Enthusiasts insist that it is a great way of exploring remote countryside, villages and even towns, and at any rate it is worth witnessing the incredulity on a local farmer's face as up to 150 scantily clad expatriates and Syrians run past. A few hashes include an overnight camping stop. To find out more, you should phone the British Embassy, ☎ (011) 3712561.

Shopping

Damascus is especially known for its brocades of silk with gold and silver threads; its tablecloths, both embroidered and printed; its inlay and silver filigree work; its copper and brassware; and its hand-blown glassware. These and many other tempting goods can be found in the souks of the Old City, at the artisans' bazaar by the Tekkiye Mosque and in hotel shops (the best of these is Haddad at the Cham Palace). Not everything will be marked and even when they are you should bargain; without much effort you should be able to get a reduction of 20 per cent to 25 per cent on even marked prices. Note, however, that some shops taking charge cards (especially American Express) will impose a percentage of about 8 per cent on the bill. Most shops close on Fridays, the Muslim day of rest, though Jewish shops will close on Saturdays, while Christian shops and the gold souks will close on Saturday afternoons and Sundays.

The **souks of the Old City** are of course one great shopping area, and as you follow the itineraries from place to place you will be passing through most of them, their specialities noted. The souks begin shutting down at about 7.30pm.

Between Souk al-Hamidiye and Straight Street is Harikah Street. Just after the round-about on the north side is the gold souk. Farther on, on the left after the Singer sewing shop, look for **Toukatelian Pearls** on the second floor. Tables heave under mounds of cultured, freshwater and seed pearls ready to be strung. Prices are excellent. Beyond, towards the Azem Palace, is the converted **Azem School** for antiques, jewellery, brocade and curios.

The **Souk al-Hamidiye** (*see* p.63) is a general bazaar selling shoes, clothing, carpets, jewellery, brassware, inlay work, musical instruments and all manner of tourist

gewgaws. Take the first right at its west end for some good carpet shops, most notably **Issam Al-Lahham** on the west side, and **Ali Baba** on the east (prices are fixed). Where the souk becomes uncovered look for **Tony Stephan** for a wide selection of brocade gifts and copperware. At the east end of the Hamidiye by the Roman arch is a shop called **Kahwaji Bazaar**, which apart from the view it offers from its roof, is well worth visiting for its carpets, kilims, old traditional costumes, Roman coins, oil lamps, tiles and Bedouin artefacts.

Running south from the Roman arch is the long **Souk al-Haiyatin** (*see* p.79), meaning souk of the tailors, a cloth bazaar, good for tablecloths, while towards its south end you can buy Arab headgear as well as the lengths of the cloth used for making it, which you might have ideas for putting to a variety of other uses.

From the south entrance to the Umayyad Mosque towards the Azem Palace is the **Souk al-Silah** (*see* p.73) with many goldsmiths. In the square just west of the Azem Palace is one of the best shops in Damascus, **George Dabdoub's Azem Palace Bazaar** (*see* p.80), good for such things as Russian icons, Persian carpets and Damascene silk tablecloths. As this is a Jewish shop, it is closed on Saturdays. Prices are high, so bargain hard here and at its other branch in the Sheraton. South from the Azem Palace to Straight Street is the **Souk al-Bazuriye** (*see* p.81), selling spices, nuts and sweetmeats.

Straight Street (*see* p.82) is the best place for buying copper and brassware. There is a flea market at its western end, while sheepskins are sold just outside it, south of the Sinan Pasha Mosque. Two thirds of the way along Straight Street, on its northern side, is **Bazar Nazir** for carpets. A tiny front belies a vast shop. It pays to know what you're looking for; bargaining may or may not be successful. Outside Bab Sharqi is **Nassan's Palace**, the oldest merchants in Damascus and one of the best places for buying brocade. They also have a shop at the Meridien Hotel. Just before reaching Bab Sharqi and heading north on the street towards the House of Ananias you come to **Giovanni**, 5 Hanania Street, an Aladdin's cave run by the Haddad family, who also have a shop at the Cham Palace Hotel. Here you will find a wide range of exquisite quality goods, including inlaid furniture, old brass lamps and trays, patterned silks, Byzantine glass, antique terracotta, silver jewellery and filigree tea and coffee sets, samovars, *narghilehs* and *galabiyyas*.

Damascus ℂ (011–)   **Where to Stay**

There is a tourist information counter in the airport arrivals hall, but it is unlikely to be of any use in helping you find a place to stay. There are accommodation counters at the airport, but only for the top-class hotels. Otherwise, to obtain information on the full range of hotels, go to the Tourist Information Office on 29 May Street (*see* p.52).

Generally speaking, the cheapest hotels are found between Martyrs' Square and the Citadel; mid-range hotels in the vicinity of the Hejaz railway station and in the triangle formed by Al-Ittahad, Port Said and Yousef al-Azmeh streets; while top-class hotels like the Syrian-owned Cham Palace are north of here or if foreign-owned (Meridien, Sheraton) are towards the western outskirts of town. As the cheapest and the mid-range hotels are all within about a 10min walk, it is fairly easy to have a look at several before choosing one. The cheapest hotels especially should be examined carefully for cleanliness, hot water, functioning toilets, fans, etc., before accepting a room.

very expensive

★★★★★**Damascus Sheraton Hotel**, Umayyad Square, POB 4795, ℂ 2229300/3, ✆ 2243607. All the usual international-class facilities you would expect, including a plethora of restaurants, café and bars, the biggest swimming pool in Syria, a business centre, bank, fitness centre, tennis courts, car hire and shops. Architecturally it is reminiscent of a war memorial, its public spaces claustrophobic and without intimacy or charm. It is also a long way west (3km) of the Old City, making you dependent on taxis.

★★★★★**Hotel Meridien Damas**, Al-Quwatli Street, POB 5531, ℂ 3718730, ✆ 3718661. Again, all the usual de luxe stuff, including several restaurants and cafés, a discotheque and a panoramic bar on the ninth floor (beautiful views of Salihiye and Kassioun at nightfall); a large heated pool, health club, tennis courts, bank, business centre, travel agency, car hire, hair salon and shopping arcade. Architecturally and in ambience the place ranks as a better class of lower income housing. Located near the pleasant residential Abu Rumaneh district on the north bank of the Barada, the hotel is 2km west of the Old City, making it something of a tiresome walk, but at least it is reasonably close (750m) to the National Museum on the south bank of the Barada.

★★★★★**Cham Palace**, Maisaloun Street, POB 7570, ✆ 2232300, ✆ 2212398. Facilities include four restaurants, including the only revolving restaurant in Syria, two bars, cafés, disco with live entertainment, bowling, swimming pool, fitness centre, hairdresser and beauty parlour, business centre, travel agent, car hire and shopping arcade. Rooms are sound-proofed and the bathrooms are panelled with marble. Being part of the Syrian-owned Cham chain, the service is a bit hapless, but the internal architecture is a delight, a screen of plants spilling from rising terraces down to the illuminated pool at the centre of the foyer. There is a pleasing variety of places to eat, drink, be entertained or just sit, and the food is good. Its downtown location puts it reasonably close to the Old City.

★★★★★**Semiramis Hotel**, Victoria Bridge, POB 30301, ✆ 2233555, ✆ 2216797. Recently refurbished, it is completely over-decorated and on a busy corner, but within walking distance of the old city. It has good facilities: car hire, swimming pool, restaurants, bars, a night club with belly dancers and Arabic music.

expensive

★★★★**Omayad Hotel** (also known as the New Omayad), 4 Brazil Street, POB 7811, ✆ 2217700/1/2/3, ✆ 2213516. Before the days of the Sheraton, Meridien and Cham Palace, this was the top hotel in Damascus, and it remains a very pleasant place. There is a rooftop restaurant and bar, car hire, and the air-conditioned rooms have TV, video and a fridge. Its central location places it within a kilometre of the Old City and the National Museum.

★★★★**Fardoos Tower**, between Maisaloun and Fardoos streets, POB 30996, ✆ 223 2100, ✆ 2235602. A new place and fairly comfortable with TV and minibar in the rooms, several restaurants, including an open-air terrace, bar, travel agents and shopping.

moderate

★★★★**Al Majed**, east of Yousef al-Azmeh Square, ✆ 2323300, ✆ 2323304. Lavishly decorated to Middle Eastern tastes, the place is very clean, excellent value, with restaurant and well-equipped rooms.

★★★★**Damascus International Hotel**, Bahsa Street, POB 5068, near Yousef al-Azmeh Square, ✆ 2312400, ✆ 2319966. Air-conditioned rooms with minibar and satellite TV. Restaurant, bars and shops. Central downtown location, 500m from the Old City.

inexpensive

★★★**Omar Khayam Hotel**, on the northwest corner of Martyrs' Square, ✆ 2312666. Built in 1928 in Art Deco style, this is an agreeable if down-at-heel place conveniently close to the Old City.

★★★**Orient Palace**, opposite the Hejaz railway station, ✆ 2231351, ✆ 2211512. Another and better 1920s establishment, an atmosphere of clapped-out opulence, with an enormous marbled hall and gilt chairs, and wonderful high rooms with balconies.

★★★**French Tower**, 29 May Street, ✆ 2314000, is a clean, comfortable, well-run place, good value for money, rooms with TV, minibar, shower, some with balcony.

★**Salam**, south off Mousalam al-Baroudi Street and back from the Tekkiye and Selimiye mosques, ✆ 2216674, is clean, pleasant, with fridge, TV and shower in rooms.

★★**Sultan Hotel**, Mousalam al-Baroudi Street, POB 221, ✆ 2225768, is between Hejaz Square and the Tekkiye Mosque complex. It has an unpromising entrance but is in fact clean and has character; all rooms have hot water. A friendly place with helpful management (tours and car hire arranged), the Sultan is popular but small, so you should try to book in advance.

cheap

★**Al Rabie**, Bahsa Street (go down steps into vine-shaded street north off Al-Ittahad Street, a short distance east from Yousef al-Azmeh Street), ✆ 2318374, ✉ 2311875. This is an old Ottoman house arranged around a spacious courtyard overhung with vines and with a fountain playing in the middle. An oasis of peace, relaxation and idleness, it seems completely removed in time from the modern world, and in that sense it is the most agreeable place to stay in Damascus. Apart from electric lighting and hot water, however, almost nothing has been done since the fall of the Ottoman Empire, and so accommodation is very simple, verging on the decrepit. For the most part it is backpackers who stay here, but frankly any millionaire with a taste for atmosphere and who is not too fussy would be very happy at Al Rabie. In summer when the place is busy (it is wise to book ahead) some sleep out in the courtyard, but there are two floors of rooms, some quite large, some with their own toilet and shower, and prices vary accordingly, from dirt cheap to cheap. No alcohol is permitted; tea, coffee and breakfast are served in the courtyard. The location is excellent, very close to the Old City, and the family who own it are very helpful, very much on the ball, and can arrange tours, car hire, find you a driver, get you to the airport and make onward hotel bookings throughout Syria and Lebanon.

★**Al Haramain** is in the same street as Al Rabie, nearer the steps down from Al-Ittahad Street, ✆ 2319489, ✉ 2314299. Also an Ottoman period house and run by the same family as Al Rabie, but here the courtyard is covered over and much smaller, in fact lends little atmosphere to the place and serves as hardly more than a grand entranceway. Al Haramain is somewhat spruced up, however, and cleaner, and alcohol is permitted upstairs. The clientele is the same as at Al Rabie, and the helpfulness is there, but the charm is lacking.

In the Tabbaleh area of Damascus, that is just outside the Old City and south of Bab Sharqi, good clean simple accommodation can be had at **St Elias Monastery**, ✆ 5432512/5421507, ✉ 5423603, and next door at the **hostel of the Memorial Church of St Paul**, ✆ 5433377, ✉ 5420317.

Damascus ✆ (011–)   ***Eating Out***

Restaurants tend to be dead before 9pm, after which there is a sudden influx of Syrians, all of whom love to dine late. The categories 'expensive', 'moderate' and 'inexpensive' are relative—in comparison with a restaurant meal in Europe or North America, an 'expensive' dinner in Damascus can be had at a very moderate cost. Here expensive means from SL500 (though more likely from SL750) to over SL1000 per person without drinks; moderate means from about SL250 to SL500; and inexpensive is below, sometimes very much below, SL250.

expensive

Some of the more sophisticated and expensive restaurants are those in the Sheraton, Cham Palace and Meridien hotels. The Sheraton is considered the smartest place to go; it is certainly the most vulgar and lacks atmosphere. The Cham Palace has the only revolving restaurant in Syria: the views across to Salihiye at sundown and at night are spectacular, and the food is good—as long as you are sitting down. Oddly, though the Meridien is French, its food in Damascus as well as in its other hotels in Syria is disappointing.

The fashionable Abu Rumaneh district in northwest Damascus, that is west of old Salihiye, has numerous smart and expensive restaurants devoted mainly to French cuisine. **Al Farès (Chevalier)**, Abdel Malek bin Marwan Street, ✆ 3333574, set in pleasant surroundings and serving mostly French but some Italian and Arab cuisine, is notable for seafood. Immediately adjacent to Al Farès is **Al Koh (Chaumière)**, ✆ 333 8883, with equally good meze and steaks, but no alcohol. **Al Motaa (Joy)**, Abdel Malek bin Marwan Street, ✆ 3335697, has Arab and French cuisine and is noted for its good mezes and tinkling pianist.

In central Damascus the **Club d'Orient**, Mrewed Street near Yousef al-Azmeh Square, ✆ 2213004, is where Damascene society goes: eat good meze and steaks among the diamonds and furs.

The following restaurants are all in the Old City. The **Umayyad Palace**, ✆ 2220826, is in a beautifully restored Ottoman building along a narrow alleyway off the street that runs along the south side of the Umayyad Mosque. Antique ornaments, live music and Whirling Dervishes make this easily the most atmospheric restaurant in Damascus, much favoured by tourist groups. Lunch buffet of meze, main course and pudding is excellent and moderately priced (no alcohol or entertainment); dinner with entertainment is more.

Elissar, near Bab Touma, ✆ 5424300, occupies the 19th-century palace of Ibrahim Pasha, with seating in a lovely central courtyard (covered in winter) or in a fabulously decorated banqueting room (where they usually stuff the tourist groups). French main dishes are preceded by Arab mezes, while upstairs **La Terrasse**, one of the most elegant restaurants in Damascus, serves exclusively Arab cuisine. **La Guitare**, south off Straight Street near Bab Sharqi, ✆ 5419823, has a laid-back atmosphere and Italian cuisine. **Casablanca**, on Hanania Street north off Straight Street near Bab Sharqi, has a cosy elegance about it, Western food, fish a speciality, and a pianist in the evening.

moderate

Still in the Old City, **Abu al Azz** is just north off the Souk al-Hamidiye as you approach the Umayyad Mosque, ✆ 2218174. Passing through the narrow entrance, you go upstairs to a spacious restaurant on two floors high above the chaos of the bazaar. Here the walls are decorated with marble mosaic and the wooden ceilings are painted and carved—and two Bedouin-style tents have been erected. The cuisine is Arab, the music is Arab, and the dancers are Whirling Dervishes. Dinner is moderate, lunch is inexpensive though no alcohol is served then. The **Umayyad Palace** (*see* above) falls into the moderate category at lunchtime (also no alcohol then). **Old Damascus**, in a street running east from behind the Citadel to the Umayyad Mosque, ✆ 2218810, inhabits an old Damascene house, has Arab cuisine, Syrian music and no Whirling Dervishes nor alcohol. It is a far lesser version of the Umayyad Palace, is mechanically geared to tourist groups and has little in the way of atmosphere.

inexpensive

Again in the Old City, one of the most pleasant places to dine is at the **Zeitouna** in Zeitoun Street, south off Straight Street, a short walk from Bab Sharqi (signposted beyond La Guitare), ✆ 5431324. Tables are set round the fountain in the courtyard of a beautiful old Damascene house, no gimmicks, merely charm, atmosphere and authentic surroundings. **Alf Leyla Wa Leyla** (A Thousand and One Nights) is on the street running east from the Umayyad Mosque, ✆ 5423021, in an old building with open courtyard and beautifully decorated liwans, though the place is rather run down. The cuisine is Arab; music in the evenings. **Abu al Azz** (*see* above) serves inexpensive lunches.

In the centre of town, **Abu Kemal**, 29 May Street, a couple of doors north of the Tourist Information office, serves an excellent range of Arab and Western meals. **Al Arabi**, in the pedestrianised street running south from the southeast corner of Martyrs' Square, has an Arab menu and is an agreeable place to sit out. In fact there are two Al Arabi restaurants in this street; the one farther up from Martyrs' Square is better.

There are plenty of little places, for example around Martyrs' Square and in the Souk al-Hamidiye, where you can pick up a snack of flat bread (*khubz*), *shawarma*, *kofta*, falafel, beans, peppers and salad very cheaply, or (unpasteurised) yoghurt, milk pudding and *kaimak*, a sticky ice cream, while in addition to water, watersellers wandering about the streets also sell a variety of fruit drinks, including pomegranate juice.

The **Nawfarah Café**, at the bottom of the steps on the east side of the Umayyad Mosque, is the most charming place in Damascus to pass the time over a glass of tea, a cup of coffee, to puff away on a *narghileh* and join a circle round a storyteller—the tale is in Arabic, of course, but the gasps and laughter from the gathering are entertainment enough. This is also the place to observe (if you return here over the years) how much Damascus is changing, here pleasantly so, as prosperity grows. The young women, as elsewhere in the world, are taking the lead in seizing their opportunities to throw off the restrictions of the past, and though it is only a small sign, it is remarkable how many, confident and laughing, Christian and Muslim, come to sit here for a coffee and a puff on the *narghileh*, the young men saying, 'Well, they are modern.' 'And the veil?' you ask, for the girls at the next table are all Muslim. 'They must wear the veil if they are traditional. If their husbands told them to wear the veil, they must'—and then, reflecting, 'But these girls are modern, I don't think we could tell them, and anyway we wouldn't,' and they seem quite happy with the modernness of the girls.

An enormous new marble complex has been built on the Umayyad Circle, including opera house, theatre and accommodation, which has improved somewhat the feeble state of the performing arts in Damascus, previously limited to occasional performances in the Sheraton by travelling theatre groups and to infrequent concerts and Shakespearean productions in the incongruous if spectacular setting of the Azem Palace. But most cultural activities of any note take place at the various foreign cultural centres—films, theatre, concerts, lectures, exhibitions: the British Cultural Centre, Maser Street, Abu Rumaneh, ℭ 3310631; the American Cultural Centre, 87 Ata al-Ayubi Street, ℭ 3338413; the French Cultural Centre, Bahsa Street, ℭ 2316181; and others.

Damascus is not exactly *mondain*; in fact about the most exciting thing going is at the **Officers' Club**, immediately west of the Meridien, which of course you cannot enter, but where they play Bill Haley's 'Rock Around the Clock' and other such favourites late into the night. Otherwise the city goes pretty quiet; no street life after dark, no gaiety, few hangouts of any kind. The cinemas show censored and puerile rubbish, and the nightclubs are tawdry affairs. The entertainments at the top hotels are just as stupid but more expensive. The city's cosmopolitanism hardly extends beyond the use of French and a fair number of Filipino, Russian and Eastern European tarts. At the Sheraton or Meridien nightclubs, for example, there is likely to be a mind-numbing crooner to put you in the mood for a *troupe folklorique*, about as *folklorique* as a Las Vegas barn dance and a good deal more tepid. Things look up only if they have lashed out on a belly dancer, usually imported from Egypt. If you can stand the pace, it goes on from 11pm to 2.30am, and requires reservations and lots of money.

The nightclubs in town, behind the Cham Palace for example, try to keep your eyelids open until as late as 4am. For your entry fee you get a drink and a meze and, if you have a few ferrets down your trouser leg, perhaps a bit of entertainment. The places are dark and intimate, with a minute stage on which a belly dancer briefly shimmies before giving way to some international set last seen at a Salvation Army mardi gras.

The **Moulin Rouge** is on the east side of 29 May Street. It cranks up at about 10pm and though it does not throw you out till 3am the show is over by midnight. The decor is tatty, the atmosphere stuffy, the performances miserable. Instead what you get for atmosphere are Filipinos, but they seem as dejected by the entertainment as you are.

The **Casino Al Jawhara**, on Port Said Street, costs a bit less than the others, opens more briefly, from 10pm to 2am, but is more to the point. A number of young girls dance rather aimlessly on the stage, vaguely directed by an older madam. Their job is to work up the men at the tables, soliciting money in exchange for dedications. They do not try very hard, instead dance a bit and laugh a lot between themselves, the whole thing more like a village wedding celebration. And the men laugh with them, while sitting at their tables and playing a longer game are Serbian, Bosnian and Ukrainian hostesses, loose, laid back, slightly lunatic and waiting.

Apart from enjoying the skin trade at the Casino Al Jawhara, about the most entertaining thing you can do in Damascus is go up to Mount Kassioun for the view and hope they have installed a funfair there so that you can ride on the dodgems.

Getting Around	102
Shahba	103
Qanawat	107
Bosra	110
Deraa	117
Ezraa	119

The Hauran and the Jebel al-Arab

The Roman theatre, Bosra

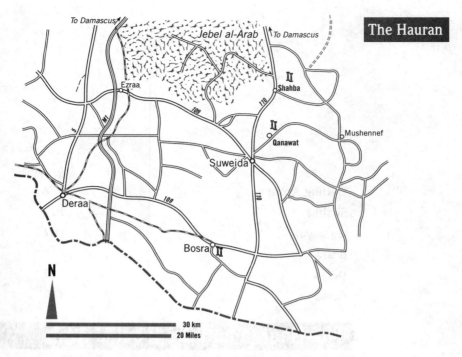

South of Damascus lies the Hauran, a fertile region possessing the finest Roman remains in Syria after Palmyra. The landscape rises gradually towards the Jebel al-Arab, a basalt massif peaking at 1800m which stands like a bastion against the eastern desert. Roman legionaries stationed on its heights deterred Bedouin incursions, ensuring security and prosperity on the plain below, and the Hauran soon became, like Egypt though on a smaller scale, a breadbasket of empire. Bosra, in the western lee of the Jebel, was a thoroughfare for the wealth of trade brought by caravans linking the Mediterranean, the Euphrates and the Red Sea. The outstanding artefact of those days of plenty and pleasure in the Hauran is Bosra's amphitheatre, one of the most intact in the whole of the Roman world.

The Arab invasion of the 7th century AD, however, marked the beginning of the Hauran's decline. Over the next 500 years, the area was exposed to the conflicting ambitions of Cairo and Damascus, while, lying close to Palestine, its ground was frequently fought over by Crusaders and Muslims. Depopulation and agricultural neglect spared what remained of the Roman past; with few inhabitants to put the ancient stones to other uses, they were left to endure the slower alterations of the elements and time.

The striking feature of these Roman monuments is their blackness. It is as though you have entered into a photographic negative of the classical past. The honeyed marble we associate with Graeco-Roman architecture is here replaced by blocks, columns and architraves of black basalt hewn from the volcanic landscape. This same stone is used to create the characteristic black and white *ablaq* seen in the Islamic architecture of Damascus.

Striking also are the blue-eyed and sometimes fair-haired people who sought refuge in the black wilderness of the Jebel during the 18th and 19th centuries. These are the Druze, a mountain people from southern Lebanon whose strange and hermetic faith links them only tenuously to Islam. The name Jebel al-Arab is in fact a recent government innovation; previously it was known as the Jebel Druze, and it continues to be something of a world of its own.

The Druze

The Druze trace the origins of their faith to the Cairo-based Fatimid Caliph al-Hakim (996–1021), whose behaviour was erratic, to say the least. The Fatimids, who were Muslims of the Shia sect, had shown themselves tolerant of other religions, and the caliph himself was born of a Greek Orthodox mother and raised by Christians. But suddenly al-Hakim reacted against his early influences, and in the course of ten years, from 1004 to 1014, he ordered the destruction of 30,000 churches in Egypt, Palestine and Syria, including the Church of the Holy Sepulchre in Jerusalem (a contributory cause of the Crusades). Jews were similarly dealt with.

Then the persecutions stopped, al-Hakim instead outraging his co-religionists by allowing himself to be proclaimed divine by his follower Mohammed ibn Ismael al-Darazi in 1016. While restoring freedom of worship to Christians and Jews, the caliph forbade Muslims to fast at Ramadan or undertake the pilgrimage to Mecca, and substituted his own name for that of Allah in the mosque services. As the fury of Cairo's Muslims turned against al-Hakim, and the caliph in turn burnt half the city down, claiming the assistance of Adam and Solomon in angel guise as he lopped off the heads of the well-to-do, Darazi fled to Lebanon where he founded the Druze sect in his own name.

Al-Hakim's departure from this world is cloaked in mystery. Each night in the company of a mute slave he would ride a donkey in the Moqattam Hills outside Cairo to observe the stars for portents. One dawn in 1021 he failed to return, some historians suspecting he was assassinated by his ambitious sister Sitt al-Mulk. The Druze, believing al-Hakim to be a manifestation of the divine, say that he underwent *ghayba*, a concealment from the world, and that he will return as their messiah.

Some would say that the Druze are not Muslims at all but are a departure from Islam with which they have no more than a historical link. The Druze reject much of *Sharia*, that is the canon law of Islam. They assemble on Thursdays, not Fridays, and non-Druze are forbidden to enter their places of worship. Their sect is secretive, with several stages of initiation in which guidance towards divine enlightenment is given as the will of al-Hakim. They believe in reincarnation, are monogamous and will marry only fellow Druze. Obedient to their elders and tightly knit, they have been remarkably successful in preserving their identity against outside pressures. Twenty years after the death of al-

Hakim, entry to their sect was closed, and they believe that their numbers have remained the same ever since. There are perhaps 600,000 Druze, living chiefly in southern Lebanon but also in Syria and Israel, while some have emigrated to the United States.

In Lebanon the Druze and the Maronite Christians have been traditionally hostile. Decades of communal warfare accompanied Maronite expansion into Druze territory during the 19th century, culminating in the massacre of 10,000 or more Maronites in 1860. French military intervention caused many Druze to withdraw to the Jebel al-Arab, where during the later French occupation of Syria the Druze led the 1925 revolt which spread to Damascus itself.

At one time the blue eyes and fair hair of many Druze gave rise to the fanciful European belief that these must be the descendants of Crusaders, notwithstanding that their sect came into being 70 years or more before the First Crusade. Nevertheless, many Druze women wear costumes straight out of troubadour times. They do not veil their faces, but instead they wear wimples beneath high conical headdresses, while from long tight bodices, which give charm and slenderness to their figures, their brilliantly coloured voluminous skirts gracefully sweep the ground. It may be that their style influenced medieval Europe rather than vice versa. The older men, the Initiates, wear a white turban and are often magnificently moustached. The stock of which the Druze are comprised has probably been native to the region for as long as any other, and in fact it is not only among the Druze that you encounter the startling light eyes and, especially among children, blond hair, but here and there throughout Syria, particularly along the coast and in the mountains behind.

Getting Around

By car: it is far easier to explore the Hauran and Jebel al-Arab by car, as attempts to do so by public transport will limit you to one or two destinations in a day.

Exploration of the Jebel al-Arab and the Hauran can be accomplished in one or two day-long excursions from Damascus, though you can also overnight at Bosra, Deraa or Suweida. The main sites are Shahba, Qanawat and Bosra, which by car can be covered in a long day's loop: Damascus to Shahba (87km); Shahba to Suweida (19km), from where you go up to Qanawat and back again (8km in each direction); Suweida to Bosra (32km); Bosra to Damascus via Deraa or Suweida (148km either way)—total 302km. Two day-long excursions will give you more time at the sites, especially if you want to include Mushennef (25km from Shahba, then 20km to Qanawat and 8 km to Suweida, or from Suweida to Qanawat and then 20km farther to Mushennef), stop at Suweida for its museum, and visit Ezraa (just off the Deraa–Damascus highway south of Damascus).

By bus, microbus and taxi: if travelling by bus or microbus, accept in advance that you will only be able to visit one or two sites in a day. Note that the flow of buses and microbuses back to Damascus from the Jebel or Bosra ceases around dusk.

There are direct bus or microbus services from the Baramkeh station in Damascus to Shahba (1hr), Suweida (1½hrs), Bosra (2hrs), Deraa (1½hrs) and Ezraa (1hr). The Deraa station in Damascus does not serve Bosra directly; you have to change at Deraa. Travelling from place to place within the region is problematic, however. In particular there is no reliable public transport between Suweida and Bosra or Deraa, though there is a microbus service between Suweida and Ezraa, and for something under LS500 you can take a taxi between Suweida and Bosra. Quite apart from the fact that waiting for buses or microbuses will make your progress slow, the lack of connections also means that you will have to divide your exploration of the region in two, devoting at least a day to each part if you want to visit all the principal places. Shahba, Suweida and Qanawat would form one part of the excursion, Bosra and Ezraa the other, and between the two you would either have to return to Damascus or you could stay overnight at Suweida. Or you could visit Ezraa and Bosra first and stay overnight at Bosra, taking a taxi in the morning to Suweida.

By train: the train is next to useless for visiting the region. At present there is only a twice-weekly service between Damascus (Hejaz station) and Ezraa and Deraa, and no service at all to Bosra except when the Bosra festival is being held in the amphitheatre for a couple of September weeks every odd-numbered year. Moreover the train (which rarely runs on time) takes 3hrs to Deraa and 5hrs in all to Bosra, at least twice as long as by bus. However, with the recent initiation of a daily train service between Damascus and Amman in Jordan, this may change; and also it might amuse you to travel by train in at least one direction between Damascus and Deraa.

Where to Stay

Accommodation is at Suweida, Bosra and Deraa.

Shahba

Route 110 runs southeastwards from Damascus across the Hauran plain where dust clouds turn out to be small herds of sheep searching the rock-strewn land for grazing. Fields are outlined by dry stone walls, as much an excuse for clearing the land of stones as keeping out sheep. Small pyramids of stones are heaped up even amid the furrows. The soil is the colour of caked blood, but the substructure of the Hauran is limestone overlaid by basalt, its black rocks and ridges breaking through the surface like the bones of a half-buried beast, and as you approach Shahba, set upon the summit of a rugged ridge of the Jebel al-Arab, you see the worn mounds of exhausted volcanoes.

Dry though it can seem, especially in summer, the dark landscape suggests the delicious wines grown on the slopes of Mount Etna in Sicily and the slightly fizzy red wine of volcanic Santorini in the Aegean. The Romans brought not only security to the Hauran but also water, building reservoirs, cisterns and aqueducts so that even the Jebel, without natural sources of its own, celebrated the vine.

Shahba is a mostly concrete and cinder block town, walls plastered white or cream or not surfaced at all so that it has the unfinished look of a construction site. When you begin to explore you will notice that the modern grey concrete often stands upon anciently cut blocks of black basalt. From Damascus you enter Shahba through the remains of a Roman arch, one of the original city gates, and joining the traffic of goats, buses, trucks and a few blades on motorbikes, you arrive at a central circle with a nearby café. From here you will easily be able to take your bearings, for Shahba, now almost entirely inhabited by Druze, occupies the site of Philippopolis, laid out with Roman regularity on a compass grid.

Getting There

Shahba is on route 110, 87km southeast of Damascus. Buses or microbuses serve Shahba from the Baramkeh and Deraa stations in Damascus, and from Suweida (*see* p.103). Return runs to Damascus are fairly frequent until late afternoon; check the time of the last departure as this varies with season.

The city was founded by Philip, Roman emperor from AD 244 to 249, whom Gibbon describes as 'an Arab by birth and consequently a robber by profession'. Certainly his father was an Arab chief and notorious brigand in the Hauran, and Philip, a soldier elected emperor by his legions, was probably born in what was still a village on this spot. His reign coincided with the thousandth anniversary of the founding of Rome, and in 248 he dazzled the imperial capital with spectacular games and rituals, though less a celebration than a diversion from the empire's decline.

> *To the undiscerning eye of the vulgar, Philip appeared a monarch no less powerful than Hadrian or Augustus had formerly been. The form was still the same, but the animating health and vigour were fled. The industry of the people was discouraged and exhausted by a long series of oppression. The discipline of the legions, which alone, after the extinction of every other virtue, had propped the greatness of the state, was corrupted by the ambition, or relaxed by the weakness, of the emperors. The strength of the frontiers, which had always consisted in arms rather than in fortifications, was insensibly undermined; and the fairest provinces were left exposed to the rapaciousness or ambition of the barbarians, who soon discovered the decline of the Roman empire.*

> Edward Gibbon, *The Decline and Fall of the Roman Empire*, 1776–88

Philip may have designed the city as a symbolic capital, and certainly its imperial plan, with walls, gates, broad intersecting colonnaded avenues and large civic buildings, magnificently commemorated his family origins. The project remained unfinished at his death, and less than half the area enclosed within the rectangle of its walls was ever built upon. Philippopolis did not survive the empire and was resettled only in the 19th century by Druze, who have often inserted their own homes within the ancient structures. The line of the walls can be traced on all four sides; of the four gates, two have survived sufficiently to permit some reconstruction, the northern gate which you enter from Damascus and the better preserved southern gate through which you pass en route to Suweida. The gates are imperial in form, a large central arch with a smaller arch on either side.

The modern traffic circle at the centre of town was also the ancient crossroads. The street running downhill to the east passes through the walls and out towards Mushennef. Most of what survives of ancient Philippopolis lies about 100m westwards along the ascending main

street (the decumanus, as it is always called in Roman cities) still paved with basalt Roman flagstones. Like the other axial streets leading off from the crossroads, this was originally 11m wide with four metre-wide colonnaded pavements on either side. You come first, on the north side of the decumanus after 50m, to a broad flight of ancient steps surmounted by four surviving basalt columns, three rising to their full height and bearing Corinthian capitals, which formed the portico of a now vanished hexastyle **temple**. Between two of the columns is a basalt post with five stone rings set in the top and a crudely carved figure in relief facing the street; he holds what appear to be two bunches of grapes or two pine cones, in either case suggesting that he is Dionysos.

Another 50m up this main street and then turning south, you immediately come to a building with several niches and a large central exedra, probably a *kalybe*, that is a shrine designed to display statues of the imperial family, some of whom were perhaps deified on the occasion of the Roman millennium. Linked to this and extending northwards, so that the main east–west street had to pass through by means of a narrow channel between its chambers, was the **palace**.

Exploring in this vicinity north of the decumanus you see a pair of stumpy Ionic columns supporting a low architrave. A television antenna sprouts from the top, washing is strung out front and tins planted with flowers add a final bright note of domesticity. An ancient carving on the left-hand column looks suspiciously like a seven-branched *menorah* (candelabra), a reminder that part of the Hauran was given to Herod the Great, the 1st-century BC king of Judaea, as a reward for backing Octavian (later Augustus) against Mark Antony. Elsewhere at this height of the town, basalt capitals and statue pedestals lie about, while old walls serve as house foundations or sheep pens. You see blond-haired children at play, and perhaps a friendly old white-turbaned Druze will appear from a doorway to say hello or even offer a glass of the local *arak*.

On the east side of the *kalybe*, steps descend into the forum which is flagged with basalt. Another flight of steps rises from the south side of the forum to a small square temple, probably raised in honour of Philip's chieftain father, Julius Marinus. It is only barely decorated, with slender pillars carved in relief at the corners, each bearing an Ionic capital incorporating what could be a bunch of grapes. Brackets on either side of the doorway held statues, one known to have been of the emperor's father. The interior walls were faced with marble, and more statuary filled the niches.

Immediately south of this temple is the **amphitheatre**, 42m across and nine rows of seats high, small but well preserved, and the last Roman theatre built in the East. The theatre is without decoration, and you notice that everywhere decoration is minimal, owing to the difficulty of the basalt. From the top row you can see that the town is built on eruptions of basalt, cut black stone on black bedrock, the ancient stones overlaid with modern grey concrete. You also see, with some relief to the eye, that Shahba is in the midst of something of an oasis; for several kilometres around there is a fair amount of green—of trees and planted fields.

You should now return the way you came to the central traffic circle. Heading south, turn east after about 75m; this brings you to the **baths** on the north side of the street and the museum on its south side. The remains of huge arches indicates the baths, which were built on a scale far exceeding the needs, if not the pretensions, of Philippopolis. The interior was faced with marble and domed in concrete, but all this is gone now.

The **museum** has been built to give cover to the fine floor mosaics discovered here in what were the remains of a private house dating from the decades following the founding of Constantinople in 330. Though two of the mosaics have erotic themes—that depicting the marriage of Dionysos and Ariadne, the other from Book Eight of the *Odyssey*, lines 266–70, in which Aphrodite is taken to bed by her lover Ares ('Come and lie down, my darling, and be happy!'), only to find themselves ensnared in her husband Hephaistos' trap—the treatment is rather stiff and has the opposite effect. More expressive is the mosaic showing Orpheus entrancing animals with his lyre, while another of the sea goddess Tethys allows the rich depiction of Mediterranean sea life. Other mosaics from Shahba are in the museums at Suweida and Damascus.

From Shahba's central traffic circle you head south for Suweida or east for Mushennef.

Mushennef

Getting There

There are morning buses from Shahba to Mushennef, but set out early as the last bus back to Shahba usually departs by noon.

Almost all that remains of the once flourishing Roman past at Mushennef has now been put to use in modern buildings. But at the centre of the village is what Gertrude Bell, who passed this way in 1905, calls 'the most charming of all the temples of the Jebel Druze', not least, you discover, because though situated on the volcanic massif within sight of a waterless desert reaching as far as Baghdad and Arabia, the temple is reflected in its artificial lake. With such tanks as these the Romans preserved through the intense heat of the summer the water gathered during the winter snows and rains. Built during those years when the empire was ruled by the general and stoic philosopher Marcus Aurelius (AD 161–80), the dark hard stone of the temple bears surprisingly delicate architectural details. Acanthus leaves spring from the Corinthian capitals atop square pillars at each corner, and rosettes and meanders lighten the entablature.

Suweida

Getting There

Suweida is on route 110, 19km south of Shahba. Buses or microbuses run here from the Baramkeh and Deraa stations in Damascus (*see* p.103). The service is frequent throughout the day, but the last run back to Damascus is at about dusk. From Suweida there are less frequent services to Qanawat, and there is a microbus service to Ezraa. But there is no public transport between Suweida and either Bosra or Deraa. A taxi to Bosra should cost something under LS500.

In keeping with the town's ancient name of Dionysias, the region around Suweida is known for the quality of its grapes, which produce a full-bodied and fruity wine as well as *arak*, an aniseed-flavoured brandy. Little else of its ancient inheritance has survived, however, owing to the cannibalising of Roman and Nabatean ruins by the Turks when they built their barracks before the First World War, and then the overlaying of what remained by the colonial-style constructions of the French, who kept close watch on the Druze here after the 1925 rebellion. Today Suweida is the capital of the modern province of the Hauran, a charmless if busy place with tree-lined streets and ugly administrative buildings, schools and barracks, the antithesis of the little villages elsewhere in the Jebel al-Arab. There is a large Greek Orthodox population, and Suweida is the seat of a bishop. Near the main square at the centre of town stand three columns of a 1st- or 2nd-century AD Nabatean temple and, close by, the ruins of a large 4th-century basilica, including part of the apse and a few pillars.

A museum, however, 1km on the right along the road to Qanawat, displays mosaics and sculptures found at Shahba. The Roman mosaics are as fine as those in the Shahba museum (though a bit older, from mid-3rd to early 4th centuries) and have similar themes, such as Artemis bathing among nymphs at a spring and sea-borne Aphrodite gazing in a mirror and arranging her hair. The sculptures span the Nabatean to Byzantine periods, and though necessarily less polished than the mosaics, they are more powerful for having been worked in hard basalt.

Where to Stay

A luxury hotel has been planned for Suweida, but for the time being you are faced with the inexpensive (but overpriced) **Tourist**, ✆ (016) 221013, basic, clean, but falling apart, with restaurant; or the cheap **Roddat al-Jabal**, ✆ (016) 221347, extremely basic, shared rooms, cold water, filthy toilet. The hotels are near one another about 300m east of the main square where the Damascus buses stop.

Qanawat

'The temples of Kanawat shining out from green country; rolling slopes dotted with trees and vineyards,' was how Freya Stark described her arrival here in May 1928. Allowing for season, that same surprise of discovery and beauty awaits you as you come to the highest point in Qanawat and see the ruined walls and graceful columns of the so-called Serai (Turkish for palace). Until recently the scene was all the more pleasant for the grove of oak trees among the stones, but these have now been chopped down, with only a mulberry left to meditate alone. Beyond, the ground falls away into a gorge, the Wadi al-Ghar, trickling with water in spring and filled with grass through summer, which opens northwards into a plain of orchards, an

upland of the Hauran. (The Wadi al-Ghar runs west across the Hauran to join the Yarmuk River which in turn enters the River Jordan just south of the Sea of Galilee.) The modern village runs along the ridge of the far bank, but up here as on an acropolis within the *enceinte* of the Roman and Byzantine walls, the remains of the ancient basilicas that comprise the Serai stand clear, unbuilt upon, intricate in plan and marvellously decorated with wreaths of vines and flowers.

Getting There

Qanawat is 8km from Suweida. In Suweida the bus stop for Qanawat is about 200m north of the main square where the Damascus buses stop. Departures during the growing season are almost half-hourly and the journey takes 15mins, with the last bus back to Suweida at about 4pm (check). Out of season, however, the service is erratic.

The Arabic *Qanawat* recalls the city's classical name, Kanatha, but also means canals, perhaps referring to the complex system of aqueducts and reservoirs installed here as elsewhere in the Jebel by the Romans. But its history goes back farther than that. As Kenath it is mentioned in Numbers 32:42, and later it was caught up in the struggle between the Nabateans and the Jewish kingdom. At first the Romans allowed it some autonomy as a city of the Decapolis, a federation of the 1st century BC and 1st century AD which included Damascus and Amman, only afterwards imposing direct rule. It continued to flourish under Christian Byzantium, when it became a bishopric (Bosra was the seat of an archbishop), but after Syria fell to the Arabs in the 7th century, Qanawat declined.

In front of the Serai there is a black flagged square that might have been a forum. From here it is pleasant to wander through the ruins of the complex structure that rises before you, noticing details like the fallen bits of architrave, one carved with rosettes and swastikas (before the 20th century an auspicious symbol) with human faces peeping out between. You soon become bewildered, though, and intrigued, by the way the components of the Serai seem to intersect and overlay one another, and at first glance seem orientated one way, at second glance another.

The **Serai** began as two adjoining Roman structures of the 2nd century AD but were then adapted to Christian worship in the 4th and 5th centuries. To understand their relationship and evolution you should first orientate yourself by entering from the paved square on the west side and pass through the first building to the open space lined with columns set upon high pedestals. This is the atrium. To the west the building through which you came was originally a basilica orientated north–south, while to the south of the atrium, through the monumental doorway, was a second and larger basilica, also initially orientated north–south. You should now examine the two buildings in turn.

The west building may have served as a Roman praetorium, that is a barracks or governor's palace. At its north end was a columned portico, at its south end a trefoil apse. During the Christian period, however, the building was reorientated east–west to serve as a church, with an altar placed on the east side. Upon an architrave here you can make out two small roughly cut crosses. A wall was built across the trefoil apse at the south end and this area perhaps became a martyrium, a chapel for keeping a saint's relics. The building was extended to the west, creating a new entrance with three portals, this being the way you came in.

Return to the atrium. The entire area now occupied by the atrium and the basilica to its south was at first a large colonnaded courtyard, though soon the southernmost portion, no more than five metres deep, was enclosed. By looking through the window you can see a triple-ribbed apse in the south wall. Whether the purpose of this courtyard and its enclosed section was secular or religious is not known. Then in about the 4th century the courtyard was cut in half by the high wall you see today with its beautifully embellished monumental doorway, again for purposes unknown. Christians took advantage of these arrangements, however, to make a church, giving it an east–west orientation by placing a synthronon, that is a semi-circular platform that framed a bishop's throne, against the east wall. On the ground before the synthronon stands a large shallow bowl, perhaps used for baptisms. Behind the synthronon, that is outside the east wall of the church, an excavation has revealed a subterranean chapel containing sarcophagi, one elaborately carved with crosses and grapes.

The Serai

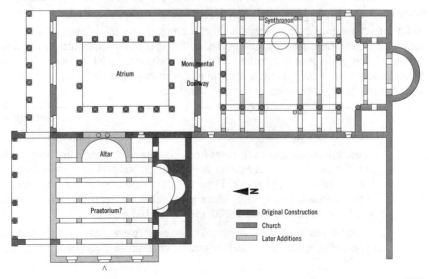

Walking Around Qanawat

A hundred metres northeast of the Serai, you come to the edge of the Wadi al-Ghar. All along this side of the wadi are the ruins of once imposing **Roman mansions**, their remains converted to houses by the Druze, who have sometimes built them into the side of the gorge so that you can walk out upon their roofs for the view. On the far bank you can see a square structure with pillars, possibly a temple or perhaps a **nymphaeum**, an enclosed water fountain. Beyond this to the north, built into the far slope, is a small **theatre or odeon**. Imagine attending a run of Seneca here.

Back at the square in front of the Serai, walk west about 50m to the first turning on your left and head south along this for another 50m to reach a ruinous **temple of Zeus**, while just to the west of it are the traces of what might have been a hippodrome. There are also underground vaults near by, perhaps a cistern. About 500m northwest of the Serai square, outside the line of the ancient walls and on the north side of the road descending to Suweida, there are the scant but richly decorated remains of a **small temple** dedicated to the sun god Helios. From its high platform there is a wide prospect over the Hauran westwards towards Mount Hermon.

Bosra

The fertility of the Hauran is most evident on the treeless plain between Bosra and the Deraa–Damascus highway where watermelons are plentiful and, until the fields are cut to stubble at the midsummer harvest, there is an Oklahoman abundance of wheat, barley, chickpeas (for *hummus*) and sesame (for *tahina*). But as for Bosra itself, the first impression is of a city blasted and blackened by war, in which a few survivors lead an improvised existence among the ruins. The place would not strike you this way if it shone as Roman ruins ought, all white and honeyed marble. It becomes fascinating, and perversely romantic, to wander through its streets and register Rome's grim determination to create grandeur from this dark, oppressive stone. If it were only blacker and did not have that dusty, dirty look. Or if this were the Jebel with its high vistas and not the plain. After a while in the black you imagine something unpleasant happening.

Yet it is tourism more than watermelons that is bringing new life to Bosra. There are interesting Islamic and Christian structures as well as Roman. The Roman theatre, in any case well preserved, has undergone restoration and is now the site of ballet, folkloric and dramatic performances in alternate summers, while in recent years a hotel has at last opened, offering an alternative to accommodation in Deraa or Damascus.

Getting There

Bosra is situated on route 109, 32km from Suweida and 40km from Deraa.

By bus, microbus and taxi: buses from the Baramkeh station in Damascus depart every 2hrs for the direct 2hr run to Bosra. The last bus back is at about 8pm but this can vary with season, so check. There are also frequent microbuses between Deraa and Bosra until late afternoon. There is no public transport between Suweida and Bosra; a taxi should cost LS400–500. (*See also* p.103.)

By train: during the Bosra Festival, which takes place every two (odd-numbered) years for two weeks in September, there is a train from Damascus via Deraa (*see* p.103).

A festival of drama, dancing and singing, staged mostly in the Roman amphitheatre, is held on odd-numbered years for two weeks in September.

History

With mountains to the west and desert to the east, the broad plain of the Hauran has been a natural north–south thoroughfare since the most ancient times. Bosra is first mentioned in the annals of Tuthmosis III (1479–25 BC), the Eighteenth Dynasty pharaoh who established an Egyptian empire by his conquests in Syria. Over a thousand years later it was briefly capital (AD 70–106) of the Nabatean kingdom, previously centred on Petra in Jordan. But it was the Romans who brought Bosra to eminence, when the Emperor Trajan extended direct rule southwards in AD 106. Bosra became the capital of the new province of Arabia, whose calendar began with the date of the city's conquest.

A caravan route led direct to the Persian Gulf, while from Antioch on the Mediterranean, and from the Euphrates via Resafa and Palmyra, Roman roads converged on Damascus to join the Via Nova Trajana running south from Bosra to Aqaba on the Red Sea. Roman forts guarded the route through present-day Jordan, a camel corps patrolled the desert's edge to ward off

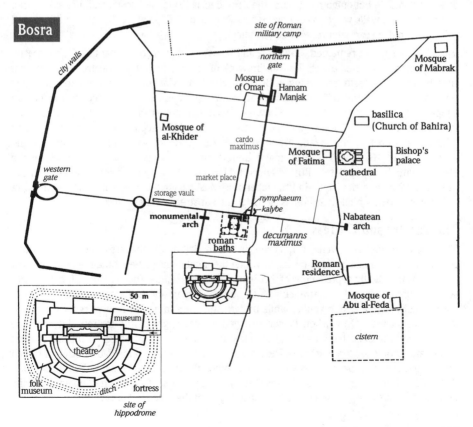

Bosra

Bedouin, while Bosra itself, the headquarters of the 5000-strong III Cyrenaica Legion, became the most celebrated fortress east of the Jordan. Zenobia sacked it in AD 268, but her career was brief and opportunistic, and she made no mark. Instead, the profits of trade and the favours of emperors have left their impress on the city to this day, its theatre, baths, market, triumphal arch and colonnaded streets attesting to its importance in the Roman imperial scheme.

Bosra later became the seat of an archbishop, to whom 33 bishops were subject, and his cathedral, now ruinous, was once one of the largest in the East. At Bosra too, so legend goes, a Christian monk first foretold a glorious future for the young Mohammed. Certainly in 632 it became the first Byzantine city to fall to the Arabs, and among its mosques is one that is perhaps the oldest in the Islamic world. Because of its position at the crossroads of trade as well as on the pilgrimage route between Damascus and Mecca, Bosra remained prosperous into the 14th century.

But Syria became a battleground when the Fatimids, who were Shia, established themselves in Cairo during the 10th century and opposed their caliphate to that of the Abbasids, who were Sunni, in Baghdad. The First Crusade was launched during this era of division, and in 1099 Jerusalem was taken. In 1147 and 1151, King Baldwin III of Jerusalem led his army into the Hauran, hoping that with the aid of its largely Greek Orthodox population he would easily be able to colonise it, but on both occasions the Crusaders failed to take Bosra, and their last hurrah before the city's walls was a cavalry raid led by Raymond of Tripoli in 1182, during the time of Saladin, who five years later recaptured Jerusalem.

The Crusader threat remained, however, and it was on that account that Saladin's dynasty, the Ayyubids, completed the earlier Muslim work of turning the Roman theatre into a fortress, thereby almost perfectly preserving it. Bosra survived the Mongol invasion of 1260, but they devastated the Hauran before their defeat by the Mamelukes, who a decade earlier had supplanted the Ayyubids in Egypt and now extended their power throughout Syria, driving the last Crusaders from the Syrian mainland in 1291. Continuing insecurity caused both trade and pilgrimage routes to shift gradually westwards (the Hamam Manjak, baths built by the Mamelukes in 1372, was the last major undertaking), leaving Bosra, like the rest of the Hauran, largely depopulated. But whereas the Druze, who emigrated from Lebanon in the 18th and 19th centuries, settled in the Jebel, it is Muslims for the most part who live in Bosra today, some having built their homes along its ancient streets and avenues.

The Theatre and Fortress

The mid-19th-century traveller J. L. Porter described visiting the fortress of Bosra, powerfully built and encompassed by deep moats, in which the inhabitants gathered their flocks to protect them from the nightly depredations of the Bedouin. Apart from the sheep, your visit today is not so very different from his. Entrance was through a single door at the east, which led on to courts, halls, staircases and vaults, while underneath were immense reservoirs for water and vaulted magazines. Only when Porter emerged at the height of the fortress did he come 'suddenly and unexpectedly to one of the most interesting ruins of Bosra—a theatre of great extent and exquisite workmanship'. The six lowest tiers of seating remained in place out of an original 37, providing places for 6000 spectators when the theatre was built in the 2nd century. At least 20 of the 60 or so Doric columns that ran round the top of the theatre remained; during performances a sun shade was probably suspended from these above the cavea.

Now the entire seating and many of the columns have been restored. Though the gleaming Corinthian columns behind the stage are mostly copies, they suggest the way in which the scaenae frons or stage building was once richly embellished, tiers of columns rising up against its façade, its surface covered with coloured marble and adorned with statuary like some great palace. At the top a roof slanting sharply out towards the audience served as a sounding board for the actors' voices. On either side of the stage are the vomitoria, through which the audience disgorged when the show was over. As many of these would have been soldiers, you wonder what the entertainments were, the unusually large arena in front of the stage perhaps allowing for circuses and gladiatorial combats.

A few minor Arab structures have been cleared from within the theatre, but otherwise the largely Ayyubid fortifications (late 12th and early 13th centuries) encasing the theatre remain. The Umayyads began the defensive works, while the Seljuks (late 11th century) built the two powerful towers at the west and east of the stage (this last containing a small archaeological exhibit), and a third along the outer arc of the theatre. The Ayyubids added four further towers along the outer arc (the one to the southwest now contains a folklore museum, and there is a café on the terrace), and they further strengthened the outer diameter by building the central bastion between the two Seljuk towers.

The Old City

Like Shahba, but on a greater scale and more intact, Bosra is laid out on a grid pattern, its streets running approximately north–south and east–west. The city was enclosed within a rectangle of walls, their line still evident to either side of the western gate. Along what would have been the southern perimeter is the theatre-*cum*-fortress.

Emerging from the theatre, walk counterclockwise; this brings you to a paved Roman street running north. The street is cambered, with raised colonnaded pavements on either side, and

Restoration of colonnade (after Butler)

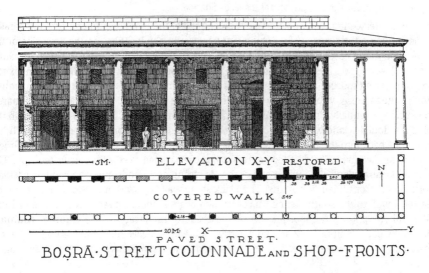

BOSRA·STREET COLONNADE and SHOP-FRONTS·

at the end of it is a **monumental arch**, its large central arch flanked by two smaller ones. This was erected early in the 3rd century in honour of the III Cyrenaica Legion which garrisoned the city. Passing through the arch, you come to the east–west axis of the city, the main Roman street, the decumanus, of Bosra, almost a kilometre long. Column bases and sometimes entire columns with Ionic capitals stand at intervals along its pavements, reminding you that where now families inhabit simple houses of stone along the way, grand colonnades once ran from one end of this thoroughfare to the other.

If you walk about 75m west along the decumanus from the monumental arch, you come on the north side of the street to a raised portico, beneath which, as you can see by peering through the openings just above street level, is an enormous **underground vault** over 100m long, constructed in the 2nd century AD and used for storing trade goods. You can enter the vault at its western end by a flight of ancient steps. A bit farther west, where now there is only a circular space, was a crossroads marked by a tetrapylon. In another 200m you come to the 2nd-century AD **western gate**, in Arabic the Bab al-Hawa or Gate of the Wind, with a single huge arch surmounted by a barrel vault. To the north and south are much damaged stretches of the city's Roman wall.

If you return again to the monumental arch and walk about 75m east, you come to a 3rd-century **Roman baths** set back a bit on the south side of the decumanus. An eight-columned portico leads into the dressing-room, whose dome has collapsed, and then beyond into the frigidarium (cold room) and the tepidarium (warm room), which has a caldarium (hot room) on either side. The hamams so associated with the Middle East and Turkey derive from Byzantine and Roman baths such as these.

Just to the east of the baths is the intersection of the decumanus and the cardo maximus (the main north–south street), marked at its northwest corner by four black lichen-splotched columns, 13m high, which were once part of a nymphaeum or public water fountain. For all the difficulty of working in basalt, their Corinthian capitals are generously detailed. A column on the northeast corner opposite and a wall with three rows of niches are all that survive of a *kalybe*, a shrine for the display of statues as at Shahba.

From this intersection, walk north. Past the columns of the nymphaeum and running parallel to the cardo are the remains of a Roman marketplace. In about 300m, on the west side of the street, you come to the **Mosque of Omar**, said to have been built by the second caliph (634–44), who took Bosra and conquered Syria in 636, which would make it perhaps the oldest surviving mosque. More likely it was built a century later, and certainly it was much rebuilt under the Ayyubids during the 12th and 13th centuries. The square-plan minaret, however, is essentially Umayyad and is one of the first minarets to have been built, though the spiral mullioned windows at the top may be an Ayyubid elaboration. The mosque, which has only come back into use in recent decades, is built of ancient stones, many inscribed in Greek, and column sections. The arcaded courtyard has been roofed over with corrugated iron. The internal arrangement of columns and arches is strong and handsome, the capitals various: Doric, Ionic, Corinthian, Byzantine. The black stone walls are without decoration, except on the *qibla* wall to the south, facing Mecca, which bears a finely carved stucco frieze of Kufic calligraphy. Opposite the mosque, on the east side of the street, is the **Hamam Manjak**, Mameluke baths built in 1372 and now partly restored. This was the last major undertaking in Bosra before the city's eclipse. The original Roman cardo maximus continued straight on to the northern gate; instead you must follow the present street as it bends first to the east, then north again, so that it brings you just to the east of the gate. The camp of the III Cyrenaica Legion was probably just outside this northern gate.

Returning the way you came, walk about 100m south of the Mosque of Omar and then turn east, which in about 200m will bring you to the vicinity of a basilica and the cathedral. The basilica, originally a civic building of the 3rd century, was later converted to Christian worship and is also known as the **Church of Bahira**. Its western and eastern ends have high round arches of great span, though these may have been added later as there is the suggestion of a pediment at the bottom of the west arch. At the east end of the basilica there is a semi-circular apse. A pair of circles over the west door may have been cut with crosses or some other Christian device, but in any case have been chiselled out.

Mohammed and the Monk

Legend says it was here in about 581 that the Nestorian monk Bahira met the 12-year-old Mohammed, who was returning from his first journey with a camel caravan into Syria. The Nestorians had been declared heretical by the Council of Ephesus in 431 for their belief that the human and the divine persons of Christ were separate, not one, as Christian orthodoxy has maintained since the Council of Nicaea in 325. (The Nestorian Church in fact survives to this day; Baghdad is its patriarchal seat, though the patriarch himself, along with a good many of his followers, has long preferred living in America.) Some would argue that in seeing the human and divine persons of Christ as separate, the Nestorians, who were active throughout the East and in Arabia itself, opened the way to Mohammed's teaching that while Jesus is a 'Spirit from God' and the 'Word of God', he is certainly not the 'Son of God' nor in any way divine, but is instead unequivocally human.

In any case, after conversing with Mohammed and noting the precocity of his intellect, Bahira is said to have accidentally seen between his shoulders the seal of prophecy (a large mole, said unbelievers), and to have declared that Mohammed would have a great future. In later years, Mohammed held Syria in the highest regard, saying, 'Joy be to the people of Syria, for the angels of the kind God spread their wings over them.'

Just to the south of the basilica is the **cathedral** of Bosra, very ruinous, the most damage having been done in the past hundred years or so, its stones removed for building material. Mid-19th-century illustrations of the cathedral show its walls and central drum intact, but now hardly anything stands but its apse, which along with its adjoining chambers is being restored. The importance of the cathedral, built in 512 and dedicated to the Syrian saints Sergius, Bacchus and Leontius, lies in its innovativeness, being an early attempt to make the transition from square plan to circular dome that characterises Byzantine churches, most especially its direct successor, the Church of SS. Sergius and Bacchus in Constantinople, built by Justinian in 527. Another Syrian example of this experimentation is the centralised church at Resafa, built during the 520s.

Just west of the cathedral is the **Mosque of Fatima**, named after Mohammed's daughter. The Shia trace their origins to her husband, Ali, and this mosque was built by the Fatimids,

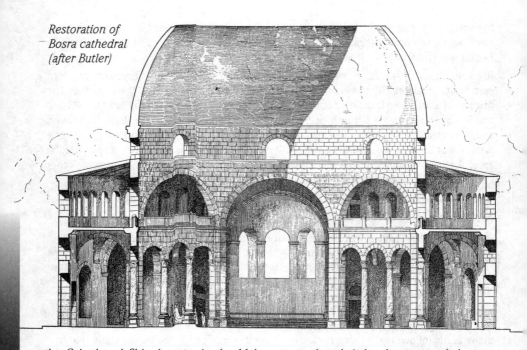

Restoration of Bosra cathedral (after Butler)

the Cairo-based Shia dynasty, in the 11th century, though it has been extended more recently. The minaret, while similar to that at the Mosque of Omar, has a more slender grace.

If you walk northeast beyond the basilica you come in about 250m to the **Mosque of Mabrak** with its adjoining madrasa. Legend variously has it that Mohammed's camel knelt at the exact spot where the mihrab now stands, or that it was a camel of Omar's, carrying the first Koran into Syria, in either case serving to make the mosque a place of pilgrimage. That part of the mosque containing the mihrab dates to 1136; very fine carved stucco work decorates its north wall. The madrasa, adjoining the mosque to the east, is the oldest in Syria and was added some-time during the 12th or 13th centuries during the Ayyubid period. Saladin, who was an orthodox Sunni Muslim, instituted madrasas, that is theological schools, as a corrective to the Shia teachings of the Fatimids, whom he had overthrown. Returning to the cathedral, you can now work your way south to the **Nabatean arch** which stands at the eastern end of the decumanus. Though it served to terminate the Roman city, it probably stood at the entrance to a sacred enclosure, the remains of its temple buried somewhere off to the east. South of the arch lie the remains of the once considerable residence of the Roman governor of Provincia Arabia, and south beyond that is the remarkable sight of an enormous **cistern**, 120 by 150m and originally eight metres deep, the sole supply of water within the walls and one of the largest that the Romans constructed in the East.

Where to Stay

expensive

★★★★**Bosra Cham Palace**, just south of the Roman theatre, ✆ (015) 790881, 📠 (015) 790996. Two restaurants, café, bar, swimming pool, tennis courts and business centre. TV and minibars in rooms. Built to capture the tour group trade, this is the only hotel in Bosra.

cheap

For true grandeur and atmosphere, however, there is the humble **hostel** on the top floor of the central bastion of the citadel/amphitheatre. It amounts to dormitory accommodation with shared shower and toilet, all very clean.

Eating Out

There is a café in the amphitheatre and several simple cafés and restaurants in the square outside, though these charge tourist prices. Less inflated are the few eateries along the road running west. Otherwise there are the café and restaurants at the Cham Palace.

Deraa

Deraa, on the Damascus–Amman highway, lies just north of the border with Jordan. Its accommodation and transport facilities are the only reasons for being here.

Getting There

By bus and microbus: there are frequent buses and minibuses between Deraa and the Baramkeh and Deraa stations in Damascus, the journey taking about 90mins. The bus and microbus station at Deraa is 3km east of the town centre (taxis and shuttle buses into town), which would be a nuisance if you actually wanted to visit Deraa; instead from the same place you can take a microbus to Bosra in about 45mins, or to Ezraa (changing at Sheikh Miskeen) in about the same time. *See also* p.103.

By train: at the moment there is a twice-weekly service between Damascus and Deraa via Ezraa, but it is hardly practical for visiting the region (*see* p.103). The service is extended to Bosra and becomes daily during the Bosra festival (*see* p.111). Things may change now that after 30 years a daily train service has been restored between Damascus and Amman in Jordan. The train station is smack in the centre of town; indeed the construction by the Ottomans of the Hejaz railway between Damascus and Medina in the early 20th century almost wholly explains why Deraa exists at all. The station is worth a look for the clapped out steam locomotives and dilapidated vintage carriages standing on the sidings.

To and from Jordan: you cannot board the Damascus–Amman Karnak bus at Deraa (check if you can board the train). Instead, to cross the border you will have to take a service taxi from the bus station to Ramtha, just inside the Jordanian border, from where you can catch a bus to Amman.

Deraa does have one claim to fame: here Peter O'Toole was stripped and beaten after refusing the homosexual advances of José Ferrer. Or so it was when O'Toole played T. E. Lawrence and Ferrer played the Turkish commandant at Deraa in David Lean's film *Lawrence of Arabia*. The Deraa incident of November 1917 was taken straight from Lawrence's *Seven Pillars of Wisdom*, his account of the Arab campaign, where it is a kind of Passion, 'the bang' (as Lawrence described it to a friend), around which not only the book is structured but so much of the mythologising of Lawrence's life.

Lawrence, then based in Azraq (now in northern Jordan) walks down the main street of Deraa, disguised in Arab robes, to spy out the Turkish-garrisoned town for future attack and is grabbed by a soldier who tells him 'the Bey wants you':

> *They took me upstairs to the Bey's room; or to his bedroom, rather. . . .*
> *He flung himself back on the bed, and dragged me down with him in*
> *his arms. When I saw what he wanted I twisted round and up again,*
> *glad to find myself equal to him, at any rate in wrestling.*
>
> *He began to fawn on me, saying how white and fresh I was, how fine*
> *my hands and feet. . . . I was obdurate, so he changed his tone, and*
> *sharply ordered me to take off my drawers. When I hesitated, he*
> *snatched at me; and I pushed him back. He clapped his hands for the*
> *sentry, who hurried in and pinioned me. The Bey cursed me with*
> *horrible threats: and made the man holding me tear my clothes away,*
> *bit by bit. His eyes rounded at the half-healed places where the bullets*
> *had flicked through my skin a little while ago. Finally he lumbered to his*
> *feet, with a glitter in his look, and began to paw me over.*

Lawrence goes on describe how he is beaten, bitten and kissed, how a fold of his flesh is pierced through with a bayonet, and how then he is whipped, until finally:

> *. . . In Deraa that night the citadel of my integrity had been irrevocably*
> *lost.*

Yet an interesting feature of the Deraa incident is that it never happened, that on almost every count, including place, date and even such details as Lawrence's supposed bullet wounds, it was a fabrication. That is the conclusion of several well-researched biographical enquiries. If some sort of sadistic sexual encounter took place, it was more likely at Azraq with Sharif Ali (Omar Sharif in the film), possibly the mysterious S. A. to whom Lawrence dedicated his book:

> *I loved you, so I drew these tides of men into my hands*
> *and wrote my will across the sky in stars*
> *To earn you Freedom, the seven-pillared worthy house,*
> *that your eyes might be shining for me*
> *When we came.*

But what was Lawrence's motive for inventing the Deraa incident? Behind the romance of the desert campaign there was failure. At about the time Lawrence claimed to have been humiliated by the Turkish bey, General Allenby was advancing on Jerusalem and needed Lawrence to cut the Turkish supply line across the Yarmuk River, but in this he failed. After the war, when Lawrence was writing his book, the Arab cause was betrayed by France and Britain at the Versailles Conference, with Lawrence, as advisor to Churchill, playing his part in that betrayal. And there was in a sense a deeper betrayal, for in the desert Lawrence had discovered and become excited by his own homosexuality and yet had to keep it secret from almost everyone. Guilt, disguise, deceit and a need for punishment pervaded Lawrence's life. Certainly in later years he frequented Chelsea beating parties and had himself birched by soldiers. Yet Lawrence also felt the need to reveal the truth about himself, however obliquely, and often transposing it onto a heroic plane. The Deraa incident, placed at the heart of his book, was both lie and truth, punishment and gratification, humiliation and self-heroisation. Much of what Lawrence wrote needs to be read in this way.

Where to Stay
inexpensive

Along Deraa's main street, a block south from and parallel to the railway line, is the cheap **Al Ahram Hotel**, ✆ (015) 230809, its rooms considerably varying in quality, so check first; and the inexpensive **Orient Palace**, ✆ (015) 238304, a comfortable and clean place to stay, indeed the best on offer in Deraa, its rooms equipped with fan, heater, fridge, toilet and shower, while its restaurant is the best in town. A new hotel is being built across the tracks opposite the post office.

Ezraa

Not all the inhabitants of the Hauran are Druze or Muslims. Despite the vicissitudes of 1500 years, Christian communities survive, and at Ezraa they worship at their original churches of St George and St Elias, of interest both for their age and their place in the evolution of Byzantine architecture.

Getting There

Ezraa is 80km south of Damascus, 25km north of Deraa and 37km west of Suweida. If travelling along the Damascus–Amman highway, look out for the massive grain silo complex to the east; Ezraa lies close by

By bus and microbus: Ezraa is served by bus or microbus from the Baramkeh and Deraa stations in Damascus; by microbus from Deraa (change at Sheikh Miskeen); and by microbus from Suweida. *See* p.103.

By train: travel by train is entirely impractical (*see* p.103).

Ezraa stands on a projecting tongue of lava just east of the Deraa–Damascus highway (look out for the massive grain silo that rises near the town) and was once an important Roman city, while in Christian times its bishops attended several ecumenical councils, including that of Chalcedon in 451. In 1182 it was sacked by King Baldwin IV of Jerusalem (immediately before Raymond's cavalry raid on Bosra), in the company of the Latin patriarch who had brought with him the True Cross. The Crusaders were mistaken in thinking that the Hauran, still largely Christian, would welcome them; Ezraa's Greek Orthodox inhabitants had fled with their property and cattle to strongholds in the rocky defiles, and Baldwin's success here, snatched while Saladin's back was turned, proved fruitless.

The Greek Orthodox **Church of St George** (Mar Girgis) is at the north end of town; from the outside it is rectangular in plan and over its west entrance is a long inscription in Greek indicating that a pagan temple had once stood on the spot but was replaced by this church in the year 410 of the Bosran calendar (*see* p.112), that is AD 516, making it probably the oldest continuously used church in Syria. It has similarities to the slightly earlier cathedral at Bosra, for if you ignore the projecting apse and side chambers you are left with a square, though inside this is inscribed not a circle but an octagon (the corners of the square being chopped off), making the transition from the square plan to the circular dome less difficult. Within the octagon, in turn, are eight piers which carry lofty arches, the stonework rising to a sixteen-sided drum with a modern and metal-clad pointed dome, replacing the more hemispherical original which collapsed in 1912.

The **Church of St Elias** (Mar Elias) near the centre of town is Greek Catholic and dates from 542. It was long left to ruin and has only recently been restored. The interior plan is of a cross set within a square, which became typical of Greek churches and is followed to this day.

The Anti-Lebanon

Maalula

Getting Around	124
Up and Around the Barada Valley	125
The Mountain Resorts of Zabadani and Bludan	125
Ancient Sites at Suq Wadi Barada and Burqush	126
Along the Flanks of the Anti-Lebanon	127
Maalula	129

West of Damascus and lying against the Mediterranean is Lebanon, a small and mountainous country. Lebanon takes its name from a high range, rising to over 3000m, which runs north–northeast in a line parallel to the coast. Inland from this is the Bekaa Valley, with the great temple of Baalbek on the east bank of the Litani River, and then another range, parallel to the first and somewhat lower, called the Anti-Lebanon, its peaks and ridges more or less marking the

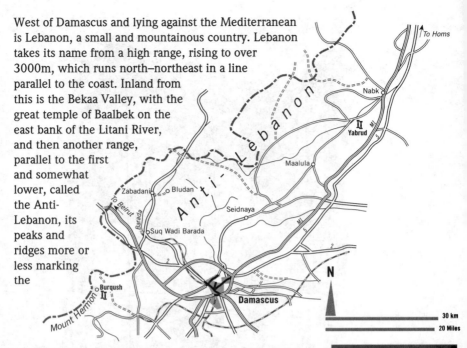

Lebanese-Syrian border. The famous cedars grow atop the westernmost range, and snows settle on the heights of both.

The Anti-Lebanon

Together they act as a barrier between the sea and southern Syria, so that Lebanon is green while just east of Damascus the vast desert begins.

The mountains also act as a barrier to transport and are traversed by only one major road, that between Damascus and Beirut. South of this road, the Anti-Lebanon rises to its highest point, the 2814m Mount Hermon, source of the River Jordan, which flows first into the Sea of Galilee (Lake Tiberius) and then into the Dead Sea. The Golan Heights, between Mount Hermon and the north-eastern shores of the Sea of Galilee, are in effect the southern expiry of the Anti-Lebanon. They have been occupied by Israel since the 1967 war, except for a demilitarised north–south strip passing through Qunaitra which has been under joint UN-Syrian control. Entry to this demilitarised zone requires a permit from the Syrian Ministry of the Interior (see p.xxx[Dam]): the reason for visiting is to see proof of the destruction wreaked on Qunaitra by the Israelis; left unsaid is the destruction the Syrians would have wreaked on Israel had things gone their way instead. The southern limit of the Golan Heights is marked by the Yarmuk River, which forms the border, west of Deraa, between Syria and Jordan. By the Arab victory over the Byzantine army at the Yarmuk in 636 Syria fell to Islamic rule.

'The faithful have located almost all the Adamical and Noachian patriarchs around Damascus,' Sir Richard Burton drily observed, and the mountains especially are filled with their bones: on Hermon the tomb of Nimrod, descended from Noah via

Ham and Cush; above the Barada valley the tomb of Abel; and just over the border in Lebanon at Nebi Shiit the tomb of Seth, third son of Adam.

High places are often holy places; and while history rushes through valley and plain, old ways of life find refuge on high ground. This chapter explores a number of ancient holy sites and Christian villages in the Anti-Lebanon, and some cool mountain resorts as well, beginning with the valley of the Barada River which waters Damascus, and continuing northwards along the eastern flanks of the range towards Homs.

The Sacred Mountain

Except for two or three months during late summer and early autumn, when it is berry-brown all over, Mount Hermon takes on a venerable appearance, its slopes like the grey hairs of an old man, its snowy triple crest like a gleaming white turban, or so the Arabs say, explaining their name for it, Jebel al Sheikh, the Mountain of the Sheikh. The Dog River, which flows into the Mediterranean north of Beirut, was once wrongly thought to have its origin here, and fabulous belief made the mountain the source of an underground river which rose over 1000km eastwards and emptied into the Persian Gulf. Its snow-caps visible from both sea and desert, the mountain was invested with preternatural powers. In Psalms 133:3 the dew of Mount Hermon is compared to the Lord's blessing and life evermore; indeed Hermon's very name means sacred.

The remains of a Graeco-Roman temple and older stones for sacrifices to Baal lie side by side upon the highest peak, a tough seven hours up from Arné and five hours down again, though the summit is off-limits now. Some say this was the mountain of the Transfiguration, recorded in the gospels of Mark, Luke and Matthew (17:1–3): 'And after six days Jesus taketh Peter, James, and John his brother, and bringeth them up into a high mountain apart, and was transfigured before them: and his face did shine as the sun, and his raiment was white as the light. And behold, there appeared unto them Moses and Elijah talking with him.' Its view has been famous, southwards the valley of the Jordan River and the Sea of Galilee, westwards the Mediterranean from Carmel to Tyre, northwards the great arc of the Lebanon and Anti-Lebanon ranges with the Bekaa between them, and below in a vast eastern sweep the gardened plain of Damascus giving way to the wheatfields of the Hauran, and beyond the dark Jebel al-Arab the blank wilderness of limitless desert.

'What a multitude of wondrous events does memory crowd together in this narrow space!' exclaimed the Reverend J. L. Porter in 1855 (*Five Years in Damascus*) from the mountaintop. 'Through these mountains and plains roamed the patriarchs with their flocks and herds. This country was witness to the prowess of Samson, the valour of David, and the wisdom of Solomon. Here God's ancient people were cheered by revelations of eternal truth from on high; and they were awed and solemnised by wonderous manifestations of Divine power and love. The feet of the Son of God and Saviour of the World trod these cities and villages, while their inhabitants beheld his miracles, his sufferings, and the heavenly purity of his life . . .'

But for Sir Richard Burton in 1872 (*Unexplored Syria*), not long after his rather more strenuous adventures in the Andes and in Central Africa where he had sought the source of the Nile, Mount Hermon was far from being the 'mighty and majestic Mont Blanc' he had been led to expect, and was instead 'a commonplace hogsback'. The discrepancy was due to 'a complaint which may be called 'Holy Land on the Brain' . . . no obscure cerebral disorder . . . it rather delights to announce its presence, to flaunt itself in the face of fact . . . As might be expected, it visits the Protestant with greater violence than the Catholic, whose fit assumes a more excited and emotional, a spasmodic and hysterical, form, ending, if the patient be a man and a poet, in a long rhapsody about himself, possibly about his childhood and his mother.'

Getting Around

By car: two looped daytrips from Damascus will enable you to visit all the places covered in this chapter. The first excursion takes in the valley of the Barada River, with Roman remains at Suq Wadi Barada, and on up to the mountain resorts of Zabadani and Bludan, a round trip of 116km, though you can combine this with a visit to Burqush, a Roman and early Christian site on the lower slopes of Mount Hermon, which will add about 36km more to your round trip total. Instead of returning to Damascus you could continue into Lebanon, visiting Baalbek and Beirut.

The second loop heads northwards from Damascus along a minor road which hugs the eastern flanks of the Anti-Lebanon and brings you to the Christian villages of Seidnaya (28km) and Maalula (a further 28km), and then to Yabrud (12km), from where in 8km you join the Damascus–Homs highway (route EM5) at Nabk, whence it is a fast 81km back to Damascus, the entire round trip amounting to 157km. You can easily combine this with a visit to the Roman temple at Dumeir along the Damascus–Palmyra road (*see* p.276). Onward journeys to Palmyra (*see* p.277) and Krak des Chevaliers (*see* p.176) also suggest themselves.

By microbus and service taxi: travelling in this way from Damascus you can visit most of the places mentioned in this chapter, though not Burqush. Microbuses for Ain al-Fijeh, Suq Wadi Barada, Zabadani and Bludan in the Barada valley depart from the Baramkeh station in Damascus. Microbuses for Seidnaya, Maalula and Yabrud depart from the Maalula station in eastern Damascus.

By train: in summer there is a daily narrow-gauge train from the Hejaz railway station in Damascus up the Barada valley to Ain al-Fijeh, taking 1½hrs. Departure from Damascus is at about 8am, and from Ain al-Fijeh at about 5pm. Additionally there is a year-round Friday and Sunday service up to Zabadani, taking 3hrs. Departure from Damascus is at about 8am, from Zabadani at about 4pm. The services, however, are erratic and cancellations are frequent, as the carriages are drawn by wonderfully ancient Swiss-built steam engines. Originally they went right over the Lebanese border and down to Beirut, with another branch following the Bekaa valley down to Homs.

Where to Stay

There is accommodation at Zabadani, Bludan (*see* p.134), Seidnaya (*see* p.137) and Maalula (*see* p.140).

Up and Around the Barada Valley

The rivers of Damascus, says the Bible (II Kings 5:12) are the Abana and the Pharpar, 'better than all the waters of Israel'. There is some learned and pointless controversy as to whether the Pharpar is the Awaj, the Crooked River, which begins as several fountains bursting from the rocks on the lower flanks of Mount Hermon and meanders through fields and groves around the south of the city before exhausting itself in the sands out near the international airport. But there is no argument that the Abana, meaning stony, is the Barada★, which after tumbling ice-cold down from the Anti-Lebanon flows through Damascus itself and is the very reason for the city's existence. The Barada, too, expires east of the city in a vague marsh on the fringe of the desert, the haunt of migratory duck in winter, drying up altogether during summer.

The Mountain Resorts of Zabadani and Bludan

To escape the summer heat of the city, Damascenes parade up the valley of the Barada, the better-off going by car, the hoi polloi by train, to mountain resorts in the Anti-Lebanon, what the French call *stations climatiques*. 'Between the solstice and the autumnal equinox all the English, and most of the Europeans, exchange the fetid City of the Caliphs for a villeggiatura,' wrote Burton in the 1870s, who as British consul retreated to Bludan above Zabadani: 'fast riding will cover the distance in four hours; whereas mules take ten, and camels rarely arrive there before the second day.' The narrow-gauge railway that in summer now climbs up the valley from Damascus (690m above sea level) to Zabadani (1180m), a distance of 50km, is better than a donkey and even quicker than a horse, though not by much, taking three hours to crawl alongside the picturesque 'old' Zabadani road. You ascend first to **Ain al-Fijeh** (25km), where a source which once trebled the flow of the Barada has been piped to supply Damascus with its drinking water. (*Ain* is Arabic for spring; *Fijeh* is a corruption of the Greek *pigi*, also meaning spring, and so Ain al-Fijeh is the Spring of the Spring). Then you climb more steeply along the green valley strip between bare walls of orange rock where there is barely enough room for the road and the railway to pass. At **Suq Wadi Barada** (35km) (*see* below) you cross a splendid gorge and head north to **Zabadani**, a sizeable resort town on a rising slope amid exuberant vegetation. Signposts indicate the source of the Barada issuing from a small lake near by, a favourite spot for picnics. Just below is the plain of Zabadani, probably itself once a mountain lake, now planted with apple, apricot and walnut trees, the horizon closed to the south by the flanks of Mount Hermon, often snow-striped into early summer.

Bludan, 7km distant and reached only by road, clings to the eastern slopes of the Zabadani valley at an altitude of almost 1400m. Once a little village with a mixed Greek Orthodox and Roman Catholic population, Bludan is now a popular resort. The bottled mineral water labelled Boukein and served all over Syria comes from one of the numerous little sources in this area. The refurbished Grand Hotel de Bludan is renowned for its excellent table and makes a good place to enjoy an *arak* with a delicious meze.

Unless you have booked well in advance, however, overnight accommodation is difficult to get anywhere in the Barada Valley during summer; for the traveller it is in any case a place to

---

★ *Barada, from the root brd, means to be or become cold; to cool; to soothe or alleviate a pain—thereby allowing the accurately descriptive epithet Cold River.*

come for the day, making a picnic of it, taking a country walk, and seeing how Damascenes enjoy themselves. (Rusticated cafés with names like 'Paradise', pebble-dash houses in gaudy colours, canopied swing-chairs and blasts of pop music are also part of the ambience.) In addition, there is a bit of archaeological sightseeing to do along the way.

Where to Stay

In Zabadani there is the inexpensive ★★**Tourism**, ✆ (013) 223100, on the main street just down from where it is crossed by the railway line, clean and comfortable enough, with TV, fridge, fan, toilet and shower in the rooms.

In Bludan there is the expensive ★★★★**Grand Hotel**, ✆ (013) 227551–3, with swimming pool and tennis courts (and a good place to come for lunch), the moderately-priced and characterless ★★**Akel Hotel**, ✆ (013) 228604, and the inexpensive ★**Al-Sahl al-Akhdar**, ✆ (013) 238526, some rooms with balcony and view.

Ancient Sites at Suq Wadi Barada and Burqush

Getting There

From Damascus, you reach the turnoff in 17km, exiting right, i.e. north, then crossing to the south; from Suq Wadi Barada head west along the Zabadani road for 2km, then turn south, and after 4km you come to the Damascus–Beirut highway. Turn east, as for Damascus, and after 9km on the highway you will reach the turnoff for Burqush. From the highway turnoff, drive 4km to the T-junction where you turn left, then immediately right; after another 4.5km turn right. There is a military checkpoint 2km before the site; you must leave your car here and walk.

Suq Wadi Barada (35km from Damascus) stands on the site of ancient Abila, important from Hellenistic to Byzantine times for its position on the Baalbek–Damascus road, and along with Damascus, Qanawat and Amman, included by the Romans in the autonomous league known as the Decapolis. The ruins of the city are about you, its lintels and capitals built into the walls of present-day houses, nothing remaining *in situ*. As a bishopric, it was represented at the Council of Chalcedon in 451; in the 7th century it was the site of an annual Easter fair and pilgrimage, people from all over Syria combining a trade in luxury goods with blessings from the local priest, renowned far and wide for his learning and sanctity. Into this happy situation burst the Arabs after capturing Damascus, catching Abila's merchants and pilgrims by surprise, the plundered fair recalled in the name Suq Wadi Barada, the Fair of the Valley of the Barada.

The origin of the ancient name, Abila, survives in the local tradition that Abel (Habil) was buried by his brother Cain atop Nebi Habil, the lofty hill overlooking Suq from the west. The murder— the first of all murders—took place not here, the locals hasten to add, but at Zabadani★, Cain carrying Abel on his back for 40 years, not knowing what to do with him. 'His soul prompted him to slay his brother,' as the Koran says (Sura 5:30); 'he slew him and thus became one of the lost. Then Allah sent down a raven, which dug the earth to show him how to bury the naked corpse of his brother.' The indefatigable Porter found the remains of a Roman temple on the summit, now gone; instead the tomb is marked by a Druze sanctuary on military land.

★ *Another legend* does *place the first fratricide at Abila, while both the crime and the tomb are* claimed *for Mount Kassioun above the Damascus suburb of Salihiye.*

About a kilometre upstream from Suq Wadi Barada the gorge turns sharply left. A series of Roman tombs are cut into the north flank of the gorge, and between these and where the gorge turns to the right again, there are the remains of an ancient aqueduct and, above it, the cutting of a Roman road about four metres wide and over 150m long; both the road and tombs were cut high up to avoid the flood waters of the river, so you need to do some scrambling to reach them.

More out of the way are the Roman and Byzantine ruins at **Burqush**, on a 1580m shoulder of Mount Hermon with magnificent views towards Damascus and the Hauran. The site lies 17km south off the new Damascus-Beirut highway. The sacred Mount Hermon attracted numerous ancient temples and early Christian monasteries and churches, but as the mountain now attracts the military, a visit is practicable only to the Burqush site. You come immediately to a massive platform, partly created by cutting away the narrow ridge, the rest of the terrace resting upon a chambered substructure. Upon this platform are the remains of a large 6th-century Christian basilica; all about, the ground is strewn with huge blocks and numerous capitals of various types. None of these sizeable pieces of masonry was locally hewn but instead had to be transported to the site. The effort was remarkable, but the history of the place is unknown, save that it had long been a place of worship, for the basilica stands in turn upon the podium of a Roman temple, and there is evidence that religious buildings have stood here since before Hellenistic times. About 50m north are the foundations of a Roman temple with a semicircular apse, and the remains of other religious buildings can be seen in the vicinity.

Along the Flanks of the Anti-Lebanon

The three villages visited here lie in the western foothills of the Anti-Lebanon, east of the Damascus–Homs highway. Each was probably Christian even before the Edict of Toleration in 313, and Seidnaya and Yabrud, and possibly Maalula too, were represented at the First Ecumenical Council, convened by the Emperor Constantine at Nicaea in 325. Maalula is one of the few places where Aramaic, the vernacular of Palestine and Syria during late Old Testament and New Testament times, can still be heard while, except in Yabrud, Christianity remains the faith of the overwhelming number.

Seidnaya

When Henry Maundrell, chaplain to the community of English merchants at Aleppo, returned from a pilgrimage to Jerusalem in 1697, he travelled inland to Damascus and then over the mountains to Beirut rather than continue northwards via Homs. Nevertheless, he thought Seidnaya worthy of a diversion, its miracle-working icon of the Virgin Mary then making it the most famous place of pilgrimage in the East after Jerusalem itself. In the event, he found that its fortress-like **convent** was 'of very mean structure, and contains nothing in it extraordinary, but only the wine made here, which is indeed most excellent. This place was first founded and endowed by the emperor Justinian. It is at present possessed by twenty Greek monks, and forty nuns, who seem to live promiscuously together, without any order or separation'. About 50 years later the Greek Catholic monks were thrown out by the Greek Orthodox nuns, since when the two denominations, which are about evenly represented in the village, have exchanged promiscuity for a war of verbal abuse. Otherwise nothing has happened since that would have improved Maundrell's opinion of the place, nor is the sweet-tasting wine much good.

The convent and its village, more a town now, stand upon a low spur projecting from the steep flank of mountain behind, charmless new concrete houses and apartment blocks looking out over a dull plain with a view of hills beyond. That the convent was founded by Justinian is legendary, and it has been so much rebuilt that its stones carry little historical interest. Yet it is good to make your way through its maze of passages to the Chapel of the Virgin, where after taking off your shoes you step into a half-domed room, delightful for its pale blue ceiling crudely painted with silver stars. The walls are encrusted with blackened icons, some said to date from the 5th to 7th centuries, hung with shimmering votive simulacra of tin feet, eyes, hands, etc. You notice then the shrine, brass doors opening upon a recess in the wall, and here men and women kneel and pray silently and fervently, their fingers stroking the miraculous icon within, the room scented with burning candles. The belief is that the icon was painted by St Luke the Evangelist, for whom the Virgin Mary seems to have been a frequent sitter; the Coptic monks of St Paul's on the Red Sea also claim one of Luke's originals, as did the cathedral at Tartus, while the most famous was the Hodegetria (the Virgin 'showing the way', that is pointing at the infant Christ on her lap) that was carried along the ramparts of Constantinople at times of siege and was lost when the city fell to the Ottomans in 1453.

Most impressive at first exposure is the universal and immediately recognisable scent of Christianity, the burning candles appealing to that primal sense, the olefactory, with its powers of arousing memories and associations. Then another impression steals upon you, the presence of women. Here there are women coming to worship, mostly women, smartly got up, lipsticked and high-heeled, their knees showing beneath their hems, a refreshing contrast to the veiled and *izzar*-cloaked shadows so often encountered in the cities, towns and villages on the plain. And women in attendance, snuffing out the candles, making sure no one runs off with the icons—these indeed are robed in black, their scrubbed pale faces like bare bottoms poking through the back flap of a pair of longjohns, but women; all of them, like the Mary they come to venerate, primary to the Christian drama, and even more than the men playing a part in their religion. A number of Muslims are likely to be among the Virgin's devotees here, for often such shrines operate at the level of folk religion, which is ecumenical in seeking cures and blessings. Down below in the village, from a small mosque comes the call to prayer. But up here you are amid a more ancient worship.

Another way of looking at it is the Reverend Porter's, writing from the still greater heights of mid-19th-century Victorian Protestantism: 'None but a people sunk almost to the lowest depths of moral degradation would tolerate the disgraceful pictures that cover the walls of this convent; and none but a people who had either forgotten or discarded the process of reflection and of reason would credit for a moment the absurd and contradictory tales and legends related of the goddess that is there worshipped.' Porter's rise to apoplexy begins when he sees over the door to the convent church a painting of the Virgin between the Archangels Michael and Gabriel, and in Arabic 'the blasphemous title 'Mother of God', though the orthodoxy of the term Theotokos, literally 'God-bearer', was accepted at the councils of Ephesus in 431 and Chalcedon in 451. Within the church, 'the whole of the walls, pillars, and wooden altar-screen are adorned, or rather disfigured, by paintings', and he singles out for attention the Day of Judgement, 'with numerous little devils, fearful in form and terrible in countenance, mounted on the backs of spirits and belabouring them with heavy sticks; while in another place is a long range of women exposed to the attacks of huge serpents, which gnaw such members as were most guilty'. You will have to look closely for yourself—the painting is just beside the entrance, for 'more minute details I cannot give; they are too disgusting to be even thought of. . . . I have visited most of the principal picture galleries in Europe, and I have seen many paintings that did not manifest a very pure taste or a very high standard of moral feeling; but it has never been my lot to see such disgusting obscenity as that exhibited on the convent walls of Seidnaya'.

Where to Stay

There is one hotel, the inexpensive **★Seidnaya Touristic**, ✆ (012) 5950358, on the western edge of town, with clean simple rooms with shower and toilet, some with balcony, and a restaurant.

Maalula

As you drive north from Seidnaya, you see that the Damascus–Homs highway passes along an undulating valley between two ranges of hills, the escarpment of the Anti-Lebanon on your left, red stone jutting out over the valley, slopes of scree beneath, and on your right the continuous dun slopes of the parallel range. The valley is cultivated in places, but after spring hardly anything is green. Then farther along the flanks of the Anti-Lebanon you come to **Maalula**, a glimmering mosaic of white and pale blue houses climbing against the scarred escarpment, abundant terraces of poplars, walnut trees and vines spilling out before it. The village is inhabited mostly by Greek Catholics, the rest being about equally Greek Orthodox and Muslim, and all have in the recent past spoken Aramaic, though Arabic is now quickly gaining ground and the old language is more understood than put to daily use. Two nearby villages, Jubb Adin and Bakhaa, also have some knowledge of Aramaic, and it is spoken among some communities in northeast Syria near the Iraqi border.

A steep path ascends at the left side of the village to the top of the escarpment, flat rooftops fanning out like a deck of cards below, and near you a small whitewashed Greek Catholic monastery encompassing the **church of St Sergius** (Mar Sarkis), named for one of the most famed of Eastern saints, who was martyred at Resafa (*see* p.259). You stoop through the low monastery door where there is a curio shop with a chatty monk who hands out small glasses of sweet red wine. At the back of the court is the ancient church, probably at least partly dating to the 7th century or earlier and containing a number of 13th-century icons. Beyond the monastery there is a restaurant blasting Arab pop music, part of the Safir Hotel, and a bit farther along you come to the top of a narrow high-walled **gorge**, something like the *siq* at Petra, which cuts down through the escarpment. The gorge is littered with the beer and Pepsi cans of the faithful or curious, some of whom have thoughtfully brought buckets of paint to mark their names on the rock walls. Once spanned by a natural arch which fell early in the 19th century, the defile is cool and shady as you descend, and there is the trickle of the tiny stream that has done all this work.

You emerge by a Greek Orthodox monastery, within it a **chapel of St Thecla** (Mar Taqla), but despite the antiquity claimed for its foundation, its buildings are new or renovated and of no interest. That Thecla of Iconium, now Turkish Konya, ever existed is doubtful, while elements in her tale suggest a more ancient pagan cult that was perverted to Christian ends. The legend goes that she was converted to Christianity in her native city by St Paul, where-upon she broke off an engagement to marry and devoted her maidenhood to God. She was young and beautiful and her loss to the world of men seems to have been too great to bear. Her fiancé had her flogged, and when this failed to win her he obtained a sentence of death by fire, but Thecla was saved by a thunderstorm and escaped. Another frustrated admirer tried to prise her from chastity by the threat of wild beasts, but again she got away, finally with-drawing to a cave on this spot. When her persecution was yet again renewed at the age of 90, this time by local medical men jealous of her healing powers, the rocks opened up—the very gorge you have just come down—and swallowed her. (In fact the people of Maalula, having a gorge and in it a cave, also wanted a Thecla to go with it; the more widely reported version of the legend has her buried in her cave at Seleucia, present-day Silifke in Turkey.)

One pagan association that suggests itself is that of Adonis and Astarte (the Greek Aphrodite), who loved in the mountains of Lebanon, her shrine, J. G. Frazer says in *The Golden Bough*, standing 'among groves of noble walnut trees on the brink of the lyn ... a little way off the river rushes from a cavern' (the reference is to Afqa, *see* p.322). Another is that of Attis and Cybele (the Greek Artemis), again a story of mountain passion, this time in Anatolia. Both are dramas of fertility, death and resurrection, both concern the seasons of cultivation and of man, both speak of waters rushing from rocks—'in these copious fountains, with their glad promise of fertility and life, men of old saw the hand of God'. And Frazer adds: 'To live and to cause to live, to eat food and to beget children, these were the primary wants of men in the past, and they will be the primary wants of men in the future so long as the world lasts.'

As the life of Thecla can be read as a perversion of the Astarte and Artemis myths, so it is also an instance of the threatening and subversive nature of early Christianity. The ancient world was 'grazed thin by death', as St John Chrysostom put it. Average life expectancy was 25 years, and only four men in every hundred lived beyond the age of 50, and fewer women. For the population of the Roman Empire not to decrease, every woman had to bear five children. Paul preached resurrection, yet an excess of Theclas could mean the extinction of the human species. True resurrection, said Paul's opponents, is 'that which takes place through the nature of the human body itself, and which, through human means, is accomplished every day'. But for Christians awaiting the Second Coming, and meanwhile eager to avoid any worldly temptation and sin, the collapse of human society was irrelevant. Chastity was venerated for the sake of gaining access to the next world, while Thecla and Christians generally, perceived as anti-social in the most fundamental sense, were persecuted for the sake of the world of the living. Persecution ended not when emperors became Christians, but when Christians, having become emperors, again concerned themselves with the living.

Where to Stay

Maalula has only the expensive ★★★★**Safir Hotel**, ✆ (012) 770250, 📠 (012) 770255, an eyesore at the top of the cliffs, with swimming pool, sauna, tennis, restaurant and bar.

Yabrud

Descending now to the Damascus–Homs highway, you head north to Nabk. Here a minor road leads back again against the Anti-Lebanon to the market town of Yabrud, where evidence has been found for the continuous habitation of the site over the course of 100,000 years. A number of Roman tombs are cut into the limestone walls of a gorge, 3km behind the town to the west, the present-day inhabitants of Yabrud translating these into the shops of an imagined ancient souk. Today the dwellers within Yabrud's white houses, set amid blooming gardens and orchards, are homo sapiens belonging mostly to the Muslim tendency, though many Greek Catholics also live here. Judging from the various systems of masonry seen in its walls, the Greek Catholic Cathedral of Constantine and Helena has been several times restored. The interior is clearly recent, though there is a good collection of old icons to the right of the altar, and here and there you notice elements of a previous temple of Jupiter used in its construction.

Norias at Hama

The Orontes and the Central Plain

Getting Around	133
Detour to Kadesh (Tell Nebi Mend)	134
Homs	138
Hama	142
Along the Orontes Valley to Jisr al-Shugur	149
Shaizar (Qalaat Shaizar)	150
Apamea (Qalaat Mudiq)	150
The Steppe Eastwards of Hama	154
Hama to Aleppo	156

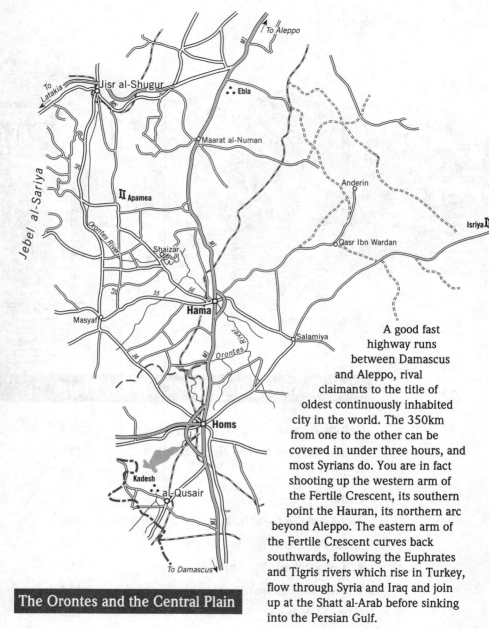

A good fast highway runs between Damascus and Aleppo, rival claimants to the title of oldest continuously inhabited city in the world. The 350km from one to the other can be covered in under three hours, and most Syrians do. You are in fact shooting up the western arm of the Fertile Crescent, its southern point the Hauran, its northern arc beyond Aleppo. The eastern arm of the Fertile Crescent curves back southwards, following the Euphrates and Tigris rivers which rise in Turkey, flow through Syria and Iraq and join up at the Shatt al-Arab before sinking into the Persian Gulf.

The Orontes and the Central Plain

The Fertile Crescent did not seem like this when you read about it in school books. The roadside is bright with non-biodegradable plastic bags, looking like large deranged flowering weeds. Syrians drive fast, and they travel light, jettisoning their rubbish out onto the Fertile Crescent.

Northwards from Homs you are running along the central Syrian plain. The annual rainfall here is 500mm, an improvement on the 200mm that falls each year just to the east where cultivation gives way to stony steppe and finally desert. The difference is sufficient to make this plain the country's principal agricultural area; as well as plastic bags, your view takes in fields of grain, cotton and sugar beet interspersed with pistachio trees, olive groves and vineyards.

To the west is the coastal range, the Jebel al-Sariya. Between plain and mountains is the blood red soil of the Orontes River valley, filled with gardens, orchards and more plastic bags. After rising in the mountains of Lebanon and spilling down into the Syrian plain, the Orontes carves a channel northwards before crossing the border into Turkey where it describes a final arc westwards past Antioch (Antakya) and flows into the sea. Throughout history the Orontes has been both prize and avenue, a frontier for Crusader armies and the backbone of the Seleucid Empire. Earlier still, Kadesh, a fortress of great strength on the left bank of the Orontes south of Homs, was an important strategic goal of those warrior pharaohs Tuthmosis III and Ramses II in their campaigns to dominate Syria.

As well as Damascus and Aleppo, most of Syria's other important cities, past and present, lie along this stretch—Kadesh, where the Egyptian Pharaoh Ramses II fought his famous battle against the Hittites; Homs astride the direct caravan route between Palmyra and the sea; orthodox Hama, where women, instead of throwing their plastic bags away, sometimes wear them over their heads; Apamea, where the Seleucids trained their elephants for war; Ebla, like a gigantic Troy, still hardly excavated, but already one of the most exciting finds in the history of Middle Eastern archaeology.

Getting Around

Over most of the approximately 350km between Damascus and Aleppo the M1 is a four-lane divided highway, making for fast car and bus journeys (comparing favourably with rail and air travel) between the two cities.

But this chapter takes things more slowly. Following the M1 north from Damascus you come to Homs (157km), just south of which you can make a 50km detour to Kadesh. (For journeys east and west from Homs, *see* **Palmyra and the Syrian Desert**, p.261, and **The Mediterranean and the Jebel al-Sariya**, p.159.) North from Homs is Hama (47km) from where you can head northwest along the Orontes valley or east to visit several sites in the desertic steppe (*see* routes below). But continuing north from Hama along the M1 you reach the turnings for Maarat al-Numan (60km) and for Ebla, known also as Tell Mardikh (26km), both places just off the main highway. Also from Maarat al-Numan you can visit the Dead Cities of the Jebel Riha (*see* p.235). Then finally you come to Aleppo (53km).

From Hama, the Orontes valley road (route 56) branches off to the northwest for Shaizar, known also as Qalaat Shaizar (28km), Apamea, known also as Qalaat Mudiq (27km), with the possibility of a detour to Masyaf (*see* p.174) along the way—and Jisr al-

Shugur (52km), from where the M5 runs west to Latakia (75km) and east to Aleppo (104km) bringing you close to Ebla en route.

Also from Hama you can strike off eastwards on a surfaced road to Qasr Ibn Wardan (56km) and Anderin (25km), returning the way you came; with four-wheel drive you could also visit Isriya.

Several **trains** a day run between Damascus and Aleppo in about 7hrs, stopping at Homs and Hama. Syrian Arab Airlines also flies several times daily between Damascus and Aleppo.

Where to Stay

There is accommodation at Homs (*see* p.142), Hama (*see* p.148) and Slenfeh (*see* p.153).

Detour to Kadesh (Tell Nebi Mend)

Homs sits at one of the great crossroads of Syria. In the desert to the east lies Palmyra and beyond it the Euphrates; westwards lies the Mediterranean. From Homs to the sea at Tartus runs a corridor between the high mountains of Lebanon to the south and Syria's coastal range, the Jebel al-Sariya, to the north. Known as the Homs Gap, this corridor was guarded midway along by the greatest of the Crusader castles, Krak des Chevaliers. From at least Roman times onwards, Homs (Emesa) has stood at the eastern entrance to this gap, where the Orontes River, which rises in Lebanon's Bekaa valley, curls down into the central Syrian plain. But long before that, another city, farther upriver, dominated this crossroads—ancient Kadesh.

For most of its distance, the highway north from Damascus to Homs runs through undulating country just east of the Anti-Lebanon range (where minor roads lead to Seidnaya, Maalula and Yabrud; *see* **The Anti-Lebanon**, p.121). Where the mountains fall away and about 20 kilometres before reaching Homs, route 413 heads 20km southwest to Al-Qusair, at which you turn northwards and in about 3km see a village upon the mound of Tell Nebi Mend. Here archaeologists from the University of London are uncovering the Bronze Age fortress-city of Kadesh, where in May 1275 or 1274 BC Ramses II fought the Hittites in a battle as celebrated as those of Armageddon and Troy, and the first in history that it is possible to describe in any detail.

Getting There

Tell Nebi Mend is difficult to get to without a car. At Homs you might be able to get a minibus or service taxi to Al-Qusair, but you must check first that you will be able to get back the same day.

Visiting the Site

There is little to see here in the way of ruins, rather you come to appreciate the topography of the site. (For assistance, seek out the site guard, Abu Zaki, at whose house Peter Parr, the archaeologist leading the dig, stays when at Tell Nebi Mend.) The mound of Kadesh stands on the left bank of the Orontes within the angle caused by the tributary stream, the Nahr Mukadiye, that joins it from the southwest. Ramses, at the head of the Amun division and with the divisions of Re, Ptah and Sutekh strung out behind him, advanced from the south along the course of the Orontes. Egyptian scouts could find no trace of the enemy, while two men claiming to be deserters from the Hittite ranks said King Muwatallis had withdrawn his army northwards towards Aleppo.

In fact the Hittite army was on the far side of Kadesh. As the divisions of Amun and Re moved northwards along the west side of Kadesh, the Hittites moved southwards along the east side of the city, keeping it between themselves and the Egyptians so as to remain unseen. Ramses and his Amun division pitched camp northwest of the point where the Nahr Mukadiye joins the Orontes, while the Re division lingered south of the tributary. These divisions were in turn separated from those of Ptah and Sutekh which were still 10km or so upstream. Suddenly, fresh information made Ramses aware of his dangerously divided situation. An Egyptian account describes what happened next: 'The Hittite king came, together with his numerous countries that were with him, and they crossed the ford of the Orontes on the south side of Kadesh. They came forth from the south of Kadesh, and they cut through the division of Re in its middle, while it was on the march, not knowing and not drawn up for battle.' The Hittite cavalry cut the Re infantry to pieces, then plunged northwards into Ramses' camp, driving the fleeing remnants of the Re division before them and sending also the Amun division into flight.

Ramses, with his household troops and immediate officers, was now entirely surrounded just north of the tributary. With terrific courage and presence of mind, he hurled himself at the weakest point in the Hittite line, between his camp and the Orontes, driving his enemies into the river. Muwatallis, with 8000 of his infantry on the east side of the river, saw the chief of his bodyguard and his own royal brother killed in the action. Had he nevertheless continued the encirclement from the south and west, Ramses would have been lost. Instead, Ramses' furious onslaught was just enough to make Muwatallis hesitate; the encirclement was not pressed, and instead the Hittites, in a lapse of discipline, pillaged the pharaoh's camp. The diversion allowed Ramses to fight bravely on with his scanty forces for a further three hours until his position was rescued by the division of Ptah, which at last reached Kadesh from the south. The city was never taken, and Ramses was happy enough to return home with his salvaged army, but for the rest of his long life he never ceased to celebrate the events at Kadesh on monuments all over Egypt.

The battle of Kadesh was the last to be won, if that is the word, by the Egyptian Empire and all but brought to a close the history of superpower conflict, summarised below, that was focused here during the second half of the second millennium BC.

Armageddon, Kadesh and Troy: A Bronze Age Tale of Three Cities

The Bronze Age, the period from about 3100 to 1200 BC, is so named for the introduction and widespread use of that metal combined of copper and tin. Harder than copper alone, bronze tools and weapons were the high technology of the day, their possession essential to any advanced society. In particular, control over the sources of copper and tin was a strategic necessity for the wielding of military power.

Anatolia (Turkey) and Egyptian Sinai had copper. Both may have produced usable amounts of tin, though Cornwall and the Danube to the west and Afghanistan to the east were its principal sources. Mesopotamia had no metals at all. In consequence the channels for trade in one or other of these vital metals passed across the Dardanelles in northwestern Anatolia and variously through eastern Anatolia, along the Euphrates and Tigris rivers, and along the Syrian coast and its interior. The Egyptians had a further need, for they had hardly any trees, and so they also traded with Lebanon and Syria for the timber from which they made their furniture, roofed their houses and built their fleets.

The rival powers inhabiting Anatolia, Mesopotamia and Egypt each sought to dominate either the areas in which these natural resources could be obtained or at least the routes of trade along which they passed. Syria therefore became a great-power battleground.

Tuthmosis III: From Kadesh to New York

The battle of **Armageddon** (Megiddo in northern Israel), fought in about 1479 BC, was the opening shot in a series of Bronze Age superpower contests that would extend over more than two centuries. The aggressive 16th- to 14th-century kingdom of **Mitanni** was centred between the Tigris and Euphrates rivers in northeastern Syria and up into Anatolia. By way of opposing Egyptian interests, the Mitanni gave support to the kingdom of Kadesh, which became head of a coalition of local Palestinian and Syrian principalities. The New Kingdom Pharaoh Tuthmosis III (1479–25 BC) launched his career, and indeed launched Egypt's imperial age, by defeating the king of Kadesh at Armageddon, the very name becoming a byword for decisive battles.

In a subsequent, sixth, campaign (he fought 17 Asian campaigns in all), Tuthmosis marched from the coast up the Homs Gap; in an account from his own annals, 'His Majesty arrived at the city of Kadesh, overthrew it, cut down its groves, harvested its grain.'

Astonishingly, you can still gaze upon the face of this man, the first to build an empire in any real sense, but for that you will have to go to the Mummy Room in the Cairo Museum, though his obelisks, talismans of empire ever since, can be seen on London's Embankment, in New York's Central Park, at the Church of St John Lateran in Rome and in the Hippodrome at Istanbul, the inscription on this last illustrating the full extent of his Asian triumphs: 'Tuthmosis, who crossed the Euphrates with might and with victory at the head of his army'.

Yet within Tuthmosis' lifetime a more powerful empire was emerging in the north, this time in north-central Anatolia. The **Hittites**, whose capital was at Hattusas, present-day Boğazköy, east of Ankara, opened their imperial period in about 1450 BC with victories as far west as the Aegean and, in the east, against the Mitanni. The final blow against Mitanni was struck around 1350 BC by Suppiluliumas I; its capital was destroyed, and the Hittites occupied Syria as far south as Kadesh.

The Widow of Tutankhamun

So great was the fame of Suppiluliumas that even Egypt nearly entered the Hittite orbit in one of the great might-have-beens of history. The boy-king Tutankhamun (1336–27 BC) had just died and his young widow, eager to retain her position, entreated Suppiluliumas to send one of his sons to be her husband and rule as pharaoh. But 'they killed him as they were conducting him to Egypt', a Hittite text informs us, 'they' presumably the supporters of Ay, a military man and Tutankhamun's *éminence grise*, who now succeeded him to the throne. Instead of an alliance, perhaps even a union, between the two superpowers of the day, the murder of the Hittite prince contributed to nearly a century of enmity that encompassed the later battle of Kadesh fought between Ramses II and Suppiluliumas' grandson Muwatallis.

The Hittites Struggle on Two Fronts

Again and again, in reliefs at Abydos, Karnak and the Ramesseum, on the pylons of the Temple of Luxor and within his rock-hewn temple at Abu Simbel, Ramses II (1279–13 BC) proclaimed a great victory, though over whom and where remained a mystery until the decipherment of Egyptian hieroglyphs early in the 19th century and, towards the end of the century, the significance of certain inscribed stones found at Hama was recognised.★ At the Temple of Luxor, for example, an outsize Ramses is shown charging into a mass of enemy chariots, driving them back into a river which loops around a fortified city. The city, we now know, is **Kadesh**, the river the Orontes, the enemy the Hittites, the date late May 1275 or 1274 BC, that is about a generation before the date usually given for the Trojan War, about 1250 BC.

That proximity of dates between the events at Kadesh and at Troy may be more than fortuitous; according to the Egyptian account of the battle of Kadesh, Ramses was opposed by the Hittite king Muwatallis who 'had gathered to himself all lands as far as the ends of the sea', numbered as 'sixteen nations', among them—and here mentioned in history for the first time—the Dardanians, a name by which Homer was later to describe the Trojans. The Egyptians were in no doubt that in the Hittites they faced a formidable opponent of imperial dimensions. Indeed for all his boasting, Ramses' famous triumph was no more than a small victory snatched from the jaws of a greater defeat: his forces were surrounded and faced annihilation from which he escaped by bravery and a momentary lapse in Hittite competence, for the Hittites maintained their authority in northern Syria, and Muwatallis even immediately extended it southwards to the region of Damascus.

But the Hittite Empire was under strain from having to maintain control over trade gateways at opposite ends of Anatolia. While Muwatallis was engaged against Egypt, the **Assyrians** reached northwards from Babylon and grabbed Mitanni for themselves, denying the Hittites access to important copper mines. It was this irruption of Assyrian power, inimical to the interests of both Egypt and the Hittite Empire, that probably brought about the famous treaty between Ramses II and Hattusilis III found at the temple of Karnak in Upper Egypt:

> *The covenant of Ramses, Beloved of Amun, Great King*
> *of the land of Egypt, hero, with Hattusilis, Great*
> *King, King of the land of Hatti, his brother,*
> *providing for good peace and good brotherhood in the*
> *relations of the Great Kingdom between them for ever . . .*

which divided Syria into spheres of influence and was sealed by Ramses' marriage to a Hittite princess. Though the eastern tin route remained in grave danger, the Hittites, by virtue of their treaty with the Egyptians, were still able to maintain control of the Syrian ports and struck back by forbidding commercial relations between them and Assyria.

But in western Anatolia, territories along the Aegean coast were slipping from Hittite control. The Hattusas archives record the growing power of a western state they call Ahhiyawa, which might be Homer's Achaeans, the name he gives to the people we would now call the

---

★ *Ramses' inscriptions in fact refer to a people the Egyptians called the Hatti. That the Hatti were the Hittites, and that the Hittites once had a great empire, was recognised only after scholarly study of the Hama stones (see p.145).*

Mycenaean Greeks. It is possible to conjecture that while Hattusilis III was struggling to maintain the Hittite position in Syria, the trade route in the northwest was threatened by the activities of the Mycenaeans. These events could have been the background to a 'Trojan War'; the war itself, as it was recalled in later centuries, may well have been a compression of a series of conflicts between the Hittites and their allies on the one hand and the Mycenaean Greeks on the other.

Trojan Heroes Fighting at Kadesh?

At about the same time as the battle of Kadesh, the Hittite archives at Hattusas record a treaty with a king Aleksandus of Wilusa in the west, which recalls Homer's prince Alexandros, the name by which Paris, abductor of Helen and son of King Priam, is most commonly known in the *Iliad*, while Wilusa could be Ilios, the name Homer gives to **Troy**. The treaty obliged Aleksandus to contribute infantry and chariots to Muwatallis' campaigns against the Egyptians and the Assyrians; Ramses listed the Dardanians, the name Homer later applied to the Trojans, as being among the 'sixteen nations' arrayed against him; and so with a bit of fancy one can imagine the young Paris fighting on the Orontes, and then a generation later the grizzled man of war fighting for his native city of Troy against the Greeks at the opposite end of the Hittite Empire.

After 1250 BC, the date usually accepted for the fall of Troy, the Hattusas tablets are ominously silent on the northwest. From Egyptian records it is clear that Ahhiyawa was growing stronger and for a while was even ranked as a great power. The Assyrians, meanwhile, continued their pressure against the Hittites' eastern frontiers. But when, in the 1180s BC, the Hittite Empire suddenly disintegrated, the end came not from those familiar quarters. Instead far to the northwest a great migration was underway, sweeping over the whole of the Aegean and Eastern Mediterranean world, and dashing itself on the shores of Egypt, which alone withstood the tidal wave, though its loss of influence in Syria meant that its imperial days were also numbered. These were the **Sea Peoples**, who in destroying such Syrian coastal cities as Ugarit (*see* p.197), cut the Hittite Empire's lines of trade and brought about its collapse.

The Hittites at Kadesh may have had the advantage of a new strategic resource, iron. With the empire's fall, so fell Anatolia's monopoly on making iron weapons, and the knowledge was soon disseminated throughout the ancient world, perhaps by the Sea Peoples themselves, bringing about the end of the Bronze Age and the beginning of the Age of Iron.

Homs

Homs is Syria's third largest city and also its most important oil refining centre. The sight of Bedouin tents and, off to the west, a giant oil refinery meet you as you enter the extensive plain of Homs, the mountains so distant as to be unnoticeable. At the intersection once of caravan routes, now pipelines from Iraq (shut down since 1982) and northeastern Syria converge on the city, from which another pipeline runs through the Homs Gap to the port of Tartus. 'A dusty, unattractive town of basalt houses,' said *Cook's Handbook* in 1934, since when oil and sugar refineries, a plant for treating phosphates from Palmyra, and spinning and weaving mills have not improved Homs but have simply helped it grow bigger. While its importance for the economic development of Syria is undoubted, Agatha Christie's remark just before the Second World War, that 'there is not very much to see', remains true for today's traveller. Yet something of the past remains, and if you have a few hours to spare, then a walk through the old souks and the Christian quarter will repay you with their traditional atmosphere.

Getting There

By train: there are four daily trains in each direction running between Damascus and Aleppo and calling at Homs and Hama along the way, two in each direction serving Deir ez Zor and Qamishli. The railway station is 1.5km southwest of the clock tower roundabout at the west end of Al-Quwatli Street, Homs' main street. There is a second, more distant, station for trains to Latakia.

By long-distance bus and microbus: the Karnak, ordinary bus and microbus stations are adjacent to one another, 1.5km north of the east end of Homs' main street, Al-Quwatli Street. The new Pullman station for luxury coaches is 750m farther north. Homs is an important crossroads of Syria, services linking it with Damascus, Aleppo, Tartus, Latakia, Palmyra and Deir ez Zor. Note however that many buses get quickly booked up for, or are set aside for, the entire journey (for example from Damascus all the way to Deir ez Zor via Homs and Palmyra or from Damascus to Palmyra via Homs), so you should book a day in advance if possible. There are frequent microbuses between Homs and Hama, and also between Homs and Krak des Chevaliers (Qalaat al-Husn).

Tourist Information

There is a tourist kiosk 50m east along Al-Quwatli Street from the clock tower roundabout, on the south side. Officially open from 8.30am to 2pm and 4pm to 9pm, it is hardly even open then, which makes no difference as it is all but useless anyway.

Orientation

The road from Damascus comes into Homs from the south and brings you to a roundabout with a clock tower. Another street, joining the roundabout from the southwest, brings you up from the railway station. Running east from the roundabout is Al-Quwatli Street, the main thoroughfare of the modern town. Most hotels are on it or just off it. There is a small tourist booth about 50m east along Al-Quwatli Street in gardens on its south side, while on the north side, about halfway along, is the new provincial museum. In all, Al-Quwatli Street is about 500m long; at its east end it joins the road north to Hama. To the southeast of Al-Quwatli Street is the old quarter, once the walled city, though its walls are almost all gone now. The Great Mosque of al-Nuri, the Church of Umm al-Zunnar, the Church of St Elias and the citadel are all here. The Mosque of Khalid Ibn al-Walid is about 500m north of Al-Quwatli Street, set back in a park on the east side of the Hama road. The bus stations are farther north along the Hama road.

History

As Emesa during Roman times, the city enjoyed some fame and opulence. Its fortunes were tied to those of Palmyra, for so long as that desert metropolis flourished Emesa was a natural stage for caravans westwards. Fortune's other avenue was Julia Domna, daughter of the high priest of Emesa, whose stars foretold she would marry a king. Septimius Severus, with his eye to rising above his position as commander of a Roman legion in Syria, married her and lo! by a coup in AD 193 became emperor. As well as lucky, Julia was also beautiful and intelligent, and in Rome became the patroness of every art and, at some expense to her chastity, the friend of every man of genius. Her two sons, Caracalla and Geta, became emperors in turn, and Emesa and Syria for some time enjoyed the favours of the imperial house.

Then in 218 a grandnephew of Julia Domna also became emperor. This was Elagabalus, who while hereditary high priest at Emesa and only 14 was raised to the purple by the Syrian legions. His name derived from Baal, whose emblem was a large black stone kept at his temple. The stone and Elagabalus came to Rome together, the one set in precious gems and placed in a chariot drawn by six milk-white horses, the other walking backwards before it, the better to enjoy the divine presence, the streets strewn with gold dust as they made their way to Rome's Palatine Hill where the stone was installed in a temple of Baal. But Elagabalus was more than lavish and superstitious; he was also degenerate and cracked. After experimenting with his inadequate manhood on a succession of concubines and wives, and ravishing a vestal virgin, he took on women's clothes and manners, appointed his lovers to the highest posts in the empire, and even made one of them his husband. This was not to the taste of the Praetorian Guard, who after four years killed Elagabalus, dragged his corpse through the streets of Rome, dumped his body in the Tiber and returned the black stone to Emesa.

Even there the stone was to be venerated once again by an emperor, in 272, when Aurelian sought Baal's support before his decisive battle against Zenobia. But with her defeat and Palmyra's fall, Emesa declined. (Thanks to Aurelian, however, the influence of Elagabalus' deity rose to new heights at Rome, where it had become specifically associated with the sun, and in 274 the emperor established a massive temple of the Unconquerable Sun as the focal point of the state religion. Such was the cult's success that to counter it the early Church appropriated the sun's birthday, 25 December, making it the birthday of Christ.) Christianity established itself early in Emesa and 3rd- to 7th-century catacombs have been found beneath houses in the old quarter in the east of the city, though for fear of collapse they cannot be visited. A significant Christian population still inhabits the old eastern quarter.

Homs became important again after the Arab conquest, when it was settled by companions of the Prophet who opposed their puritanical version of Islam to the easier ways of the Umayyad court in Damascus. But by the 18th century Homs had sunk into decrepitude. 'There are to be seen in this town,' reported John Green in his *Journey from Aleppo to Damascus*, 'an infinite number of curious works of marble, and ruins of very magnificent buildings, though at present they are for the most part level with the ground. This devastation is owing, in a great measure, to the Arabs of the neighbouring deserts of Syria, or Arabia, who extort large sums of money from the inhabitants. To avoid which, great numbers of them have left the city, and retired to other places, where they may be more secure.'

A Tour of Homs

At the east end of Al-Quwatli Street where it meets the Hama road, turn south and this brings you, past modern souks, into the old quarter. Almost immediately to the east is the **Great Mosque of al-Nuri**, which probably stands on the site of the Baal temple and a later church of St John. Among the oldest things in the city are some Roman columns used in the construction of the much rebuilt mosque named for Saladin's predecessor Nur al-Din. To the southeast of the mosque are the **old covered souks**, as animated as those of Aleppo and Damascus and saved by the provincial status of Homs from being at all touristic.

Apart from the old souks, one of the few remaining areas of Homs to preserve its traditional character is the **Christian quarter**, which lies to the east. There are numerous buildings of

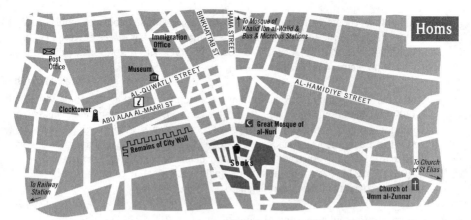

N

250 metres
200 yards

the Mameluke period here, though mostly in a sad state of dilapidation, and a number of churches with ancient histories. About 500m east of the Al-Nuri Mosque is the **Church of Umm al-Zunnar** (the Virgin's girdle), so-named after a textile belt discovered under the altar in 1953 and quickly claimed by the Syrian Orthodox Patriarch of Antioch to have belonged to the Virgin Mary. A 4th-century church stood on this site, though the present building dates only from the end of the 19th century. Turn right on leaving the church, then take the first right, and in 250m eastwards you come to the **Church of St Elias** (Mar Elian), parts of its crypt dating back to perhaps the 6th century, named after a 3rd-century Roman officer and son of the governor of Emesa, who was martyred for his faith at the hands of his own father. In 1970 a series of fine murals were discovered in the crypt beneath a coat of plaster. These are accompanied by inscriptions in Greek and Arabic and depict Christ enthroned between the Virgin and Mary Magdalene on one side and John the Baptist and possibly St Elias on the other. There are medallions of various saints and prophets, while the Evangelists Matthew, Mark, Luke and John are depicted in side niches. There are traces also of what might be 6th-century paintings, in which case they are possibly the oldest extant church paintings in Syria.

What remains of the **citadel** (*qalaat*), destroyed in the 1830s by Ibrahim Pasha, son of Mohammed Ali of Egypt, is at the southwest corner of the old city, but the mound is now off-limits. The Orontes passes northwards about a kilometre to the southwest of here. One of the few surviving stretches of the Arab **city wall** is near the northwest corner, two blocks south of Al-Quwatli St. The Ottoman-style **Mosque of Khalid Ibn al-Walid** is 500m north up the Hama road from Al-Quwatli Street. More impressive outside than in, the mosque is set back beyond flowerbeds on the east side of the road and is immediately recognisable by its black and white *ablaq* with two pencil-thin minarets and several metal domes. It was built immediately before the First World War but contains a tomb said to be that of Khalid, conqueror of Syria, whom Mohammed had called the Sword of Islam.

Where to Stay
expensive

Southwest of the town centre and near the Damascus–Aleppo railway station is the **★★★★Safir**, ✆ (031) 412400, ✉ (031) 433420, with air conditioning, bath, TV and minibar in all rooms, restaurants, café, health club, swimming pool and tennis courts. Farther distant, to the south of town on the Damascus road, is the ★★★★**Homs Grand** (Homs al-Kabir), ✆ (031) 412600, 📠 (031) 423021, with ditto rooms, restaurants, café, but no recreational facilities.

inexpensive

At the Karnak bus station 1.5km north of the towon centre is the ★★**Karnak**, ✆ (031) 233099, which despite its location is quiet, clean and usually empty. Rooms have air conditioning and bath. Coming into town, the standard markedly drops. The ★★**Grand Basman**, Abu Alaa Street, ✆ (031) 225009, has clean if spiritless rooms with bath, but is overpriced; ★★**Raghdan**, near the middle of Al-Quwatli Street, ✆ (031) 225211, has rooms of varying quality from shabby to more shabby and is more overpriced than the Grand Bagman.

cheap

★★**Semiramis**, mid-way along Al-Quwatli Street, ✆ (031) 221837, with shower and toilet in rooms but no air conditioning or fan, is a rather run-down place though at the top of this category in price. ★**Al-Nasr al-Jadeed**, along the western stretch of Al-Quwatli Street, ✆ (031) 227423, is cheaper, cleaner, friendlier, has fans in rooms, but toilets and showers are shared. There are other hotels along or just off Al-Quwatli Street, but beyond those already mentioned lies the abyss.

Eating Out

There are simple restaurants, snack bars and cafés along Al-Quwatli Street or close by. Perhaps the best of these restaurants, and serving alcohol, is the **Toledo** on Abu Alaa Street a block south. Both the Karnak bus station and the Damascus–Aleppo railway station have decent restaurants where alcohol is served, but they are little frequented and out of the way. Otherwise there are the expensive restaurants at the Safir Hotel.

Hama

It is exactly as John Green said of Hama in 1736: 'One can see nothing of it before he comes just to it.' By this point in its course the Orontes has worn a deep bed through the monotonous plain, and it is only as you come to the valley escarpment that you discover beneath you the whole sunken city hidden along the river banks. The place once had a reputation for picturesqueness, being hardly touched by the modern world, so that until very recently travellers have echoed Green's description that 'it contains some beautiful houses and mosques, which are built of black and white stone. The Orontes turns eighteen great wooden wheels, which raise the water and throw it into canals borne upon great arches, whereby it is conveyed into the gardens without the town, as well as the fountains within it. There are some pretty good bazaars in Hama, where there is a trade for linen, which is manufactured there, and sent to Tripoli to be exported into Europe. There is a very pleasant garden by the riverside, full of orange trees'.

Yet just as Hama lay in its motionless lower world, escaping time and the changing winds of the encircling plain, so it remained enclosed within an atmosphere of intense belief and fierce intolerance. Its inhabitants are 'notoriously farouche', Robin Fedden (*Syria*) was writing in 1946, and 'hostile to all ideas and persons unfamiliar. Their mood is expressed in sudden violences and rash riots'. It was against that background that the events of 1982 occurred.

The 1982 Uprising in Hama

In 1970 the then air force general and defence minister Hafez Assad ousted the civilian Baathist leadership that had been responsible for the debacle of the 1967 war against Israel and the failure of Syria's armed intervention in Jordan on behalf of the Palestinian uprising in 'Black September' 1970. President Assad, as he became, though belonging to the minority Alawi sect, broadened his Baathist regime and was fairly successful in making himself the representative of all Syrians, not just of a particular interest or group. Conservative Sunni Muslim opinion, however, centred especially in Hama, remained against him, especially after his 1973 constitution failed to make Islam the state religion. Assad responded in kind to the terror campaign led by Muslim fundamentalists, which culminated in his suppression of an armed uprising in February 1982, when the Muslim Brotherhood held Hama for four days. The revolt was crushed and parts of the city were destroyed at the cost of between 8000 and 25,000 lives. The pall this has cast over the city can be imagined, but the suppression of militant fundamentalism was not altogether regretted by the Syrian population at large, at least a quarter of whom are Christian or non-Sunni Muslims, nor by those many Sunni Muslims who would prefer not to live under a fundamentalist regime.

There is little sign of Hama having been razed, instead there is much construction going on in stone and concrete, a familiar enough sight anywhere in Syria. Except down by the river, the impression is of an entirely ordinary, often tatty, town, Syria's fourth largest in fact and the centre of its iron and steel industry. But some things hardly change. In and around Hama you notice the frequency with which women veil themselves. Some wear a full black robe from the top of their heads to their toes. Others wear a mini-version over the head and face only, which is then tucked into a buttoned-up overcoat worn even in the fiercest heat. And occasionally you will see a woman in a light summer dress, Western-style, with stockings and smart high-heel shoes, but with a black plastic bag over her head, as though all dressed up for her own hanging.

The best thing to do is to have lunch down by the riverside, where amid the diversion of the scene you can also consider the history of this ancient place. The Homs–Aleppo road crosses the Orontes at the centre of town, the tourist office overlooking a park along the right bank of the river. About a kilometre upstream from here you come to two pairs of *norias*, or waterwheels, known as the **Four Norias of Bechiriyat**, which turn at various speeds like the works of a gigantic clock. A café and restaurant overlooking the *norias* is the place to settle in for a meal or drink and enjoy the most entertaining sight in Hama. Being of wood and mounted on wooden blocks upon stone piers, the *norias* make a rising and falling drone like an attacking squadron of Baron von Richthofen's flying circus. Boys swim about in the river (there are no girls in sight, none even watching) and catch hold of the blades, riding the wheels upwards and then leaping back into the water, or sometimes clambering onto the tops of the 15m-high stone supporting piers from where they dive or cannonball into the Orontes. More idly, they fix themselves within the framework of the wheels and just go round and round with the *norias*, a dip per revolution. There may be a party of French sitting on this terrace, most likely drinking mineral water, though cans of American lager trundled in from Beirut and *arak* are also served. It is only the visiting Saudis and Kuwaitis who down bottles of Johnny Walker.

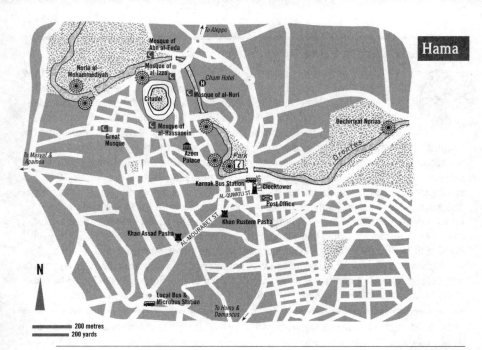

Hama

Getting There

By train: at least two trains daily in each direction link Hama with Aleppo, Homs and Damascus. The railway station is 1.5km west of Sadik and Al-Quwatli streets at the centre of town, a local bus running between the two.

By long-distance bus: the bus stations for all Karnak and Pullman services to and from Homs, Damascus and Aleppo are on the south bank of the Orontes within 50–100m of the clocktower at the centre of town, where Sadik Street (the main Homs–Aleppo road) is carried over the river by a bridge.

By local bus and microbus: the local bus and microbus depots are across the road from one another on Al-Mourabet Street, a kilometre southwest of the town centre (follow Al-Mourabet Street out from Khan Rustem Pasha), to which they are linked by local bus. There are microbuses to Masyaf (*see* p.174) and along the Orontes to Shaizar, Apamea (Qalaat Mudiq) and Jisr al-Shugur, and to Aleppo, as well as frequent runs to Homs.

Tourist Information

The Tourist Office (*open daily 8–2, closed Fri*) is on the north side of the Orontes in the park along Sadik Street (the main Homs–Aleppo road).

History

Throughout the last half of the second millennium and the first half of the first millennium, Hama's periods as an independent kingdom alternated with subjection by the Mitanni, the Hittites and the Assyrians. As Hamath, Hama is several times mentioned in the Old Testament as the northern limit of Israelite activity, and in II Samuel 8:10 its king yields allegiance to King David. But as so often happens at continuously inhabited places, nothing survives of these

144   *The Orontes and the Central Plain*

times, apart from such references and the evidence of excavations, particularly at the citadel hill, nor of the classical period, when it was known as Epiphania after the Seleucid Antiochus IV Epiphanes, nor even of the Byzantine or early Arab empires. It flourished under the Ayyubids, when its oldest extant *norias* were built, while its oldest mosques date from the 12th and 13th centuries when Hama was disputed by rival dynasties at Aleppo and Damascus. The Ottomans left their mark with a pair of khans and the beautiful Azem Palace, rivalling that at Damascus.

The Hama Stones and the Discovery of the Hittite Empire

For all Hama's lack of ancient ruins, it was the discovery here of a number of inscribed basalt stones that led to nothing less than the realisation that there had once been such a thing as the Hittite Empire. On monuments all over Egypt, Ramses II had repeatedly broadcast his rather dubious victory at Kadesh (*see* p.134) over a people his inscriptions called the Hatti. But nothing connected the Hatti to the Hittites, who until then were known only through several slighting and confused Old Testament references. In Joshua 3:10 for example they appear among a mostly humdrum list of local peoples when the Israelites enter the Promised Land: 'And Joshua said, Hereby ye shall know that the living God is among you, and that he will without fail drive out from before you the Canaanites, and the Hittites, and the Hivites, and the Perizzites, and the Girgashites, and the Amorites, and the Jebusites'. Later, in II Samuel, King David's lust fixes upon Bathsheba, wife of Uriah the Hittite, a mercenary in the king's service. On every count Uriah is dispensable and David, to freely gratify himself, arranges for Uriah's death in battle. There is nothing in these biblical accounts written hundreds of years after the fall of what we now know to have been the Hittite Empire to suggest the true history of Uriah's people nor to locate them anywhere other than within the bounds of the Jewish kingdom. Yet their seeming insignificance is contradicted in II Kings 7:6 when 'the kings of the Hittites and the kings of the Egyptians' are mentioned in one breath.

The stones at Hama were noticed in 1812 by the Swiss adventurer, John Lewis Burckhardt, who was also the first modern European to come upon Petra in Jordan and Abu Simbel in Egypt. 'In the corner of a house in the bazaar,' he wrote in *Travels in Syria*, 'is a stone with a number of small figures and signs, which appear to be a kind of hieroglyphical writing, though it does not resemble that of Egypt.' But the stones remained in obscurity until 1870 when the American consul in Beirut came upon them again and published a facsimile of the inscriptions on one. An attempt was made to purchase a stone embedded in a wall, but its owner would not part with it owing to the income it provided, deformed people being willing to pay for the privilege of lying upon the stone in the hope of a cure. The following year Sir Richard Burton visited Hama to inspect the stones and published a series of facsimiles in his *Unexplored Syria*. But despite speaking 28 languages, one of which, said his detractors, was pornography (he translated *The Perfumed Garden* and *The Kama Sutra*, as well as *The Thousand and One Nights*), the language of the stones eluded him. He urged, however, that the stones be bought at government order, and this is what happened; they were prised from the walls of shops and houses, lifted from lanes and gardens, and delivered to the museum at Constantinople, with casts sent to the British Museum, so making them available for scholarly study.

When at the close of the decade British Museum excavators found similar inscriptions at Carchemish on the Euphrates (now just over the border in Turkey), A. H. Sayce, the Oxford Professor of Assyriology, travelled to the Karabel Pass at the opposite end of Anatolia, almost within sight of the Aegean between Sardis and Smyrna (now Izmir), to see for himself a relief that Herodotus had described more than 2000 years before: 'The carved figure is two metres high and represents a man with a spear in his right hand and a bow in the left, and the rest of his equipment to match—partly Egyptian, partly Ethiopian. Across the breast from shoulder to shoulder runs an inscription, cut in the Egyptian sacred script: "By the strength of my shoulders I won this land".' In fact Herodotus' translation of the 'Egyptian script' was pure invention, but the relief with its pointed helmet that he took to be of an Egyptian pharaoh was not unlike that seen in 1834 by the Frenchman Charles Texier carved on the King's Gate at Boğazköy, those then still mysterious ruins east of Ankara which would later be recognised as Hattusas, capital of the Hittite Empire. While Sayce was no more able to decipher the inscriptions at Karabel, Boğazköy, Carchemish and Hama, he saw their similarity and made the star- tling proposal 'that in pre-Hellenic days a powerful empire must have existed in Asia Minor which extended from the Aegean to the Halys [the modern Kizilirmak which flows near Boğazköy] and southward into Syria . . . [possessing] its own special artistic culture and its own special script'.

Making a series of inspired connections, he identified the descendants of this once great empire as those biblical cuckolds the Hittites, further venturing that they were one and the same people as the Hatti who at Kadesh had checked the ambitions of Ramses II. By pointing to a Hittite homeland not in Palestine but much farther to the north, with the Orontes as its southern limit, he renewed interest too in the massive ruins at Boğazköy, which Hugo Winckler of the German Oriental Society began excavating in 1906. Almost at once he hit upon the Hittite royal archives, its tablets inscribed in Babylonian cuneiform, the diplomatic language of the day, which told him this was indeed the impe- rial capital, called Hattusas. Soon one such tablet came into his hands which not only could he understand at sight but with whose contents he had been familiar for years:

> The covenant of Ramses, Beloved of Amun, Great King
> of the land of Egypt, hero, with Hattusilis, Great King,
> King of the land of Hatti . . .

'Here was something,' said Winckler, 'that might perhaps have been yearned for in jest, a gift from the fairies'—it was the Hittite copy of that peace treaty between the coequal 'brothers' Ramses II and Hattusilis III, successor to Ramses' royal adversary at Kadesh, its cuneiform matching word for word the Egyptian hieroglyphic version long known to scholars on the temple walls at distant Karnak. Thanks in part to the stones of Hama, the Hittite Empire, lost to the world since before Homer's time, had re-entered history.

Following the Orontes through Hama

The muddy brown Orontes flows along a narrow and twisting course through Hama, its banks sometimes thick with overhanging trees and bushes, elsewhere bordered by parks and play- grounds or by mosques and houses whose very feet touch the water.

The starting point for a tour of Hama is at the centre of town where a bridge carries the Homs–Aleppo road (Sadik Street) over the Orontes. Immediately west of the bridge, the river turns northwards, a park on its right bank, with several *norias* in view. About 600m downstream, on the left bank, is the citadel (*qalaat*). Here the river bends westwards again for 400m before resuming its northerly progress. The Four Norias of Bechiriyat apart (*see* p.143), everything worth seeing lies along or close to these two stretches of the Orontes, where at night there is something of a funfair atmosphere at the many open-air restaurants and cafés.

About 350m downstream, on the left bank, is the Beit al-Azem or **Azem Palace**, which houses the **museum**. Built by Assad Pasha al-Azem, governor of Hama until his transfer to Damascus in 1743 (where you can visit his grander though similar residence of the same name), this is one of the finest examples of Ottoman architecture in Syria. The swept and spotlessly clean open courtyard is paved with tiles, planted with a few trees for shade and decorative effect, and a fountain plays at its centre. At one end is the liwan, a high-roofed room entirely open on one side to the courtyard, divans set against its three walls, so that its occupants could recline here, enjoying the mingling of indoors and outdoors, which comes naturally in a climate such as Syria's. Unlike the Azem Palace in Damascus, the one at Hama has a second courtyard on the first-floor level to take advantage of the cool breezes and lovely views across the Orontes. The interior rooms maintain this outdoors effect, with fountains and painted panels of birds and fruits and cypresses. The upper levels were badly damaged during the 1982 fighting but are being restored. Roman and Christian remains are displayed in the lower courtyard, while a room off to the river side of the courtyard contains, most notably, a 4th-century AD floor mosaic found in a village house west of Homs depicting a group of women musicians playing various instruments.

Between a pair of *norias* and a small bridge 100m farther north along the same side of the river is the **Al-Nuri Mosque** begun in 1172 by Saladin's predecessor, Nur al-Din. The typically Syrian square-plan minaret in contrasting bands of limestone and basalt is original, as is the intricately worked wooden minbar inside the prayer hall. Opposite, but destroyed in 1982, was the Beit Keilani, a large rambling house with rooms overhanging the river and its own *noria* (explaining why there are now 17 *norias* in Hama, when 250 years ago Green counted 18). After the Azem Palace, it was the finest residence in Hama; now the Cham Hotel occupies the site. Beyond the Al-Nuri Mosque, where the Orontes bends westwards and still on the left bank, is the 15th-century **Al-Izza Mosque** of the Mameluke period.

Across the river is the **Mosque and Mausoleum of Abu al-Feda**, also known as Al-Hayyat, Mosque of the Snakes, for the interlaced stonework of its windows. In 1289, at the age of 16, Abu al-Feda fought in the army of the Mameluke Sultan Qalaun at the fall of Tripoli; in 1291 he was at the fall of Acre, recording that 'we men of Hama were stationed, as usual, on the far right flank of the army'. As a vassal of the Mamelukes, he ruled Hama as emir from 1310 until his death in 1331. Being himself a poet and geographer, he proved also a generous patron of literature and science. But he is best known for his historical works, especially for his eyewitness accounts of the last years of the Crusader presence in the Middle East: 'After the conquest of Acre,' he wrote, 'God struck fear into the hearts of those Franks still remaining on the Syrian coast. Thus did they precipitately evacuate Sidon, Beirut, Tyre and all the other towns. The sultan (Qalaun's successor, Khalil) therefore had the good fortune, shared by none other, of easily conquering all those strongholds, which he immediately had dismantled. With these conquests, all the lands of the coast were fully returned to the Muslims, a result undreamed of. Thus were the Franks, who had once nearly conquered Damascus, Egypt and many other lands, expelled from all of Syria. God grant that they never set foot here again!'

If you now continue along this westward-flowing stretch of the river you come on the left bank to the **largest of the *norias***, called Al-Mohammediyeh, dating from the 14th century. This and all the other *norias* of Hama were owned by one or other of four great families who well into the 20th century ran Hama, often ruthlessly, as their feudal domain. There is a story of the head of the Azam family who coveted a neighbour's garden. An offer was made, but the neighbour refused to sell. So the Azam notable had one of his own slaves killed, dismembered and then secretly buried at no great depth in his neighbour's garden. A few days later he joined his neighbour for coffee on the very spot, but soon complained of the smell. The Azam insisted that the ground be dug up and, when the body was found, charged his neighbour with the crime. In compensation for his murdered slave, the Azam was given the garden.

The *norias* were introduced by the Byzantines specially to overcome the great depths of the Orontes' banks. (A mosaic at the National Museum in Damascus, dated AD 469, provides the earliest evidence of a *noria* at work on the Orontes—*see* p.59.) The water is lifted to the tops of the stone piers and discharged into aqueducts to irrigate the town's gardens and surrounding fields, though these days the *norias* are just for show; the gardens along the banks of the Orontes are watered by motorised pumps.

You can now return to the **citadel** (*qalaat*), these days with a park and café on top from where there is a good view over the city. The citadel hill was possibly once part of the ridge which juts out into the valley at this point; if so, the task of cutting it free was a mammoth undertaking of ancient times. A few stone fragments lie about, but otherwise all the cut stone of its fortifications has been removed and put to building use below. The **Mosque of al-Hassanein** stands just to the southwest of the citadel hill, near the road to the summit; it was rebuilt by Nur al-Din after an earlier mosque on the site was felled by an earthquake. About 100m to its west is the **Great Mosque**, almost totally destroyed in 1982 and now being rebuilt by the Antiquities Department, though it seems impossible that its earlier interest can be recreated, for it had once been the site of a pagan temple, then a Byzantine church, whose doors and windows were traceable in the walls of the mosque. Like its contemporary, the Great Mosque of the Umayyads in Damascus, its broad courtyard, with a treasury elevated upon Corinthian columns, was surrounded on three sides by porticoes with Byzantine shafts and capitals, on the fourth by a basilical prayer hall.

Finally, there are two Ottoman khans along Al-Mourabet Street near the souks southwest of the bridge where the Homs–Aleppo road (Sadik Street) crosses the Orontes. The **Khan Rustem Pasha**, no more than 200m from the bridge, dates from 1556 and is being restored. Rustem Pasha, for whom Sinan built one of his finest minor mosques in Istanbul, was twice Grand Vizier under Suleiman the Magnificent and husband of the sultan's favourite daughter, Princess Mihrimah. The **Khan Assad Pasha** of 1738 presents its huge façade another 200m down the street; it is now a technical school.

Where to Stay
expensive

The ★★★★★**Apamée Cham Palace**, ✆ (033) 277429, ✉ (033) 511626, is the large modern blot on the landscape overlooking the Orontes opposite the Al-Nuri Mosque, but with good views of Hama if you are inside looking out. Restaurants, bars, outdoor swimming pool, tennis courts and all the rest of it.

★★★**Hama Tower** is on the 10th and 11th floors of a new tower block near the Karnak bus station less than 100m northwest of the clocktower at the centre of town, ✆ (033) 226864, 📠 (033) 521523. Clean, comfortable if rather bare rooms with air conditioning, shower and toilet; those on one side with balconies and fine views over Hama. Small restaurant. Less expensive still is the ★★**Noria**, 100m west of the clocktower on Al-Quwatli Street, ✆ (033) 511715, 📠 (033) 512414, a friendly, clean and comfortable hotel with restaurant, rooms with air conditioning, fridge, TV, toilet and shower.

cheap

Immediately west of the clocktower on Al-Quwatli Street are two excellent, friendly and clean hotels, the ★**Cairo**, ✆ (033) 237206, 📠 (033) 512414 (the same owner as the Noria), and the ★**Riad**, ✆ (033) 517776, 📠 (033) 510788. A variety of rooms is available in each with private or shared facilities, and there is also dorm accommodation. Both are also very helpful in providing travel information and arranging tours.

Eating Out

The **Al Boustan** and **The Four Norias** restaurants at the Four Norias of Bechiriyat, east along the Orontes, are delightful for the antics of the boys leaping off the water-wheels. Beer and stiffer drinks are served. The **Al-Rawda Restaurant** by the Al-Nuri Mosque offers townscape river views, while the **Sultan**, also near the Al-Nuri Mosque, sits you right up against two norias and serves quality Arab food, though no alcohol.

Along the Orontes Valley to Jisr al-Shugur

Getting Around

Without a car, you will have to rely on local buses and microbuses, which run from Hama to Shaizar, Apamea (Qalaat Mudiq) and Jisr al-Shugur (linking with Latakia and Aleppo), as well as to Masyaf.

Downstream from Hama as you take the road to Apamea, the Nahr al-Assi, the Orontes, loses its muddy colour and flows a clear green. The villages along the way tend to be on hilltops or ridges rather than occupying the rich soil of the Ghab, a marshland until the 1970s, whose few inhabitants made a poor living raising buffalo and catching catfish, but and now the fertile valley region extending northwards to Jisr al-Shugur. Tuthmosis III hunted elephants here on his way back to Egypt after his eighth Asian campaign. The Egyptian report is of a herd 120 animals strong; in the course of the hunt, the pharaoh was only saved from a charging elephant when one of his generals lopped off its trunk. The unhealthy marshes have been drained, the Orontes has been channelled through artificial embankments and several dams have been built, causing nearly 80,000 hectares to be brought under cultivation, their fruit orchards and grain fields creating the colourful patchwork that you now see as you look out from the headlands of Shaizar and Apamea.

Though this route takes you to Jisr al-Shugur from where you can head west to Latakia or east to Aleppo, you can also branch off onto minor roads that will take you into the Jebel al-Sariya, the mountain range separating the Mediterranean from the Orontes valley. From Hama, Shaizar or Apamea you can easily reach Masyaf (*see* p185), eyrie of the Assassins, while 18km south of Jisr al-Shugur there is a new road up to Slenfeh and so down to the Crusader castle of Saône (Qalaat Saladin) (*see* p203).

Shaizar (Qalaat Shaizar)

There are sheep in the fields and wandering along the road as you approach Shaizar, 28km northwest of Hama. A couple of broken-down *norias* stand in the river which here runs between walls of rock; on the left bank, raised upon a narrow rocky ridge, is the *qalaat* of Shaizar, a frontline Muslim bastion against the Crusaders, who for a time held nearby Apamea and whose castles controlled the passes through the Jebel al-Sariya rising to the west. The name derives from the Roman Cesara, but the importance of the site, which commands a crossing point in the river marked by an old Turkish bridge, only really dates from 10th-century Byzantine attempts to regain control of the Orontes. The fortress, however, is an entirely Arab and Mameluke work of the 11th to 13th centuries. Its ruinous condition is owed to war, earthquake and not least its occupation until recent decades by an Arab village whose inhabitants recycled its stones.

Though not as well built as the castles of the Crusaders, Le Grand Césaire, as the Franks called it, nevertheless successfully withstood their several assaults, at times undertaken in combination with the Byzantines, owing to its impregnable position and the stoutness of its defenders. The fortress belonged to the Munqid family, one of whose members was the 12th-century Emir Usamah al-Munqid, a distinguished diplomat and man of letters, who became a personal friend of both Saladin and King Fulk of Jerusalem and admired the Crusaders' martial prowess but abhorred their lack of refinement, writing, 'Among the Franks we find some people who have come to settle among us and who have cultivated the society of the Muslims. They are far superior to those who have freshly joined them in the territories they now occupy'. That was precisely the irony of the Crusades. Those who stayed longest in the East and most appreciated its culture and learning were insufficient in number to maintain their hold there. Because they had always to rely on fresh waves of Crusaders, who ignorantly detested everything Arab civilisation had to offer, the friendship and understanding between the two worlds that might have given the Crusader states some permanence was incessantly undermined.

The fortress stands upon a spur separated from the plateau by a man-hewn channel like that at Saône, and so you must enter by a ramp which passes over a series of arches like that at the Aleppo citadel. This part of the castle, built in 1290, is skirted by a *glacis*, reminiscent of 'The Mountain' at Krak des Chevaliers, though on a much smaller scale. A passageway leads to an open area littered with the debris of the evacuated village; there are vaulted cellars to see but not much else except, from the fortress heights, good views over the plain and down into the Orontes gorge.

Apamea (Qalaat Mudiq)

Once a great city of antiquity, later both an Arab and Crusader citadel, Apamea is impressively sited on a promontory above the right bank of the river, 27km northwest of Shaizar. High yellow grasslands roll away eastwards; to the west the Jebel al-Sariya rises blue in the heat haze; and below, the long green valley of the Orontes promises richness. In Seleucid times these grasslands and valley slopes, lusher then than now, quartered the empire's 600 war elephants and pastured the famous stud of 30,000 mares and 300 stallions which supplied the imperial cavalry. Now and especially in the hot sun and heavy humidity of summer you survey the worn landscape and notice large stones lying about in the plateau fields, and you search in vain for trees that might limit the erosion while offering shade and coolness.

History

Together with Ionia on the Aegean coast of Asia Minor and Babylonia between the Tigris and Euphrates rivers, northern Syria was one of the great nerve centres of the Greek empire in Asia established by Alexander the Great's general, Seleucus I Nicator (ruled 312–280 BC). Settled with veterans and colonised with Greek-speaking cities, northern Syria became a second Macedonia. To four cities he founded along or near the Orontes Seleucus gave imperial names: Seleucia, at the very mouth of the river, was the port for Seleucus' capital city of Antioch (Turkish Antakya), named after his father, while Laodicea, today's Latakia farther down the Mediterranean coast, he named after his mother. This in turn served as a port for Apamea, named after Seleucus' Persian wife, which was an important military base on the middle Orontes. Taken together, these favoured cities formed the backbone of the Seleucid Empire, which was to endure until they each fell to Pompey in 64 BC and Syria was made a Roman province.

In fact almost nothing of the Seleucid period survives above ground either here or elsewhere in Syria, usually because the Romans built amply upon what the Seleucids had founded. For the Romans too Apamea was a military headquarters, and from here Mark Antony launched his victorious Armenian campaign of 34 BC, Cleopatra accompanying him as far as the Euphrates and then returning to Egypt through Apamea, Homs and Damascus. And so at Apamea what you see are the remains of a Roman city, principally of the 2nd century AD, when its population stood at about 200,000 (comparable to that of Antioch and Palmyra, while the population of Rome was at least a million). Belgian excavation work has been continuous since 1930 and recently the Syrian Antiquities Department has undertaken extensive restorations. Though these efforts fall far short of turning Apamea into another Palmyra, they should be measured against the five-sentence description of the site given by Baedeker in 1912, which spoke of 'shapeless ruins'.

Visiting Apamea

The modern village of Qalaat Mudiq is on the broad plain of the Orontes valley. Above it, rising from the eastern escarpment, is the citadel, beyond which, just to the north, a road runs up to the Apamea site. But first stop at the enormous **Ottoman khan** amid the village. The khan is 16th-century and was built to service the pilgrimage trade to Mecca. It is 80m square, its vast courtyard blanched with sun but relieved by flowers, vines and palms. Long vaulted chambers, cool and half-lit by indirect sunlight, enclose the courtyard on all four sides. Only recently restored, the khan has been made into a simple but effective **museum** of finds from Apamea and its vicinity. Often very fine examples of capitals, including Corinthian and Byzantine basket-style, stand against the walls, while excellent mosaics, both pagan and Christian, are set into the floors, their subjects including Adam, Aphrodite and Socrates (this, of the late 4th-century AD when Apamea was a centre of neo-Platonism, is especially fine), and some mosaic inscriptions referring to St Paul.

The Seleucid **citadel** now bears a ruinous Arab and Mameluke fortress, Qalaat Mudiq (Castle of the Straits), of the 12th and 13th centuries. The Norman Crusader Tancred, cousin of Bohemond, seized the citadel from the Fatimids in 1106 but it fell to Nur al-Din in 1149. The panorama over the Orontes from here is marvellous. Beneath you, to the south, you get a good bird's eye view of the khan, and nearer, on a lower spur of the citadel, is a rather ordinary **Ottoman mosque** of the late 16th century. Northwards you see the best preserved section of Apamea's **walls**, running round the north and west sides of the city. If also you look southeast-wards from the citadel you can make out the 2nd-century AD **theatre**, perhaps once the largest in the Roman world, though most of its stones have been carried away for domestic buildings.

The modern road from the citadel passes the theatre where it then heads due east, following the line of a decumanus, one of several east–west axes of the Roman city, and intersects the cardo maximus, the grand north–south **colonnaded avenue** completed during the reign of Marcus Aurelius (AD 161–80). At 1.85km, it is over a third longer than the colonnaded way at Palmyra and is also much broader, 37.5m to Palmyra's 25m. It is this you come to see, the re-erected columns marching across fields of grass and asphodel, paving stones rutted by long-silent traffic, doorways that once ushered you into the grand civic and religious buildings along its length now opening onto vacuity.

Apamea

From this intersection and walking north along the colonnaded avenue you come in about 100m to a **nymphaeum**, a public fountain in the form of an exedra once decorated with statues, set back behind the columns on the east. Another 150 metres or so farther on, but set back behind the west side of the avenue, is a long and narrow open space, the not yet entirely excavated **agora**. The column bases all about are richly carved. There is a hill behind this to the west and over it are the remains of the **Temple of Zeus**, erected during the reign of Hadrian (AD 117–38) and demolished by the Christians in the late 4th century. It had been an oracular shrine, uttering lines of Homer which taken out of context were suitably ambiguous. If you head now directly back to the colonnaded avenue, you face, along its eastern

1 Ottoman khan 2 Citadel 3 Ottoman mosque 4 Theatre 5 Cardo maximus 6 Decumanus 7 Nymphaeum 8 Agora 9 Temple of Zeus 10 Honorific column 11 Baths 12 Circular church 13 Church of SS. Cosmos and Damian 14 Roman houses 15 Cathedral

side, a stretch of **columns with spiral fluting**, the direction of the spiral on one column alternating with that on the next. It is a feature almost exclusive to Apamea and creates a remarkably ornate effect, especially if looked at from an angle so that the shafts partly overlap one another. The capitals are Corinthian and the entablature is also elaborately worked, while here and elsewhere along the colonnade some columns have projecting consoles, as at Palmyra, upon which statues of eminent persons stood.

About a kilometre north from the intersection where you began your walk you come to another intersection, this one marked by the base of an honorific column. About 150m beyond this, on the east side of the colonnaded avenue, are the remains of sizeable **baths**, built at the end of Trajan's reign, in AD 117. Trajan ordered the rebuilding of the city after an earthquake in AD 115, the task beginning at this northern end of the colonnaded avenue and progressing southwards over the decades. In consequence, the columns and their entablatures here are more soberly classical, while as you return southwards you notice that they become more ornately Syrian.

The remains elsewhere at Apamea are less interesting, but if you wish to continue your exploration of the site you should now start again at that first intersection where the modern road crosses the colonnaded avenue. About 50m south, on the west side, are the circular foundations of a mid-6th-century **church**, while in 50m more but on the opposite side are the remains of the contemporary **Church of SS Cosmas and Damian**, who were buried at Cyrrhus, though some of their relics were kept here. The saints were apparently twin brothers who practised medicine without charging fees and were martyred for their faith. Perhaps it was the notion of free health care that made their cult enormously popular and widespread, churches bearing their name offering a process called incubation, by which the sick stayed overnight, hoping that they would be favoured with a dream that would lead to their cure.

Again from the intersection of the modern road with the colonnaded avenue, but this time following the decumanus eastwards, you come in about 400m to excavations revealing three **Roman houses** to the north and a 5th- to 6th-century **cathedral** to the south. Fourth-century pagan mosaics found beneath its floors can be seen in the local museum, testimony to Apamea's reputation as a centre of neo-Platonist philosophy during the 3rd and 4th centuries AD.

To Jisr al-Shugur

Getting There

Jisr al-Shugur is served by buses, microbuses and trains running between Aleppo and Latakia, as well as by buses and microbuses running along the Orontes valley from Hama. The train journey between Latakia and Aleppo is especially recommended for the beautiful and dramatic landscapes en route.

Route 56 crosses to the west side of the Orontes valley and runs northwards along the flanks of the Jebel al-Sariya. You are now along the eastern picket of Crusader country. At about 18km south of Jisr al-Shugur, a new road climbs into the mountains to **Slenfeh**, a 1200m-high resort village of grey concrete box houses (with the moderate ★★**Grand**, ✆ (041) 750606, and the inexpensive ★**Tourist** hotels, both usually open only in summer) beneath Nebi Yunes, at 1602m the highest peak in the coastal range, and so down towards Saône (Qalaat Saladin) and Latakia. Three kilometres farther north on route 56, that is 15km south of Jisr al-Shugur, and you are below **Qalaat Burzey**, an almost entirely ruinous though wonderfully romantic 12th-century Crusader castle clinging to a rocky crag 500m above the floor of the Orontes valley.

Despite its seeming impregnability, it fell to Saladin during his remarkable 1188 campaign when he took Latakia on 22 July, Saône on 29 July and Burzey on 23 August. There is no path and it is a steep climb over difficult ground.

Jisr al-Shugur, 52km north of Apamea, is a busy and not unattractive market town, many of its houses painted blue, amid orange trees, maize and sunflowers. The place has certainly improved since Henry Maundrell came this way in 1697; 'Shoggle,' as he called it, 'is a pretty large, but exceeding filthy town, situated on the river Orontes: over which you pass by a bridge of thirteen small arches to come at the town. The river hereabouts is of a good breadth. Its waters are turbid, and very unwholesome, and its fish worse; as we found by experience, there being no person of all our company that had eaten of them overnight, but found himself much indisposed the next morning.' Jisr means bridge, which here is built of Arab stones laid upon Roman masonry and projects southwards to withstand the force of the current. From Jisr al-Shugur the M5 runs west to Latakia (75km) and east to Aleppo (104km) bringing you close to Ebla en route.

The Steppe Eastwards of Hama

From Hama a surfaced road leads to the Byzantine sites of Qasr Ibn Wardan in 56km and Anderin in a further 25km. To reach Isriya from Qasr Ibn Wardan or Anderin (40–50km) you will need a four-wheel drive; or you will have to backtrack to Hama from where it is 120km along paved roads to Isriya via Salamiya. Each of these places is evidence of the more flourishing conditions of the Syrian steppe 1500 and more years ago, not only because the climate was kinder but also because of practical organisation.

Anderin and Isriya are likely to be of interest only to the specialist, the adventurous or the perverse.

Getting Around

Without a car, forget it. In Hama you can hire a taxi for the excursion, having your hotel make the arrangements for you (the Noria, Cairo and Riad hotels are particularly helpful), or by dealing directly with the driver. There is a paved road to Qasr Ibn Wardan and on to Anderin; and from Hama there is another paved road via Salamiya to Isriya which has recently been extended all the way to Resafa (*see* p.244). Note that between Salamiya and Resafa there is almost no traffic. Therefore, quite apart from carrying sufficient petrol and ensuring that your vehicle is sound, also carry a good supply of food and water, as you are likely to have to wait a very long time indeed if you break down before anyone comes along. To travel directly between Qasr Ibn Wardan or Anderin and Isriya across the steppe you must have four-wheel drive— and do not expect *anyone* to come along if you break down.

Qasr Ibn Wardan

Qasr Ibn Wardan is one of the most remarkable sites in northern Syria, its towering, broken walls rising up like a vision of some great city on the edge of the desert. Yet as you draw closer you see this is not a city at all, instead a palace, a church and a barracks, though they form a monumental ensemble. They are dated by inscriptions to 561–4, that is to the closing years in the reign of Justinian, whose policy was to restore to the Byzantine Empire most of the territory lost since the zenith of Roman power in the 2nd century AD. To secure Syria against the Persians, great fortresses such as Resafa and Halabiye were built along the Euphrates. Qasr Ibn

Wardan, on the other hand, is somewhat mysterious; probably it was meant to provide strategic depth and also to control the desert Bedouin, yet there is an elegance about it, a sumptuousness, that reminds you of the pleasure dome aspects of the Umayyads' two Qasr al-Heirs.

The three buildings stand on a slight elevation, the church and palace close together to the north, the barracks 100m to the south. The **barracks**, once a high-walled quadrangle 50m square, is now, except for a 10m-high section containing the sole entrance gate, almost entirely an indistinguishable heap of ruins down to foundation level.

The **palace**, also 50m square and built around a great courtyard, is likewise largely a pile of rubble. But the central section of the southern side, itself impressively massive and consisting of two storeys of vaulted halls and chambers, has survived well enough and has recently been somewhat restored by the Syrian Antiquities Department. This was the most important part of the palace, being its entrance with audience chamber and residential quarters. It reminds you of the Bucoleon, that ruined sea-pavilion of Justinian's Great Palace at Constantinople, its gaping windows and terraces overlooking the Sea of Marmara, but here at Qasr Ibn Wardan the remains are more substantial and the view is of the desert.

The comparison with the architecture of Constantinople is appropriate, for both here at the palace and at the adjoining church the direct influence of the imperial capital is apparent, not only in architectural forms but also in the techniques and materials used. The masonry work is not the usual Syrian stone but instead alternating bands of brick and squared basalt, reminiscent of the metropolis, with even the bricks having the quality and colour of those used in the Church of Haghia Sophia. Quite simply, Qasr Ibn Wardan would not have been out of place in Justinian's Constantinople, while in Syria it is practically the only example of wholesale importation of Byzantine metropolitan architecture.

In consequence, there is debate over who built the ensemble at Qasr Ibn Wardan and for whom. The controversy centres particularly on the **church**, also well enough preserved though its mosaics are gone and the dome has fallen. There has been a suggestion that it might have been built by an architect called Isidoros, nephew of that Isidorus who with Anthemios of Tralles built Haghia Sophia, but this has been countered by observations that many of its features are eccentric, its proportions uncommonly tall, for example, and the main structural arches slightly pointed rather than semicircular. Also, instead of resting directly on these arches, the dome is raised awkwardly upon a drum, the pendentives, those triangular sections of a hemisphere that make possible the transition from a square plan to a circular dome, springing within the drum rather than below it. This reveals an imperfect assimilation of those architectural principles that had recently achieved marvellous expression in the Constantinople churches of Haghia Sophia and SS Sergius and Bacchus, nor is the carving round the doors and of the capitals up to metropolitan standards. The architect of Qasr Ibn Wardan, therefore, was probably not from Constantinople, but instead was a Syrian imitating but not quite expert at Byzantine forms.

All the same, this almost unique attempt to bring Constantinople to the steppe raises the question for whom was it meant, to which the answer remains a mystery. That Qasr Ibn Wardan must have served as the residence of some important military commander seems obvious, yet its construction was begun at the same time as a 50-year peace was agreed with the Persians, and you wonder if it was not meant to be the site of an Eastern durbar and to receive the visit of an emperor or his most brilliant general, though a year after it was completed both Justinian, then a very old man, and his great general Belisarius died.

Anderin

Founded perhaps in the 2nd century AD, Anderin became a sizeable Byzantine city with 10 churches and a **barracks**, which at 80 metres square was even larger than that at Qasr Ibn Wardan and built just earlier, in AD 558. The houses were built of sun-baked bricks and these have now entirely disintegrated, so what survives here and there are tower-like structures of local basalt, in fact the angles of walls of the more important buildings. Even these remains are being rapidly pilfered, the barracks now a jumble of stone, a large 6th-century triple-naved church, perhaps the **cathedral**, reduced to barely more than a few blocks of masonry, so that a visit to Anderin is for those who, if not looking for stones to take away, at least appreciate the desolation of their absence.

Isriya

Provided you have four-wheel drive, you can reach Isriya directly eastwards across the desertic steppe from Qasr Ibn Wardan or Anderin (40–50km), or from Hama you can take a paved road via Salamiya (since the 19th century settled by Ismaelis from the Jebel al-Sariya, *see* p.175) to Isriya from where there is a newly surfaced road all the way to Resafa (90km). What you find is an early 3rd-century AD **Roman temple**, or rather a stout cella of limestone blocks with an elaborately carved portal at the east end and Corinthian pilasters in relief on the north and south temple walls in a manner known as pseudo-peripteral, meant to suggest a fancier surround of free-standing columns. Behind the portal and to the right is a winding staircase leading up to the roof. From here upon the citadel mound of a now vanished Roman town you can look out over the once fertile wasteland, a crossroads for caravans between Resafa and Homs and between Qinnasrin (ancient Chalcis ad Belum, southwest of Aleppo) and Palmyra.

Hama to Aleppo

Between Hama and Aleppo the earth becomes meat-red, veal when dry, venison when moist. Fields are striped with rainbows of green and the water trickling through them is the colour of blood. Closer to Aleppo you see beehive houses made of mud and straw, women fluttering from one to another like bats. Also pistachios are grown on these plains and are sold raw along the roadside.

Getting Around

Trains and long-distance buses travel non-stop between Hama and Aleppo. Unless you have a car, the only practical way of reaching Maarat al-Numan and Ebla (Tell Mardikh) is by local bus or microbus from Hama or, more conveniently, Aleppo.

Cannibalism at Maarat al-Numan

After capturing Antioch, the First Crusade led by Count Raymond of Toulouse marched up the valley of the Orontes to a point just north of Jisr al-Shugur and then southeast to Maarat al-Numan, just off the M1, about 75km south of Aleppo. From there in January 1099 they would continue southwest, crossing the Orontes between Shaizar and Hama, passing through Masyaf, then south to what was still Husn al-Akrad, the Castle of the Kurds, now Krak des Chevaliers, and so through the Homs Gap to the Mediterranean, following its coastline to a point just north of present-day Tel Aviv and then eastwards to Jerusalem, which the Crusaders captured on 15 July.

It is a wonder they got there at all. At Antioch, food had been short and Raymond led several raids into the interior to obtain provisions. There were arguments too. Raymond disputed Bohemond's claim to Antioch and hesitated to march on to Jerusalem until the matter was settled. But the troops were growing restless, tempers were fraying and open fighting between the factions was growing more likely. To give their soldiers something to do and to protect the eastern flank of the Crusade's line of march, and yet to avoid straying too far from disputed Antioch, Raymond and Bohemond attacked the fortified Muslim town of Maarat al-Numan, entering it at dawn on 12 December 1098 and slaughtering the men and selling the women and children into slavery.

But food supplies were quickly exhausted and numbers of Crusaders began dying of starvation, one of the commanders later explaining in an official letter to the pope that 'a terrible famine racked the army and placed it in the cruel necessity of feeding itself upon the bodies of the Saracens'. The Turks who controlled northern Syria at the time were impressed at the Crusaders' tenacity under such conditions, though often afterwards in their epic literature they described the Franks as fanatical man-eaters, taking to cannibalism out of perverse pleasure rather than necessity. Raymond, with yet another problem on his hands, abandoned his claim to Antioch, and to show there would be no turning back burnt Maarat al-Numan to the ground. Then walking barefoot, as after all this was a pilgrimage, he led the Crusaders on to Jerusalem.

Maarat al-Numan

A dull if busy market town 60km north of Hama, a sprawl of greyish limestone on the tedious plain, Maarat al-Numan hardly tempts the traveller's appetite as he hurtles along the M1 a kilometre to the east. In John Green's *A Journey from Aleppo to Damascus*, published in 1736, there is at least the intriguing information that the name translates to mean 'the Disease of Ostriches', which would be true enough if it were called Al-Marad al-Naaman, but alas Maarat derives from the Greek name for the place, Arra, while Al-Numan Ibn Bashir was no bird but a follower of the Prophet who became governor of the region after the Arab conquest.

All the same, Maarat al-Numan is worth visiting for its khan-cum-museum, which you reach by heading first for the central square with its large mosque, whose towering **minaret** was built in the 12th century (the town reverted to Muslim control in 1135) to rival that of the Great Mosque at Aleppo. A short walk to the southeast brings you to the 16th-century **Khan Murad Pasha**, at over 80m square the largest in Syria, which houses the **museum** (*open daily 9–2 and 4–6 summer, 9–2 and 3–4 winter, closed Thurs; adm*), containing artefacts from the surrounding area, and most notably a fine collection of 5th- and 6th-century Byzantine mosaics.

Ebla (Tell Mardikh)

The turnoff for Ebla (signposted Ibla) is about 26km north of Maarat al-Numan. You drive east off the highway and in 3km, after passing through a village, the road rises over a gap in the *tell*, which is in fact a vast circular stone wall hidden by a deep covering of earth. As you dip down the other side, the sensation is of entering the caldera of a very old and worn volcano. Here and there are patches of excavations, as though a small team of extremely slow and underpaid cleaners have been called in to brush away the dust of millennia, and interesting mostly to witness what a patient rather than obviously glamorous business archaeology is.

An Italian team led by Paolo Matthiae of the University of Rome began excavating here in 1964. They discovered a great Bronze Age trading city of the late third and early second millennium BC, whose links extended west into Anatolia and east into Mesopotamia, while it dominated the then more fruitful plains and urban centres of northwest Syria. In about 2300 BC it became subsidiary to the Akkadian Empire of Mesopotamia and was then eliminated as a power altogether by the Hittites in about 1600 BC.

More important than the structures and artefacts found during the excavations has been the discovery of Ebla's royal archives in 1975. These have aroused both scholarly and political controversy, and because the information they contain may have been subject to distorting inter-pretations (or may simply be unpalatable), it now seems to some that the Italians are, by taking so long to translate the material, effectively suppressing their contents. The problem in a nutshell is that the archival tablets inscribed in cuneiform mention names such as Ab-ra-mu, Da-u-dum, Mi-ka-ia, Ish-ma-il and Ish-ra-il, similar enough to Abraham, David, Micah, Ishmael and Israel. Further, one tablet was claimed to list the cities of Sodom, Gomorrah, Admah, Zeboim and Zoar in the same order as they are found in Genesis 14:2, which was written many centuries later— though subsequently the claim was shown to be false, the names of three of the cities having been misreadings. Nevertheless, the various inscriptions suggest, say some scholars, a certain common cultural tradition between Ebla and the world of the Old Testament, while Matthiae says flatly that 'the unscientific polemics about their contents, almost always based on quite unfounded information, have sometimes reached grotesque proportions'.

Matthiae is in a delicate political position, his Ebla in danger of being taken as something of a Zionist plot by the Syrian authorities, who dread the implications that could follow on the supposition that early Jews were Syrians or early Syrians were Jews. To be fair, they have not been calmed by the crackpot claims of various Christian and Jewish fundamentalists in America and elsewhere, but the Syrians have also been driven to absurdities themselves, as when Dr Afif Bahnasi, Director General of Antiquities, said of Ebla that 'this kingdom, which goes back 4500 years, is an Arabian kingdom', when in fact the Arabs do not appear in history until the begin-ning of the first millennium BC, 1500 years after the Ebla tablets. At any rate, even more slowly than the Italians dig at Ebla do the Italians now translate the tablets they have found.

Much of the **citadel**, rising higher than the surrounding walls, has been excavated, revealing a royal palace with courts and stairways, ceremonial chambers, handsome architraves of well-cut basalt blocks, numbers of pulverising bowls and grinding trays, and quantities of potsherds. To see the base of a **monumental gateway** walk over to the southwest arc of the rim where the earth has been dug away down to the masonry. But the best way to sense the scale of the place and to feel your way back into its time is to walk along the top of the ramparts right round Ebla, imagining it with a population of perhaps 30,000, and looking out to the horizons it once knew.

Getting Around	162
Krak des Chevaliers (Qalaat al-Husn)	163
Exploring the Southern Jebel al-Sariya	171
Safita	172
Husn Suleiman	173
Masyaf	174
Tartus	176
Arwad	181
Amrit	182
Margat (Qalaat Marqab)	184
Exploring the Northern Jebel al-Sariya	188
Saône (Qalaat Saladin)	190
Latakia	193
Ugarit (Ras Shamra)	197

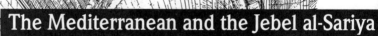

The Mediterranean and the Jebel al-Sariya

Cathedral at Tartus, after Enlart

The Mediterranean and the Jebel al-Sariya

One of the astonishing things about travelling through Syria is the way land-scapes and historical periods so completely change by the hour. It is a fast drive from the Roman colonnades and dry desert heat of Palmyra to the humidity and splashing medieval *norias* of the Orontes. Then there is the freshening climb through the high pine-scented slopes of the Jebel al-Sariya, sea-clouds catching at the summits, Crusader and Ismaeli castles besieged by sunflowers and this-tles, plunging valleys patterned green with terraces of tobacco (that wonderful leaf called Latakia once used in Camel cigarettes and still found in the finest pipe tobaccos), and so the descent through olive groves to ports from which the Phoenicians sailed out upon the blue Mediterranean horizon.

The narrow littoral and the Jebel al-Sariya, those mountains rising just behind, are the doorway between the Syrian interior and the wider Mediterranean. The Phoenician port of Arwad and its dependency Jeble, and the pre-Phoenician port of Ugarit (Ras Shamra), were major mercantile and political players in the world of the second and first millennia BC. With incalculable cultural effect, though purely in the cause of efficiency and profit, the inven-tory-keepers of Ugarit were among the first to adopt and develop the alphabet, consigning it westwards along with their cargoes to the Greeks. Latakia, modern Syria's foremost port, first rose to importance under the Seleucids as the sea-gateway for Apamea, their military headquarters on the Orontes. The Crusaders built castles to control the mountain passes, Krak des Chevaliers (Qalaat al-Husn), Margat (Qalaat Marqab) and Saône (Qalaat Saladin) being the three greatest fortresses to be seen anywhere in the Crusader East, while at Tartus their cathedral stands as the finest survival of Crusader religious archi-tecture outside Jerusalem.

Not only do history and landscape mark off this part of Syria, but so do the look and bearing of the people. Your attention is caught by groups of girls and boys walking home from school along these coastal and mountain village roads. The girls often have light brown hair, sometimes very long and hanging well-brushed down their backs. Some are extremely attractive and a few are quite flirtatious with their glances and their smiles. This open femininity is a striking feature in this part of Syria and is largely missed inland once over the moun-tains and into the Orontes valley, and in Aleppo and Damascus.

Perhaps this is because the Jebel al-Sariya has long been a refuge against Sunni orthodoxy, the mountains home to Ismaelis and Alawis, heterodox sects whom the more orthodox would be reluctant to accept, along with the Druze, as Muslims at all. Among Sunni Muslims, the Ismaelis had a reputation, reports Gertrude Bell in *Between the Desert and the Sown*, for 'worshipping women', with every female child born on the 27th day of the month of Ragab held to be an incarnation of the divinity. Such a girl-child was called the Rozah, and while the Ismaelis read the Koran, they also had other sacred books, one of which, according to Gertrude Bell's Sunni informant, was 'all in praise of the Rozah, describing every part of her with eulogy'. 'The creed seems to spring from dim traditions of Astarte worship, or from that oldest and most universal cult of all, the veneration of the Mother Goddess; but the accusations of indecency that have been brought against it are, I gather, unfounded.'

Getting Around

The area covered in this chapter is approximately defined by the Orontes valley to the east and the Mediterranean coast to the west, along which runs the old two-lane route 1, now supplemented by a modern four-lane divided highway, which comes up from Lebanon, passes through Tartus, Baniyas and Latakia, and continues northwards to Antakya in Turkey. The region's southern boundary is the new four-lane divided highway between Homs and Tartus, all but replacing the old route 3 that slices through a slight bulge of Lebanese territory, while its northern boundary is route M5, also recently upgraded, between Latakia, Jisr al-Shugur and Saraqib, where it joins the M1 Damascus to Aleppo motorway. This chapter covers the region from south to north.

There are fast and frequent buses and microbuses along these main routes but less frequent services, if any, along minor routes. As always, the best way to travel is by hired car, and this is especially true for exploring the mountain routes with their beautiful scenery, out-of-the-way villages and less accessible castles and other sites, difficult and time-consuming if you have to rely on public transport. An alternative is to bring a well-equipped bicycle with you to Syria, cycling being an excellent way of covering the fairly short distances between fascinating spots both in this coastal and mountain region and in the adjacent highland region (*see* **The Northern Highlands**, p.223). Or, like T. E. Lawrence, you could walk.

Tartus can be reached by rail from Damascus in 3hrs 40mins, the line passing through Homs from where the journey time is 1hr 45mins. Latakia can be reached by rail from Aleppo in 3hrs, the line passing through Jisr al-Shugur which is 2hrs from Aleppo. There is no railway line between Tartus and Latakia, though one is intended.

The port of Latakia is fitfully served by passenger ships from Libya, Egypt, Cyprus, Turkey and Greece, while cruise ships sometimes call at Tartus.

Where to Stay

There is accommodation at Krak, Safita, Tartus, Baniyas, Slenfeh (*see* pp.171, 173, 180, 184 and 153), Latakia (*see* p.196), Ras al-Bassit and Kassab (*see* p.200).

The Crusaders' Need for Castles

Though this guide concentrates on the more remarkable castles in Syria, their number throughout the Holy Land was great. T. E. Lawrence on his walking tour visited 49, almost all of them built by the Crusaders. Each was a considerable investment in stone, often large and elaborate, and continuously improved by the latest innovations in military science. Combining an unerring eye for strategic advantage with a sure feeling for elegant economy in architectural form, the Crusaders impressed strangely and beautifully the genius of France on the coasts and mountains of the Levant. But why did they build so many castles? The answers lay in geography, manpower and the feudal system.

The Latin states were long and narrow, lacking defence in depth. The Principality of Antioch, the County of Tripoli and the Kingdom of Jerusalem stretched 700km from north to south, yet rarely were they more than 80 to 120km broad, the County of Tripoli perilously constricting to the width of the coastal plain, only a few kilometres broad, between Tartus and Jeble. The inland cities of Aleppo, Hama, Homs and Damascus all remained in Muslim hands, while Mesopotamia and Egypt were recruiting grounds for any Muslim counterthrust, as the campaigns of Saladin and the Mamelukes would show. For the Crusaders, the natural defensive line was the mountains, and they built castles to secure the passes.

Stones more than soldiers were pressed to this purpose as the Crusaders were chronically short of men. When the First Crusade sacked Jerusalem in 1099, the Christian knights who stepped through blood and corpses to kneel at the Holy Sepulchre numbered only 1200, their foot soldiers amounting to only ten times more. The deed done, most returned to Europe; the Kingdom of Jerusalem was thereafter defended by 300 mounted knights. Despite successive Crusades, at no time during the entire history of the Crusader states were they able to put more than 2600 horse in the field. Moreover, though there was still a large local Christian population, these were Orthodox, the Crusaders a Latin minority.

Outnumbered and insecure, the Franks, as they were known locally, of necessity housed themselves in fortified towns or in castles. Nevertheless, the Crusader states could survive only as a going concern, and the Franks set about organising their possessions along familiar European feudal lines. Castles were as much centres of production and administration as they were military outposts; you can picture them as battlemented country houses, containing corn mills and olive presses, and surrounded by gardens, vineyards, orchards and fields, their lands in some cases encompassing hundreds of villages and a peasantry numbering tens of thousands. Wood to Egypt, herbs, spices and sugar to Europe, were important exports; indeed throughout the 12th and 13th centuries Europe's entire supply of sugar came from the Latin East.

But in times of war, agriculture was always the first victim. Were it not for Western subvention and the taxes imposed on trade between the Muslim East and Europe as it passed through the Crusader states, they would have collapsed sooner than they did. Throughout the 200 years of the Crusader venture, Venice, Genoa and other Italian merchant cities carried on a greater wealth of trade with the Egyptian port of Alexandria than with all the Crusader ports combined. The Muslim rather than the Christian East was the real Eldorado. The Latin rulers were always strapped for cash, the bulk of their revenues going towards the upkeep of mercenaries, knights and castles. It was a vicious circle; insufficient land and manpower making castles a necessity; the cost of knights and castles greater than the productivity of the land could justify.

Krak des Chevaliers (Qalaat al-Husn)

Open daily 9–6 in summer, 9–4 in winter, 9–3 during Ramadan; adm.

In 1909, when T. E. Lawrence was not yet 'of Arabia' but merely of Oxford and still only 20, he went on a summer's walking tour of Crusader castles. Writing home after spending three days at Krak des Chevaliers, he described it as 'the finest castle in the world: certainly the most picturesque I have seen—quite marvellous'. What especially impressed him was that it was 'neither a ruin nor a show place . . . and were Baybars to reappear he would think it as formidable as of old'. Nor does it have the feel of a show place now, though the French did some restoration work in 1936. Best of all is the genius and grace of its construction; at no other castle will you so immediately understand and admire the way the Crusaders' military architecture functioned as at Krak. As you travel west on the Homs–Tartus highway, you notice the trees bent eastwards, forever blown by draughts of Mediterranean air sucked through the Homs Gap by the rising desert heat behind you. This is the only point between Turkey and Israel at which the otherwise unbroken line of coastal mountains allows access between the sea and the interior. The landscape is broad, the earth brown and strewn with boulders, though cultivated here and there. To the south, between the highway and the site of Kadesh at Tell Nebi Mend (see p.134), is the Buhayrat Homs or Homs Lake, originally created when Egypt's pharaohs built a dam across the Orontes, which flows down from Lebanon's central Bekaa valley. At 40km the mountains begin to close in, the Lebanon range rising like a wall; here, before the gap opens up towards Tartus and forms the wonderfully fertile Buqeia plain (la Bocquée of the Crusaders), you see off to the north a spur of the Jebel al-Sariya crowned by Krak des Chevaliers.

Turning off the highway you approach the castle along a 10km road rising gently through a wheat plain, passing through Hwach, a prosperous Orthodox Christian village, the uncovered heads and faces of the women and couples walking hand in hand, providing a contrasting sense of alertness and liveliness to the torpor of the Sunni Muslim village on the slope immediately below Krak. This village, Al-Husn, was built to accommodate the families which inhabited the castle until 1934, when they were cleared out by the French.

Getting There

By car you follow the Homs–Tartus motorway westwards; the turning, north, is at 40km, signposted Hosn Citadel. It is then another 10km up to the castle. Only Homs offers direct access to Krak: there are frequent microbuses taking about 1hr (ask for Qalaat al-Husn). If staying at Hama, travel first to Homs (about 45mins). From Tartus, take a bus or microbus bound for Homs and ask to be let off at the turning for Qalaat al-Husn; from there you will have to walk or wait for a microbus from Homs. Taxis and microbuses are usually to be found at the entrance to Krak looking for departing custom, though they try to get away by mid-afternoon, so check that you will have transport when you need it (the restaurant here can phone for a taxi if necessary).

History

Krak des Chevaliers not only overlooks the Homs Gap but stands near the outlet of the Bekaa valley where it spills the Orontes river onto the plain of Homs. And so, like Kadesh, once the contested prize of Egyptians and Hittites, the site occupied by Krak has long been at the crossroads of history, and indeed the Egyptians may well have had an outpost here. But the first fortress known certainly to have been built on the spur was the work of the Emir of Homs in 1031, who garrisoned it with Kurds. Husn al-Akrad, meaning Citadel of the Kurds in Arabic, probably accounts for its later name, Krak des Chevaliers (Krak of the Knights), given it by the Crusaders.

The First Crusade came this way in February 1099 after its massacre of the inhabitants of Maarat al-Numan, Count Raymond of Toulouse leading his army to the sea via the Homs Gap

*1 Entrance tower 2 Stables 3 Moat 4 Glacis ('the Mountain')
5 Stables 6 Postern gate 7 Court 8 Loggia 9 Banqueting Hall
10 Stores chamber 11 Chapel 12 Café 13 Keep 14 Warden's
tower*

and briefly occupying the site. But no sooner had they continued on to Jerusalem than the Emir of Homs recovered the citadel and not until 1110 was it retaken by Tancred of Antioch, to become the eastern outpost of the County of Tripoli (present-day Trablus in Lebanon). Nothing survives of the Kurdish fortress nor of the earliest Crusader work. Instead what you see was built and expanded in phases by the Knights Hospitaller from 1144 onwards, with subsequent Mameluke additions.

The castle's control of this strategic crossroads and its forward position, so close to Homs and Hama and nearly intersecting the interior route between Damascus and Aleppo, caused one Saracen chronicler to describe it as 'a bone stuck in the very throat of the Muslims'. Yet despite repeated attempts against it, Krak held firm, and even Saladin, after his great victory over the Kingdom of Jerusalem at Hattin in 1188, took one look at its defences and marched off northwards to storm the spectacular walls of Saône. Krak was not taken, it was given away. During the last years of the Latin states even the Hospitallers could not raise sufficient manpower and the castle, which could house 2000 men, was reduced to a garrison of fewer than 200 knights, a lonely outpost facing a still-gathering enemy. The waiting was terrible, and it became an immurement. Finally, after Krak had been in Christian hands for 161 years, and after a month's siege, the remaining knights accepted the Mameluke Sultan Baybars' offer of safe conduct and in 1271 rode to Tartus and the sea for the last time.

Hospitallers and Templars

The Hospitallers derived their name from the Hospital of St John in Jerusalem, where their original function was to care for Christian pilgrims, but by the 1130s they had taken on military duties. A similiar military Order, the Templars, taking their name from their headquarters in the Temple quarter of Jerusalem, had been founded in about 1119, its original duty to protect the pilgrimage routes. Both Templars and Hospitallers received donations of property in Europe which soon made them wealthy, while young men of noble families seeking to fulfill the moral and religious obligations of knighthood rushed to their standards.

Very quickly the undermanned and under-financed Crusader states were selling or giving frontier strongholds to the Orders, the Templars undertaking the defence of

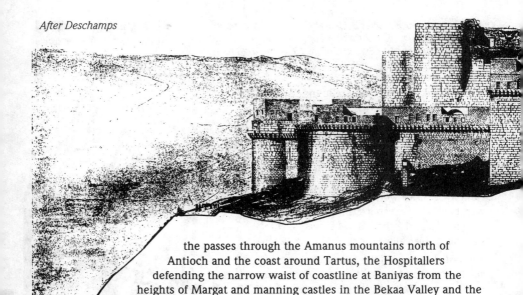

the passes through the Amanus mountains north of
Antioch and the coast around Tartus, the Hospitallers
defending the narrow waist of coastline at Baniyas from the
heights of Margat and manning castles in the Bekaa Valley and the
Homs Gap, including Krak des Chevaliers.

Examining the Outer Defences

Instead of immediately entering Krak, you should follow the road that runs counterclockwise round past the west flank of the castle. The road rises along the shoulder of a ridge to the south (surmounted by a rest house) and you see Krak behind you on its spur like a vast battleship on station, forever cresting a giant wave. The great castle hangs in magnificent suspension above the plain beyond, which in summer is lucent with the greens and yellows of figs, olives, maize, prickly pears, vines, sunflowers and eucalyptus. Yet at the change of seasons Krak can be all but invisible in the lowering clouds, and in winter the landscape takes on the sombre grey of moorland and is sometimes streaked with snow. You may have long associated the Crusaders with polished skies and burning sun—it is odd to think of them shivering and getting their armour rusty.

From here you get a good overall impression of the defences, an encircling curtain wall with a line of round towers, Crusader-built, along its western flank. Within this and rising higher, a tighter ring of walls and towers surrounding a central court, all this also Crusader work. The square or partly square towers of this inner ring are earliest in date, as are signs of rough bossage; round towers and smoothly dressed stone were later Crusader innovations. Also belonging to the later period of construction at Krak are the gigantic taluses, those massive slopes of masonry, against the external faces of the south and west inner walls.

These circles of outer and inner defences constitute the concentric system which allowed for successive stages of retreat if need be, the defenders always having the advantage of dominating the attackers from a greater height. Notice that the southern area of the inner defence ring is highest of all, this being the keep, the final redoubt. The castle follows the form of the spur and is pointed northwards; it is broadest at its southern base where the spur connects with the ridge upon which you stand. Krak was most vulnerable at this

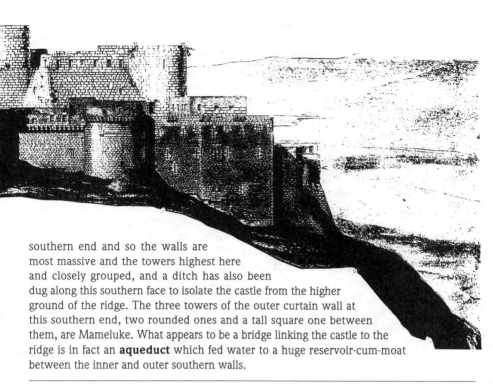

southern end and so the walls are most massive and the towers highest here and closely grouped, and a ditch has also been dug along this southern face to isolate the castle from the higher ground of the ridge. The three towers of the outer curtain wall at this southern end, two rounded ones and a tall square one between them, are Mameluke. What appears to be a bridge linking the castle to the ridge is in fact an **aqueduct** which fed water to a huge reservoir-cum-moat between the inner and outer southern walls.

The Inner Ring of Defences

You can now return to the entrance on the east side of Krak. The two square towers to the south along this flank are Mameluke work, but the **entrance tower**, once approached over a moat and drawbridge, is late Crusader, though it bears an Arabic inscription recording Baybars' restoration of the castle. You enter a dark, vaulted passage, ascending steeply; several times it switches direction at 90 and then almost 180 degrees, and at these elbows, open to the sky, you are stunned by the sun, where once arrows, blocks of stone and burning pitch would have been loosed upon your head. Along the way, an intruder would also have had to force four gates and, at the uppermost, at least one portcullis. This leads into the small court at the heart of the castle.

But either now, as you are climbing up the entrance passage, or later you should make a ground-level clockwise circuit of the inner and outer walls. To do this, leave the entrance ramp where it makes its almost 180-degree bend. A gateway leads south to the outer ward, that space between the inner and outer circle of walls, bringing you to the inner moat which served also as a reservoir, frogs splashing about in its thick greenish water. From this and rising all along the south face of the inner wall is a gargantuan **talus**, a masonry slope 25m thick at its base, which at the final siege the astonished Muslims called 'the Mountain' and never attempted to take. This side of the castle, facing the ridge to the south, was the most vulnerable and so the most comprehensively defended, though the intention behind this remarkable talus is unclear. Possibly it was a buttress against earthquake, which in 1170 had caused damage to the early Crusader castle; and possibly it was to prevent mining, though this inner part of Krak stands on solid rock. T. E. Lawrence thought it was to prevent assailants from pressing against the wall and so ducking beneath the line of fire. He attempted to climb it barefoot but got only halfway up, and there was nobody dropping boulders on his head at the time. Above it between the central and eastern towers is the **keep**, while at the western corner is the Warden's Tower, which you can later visit from the court.

Along the south side of the moat and against the outer wall is a 60m-long chamber faintly lit by skylights, most likely once a stables. You can also look inside the three towers along this south outer wall, the central square tower built by the Mameluke Sultan Qalaun in 1285, the round towers by Baybars; Crusader towers had stood at these positions earlier and it was the round tower to the west that Baybars successfully mined in 1271. You can now walk northwards between the inner and outer walls along the west side of the castle, noticing the talus against the inner wall as you pass the four round towers in a line that strengthened the outer wall. The square tower towards the north end of the inner wall where the talus ends and with a postern at its base is early Crusader work which underwent several alterations, as you can see by the ascending relieving arches, 'relieving nothing', as Lawrence said. This seemingly decorative effect is striking, though originally the arches concealed machicolations, that is slits at the top from which projectiles could be directed against attackers. But as the tower was successively raised, so the machicolations were filled in. (Machicolations took various forms, for example a box-like projection on corbels, but often elaborated with an eye to style as much as anything else; you will notice them all around Krak and at other Crusader castles. The box machicolations along the outer face of the western curtain wall were described by Lawrence as resembling 'the latrines common in France in appearance, but are defensive in intention', suggesting that certain unorthodox projectiles were sometimes dropped on the enemy.)

After an angle in the outer wall you come to a fifth round tower, atop which the Crusaders had a windmill for grinding corn. Beyond this a gap has been made in the walls through which the villagers, who inhabited Krak until 1934, came and went. The knights would make sorties against the enemy by slipping out through the postern gate between the next pair of towers at the rounded north point of the castle walls. You can now return to the entrance ramp by retracing your steps or continuing clockwise to the square tower midway along eastern wall of the inner defences, a passage leading you to the top of the entrance ramp with its portcullis and so through to the court.

The Castle Interior

You are reminded again of the image of a battleship when you enter the **court**, so narrow and economical a space for so many hundreds of knights to have passed through in the course of a medieval afternoon. Opposite is a **loggia**, where the light sifts through fine stone tracery reminiscent of Rheims, an elegant 13th-century Gothic addition, its roof divided into seven diagonally ribbed vaulted bays. 'Grace, wisdom and beauty you may enjoy, but beware pride which alone can tarnish all the rest', reads the Latin inscription on the window on the extreme right of its rear wall, where two doorways admit you to the long narrow **banqueting hall** beyond. You are stepping back a century, but the style remains Gothic. Austere and dimly lit, the place hardly lends itself to carousing, though once it must have sung with French voices. Farther within and gloomier still is a huge nave-like **chamber**, 120m long, running in a great arc round to the chapel, and at one time filled with kitchens and bakeries, granaries and storage jars, for siege was always expected and the major castles were stocked with provisions to last up to five years.

Back across the court is the 12th-century **chapel**, built sometime in the first decades after the Hospitallers took possession of the castle and when the Romanesque was still in favour. Beneath its barrel vaulting which would ring to the Latin mass, the church has a monastic simplicity enhanced by the absence of Christian decoration, only traces of painted rosettes adorning the north wall. The Muslims turned the chapel into a mosque, and in the south wall between two minbars a mihrab indicates the direction of Mecca. Turning in his grave beneath the floor is Geoffrey de Joinville, a model of chivalry to whom Richard the Lionheart granted the arms of England to quarter with his own, and uncle of Jean de Joinville, chronicler of St Louis' farcical Seventh Crusade, whose defeat at Damietta in Egypt was masterminded by Shagarat al-Durr.

Now climb the staircase built across the original door of the chapel during the final siege to reach the **northern ramparts**. The square tower to the northwest is the one with arched machicolations seen during your earlier perambulation between the inner and outer walls. This and the scene immediately around you gives a sense of how the castle must have been when the Hospitallers acquired it in 1144: no curtain wall, instead the central court surrounded by a roughly bossed wall is strengthened by square towers having a shallow projection.

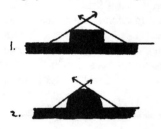

A drawing by T.E. Lawrence of square and rounded towers, showing the defensive and offensive advantages of the latter

The importance of round towers projecting well out from the wall is that they permit the defenders in the towers a continuous 180-degree sweep as they direct projectiles at the enemy. Also a projecting rounded tower of the same diameter as a projecting square tower presents less of an obstruction to the defenders on the adjoining walls, whose sweep is likewise broadened. This is because a rounded tower has no corners. An enemy could have hidden behind the corner of a square tower for protection against attack from the ramparts of an adjoining wall, but a round tower offers almost nowhere for the enemy to hide. This explains why almost all the early square towers at Krak (though not this one) were subsequently rounded off on the outside and why later Crusader towers were invariably round; it also in part explains the Crusaders' military superiority over the Muslims; and of course it allows you to distinguish between earlier and later Crusader work. The Byzantines had usually built square towers, as did the Arabs, the Citadel at Aleppo being an example of this, as is the jerry-built castle of the Assassins at Masyaf.

A vaulted chamber within this tower now contains a **restaurant-café-bar**. From these ramparts you can look out west-northwest and if the day is clear see the Templar fortress of Safita. This intervisibility between castles was another Crusader advantage: for example from Krak the knights could literally keep on eye on Homs and could signal to Safita, which in turn was within sight of Tartus—an almost instant visual telegraphic system over a distance of nearly 100km.

You should now descend to the court again and cross it to a flight of steps which take you up to the line of three **southern towers** sitting above 'the Mountain'. Notice the often delicate architectural detail superimposed on structures built of huge blocks of stone, for here in airy yet powerfully built accommodation lived the upper echelons of the garrison. The middle and southeast tower both present rounded faces to the high ground to the south, the direction from which an attack was most likely to come (another advantage of round towers is that they are structurally stronger and present a glancing angle to objects catapulted at them). The central tower has large mullioned windows, though not on its south side, where there is only a single large loophole for loosing arrows. A massive central pillar runs up through the centre of the tower, giving additional support to each storey. A keep links these southeast and central towers; from its flat roof the defenders could in turn fire catapults at the besiegers. When Lawrence stayed at Krak, the governor of the province had his residence and his harem here, 'also cows and fleas, etc.'.

The Hospitaller standard fluttered from the top of the round southwest tower, a lighter construction known as the **Warden's Tower**, whose purpose was primarily residential. A spiral staircase rises to a graceful and voluminous chamber, the Grand Master's apartment, dating from the mid-13th century, with delicate pilasters, Gothic ribbed vaulting and a frieze of five-petalled flowers, like the rosettes in the chapel but here carved in stone. From its roof there is a splendid view of the concentric circles of Krak's defences spiralling around you, as if you had been swallowed by a giant nautilus—though that is to deny the sense of command, for now at last you stand upon the bridge of the great battleship that is Krak des Chevaliers, sailing high above the rolling waves of a magnificent landscape. In summer the prospect must have reminded the Crusaders of Provence, but at the change of seasons the sky goes dark with storms, and you hear the thunder roll up through the crooked entrance ramp and reverberate within the chambers of the castles' core; a heavy rain beats against the talus and pits the moat below; and lightning bleaches all the sky and land about—the Scottish Highlands it can seem then, more Macbeth than Bohemond.

The Fall of Krak

From here you can reawaken the scene on 3 March 1271, as the Grand Master watched the Egyptian army under Baybars, accompanied by a contingent of the Assassins, approaching from the south. First they overwhelmed a triangle of outer defences, no trace of which remains today, against the tenacious resistance of the knights. Then they successfully mined the southwest tower of the curtain wall, causing it to collapse, the Muslims rushing through to the outer ward, surprising and killing a number of the garrison. At this point they faced 'the Mountain' and the moat, defended by fewer than 200 Hospitallers in the towers and along the ramparts above, and could advance no farther. Instead Baybars resorted to stratagem, delivering a forged note purportedly from the Grand Commander at Tripoli, urging the knights to surrender. Their defences and supplies might have allowed them to hold out for years, but it must have seemed to them that Krak was drifting anchorless and rudderless upon an irresistible Muslim tide. Weary, dejected and demoralised, Krak more a prison than a stronghold, on 8 April the Hospitallers accepted Baybars' offer of safe conduct to the sea. Within 20 years the few Crusader possessions along the coast would fall and the 200-year European adventure in the Holy Land would end.

There is a restaurant-café-bar in a tower on the north ramparts of the castle. Outside, not far from the castle entrance, is **La Table Ronde**, ✆ (031) 734280, a restaurant primarily but also offering cheap accommodation in four rooms, each with three or four beds, or you can camp in its grounds. The inexpensive **★★Amar Tourist Resort**, ✆ (031) 733203, open June–Sept, clean and friendly, with restaurant and pool, has two double rooms with shower and toilet, and 17 three-room apartments sleeping four; all rooms have balconies. If you have your own transport or care to walk the 7km along the road to the Monastery of Saint George (*see* below), you come first to the cheap **★Al-Naaim** hotel and restaurant, ✆ (031) 730422/735224, open June–Sept, with six rooms, each with shower and toilet, two with balconies and views of Krak. The terrace restaurant at this clean and friendly place also has beautiful views towards Krak. Closer to the monastery is the moderate **★★★Al-Wadi**, ✆ (031) 730456, 📧 (031) 730399, open year-round: rooms with fan, TV, fridge, shower, toilet and balcony; there are restaurants, bar, tennis courts and pool.

The Monastery of Saint George

Open daily 9–8; free.

The Greek Orthodox Monastery of Saint George (Deir Mar Girgis) is visible from the ramparts of Krak des Chevaliers, lying off to the northwest in that deep and beautiful valley that plunges away beneath the castle. It is as much if not more for the peaceful setting (also the accommodation; *see* under Krak) that you make your way down to the monastery, first returning from Krak to the road running north from the Homs–Tartus highway, turning left to follow it north, then at 1km bearing left at the fork, arriving at the monastery in a further 3km (7km in all from Krak). The Wadi Nasara, or Valley of the Christians, has been home to Orthodox Christians since the earliest times. Of its 31 villages, 27 are Christian and four Alawi; the only Muslims in the area are the Sunni inhabiting Al-Husn, overlooking the valley immediately below Krak. The monastery was founded in the 6th century during the reign of Justinian, but there is almost nothing of Byzantium in evidence. As you enter the first courtyard, the chapel on your right dates from 1857 and contains a finely carved iconostasis. The lower and older courtyard beyond has some remains of the Byzantine monastery, and by going down steps you enter a 13th-century chapel with an ebony iconostasis, its icons depicting the life of Saint George. The feasts of Saint George on 6 May and of the elevation of the Holy Cross on 14 September are attended by pilgrims from all over Syria and Lebanon.

Exploring the Southern Jebel al-Sariya

Instead of following the Hospitallers' route of withdrawal from Krak des Chevaliers to Tartus, you can instead explore the southern reaches of the Jebel al-Sariya, visiting Safita, Husn Suleiman and Masyaf, from where along a dramatically beautiful road you can reach the coast at Baniyas via Qadmus, and so south to Tartus or north to Latakia. Interestingly, the 1912 Baedeker devotes a bare five sentences to Krak des Chevaliers and only one to Safita, saying 'it is not easily reached owing to the unsafe state of the country'. Husn Suleiman and Masyaf it passes over in silence. Nowadays you need be concerned only about getting lost among the confusing web of roads between Krak, Safita and Husn Suleiman. Look out for the yellow signs that indicate historic sites; even if they are in Arabic, you know when (and if) you see one that you are on the right track. But also you should not hesitate to ask for directions. People will often go out of their way to help you, and you may be invited in for coffee accompanied by happy conversation in whatever combination of Arabic, French, English and sign language that can be mustered between you. The landscape is appealing, almost Provençal in the south, while running north along the ridges towards Masyaf you could be in the Cévennes. There are many lovely spots to enjoy a picnic, especially in spring when the valleys are covered with wildflowers.

Safita

You approach Safita through ascending terraces of orchards and olive groves, the town of stone-built houses painted white and pink clustering about the solid mass of a Crusader keep, 27m high and illuminated at night, rising from a mount. This is almost all that remains of Chastel Blanc, the White Castle of the Templars, an outpost of Tartus against Assassin territory to the northeast and contributing to the defence of the Homs Gap.

Getting There

If driving from Krak, head west about 15km, then north about 7km; from Tartus the distance is 30km southeastwards. Microbuses run regularly to Safita from Tartus, less frequently from Homs. At Safita the microbus station is just to the east of the castle, though some go to the bus station. Long-distance buses serve Safita from Damascus, Latakia and Homs. The bus station is adjacent to the Safita Cham Palace hotel. Note that as Safita is a summer mountain resort, services fall off out of season. Taxis can be found at both the bus and the microbus stations and can be rented for the half-day or day to visit Krak des Chevaliers and other places in the region.

History

The Crusaders probably first built a castle here in 1112 but it was largely destroyed by Nur al-Din in about 1171 when he also briefly occupied Tartus. Saladin's lightning campaign along the coast in 1188 following his victory at Hattin and conquest of Jerusalem the previous year persuaded the Count of Tripoli to place the Templars in charge of Tartus, which now became their headquarters, the keep at Safita as you see it today being their work and probably dating from the first years of the 13th century. Though 700 Templar knights garrisoned Chastel Blanc at the approach of Baybars in February 1271, they were ordered to evacuate the castle by the Master of the Order in Tartus, isolating Krak des Chevaliers, which fell two months later.

The Castle

No fixed opening hours nor an entry fee as the castle is a church; if it is not open, the adjacent restaurant will have the keys.

Originally there was an encircling or rather oval-shaped wall, having a pronounced talus, which extended as far as 40m out from the keep at its centre, and an inner wall of irregular shape. Dwellings now entirely occupy the *enceinte* and incorporate architectural fragments of the defences. A portion of the east gate in the outer wall can still be seen if you follow the cobbled road leading into the town from the rear of the keep.

There had possibly been a Byzantine fortress here (and indeed Gertrude Bell, who found a Phoenician coin at Safita, supposed it had been an inland stronghold of that merchant nation), but the arrangement is typically Frankish, the well-built tower especially so. The façades are blank except for arrow-slits and the machicolation above the entrance, which is on the west side. The surprise as you enter is to discover that the ground floor was built as a church, its high and dimly-lit vaulted nave rounded off by an apse at the east end with a sacristy on each side. Never turned into a mosque nor deconsecrated, the church now serves the Greek Orthodox community who moved here from the Hauran in the 19th century and share Safita with Alawis. A staircase to the right of the doorway takes you up to the first floor, which served as an armoury and housed the garrison. A further staircase leads to the open terrace at the top of the tower, in part still crenellated, with panoramic views of the town and the surrounding landscape, ranging as far as Krak des Chevaliers on its spur along the horizon to the southeast and a glimpse of the Mediterranean to the west.

Where to Stay

expensive

★★★★**Safita Cham Hotel**, ✆ (043) 525982, ✉ (043) 525984. Charmless and intrusive, with pool, sun terrace, disco, restaurant and bar. Situated off the western end of the main street, it has good views over the town.

inexpensive

The **Safita Bourj** hotel, ✆ (043) 521932, 1km east from the roundabout which itself is just east of the castle. Rooms with fan, bath, toilet and balcony (with shower instead of bath, rooms rates fall into the cheap category). The place is modern, clean, characterless and liable to be inhabited by noisy families. No breakfast served, indeed no restaurant.

cheap

The **Syaha** (Tourist) hotel near the roundabout to the east of the castle has fairly clean and simple rooms with cold water showers; the toilets however are filthy.

There are ample private apartments to rent by the night or longer for the price of an inexpensive hotel room (sometimes less). Ask at any café and an owner will be found.

Eating Out

Al Bourj next to the castle keep at the top of the hill has indoor seating and an outdoor terrace with marvellous views over the town and the surrounding mountains. Prices are inexpensive for drinks (including alcohol), mezes and meals.

Husn Suleiman

Though the name means Suleiman's Citadel, this is neither a fortress nor has it anything to do with Suleiman, rather its ruins are of Baetocecea, a Roman cult centre dedicated to Zeus following the earlier worship here of Baal. Altitude accounts for Baal and Zeus, both sky gods, for Husn Suleiman lies at the head of a valley high up in the mountains. That Astarte was also venerated here in Roman times is perhaps owed to the clear spring that breaks from the rocks outside the temple and flows down the valley of green turf and poplars. 'The site must be well worthy of careful excavation', wrote Gertrude Bell, though she probably would not have minded to learn that nearly a century later it had not been, for 'no additional knowledge will enhance the beauty of the great shrine in the hills'.

You will need your own transport to reach Husn Suleiman. By car from Safita, just head north 7km, then east 20km; or from Masyaf drive about 30km southwest.

Exploring the Ruins

The cella stands at the centre of a huge grey-walled compound, 134 by 85m, with gates built of massive blocks of stone in each side. The northern gate with its propylaeum is the most elaborate, the gigantic lintel beneath a relieving arch of its outer portico reminiscent in its scale and execution of Baalbek in Lebanon, Gertrude Bell speculating that the same architect was at work at both places. The cella, largely ruinous, is raised upon a stone-built platform preceded by a flight of steps, an altar for sacrifices at the base. Six free-standing columns formed a portico to the cella which otherwise was pseudo-peripteral, that is the columns along its sides and rear are engaged, creating only the effect of peripteral columns seen for example at Palmyra's Temple of Bel. The date of construction is probably late 1st-century AD, Roman dressing on Phoenician form, with an interior staircase to the right of the entrance once giving ceremonial access to the roof.

A second compound across the road to the northwest has acquired the name al-Deir, meaning the monastery, as perhaps it became in Christian times. It encloses a small Ionic temple with an eagle over the lintel, and there are traces within the north area of the compound of a Christian basilica.

The mountains form an amphitheatre round the site, their slopes bare yet here and there a grove of oak or other deciduous trees upon their crests. Important though timber has always been for shipbuilding and roof beams, such groves as these have survived for centuries. The Phoenicians worshipped sacred trees and the Alawis, who have retained so many pagan beliefs, have preserved these groves against man and goat. They bury their dead on mountain tops where in afterlife they are the protectors of the trees rooted among their bones.

Masyaf

Running north along the high ridges towards Masyaf, the land falls away deeply on either side; if you are approaching from Hama, then already from a distance you can see the castle of the Assassins standing out against the rising flank of the Jebel al-Sariya. This mountain country of the Ismaelis ran back towards the coast, overlooking Tartus, Baniyas and Jeble, while on this side it hovered over the Orontes Valley. Their principal strongholds were at Masyaf and Qadmus on the direct Masyaf–Baniyas road, no trace of which now survives; in all they are believed to have had 10 castles.

Masyaf was particularly favoured by the sect's late 12th-century leader in Syria, Rashid al-Din Sinan (died 1193), who became famously known to the Crusaders as the Old Man of the Mountain, a title they conferred also on his successors. From here in his jerry-built eyrie, its walls almost superfluous, he defended Ismaeli autonomy at long range, by choice assassinations of knights and emirs alike. We owe to this militant branch of the Ismaelis our word assassin, from their supposed habit of taking hashish (*hashhashin* is the Arabic for 'consumers of hashish'), by which, it was thought, they prepared themselves for their daring attacks. Today along the market streets of Masyaf there is an air of purposeful peasant trade, their descendants handsome, the girls addicted to no more than flirtatious glances and bubble gum.

If travelling by car, Masyaf is 40km west across the Orontes valley from Hama; 50km east along a magnificent mountain road from Baniyas; or about 30km northeast of Husn Suleiman. Masyaf can also be reached by microbus from Hama, less frequently from Baniyas and Apamea.

Eyrie of the Old Man of the Mountain

Open daily 9–6 in summer, 9–3 in winter; adm; if locked ask around for the caretaker.

The castle is on the east side of town, impressively set upon a rocky ledge overlooking the Orontes, its site earlier chosen by the Seleucids, Romans, Byzantines and even briefly the Crusaders for their defences. The Crusader work is recognisable by regularly laid lower courses of well-cut stone; the Ismaelis, who possessed Masyaf from about 1140, took less care, their walls a jumble of small irregular stones, found blocks and ancient columns. The plan is a central keep surrounded by a curtain wall buttressed by square towers, much of it overgrown and in a bad state of repair.

The Assassins

The term Assassins describes a militant branch of the Ismaeli sect originating in Persia in the late 11th century. The Ismaelis in turn are usually considered to be a branch of Shia Islam, though they continue certain pre-Muslim beliefs, in particular dualism, a system (found also in Christian history as Gnosticism) that explains evil not as the absence of good but as part of the essence, along with good, of both the world and its Creator, who himself may be an emanation of an ultimate and unknowable God. Within man, however, who like the world contains within him a mixture of good and evil, there is a particle of the divine, a spark which, given possession of the secret knowledge, can reunite man with the unknown God.

The Ismaelis claimed to possess this knowledge. So did that branch of the Ismaelis, the Assassins, whose particular glimpse of knowledge was described by Marco Polo, who passed through Persia at the time. The Assassins used drugs to convince novices that they had entered a garden of delights where fountains flowed with milk, honey and wine, and where *houris*, those maidens of paradise, were likewise on tap. Brought back to their normal state, the initiates were told they had indeed visited paradise, which would certainly be forever theirs provided they gave absolute obedience to the commands of the Assassins' *imam*.

The Assassins spread into Syria during the turmoil and fragmentation of the last decades of the 11th century when the country was nominally under the control of the Shia Fatimids of Egypt but subject also to pressure from the Seljuk Turks and the Byzantines. The Assassins' antipathy towards orthodox Sunni Islam, however, took militant and murderous form, and led them also to ally with the Crusaders. Soon they were obliged to retreat from the cities into the Jebel al-Sariya, where from such strongholds as Qadmus, Qalaat al-Kahf and Masyaf they employed a strategy of assassination to influence and control anyone, Muslim or Christian, who might threaten their independence.

A Sunni *qadi* of Aleppo and a Latin patriarch of Jerusalem were among the Assassins' victims. But their most famous attempt was against Saladin in 1176. As the champion of orthodoxy and leader of the Muslim resurgence, Saladin had already overthrown the Fatimids in Egypt and was now in full cry against the Crusaders and the Assassins. He entered the Jebel al-Sariya to lay siege to Masyaf, but his soldiers reported mysterious powers about, while Saladin was disturbed by terrible dreams. One night he awoke suddenly to find on his bed some hot cakes of a type that only the Assassins baked, and with them a poisoned dagger and a threatening verse. Convinced that Rashid al-Din Sinan, the Old Man of the Mountain, had himself entered his tent, Saladin's nerves gave way. He sent a message to Sinan asking for forgiveness and promised not to pursue his campaign against the Assassins provided he was granted safe conduct. Saladin was pardoned and hastened back to Cairo.

The Assassins' headquarters in Persia fell to the Mongols in 1260, while the strictly orthodox Mamelukes helped to extend Sunni control over most of the country from its centres in Aleppo and Damascus. In 1270 the Mameluke Sultan Baybars put down an Assassin revolt and in the following year he was able to command an Assassin contingent at the final siege of Krak des Chevaliers. By 1273 the Assassins ceased to have a political identity altogether. Soon their version of the Ismaeli sect became one more minority, along with the Christians and Alawis, of the Jebel al-Sariya, where throughout the Ottoman period, provided they did not cause trouble and paid their taxes, they were generally left alone. In the 19th century many Ismaelis left the mountains to settle at Salamiya (*see* p.156), a town on the desert road to Isriya, and those who remain are greatly outnumbered and facing displacement by the Alawis.

From Masyaf you can now follow the road to the coast at Baniyas through magnificent mountain country, passing the site of the vanished Assassins' castle at **Qadmus** along the way (from where, by following a spur road, you can reach **Qalaat al-Kahf**, another Ismaeli castle, set between wild gorges and badly ruined). From Qadmus you run along the southern brim of a deep valley, flocks of goats crawling like centipedes far below. A narrow stream, too slight it seems for the task it has accomplished, winds along the bottom, the precipitous mountain slopes carved round and smooth like wood, terracing following the contours like the grain. And then suddenly from a great height still you look down upon a sloping plain of silvery olives and spikey palms and the shining blue Mediterranean.

Tartus

Between Krak des Chevaliers and the sea, the Homs Gap opens onto broad rich farmland, called by the Crusaders *la Bocquée*, intersected by several ridges linking the mountain ranges to north and south. As you climb over the final brow you see Tartus down below, the island of Arwad seemingly close offshore, and between the two, numbers of ships riding at anchor. The oil pipeline and new road and rail links with the interior have transformed this once sleepy fishing port, and though it is still a distant second to Latakia, there is considerable industrial expansion to the north and a proliferation of concrete apartment blocks all around the city. Yet instead of an air of busyness, Tartus has a dull and listless atmosphere. Concrete is the blight of Syria, remorselessly replacing character with vacancy and ugliness.

The highway from Homs brings you to the south of the city; you should head straight for the sea and then turn northwards, arriving in about 1.5km at the old quarter within the remains of the Crusader citadel, compact and interesting to walk about, with character still, its houses fixed into medieval arches, walls and bastions, fending off the concrete mixer. These are the remnants of Tortosa of the Templars. The Cathedral of Our Lady of Tortosa is to the southeast, 100m beyond the citadel's outer defence walls, and it is this that you especially come to see.

Getting There

By train: there is a daily train from both Damascus and Latakia. The station is 1km southeast of the citadel.

By bus and microbus: the regular bus and microbus station is by the railway station, with services to Aleppo, Latakia, Baniyas, Safita, Amrit, Homs, Damascus and elsewhere.

By luxury coach: coaches link Tartus with Aleppo, Latakia, Homs and Damascus (also Tripoli and Beirut in Lebanon). The various companies have their stations 500m east of the citadel.

By service taxi: these make runs between Tartus and Damascus, Homs and up the coast to Latakia, also to Tripoli and Beirut in Lebanon, as well as elsewhere depending on demand. You find them gathered to the immediate southeast of the old town, at the intersection marked by a clock tower, halfway between the citadel and the railway station.

Tourist Information

The Tourist Office, open from 8am to 2pm, closed Fridays, is on Khaled Ibn al-Walid Street, which runs from the northeast corner of the citadel to the luxury bus stations.

History

Nothing remains of the Phoenician foundation, its classical name Antaradus (a compression of anti-Aradus) indicating its position as the mainland complement to the more important settlement opposite on Arwad (Aradus). A chapel, reputedly the first dedicated to the Virgin, is

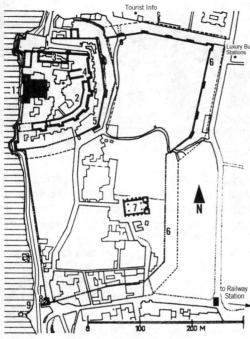

1 Keep 2 Inner citadel wall 3 Banqueting hall 4 Chapel 5 Outer citadel wall. 6 City wall 7 Our Lady of Tortosa 8 Crusader tower 9 Ferries to Arwad

known to have been built here in the 3rd century, long before the Roman Empire officially tolerated Christianity. When two centuries later the chapel was felled by an earthquake, the disaster was proclaimed a miracle, for the altar had survived. An icon of the Virgin, yet another painted by St Luke (*see* p.128), further enhanced the air of veneration attendant to this spot. The Crusaders built upon this history when they began construction of Our Lady of Tortosa in 1123 to house the miraculous altar and receive the prayers of pilgrims.

Following Nur al-Din's brief occupation of the city in 1152, the Count of Tripoli (Trablus down the coast in Lebanon) placed Tortosa in the care of the Templars, who greatly improved its defences. Nevertheless, Saladin seized the city, destroying most of it, including much of the cathedral, early in July 1188 before carrying his campaign northwards, the Templars escaping destruction by bolting themselves ignominiously inside the keep. Thereafter the cathedral was rebuilt and Tortosa remained continuously in Templar hands, even after the Hospitallers had surrendered their great fortresses of Krak des Chevaliers to Baybars and Margat to Qalaun. Indeed, except for the Templars' Château Pelerin (Athlit) in present-day Israel, which outstayed it by 11 days, Tortosa was the last Crusader toe-hold on the Levantine mainland, abandoned by the knights on 3 August 1291, though they clung to the offshore island of Arwad for 11 years longer.

Looking Around Tortosa of the Templars

A surviving 100m section of the citadel wall faces the Mediterranean and was once washed by the sea where now runs an esplanade. If you position yourself here, you can get some idea of the triple circuit of Tortosa's defences. The remains of the **keep** in which the Templars crowded while Saladin sacked their city lie behind the talus at the southern end of this surviving sea-wall (notice the postern, from where perhaps in 1291 the garrison sailed away). Fifty metres to the north a square bastion marks a corner of the **inner citadel wall** which first extended eastwards and then curved round in a semicircle, returning to a now vanished section of the sea-wall 50m south of the keep. It is difficult to trace the line of this inner wall, which survives only in remnants among the tangle of streets and jumble of habitations that fill the citadel enclosure, and where you still see quite a few men wearing the old baggy Turkish trousers—like elephants with a hernia. If you thread your way in, then behind the keep you come to a little square with a leafy café immediately east of the keep. On the north side are slight traces of a 13th-century **banqueting hall**, while to the northeast are the remains of a **chapel**.

The **outer citadel wall** likewise forms a semicircle and is easier to follow. Again standing with your back to the sea and facing the talus slope of the keep, the southern limit of this outer wall is met at the square tower 100m to the south, its northern limit just beyond the square bastion mentioned earlier. You can follow this northern section of the outer citadel wall as it runs eastwards. In about 200m it curves southwards to complete the semicircle. But continuing eastwards for a farther 200m is the line of the **city wall**, which also then turns to the south and then back to the sea at a point about 400m south of the talus and keep where there is now a free-standing square Crusader **tower**.

Within the city wall but 100m to the southeast of the outer citadel wall is the **Cathedral of Our Lady of Tortosa**, now doubling as a **museum** (*open 9–6 in summer, 9–4 in winter, closed Tues; adm; see also 'Photography', p.20*). (Or from the keep of the citadel walk 200m south along the seafront road, then take the road that heads due east, in 200m bringing you to the front of the cathedral. If in doubt, you can ask for the *kanisa*, church, or the *mathaf*, museum.) It has known worse days, Henry Maundrell observing in 1697, 'Its walls and arches and pillars are of a bastard marble and all still so entire that a small expense would suffice to recover it into the state of a beautiful church again. But, to the grief of any Christian beholder, it is now made a stall for cattle; and we were, when we went to see it, almost up to our knees in dirt and mire'. As you can see by the octagonal minaret added at the northwest corner, the cathedral has served also as a mosque, while the Ottomans used it as a barracks.

You enter from the west, where the cathedral presents a blank wall pierced only by a small door, above which is a triangular arrangement of windows with slightly pointed arches. The impression is more of a fortress than a church, and you notice the vestiges of corner towers that also would have served a defensive purpose. This is a 13th-century reworking of the façade undertaken in anxious times when clearly efficacy rather than style determined the cathedral's outward appearance. Not that it was of any help to 18-year-old Raymond, heir to the thrones of Antioch and Tripoli, who in 1213 was stabbed to death outside this door by two Assassins.

Step inside and you discover a medieval French cathedral, the most graceful religious building of the Crusaders in Syria. It is bare of Christian ornament, and its empty volume swallows the whispers of occasional visitors. Undazzled by detail, your eyes follow the trajectories of massive arches which soar from acanthus capitals, and you are impressed with the sense that Our Lady of Tortosa was built by men who meant to stay forever in the Holy Land.

The plan is basilical, a barrel-roofed nave with side-aisles and three apses at the east end, its features marking the transition from the Romanesque to the Gothic. Engaged columns articulate the piers, those columns from which the rounded transverse arches spring having capitals of stubby acanthus, while more florid Corinthian capitals top those columns supporting the slightly pointed arches dividing the side-aisles from the nave. Apart from these features, and the worn and pitted amber stone itself, there is no sign of decoration except for a headless bird at the top end of the north aisle, probably representing the Holy Ghost, and some traces of *ablaq* on the transverse arches. Altogether, the feeling is similar to that in the chapel at Margat, though here at Tortosa the scale is grander, the proportions more graceful.

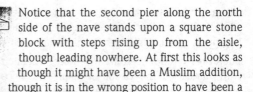

Notice that the second pier along the north side of the nave stands upon a square stone block with steps rising up from the aisle, though leading nowhere. At first this looks as though it might have been a Muslim addition, though it is in the wrong position to have been a minbar, and on closer inspection you can see that it was allowed for in the original construction. The block is pierced by a transverse vault. This probably gave access to the earlier Byzantine chapel which was then entirely built over during the Templars' final reconstruction programme.

The museum displays exhibits from along this coast, though their arrangement betrays no sense of chronology or typology. In the north aisle you see a few *amphorae* and the like, encrusted and dredged from the sea, and some traditional costumes. In the nave are coins, architectural and sculptural fragments and glassware embracing the classical to Arab periods. The miscellany continues along the south aisle and includes items from Ugarit. In the central apse are funerary pieces including bronze coffins and a large marble Roman sarcophagus of the 2nd century AD bearing reliefs, thoroughly vulgar in style, of nymphs and winged cupids holding bowers.

Where to Stay
inexpensive

The ★★★★**Grand Hotel**, ✆ (043) 315681, 🖷 (043) 315683, 1.2km south of the citadel and on the sea front, is a bit faded as all grand hotels should be but still the best in town. Rooms are well furnished and have air conditioning, bath, fridge and TV. There is a café and restaurant. ★★**Al-Bahr**, ✆ (043) 221687, also on the corniche, about 750m south of the citadel, is fairly new; restaurant; rooms with fan, bath and small balcony.

cheap

The ★★**Blue Beach**, ✆ (043) 220650, and the ★★**Ambassador**, (043) 220183, are next to one another on the sea front just south of the ferry harbour for Arwad, i.e. 300m south of the citadel. Both have clean bare rooms with bath and fan, some with air conditioning. The Blue Beach is the friendlier of the two. ★**Daniel**, ✆ (043) 220582, is on Al-Wahda Street which runs back from the sea front (immediately north of the Blue Beach and Ambassador hotels) towards the clocktower. Rooms vary in quality so check first, but most are clean and have bath and fan. Breakfast is available; the staff are friendly and helpful. If you get a good room here (though the place is often full), then you will be better off here than at the Blue Beach or the Ambassador and at a lower price. ★**Republic**, ✆ (043) 222580, almost next door to the Daniel, is fairly clean; rooms with fan, shared showers.

Eating Out

There are plenty of restaurants along or just off the corniche. For a good seafood meal at a moderate price in atmospheric surroundings, try **The Cave** on the corniche; it is built into the wall of the citadel with dining in a vaulted chamber.

The island looks much farther off when viewed from Tartus than it had seemed when coming down out of the Homs Gap, but the distance is only 3km and one of an almost non-stop succession of launches will bob you past the scores of ships lying at anchor in the straits and land you there within 20 minutes. This is the only inhabited island off the Syrian coast, and it is very small, an 800m-long triangle pointing north. The Hebles islands to the south are even smaller, and nobody lives there and nothing is grown, but in summer the youths of Arwad will sometimes take a boat to them for a swim in their exceptionally clear waters.

Arwad's prosperity has always depended on being opposite Syria but not of it. Along with Byblos, Sidon and Tyre to the south, Arwad was one of a tetrarchy of important Phoenician cities and possessed the best harbour between Tripoli and the mouth of the Orontes. Arvad, as the Phoenicians called it, colonised the mainland as far north as Jeble and eastwards nearly to Homs. During the Seleucid period Arwad (Arados in Greek) preserved a large measure of autonomy and flourished commercially, not least from the manufacture from mussels of purple dye, when for want of space but no lack of wealth its houses rose to many storeys. But the Romans subordinated Arwad to Tartus, and the island declined. Little of its ancient past survives today, but there are other good reasons for visiting the place.

Getting There

The harbour for Arwad (sometimes known as Ruad) is opposite the free-standing Crusader tower south of the citadel at Tartus. Motor launches to the island are frequent and inexpensive, the crossing taking no more than 20 minutes. The last launches return just before dusk.

Visiting the Island

As you sail into the arms of its harbour, which protectively faces away from the open sea and towards Tartus, you notice that the central jetty, which is a low natural promontory dividing the basin in two, carries great blocks of ancient foundations and walls. A lone classical column with capital also stands here. More huge blocks, probably remnants of the Phoenician walls, can be seen along the west and southwest sides of the island. Otherwise it was left to the Crusaders to give Arwad two centuries of importance again. Today many younger islanders, mostly Sunni Muslims, tell you that they too would like to sail away westwards, as emigrants to America.

For the visitor, Arwad is delightful, owing in part to the greater difficulty of transporting cement to the island, but also to the crossing and the day-out atmosphere of the place, with the laughter of pretty girls with eyes as blue as glaciers and old women in black being manhandled on and off the launches and people sitting around at harbourside cafés enjoying grilled fish and glasses of *arak*. But also it can be a fairly filthy place; with nowhere to dispose of rubbish, it is piled up on the shore for the tides to carry out to sea—or to Tartus. A fishing town covers Arwad so completely that houses even grow on the ancient Phoenician sea walls. On the south side the sound of hammers on wood signals a shipyard, a reminder that the island contributed towards the fleet that Xerxes sent against the Greeks at Salamis. There are no streets, only twisting lanes and narrowing passages, and in their midst a Crusader castle (*see* below) from where the escaping Templars from Tortosa clung to a view of Christendom's lost prize for 11 years longer, until 1302.

Near the central jetty where fishermen mend their nets are the cafés and restaurants, and behind these are the walls of a small **Muslim castle** with round towers, slit merlons, boxed machicolations, a parapet on corbels running round the inside. Just south of the Muslim castle, a market twists back into the town, selling daytrip gewgaws as well as fruit, vegetables, eggs and other foods brought over from the mainland for the locals, as they have no space to grow anything. If you follow this back towards higher ground near the west side of the island you come to the **Crusader fortress**, probably 13th-century, with massive round corner towers. This was the last outpost of the Templars; now it is the local museum (*open daily 9–4, closed Tues; adm*). Next to its gate is carved a lion and palm in relief, the crest of the Lusignans. For some decades after the Templars' departure, raids against Syria were mounted from Cyprus, and both Tortosa and Arwad were briefly held, this crest perhaps a memento. If so it appears that the Muslims, with dark humour, later added a chain, tethering the royal beast to the palm he had vainly sought to rule.

The End of the Templars

As the Templars made this crossing and looked back along the receding mainland, the devastation was already beginning. For some months after the fall of Tortosa in 1291, Mameluke troops laid waste to the coastal plain. Orchards were cut down and irrigation systems wrecked, while native Christians fled into the Jebel al-Sariya. The only castles left standing were those far back from the sea and Margat, high upon its mountain. Anything that might be of value to the Crusaders should they ever attempt another landing was destroyed.

Muslim bitterness towards the Crusades was matched by recriminations in Europe. With the Mameluke seizure of Arwad in 1302, the Templars became little better than refugees in Cyprus, France and elsewhere. Soon they became hunted men. Their purpose had been the defence of the Holy Land, yet in 1291 they had lost Acre (in present-day Israel), Christendom's last great stronghold, as well as Tortosa. They had grown powerful and far wealthier than the Hospitallers, for the Templars had long been the chief money-lenders in the East, a role that won them many enemies among the Christians, even as it earned them Muslim friends. The interest many Templars took in Muslim learning and religion, and perhaps in some of the heterodox cults which then as now found a home in Syria, helped fan the rumours that their Order conducted secret, obscene and blasphemous initiation rites. In 1307 the king of France arrested and charged the Templars there with heresy, and a year later Cyprus followed suit. Under torture, most of the knights confessed. In 1312 the pope suppressed their Order and granted their property to the Hospitallers, and in Paris, two years later, the Templar Grand Master was burnt at the stake.

Amrit

The strange ruins of Amrit, ancient Marathos, begin 7km south of Tartus on the coastal road to Tripoli and cover an area 3km long and 2km wide. Along this road in 333 BC came Alexander after his great victory over the Persians at Issus near Iskenderun in present-day Turkey. From Amrit he sent his general Parmenion to Damascus, there to take possession of Darius' baggage and treasure, which included, according to one source, over 2000 kilos of gold. Meanwhile

Alexander received a message from Darius, ceding Asia Minor in return for peace. This had been limit enough for Alexander's ambition at the campaign's outset, but from Amrit he answered the Persian king that 'everything you possess is now mine'. Here was the moment when Alexander first laid claim to a vast Eastern empire, and it marks the beginning of that 1000-year Hellenistic, Roman and Byzantine imperium to follow.

Arwad, whose cult centre Amrit was, had immediately come to terms with Alexander, and so he paused here in some ease before marching south against Byblos, Sidon and Tyre. The conquest of Egypt would follow, and having secured his flank and rear he would turn east again to destroy the Persian Empire. Yet even as he looked around Amrit, Egypt and Persia were presaged in the architectural mix around him, the only site in Syria where this particular blend of Phoenician syncretism remains evident.

Getting There

Microbuses depart from near the railway station at Tartus for Al-Hamidiye, 17km down the coast; ask to be let off at Amrit or Nahr al-Amrit (the River of Amrit), 7km south of Tartus. To return, just flag down a microbus on the road. Note that there are two roads south from Tartus, one along the coast, the other a kilometre inland. Either can serve as an approach, but the directions that follow start from the coast road.

Exploring the Ruins

First, just east of the coast road, you come to a **temple compound** of the Persian period, 6th to 4th centuries BC, cut from solid rock on three sides, while on the fourth, now open to a salty marsh-plain, was a wall and gate. This enclosed a sacred lake fed by a healing spring; at its centre on a low mass of rock stands a tiny **naos** with an Egyptian-style cavetto cornice dedicated to the Phoenician god Melkart or Moloch (variant Molech), a solar divinity known as 'protector of the city' to whom children were sacrificed by fire (as anyone who has seen D. W. Griffith's film *Intolerance* will know, or who is familiar with the Bible, e.g. Jeremiah 33:35, referring to the practice in Jerusalem: 'And they built the high places of Baal, which are in the valley of the son of Hinnom, to cause their sons and their daughters to pass through the fire unto Molech; which I commanded them not, neither came it into my mind, that they should do this abomination, to cause Judah to sin'). The typically Phoenician plan of this sacred area was to be repeated and developed elsewhere in Syria, for example at Husn Suleiman and the Temple of Bel at Palmyra, where in each case a relatively small temple is set within the walls of a vast sanctuary. Immediately east is a *tell*, whose remains go back to the late 3rd millennium BC, and north of this, across the stream called Nahr al-Amrit, are traces of a probably Hellenistic **stadium**.

Next to see, 700m farther south and again east off the coastal road, are two 4th-century BC monolithic cylinders, 7 and 4m high, known locally as **the Spindles**, *maghazil*, with burial chambers below. At the base of the higher tower are four sculpted lions, Persian in style, and atop it a rounded cap, while atop the shorter tower is a five-sided pyramid. A farther kilometre south and off to the west of the road is a great black cube built of massive blocks and containing two burial chambers, one above the other. The locals call this *Burg al-Bezzaq*, parochially explaining that *bezzaq* means snail, which it does, though they have no idea why this funerary monument should therefore be the 'Tower of the Snail'. But *bezzaq* also means the Egyptian cobra, a pharaonic motif that might have been employed along the now fallen cornice. This **Tower of the Cobra** was surmounted by the pyramid that now lies near by.

Baniyas

Getting There

Baniyas is about 38km north of Tartus, 50km south of Latakia and 50km west of Masyaf. Microbuses ply between Baniyas and Tartus, Latakia and Masyaf. There are occasional microbuses running close by Margat (Qalaat Marqab).

Factories, refineries and industrial plants of one sort or another line your way north out of Tartus and again on either side of Baniyas, where there are also anti-aircraft guns along the shore. Between the two, the coast is straight and dull, its beaches dust and stone. Villages crest fine foothills which fall away in a gentle olive-clad decline to the coastal plain where concrete boxes erupt from groves.

Baniyas was the Crusader Valénie, wrecked along with much of this coast by the Mameluke troops of Sultan Al-Ashraf Khalil after the fall of Tartus and the long neglect that followed. The little river that flows into the sea here, and that has carved the terrific valley you drive along between here and Masyaf, was the boundary between the Kingdom of Jerusalem and the Principality of Antioch. In the late 17th century Baniyas was described by Maundrell as 'at present uninhabited; but its situation proves it to have been anciently a pleasant, its ruins a well-built, and its bay before it, an advantagious habitation'. Repopulated as recently as the French Mandate, you realise as you stand by its small curved harbour that for a few decades it must have been a charming place. The town is set within a deep indentation where the mountains splay on either side and Margat looks down from its titanic acropolis. But the remaining old houses along the unused harbour are crumbling and being torn away to be replaced by blank concrete. Back from the harbour, the cement mixer has wrought a horrible revolution. Nothing of beauty, character or interest remains, and today Baniyas is a dump.

Where to Stay

There are two small tolerable hotels at Baniyas, both cheap, the ***Baniyas**, ✆ (043) 710173, and the ***Homs**, ✆ (043) 710408.

Margat (Qalaat Marqab)

As you approach Baniyas from Tartus, you cannot fail to see the brooding bulk of Margat upon its mountain height, 'a castle', wrote the young T. E. Lawrence, 'about as big as Jersey I fancy: one wanted a bicycle to ride round it'. At night it is floodlit, floating vast against the black sky like an intergalactic mother-ship. Called Qalaat Marqab by the Muslims, the Castle of the Watchtower, it commanded both the coastal plain, here constricted to a narrow strip, and the valley running back through Assassin territory towards Masyaf. Sold to the Hospitallers by the

Principality of Antioch in 1186, Margat was completely rebuilt in accordance with the latest concepts in French military architecture, Lawrence remarking that it looked like an 'unrestored Carcassonne'. Ruinous in parts, some appreciation of its concentric plan is

gained if you have already visited Krak des Chevaliers, though its broken walls of sombre black basalt even now contribute to a sense of impregnability. Already by 1188 it seemed so formidable to Saladin that he chose to march by, while in 1191 it was to Margat that Richard the Lionheart first came when he landed in Syria from Cyprus at the outset of the Third Crusade. Yet though Margat was equipped to withstand a five-year siege, it fell to Sultan Qalaun in 1285 after five weeks.

Getting There

Margat is 6km from Baniyas and is reached by first taking the old coast road south and then switchbacking up the mountain. Occasional microbuses run up close by Margat (Qalaat Marqab) from Baniyas.

Visiting Margat

Open 9–6 in summer, 9–4 in winter; adm.

Driving up the mountain flank, you pass villages of stone still holding their own against concrete. The slopes are terraced right to their ridges, planted with olives mostly, ribs of chalk showing through the soil, with here and there some prickly pear and palms. The final approach brings you up beneath the eastern walls towards the massive southern defences. Just here, where the road runs alongside a half-buried masonry outwork to the right and with Margat still looming above you, you should pause. The castle is triangular in plan, and you notice at its southern point several bands of white marble in the stonework, a Mameluke touch, for this was rebuilt by Qalaun after he had successfully mined the Crusader defences and brought them down. Mining in those days was accomplished by digging a tunnel beneath wall or tower, propping up the excavation with wooden beams as the task progressed. By lighting a fire and destroying the beams, the tunnel would collapse and bring down the defences above it. This Qalaun had done to the subsequently rebuilt white-banded outer enclosure wall with its projecting round tower, but he had also dug other mines which he invited the Hospitallers to inspect for themselves. Seeing the hopelessness of their situation, they accepted his pledge of safe passage and on 25 May 1285 rode off to Tartus and Tripoli.

You now continue clockwise round to the west gate tower. The keeper occupies a white-washed chamber above the entrance vestibule, a good breeze kicking through his window from which there is a superb view over the Mediterranean. Once through the gate tower you should turn right (south), following the line of the west wall for about 25m, where you reach an inner gate with steps leading up to the triangular **inner court**, beneath which a great cistern stored water for the garrison. Surveying the court clockwise, starting from your left (east), you see store-rooms, a chapel, a barracks which adjoins a high round keep, and to the west of this a two-storey great hall. Nearer to you, against the west wall, a restored building houses a café.

The **round keep,** late 12th-century with walls up to 5m thick, is typical of Hospitaller work; if they could not build in the round, then as at Krak des Chevaliers they would round off the earlier square towers they had inherited. From its top you get the clearest idea of the castle's concentric defences as well as a magnificent panorama over mountains, coast and sea.

The principal entrance to the **chapel** is from the west, up a flight of steps and through a slightly pointed arch set upon slender engaged (and now broken) columns bearing simple acanthus capitals. There is a similar entrance on the north side, level with the court, the columns here intact. Built in the late 12th century, the architectural style is transitional, Gothic but with a lingering sense of Romanesque. Inside, the chapel compares in austere elegance to the cathedral at Tartus, though on a smaller scale and less elaborate. Nevertheless, it gains a sense of spaciousness by having no aisles and so no internal columns. Instead you are aware of its three lofty pointed arches, one with black and white *ablaq* delimiting the apse, the second midway along the nave undecorated but supported by engaged columns with restrained acanthus capitals and the third supporting the façade. The rhythm continues along the side walls which have two arches each, and in each there is a pointed arched window as there is also in the apse. There is no trace of decoration otherwise, and probably its handsome-ness always resided in the simplicity, height and strength you see today.

You can now walk round the **southern perimeter** of the castle, between the inner walls surrounding the court and the outer enclosure walls rebuilt by Qalaun. Also, returning towards the west tower gate you can explore the **northern precincts** of Margat, entirely ruinous but all the more enjoyable for that up and down tunnelled stairways that now lead nowhere, or lead into some vast vaulted chamber you can barely get out of—popping out upon an upper level, open now and splashed in sunlight where sunlight was never meant to be—and all the while delighting in varying high views of the sea and the valley hinterland.

The Mamelukes

In 1171 Saladin overthrew the Shia Fatimids in Cairo and established in their place his Ayyubid dynasty which in the name of Sunni orthodoxy ruled over both Egypt and Syria. But in 1249, as St Louis, the king of France, landed in Egypt at the head of the Seventh Crusade, Sultan Al-Salih Ayyub lay dying in Cairo. The invasion was repulsed by the sultan's elite Mameluke force, and they soon took advantage of their military strength to insinuate themselves into a position of political authority. Mameluke means white slave, and the Mamelukes were a slave militia, at this period mostly pagan Kipchak Turks captured as children in the southern Russian steppes. Brought to Cairo to serve the Ayyubid regime, they were converted to Islam and trained to become the outstanding warriors of their age.

A branch of the Ayyubids clung on to power in Damascus but were swept aside by the Mongol onslaught of 1260. In September of that year, however, a Mameluke army from Egypt defeated the Mongols at Ain Jalud in Galilee, and apart from the territories of the Crusaders and Assassins, all of present-day Egypt, Israel, Jordan, Lebanon and Syria was theirs. The Mameluke sultanate was non-hereditary, supreme power going to the strongest among the military elite. (Indeed, Mamelukes could only be bought, never born; the free-born children of Mamelukes were disqualified from joining the slave elite.) Formidable in the field and highly centralised in its administrative organisation, the sultanate now turned its attention towards the Crusader states.

Baybars had been one of the leading Mameluke commanders at Ain Jalud; within two months he was sultan (1260–77). In 1268 a Mameluke army under Baybars' personal command took Antioch; Mameluke campaigns in the Jebel al-Sariya between 1265 and 1271 cost the Assassins their castles and made them the sultan's subjects; and with that accomplished, in 1271 Baybars took Krak des Chevaliers.

The Mongols again invaded Syria in 1280, sacking Aleppo before withdrawing. Qalaun (1280–90) was now Mameluke sultan and in the following year he advanced into Syria to meet another Mongol attack. Eager to protect his flank, Qalaun agreed a truce with the Hospitallers at Margat, and in October 1281 won a desperately fought battle against the Mongols outside Homs. Concerned about the ambitions of Genoa, which sought territory at the expense of the County of Tripoli, the better to interfere with the profitable trade that the Mameluke sultanate enjoyed between India and the Far East on the one hand and Europe on the other, Qalaun resumed his offensive against the Crusaders, taking Margat in 1285, Latakia in 1287 and Tripoli in 1289. He died on the eve of his campaign against Acre, the last great Crusader city, which fell to Qalaun's successor, Al-Ashraf Khalil, the following year, in 1291, as did Tortosa.

The context of the Mameluke campaigns in Syria went well beyond the Crusader presence. The Mongol threat and the ambitions of the Italian merchant states worried the Mamelukes at least as much. As for defending 'Muslim' Syria against its enemies, it should be understood that the orthodox Sunni Muslim Mamelukes imposed their rule on a country divided along complex ethnic and religious lines. The larger towns, such as Aleppo, Hama, Homs and Damascus, were predominantly Sunni Muslim, but much else of Syria was Ismaeli, Alawi and Greek and Syrian Christian Orthodox, not to mention Druze and Maronite Christian in the Lebanon ranges. In fact the Mamelukes, like the Ottomans later, never succeeded in establishing more than nominal rule over the coastal mountains, and in time they came to be resented throughout the country.

You wonder if it was as odd for Qalaun as it is for you to stand upon the heights of Margat, overlooking terraces of olives sloping away to the Mediterranean—Qalaun, the Turkish slave from southern Russia who never learnt to speak Arabic fluently and who ruled from Cairo in the name of an orthodoxy he had been obliged upon purchase to accept and that many of his subjects strenuously resisted. There are Mameluke monuments to see in Damascus, though the finest are in Cairo, among them the beautiful mosque-madrasa-mausoleum complex of Qalaun himself, decorated with more than a touch of Crusader

Gothic style. Meanwhile, on the slopes beneath Margat, you see the local people bending more to their olive terraces than to history.

Jeble

Four centuries after the Crusaders were driven from this coast, the devastation wrought by the Mamelukes was still apparent, Maundrell observing that 'many ruins of castles and houses, which testify that this country, however it be neglected at present, was once in the hands of a people that knew how to value it, and thought it worth the defending'.

The seaside town of Jeble stands almost exactly halfway between Baniyas, 24km to the south, and Latakia, 28km to the north. As Gabala it was a minor Phoenician port subject to Arwad and has since passed through the usual hands. 'It makes a very mean figure at present,' said Maundrell, comparing what continued to be into this century an impoverished village with those traces, amid which it squatted, of a much greater past. Recent growth has obliterated more of that past, to no great advantage. What principally survives is the ruinous and over-grown **Roman theatre** at the centre of town near the sea. At 90m across, it was comparable in size and capacity to the theatre at Bosra, with well over 30 rows of seating (over 20 surviving in whole or in part) rising upon massive vaults. Later the Crusaders made it into a fortress. Some of its marble stones can be seen in the nearby **Mosque of Sidi Ibrahim Ben Adham**, named after the Muslim saint whose tomb lies within. He is said to have been a sultan of Afghanistan who renounced his throne and lived out the last 20 years of his life at Jeble, devoting himself to poverty and prayer until his death in 778. The much rebuilt mosque in turn stands on the site of a church built by Heraclius, the 7th-century Byzantine emperor who recovered Syria from the Persians, only to lose it to the Arabs.

A café on the edge of a low cliff overlooking the Mediterranean, just south of the two small fishing harbours, is a pleasant place to pause for refreshments.

Exploring the Northern Jebel al-Sariya

These mountains go under different names in several places, as they run along upon the coast, and are inhabited by rude people of several denominations. In that part of them above Jebilee, there dwell a people, called by the Turks, Neceres, of a very strange and singular character. For 'tis their principle to adhere to no certain religion; but chamelion-like, they put on the colour of religion, whatever it be, which is reflected upon them from the persons with whom they happen to converse. With Christians they profess themselves Christians; with Turks they are good Mussulmans; with Jews they pass for Jews; being such Proteus's in religion, that no body was ever able to discover what shape or standard their consciences are really of. All that is certain concerning them is, that they make very much and good wine, and are great drinkers.

Henry Maundrell, *A Journey from Aleppo to Jerusalem at Easter* AD *1697.*

From Jeble you can continue straight up the coast almost to Latakia, where Route 30 heads east into the mountains to the Crusader castle of Saône (Qalaat Saladin). But there are also some minor roads through these northern reaches of the Jebel al-Sariya which carry you through especially beautiful and unspoilt scenery and introduce you to a few curiosities along the way. About 7km north of Jeble a road climbs up into the mountains and after about 10km passes through **Qirdaha**, birthplace and family home of the Syrian president Hafez Assad, who is an Alawi, that sect known also as Nosairis, Maundrell's Neceres.

From here you can continue a farther 10km or so eastwards to **Qalaat al-Mehelbeh**, a remote and ruinous Crusader castle that was dependent on Saône and like it, three days later, fell to Saladin in 1188. To find it, you may have to ask the way to the village of Mehelbeh, where you can see the castle outlined against the sky atop a summit called Jebel Arbaine. It is then a 20-minute walk up to the entrance on the south side of the crumbling fortifications. The scenery is grand, the castle an excuse more than anything for coming this way. If you follow the goat paths down from its western defences you soon discover an Alawi shrine, the burial place of a 13th-century holy man, set by a spring within a copse of oak and built partly of material from the castle.

Returning almost halfway to the coast again, you can pick up a mountain road running north-wards towards Haffeh and Saône (Qalaat Saladin), and then either go down to Latakia or continue eastwards over the mountains, taking the main road to Jisr al-Shugur or backroads to Slenfeh (*see* p.153), which lies beneath **Nebi Yunes**, at 1602m the highest peak in the Jebel al-Sariya, and Qalaat Burzey (*see* p.153), and so into the Orontes Valley.

The Alawis

Syria's coastal mountains, the Jebel al-Sariya, are named after the Nosairis, followers of Mohammed Ibn Nosairi, their 9th-century leader. Better known as the Alawis, for their belief that Ali, son-in-law of Mohammed, was an emanation of God, they are an extremely heterodox variant of Shia Islam. Indeed some Muslims would deny the Alawis are Muslims at all. However, the Alawis have been declared a legitimate branch of Islam by the Lebanese leader of a Shia sect that is also the state religion of Iran.

Alawi religious practice has been variously described as including elements of Phoenician paganism, Babylonian star-worship (they are said to believe that the Milky Way is made up of the deified souls of true believers), Ismaelism and Christian Gnosticism. Gertrude Bell reported her conversation with the Sunni *qadi* of Homs: 'I began by asking about the Nosairis, but the *qadi* pursed his lips and answered: 'Some of them pretend to worship Ali and some worship the sun. They believe that when they die their souls pass into the bodies of other men or even animals, as it is in the faiths of India and China.'

Typically, ill is spoken of that which is not understood, and in fact no one can be entirely sure of Alawi beliefs and practices, for they worship in secret, meeting at night in secluded places. It is said that they celebrate certain Christian holidays, including Christmas and Easter, though in their own way, and that they perform a mass-like cere-mony which includes a reference to 'body and blood' being 'eternal life'. Initiates ascend through three stages to the inner knowledge of the sect, often also joining the ruling oligarchy of the community which is dominated by clans. The rest of the community constitute the uninitiated mass, among which, unlike the Druze, are women, who can never be initiates and who indeed are not credited with having souls (perhaps explaining why Alawi women are so pleasant). As a small ethnic group, perhaps originating as a south Arabian tribal people who have mingled with the local population, clan solidarity and the mountain fastnesses of coastal Syria have allowed them to fashion a cult from almost every religion they have come into contact with over the past 2000 years even while professing the dominant religion of the times in order to escape persecution.

The Mameluke Sultan Baybars forced the Alawis to build mosques in their villages, but he could not force them to pray in them. Instead, they used the buildings as stables for their cattle and beasts of burden. Nor did the Ottomans have greater success and allowed them to enjoy a certain geographical toleration, the toleration of necessity accorded to a people living in remote mountain areas. That also meant, however, that the Alawis were excluded, far more than the Christians, from all important official and professional positions. Comprising about six per cent of the population of Syria (and found also in Turkey, where recently they have suffered attacks from Sunni fundamentalists, and Lebanon), they remained an almost entirely peasant people with no hope of advancement, though the French, for their own reasons of divide and rule during the Mandate, flattered the Alawis by organising the region centring on Latakia into a separate state.

Exclusion turned out to be the making of them. Impoverished and denied other routes of advancement, Alawis joined newly independent Syria's armed forces in disproportionate numbers, and through a series of coups have since the 1960s supplanted the majority Sunnis as the holders of military and political power, their exceptional communal solidarity helping them to maintain their dominance in a country of religious and ethnic factions.

Saône (Qalaat Saladin)

The Crusader castle of Saône was named after Saladin only in 1957 to commemorate his capture of it in 1188; until then its Frankish name had been only slightly arabised to Sahyun.

Coming from Latakia, you follow the meanderings of the Nahr al-Kabir past plane trees and cattle watering in the gravel shallows, and then into gorse-covered hills. The scent of Aleppo pine hangs in the air as you pass through Haffeh and switchback up into high mountain country tufted with holm oak. Here in this remote landscape your eyes are taken by far views to Nebi Yunes (*see* p.189) rising above the Orontes valley and westwards across the falling waves of the Jebel al-Sariya to the sea. Then suddenly you see it, mysterious and powerfully couchant, half-submerged like some colossal Mayan temple in a wild exuberance of forest, Saône upon its narrow ridge between two deep ravines.

Getting There

Saône is about 28km northeast of Latakia via the village of **Haffeh** on route 30. At the far (east) end of Haffeh a sign indicates to the right the turning for 'Qalaat Saladin', reached in 7km. Microbuses run between Latakia and Haffeh from where, unless you can get a ride, you will have to walk, as indeed does the keeper. Make sure you are back at Haffeh before nightfall to catch the last microbus. There are occasional microbuses between Slenfeh and Haffeh. There is a café at the castle and a restaurant at Haffeh, but no accommodation.

Arriving at Saône

The road plunges towards the northern ravine, switches and climbs again, and then runs you below round towers and a huge square keep hanging over the sheer wall of a terrific gorge. A million years of winter torrents might have worn this channel through the rock, yet it was cut by the Byzantines, who first built here, and enlarged by the Franks to isolate their fortress from the body of the mountain to the east. To support their drawbridge over the **channel**, which is 156m long, 28m deep and from 14 to 20m broad, they left a single **needle of stone**, greater than any Egyptian obelisk, 'the most sensational thing in castle-building I have seen', said T. E. Lawrence. (It is best to see the channel and needle around noon when the sun is directly overhead; at other times they are in deep shadow.) Either here at this precipitous northeast corner or west along the northern flank where the walls narrow upon the lower courtyard, Saladin's troops clambered up and over Saône's defences. The postern drawbridge that once perilously crossed the rock-moat is gone now; instead you continue round to the south flank of the castle with its massive square projecting towers to the main **entrance gate**. The dog's-leg entrance, once protected by a portcullis, is through the third square tower along, bringing you into the castle compound where carline thistles and blue eryngo deploy their spiny defences and the small yellow flowers of restharrow and woundwort grow among the shattered walls.

Purpose, History and Plan of Saône

It seems a lost place for such a castle to be, seemingly not astride a route to anywhere, though both in the past as now the route from Aleppo to the coast crossed the Orontes at Jisr al-Shugur and then climbed up through the Bdama pass. Here it divided, one route heading for Latakia, as the main road does now, the other looping south through Haffeh. It seems to have been this latter route that Maundrell took in the spring of 1697 after coming up to Bdama from 'Shoggle' (Jisr al-Shugur), preferring to reach the Mediterranean well south of Latakia at Jeble. After leaving Bdama, he writes, 'Our road here was very rocky and uneven, but yet the

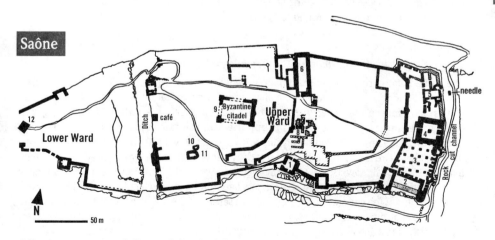

1 Entrance gate tower 2 Cistern 3 Stables 4 Keep 5 Postern gate 6 Cistern 7 Mosque 8 Muslim palace and baths 9 Byzantine citadel 10 Byzantine chapel 11 Crusader church 12 Byzantine Chapel (after R.C. Smail)

variety which it afforded made some amends for that inconvenience. Sometimes it led us under the cool shade of thick trees; sometimes through narrow valleys, watered with fresh murmuring torrents; and then for a good while together upon the brink of a precipice. And in all places it treated us with the prospect of plants and flowers of diverse kinds, as myrtles, oleanders, cyclamens, anemones, tulips, marigolds and several other sorts of aromatic herbs.'

The castle, therefore, though Maundrell seemed unaware of its existence, stood near this more southern route from where it could also help protect the fertile plain around Latakia. First it was the Byzantines who built here when they briefly reasserted their control over northern Syria during the late 10th century, but in its present form Saône dates from the early 12th century, the personal enterprise of Robert of Saône and more so of his son William, feudal lords who held extensive lands from the Prince of Antioch. Robert, who was Tancred's right-hand man, was captured in 1119 while leading an expedition against Damascus, whose commander demanded he convert to Islam. When Robert refused, the commander drew his sword and cut off his head, throwing Robert's body to the dogs but setting the Lord of Saône's skull with jewels and keeping it as his drinking cup. To William then, from 1120 onwards, fell the largest share in building the castle you see today. When it fell to Saladin in 1188, Saône had been in Crusader hands for only about 70 years, nor was it ever to revert to the Franks. And so what is preserved here is an early Crusader castle, without the extensive remodelling of features undertaken by the Hospitallers, for example, at Krak des Chevaliers.

Once through the entrance gate tower in the southern walls, you are in the upper ward where you can get your bearings. The castle has the shape of a long slender lance-head, coming to a sharp point where the two ravines, torrential in winter and spring, converge at its western end. Its keep is along the castle's broad flat eastern end which overlooks the rock channel that separates the fortified spur from the higher mountain ridge. The entire position slopes from east to west: the lower ward to the west relied on the steep ravines for defence and was protected by less powerful walls and towers; while the upper ward, the heart of the castle, was stoutly defended, especially along the line of the rock channel where it was most vulnerable to bombardment from the high ground to the east.

Exploring Saône

Open daily 9–6 in summer, 9–4 in winter; adm.

The castle is fairly ruinous, more so than Margat and far more so than Krak des Chevaliers (though all the same it is instructive to compare the surviving features at Saône with those later castles), and indeed the lower ward is more a briar patch than even a ruin. Having passed through the entrance gate tower into the **upper ward**, you should proceed counterclockwise, first following the line of the southern walls eastwards (i.e. to your right). That the **towers** along this wall are square is itself indicative of early Crusader work, as is the pronounced bossing of the masonry blocks. The towers, however, are well made and their condition compares favourably to the inferior Byzantine work you come across later. In the lower chamber of the first tower to the east (right) of the entrance tower, you can see several of the 380-kilo **stone balls** hurled into the castle by Saladin's mangonels. Beyond the farthest tower is a **cistern** at the southeast corner, while north of this and along the east wall is a pillared hall that served as a **stables**.

North again and overlooking the rock-cut channel is the **keep**, its walls 5m thick, pierced by small loopholes and topped with crenellations. The squat appearance of this and other Syrian keeps is due to the lack of wood, the upper floors having to be supported by heavy stone vaulting below, not lighter wooden beams, the weight of the structure limiting its height. You see this when you go inside, the gloomy lower storey rising 11m to a vaulted ceiling supported by a powerful central pillar. A stairway leads to the upper storey and onto the roof with wonderful views down into the channel. Just north of the keep is the **postern gate**, originally entered over the channel by a drawbridge; now you look out into space except for the needle rising up from the floor of the channel far below.

You should now peer over the walls at their northeast corner, possibly the point where Saladin's men got up. It is almost a sheer drop and seems an impossible climb, not that the alternative argument, that they got up over the north wall farther to the west, is any more attractive to anyone prone to the slightest vertigo. Latakia had fallen to Saladin on 23 July 1188 and by 27 July he had laid siege to Saône. He placed mangonels on the high ground across the channel to the east and others on the ridge across the north ravine, each device bombarding the castle with heavy stone balls. Saône was the largest of the Crusader castles, hardly an advantage on this occasion as the defenders, as usual, were short of men and unable to man the circuit of its defences adequately. The knights fought bravely and made at least one sortie, and it was perhaps at the very moment that Saladin's soldiers stormed through a breach; at any rate, resistance was brief and on 29 July the garrison surrendered.

You can now walk west across the upper ward, noting a large **cistern** at 150m along the north wall and towards the south wall a late 13th-century **mosque** and minaret built by Qalaun. Between the two, and almost opposite the entrance gate tower, are an early 13th-century **Muslim palace and baths**. About 50m west of these and at the centre of the court is the badly ruined 10th-century **Byzantine citadel**, probably the oldest structure at Saône. Its poor state of preservation is probably in part due to its construction, its smaller blocks of stone comparing unfavourably to Crusader work and having the inferior effect of courses of brick. To its south are the remains of a small **Byzantine chapel** up against the side of a larger **Crusader church**. Just to the west and occupying a Crusader building is a **café** offering wonderful views beyond; the line of walls to its north and south, and the traces of a ditch behind it, indicate the division between the upper and lower wards.

You can wander off into the **lower ward**, entirely overgrown, coming to another **Byzantine chapel** at about 100m west of the café. Some argue that it was at this point, where the north and south walls come closest together, that Saladin's troops broke through the north wall and took possession of the lower ward, causing the defenders in the upper ward to surrender. Amid the vegetation lie traces of a town that soon filled this lower portion of the castle compound after Saône's fall.

Latakia

Latakia is a useful base for visiting Saône (Qalaat Saladin) in the mountains to the east and Ugarit (Ras Shamra) to the north, nor is it impractical to make a day's excursion south along the coast to Tartus and back (about 90km each way), taking in Jeble, Margat (Qalaat Marqab) and Arwad. The place is relaxed, open and quite Western and has a fair selection of hotels in all categories, including luxury beach resort hotels a few kilometres north. There is a faintly atmospheric touch of the Levant in the old quarter in the vicinity of Al-Quds (Jerusalem) Street, the continuation of Al-Ghafiqi Street, which runs west from Al-Yaman Square near the railway station. Otherwise there are very few remains of Latakia's past, and you are missing little if you do not pause to see them. Instead take your cue from Latakia's role as a transshipment point: you are here because you have somewhere else to go. To reduce Syria's dependence on Iskenderun in Turkey and Beirut and Tripoli in Lebanon, recent decades have seen Latakia developed into a major port, its modern facilities extending north of the old harbour, an outlet especially for the agricultural produce of the Orontes valley and the Gezira in northeast Syria. In fact Latakia itself is set in a fertile plain growing cotton, tobacco and a variety of fruits, as you are reminded by street corner stalls selling watermelons, cantaloupes, peaches, plums and apples.

Getting There

By air: at the moment, two flights a week, both on Friday, wear out the runway at Al-Basil International Airport (named for Hafez Assad's dead son): one from Cairo, the other from Damascus, both operated by Syrian Arab Airlines.

By train: the railway station is on the east side of town at Al-Yaman Square, about a kilometre east from Baghdad Street along Al-Quds (Jerusalem) Street. There are several trains daily between Latakia and Aleppo via Jisr al-Shugur, a journey well worth it for the beauty of the scenery. A line is intended between Latakia and Tartus.

By sea: depending on the season, and whether shipping companies think it is worth their while, there may be sailings between Latakia and Libya, Egypt, Cyprus, Turkey and Greece.

By long-distance coach: the new station for luxury Pullman coaches is just behind the railway station near Al-Yaman Square with services to Aleppo, Deir ez Zor, Hama, Homs and Damascus; also to Tripoli and Beirut in Lebanon.

By bus and microbus: old buses use the old bus station on Ramadan Street about 600m west of Jumhuriya Square and serve Aleppo, Tartus, Homs and Damascus. There are also several microbus stations in this general area: for Aleppo, Damascus and Beirut, close to the old bus station; for Haffeh (for Saône/Qalaat Saladin), Kassab and Jeble, in the area north of the Tourist Office, in al-Jalaa Street east of Assad stadium; to Baniyas, Tartus, Safita, Hama and Homs, just north off Jumhuriya Square. For Ugarit (Ras Shamra) via Blue Beach, the microbus station is in Antakiah Street just north off the western end of Ramadan Street at the Assad statue.

Tourist Information

The Tourist Office is on Ramadan Street, 350m west of Jumhuriya Square; open 8–6, closed Fridays.

Looking Around the City

The Phoenicians founded Latakia, but it became important only during Hellenistic and Roman times, Seleucus I Nicator (ruled 312–280 BC) favouring it with his mother's name, Laodicea, and establishing its street-grid still evident between the railway station at Al-Yaman Square on the east side of town and the old port to the west. It is at Al-Yaman Square that you can first take your bearings. One of the few more substantial survivals from classical times is a **Roman arch**, in fact a four-sided gateway, its position indicating the Roman cardo maximus or main

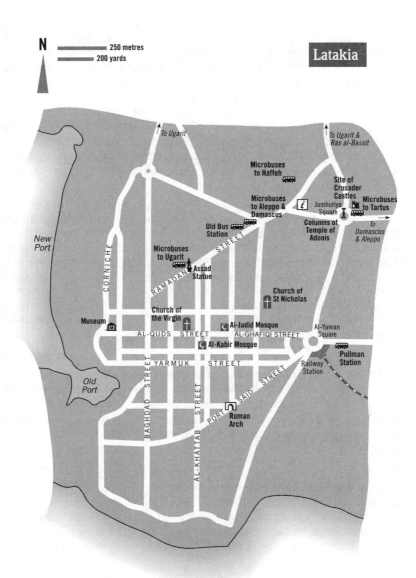

N

250 metres
200 yards

To Ugarit

To Ugarit &
Ras al-Bassit

Microbuses
to Haffeh

Site of
Crusader
Castles

Microbuses
to Aleppo &
Damascus

Jumhuriya
Square

Microbuses
to Tartus

Old Bus
Station

Columns of
Temple of
Adonis

To
Damascus
& Aleppo

New
Port

CORNICHE

RAMADAN STREET

Microbuses
to Ugarit

Assad
Statue

Church of
St Nicholas

Museum

Church of
the Virgin

Al-Jadid Mosque

Al-Yaman
Square

AL-QUDS STREET

AL-GHAFIQI STREET

Al-Kabir Mosque

Pullman
Station

YARMUK STREET

BAGHDAD STREET

Railway
Station

Old
Port

AL-KHATTAB STREET

PORT SAID STREET

Roman
Arch

north–south street. You find this in the south of the old town along Port Said (Bur Said) Street about 500m southwest from Al-Yaman Square. About 700m north of Al-Yaman Square, at the centre of the traffic whizzing round Jumhuriya Square, are four monolithic Corinthian columns, all that remain of a Roman **temple of Adonis**. Two Crusader castles stood upon the hill immediately to the east of Jumhuriya Square, but no trace of them survives.

Latakia was a lovely city in Crusader times, with many Byzantine churches and palaces, but when it fell to Saladin on 22 July 1188, the Muslim chronicler Imad al-Din, who was with the army, wept at its pillage and ruin. Though soon regained by the Franks, Qalaun took advantage of an earthquake to breach its defences in 1287. Walking west from Al-Yaman Square along Al-Ghafiqi Street, you come in about 500m to the 18th-century **Al-Jadid Mosque**, from where you can again take your bearings to visit a few other places of interest. The mosque stands on the corner of the cardo maximus, so that the Roman arch mentioned above is about 500m due south. One block up from Al-Ghafiqi Street (which farther east becomes Al-Quds Street) and parallel to it is Maisaloun Street; about 200m east along it is the Greek Orthodox **Church of St Nicholas**, possibly Byzantine, with a good collection of 17th- and 18th-century icons. Now going about 400m west along Maisaloun Street you come, amid the souk to the south, to the **Church of the Virgin**, also Greek Orthodox and possibly Byzantine, though its ornate marble iconostasis belongs to the 18th century.

Again from the Al-Jadid Mosque on Al-Ghafiqi Street, if you go one block south and then west about 150m you come to the 13th-century **Al-Kabir Mosque** or Great Mosque with a good façade. Finally, by following Al-Ghafiqi Street, which then becomes Al-Quds Street, all the way to its western end you arrive at the **museum** (*open daily 8–2, closed Tues; adm*), displaying artefacts from Ugarit and medieval armour, and itself housed in a 16th-century khan that has seen service as a tobacco exchange and residence of the governor of the Alawi state during the French Mandate.

Where to Stay

Latakia's luxury hotels are in the Blue Beach area, 6–10km north of town.

very expensive

★★★★★**Cote d'Azur de Cham Hotel**, on the Mediterranean, 8km north of downtown Latakia, ✆ (041) 428700, ✉ (041) 428285. The hotel is a self-contained resort with 600m of private sand beach with watersports facilities, swimming pool, tennis courts and mini-golf. All the rooms have kitchenettes, air conditioning, TV and video, and there are indoor and outdoor restaurants, a bar, disco and, on the beach, a snack bar. Despite the impressiveness of the set-up, there is a Third World haplessness about the place.

expensive

★★★★★**Le Meridien Lattaquie**, on the Mediterranean, 10km north of downtown Latakia, ✆ (041) 428736, ✉ (041) 428732. A strikingly designed resort hotel looking something like an Aztec pyramid with private sand beach, swimming pool, tennis courts, restaurants, bars and disco, its rooms air-conditioned and equipped with TV and video but not kitchenettes. The service is better here than at the Cote d'Azur, but not by much.

moderate

★★★★**Riviera Hotel**, Ramadan Street near the Tourist Office, ✆ (041) 421803, ✉ (041) 418287. A fairly new businessmen's hotel; the air-conditioned rooms have bath, TV and a fridge.

inexpensive

★★**Haroun Hotel**, on Jumhuriya Square at the northeast end of Ramadan Street, ✆ (041) 427140, ✉ (041) 418285. Not as cheerful as the Riviera but considerably cheaper, and the rooms still have bath, TV and fridge.

★★New Omar Khayam, ✆ (041) 228219, ✉ (041) 475252, on Al-Jalaa Street near Assad stadium, in the area north of the Tourist Office. Rooms with air conditioning, bath, TV, fridge; restaurant and rooftop terrace. Recommended over the Haroun.

★★Al Gondoul, ✆ (041) 477681, on the corniche (Jamal Abdul Nasser Street) with views overlooking the port and a terrace restaurant. Rooms with shower, balconies, some with air conditioning.

cheap

★Latakia, ✆ (041) 479527, Arwad Street, just north off Ramadan Street at the Assad statue. The best in its category. A variety of rooms available, some with balcony and bath, all clean. Friendly and helpful manager.

Latakia's cheapest hotels cluster about the western end of Ramadan Street in the vicinity of the Assad statue and especially in the area just north of the mosque. The Latakia (above) is the best of these, otherwise they are much of a dim muchness.

Eating Out

Apart from the usual run of downtown or resort hotel restaurants, try the **Plaza**, on the corniche just north of the museum, an attractive moderately priced restaurant serving a good range of Western, Arab and seafood dishes. Evenings only, from 8pm.

Ugarit (Ras Shamra)

Ras Shamra, meaning Cape Fennel in Arabic, is 14km north of Latakia, though almost as soon as excavations began in 1929 the site reclaimed its ancient name, being recognised as Ugarit, the great trading city so often mentioned on the clay tablets of the foreign office archives discovered earlier at Amarna, the 14th-century BC capital of the Egyptian Pharaoh Akhenaton. Except during the Second World War, the French excavations have been continuous, yet Ugarit is of such considerable extent that only a quarter of the whole has been revealed. Its artefacts have been removed to the National Museum at Damascus and the Louvre at Paris, but that does not lessen the fascination of walking about its silent streets, exploring a city of stone-built palaces, temples and houses possessing almost the intimacy of Pompeii and nearly twice as old.

Getting There

Microbuses depart from the Antakiah Street station north off Ramadan Street near the Assad statue.

History

Artefacts removed from the very base of the *tell* show that the site was already settled in the 7th millennium BC, during the Neolithic period. In the early Bronze Age, 4000 years later, Ugarit was supplying metalless Mesopotamia with copper from Cyprus. At about 2000 BC Ugarit was occupied by Canaanites, whom the Greeks later called Phoenicians, a Semitic people who are presumed to have migrated to the coast from Arabia via Mesopotamia. For the next few hundred years the city flourished under a local dynasty which controlled the coast between Jeble up to the present-day Turkish border, a sufficiently fertile region that agricultural produce was an important export and timber was shipped to treeless Egypt, while most importantly the manufacture of bronze became a speciality.

From the 16th century BC Ugarit's prosperity greatly increased as it traded with, while at the same time fended off the attentions of, the burgeoning empires of New Kingdom Egypt to the south and the Mitanni and later the Hittites to the north. Despite large-scale destruction caused by a tidal wave in the mid-14th century BC, the city recovered and enjoyed renewed wealth, the remains of palaces, temples and dwellings that you see today dating from this golden age of the late 14th century to the early 13th century BC. This was also the moment when the alphabet first appeared at Ugarit, probably introduced from Sinai, where a 30-character version was employed by uneducated turquoise miners for whom hieroglyphics proved too complicated, an ironic beginning for the most revolutionary and expressive of mankind's inventions. Not that Ugarit produced a nest of litterati: the alphabet's functional simplicity appealed to the tradesman's mind and it was used for inventories and tax assessments and found its way into more imaginative use only when it was adopted for religious texts (those found at Ugarit exhibiting close parallels with the Book of Job and the Psalms). Meanwhile, diplomatic correspondence, such as that found at Amarna, continued in Babylonian syllabic cuneiform, where tablets record appeals from Ugarit to the Egyptian Pharaoh Akhenaton to appease the encroaching Hittites with gifts—a threat the Egyptians would soon seek to counter instead by force of arms at Kadesh (*see* p.134).

During the 13th century BC, Ugarit's trading links with the Aegean increased and with its exports passed also the alphabet to Greece (*alpha* and *beta* being of course the first two letters of the Greek alphabet). Not a moment too soon: around 1200 BC Ugarit was overwhelmed by the Sea Peoples, its centrally regulated palace-based economy destroyed and replaced afterwards by a humbler village-based economy lacking the concentration of wealth and the technological means to make a mark in the new Iron Age world. A last message has been found from the king of Ugarit to the king of Cyprus: 'Ships of the enemy have come, some of my towns have been burned and they have done wicked things in our country. All my troops are deployed in Hittite territory, and all my ships are standing off the Lycian coast, so the country is at the mercy of the enemy. Seven enemy ships have appeared offshore and have done evil things. If there are more hostile ships on the way, please inform me and of what kind.' The letter was still in the oven waiting to be baked when Ugarit was burned.

Looking Around the Town

Perhaps the most enjoyable thing to do at first is simply to walk and clamber about, along paved streets and atop solid stone walls, noticing door jambs and grinding stones, surprising lizards basking in the sun and watching brilliantly coloured frogs hopping about the palace. You need to look out for mottled vipers lurking amid the grass and flowers on uncleared ground, but the frogs confine themselves to the excavations, as though only the palace is really good enough for them, pressing their bellies against the warmth of stone and not having to worry about the snakes. Meanwhile you are getting a sense of the disposition, running roughly west to east, of the royal quarters, the residential area, the acropolis, the commercial district, piecing the city together before exploring it in greater detail.

The site is a large *tell*, a mound of earth and debris and successive layers of ruins that has accumulated over the millennia, and here and there it has been cut down to reveal the

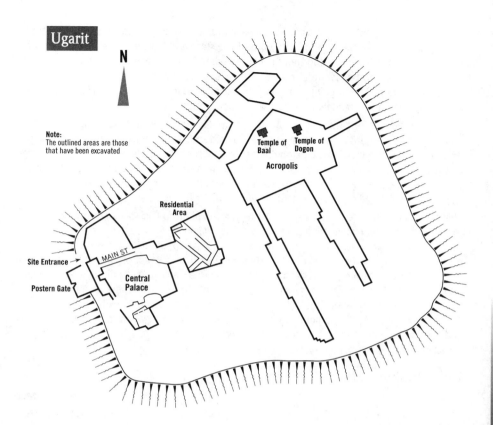

Ugarit

Note:
The outlined areas are those that have been excavated

Temple of Baal
Temple of Dogon

Acropolis

Residential Area

Site Entrance →

MAIN ST

Central Palace

Postern Gate

13th-century BC level. The present-day **site entrance** is on the west, where there is a ticket office, the main street of the city stretching away ahead of you towards the east.

But instead of entering here, look off to your right (south), where you will see a sloping stone **wall**, a thick talus that was part of the city's western defences, which is pierced by a graceful beehive-shaped 15th-century **postern gate** of massive hewn stones, beautifully fitted together. This is flanked on its north by what must have been a sizeable **tower**, judging from the 5m-thick walls at its base. The postern gave on to the palace quarter, which lies just within. Passing through the postern from outside the west walls, the ancient entrance crooks to the left, takes you up a flight of steps and turns right, so that you are by the ticket entrance and are again facing the main street of the city running east.

So standing by the ticket office at this western entrance to Ugarit and looking along the east-ward-running **main street**, you see on your right (south) the **central palace** (there are subsidiary palaces to the north of the main street and to the south of the central palace), which you enter over flagstones between two column bases. Turning right (south), you come to the **main courtyard,** with evidence of runnels in the paving by which water was distrib-uted throughout the complex. The area covered by the palace is immense, nearly 10,000 square metres covered by 90 rooms arranged around five large courtyards, and having as well an interior garden and 12 staircases. The royal apartments were probably on an upper storey, now gone; but in addition, the palace housed the state archives with the facilities also for making its own clay tablets and had to accommodate an extensive civil service, as well as have storerooms and workshops for royal craftsmen—it was in fact a self-contained administrative institution. The large open area at the far (east) end of the palace was the **garden**, once equipped with verandahs, pavilions and ivory furniture.

If you now return to the main street, lined with well-laid stone walls, and walk east along it, you come to what must have been a wealthy **residential area** with a number of spacious dwellings, though built of smaller stone blocks than at the palace, these held in place by large blocks at door jambs and corners. You may notice an oven at one, a water trough at another, while in several there are grinding stones. A number of these houses contain sepulchral cellar vaults with well-fitted stone lids—it would appear that generation lived upon generation.

Northwards beyond the residential area is the highest point in Ugarit, its **acropolis**, reached from the main street by following the path that runs diagonally left across unexcavated ground. As you are about to climb the acropolis you see, to the right of the path, a broad and extremely deep trench, dug by the excavators to explore more ancient strata of Ugarit's past. On the northwest part of the acropolis is the **Temple of Baal**, the Canaanite god of the heavens, while on the southeast part of the acropolis is the **Temple of Dogon**, god of the underworld. From the top of the acropolis you can look out southwards over the **commercial quarter**, while 1.5km northwards lay the harbour, 'a lovely little bay of deep-blue water framed in white sand and low white rocks', wrote Agatha Christie, who spent Christmas here in 1938 with her archaeologist husband Max Mallowan. This is now a military area and off-limits.

Ras al-Bassit

Getting There

There are occasional microbuses from Latakia and more frequent ones to Kassab, a mountain village 25km to the northeast, right on the Turkish border, from where you will have to take a taxi down the tortuous road to Ras al-Bassit.

From Kassab you can walk across the border and get a dolmuş (a Turkish service taxi) to Antakya (Antioch).

Close to the Turkish border and 55km north of Latakia, the half-moon bay and black sand beach of Ras al-Bassit has been developed as a resort. Though the waters are clear and the surrounding scenery magnificent (just into Turkey rises 1728m Jebel al-Aqra, the Mount Casius of antiquity, sacred to the Phoenicians and climbed by the emperors Hadrian and Julian the Apostate to worship Zeus), it becomes terribly crowded in summer, is becoming uglier with concrete every year and is well into acquiring a bloom of rubbish.

Returning to the main road and continuing north takes you over the border into Turkey and down into Antioch (Antakya) on the lower reaches of the Orontes.

Where to Stay

At Ras al-Bassit there are beach bungalows to rent in summer, while at Kassab in the mountains above there are several decent inexpensive hotels.

The citadel

Aleppo

Getting There	205
Getting Around	207
Tourist Information	207
The Aleppo Museum	209
Khan al-Gumruk	211
The Great Mosque	212
The Citadel	214
The Jdeide Quarter	217
Where to Stay	219
Eating Out	222

Aleppo does not abound like Damascus in ancient and beautiful monuments; but surpasses it in bigness, trade and consequently in wealth, which advantages have rendered it one of the most famous cities of the Turkish Empire.

The Arabs call this city Haleb, which they say signifies milk or milking. To account for this etymology they pretend that when Abraham passed through Syria, in his way from Harran to Canaan, he was very liberal in bestowing the milk of his cattle on the poor of those quarters.

The city is of an oval figure, about three miles in compass, but neither its walls nor towers appear to be of any great defence. The entrance is by ten gates, some of which are very handsome . . . . The houses make no great appearance on the outside, but those belonging to the richer sort are adorned on the inside with paintings, gildings and marble. The handsomest of all the mosques was formerly a church, supposed to be built by St Helena. The number of Catholics is great here, although the Mohammedan be the established religion.

John Green, A Journey from Aleppo to Damascus, 1736.

The northern plains are treeless and featureless, the start of that great flatness reaching eastwards into Mesopotamia. In summer they burn; in winter they can be sharply cold. There is a feeling of vacancy, of primitiveness, and then quite suddenly you fall upon Aleppo, hidden in a bowl. The city has been likened to a saucer with the Citadel mound rising at its centre like an upturned teacup. The observation is quaint, and was made of course by an Englishwoman, Gertrude Bell, but arriving off the plains the sensation is an Alice in Wonderland one, the city and its parks in a hollow below you as you wind your way down from the rim.

Except to fill up a hole in the landscape, Aleppo at first sight does not impress you with a reason for being, yet it vies with Damascus for being the oldest continuously inhabited city in the world. But while Damascus is immediately dramatic, a place where the mountains meet the desert, its oasis the natural terminus between two worlds, Aleppo is a sunken crossroads, a hidden shelter, in the midst of a lonely plain. Not being a goal in its own right, Aleppo's prosperity has always depended on commercial effort, giving rise to the Damascenes' jibe that the Aleppans are bourgeois and have no sense of style, to which the Aleppans retort that they are men, the Damascenes women and lazy.

Periodically, Aleppo (Halab) has attracted people of enterprise who have left their mark on the city. The Venetians opened a trade counter here in the 13th century and were joined by the French and English in the 16th century ('Her husband's to Aleppo gone', writes Shakespeare in *Macbeth*, I, iii, 7) and in the following century by the Dutch. Many Armenians settled here even before the First World War when they fled the Turkish massacres in their tens of thousands, making Armenian the second language of the city, both spoken and written up on shop fronts.

But enterprise has not always been enough. Aleppo's outlets to the Mediterranean lie some way off, at Latakia and at Antioch (Antakya) and Alexandretta (Iskenderun), these last two in some measure severed from it in 1939 when the French gave the Hatay to Turkey. The Euphrates trade has not been constant either, as the careers of Palmyra to the southeast and Cyrrhus to the northwest have shown, while nowadays the closed border with Iraq has also hurt Aleppo's traffic. Even in 1736 John Green was writing, 'The great trade for all sorts of merchandises brought hither from Persia and the Indies makes the place very populous; but that trade is observed to decline, since the way to the Indies by sea has been found out by the Europeans, who prefer it to that by the Euphrates and Tigris.' Vulnerable to the vicissitudes of history, the city has more often been of secondary importance, as it is today after Damascus.

Today there is a stale whiff of cosmopolitanism about Aleppo. It lingers at the Baron Hotel whose doors once opened onto a wider world. Apart from the society of Armenians and other minority Christians—the Maronites, the Greek Orthodox, the Greek and Syrian Catholics—a lugubrious uniformity and narrow insularity pervades the town, whose majority Muslim population is far more conservative than that of Damascus.

But there is charm in Aleppo's souk area where an atmosphere of the Middle Ages survives. It is not roofed over in tacky corrugated tin as at Damascus but limestone-vaulted, its passages totalling over 30km in length, making it the largest covered bazaar in the Middle East, where the dust of spices floats on the gloomy submarine light.

History

The recorded history of Aleppo goes back to the early 2nd millennium BC when it appears in the Hittite archives in central Anatolia and those of Mari on the Euphrates. In the middle centuries of that millennium the Amorite kingdom of Yamkhad with its capital Halap, as Aleppo was called, became the focus for Hittite ambitions towards Mesopotamia which culminated in their overthrow of the Amorite dynasty at Babylon in 1595 BC. In the centuries that followed, the Hittites and Egyptians fought to establish their spheres of influence in Syria, the Hittites eventually confirming their rule over most of the country at the battle of Kadesh (see p.134) against Ramses II in 1275 or 1274 BC. Within two centuries, however, the invasion of the Sea Peoples saw the destruction of the Hittite Empire, whose cultural influence in northern Syria nevertheless survived in the form of a series of small Neo-Hittite states, of which Aleppo was one. Reminders of this period are those repulsive black statues on display in the city's museum.

From the 8th to the 4th centuries BC the Assyrians and then the Persians dominated northern Syria. In 333 BC the arrival of Alexander the Great marked the beginning of Greek rule which continued for nearly 300 years in the form of the Seleucid Empire. During this time, Aleppo, given the Macedonian place-name of Beroia, was an important trading city on the route between the Euphrates and Antioch and was given a typically Hellenistic grid plan based on the 5th-century BC ideas of Hippodamus of Miletus (see p.83) which can be detected as you wander about parts of the old city today.

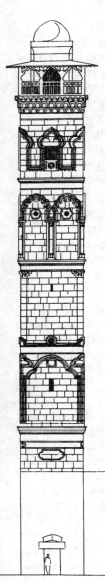

In 64 BC Pompey brought Syria under Roman control which continued in transmuted form under the Byzantines at Constantinople until Aleppo fell to the Arabs in AD 637. Of Roman Aleppo, however, only a few recycled blocks remain, while the principal Byzantine monument is the much battered and amputated cathedral, said to have been founded in the early 4th century by St Helena, mother of Constantine the Great, now a madrasa. Yet these 700 years of Roman and Byzantine rule were for the most part an era of security and great prosperity for northern Syria, as witnessed by the remarkable development of the marginal limestone highlands in the north-west of the country (*see* **The Northern Highlands**, p.223), which depended on the markets of Aleppo as well as of Antioch for the export of olive oil. But with the shift in the trade routes southwards through Palmyra and north through Cyrrhus, Aleppo declined commercially and its principal function was as a military station inside the Euphrates frontier.

The city declined further after it surrendered to the Arabs in 637. Its ancient name was revived in the form of Halab, by which it is still known in Arabic, but to the Umayyads in Damascus and later the Abbasids in Baghdad, Aleppo was only of secondary importance. However, in the 10th century Aleppo's peripheral position was turned to good account when it became virtually independent under the Hamdanid dynasty, Arab refugees from Iraq. On the basis of the flourishing trade which they took care to direct through their city, they established a prosperous court that was celebrated for its liberal outlook and cultural brilliance. But it was a brief moment, for in 962, during the Byzantine reconquest of northern Syria, the Hamdanids were overthrown and the city was sacked. The one outstanding survival from the Arab period is Aleppo's Great Mosque of the Umayyads, later much altered by the Mamelukes.

During the next two centuries Aleppo became a focal point in the struggle between Christendom and Islam. In 1023 it fell to the Mirdasids, a Bedouin people, and then in 1070 was conquered by the more ambitious Seljuk Turks, who a year later defeated the Byzantine imperial army at Manzikert in eastern Anatolia. Turkish tribes were soon ravaging the whole of Anatolia as far west as the Aegean and, faced with this threat to its very existence the Byzantine Empire appealed to the West for help. The response came in the form of the First Crusade, whose soldiers encircled Aleppo in 1098 and, though failing to take it, crippled its trade with the coast. In 1124 the Crusaders again laid siege to the city and it was saved only by a Seljuk force from Mosul in Iraq. Among these was Zengi, who with his son and successor Nur al-Din rebuilt the city's defences and established its first Sunni madrasas in their determination to make Aleppo a centre of military resistance against the Christians and a stronghold of spiritual orthodoxy against such heterodox Muslims as the Ismaeli Assassins who now withdrew to the coastal mountains.

The Muslim cause was dramatically advanced by Saladin, who succeeded Nur al-Din in 1176. Within a decade Saladin had united the entire Muslim world from Cairo to Baghdad, while in

1187 he recaptured Jerusalem from the Crusaders. At his death in 1193, Saladin's Ayyubid dynasty was perpetuated at Aleppo by his son al-Zaher Ghazi, who became governor of the city. Ghazi continued to refortify Aleppo while renewing its prosperity, circumventing the Crusader-controlled ports by initiating trading relations with Venice, so that Aleppo enjoyed a political and cultural renaissance that lasted until the Mongol invasion of 1260. To Ghazi is owed much of the Citadel in its present form and the loveliest of Aleppo's mosques and madrasas, the Faradis Madrasa in the southern quarter.

Though the Egyptian-based Mamelukes saved Syria from Mongol domination, for the next 75 years east–west trade was diverted northwards, passing through Mongol lands to the Black Sea and so to Constantinople, leaving Aleppo a commercial desert. But when the Mongol Empire broke up into several parts, and one of these, the Ilkhanate, which controlled Iran and Iraq, converted to Islam and made peace with the Mamelukes, trade again flowed through Aleppo. It is to the late Mameluke period during the 15th and early 16th centuries, and to the Ottoman period from 1516, that Aleppo's great khans belong, the city's fortunes owing much to Jews expelled from Spain by the Christian Reconquista in 1492, for it was largely they who financed the caravan trade. Aleppo's population at this time exceeded that of Damascus, but trade and population diminished through the 18th century as Europe abandoned its dependence on the overland trade routes through the Middle East in favour of its sea routes to India and China.

Aleppo's population and economic activity rose again with the influx of Armenian refugees from Turkish genocide during the First World War, but the old patterns of trade between Anatolia and Mesopotamia, first recorded in archive tablets 4000 years ago, have been interrupted, as in 1939 when France, then the colonial power in Syria, ceded the Hatay and with it Aleppo's natural Mediterranean outlet, Antioch, to Turkey, and in 1982 when the border with Iraq was closed. Meanwhile Damascus has enjoyed all the benefits and much of the spoilation of being the nation's capital, leaving Aleppo more in touch with its medieval past.

Getting There

By air: in addition to Syrian Arab Airlines' daily flights between Aleppo and Damascus, Aleppo's airport also handles international flights serving the Middle East and Turkey, but flights between here and Europe are few. Most **airline offices** are on or immediately off Baron Street, for example Air France, BA, KLM, Alitalia, Lufthansa, Gulf Air, THY Turkish Airlines and Syrian Arab Airlines. Most **travel agencies** are also found on or close by Baron Street.

By train: the railway station (Baghdad station) is at the northwest of the city, just north of the public park flanking Al-Jabri Street, which at its southern end runs parallel to and west of Baron Street. From Baron Street the railway station is 1km. Aleppo is linked by daily rail services to the Euphrates valley, the Gezira, Latakia, Homs and Damascus, and there is also a weekly service to Turkey, calling at Iskenderun, Adana, Tarsus, Konya, Ankara and Istanbul, normally taking about 36hrs in all.

If there is one railway journey worth making in Syria it is that between Aleppo and Latakia. The line winds its way through beautiful mountain scenery and across high bridges spanning dramatic gorges and is far more interesting than travelling by road.

First-class bookings on all services should be made at least a day in advance.

By long-distance bus: the Karnak bus office is on Baron Street, just south and across from the Baron Hotel. The Karnak bus station for destinations throughout Syria is behind, on Al-Walid Street. The station for buses for Turkey and Lebanon is on the south side of the same block, on Al-Maari Street. Luxury buses and ordinary buses have stations immediately south of Ibrahim Hanano Street (south of the Aleppo Museum) for destinations throughout the country. The station for Aleppo's city buses is also here. There is yet another station on the east side of the city where ordinary buses and microbuses serve points east of Aleppo, e.g. Raqqa and Deir ez Zor, but such a nuisance to get to that you are better off taking a Karnak bus or luxury coach from the centre of town. If you find yourself arriving at the east bus/microbus station, it is a 3km walk or city bus or taxi ride to the centre.

By microbus and service taxi: apart from the microbus station on the east side of the city serving destinations to the east, e.g. Raqqa and Deir ez Zor (*see* above), there is a microbus station by the bus stations south of Ibrahim Hanano Street serving points northwest of Aleppo, e.g. to Daret Aazah, which is as close as you can get (6km) to Saint Simeon (Qalaat Samaan). Also service taxis from here cover the country and go to Beirut as well.

Orientation and Itinerary

Though the history of Aleppo reaches back to the earliest millennia of urban settlement, next to nothing of its more distant past survives except in the Graeco-Roman grid of its principal streets, overlaid now within its walls by what is essentially a medieval city. It is in this **old city** and in the **Jdeide quarter** to the north, the 'new' quarter of late Mameluke times, largely settled by Christians, both Armenian and Maronite, that almost everything of interest lies.

Of course the city has extended well beyond these limits, and it is from the west of the old city, now Aleppo's **downtown area**, that you can most conveniently begin your tour, which is best done on foot. The **Baron Hotel** is here, a landmark in its own right, on **Baron Street** which runs from north to south, where there are numerous travel agencies and airline and car hire offices. A short walk from the hotel, at the south end of Baron Street, you come on the west to a park, where the **tourist office** is, and on the east the **Aleppo Museum**. Follow the crossroads here east towards **Bab al-Faraj Square**, unmistakable for the large clocktower in the midst of it, built by the Ottomans in 1899. Just before the square turn hard right into Al-Kalleseh Street, which takes you south along the old city walls to **Bab Antaki**, the Antioch Gate.

Bab Antaki is one of the main gates into the old city. From it, **Souk al-Attarine Street** runs straight eastwards through the **souks**, past the **Khan al-Gumruk** to the south and the **Great Mosque** and other khans to the north, and in about 800m brings you to the **Citadel**, from where you can reach the southern quarter.

One way of reaching the **Jdeide quarter**, which lies north of the old city, is to make for **Bab al-Faraj Square** with its clocktower and from there head north for 150m or so, crossing Al-Khandak Street, the eastward extension of Al-Quwatli Street. The quarter lies beyond, to the northeast. You could also strike north from the Great Mosque.

Getting Around

On foot: walking is the most convenient way of getting around downtown Aleppo, the Old City and the Christian quarter to its north.

By bus: the local city bus station is towards the south end of Baron Street, that is south of the Tourist Office and the Aleppo Museum and immediately south of Ibrahim Hanano Street. The city buses, however, are unlikely to be of convenient use to the visitor: better to walk or take a taxi.

By taxi: taxis are cheap but hardly necessary unless you get tired or are staying in a hotel away from the Baron Street downtown area.

By car with driver: this amounts to coming to an arrangement with a taxi driver for a half day or day and is a good way of visiting places like Qalaat Samaan (*see* p.229). Your hotel can make the arrangements for you.

Car hire: there are car hire agencies along Baron Street (*see* p.4 for general advice). For Europcar, contact their desk at the Pullman Shahba Hotel in the west of the city, ✆ (021) 667200.

Tourist Information

The Tourist Office is in the gardens at the intersection of Baron Street and Al-Maari Street, opposite the Aleppo Museum, and is in theory open daily from 9am to 2pm, closed Fridays. You will not be rewarded, however, if you actually find it open: they have little information to impart and provide only a very poor map of the city.

communications

The **Central Post Office**, open daily 8–5, is at the conjunction of Al-Jalaa and Ibn Khaldoun streets at Al-Quwatli Street. Letters and parcels (for procedure, *see* 'Communications', Damascus, p.53) can be sent from here, and you can receive letters sent to you here addressed as follows: Your name, Syria, Aleppo, Poste Restante.

The Central Post Office is also the place from which to make **long-distance phone calls** and send **faxes**. This section stays open until 10pm. Bring your passport (*see* 'Communications', Damascus, p.53). Phone cards are also sold here, and there are phone-card telephones outside the building.

With greater efficiency and at hardly greater cost, you can also make international phone calls and send faxes from DHL (open 9.30am–11pm), whose office is just south of Al-Quwatli Street in the street parallel to and immediately east of Baron Street, where of course you can use their courier service too.

health and emergencies

For minor ailments, seek advice and medication from a pharmacist. Otherwise ask your hotel to recommend a doctor or hospital, or to put you in touch with the police. The Aleppo University Hospital, ✆ (021) 236120, is in the western part of the city opposite the Pullman Shahba Hotel.

The Emergency Police Station (announced in English and with red police cars parked outside) is on the northeast corner of the intersection of Al-Quwatli/Al-Khandak and Al-Tilel streets near the Christian quarter, 250m north of the clocktower square. In an emergency: police, ✆ 112; ambulance, ✆ 110; fire, ✆ 113; traffic police, ✆ 115.

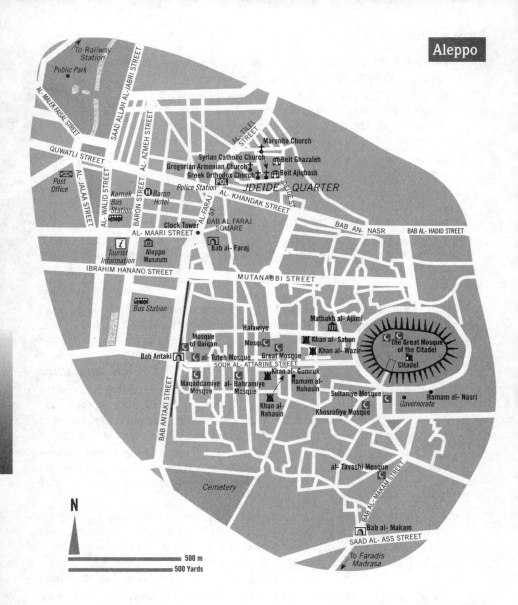

maps and publications

The Tourist Office at the southwest corner of the intersection of Baron and Al-Maari streets might have a free but rather poor map of Aleppo. You will be better off buying one of those maps of Syria, which include maps of Damascus, Aleppo and Palmyra, at the bookshop of one of the top hotels.

The Commercial Bank of Syria on Baron Street north of Al-Quwatli Street and on Mutanabbi Street east of Bab Antaki Street will change both foreign currency and travellers cheques, as will the branches at the top hotels. At other branches of the bank and at the exchange kiosk at the intersection of Al-Quwatli/Al-Khandak and Al-Faraj streets you can change cash only.

The Aleppo Museum

Open daily 9–4, closed Tues; adm.

The museum, a modern building, is at the south end of Baron Street. Most exhibits are labelled in English and Arabic, some in French and Arabic. Exhibits do get changed about and at various times some rooms will be empty, making it impossible to offer a proper room-by-room description (there is a guide book on sale at the entrance). In theory, its chronological sequence is followed by moving in a counterclockwise direction indicated by arrows. The museum is arranged as a hollow square of two storeys round a central courtyard. All historical periods are contained within the museum, though the emphasis is on Iron Age and classical material, and there is a good Islamic collection. The modern art gallery is for the most part a joke.

At the **main entrance** to the museum are portions of a temple gateway and several statues carved from basalt, such as the ludicrous female sphinx with popping white eyes. These are from **Tell Halaf**, an Iron Age Neo-Hittite settlement in the Gezira, and date from the 9th century BC. There are further statues from Tell Halaf inside the museum.

On the **ground floor**, the first hall contains exhibits from the Bronze Age site of **Mari** on the Euphrates, including a bronze guard lion of the 18th century BC in pronounced Babylonian style, a statue of King Lamgi-Mari in case 2, several larger statues including a remarkable one of a spring goddess holding a vase, and a sampling of cuneiform tablets found in the palace archives. Also in this room are discoveries made by Max Mallowan, Agatha Christie's husband, in the late 1930s at the Gezira Bronze Age site of **Tell Brak**, including votive offerings from the Eye Temple.

After this is a room containing various Bronze Age objects from **Hama** and **Ugarit**, including Mycenaean and Cypriot pottery and Twelfth Dynasty Middle Kingdom Egyptian or Egyptian-style figures.

Beyond this is a hall running along the rear of the building devoted to various Iron Age sites, including **Tell Arslan Tash** and **Tell Hajib** in the Gezira and **Tell Ahmar** on the Euphrates close to the Turkish border. But best—because worst—of all are the 9th-century Neo-Hittite statues from Tell Halaf, west of Haseke in the Gezira. Like the statues at the museum entrance, these are great basalt things, all of them heavy, squat, ugly and stupid-looking. The style derives from the Assyrian but is crudely executed; instead of achieving monumentality, it achieves only moronitude. Hadad, Ishtar and female sphinxes, the whites of their eyes painted in with large black spots for their irises, each have a comic-book look, of idiocy usually, a glum idiocy—Iron Age Cabbage Patch dolls.

Turning the corner, you enter another hall, this one running along another side of the building. The objects here are from **Aleppo**, **Ebla**, **Ain Dara** and elsewhere. There are beautiful impressions from cylinder seals showing court scenes and wild animals dancing.

Going upstairs you pass a **mezzanine** with nothing in it and then come to the **first floor**, in part devoted to photographs and jetsam from various **recent foreign expeditions** at northern Syrian sites. A gallery of **modern art** is also up here, a laughable exercise apart from the work of Fathi Muhammed.

Another hall is devoted to **Greek**, **Roman** and **Byzantine** objects from such sites as **Palmyra**, including coins and mosaics and best of all some graceful Byzantine glassware.

The final hall contains the **Islamic Arts Museum**. There is some very fine pottery and faience, lovely glassware (better than the Byzantine), an astrolabe of the 12th or 13th century, illuminated Korans, coins and a scale model of Aleppo. Apart from the amusement value of the dopey Neo-Hittite stuff downstairs, this is the most satisfying hall of the museum.

Bab Antaki

Bab Antaki, the Antioch Gate, set in the western wall of the old city and the only one still preserved, is an Ayyubid construction dating from the 13th century. Through an earlier gate here the Arabs entered Aleppo in AD 637, while in Roman times a triumphal arch is thought to have stood on this spot. What was perhaps once a guardroom in the gate is now a workshop for smiths who summer and winter sweat like Beelzebubs round a blazing forge making pots and metal implements. Even in summer, when their work is terrifically hot, they ignore the jangle of the waterseller's cups, preferring their own jugs of warm water, explaining that drinking cold water would make them ill.

Just in from the gate you see a street rising on the left (north), and this runs along the **ramparts** from where there are good views over the northwest corner of the city. You are in fact standing upon the mound of an ancient village incorporated by the Hellenistic Greeks into Beroia, their name for Aleppo. There are some interesting **doorways** along this rampart street, some wooden and studded with iron bolts, others painted with Mecca pilgrimage scenes. At 50m on your right (east) is the small Mameluke **mosque of Qaiqan**, the mosque of the crows.

Into Souk al-Attarine Street

Starting again from Bab Antaki, a winding passage leads eastwards into the souks. At first, as you pass shops selling metal goods, the way is uncovered; then where it is roofed over with corrugated galvanised tin the wares are mostly cloth; and finally where you pass under stone vaultings the market becomes more various, and there are confectioners, grocers, butchers, spice stalls and little eating places, and the thoroughfare is full of donkeys.

At about 20m in from the gate, where the street straightens out, **Souk al-Attarine Street** follows the route of the decumanus and continues dead east to the Citadel. Just at this point is the **Al-Tuteh Mosque** on your left (north). This Ayyubid mosque of the mulberry tree bears a fine 12th-century Kufic inscription and is in part built of blocks from the Roman triumphal arch that stood at Bab Antaki. An earlier 7th-century mosque on this site is thought to have been built to commemorate the taking of the city and was the first in Aleppo.

As you walk eastwards along Souk al-Attarine Street, you notice a series of straight streets intersecting from the south, obvious reminders of the original grid plan of Hellenistic Beroia. About 150m east of the Al-Tuteh mosque you come to a series of Islamic buildings off to the south. The first, set back 50m, is the **Madrasa Maqaddamiye**, the oldest theological school in Aleppo, formerly a church. A bit farther along, on Souk al-Attarine itself, is the 16th-century Turkish **Al-Bahramiye Mosque** with a tall minaret, while behind this to the south is the ruinous **Maristan Nuri**, a hospital founded by Nur al-Din in the mid-12th century.

Khan al-Gumruk

About 400m east from Bab Antaki (and halfway to the Citadel) a high dome over Souk al-Attarine marks the entrance to the **Khan al-Gumruk** which extends to your right (south), the largest khan in Aleppo and one of the finest. Built in 1574, it still houses well over 300 shops, many arranged round its central court. Khan al-Gumruk means customs house, *gumruk* passing into Turkish and Arabic from the Greek *emporikós*, meaning commercial, from *emporía*, meaning traffic, trade, commerce or business—the origin of our word emporium. Here duties were once imposed on imported and exported goods, and here the French, English and Dutch had their banking houses and consulates.

The English Factory

With the founding of the Levant Company by Queen Elizabeth I in 1581, the English opened their main Syrian trade counter at Aleppo, the depot for Persian silks and the terminus of the annual caravan from Basra on the Shatt al-Arab. Aleppo was already the most important European market in Syria, the French having set up their trade counter here earlier in the century, while the Venetians had already done so in the 13th century, bypassing the Crusader ports. Within a century the English 'factory', as it was called, numbered about 50 merchants and was the most important in the city.

Profits could be enormous but were paid for by years of privation. The English and other nationalities were each compelled by the Turkish sultan to live in their own khan, as much for their safety against the sometimes violent prejudice of Muslims against unbelievers as anything else, and they were not permitted out at night. There round a central courtyard they kept their goods locked up below and had their living apartments upstairs. Relations with Muslim men were confined to business dealings and with Muslim women were non-existent. It was a bachelor life; 'our delights are among ourselves', wrote one 17th-century merchant, by this referring to the off-hours spent in the khan library or drinking, with occasional forays into the surrounding countryside for hunting and sometimes even games of cricket. Others might undertake the perilous pilgrimage to Jerusalem, as did Henry Maundrell, chaplain to the English merchants of Aleppo, in 1697. He and others also made various astronomical observations that helped towards the more accurate charting of Syria, while it was from Aleppo that the first Europeans set out to rediscover Palmyra, culminating in Robert Wood's marvellously recorded expedition of 1751.

The Aleppo trade went into decline during the 18th century and the English factory was closed in 1791.

Khan al-Nahasin

A few steps farther east and adjacent to the Khan al-Gumruk, the **Khan al-Nahasin**, which means khan of the coppersmiths, was in fact built in 1539 by the Venetians to protect their goods and house their consul. The entrance is round the east side. A tree grows in the courtyard, across which, on the south side, is the **oldest continuously inhabited house in Aleppo**, which thanks to Adolphe Poche, the lately deceased Belgian consul who lived there, has been maintained almost exactly as it was four centuries ago and is filled with antiques of old Aleppo as well as archaeological treasures from around Syria. When the Venetian Republic fell to Napoleon at the end of the 18th century, Adolphe Poche's greatgrandfather, the Austrian director of a trading company, married the last Venetian consul's daughter. Adolphe Poche was born in the house in 1895 and as well as becoming Belgian consul in 1939 was also a doctor, scholar, historian and archaeologist. Now to gain admission to the 16-room house you will have to apply to the present Belgian Consulate in the Khan al-Kattin, immediately south of the Khan al-Wazir (*see* p.214).

Opposite the east entrance to the khan is the **Hamam al-Nahasin**. Beneath its modern accretions and still open to the great unwashed is a 12th- or 13th-century baths.

Past the Khan al-Gumruk, Souk al-Attarine Street is given over to cloth and gowns with tailors at work in the passages behind to the south, while off to the north are the gold souks. Towards the eastern end, just before you emerge at the Citadel, are sheepskins and tent trappings. From the Khan al-Gumruk it is a 100m walk north to the west entrance of the Great Mosque.

The Great Mosque

There are four entrances to the mosque, those on the south and east sides leading directly from the souks, that on the north side (with a cupola and fine Mameluke stalactite carvings) from a large square, while non-Muslims must enter through the west entrance. This **visitors' entrance** is near the northwest corner of the mosque and close by the large square in which rises, entirely detached from the mosque, an enormous four-sided **minaret**, 45m high. It looks like something that might have been raised outside a Victorian railway station, but it was built by the Seljuks in 1092. They had taken Aleppo in 1070 and their great victory over the Byzantines at Manzikert in eastern Anatolia in 1071 gave them control over the whole of Syria. The Seljuk advances into Syria and Anatolia were one reason why Pope Urban II preached the First Crusade at Clermont-Ferrand in 1095, and three years later the Crusaders were camped outside the walls of Aleppo, though they never succeeded in taking the city. The minaret is handsomely proportioned, none of its four sides decorated in quite the same way but each divided into four registers, the registers separated by finely carved Kufic inscriptions.

The **Great Mosque** stands on what had been the agora of the Hellenistic city, which in Christian times became the garden of the Cathedral of St Helena (*see* the Madrasa Halawiye below). Founded in about 715 by the Umayyad Caliph al-Walid I, who 10 years earlier had founded the Great Mosque at Damascus, the Aleppo mosque was completed by al-Walid's successor, Caliph Suleiman, in about 717. Similarities between the two mosques are evident, though the Aleppo mosque was rebuilt by Nur al-Din after a fire in 1169 and the Mamelukes made subsequent alterations. But the results have not been happy and Aleppo's Great Mosque possesses little of the grace and none of the aura of the Great Mosque in Damascus.

From the west entrance you step into a large **court**, the pillared **arcades** on three sides being Mameluke substitutions for the original colonnades as seen at Damascus. The pattern is echoed along the south side of the court by a series of arches in the **façade of the prayer hall**, though these have been closed by fretted partitions which, like everything else that has been painted here, have been painted 20 times too often, destroying any delicacy they might once have had. Otherwise, the façade is highly decorated with intricately cut and variously coloured stone, and this is especially true of the main door, a fine composition of inlaid basalt and carved white marble. The finely worked façade and the flanking arcades make a strong impression by daylight when the sun bounces off the white flagstones of the court, but the strips of green neon lights and bare white bulbs that illuminate the court at evening prayers make you feel the only thing missing are the funfair rides.

The **interior of the prayer hall** is long and shallow, its heavy piers and vaulting, again Mameluke additions, hung with absurd and nasty ballroom chandeliers. At the centre is a small dome, its squinches luridly decorated, while in the *qibla* wall the mihrab has been painted brown and is arched with neon strips. To the left of this through brass bars and murky glass, as though it were a large aquarium full of dead fish, is a reliquary draped in beautiful gold-embroidered cloth. In rivalry with Damascus, whose Great Mosque supposedly possesses the head of John the Baptist, this reliquary is said to contain the head of Zachariah, his father. The chamber is faced with fine tiles.

Cathedral of Saint Helena

Outside and opposite the west entrance of the Great Mosque there is a court surrounded on three sides with student cells. The west side, straight ahead of you, presents two liwans. The liwan on the right is glassed-in and is supported by a pair of classical columns with capitals. The capitals are too small for the columns and clearly do not belong to them. The liwan on the left is filled in with stone into which are set two doors and above them a window. A door between the liwans leads, if you find it open, into the **Halawiye Madrasa**, founded in 1124, but usually it is closed up and the general appearance of the place is one of neglect.

But then a sense of discovery steals upon you, for as you stand back in the court you see that the left liwan is surmounted by a low broad dome, unmistakably Greek in shape and set upon an octagonal drum whose sides are pierced by windows. If it is open, or by peeping through a crack in the left liwan door, you see that the drum is supported by handsome porphyry columns with richly carved Corinthian capitals, and you realise that this left liwan is a survival of the 6th-century Byzantine **Cathedral of St Helena**, named after the mother of the Emperor Constantine the Great, who made a pilgrimage to the Holy Land in 326. Though the Great Mosque had been built in its gardens, the church itself continued as a place of Christian worship until 1124 when a besieging Crusader army violated certain Islamic holy places outside the city walls and in retaliation Aleppo's Seljuk defenders converted this to use as a madrasa. The beautifully carved wooden mihrab, perhaps Egyptian work, inside the right liwan dates from 1245 when Nur al-Din further remodelled the building.

The cathedral-cum-madrasa is a simple and shabby place now and it speaks to you only in whispers, but the long and changing history of Aleppo that it relates will make it more appealing for some than anything else in the city.

Khan al-Sabun and Khan al-Wazir

There are two old caravanserais to visit 100m due east of the minaret of the Great Mosque. The first is the **Khan al-Sabun**, a Mameluke masterpiece of the late 15th or early 16th centuries decorated with fine floral and geometric stone carving both inside and out, though unfortunately much of the interior is taken up now by a warehouse which obstructs any general impression. Across a small square immediately east of the Khan al-Sabun is the 17th-century **Khan al-Wazir**. You enter from the west through a monumental gate of black and white *ablaq* and pass into a large court, well preserved except on the north side. On the north side of the square between the two khans is a small 12th-century palace, the **Matbakh al-Ajami**.

Khan al-Wazir

The Citadel

History

Though you smile at the assertion of early Arab writers that the mound is supported by a thousand columns, you are tempted to agree with the implication that so sudden a hill must be artificial. Debris has accumulated and the 55m-high mound has been shaped over time, but it is in fact a natural feature. At first its use was religious, the Neo-Hittites raising a temple upon it in the 10th century BC. Here also, goes the belief, Abraham paused to milk his cow. Not until the Seleucid period did it become a citadel. Thereafter for over a millennium its function is obscure, though there are cisterns thought to be Byzantine and the remains of a church now incorporated into a mosque.

The Hamdanid court was housed here during the 10th century and during the reign of Saladin's son Ghazi (1193–1215) it became both residence and fortress. The Citadel suffered from the Mongol onslaughts of 1260 and 1400, this last under Timur (Tamerlane), and had to be much rebuilt. But as 15th-century Aleppo had so grown that it entirely encircled the mound, the Citadel lost its effectiveness as a defensive bastion, and the Mamelukes instead concentrated their works on building state apartments.

The present complex, therefore, dates from several periods, though essentially what you see is Ghazi's work: the encircling moat, the paved *glacis* and the monumental gate.

Visiting the Citadel

Open daily 9–6 in summer, 9–4 in winter, closed Tues; adm. The entrance to the Citadel is on the south side of its mound.

The **sole entrance** to the Citadel is on the south through an outer tower, originally 13th-century but rebuilt by the Mamelukes early in the 16th century. This defended the rising stone-arched **bridge** (originally a drawbridge) spanning the 22m-deep **moat**, dry but once capable of being filled with water. Once across this, you ascend a **stairway** raised on several slender arches and can look up at the stone-faced *glacis*, much of it missing now but still rising in parts to two-thirds the height of the mound and pinned to the bedrock by lengths of Roman and Byzantine columns. The outer tower, moat, *glacis* and the monumental gateway before you all date from the rule of al-Zaher Ghazi. Today they present a magnificent architectural ensemble; in their time they also presented a formidable outer line of defence, any would-be attacker being exposed to fire both from the line of walls set with square towers, though these lack much salient, and particularly from the **monumental gateway**, almost a fortress in itself, with arrow slits and a line of box machicolations, though decorated too with a horizontal calligraphic band, a 13th-century commemoration of Mameluke reconstruction work. (To visit the throne room within the monumental gateway, *see* below.)

Assuming the attackers could then have forced the gateway, they would have been faced with a **bent entrance** of daunting complexity, wriggling right, left, left, right, right and left before giving onto a court. Such bent entrances were an occasional Byzantine device, but they became commonplace among the Crusaders and their Muslim adversaries. The twists and turns slowed down the momentum of attack; the short passages made it impossible to drive even a short battering ram against the inner gates; while the alterations in darkness and brightness meant that the attackers would be momentarily blinded while their eyes adjusted to the varying levels of light. The most ingenious example of this is at Krak des Chevaliers, but the Citadel runs a close second. You pass through three gates in all, and you should notice the **carved figures** at each, entwined dragons over the first, two lions facing one another over the second, while flanking the third is another pair of lions seen face-on. Such apotropaic devices were known in the most ancient times, their purpose then as here being to ward off danger.

Emerging into the **court** you see on your right, below, a **cistern** and a series of brick **vaults**, perhaps dungeons, all thought to be Byzantine. Stepping into the daylight you find yourself atop the mound. Several of the structures here are ruinous but are undergoing excavation and restoration. A rising path leads northwards to steps on your right (east), which in turn lead to the remains of a 13th-century **Ayyubid palace** destroyed by the Mongols. From here continue round southwards back to the monumental gateway tower, this time to an upper storey doorway. Not only will you find the **toilets** within, but also by passing through an impressive stalactite portal you enter a vast **throne room**, newly restored, belonging to the Mameluke period. The walls are panelled, and the slender piers sheathed in wood support a beamed and coffered ceiling, elaborately carved, inlaid and painted. Rising through the centre of the ceiling is an octagonal drum, its sides filled with stained-glass windows so that the entire chamber is suffused with softly coloured sunlight.

Emerging from the monumental gateway and returning the way you came, you continue northwards and come on your left (west) to the **Mosque of Abraham**, built by Nur al-Din in 1167, the very spot where Abraham supposedly milked his cow and so bequeathed Aleppo its name, as Halab in Arabic is composed of the same root letters as the word for milk. A church once stood here, two of its columns evident still in the north wall of the mosque, and as if the cow was not enough, it contained, as did the principal church of Damascus, not to mention several other places, the head of John the Baptist.

At the top of the path you come finally to the **Great Mosque of the Citadel**, rebuilt by Ghazi and great in appeal if not in fact in size. A doorway leads into a stone-paved **court** with a fountain and three evergreens. Arcades surround the court on three sides, the arches to east and west strong and handsome, while through arches with stone tie-beams on the south is the prayer hall. A cavetto cornice, which like the tie-beams suggests Cairene influence, runs round all four sides. Altogether, the court is severe but beautifully balanced, like a Japanese garden. In the northeast corner is a contemporary **minaret**; from it or from the parapets of the mosque there are wonderful panoramic views over Aleppo. Within the **prayer hall**, which runs the length of the court but is only an arch deep, are two plastered vaults on either side of a central brick dome which stands on an octagonal drum pierced by eight rectangular windows. The squinches are plain, and there is only a simple lozenge decoration where the arches leave the south wall and the opposite north pillars. The mihrab also is plain but for some simple geometric carving round the arch. Yet it is precisely this restraint in decoration and the handsomeness of the architectural proportions that create a cloister-like and contemplative mood that is deeply affecting and make this mosque a jewel of the Ayyubid period.

Near the mosque, opposite a **café**, are the remains of **barracks** built by Ibrahim Pasha, the great Egyptian general and son of Mohammed Ali, who in the early 19th century conquered Syria and most of Arabia and would have overthrown the Ottoman Empire as well but for British intervention. Also near by is a recently installed **amphitheatre** intended for civic entertainments.

From the Citadel Through the Southern Quarter

This section begins with a few places just south of the Citadel and then continues southwestwards to the Faradis Madrasa 2km distant, which you might prefer to reach by taxi.

Immediately opposite the entrance to the Citadel is the large white **Governorate** and to the east of it is the 14th-century **Hamam al-Nasri**, recently renovated and in service once more as the finest baths in Syria.

The street running southwards along the west side of the Governorate brings you in a few metres to the **Sultaniye Madrasa** on your left (east). This is known also as the Zahiriya, for it was begun by al-Zaher Ghazi and completed a few years after his death in 1215, his remains interred in the chamber to the left of the prayer room.

A bit farther along this street and off to the right (west) is the **Khosrofiye Mosque** with a typically pencil-shaped Turkish minaret and five domes over the portico. Dating from 1537, this was the first Ottoman mosque in Aleppo and was built for its governor by Sinan, who later in his long and brilliant career would build the Suleymaniye, the finest imperial mosque in Istanbul.

From here you can decide whether to walk the 2km (in each direction) or take a taxi to the Faradis Madrasa beyond the southern cemeteries at the far end of Bab al-Makam Street, which runs southwestwards through the gate (bab) in the southern walls from which it takes its name. From the Sultaniye Madrasa and the Khosrofiye Mosque you first follow the street running southeastwards, which then runs into Bab al-Makam Street. About 100m along from this junction you pass on your right (west) the 14th-century **Al-Tavashi Mosque** with slender columns adorning its façade, and in another 200m you come to **Bab al-Makam**, another of Ghazi's constructions, later rebuilt under the Mamelukes.

From the small square outside the gate it is another 800m along the street continuing southwest to one of the finest of Aleppo's religious buildings, the **Faradis Madrasa**, the School of Paradise, built by Ghazi's widow in 1235. A stalactite portal leads via a dark and twisting passageway into a bright open court. Round three sides run arcades of ancient columns and on the north rises a great liwan, these and the sky above reflecting in the courtyard pool, the effect wonderfully peaceful. Within the triple-domed prayer hall to the south, the central mihrab, inlaid with poly-chrome marble and banded with arabesques, achieves a marvellous but restrained beauty.

The Jdeide Quarter

The Jdeide quarter, the traditionally Christian 15th-century 'new' quarter of the late Mameluke period, lies north of the old city. The principal monuments here are two fine houses, the 18th-century Beit Ajiqbash and the 17th-century Beit Ghazaleh, though also the quarter is a generally atmospheric place to wander about, especially at night. You walk down narrow streets, often cobbled and arched, between the blank stone façades of the great houses built by wealthy Christian merchants, their strong wooden doors studded with bolts or entirely clad in metal. Vast upper windows overhang the street and at night you are aware of being watched from darkened rooms within, a glimpse of young girls darting away from half-open louvred shutters and then giggling in the silence.

To reach the Jdeide quarter you can head north from the Great Mosque, crossing Al-Khandak Street, the quarter lying off to the north and west; or you can get there from the clocktower in Bab al-Faraj Square between downtown and the old city, again crossing Al-Khandak Street (the eastward extension of Al-Quwatli Street) but this time near the Emergency Police Station (written in English) at the northeast corner of the intersection with red police cars outside, the quarter in this case lying off to the northeast. Entry to the quarter is described as if coming from this latter direction. Coming up from the clocktower and crossing Al-Khandak Street, so that the Emergency Police Station is on your right, continue about 150m north along Al-Tilel Street until you come to the first street on your right (east). Follow this street southeastwards and in about 150m you come to the 15th-century **Gregorian Armenian Church**, its black doors posted with death notices, while inside are paintings and icons. Now continue due east, passing the 19th-century **Greek Orthodox Church** and the **Syrian Catholic Church**, both on the north side of the street, until you come to the intersection with Jdeide Street (the street by which you would have entered the quarter had you walked north from the Great Mosque).

On the northwest corner of this intersection is **Beit Ajiqbash**, built in 1757 for a Christian merchant family of that name and now the **Museum of Popular Traditions** (*open 8–2, closed Tues; adm*). Passing through an arch you enter a planted court with fountain. You should note the stone carving round the court, which is superb, as though a continuation of

Beit Ajiqbash

that north Syrian craftsmanship found for example at Qalaat Samaan. On the south side of the court and opening northwards to enjoy the summer shade is a high liwan where the comforts of both outdoor and indoor life could be combined. Dwelling rooms run round the court and there is no sense of confinement as in a Muslim house where women were kept in a separate *haremlek*. On the north side is a grand salon with beautifully carved wooden wall panels and a carved and painted woodwork ceiling. The place is furnished to the period with the usual inlaid chairs, chests and tables, while in the cool stone cellars are metal trays, pots, coffee urns and charcoal burners. The huge wooden mortars and pestles are for grinding coffee.

Now walking north along Jdeide Street you come in about 75m to **Beit Ghazaleh**, also the house of a Christian merchant family but this time dating from the 17th century, though the plan and decorations are similar to Beit Ajiqbash. It is not in such good repair, however, and is used as an Armenian school.

Immediately north from Beit Ghazaleh, both the first and second streets off to your left (west) will take you to the late 19th-century **Maronite Church** and the adjacent and smaller mid-19th-century **Greek Catholic Church**, both giving on to a square. Walking west out of this square brings you into Al-Tilel Street, into which you should turn left (south) to return to Al-Khandak Street and Bab al-Faraj Square with the clocktower. Or facing the Maronite Church, with the Greek Catholic Church on your right, you can return to the Gregorian Armenian Church by taking the lane on your right (south), turning left at the T-junction at the bottom, and so back to Al-Tilel Street. But now, having got your bearings within the quarter, you might wish to wander about it for a longer while yet.

Sports and Activities

Sport and other recreational activities are largely confined to what you can find at the luxury hotels; the pool and tennis and squash courts at the Chahba Cham, for example, are open to non-guests for a fee.

Shopping

Though the Aleppo souks are far more atmospheric than those of Damascus, they also close down earlier, at about 6pm, perhaps a reflection of the more sober business side of Aleppan life, whereas Damascenes throng their souks in the spirit of a popular entertainment until 7.30pm or so. As at Damascus, Muslim shops are closed on Fridays (when the souks as a whole are largely dead), Christian shops and the gold bazaars from Saturday noon and on Sunday. Souk al-Attarine Street, running from Bab Antaki in the west to the Citadel in the east, is at first uncovered and here sells **metal goods**, mostly tools and pots. Then where it is covered with sheets of corrugated metal, lengths of **cloth** are sold. Where it becomes stone-vaulted, the shops are more varied, selling **confectionary, nuts, food** and **spices** (attarine means spices). Along the Khan al-Gumruk you will find **copper** and **brass**. More metal utensils are sold along the west side of the Great Mosque, while between Souk al-Attarine Street and the south side of the mosque, **clothing** is sold. East of the Khan al-Nahasin on the south side of Souk al-Attarine Street are **tailors** and wool and cotton merchants. On the east side of the Great Mosque are shops selling **silks, cotton, carpets** and **gold**. Continuing east along Souk al-Attarine Street you pass by shops selling **robes**, tent trappings and finally, just before reaching the Citadel, **sheepskins**.

Aleppo ✆ (021–)   ### Where to Stay
                                                               very expensive

★★★★★**Chahba Cham Hotel**, on the Damascus road, 3km west of the Baron Street downtown area and the Old City, ✆ 248572, ✉ 235912. Set in its own gardens, this is Aleppo's only five-star hotel. The lobby, with its pair of monumental columns, might some day make an interesting ruin. There are three restaurants, one a supper club, another with top-floor panoramic views across the bowl of the city, plus cafés, bars and a discotheque. The rooms have TV, video and minibar. Among the range of further *divertissements* are an outdoor pool, tennis and squash courts, fitness centre, sauna, jacuzzi, barbershop, beauty parlour, business centre, bookstall and a shopping arcade.

expensive

★★★★**Pullman Shahba Hotel**, POB 1350, ✆ 667200, ✉ 667213, on the Damascus road near the university and in an attractive residential neighbourhood, 2km west of the downtown area and the Old City. The full range of facilities include a swimming pool and rooms equipped with TV, video and minibar, but less over-the-top and more pleasant than the Cham. It provides a bus service into town.

★★★★**Amir Palace Hotel**, Ibrahim Hanano Street, ✆ 214800, ✉ 215700, between the Aleppo Museum and the bus station. No pool, but panoramic restaurant, night-club, bar and shops, as well as rooms with TV and minibar, and with the advantage of being within walking distance of everything.

inexpensive

★★★**Tourism Hotel**, Al-Jabri Street at Al-Quwatli Street, along the east side of the large public park, northeast of downtown, ✆ 210156, ✉ 219956. Restaurant, night-club and bar. Good rooms with TV, bath and air conditioning.

★★★**Baron Hotel**, Baron Street, downtown, ✆ 210880, ✉ 218164. Some rooms with bath, no air conditioning, no TV, no video, no minibar. Nor are there tennis courts, a swimming pool, a business centre, a fitness centre, a beauty parlour, a jacuzzi, a night-club or a shopping arcade. There is however a restaurant, bar and terrace (*see* below).

★★**Ramsis Hotel**, Baron Street, across the street from the Baron Hotel, ✆ 216700. Much newer than the Baron and costing very nearly as much, the Ramsis has fairly clean, air-conditioned rooms with baths but nothing more.

★**Yarmouk**, ✆ 217510, Al-Maari Street opposite the Aleppo Museum. Rooms with fan, fridge, shower and balcony, clean and very good for the price, so that it fills up quickly. ★**Tourist**, ✆ 216583, a block north of Al-Maari Street (turn off halfway between the museum and clocktower), has rooms with shower and toilet (some cheaper ones without) and fan; very clean and friendly, also very popular, so try to book ahead. ★**Afamia**, ✆ 217078, between Baron and Al-Walid streets, north of the Karnak bus station. Clean rooms with fan, toilet and shower, some with balcony.

The Baron Hotel

For atmosphere and legend, this is the place to stay. Built in 1909 (though only finally completed, as the date engraved above the entrance indicates, in 1911) by two Armenian brothers, the Mazloumians, in what was then the new and verdant European residential area west of the Old City, the Baron was immediately celebrated as one of the first hotels in Syria to offer Western standards of comfort along with Eastern standards of hospitality. In the 1920s the terrace with its ornate lanterns was a favourite spot for shooting wild duck on the neighbouring swamp. Today it overlooks the main street of downtown Aleppo and its white limestone façade seems less imposing amid the clutter of buildings that have grown up around it. But on 1 April 1914 T. E. Lawrence wrote home from here, 'Another letter from this beautiful hotel whose face you must be getting to know by heart', and since then its lofty rooms with their louvred shutters and antique plumbing have known such guests as King Feisal, leader of the Arab Revolt, Kemal Atatürk, Theodore Roosevelt, Charles Lindbergh, Freya Stark, Agatha Christie, the spy Kim Philby, son of St John Philby, the Arabian explorer, and Paolo Matthiae, who excavated Ebla.

Nationalisation by the Syrian government has starved the Baron of the money needed to keep it up to scratch. Where once wild boar, pheasant and caviar were regularly on the menu, the Mazloumian family, who still run the hotel, have had to struggle to keep the plaster on the walls and the springs in the mattresses. Tour groups mercifully tend to avoid it, preferring the slick vacuity of Aleppo's modern hotels. But given the choice, travellers with a sense of history and a taste for faded elegance will prefer the comfortably uncomfortable Baron.

There is a 1000-year story behind the name Baron. The Armenian kingdom centred on Lake Van was overthrown by the Seljuks in the 11th century, and many Armenians then established themselves between the Taurus Mountains and the Mediterranean around Adana, Tarsus and Mersin. These Cilician Armenian feudal dynasts soon became more Westernised than their forebears, mixing and often intermarrying with the Crusaders. At the same time they acquired or gave themselves such a plethora of titles that soon almost everyone was a baron, so that the term came to mean simply gentleman and was used almost in the way we might address someone as sir. Even before the First World War, when the Turks exterminated between one and half and two million Armenians of Van, Cilicia and elsewhere, their government had launched a series of pogroms against Armenian communities throughout Anatolia, which between

1894 and 1896 saw the slaughter of a quarter of a million Armenians. Many fled into what are now Syria and Lebanon, where they were welcomed and protected by the local populations, though these countries were still then part of the Ottoman Empire. Among those to come to Aleppo were the Mazloumians from Cilicia, and with them they brought their honorific title, giving it to their hotel.

The hotel is now run by Armen Mazloumian, son of Crikor (known to everyone as Coco) and grandson of one of the founding brothers. Coco, who died recently, and his English wife Sally would reminisce about many of their famous guests. Kim Philby, the high-ranking British diplomat who as it turned out had been a Soviet spy since 1933, strove hard to drink the well-stocked bar dry, recalled Coco: 'He would come up from Beirut for a few days and start drinking at 10am and go on literally all day. I was only amazed that with all that drink inside him, he never let the cat out of the bag.' He was a charming man, remembered Sally, and 'had the kindest eyes I had ever seen'. Coco could remember Agatha Christie 'as clearly as if it were yesterday. She had a beautiful face and was extremely perceptive. When she stared at you, you felt it was with X-ray eyes. When I asked her what she was writing, she would look at me like a sphinx, but eventually she told me it was *Murder on the Orient Express*'. Coco was only a boy when T. E. Lawrence would stay at the hotel, but he recalled him 'spending hours pacing up and down the terrace. He was a short, stocky, intelligent man who always stood out from the other guests. He never bought a rug without taking my father's advice'.

Lawrence first checked into the Baron on 6 September 1909. He was 21 and had just completed a 1800km walk through Palestine, Lebanon and Syria, visiting most of the Crusader castles en route. Soon he was back, for after graduating from Oxford he worked on the archaeological dig at Carchemish, now on the Turkish border, leaving Syria only on the eve of the First World War, in which he was to turn himself into the legendary Lawrence of Arabia. In the lounge, together with a photograph of the Baron as it looked in 1911, there is a copy of the bill made out to 'Monsieur Lawrence' on 8 June 1914. It gives no room number, and when asked, the Mazloumians say 'he stayed so many times', though room 201 at the southwest corner is singled out as one of those he occupied. Certainly the 200-series of rooms on the first floor facing the front are the most agreeable. The dark wood-panelled restaurant with revolving fans lets out through French doors onto the side terrace where dinner is served in summer beneath trees twinkling with lights. The bar is comfortable, with deep armchairs and a happy array of bottles to choose from. Best of all is the terrace out front, reminiscent of the old Shepheards' in Cairo, the faint buzz of night traffic passing by below, behind you an old thermometer fixed to the wall advertising Stephens' Inks, and in French Encre Stephens, indicating *glacé* at 0°C, *tempéré* at 12°C, *chaleur humaine* at 37°C, and at 47°C *Sénégal*. This is the place to have an Aleppo-brewed *Al-Shams* in the company of one of the Baron's habitués, an interesting and solicitous man whom Armen Mazloumian will introduce as the chief of the Aleppo Mukhabarat or secret police.

Armen himself is extremely knowledgable about the Northern Highlands (*see* p.223) and has explored and photographed every one of its hundreds of sites, visiting some lying close to the frontier at risk to his life, where he has been shot at by Turkish border guards. Before rushing off to Qalaat Samaan have a word with Armen. If he has time, he may show you some of his thousands of slides of Byzantine sites in the Northern Highlands, and he can certainly suggest some out-of-the-way places to see and can arrange for a car with driver to take you round at a good price.

Eating Out

Apart from dining at the top hotels, which offer the usual expensive and bland international and Arab cuisine (the Pullman has an Italian restaurant), there are several moderately-priced quality restaurants—for example, **Al-Estiraha**, **Al-Bustan** and **Al-Khoukh**—along Al-Jabri Street which runs along the east side of the large public park to the west of the upper end of Baron Street. The Jdeide quarter is another good place to seek out restaurants, often occupying old houses there: for example, **Yasmeen House**, full of character and with interesting Arab cuisine, at the end of a lane running westwards of Jdeide Street betwee Beit Ajiqbash (the Museum of Popular Traditions) and Beit Ghazaleh. But for atmosphere, the terrace of the **Baron Hotel** is the best place of all. Drinks are served along the front, overlooking the street and providing that satisfaction of being able to watch the world go by without having to be part of it, and there is an excellent bar inside. Dinner is served on the more secluded part of the terrace round the side beneath trees and lights, or indoors through French doors in the dining room panelled in dark wood beneath twirling fans. The service is always friendly and attentive, the food simple but good.

There are numerous inexpensive restaurants and cafés along or just off Baron Street, from which women are totally absent after 10pm. The **Andalib Restaurant** on Baron Street, for example, immediately north of the Baron Hotel, has an outdoor terrace, as does **Al-Andalus** on Al-Quwatli Street. There are several cheap little eating-places just past the fruit and vegetable stalls and butchers as you enter the stone-vaulted section of Souk al-Attarine Street in the Old City, entered from Bab Antaki.

Entertainment and Nightlife

Aleppo was the first place in Syria to see a motion picture film projected, by a Turk. Things have gone downhill ever since, the cinemas along Baron and Al-Quwatli streets showing nothing but censored slush to all-male audiences. There are also numerous awful nightclubs in this area; the brothels are usually next door. The top hotels have nightclubs offering the usual crooner-belly-dancer-folklorique show.

Occasionally there are **plays** and **musical programmes** at the recently installed amphitheatre atop the Citadel. Ask at your hotel or the Tourist Office for information.

During the **cotton festival** (*Mehrajan al-Qutun*) at the end of September, which celebrates the end of the cotton harvest, cars are decorated with cotton ribbons and young women and girls wear their prettiest crisp white dresses.

Exhausted by this flurry of excitement, you can take a **Turkish bath** at the 14th-century Hamam al-Nasri, immediately east of the large white Governorate building opposite the Citadel entrance. These are the finest baths in Syria and were renovated by the Ministry of Tourism in 1985. On Mondays, Thursdays and Saturdays it is open to women from 9am to 5pm, and to men from 5pm to midnight. It is also open to men from 9am to midnight on all other days of the week.

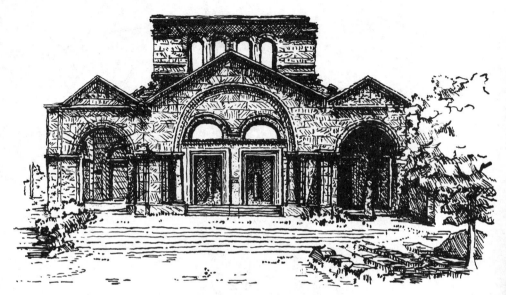

Qalaat Samaan

The Northern Highlands

Getting Around	226
North of the Massif: Cyrrhus and Ain Dara	227
The Jebel Samaan	228
Deir Samaan	228
Qalaat Samaan (Saint Simeon)	229
The Jebel al-Ala	234
The Jebel Riha	235

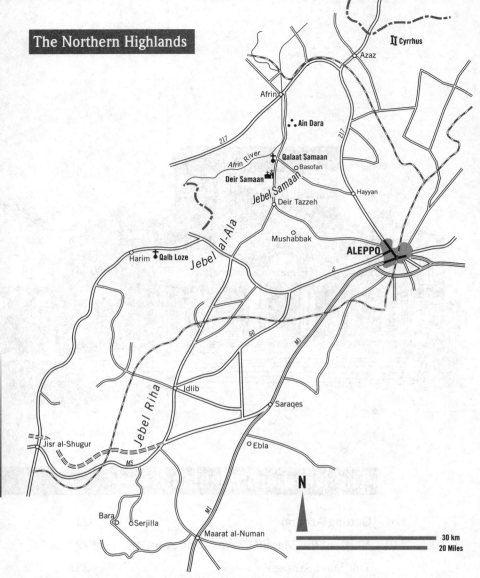

The worn and fissured limestone landscape of the northern highlands is eerily pale and colourless as though illuminated by perpetual moonlight. Pockets of red soil lie like congealed blood amid the rock where indigent peasants somehow eke out an existence, their drystone walls enclosing stony fields. Like the skeletons of beached whales, clusters of ancient churches and villas lie stranded amid horizons of boulders, the remains of wine and olive presses recalling that a thousand years ago this was a country patterned with vineyards and olive groves.

The view was familiar to Simeon the Stylite, though his gaze was aimed at higher things: wishing to be closer to God, he spent the best 38 years of his life atop a pillar 18m high. Such renown did Simeon win by his elevated piety that when he died in 459 a huge and wonderful church was built around his pillar. Both the stump of this pillar and the remains of the church of Saint Simeon can be seen at Qalaat Samaan today.

But for an olive boom, however, the activities of Simeon and other 'athletes of God' might never have been mounted in the northern highlands. Hundreds of so-called Dead Cities—villages, agricultural towns, religious complexes—are scattered on ridges and slopes across this great massif which lies between the Hama–Aleppo highway to the east and the Orontes and Afrin river valleys to the west and runs from Apamea in the south to Cyrrhus in the north. The region had been prosperous and densely populated during Roman and Byzantine times but then fell into rapid decline during the 8th century and was completely abandoned in the 10th century. Yet this collapse was caused neither by erosion nor by Arab or nomad devastation.

The land has always been marginal, and the highland villages were never agriculturally self-sufficient. But a good living could be made from the cultivation of olives for which the soil and climate are ideal. An economy of such evident wealth based almost solely on olives (the vine was very much secondary) was only possible, however, under special conditions. It took many years before newly planted olive trees would bear fruit, and so their cultivation required long-term capital investment, and then there had to be suitable channels of trade by which the olive products could be exchanged for all those necessities the highlands were incapable of producing for themselves. The Roman and Byzantine presence provided centuries of peace and security favourable to capital investment, while nearby Antioch and to a lesser extent Aleppo were ready markets.

Under these conditions both building works and saintliness flourished, most famously at Qalaat Samaan (Saint Simeon), which has been called 'the most significant Christian edifice built before the erection of Hagia Sophia in Constantinople' (H. C. Butler, *Princeton University Archaeological Expedition to Syria*, 1907–20). But once northern Syria became an unstable frontier region between Arabs and Byzantines, prosperity collapsed. God's athletes departed with the rest of the population and all that remain are their unburied stones.

> *Intercourse with females is superfluous for the angels: as immortal they have no need of increase, and as bodiless they are incapable of sexual activity. Another reason for calling them holy is that there is nothing of the earth about them: instead, separated from all earthly passions, they labour as a heavenly choir, singing hymns to their maker. They also serve by ministering to the divine will, in accordance with its commands, sent out as they are by the God of all creation to further the salvation of men.*

It is in imitation of their mode of life that so many men have embraced the service of God, shunning even licit intercourse as a distraction from the things of God and forsaking their homes and families: this they do in order to be anxious only about the affairs of the Lord and to escape all bonds that might prevent the mind from soaring into heaven and gazing in desire at the invisible and ineffable beauty of God. They fill the cities and the villages, the hilltops and the ravines. Some of them by living in community fashion in their souls the images of wisdom; others living in twos or threes, or in solitary isolation, protect their eyes from the lure of visible beauty and win for their souls the freedom to bask in the contemplation of things spiritual.

From *The Cure of Hellenic Maladies* by Theodoret of Cyrrhus (AD 393–466), who knew Simeon and other such 'athletes of God' personally.

Getting Around

It is possible to reach (or get close to) some of the sites mentioned in this chapter by bus or microbus from Aleppo, but even then it will be a time-consuming nuisance to travel this way. It would be much better (allowing you to see more and quite possibly saving you money) to hire a car or a taxi for the day. Armen Mazloumian of the Baron Hotel in Aleppo (*see* p.221) is an expert on the sites and can be very helpful in arranging transport.

Cyrrhus, which lies on the far side of the Afrin valley just beyond the massif, is 76km north of Aleppo and almost on the Turkish border (it can also be reached from Qalaat Samaan). You can take a microbus from Aleppo to Azaz, but you will have to hire a taxi for the last 28km to Cyrrhus (known locally as Nebi Uri). You will have the same problem in reaching Ain Dara, which requires taking a microbus from Aleppo to Afrin and then hoping you can pay someone to take you farther.

The limestone massif of the northern highlands has a general elevation of 400 to 500m. In three areas, however, it rises higher, and in each of these—the Jebel Samaan, the Jebel al-Ala and the Jebel Riha—there are sites particularly worth seeing. Directions are given below for reaching each area from Aleppo, though you can also go from one to the other in a loop (or approach the sites from Latakia): Aleppo, Qalaat Samaan, Qalb Loze, Harim and Jisr al-Shugur (for the Latakia-Aleppo highway).

The Jebel Samaan, rising to 870m, has the sites of Deir Samaan and its 'acropolis' of Qalaat Samaan (Saint Simeon). To reach it you take the new 30km road direct from Aleppo to Deir Tazzeh (Daret Aazah), from where it is 4km north to Deir Samaan and a farther 2km to Qalaat Samaan. Microbuses go from Aleppo to Deir Tazzeh (Daret Aazah). From there you will have to walk or hope to find someone to pay for a ride.

The Jebel al-Ala, rising to 817m, is reached by taking route 5 and then route 56 west from Aleppo towards Harim. The outstanding site here is Qalb Loze, a few kilometres east of Harim. There are buses from Aleppo to Harim, but it is then a steep hard walk up to Qalb Loze.

The Jebel Riha, known also as the Jebel Zawiye, rises to 939m and lies southwest of Aleppo, south of the Aleppo–Latakia highway and west of Maarat al-Numan (*see* p.157), which is just off the Hama–Aleppo highway, the M1. The sites especially worth visiting here are Bara and Serjilla. There are buses from Aleppo to Maarat al-Numan, but from there you will have to find someone who for a sum will give you a ride.

Where to Stay

Accommodation is in Aleppo (*see* p.219).

North of the Massif: Cyrrhus and Ain Dara

The Emperor Justinian, both out of his forethought for the safety of the state, and at the same time as showing especial honour to the Saints Cosmas and Damian, whose bodies lie close by even up to my day, made Cyrrhus a flourishing city and one of great note through the safety afforded by the strongest possible wall, by the great strength of its garrison, by the size of its public buildings, and by the imposing scale of its other appointments.

Procopius, *Buildings,* II, xi, 2ff.

Approaching **Cyrrhus** (known locally as Nebi Uri) via the border post town of Azaz, you cross over two 2nd-century AD hump-backed **Roman bridges**, the first carrying you across the Afrin river, the second, a kilometre beyond and just outside Cyrrhus, taking you over the Sabun river. Though Theodoret, the 5th-century chronicler of Saint Simeon and other Syrian holy men, was bishop here, and Saints Cosmas and Damian (*see* Apamea, p.150) were martyred and buried here, the function of the place was essentially military. Cyrrhus was founded by Seleucus I Nicator soon after 300 BC and remained important as a garrison town through the Roman and Byzantine periods as it protected the caravan route between Antioch and the bridge over the Euphrates at Zeugma (Turkish Birecik). With the Arab invasion its strategic point was lost and the place remains almost entirely uninhabited, though olive trees are being planted in an effort to revive the area.

Seldom visited and only partly excavated and reconstructed, the site is more romantic than revealing. A Roman **tower tomb** of the 2nd or 3rd century AD stands by the side of the approach road. It has a pyramidal cap with an acanthus bobble on top, while the lower storey has become the tomb of a 14th-century Muslim saint. The remains of a **theatre**, originally 115m in diameter, making it larger than that at Bosra, stands along what was the north–south cardo maximus, flagged with basalt. Behind it, to the west, is the **citadel** with good views over the countryside and northwards along the line of Justinian's **walls**.

Worth a stop if you are visiting Cyrrhus or Qalaat Samaan is **Ain Dara**, 10km south of Afrin, a 1st-millennium Neo-Hittite site most notable for its temple, probably to Ishtar, approached up steps flanked by **carved lions**—an opportunity to see in the wild, so to speak, examples of early Iron Age sculpture otherwise caged at the Aleppo Museum.

The Jebel Samaan

Describing the route to Qalaat Samaan, the 1912 edition of Baedeker advised that 'travelling is sometimes rendered unsafe by the nomadic Kurds and Turcomans who range through the greater part of northern Syria'. These days you drive towards the Jebel Samaan along the new road west from Aleppo to Deir Tazzeh (Daret Aazah), observing that where the blood-red soil has gathered in flattish basins the land is cultivated with wheat, sparkling green in early summer, but that elsewhere all is grey knuckles of rock. The absence of trees is striking, except where gnarled and tenacious olives grow within stone-walled enclosures or sometimes seem to hatch from cracks in the boulders themselves. There are still Kurds in the area, notably at **Basofan**, northeast of Qalaat Samaan, 'a village of devil-worshippers', they tell you in Aleppo, 'true Kurds, not like those Muslim Kurds'. Known as Yazidis, they are yet another of those obscure dualist sects that inhabit Syria, believing that evil is part of the Divinity, along with good; but they do not worship evil, rather they seek to appease it. It lurks in lettuce, a belief shared by tourists, but it seems to be absent from olives, and so they are trying to make a go of it in the Jebel Samaan.

At **Mushabbak**, visible off to your left (south) at about 24km along the Aleppo–Deir Tazzeh (Daret Aazah) road and reached by a kilometre-long track, there is a 5th-century Christian basilica, roofless and eviscerated, looking like the ribcage of a giant quadruped, solitary now in fields of stone but once a busy pilgrimage station along the way to Saint Simeon's church. It is your first ghostly introduction to the flourishing centuries of the Jebel Samaan, a region, wrote Butler, leader of the Princeton Expeditions of 1904–9, that was 'densely populated in comparison with almost any country district in Europe or America today which one might name in which there might be found corresponding evidences of wealth'.

Deir Samaan

In the days of its glory, Deir Samaan was an early Christian Epidauros, a small city of monasteries, hostels and bazaars, visited by many of the world's powerful and humble alike, sometimes thousands at a time, all seeking a cure for their souls or some of them, anyway, for you cannot resist the thought that many others came for the spectacle, and that for them Deir Samaan was less an Epidauros than an Orlando. The spectacle, or the cure, was provided by Simeon, and this was the base camp for the final ascent of the hill to the north where Simeon lived atop his pillar, and where, when he died, the great church was built to provide a continuing focus for pilgrimages.

The best place to get an overall impression of Deir Samaan is from that hill, Telanissos in Greek, the 'mountain of women', which is the last thing it was for Simeon, who would not allow a woman within eyeshot. But the name was there before the saint, and it became the name of the settlement at its base, a little farming community to which Simeon came. Previously he had been living down a well but had been hauled up; there are reports that he also spent a summer as a human turnip, buried up to his head in a monastery garden; now at Telanissos he lived more conventionally, in a tiny cottage, though he would seal up its door and refuse all food during the 40 days of Lent, at first standing continuously and chanting hymns to God, but in the final days having to lie down, as Theodoret tells us, 'for as his strength was gradually exhausted and extinguished he was compelled to lie half-dead'. It was

all good practice, though, as we shall see when we follow Simeon up to his hilltop pillar. Here down below you can see the remains of the **hostels, bazaars, a church and two monasteries** (Deir Samaan means Monastery of Simeon) built in the 5th and 6th centuries to accommodate gawkers and God-seekers. There is also a **monumental arch**, marking the start of the sacred way up to the hilltop church of Qalaat Samaan. (Nowadays you enter Qalaat Samaan via its ticket office at the top of the modern road to the east, but you can come *down* the sacred way from Qalaat Samaan to Deir Samaan.)

Qalaat Samaan (Saint Simeon)

Qalaat Samaan should not be regarded as a separate and distinct place from Deir Samaan (*see* p.228) but rather as its crowning feature, its acropolis. The church of Saint Simeon built round its famous pillar was still a place of pilgrimage late into the 12th century, though in the 10th century it was fortified by the Byzantines and then by the Muslims, hence *qalaat*, meaning fortress. These defence works seem not to have amounted to more than building the wall that encloses the site, so that what you otherwise see belongs almost entirely to the years 476–92 when the church, the adjoining monastery and the baptistery were built in a burst of brilliant architectural activity commemorating the life of Saint Simeon the Stylite.

Simeon the Stylite

Simeon died in 459 after spending 38 blazing summers and bitter winters wedded to his pillar (*stylos* in Greek)—or rather to a succession of pillars. Indeed at first he had no pillar at all. Initially he ordered a roofless circular

enclosure to be built atop the hill and had himself bound within it by means of an iron chain 10m long, fixed at one end to a rock and at the other to his right foot. The central octagonal court of the church, with a radius of 10 metres from the stone column base at the centre, might well mark this original ambit.

Theodoret of Cyrrhus (393–466) reports in his *Religious History* that 'As Simeon's fame circulated everywhere, everyone hastened to him, not only the people of the neighbour-hood but also people many days' journey distant, some bringing the paralysed in body, others requesting health for the sick, others asking to become fathers; and they begged to receive from him what they could not receive from nature'. Aspiring to be an angel, Simeon forbade the presence of women, however, and refused even to see his mother, while on one occasion a woman who attempted to breach this rule dropped miraculously dead on the spot.

'Since the visitors were beyond counting,' Theodoret continues, 'and they all tried to touch him and reap some blessing from his garments of skins, and he could not abide the wearisomeness of it, he devised the standing on a pillar.' The first pillar was 3m high but perhaps not quite high enough to avoid the occasional poke, for Simeon ordered that a pillar of 6m be cut. And now passion overtook mere practicality: nothing less than a pillar 11m high would do, then finally one of 18m, 'for he yearns to fly up to heaven and to be separated from this life on earth'.

It is well to appreciate that Theodoret was no fabulist and was well aware of the difficult position he had been put in by having personally witnessed events that 'beggar description'. 'I am afraid,' he tells us, 'that this narrative may seem to posterity to be a myth totally devoid of truth, for the facts surpass human nature.' Simeon did not sit or lie atop his pillar, though there was room to do so as it was surmounted by a platform. Rather he perpetually stood, often with his hands raised to the heavens in prayer, but also offering worship to God by repeatedly bending his emaciated body: 'Many of those standing by count the number of these acts of worship. Once one of those with me counted one thousand two hundred and forty-four of them, before slackening and giving up count. In bending down he always makes his forehead touch his toes—for as his stomach receives food only once a week, and little of it, he is able to bend his back easily.' In between these exertions Simeon cured the sick and resolved the strife of those in dispute, and such was his fame and the awe in which he was held that on several occasions the Byzantine emperor himself requested Simeon's intervention in the great doctrinal disputes of the time.

Indeed, Simeon was probably the best-known person in the 5th-century world: 'With everyone arriving from every side and every road resembling a river, one can behold a sea of men standing together in that place, receiving rivers from every side. Not only do the inhabitants of our part of the world flock together, but also Ishmaelites, Persians, Armenians subject to them, Iberians, Homerites, and men even more distant than these; and there came many inhabitants of the extreme west, Spaniards, Britons, and the Gauls who live between them. Of Italy it is superfluous to speak. It is said that the man became so celebrated in the great city of Rome that at the entrance of all the workshops men have set up small representations of him, to provide thereby some protection and safety for themselves.'

It is easy to mock, and Theodoret admits that some did come to mock Simeon on his pillar. But by his extreme and very visible asceticism, Simeon did manage quite literally to place himself beyond this world, to transcend its rivalries and its fears, and to transcend the human condition itself. Not unreasonably, in an age immersed in simple faith, Simeon could seem to have direct access to God and so be able to bring to bear on the world's problems something of that power and wisdom associated with the divine.

'He is as modest in spirit as if he were the last of all men in worth. In addition to his modest spirit, he is extremely approachable, sweet and charming, and makes answer to everyone who addresses him, whether he be artisan, beggar or peasant. And he has received from the munificent Master the gift also of teaching. Making exhortation two times each day, he floods the ears of his hearers, as he speaks most gracefully and offers the lessons of the divine Spirit, bidding them look up to heaven and take flight, depart from the earth, imagine the expected kingdom, fear the threat of hell, despise earthly things, and await what is to come.'

When Simeon died on his pillar-top, imperial troops took his body away, against local protests, for burial in the cathedral at Antioch. That being a hotbed of monophysitism, he was later removed to Constantinople. In death as in his lifetime, he was too potent a figure for the metropolitan authorities to ignore. They would possess his corpse, and at Qalaat Samaan they would lavish the resources of the imperial treasury on his commemorative church to ensure that his cult served imperial ends.

Visiting Qalaat Samaan

Open daily 9–6 in summer, 9–4 in winter; adm.

The best thing to do is first to get your bearings amid the complex and then simply to wander around, assimilating the architectural harmony of the church, filling your eyes with the beautifully carved details and standing by the butt of Simeon's column, pondering his lifetime and enjoying his view.

From the ticket office you mount the levelled platform on which the church and other buildings stand. You see the baptistery off to your left (south) and the church off to your right (north). You are at the top end of the sacred way, in fact, which led up from Deir Samaan, new converts initiated into Christianity at the **baptistery**, a handsome square building with an octagonal drum which supported a conical wooden roof. Steps inside (east) lead down to what was a walk-through baptismal font; the floor of the font, usually covered with dust (splash some water on it) bears a mosaic pattern of red buds on a white ground. There is a good view from here of Deir Samaan (*see* p.228) spread out below you with some beehive dwellings among the more substantial masonry remains. You can go down this way if you like after looking about Qalaat Samaan, but for the moment you can imagine the troops of pilgrims trudging up the hill and their excitement as they wade their way through the baptismal font. Now turning to face the **Church of Saint Simeon**, you approach it along the last paces of the sacred way as would have a pilgrim. The colour of the limestone is pleasing, often wearing to a handsome metallic grey, yet also great expanses of masonry respond warmly to the sunlight and glow orange. Before you is the triple-arched **narthex**, the southern entrance vestibule of the church. Normally in a Byzantine church the narthex would be at its west end, leading you into the body of the building and towards the apse at the east end. But once inside you will see that Saint Simeon is very unusual in its plan. First, however, have a good look at the carved decoration on this southern façade. The arches, pediments, columns and capitals are classical in conception, yet there is also a distinctively Syrian feel in the richness and variety of the detail, for example in the sharp, spiky quality of the carving, and in the moulding that drapes across the curves of the four window arches above, a sinuous motif that is repeated throughout the church. The resources for building Saint Simeon came from Constantinople, but the craftsmanship and exuberance is unmistakably local. Notice how the columns supporting the central round arch on either side are finished at their acanthus capitals with a lovely touch: the stonecutters have laid the fronds lightly back as though they have been caught by a breeze swirling in through the narthex. Known as blown acanthus, the effect is

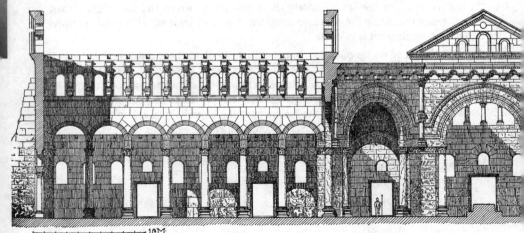

SCALE: .50CM-1M·
10M·

232

graceful, even spiritual, the breeze itself a pilgrim to the mysteries within, and it was first employed here, to be adopted throughout the Byzantine Empire.

To your right (east) are the remains of a **monastery and chapel**, presumably built to accommodate resident clergy, visitors being housed at Deir Samaan, below. You now pass through the southern basilica to the **central court**, where you see that the plan of the church is a giant cross, each arm a basilica pointing more or less towards one of the cardinal compass points—though the entire configuration is rotated somewhat clockwise from a true north–south alignment. At the centre of the court is the base on which **Simeon's pillar** stood, and indeed there is a worn, stumpy, almost egg-shaped stone upon it, the faithful having chipped away the rest, so they say, though its provenance is something of a mystery. Certainly no pillar stood upon this base when Gertrude Bell came here in 1905: 'I scrambled over the heaps of ruin till I came to the rock-hewn base of that very column, a broad block of splintered stone with a depression in the middle, like a little bowl, filled with clear rain water in which I washed my hands and face. I sat and thought how perverse a trick Fortune had played that night on the grim saint. She had given for a night his throne of bitter dreams to one whose dreams were rosy with a deep content that he would have been the first to condemn. So musing I caught the eye of a great star that had climbed up above the broken line of the arcade, and we agreed together that it was better to journey over earth and sky than to sit upon a column all your days.'

The **eastern basilica**, somewhat longer than the other three, was the church proper, where liturgical services were held. In several spots the dry earth that lies a few centimetres deep has been kicked away, revealing a beautiful flooring of blue and white geometric mosaic. The basilica's projecting apse, in this case a triple apse, was a recent innovation, first found in Syria at Qalb Loze. Until then apses had been set within the flat-backed rectangle of the basilica; thereafter the projecting apse, or chevet, became a standard feature in Syrian church architecture. You will appreciate it better if you walk round the outside, noticing also the decorative use of columns between the chevet windows and the continuous band of draped moulding.

Restoration after Butler

Curiously, this eastern basilica is not perpendicular to the court like the other three but instead twists slightly counterclockwise, as though to correct the clockwise twist mentioned above and so to bring its apses more into line with true east. This in fact it fails quite to do, and you wonder why the builders bothered, or why they did not orientate all four basilicas correctly in the first place. The answer might be that to build the western basilica an artificial west terrace had to be constructed where the hill sloped sharply away—perhaps aligning the four basilicas exactly to the cardinal points would have meant underpinning not only the western basilica but also part of the northern basilica. The cruciform plan was not an innovation here but had already been introduced with the now vanished church of the Apostles in Constantinople, built during the reign of Constantine or his successor, Constantius; at any rate, it is a nice thought to imagine that the attempt to impose this metropolitan plan here was somewhat resisted by the local topography. There is a fine view from the artificial **west terrace** over the Afrin valley westwards towards Antioch and of the hazy march of the Amanus Mountains to the northwest, across which both Alexander and the First Crusade entered Syria.

The Jebel al-Ala

From Aleppo or Qalaat Samaan you head into the Jebel al-Ala along route 5 which eventually reaches Antioch (Turkish Antakya). But before coming to the border you turn off onto route 56 for Harim, bringing you close to the object of your journey here, Qalb Loze. The road is good all the way and the landscape en route is not so much spectacular as simply incredible. The road seems laid across a churning sea of stone, not a bird, leaf, insect or any living thing moving amid the desolation. The highlands fall away to the north, where the tidal wave of rock lies exhausted before a great fertile plain pricked with the characteristic pencil-thin minarets of Turkey.

If instead you are coming up from Jisr al-Shugur to Harim, then the landscape is well-watered and soil-covered, a rolling countryside covered with olive groves. Poplars or cypresses would make it look like Italy. It is lovely and very pleasant to drive through, and though the road is not terribly good it is adequate and almost untrafficked.

Qalb Loze is signposted (as Kulb Lawze) from Harim. Follow this blue sign for 1.5km to a fork, there taking the right fork and climbing for about 5km through an increasingly stony landscape until you reach the village and church on the summit of the ridge.

Qalb Loze

An impoverished village now huddles around the church of Qalb Loze, a village of laughing children for whom you are a major entertainment. Their hair is often fair, sometimes flaxen, and their eyes are often blue or green. They are Druze, originally from the mountains of Lebanon, who for a thousand years have found refuge in this and other villages of the Jebel al-Ala and who live in isolation here far from those greater numbers of more recent Druze settlers in the Jebel al-Arab (see p.101). Qalb Loze means Heart of the Almond in Arabic, but no almonds grow here and only a few olive trees. A few men of the village are helping to restore the church; the rest, it would seem, grow stones.

The church (key from the keeper who lives near by) was built a decade or so before Qalaat Samaan, that is in about 460. To whom it was dedicated is unknown, but there was no village around it then, rather Qalb Loze may have been, like Mushabbak (see p.228), a way station for pilgrims to Saint Simeon's shrine. A single basilica, worn grey now and lichen-covered, much of the edge and depth to its carving lost to weathering, it lacks the immediate appeal and associations of Qalaat Samaan and was never so ambitious a structure. But it has a metropolitan monumentality about it and bears also the impress of local Syrian craftsmanship and innovation that is more boldly stamped on the Stylite's church.

The basilica once had this crest of the Jebel al-Ala to itself and still stands within a temenos like an ancient temple. Before going inside, you should walk round to the east end of the church to its projecting apse, or chevet, the inspiration for that at Qalaat Samaan, adorned with columns between windows

Reconstruction of Qalb Loze after Mattern

draped with moulding. The west façade of the church is flanked by towers between which rose a single enormous round arch, a prefiguring of the Romanesque, fallen now though echoed by the smaller relieving arch over the sunken portal. Entering the once timbered and now roofless nave (which you must do from the north side of the church), you are struck by the rhythm of broad round arches striding along the aisles towards the majestic semicircular apse. The interior of the nave would have been filled with sunlight streaming through its high clerestory windows, the elevation of the aisles kept unobstructively low by flat stone roofs, as you can see along the south aisle where the roofing slabs are still in place.

The Jebel Riha

Known also as the Jebel Zawiye, this is the area to visit if you want to see dead cities in the sense of complete townships and not just an isolated church or even a religious complex. The Jebel Riha lies southwest of the junction of the Latakia–Aleppo and the Hama–Aleppo highways and so can be visited en route (and included, for example, with visits to Ebla and Maarat al-Numan) as well as from Aleppo itself.

Bara can be reached in 15km from Maarat al-Numan via Basqala or in 13km from Urum al-Joz, where there are some beehive houses, on the Aleppo–Latakia highway. Serjilla is then 7km east of Bara on a dead-end road.

Bara

Today Bara is no more than a village living on the cultivation of olives and cherries, but from its position halfway up a slope it overlooks the largest dead city in Syria, a centre for the large-scale production of olive oil and wine in Byzantine times. Founded in the 4th century AD, it reached the peak of its prosperity over the following two centuries, from which period five churches, three monasteries, two pyramid-capped mausolea and numerous villas and other buildings remain, including evidence of olive oil presses built to an industrial standard. Unlike the settlements farther north, Bara did not seem to depend on trading its produce through Antioch and so continued to flourish through Muslim times and was captured by the First Crusade in the autumn of 1098 just before the siege and massacre at Maarat al-Numan. In 1123 it reverted to the Muslims who built Qalaat Abu Safian, the fortress half a kilometre to the north.

Serjilla

Serjilla lies just below the crest of the eastern slope of the *jebel*. A now dried-up stream wound down a semicircular hollow at the base of which baths were built to catch all the available water. The town fans out beyond the baths. All the slopes around were built up with terraces where you can still make out standing stones which served as supports for vines. Some of the streets are lined with pillars and these served as vine arbours. Where all is now barren and broken there was once a thriving community intensely cultivating the vine and finding shade beneath its bowers. The baths, thought Butler, were perhaps the best preserved not only in Syria but anywhere for the early Byzantine period between Constantine and Justinian, their walls adorned with paintings, their floors covered with mosaics (stolen after the departure of the Princeton Expedition). He wrote: 'The picture that this building presents to the imagination is a scene from the daily life of the inhabitants of these Syrian hill-towns during the 5th and 6th centuries—a scene suggestive of a high degree of civilisation and of not a little luxury.' A church and numerous detached villas cover the rest of the site.

Resafa

Getting Around   241

Resafa   244

The Euphrates and the Gezira

Raqqa   248

Halabiye   251

Deir ez Zor   253

Dura Europos (Salihiye)   255

Mari (Tell Hariri)   258

Into the Gezira   260

Called the Nahr al-Furat in Arabic, in the course of its 2430km journey from Turkey to the Persian Gulf the Euphrates passes within 80km to the east of Aleppo and continues southeastwards across Syria in a diagonal cut. Cut is the word, for over much of this distance the Euphrates runs between steep mud embankments, so that you see it only suddenly as you draw near. For a river so famous in history you would expect great fertility and prosperous towns, a landscape busy with activity as along the Nile. Instead the Euphrates is hidden, signs of life are meagre and the landscape is often dreary.

For 2000 years the Euphrates was a strategic prize, variously an avenue of trade and an armed frontier from Hittite down to Byzantine times. Despite this contest and perhaps because of it, the age-old irrigation network that greened the river's border-lands was maintained. Even as late as the 9th century, Haroun al-Rashid, the Abbasid Caliph celebrated in *The Thousand and One Nights*, could travel from his summer resi-dence at Raqqa all the way back to his capital at Baghdad under the shade of trees. But already the Arabs were allowing the waterwheels and canals to suffer from neglect, and in the 13th century the Mongols completed the destruction. Left untended by man, the Euphrates became a wasted river, running brown and lugubrious through its channel, its mood only changing when the melting snows and spring rains of Anatolia would cause it to race and flood from April to June.

Most neglected and isolated was that northeast corner of Syria between the Euphrates and the Tigris, the upper part of what historically is known as Mesopotamia, Greek for 'the land between the rivers', and which the Syrians call al-Gezira, 'the island'. Here along the tributary rivers of the Khabur and Jaghjagha, the hundreds of *tells*, those mounds of debris that mark ancient towns and cities, testify to an ancient fertility.

Now the Euphrates region and the Gezira (optimistically referred to as 'our California') are experiencing a drive for development that involves improving the infrastructure and increasing agricultural output. New roads and a railway now reach up into the Gezira, as well as a pipeline to carry oil back to Hama

N

60 KM
40 Miles

Qamishli

Tell Brak

Haseke

G E Z I R A

Halabiye

Deir ez Zor

Qalaat Rahba

Mayadin

Euphrates River

Dura II
Europos

Mari

The Euphrates and the Gezira

and Tartus from wells drilled since the late 1960s near the Tigris valley, while new oil fields have been opened up around Deir ez Zor. A huge dam, completed in 1978, has been built east of Aleppo at Al-Thawra, creating hydro-electric power for the entire country and backing up the river to create Lake Assad, whose waters are being used to triple Syria's irrigated area. Other dams are planned for the Euphrates' tributaries, with the intention of turning the uplands through which the Balikh and Khabur rivers flow into vast granaries, while already the regions round their lower reaches have been planted with cotton.

From the bowl in which Aleppo sits you climb up onto a flat plain extending endlessly in all directions. In winter everything turns to mud; in summer the ground bakes and the yellow stubble is grazed by long-eared sheep. By the end of July there has been a harvest of wheat, and in readiness for the next season's planting the occasional tractor coughs its way through the dust, scratching furrows in dry soil the colour of veal. Off to the south you see the railway line and perhaps a diesel drawing a string of modern carriages. It will cross to the north bank of the Euphrates just before the turning for Resafa and not recross it again until reaching Deir ez Zor.

The places most worth visiting are those ancient frontier outposts and caravan cities along the Euphrates or close to it: the Byzantine sites at Resafa near Raqqa and Halabiye towards Deir ez Zor and Graeco-Roman Dura Europos farther downriver.

Beehive Houses

You see them on the dusty plains of northern Syria, both to the west and east of Aleppo and along the Euphrates: beehive-shaped houses made of mud brick, women darting in and out like brilliant swallows, their long dresses of cobalt or intense red, their teeth capped with gold. Usually the houses are clustered into villages, but occasionally they are spread out like large tank traps on the plain. As a man grows rich he adds another beehive and yet another, until he may have a dozen or more standing round a courtyard, some inhabited by himself and his family, some by his animals, one forming his kitchen, and one his granary. Gertrude Bell remarked that they 'are like no other villages save those that appear in the illustrations to Central African travel books'. Sometimes the beehives are truncated, curving upwards only two-thirds of the way and then sliced off, flat topped instead of pointed, making them stranger still, looking like lunar landing modules.

Plastered white, to which the blown dust lends a pleasing pastel, beehive houses are well-adapted to the extremes of climate. With luck you may be invited in for a glass of tea. Through a single opening you enter the dark interior that remains at a constant temperature day and night, summer and winter. The place is swept spotlessly clean and furnished with a large chest, beautifully painted, the woman's pride.

At sunset the men lead their sheep back from grazing, the sky nacreous in the west, slate blue in the east as though waiting to thunder, the yellow grass electric bright. They are robed figures on horseback, bearing their staves like sceptres and themselves like kings, their sheep a following wedge kicking up a fine pink cloud of dust against the closing night. These figures and colours are the more dramatic for the lack of anything else to take your attention. The vast landscape rolls away like a light-sea, not an outcrop or a tree to disturb its soporific monotony (you feel kinder towards it now that the fierce heat has settled). There are only the villages, hammered by the sun during the day, beaten against the dust and gripping it like clams, now opening softly like night flowers.

These days electricity poles march across the plains and most of these villages are electrified. In addition to admiring the painted chest and enjoying the refreshing tea, you may join the returning menfolk who turn to *their* pride: colour televisions on which they watch *Benny Hill* or *Hawaii Five-O*.

Getting Around

The following itinerary heads eastwards from Aleppo to Lake Assad and then follows the Euphrates highway (route 4) to Resafa (160km to turning, then 25km along branch road). The itinerary then continues along the highway to Raqqa (190km from Aleppo), Halabiye and Deir ez Zor (315km from Aleppo). From Raqqa and Deir ez Zor you can travel up into the Gezira. Continuing along route 4 downriver from Deir ez Zor, the chapter covers Dura Europos (95km) and Mari (120km from Deir ez Zor) near Abu Kamal, close to the Iraqi border.

As usual, the best way of getting around is by car, and it is almost the only way to reach several of the sites.

Whether starting out from Aleppo or Palmyra, frequent buses or microbuses will take you to all the towns along the Euphrates highway (route 4), but not to all the sites. Unless you have hired a car or taxi, you will either have to walk or hope to get a lift to such sites as Meskene on the south shore of Lake Assad and Qalaat Jaber on the north shore; Resafa, 25km south of the highway (the turning is 30km west of Raqqa); and Halabiye, 10km north of the highway (the turning is about midway between Raqqa and Deir ez Zor).

There are good bus and microbus services into the Gezira. The Tell Brak excavation site is only a couple of kilometres from the village of that name, which is about midway between Haseke (180km from Deir ez Zor) and Qamishli (260km from Deir ez Zor) on the Turkish border.

The railway from Aleppo will take you along the Euphrates to Raqqa (in 2½hrs) and Deir ez Zor (in 4½hrs), and from Deir ez Zor into the Gezira, stopping at Haseke (in 2½hrs), Qamishli (in 3½hrs) on the Turkish border and Yaroubiya (in 5hrs) near the Iraqi border. There are at least two trains daily.

There are flights from Damascus to Aleppo (several daily), Deir ez Zor (twice weekly) and Qamishli (thrice weekly).

Where to Stay

Apart from Aleppo, the best base in the region in terms of range of accommodation is Deir ez Zor (*see* p.254).

Meskene

At 88km from Aleppo you come to the modern town of Meskene. Immediately after it there is a turning north that in a farther 4km brings you to the Meskene site. Formerly it had over-looked the Euphrates valley; now part of the site has been surrendered to Lake Assad.

Meskene's history was that of a fortified caravan crossing point over the Euphrates from the end of the 3rd millennium BC down to the Mongol invasions of the 13th and 14th centuries AD. This may have been Thapsacus where Alexander built his bridge of boats and in the summer of 331 BC crossed the Euphrates en route to his great battles against Darius at Gaugamela and Arbela, and so on to Babylon and Susa. Hittites, Seleucids, Romans, Byzantines, Arabs and Crusaders all built here. Now the lake waters lap at the **Byzantine walls**.

The principal sight is a towering 13th-century octagonal **minaret** of brick that can be seen from some way off. The minaret is Abbasid work, showing Persian influence, and can be climbed to the top by an internal staircase. It was moved here from near by in the 1970s to escape the rising waters of the lake.

Al-Thawra

Getting There

Buses and microbuses operate to Al-Thawra from Aleppo, Raqqa and Deir ez Zor. From Al-Thawra the last services are at about 4pm. To reach Qalaat Jaber (*see* below) without your own car, you will either have to walk or try to get a ride.

Returning to the highway, in a farther 20km you come to a turning north that in 5km brings you to Al-Thawra ('the Revolution'), the new town servicing the world's largest earth-fill **dam**, its hydro-electric generators and those regiments of electricity pylons marching off to the hori-zons. Though the town is mostly modern apartment blocks, they look pleasant enough and are set among gardens. At the dam, and conceived in a style that might be called Syrian Surrealism, is a **statue of Assad** bringing the future to the masses. Upriver the Euphrates spreads out into a vast metallic shimmer against the arid surroundings, like an imprisoned arm of the Mediterranean reaching into the hinterlands of Syria. Until recently, writers have always described the Euphrates as flowing brown; now the dam holds back both the waters and the mud, letting through a clear blue stream that only slowly broadens towards Raqqa.

Qalaat Jaber

North over the dam at Al-Thawra and round the northeast side of the lake, a distance of about 10km in all, is the Arab **castle** of Qalaat Jaber. Where it once stood on a promontory over-looking the Euphrates, it now stands on an island in the lake and is reached by a causeway. Built during the first half of the 12th century to oppose the Crusaders to the north at Edessa (present-day Urfa in Turkey), this too, like Meskene, was a Euphrates crossing place. Zengi, hero of the gathering Muslim resistance to the Crusaders and captor of Edessa in 1144, was killed at the castle two years later by a slighted eunuch of Frankish origin. The murder did the Muslim cause no permanent harm, however, as his son Nur al-Din eventually cleared the Crusaders from all but the Syrian coastal region, and Saladin, Nur al-Din's nephew, was to drive the Crusaders out of Jerusalem.

The Shia: Partisans of Ali

More important to Islam was the prolonged battle of Saffin fought near by in AD 656 between Ali, the fourth caliph and son-in-law of the Prophet, and Muawiya, the rebellious governor of Syria and relative of Ali's predecessor, the assassinated Caliph Othman. Wishing to avoid further bloodshed, Ali agreed to negotiations, and on the understanding that Muawiya would put aside his claim to the caliphate, so Ali put aside his. But Muawiya reneged while claiming Ali deposed.

The consequences were profound, but first for background it is necessary to go back to Mohammed himself. He was more than a prophet; he had organised the Arab tribes into an enduring political and military force that within a hundred years or so of his death in AD 632 advanced as far west as Morocco and Spain, as far north as Poitiers and as far east as the Indus. But Mohammed died without naming a successor. Ali, husband of the Prophet's daughter Fatima, advanced his claim but after some argument Abu Bakr, one of Mohammed's companions, won acceptance as caliph (*Khalifat rasul-Allah* or Successor to the Apostle of God). Abu Bakr was succeeded by Omar who was succeeded on his death by Othman, an old, weak and vacillating man, but a member of the powerful Umayyad family of Mecca. Tribal tensions within the ever-expanding Arab Empire led to revolt and his murder in AD 656.

Again Ali put himself forward as the natural inheritor of the caliphate, for not only was he related to Mohammed through Fatima, but he was a man of considerable religious learning and sincerity, while his supporters claimed that the Umayyads were no more than power-seeking opportunists. To some extent both sides cloaked political and economic aspirations in religious arguments. Ali however was opposed by Aisha, who had been Mohammed's favourite wife, along with her Umayyad family and many of Mohammed's surviving companions. Reluctantly, Ali was obliged to fight, but his decision to negotiate at the battle of Saffin won him enemies, and five years later, in 661, he was assassinated by an erstwhile follower.

But Hassan, Ali's son and successor, almost immediately conceded the caliphate to Muawiya, who became founder of the Umayyad dynasty. Now the Shia or Shi'ites (*shi'at Ali* means partisans of Ali) rallied to Ali's second son, born of Fatima and so Mohammed's grandson, but in 680 Hussein was defeated and killed by Muawiya's son Yezid at the battle of Kerbala in present-day Iraq. For the Shia, Hussein's death was a martyrdom, all the more emotive because in a sense the blood of the Prophet had been shed. To this day, some Shia mark the anniversary of Hussein's martyrdom by working themselves up into a frenzy and beating and wounding themselves in the streets.

It was on this matter of succession that Islam was riven, for the Shia refused to accept as caliph any but Ali's descendants, while the Sunni, followers of the *sunna*, the Way (represented for a century by the Umayyads, though the dynasty was later rejected by Sunni Muslims), barred the caliphate to the Prophet's descendants for all time.

Nevertheless, the Shia went on to win some notable victories as when the Fatimids took Egypt and advanced up into Syria, and to this day one-tenth of all Muslims (Iranians, most Iraqis and significant numbers in Yemen, eastern Arabia, Lebanon and Syria) still hold to the Shia conviction that with the deaths of Ali and Hussein the greater part of Islam was stained with betrayal. All the same, this division within Islam is not so great as many of the doctrinal rifts in Christianity. Though Hussein is buried at Kerbala, the Umayyad Great Mosque at Damascus (*see* p.67) claims his head (as does the mosque of Sayyidna al-Hussein in Cairo), making it a place of pilgrimage for Shia, many of them Iranians.

Resafa

Resafa offers the most spectacular standing remains anywhere along the Euphrates valley. At 160km east of Aleppo or 25km west of Raqqa you come to the village of Al-Mansura astride what is here a divided four-lane highway. Resafa is signposted off to the south and the way is paved for the whole of the 25km run across the seemingly barren wasteland. Yet here and there you are surprised by sudden strips of cultivation, dark green mirages you think at first, where water is channelled between low earth banks to irrigate sections of field. Then, just as strangely, off in the distance you see the forbidding walls of Resafa rising amid heaps of sand. You need three hours to see this improbable pilgrimage town, the Sergiopolis of the Byzantines, and the best way to begin is to follow the road right round the 2km rectangular circuit of its **walls** (there are houses and a water spigot near the road on the south side). The walls are defended by 50 **bastions and towers** of various design, with round towers at the corners. Finally you should return to the magnificent north gate.

Getting There

The turn-off for Resafa is 160km east of Aleppo, 30km west of Raqqa at a deadbeat place called Al-Mansura. It is then 25km south to Resafa. Really you need your own car. You could hop off the Aleppo–Raqqa bus at Al-Mansura, but as Resafa is on the way to nowhere, there is a very good chance that you will stand about all day at Al-Mansura and never get a passing ride. With luck, and for sufficient inducement, you might be able to persuade someone to take you there—*and back.*

History

> There is a certain church in Euphratesia, dedicated to Sergius, a famous saint, whom men of former times used to worship and revere, so that they named the place Sergiopolis, and they had surrounded it with a very humble wall, just sufficient to prevent the Saracens of the region from capturing it by storm. For the Saracens are naturally incapable of storming a wall, and the weakest kind of barricade, put together with perhaps nothing but mud, is sufficient to check their assault. At a later time, however, this church, through its acquisition of treasures, came to be powerful and celebrated. And the Emperor Justinian, upon considering the situation, at once gave it careful attention, and he surrounded the church with a most remarkable wall, and he stored up a great quantity of water and thus provided the inhabitants with a bountiful supply. Furthermore, he added to the place houses and stoas and the other buildings which are wont to be the adornments of a city. Besides this he established there a garrison of soldiers who, in case of need, defended the circuit wall.

> Procopius, contemporary 6th-century historian
> of Justinian's reign, *Buildings.*

The north gate at Resafa after Sarre and Hertzfeld

An exiguous supply of water from brackish wells was sufficient for the Assyrians to make Resafa a military camp in the 9th century BC. In time it became a minor station at the intersection of two caravan routes, the last stop on the Damascus–Palmyra route before reaching the Euphrates crossing and a detour for traffic forced from the banks of the Euphrates where they narrow due east of Resafa, becoming impassable when the river was in flood. Over 1000 years later the Roman Emperor Diocletian established a frontier fortress here to guard against the Sassanian threat, the Damascus–Palmyra–Resafa route to the Euphrates becoming the Strata Diocletiana.

During the reign of Diocletian also, in about AD 303, Resafa witnessed the torture and beheading of the commander of the imperial palace guard. The story goes that Sergius, a Christian convert who refused to sacrifice to Jupiter, was made to walk from the Euphrates in shoes lined with sharp nails and at Resafa had a hole bored through his lips through which a rope was passed to lead him to his place of execution. His martyrdom made an immense impression and he soon attracted a widespread cult, becoming the patron saint of Christians in the Roman army and of the local desert nomads and indeed of the whole of Syria. What had been the minor caravan station and frontier outpost of Resafa soon grew into the great pilgrimage centre of Sergiopolis, and the rich showered gifts on his shrine. During the reign of Justinian (AD 527–65), and in some cases before, the enclosure was filled with the adornments Procopius mentions.

Resafa was eventually sacked by the Sassanians in the early 7th century, but it was restored and favoured especially by the Umayyad Caliph Hisham, who built a palace outside its southern walls, though little trace of it survives. The town again suffered a few years later, after the Abbasid conquest of 750 (they also dug up Hisham, who was buried here, and flogged his bones, so great was their detestation of his dynasty), and a century on it was reported to be no more than a habitation for local pastoralists. A final sack by the Mongols in 1247 left it desolate. Excavations and restorations have concentrated on the churches you see today. Drifting sand heaped against the richly decorated north gate kept it remarkably preserved, while the sheer size of the cisterns and Justinian's walls, and the skill with which they were built, account for their survival during the succeeding seven and a half centuries.

Visiting the Site

The site is wide open; no adm fee.

Before entering by the north gate, you should walk the short distance to the late 6th-century **audience hall of al-Mundhir** outside the walls to the north. Until not long ago this was thought to have been the spot of St Sergius' execution and burial, the hall mistaken for a church built on the site. Al-Mundhir was chieftain of the Ghassanids, a Christianised Arab tribe who served the Byzantines by patrolling the desert between Palmyra and the Euphrates, keeping other tribes to the east and south at bay. Solidly built to a cross-in-square plan, the building is similar to a Byzantine church, having a semi-domed apse at the east end with small semi-domed alcoves on either side, the hall centrally surmounted by a cone where now the sky comes in. The place has a provincial feel to it, squat, the carvings crude, the acanthus atop the low arch-supporting pillars not much relieved though with a certain rustic charm. A frieze of low relief runs round the interior and in the apse there are pairs of monsters facing one another. (Also in the apse was found the Greek inscription, 'Long live Alamoundaros!', confirming that this was not a church but belonged to al-Mundhir, though he may well have held court here on St Sergius' feast day.) At the right of the apse, in this case in high relief and not balanced on the left side, is what could be a bird, possibly a phoenix. Restoration is underway.

Return now to the triple **north gate**, one of the finest Byzantine remains in Syria. Each rectangular portal is framed by engaged columns with deeply and delicately relieved acanthus capitals. Five arches of different sizes span the portals and the spaces between them in a rhythmical and richly ornamented frieze of crosses and grape-laden vines. In structure and style the gate has been compared to parts of Diocletian's palace at Split. For all the beauty and religious symbolism of this north gate, it was also part of an impressive defensive system. Powerful bastions rise on either side, and originally it was approached through a single outer gateway admitting to a vestibule, though this has not survived. Passing through the gate, however, you can look back and see the protected upper **gallery** running round the walls, permitting the garrison to move quickly and under cover from one tower to another.

You will also notice as you look at these walls—and if you do not notice it immediately, the effect makes itself felt on you after some while—the peculiar nature of the crystalline stone of which Resafa was built (similar to that at Halabiye). It is a type of gypsum, now worn and coloured orange by clinging dust but here and there showing through lightly. Once it must have sparkled and even blinded sight, and even now, if you look closely at its coarse and irregular crystal structure, which fractures jaggedly, the impression is of embedded mica. Take off your sunglasses and you are struck by its glare. For the townspeople of Resafa it must have been a pain in the neck.

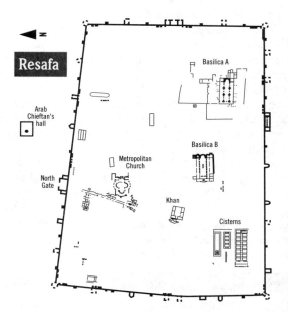

Resafa

Basilica A

Arab Chieftan's hall

Basilica B

Metropolitan Church

North Gate

Khan

Cisterns

Now looking across what was once a small city, what you see are hundreds of mounds and pockmarks as though giant moles have been at work—in fact Bedouin digging for treasure—and drifts of sand covering the devastation left in the Mongols' wake. Rising from this are the remains of three churches and a khan, cleared and in some cases partly restored by archaeologists.

From the north gate there is a discernible path, once an axis of the city though running across it at a slight southwesterly diagonal. After about 100m you come, on your left, to a ruinous though intriguing **metropolitan church**, basilical yet with swollen bays on three sides, the circular scheme continued on the east by the curved apse. Built in the late 520s, this Resafa church was a slightly later attempt than the cathedral at Bosra (*see* p.115) to make the transition from square ground plan to circular dome. Apart from its curious tetraconch (four-apsed) shape, it is noteworthy for its fine decoration, similar to that of the north gate, which can be especially appreciated in the north chapel with its slipped keystone to the left of the central apse. This church has been called a martyry in the belief that it was the burial place of St Sergius, though more recent speculation plumps for basilica B, one of the two larger basilical churches off to the southeast that you will come to in a while. They were built to service pilgrims, while the sarcophagi of bishops here suggests that this was the episcopal or metropolitan church of Resafa.

Continuing a farther 100m or so along the southward path you pass, again on your right, the remains of a Byzantine **caravanserai**. After a similar distance towards the southwest corner of the walls you come to a group of three **cisterns**, beautifully constructed and perfectly preserved underground vaults of enormous size, especially the southernmost, which is 58m long, 22m wide and held water to a depth of 13m. These are the work of Justinian or in any case were enlarged by him, and they are capable of holding sufficient water, collected during the winter rains, to supply Resafa for two years. Signs warn of the danger of going too close, and when you peep in at the top you see why: the drops are terrific.

From the cisterns you can strike off eastwards to the two pilgrimage churches, the first called **basilica B**, late 5th-century and very ruinous. The central apse contained the remains of a martyr, perhaps St Sergius, but he had become too important to remain here for long, the Emperor Anastasius I, Justinian's predecessor but one, carting him off to Constantinople.

Undeterred by the saint's absence, pilgrims came to Sergiopolis in ever swelling numbers, necessitating the construction in the 550s of the yet larger **basilica A** in the southeast corner of the city. Commonly called the Church of St Sergius, an inscription states that in fact it was dedicated to the Holy Cross. It is more entire than basilica B and recent restoration work helps convey something of its former grandeur, an effect achieved not by fine stone carving, which is all but absent here (as are the mosaics for which it was once famed), but by the striding arches that divide the aisles from the nave and which are similar to those in the church at Qalb Loze (*see* p.234) built a century earlier. Within decades of basilica A's completion, however, it was rocked by an earthquake and each of the original arches, which rose from piers, were filled in with rather shoddy stonework to create two lesser arches supported by columns. Even so, the effect is not unpleasant, ruin propped up by ruin, for the columns were brought from the earthquake-wrecked tetraconch church, several bearing episcopal inscriptions in Greek round the top, sometimes written backwards, and the acanthus capitals are good. The lack of transverse arches indicates that the roof was not of stone but rather of wood supported by beams. Beneath the partly collapsed semi-dome of the central apse, notice the bema, that horseshoe-shaped podium reserved for the clergy.

In the vicinity of the church, trenches have been dug laying bare **marble-paved streets**, and you are reminded of the crowds that once pressed here. Now there is a great silence, louder for the crunch of your foot on the ground, the clacking of a stone kicked along the paving.

Raqqa

'The river is very wide here, the country is pale and flat and shining, and the air is hazy,' wrote Agatha Christie of Raqqa in the late 1930s. Raqqa indeed means flat land in Arabic; an unattractive agricultural and commercial centre promoted to the status of provincial capital in 1960, it is the only place of any size in that immense flatness between Aleppo, 190km to the northwest, and Deir ez Zor, 135km to the southeast. But the river no longer flows broadly at Raqqa, charged with mud as it used to be, not since the construction of the giant dam at Al-Thawra from which it issues emerald green and turquoise in turn. Past Raqqa on its left bank it flows crystal clear through gravelly channels.

The dam and the great irrigation projects associated with it for this region are rousing Raqqa from the 700 years of sleep into which it fell after the Mongol sack in 1258, a fate it shared with Baghdad. There was a time when the two could justly be mentioned in the same breath, for the Abbasids founded Raqqa in AD 772, 10 years after Baghdad, and made it the second capital of the Arab Empire. Just as Baghdad was circular, built consciously as the centre of the universe, so Raqqa was nearly so, a great horseshoe wall defended by 100 towers and so thick that two horsemen could ride abreast atop its ramparts, much of it surviving still, its open end closed by the Euphrates and a now vanished riverside wall. The Romans and Greeks had forts and settlements here, the earliest said to have been established by Alexander the Great himself, though more probably by his successor, Seleucus Nicator. Nothing of these periods survives, but great efforts are being made to restore the city's walls and gates to something like their Abbasid glory.

Getting There

Raqqa is on the north bank of the Euphrates, 190km from Aleppo and 135km from Deir ez Zor.

By train: Raqqa is on the Deir ez Zor-Aleppo line and is served by two trains a day in each direction, two from Deir ez Zor, two from Aleppo, one of these having come first

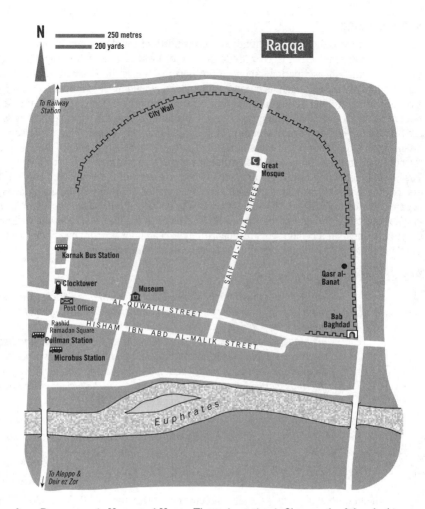

from Damascus via Homs and Hama. The train station is 2km north of the clocktower.

By bus and microbus: the Karnak bus station is just north of the clocktower; the Pullman and microbus stations are about 300m south of the clocktower. Both bus stations offer frequent departures to Deir ez Zor, Aleppo, Hama, Homs and Damascus. The microbuses serve a number of places, including Aleppo, Deir ez Zor, Al-Thawra and Al-Mansura (the turn-off for Resafa).

Tourist Information

There is a Tourist Office, unmarked, in a room behind the Karnak Hotel. You may be able to arrange journeys to local sites, e.g. Resafa, here.

There is no bank in Raqqa, so have cash on you.

Visiting Raqqa

In the east of the old city, a few hundred metres north of the downriver bridge, is the **Bab Baghdad**, or Baghdad Gate, faced with decorative brickwork and rebuilt in the 12th century, that is after the Abbasid period. About 200m north of this is the **Qasr al-Banat**, meaning Palace of the Maidens, though its purpose is unknown, a building of four liwans opening upon a central courtyard and dating from the 9th century. From here you can follow the Abbasid **wall** northwards and then continue as it describes a semicircle to the west. Within the walls is the ruinous 8th-century **Great Mosque**, built of mud brick in Mesopotamian style and recognisable by the towering round minaret restored in the 1160s by Nur al-Din, who also rebuilt the courtyard arcades. There is a small **museum** (*open 9–6 in summer, 9–4 in winter, closed Tues; adm*) containing unearthed artefacts a kilometre west of the Baghdad Gate and 300m east of the clocktower. A kilometre northeast of the walled town two **Abbasid palaces** have been excavated, one that of Haroun al-Rashid, the fabled caliph of *The Thousand and One Nights*, the other thought to be that of his successor al-Maamun (who while in Egypt to suppress a Christian rebellion took the opportunity to search for treasure by knocking a hole in the side of the Great Pyramid, which still serves as its entrance today).

Preserving the Euphrates Sites

> *The Mesopotamian method of building with sun-dried brick, which was more or less generally employed, and the extent and isolation of the sites make it questionable whether it would be worth while to undertake costly maintenance and consolidation work. At Mari, Dura Europos and Raqqa the treasures found are of greater interest than the buildings; once the excavations have been completed, plans drawn and photographs taken, the ruins can be left to their fate. It will then be the task of museums and publications to make them live once more.*

> UNESCO, Syria: Problems of Preservation and Presentation of Sites and Monuments, 1954.

Where to Stay

inexpensive

The best hotel in town is the government-run ★★★**Karnak**, ✆ (022) 232265/7, 800m west of Rashid Ramadan Square (the road soon divides; take the right fork and follow it round the curve). Clean, comfortable carpeted rooms with bath, air conditioning, TV and balcony. There is a restaurant and duty-free shop. The staff are friendly, but the place is rather run-down.

cheap

The ★**Tourism**, ✆ (022) 220725, Al-Quwatli Street, is just east of the clocktower. Rooms have fan, bath, TV and fridge; they are clean but somewhat dark. The ★**Ammar**, ✆ (022) 222612, immediately north of the clocktower, is no cheaper than the Tourism and offers less, with shared showers and only some rooms with fan; also its proximity to the clocktower and a mosque can make it a noisy place.

Halabiye

On the right bank of the Euphrates between Raqqa and Deir ez Zor, Halabiye was the greatest of the Byzantine frontier fortresses. But its importance was strategic, not commercial, so that when the frontier was lost to the Persians early in the 7th century, then soon after to the Arabs for whom the Euphrates ceased to be a frontier at all, Halabiye lost all purpose and was abandoned. Its remote isolation from population centres saved its stones from being recycled in other building works, so that apart from damage by earthquake and flood its massive walls—described by Procopius in the 6th century as 'a remarkable sight and exceptionally beautiful'—survive impressively intact.

Getting There

Halabiye is 100km from Raqqa and 65km from Deir ez Zor. To reach it, you must turn north at Tibne; at 12km the site is signposted to the right from where you follow the paved road for another 8km.

If travelling by public transport, you will have the same problem reaching Halabiye as reaching Resafa. You can get off the Raqqa–Deir ez Zor bus at Tibne, but then it is a walk of 20km in each direction (or 9km in each direction if dropped off at the tiny village of Shiha) unless you can find someone who, for payment, will take you there, wait and bring you back (which you are more likely to do at Tibne).

To reach Zalebiye (*see* below), on the opposite side of the Euphrates, cross by the shaky wooden bridge upstream (north) of Halabiye, 6km in each direction. Otherwise you will have to start again by microbus from Raqqa or Deir ez Zor. Ask to be dropped at Zalebiye, from where it is a 2km walk to the site. But as the route along the east bank of the Euphrates is little frequented, do not count on being easily able to get a ride back again to Raqqa or Deir ez Zor.

History and Plan

The Euphrates narrows here and runs between hills, making it an ideal place to control the river's traffic. At one point on the west bank the hills recede, creating a natural amphitheatre at the foot of a basalt cliff. In about AD 266 the spot attracted the attentions of the queen of Palmyra, then at the height of her power, and the fortress she founded was named Zenobia in her honour. But when the Romans occupied Palmyra in 273, they took the river fortress too. After the fall of the Roman Empire in the West, Justinian fought to recover imperial territory in Italy, Spain and North Africa, and he strengthened Byzantine defences in the East. At Halabiye, he greatly enlarged the circuit of walls and built churches, baths and stoas within, though the place never amounted to more than a garrison town. 'For all these operations,' writes Procopius, 'the masterbuilders Isidorus of Miletus and John of Byzantium gave their assistance.' This Isidorus was the nephew of the Isidorus who had been one of the architects of Justinian's great church, the Haghia Sophia in Constantinople, completed in 537. The younger Isidorus was responsible for rebuilding its dome after an earthquake caused its collapse in 558.

The stone used at Halabiye is similar to that now dulled but once peculiarly glittering gypsum employed at Resafa, that fortified pilgrim town that was also part of Justinian's forward line of defence. The plan of the Halabiye fortress is a triangle, its base a 385m run of walls along the river, its sides a north wall 350m long and a south wall 550m long rising to a citadel at the apex: this, as Procopius explains, to command the high ground to the west from which previously 'it was possible for the barbarians, whenever they attacked the city, to shoot down with impunity upon the heads of the defenders, and even upon the heads of those who stood in the middle of the city'.

But Justinian's Western ambitions put an intolerable strain on Byzantium's resources in the East, the direction of greatest threat. For all its apparent strength, Halabiye was part of an undermanned and fixed defensive system along the Euphrates, a Byzantine Maginot Line. In 610 the Sassanian Persians swept through, sacking Halabiye as they went, and by 613 Damascus and all Syria was theirs. Byzantine Egypt followed and Anatolia itself was threatened. Yet in an astonishing series of campaigns, the Emperor Heraclius inflicted defeat after defeat on the enemy, and in 629, having driven the Persians back to their capital, he returned to Constantinople in triumph. But the struggle had exhausted Persians and Byzantines alike, and within a few years the Arabian tribes, newly won to Islam by Mohammed, imposed their rule across almost the whole of the East.

Visiting Halabiye

The site is open; no adm fee.

The road brings you to the south gate and continues parallel with the river through the north gate and on for another kilometre to a number of **tower tombs**, all that remains of the Palmyrene presence.

This road between the two gates marks the original **cardo maximus** and was intersected midway along by the **decumanus** running from east to west, traces of which are evident. This crossroads can be taken as your point of reference for reaching the few ruins, mostly foundations, within the walls.

About 30m to the northeast of the crossroads are the **baths**. Following the decumanus 50m westwards you come on your left (south) to a **basilica**, one of two churches at Halabiye. To the right (north) of the decumanus is the **forum**, while a bit farther on are the more substantial remains of the second and larger **basilica**. Both churches are thought to belong to Justinian's reign.

Now continue to the north gate to follow the **walls** as they rise westwards towards the apex of the triangle, punctuated by a series of massive two-storey square **towers**. The defenders could go from one tower to another by means of galleries within the walls. Near the apex you will notice a larger structure of three storeys with vaulted ceilings, the **praetorium** or soldiers' barracks. Walls, towers and barracks; all these are Justinian's work. A final steep climb takes you up to the **citadel** with a terrific view over the whole of the fortress, out over the Euphrates and down into the *wadi* behind. Though part of Justinian's original plan, the citadel has been somewhat reworked by the Arabs. You can now return to the south gate by following the line of the south wall.

On the opposite bank of the Euphrates and within view 2km downstream is the smaller and badly ruined site of **Zalebiye**, companion fortress to Halabiye and sharing with it the same history from Palmyrene to Arab times. By crossing a wooden bridge upstream (north) of Halabiye, you can reach the site in 6km; otherwise you must first go either to Raqqa or Deir ez

Zor and follow the minor east bank road between the two. The railway also runs along the east bank and offers a close view in passing.

Deir ez Zor

A junction for journeys throughout the Euphrates valley, up into the Gezira (*see* below, p.260) and southwest to Palmyra (220km), Deir ez Zor, on the right bank of the river, also offers the best range of accommodation east of Aleppo. Also for the economic development of Syria, Deir ez Zor has recently taken on considerable importance as new oil fields, exceeding in supply those of the Gezira, are opened up in the vicinity. Though prosperous, chaotic and rapidly expanding, the pulse of the town is set by the river, which can make it an unhurried and pleasant place to stay. It is also far more attractive than Raqqa, though in Deir ez Zor, apart from the excellent new (1996) archaeological museum, there is almost nothing to see.

The **museum** (*open daily 9–6, closed Tues; adm*), which owes the quality of its presentation, also its funding, to Germany, is a delight for the way it brings the past to life. There are four principal sections: prehistory, ancient Syria, the Graeco-Roman period, and Syria since the Arab conquest. The first two sections are especially remarkable and include reconstructions of prehistoric dwellings and a Mari temple. All of the Euphrates valley and finds from the Gezira tells are represented, and everything is intelligently labelled in English.

Also worth visiting is the **Holy Martyrs Armenian Church**, a handsome understated edifice built in 1990 which commemorates the 1½ to 2 million Armenian victims of the Turkish genocide during the First World War, especially those who died in the Turkish-run death camp at Deir ez Zor (*see* p.35), some of whose bones are preserved on the lower ground level.

Getting There

By air: there are twice-weekly flights between Damascus and Deir ez Zor.

By train: the train station is on the opposite (northeast) side of the river from town, a distance of 3km. At the arrival and departure of trains, buses run between the railway booking office at the centre of town (by the Karnak bus office) and the station. There are at least two trains a day between Deir ez Zor and Aleppo, a daily train to Damascus, and three trains daily to Haseke and Qamishli towards the Turkish border.

By bus and microbus: the Karnak bus station is at the town's central 8 Azar (March) Square. The Pullman and microbus station is 1km south of the centre along 8 Azar Street. There are buses and microbuses downriver to Abu Kamal, upriver to Raqqa and Aleppo, across the desert to Palmyra and Damascus, and into the Gezira to Haseke and Qamishli. For the Palmyra and Damascus journeys in particular, you should book a day in advance.

Car hire: Europcar has an agency in town and at the Furat Cham Hotel.

Tourist Information

The Tourist Office is in a side street off Khaled Ibn al-Walid Street, about 300m east of the central square. Opening hours are from 9am to 2pm daily, closed Fridays.

money

The Commercial Bank of Syria, open from 8am to 2pm, closed Fridays, is on Al-Imam Ali Street, about 600m west of 8 Azar Square.

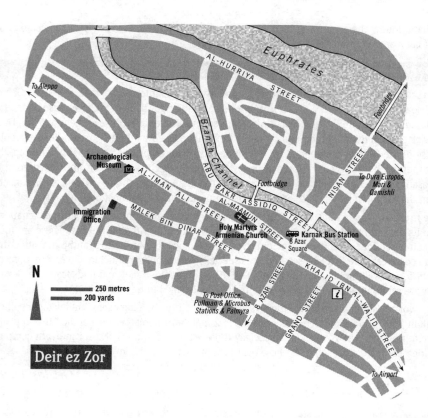

Deir ez Zor

communications

The Post Office, open 8–8, closed Fridays, is 750m south of 8 Azar Square along 8 Azar Street towards the Pullman station. The telephone office, open 8am–10pm daily, is on Al-Imam Ali Street about 200m west of 8 Azar Square.

visa extensions

The Immigration Office is on Malek Bin Dinar Street, south of the Archaeological Museum, and is open 8–2, closed Fridays. You will need three photographs. Visas are issued the same day, but get there early.

Where to Stay
very expensive

★★★★★**Furat Cham Palace**, on the Euphrates, 5km west of the centre, ✆ (051) 225418, ✉ (051) 222672. Two restaurants, snack bar, bar, disco, swimming pool, tennis courts, fitness centre, sauna and business centre—the place caters to oilmen and tour groups. The pool is open to non-guests for a fee.

★★★★**Concord,** ✆ (051) 224272, ✉ (051) 225411, on Al Hurriya Street, not so far west of the centre as the Cham but no views over the Euphrates either. Restaurants, bar, swimming pool.

inexpensive

★★**Raghdan Hotel,** ✆ (051) 222053, ✉ (051) 221169, just north of the central 8 Azar Square and overlooking the Euphrates branch channel. A clean, quiet and pleasant hotel dating from the French mandate. The rooms are high and spacious and have shower, toilet, fan, or in some cases air conditioning. There is an upstairs restaurant.

cheap

★**Al Arabi al-Khabir,** ✆ (051) 222070, on Khalid Ibn al-Walid Street, just east of 8 Azar Square. Clean basic rooms, less clean shared shower and toilet, generally a bright and friendly place, certainly better than other hotels in this category—all of which cluster round the central square and should be carefully inspected.

Eating Out

No place stands out for its cuisine and more likely you will be drawn by the river views. The **Aseel** and the **Cairo** restaurants 1km or so west of 8 Azar Square along the Euphrates branch channel, also the **Bridge** and the **Tourist Blue Beach** restaurants on either side of the suspension footbridge overlooking the Euphrates proper offer pleasant views though mediocre food at inflated prices. The upstairs restaurant of the Raghdan Hotel also has good views and the food, though ordinary, is inexpensive, also alcohol is served. There are very agreeable garden cafés on the north side of the Euphrates across the footbridge.

Qalaat Rahba

From the village of Mayadin, 45km south of Deir ez Zor along the Euphrates highway (Route 4), you can see the small 12th-century Arab **castle** of Qalaat Rahba a kilometre or so off to the southwest. The castle stands on a mound, its pentagonal keep girdled by several concentric walls. Built during the reign of Nur al-Din to help extend his control over the whole of Syria, Qalaat Rahba also served the Mamelukes but suffered damage during the successive Mongol incursions and was abandoned. Now it is rather romantically disintegrating, more appealing from afar.

Dura Europos (Salihiye)

As Halabiye was the greatest of the Byzantine frontier fortresses, so Dura Europos was the greatest border fortress of the Graeco-Roman period as well as being a caravan city and river port, so that it combined economic with strategic importance. The Eastern and Western cultural influences that met here produced a vivid art, as for example the synagogue frescoes now reconstructed at the National Museum in Damascus.

The site commands a bend in the river to the east from the height of the escarpment and is bordered to north and south by narrow ravines. Following these contours, its walls describe an irregular rectangle whose sides vary in length from 500 to 800m, only the long west wall towards which you approach being unprotected by natural features.

Dura Europos is 95km southeast of Deir ez Zor along the Euphrates highway (Route 4), from where it is both signposted and within clear view 2km eastwards.

Microbuses run between Deir ez Zor and Abu Kamal. Ask to be dropped off on the main road at Salihiye (or Dura Europos) and walk the 2km out to the site. There is usually a fair amount of traffic on the road for going on to Mari or back to Deir ez Zor, though not on Fridays. A taxi can be hired at Deir ez Zor for the day ($35) to take you both to Dura Europos and Mari. In summer especially bring plenty of water and protect yourself against the sun.

History

To Dura, meaning fortress in Old Semitic, was added Europos, the birthplace in Macedonia of Seleucus I, one of whose generals founded a colony here in about 300 BC and gave grants of land to his troops that reached all the way up into the valley of the Khabur to the north. In typical Hellenistic fashion, its streets were laid out on a rectangular grid, while its function was to protect the lines of communication between the military centres of Seleucia on the Tigris to the east and Apamea on the Orontes to the west. But the Seleucids could not hold the vast Asian empire won by Alexander the Great, and by 141 BC the Parthians had advanced westwards to the Euphrates and occupied Dura Europos, whose population, increasingly Aramaic-speaking peoples indigenous to this region, became less Western and more Eastern in habits and outlook.

During the 1st century BC, at the beginning of that era of stability owed to the new balance of power between Rome and Parthia, when Palmyra began to flourish and one stream of its trade passed this way, Dura Europos began to grow in size and increase in prosperity. In AD 165 Rome occupied the city, and with the rise of a more aggressive Persian power, the Sassanians, the Romans correspondingly enlarged their garrison. They built barracks and administrative quarters and such Roman amenities as baths and a theatre, as well as temples to those favoured gods of the legions, Jupiter and Mithras, to which the city's cosmopolitan population added a Christian chapel, a synagogue and pagan temples of their own. But in AD 256, after several previous attempts against the city, the Sassanians breached the vulnerable western wall and reduced Dura Europos to ruins.

For nearly 1700 years the site lay all but unnoticed, until 1920 when a British army detachment, engaged in skirmishes against Bedouin in the desert northwest of Baghdad, sought protection within the northwest angle of Dura Europos' ancient walls. Digging down, they suddenly uncovered a wall painting in what archaeologists would later identify as the temple of the Palmyrene gods. The survival of these paintings and those of the synagogue and the Christian chapel, all along the western wall, was ironically owed to the desperate measures taken by the inhabitants during their doomed defence against the Sassanians in 256. To strengthen the wall against mining, they had piled sand against its inner face, burying the paintings and so preserving for posterity what one archaeologist has described as 'the Pompeii of the desert'.

Excavations conducted by French and American teams from 1922 have revealed 11 temples, two small sanctuaries, the synagogue and the Christian chapel, a market, baths and numerous houses. Sculptures and paintings have been removed to museums, the wall paintings from the chapel to Yale University and those from the temple of the Palmyrene gods and the synagogue to the National Museum in Damascus.

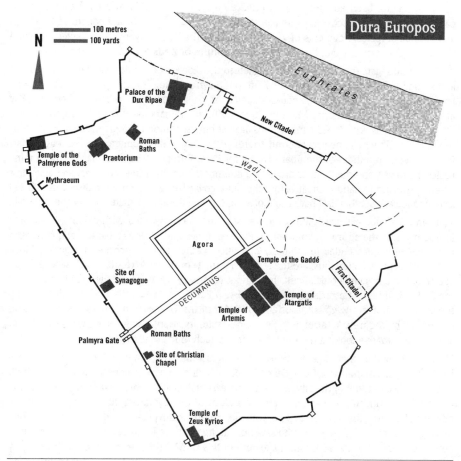

100 metres
100 yards

N

Dura Europos

Euphrates

Palace of the
Dux Ripae

New Citadel

Roman
Baths

Temple of the
Palmyrene Gods

Praetorium

Wadi

Mythraeum

Agora

Temple of the Gaddé

Site of
Synagogue

First Citadel

DECUMANUS

Temple of
Atargatis

Temple of
Artemis

Palmyra Gate

Roman Baths

Site of Christian
Chapel

Temple of
Zeus Kyrios

Visiting the Site

Note that the temporary entrance to the site is to the right of the Palmyra Gate, so that you come first to the Christian chapel. The site is open daily to sundown; adm.

Except for the walls, little remains above foundation level and it is to museums in Damascus and elsewhere that you must go to see the treasures excavated at Dura Europos. You come here more for the sense of location and will need a couple of hours to go round the site. You approach, as the Sassanians did, the **west wall**, which in some places rises to 9m and is defended by towers all along its length. The stone towers and mud brick walls date from the Seleucid period, but where you see walls of stone, these were built later by the Parthians. The track leads up to the bastions of the **Palmyra Gate**, which gives on to the **decumanus**, running from west to east, the principal thoroughfare of the city, which can be followed later.

First, about 50m to your right and opposite the section of wall between the Palmyra Gate and the first tower, are the foundations of the **chapel**, the oldest known place of Christian worship in Syria, having been adapted from a private house in about 240 and used especially for baptisms. Its walls were covered with painted scenes of Adam and Eve, a shepherd and his flock and various miracles, fragments of which are now at the Yale University Art Gallery. Beyond this, in the southern angle of the walls, was the **temple of Zeus Kyrios** (Zeus the Lord).

Again from the gate, but this time heading left to the block opposite the wall between the first and second towers, you come in about 75m to the **synagogue**. This too was converted from a house, probably between AD 165 and 200, and subsequently enlarged in 244. Its frescoes, now at Damascus in the National Museum (*see* p.59), are remarkable for their brightness and imagery, breaking with Hasidic injunctions against representation by depicting such subjects as the Exodus. Under the nearby **second tower** to the left of the Palmyra Gate, archaeologists found an eerie reminder of the final struggle for Dura Europos. The Sassanians drove a mine under the tower, and the Romans drove a countermine from the inside, attackers and defenders meeting in hand-to-hand combat before the mine collapsed. The men were discovered in full armour and carrying their last pay, a coin of AD 256 giving the approximate date for the city's fall.

You can now walk eastwards along the **decumanus**, formerly lined with colonnades, which in 300m passes the **agora** on your left, in Parthian times built over as a bazaar, and continues to a *wadi* which descended to the port, long since washed away. Opposite the agora, a block to the right of the decumanus, are the remains of the **temple of Artemis** which served as the centre of the city's chief official cult throughout its history. Near it was a temple in honour of the Syrian goddess **Atargatis** and another to two Palmyrene gods, the **Gaddé**. Overlooking the south end of the *wadi* is the original **citadel** of the Greeks and superseded in the 2nd century BC by the **new citadel**, also Seleucid despite its orientalising triple liwans, on the far side of the *wadi* overlooking the Euphrates, into which much of it has fallen.

Now following the inner edge of the *wadi* northwestwards you come to the Roman quarter of Dura Europos. The **palace of the Dux Ripae**, the commander of troops along the river, built during the last decades of the city, is against the east wall near its northeast corner. Against the north wall, 300m to the west, is the **praetorium** of the Roman military camp, and in the northwest corner the 1st-century AD **temple of the Palmyrene gods** or temple of Bel, serving the corps of Palmyrenes who saw duty along with the Romans here, its wall paintings now also in the National Museum. Just south of this is the **Mithraeum**, an early 3rd century AD centre for the worship of Mithras, whose origins were in Persia but whose cult spread throughout the Roman Empire and was especially popular among legionaries who rather liked its macho induction ceremony, which involved climbing into a pit and having a bull slaughtered over their heads. Even so, Mithraism gave Christianity a close run, and though blood is thicker than water, it is also more messy, and in the end it was perhaps squeamishness that decided the next 2000 years in favour of the baptismal font.

Mari (Tell Hariri)

At 25km south of Dura Europos and 120km south of Deir ez Zor you see Tell Hariri rising from the flatness between the road and the Euphrates. Numerous *tells* dot the landscape of the Euphrates and the Gezira, each marking some ancient though often humdrum settlement. But here in 1933 a Bedouin, looking for a stone to mark a grave, disinterred a 4000-year-old statue of the sun god Shamash, a discovery which excited the attentions of archaeologists, who at once began digging and have been digging ever since.

What had been found was Mari, a royal city state like Ebla to the west (with which it enjoyed close relations), which flourished for over 1000 years from 2900 BC, and which was a great trading centre, especially in tin for manufacture into bronze. It had links to Babylonia and the Mediterranean, and possessed an extensive irrigation system for agriculture. Excavations revealed a vast palace, its walls in places surviving to 5m and adorned with wall paintings, its 275 rooms containing shrines, a throne room, ceramic baths, an archive of 17,000 tablets inscribed in Babylonian cuneiform, statues of kings, gods and goddesses, though looking more like *nebbishes*, and a wealth of other artefacts.

In about 1760 Mari fell to Hammurabi of Babylon, who three years later razed its defences and knocked down its mud brick palace walls, filling its rooms with earth and thereby preserving their contents, including wall paintings, for our times. These are now found at the Louvre and the Aleppo and Damascus museums.

The site itself is not particularly rewarding for the visitor. About a tenth of the *tell* has been excavated, archaeologists stripping away layer after layer of mud brick, recording finds and foundations before proceeding to an earlier level. There is little that is intelligible to the layman, and even orientation is difficult, while in winter the rains turn much of the site to mud.

Getting There

Mari is situated on the east bank of the Euphrates, 25km south of Dura Europos and 120km south of Deir ez Zor.

Microbuses running between Deir ez Zor and Abu Kamal will drop you off on the main road from where the site is about a kilometre's walk. *See also* p.256.

Visiting the Site

Open daily 9–6 in summer, 9–4 in winter; adm. There is a café at the site.

From the Deir ez Zor–Abu Kemal road a track heads eastwards to the **archaeologists' quarters** on the southwest side of the *tell*. With any luck, there will be someone there who will be able and willing to explain the site. The *tell* is a low mound running diagonally from southeast to northwest and it is in the latter half that almost all the excavations have been concentrated.

The **palace** forms a square whose sides are each about 100m long. Popularly known as the palace of Zimri-Lim (1775–60 BC), who was the last king of Mari, it was actually constructed over the course of several centuries. Its **entrance**, on the north near the northeast corner, gave on to a forecourt which in turn led on to the large **eastern courtyard**. On its south side is a chamber identified as an **audience chamber or a shrine**, in which case probably to Ishtar, goddess of fertility. It was found decorated with paintings dating from 2100 BC. Beyond this, in the southeast corner of the palace, were **religious buildings**, including possibly a temple. West of the large courtyard is a somewhat smaller **inner courtyard**, a reception room on its south side leading to the **throne room**, the palace's largest room, in which the throne was placed against the west wall. West of this were the **archives**. The numerous small rooms in the southwest corner of the palace are thought possibly to have been the **slaves' quarters**, while the entire area to the west and north of the inner courtyard were the **living quarters** of the royal family.

A group of **temples**, including one to Shamash, is to the east of the southeast corner of the palace, while to the west of the palace's southwest corner, in the oldest part of the city (which is partly roofed over against the rain), is the **temple of Ishtar**, dating from perhaps 2500 BC.

Almost certainly the only reason for coming this way is to cross over into Turkey. From Deir ez Zor, route 7 runs north to **Haseke** (180km), an ugly place, and **Qamishli** (260km) on the border (the area is Kurdish). There is also a railway line. If travelling by road, you have the convenient opportunity to visit Tell Brak.

Tell Brak

Tell Brak is about halfway between Haseke and Qamishli. You head for the village of that name, which is a kilometre or so east off the new Haseke–Qamishli road (it is on the old road), from where you head southeast for 2km for the mound on the banks of the Jaghjagha River. The site is older even than Mari and reaches back to the late 4th millennium BC. Here in 1937–39 Max Mallowan excavated the so-called **Eye Temple**, dating from 3100 to 2900 BC, named after the hundreds of votive offerings bearing a representation of the eye. The British have resumed excavation of the *tell*, turning up an **Akkadian fortress** of about 2350 BC and a **Mitanni palace** of 1500 BC. The Akkadian Empire was one of the world's first, and was established by its Semitic ruler Sargon (2371–2316 BC). For a time it extended over the whole of Mesopotamia, east into Persia, north into Anatolia as far as Diyarbakir and west across northern Syria to the Mediterranean, making both Mari and Ebla subject to it.

Agatha Christie's Mystery in Mesopotamia

Mallowan's wife was Agatha Christie, who accompanied him on these digs and wrote a delightful book, *Come, Tell Us How You Live*, about her experiences. First there is the need to find a likely *tell*: 'All digging is a gamble—among seventy *tells* all occupied at the same period, who is to say which one holds a building, or a deposit of tablets, or a collection of objects of special interest?'

'We have made a day's excursion on the opposite bank of the Khabur to Tell Halaf again, and we have done two days on the Jaghjagha—a much overrated river, from the point of view of appearance—a brown muddy stream between high banks—and have marked down one *tell*—Tell Brak—as highly promising. It is a large mound, with traces of several periods of occupation, from early prehistoric to Assyrian times.'

Meanwhile, Agatha was plagued by a mystery: '"I seem," I explain, "to be always falling over to the left."' 'Max says it is probably one of these rare tropical diseases that are distinguished by just being called by somebody's name. Stephenson's disease—or Hartley's. The sort of thing, he goes on cheerfully, which will probably end with your toes falling off one by one.'

'I contemplate this pleasing prospect. Then it occurs to me to look at my shoes. The mystery is at once explained. The outer sole of my left foot and the inner sole of the right foot are worn right down. As I stare at them the full solution dawns on me. Since leaving Deir ez Zor I have walked round about fifty mounds, at different levels, on the side of a steep slope, but always with the hill on my left. All that is needed is to go into reverse, and go round mounds to the right instead of the left. In due course my shoes will then be worn even.'

In such ways does archaeology proceed.

The tetrapylon, Palmyra

Palmyra and the Syrian Desert

Getting Around   263

Approaches to Palmyra
from the West   263

Palmyra (Tadmor)   265
   Exploring the Site   271

The Desert East of Palmyra   288

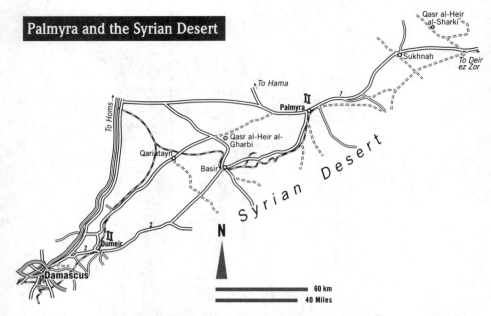

As mountains block the western and northern approaches to Damascus, you fly in from the east, the flight path carrying you over the Syrian Desert. You could be arriving at another planet, its landscape alien and contorted, as though bombarded over the millennia by asteroids. The captain announces that no photographs are to be taken, and it is then that you make out the missile emplacements, looking like the swept entrances to tombs. Such signs of life are almost welcome, and you marvel that caravans once picked their away across this fearsome desolation. Yet until the advent of roads and motorised transport in the 20th century, camel caravans still crossed the desert between Damascus and Baghdad, all stopping at Palmyra.

Baedeker's 1912 guide to Palestine and Syria tells that the journey from Damascus to Palmyra took four days by camel, five days on horseback or by carriage. Water was a problem and an armed escort was desirable. A supply of tobacco was recommended to keep the local Bedouin sweet. Happily for lunatics, there was the convenience of a famous cure en route: at the village of Qariatayn the sufferer was shackled overnight within a room; in the morning his chains would fall from him and miraculously (provided he paid his bill) the affliction would vanish.

The need for treatment is reduced these days, as the drive from Damascus, or for that matter Homs or Deir ez Zor, is less than three hours. Even so, when the sun is high and the desert is blanched of colour, there is time enough for the tedious horizons to fill with spectral things. Pairs and sometimes entire families of twisters spout suddenly from the ground like fountains, dust clouds sweep across the road and phantom pools of water levitate deliciously above the sands. In the distance, black Bedouin tents seem like the carapaces of dead beetles consumed by heat.

Yet the Syrian Desert was once an international thoroughfare, travellers finding refuge against the delirium of sand and sun at the oasis of Palmyra. To the east lay Mesopotamia and India, to the west the Mediterranean and Anatolia; offering sustenance and water to caravans navigating this perilous wasteland, Palmyra became one of the great trading centres of the ancient world. The city prospered and mimicked Rome in grandeur, then fell after briefly challenging Roman might.

Some rush to visit Palmyra's incomparable ruins as a day-trip from Damascus, which is a pity, not only because it allows so little time at the site, but because they miss the unexpected beauty of this otherwise harsh environment at dawn and evening and by moonlight. As the sinking sun drains the sky of obliterating light, the air cools and the landscape is suffused with colour. Then mountains settle into mauve and the desert gleams like the flesh of an opened fruit. Something of that pleasure must have been the reason why the Umayyad caliphs built their eastern and western palaces of Qasr al-Heir. To these they would withdraw from the pressures of city life to refresh their roots in the sundown deliquescence of the desert wilderness.

In addition to Palmyra, Qasr al-Heir al-Gharbi (West) and Qasr al-Heir al-Sharqi (East), this chapter also covers the Roman remains at Dumeir.

Getting Around

Palmyra (Tadmor in Arabic) is reached by good fast roads from Damascus, Homs, Hama and Deir ez Zor. The usual route from Damascus is via Dumeir and Basir in 243km. An alternative route from Damascus is via Qariatayn, Qasr al-Heir al-Gharbi (West) and Basir in 292km. A newly opened route runs from Hama via Salamiya in 196km. From Homs the most direct route covers a distance of 155km, though via Qasr al-Heir al-Gharbi and Basir the distance is 200km. There is only one route from Deir ez Zor, a distance of 221km, though the diversion to Qasr al-Heir al-Sharqi (East) will add a further 60km: 30km out and then back along an indistinct track over rough ground (four-wheel drive advisable and in wet weather a necessity).

Buses, microbuses and service taxis serve Dumeir from Damascus, and serve Palmyra (*see* p.266) from Damascus, Homs and Deir ez Zor. To follow the route from Hama, also to visit the Qasr al-Heir palaces, you need your own transport.

Where to Stay

There is accommodation at Palmyra.

Approaches to Palmyra from the West

As you rise out of the green basin of Damascus, the fields and orchards fall away, the factories and even the electricity pylons are gradually left behind in the haze. You are climbing almost imperceptibly onto the steppe, the empty arid prelude to the desert. The last cultivation to the northeast of the capital is around the town of **Dumeir**, once a Roman station along the Damascus–Resafa caravan route. Nowadays from Damascus you turn off the Homs highway at 24km, and after 18km along the road to Palmyra you come to Dumeir, and near its centre a Roman temple. Built in AD 245 during the reign of Philip the Arab, the temple has been much restored and stands almost intact, having passed through phases as a Christian church and an Arab fortress. The locals sometimes call it the *qalaat* and attribute it to a king who lived a thousand years called Hanna bin Manna, a play on the Arabic phrase '*wa ma tamanna*', meaning that which is wished for—the fantastical means by which such a grand building came to be in their midst. Dedicated to Zeus Hypsistos, the Heavenly God, the temple seems to have replaced an earlier shrine to Baalshamin, the Phoenician sky god, the stairways leading to the roof suggesting an open-air ritual.

A farther 5km along the way to Palmyra you come to the remains of a sizeable 2nd-century Roman military camp, about 180m square, with round towers at each corner, rounded bastions projecting from the walls and bastioned gates on each of the four sides. Though apparently stripped by the Arabs of all its marble for use at Damascus, its street plan is plain and several structures are fairly intact. The camp is just off the road leading south to a 20th-century Syrian air force base.

From here on to Palmyra, your way is alongside low brown mountain ranges, their geological structure etched on their flanks. But if you are travelling along the direct Homs–Palmyra road the landscape will be flat and more steppe than desert almost to Palmyra itself, with swathes of desiccated yellow fuzz and clusters of green succulents like sea urchins on the ocean floor. In springtime the dun horizons are enlivened by a colourful show of wildflowers. Look out for beehive houses, more typical of the steppe around Aleppo, near Furqlus, about 40km east of Homs. Ancient irrigation systems once made these plains more fertile and inhabitable than they are now, while reservoirs sustained shepherds' villages in the mountains throughout the summer months. Such was the degree of cultivation in the now desertic steppe between Homs and Palmyra that, during his months of operations against Zenobia, the Emperor Aurelian was able to feed his army of 40–50,000 men upon the produce of the country. After the fall of Palmyra in the late 3rd century AD, such villages and cultivation were abandoned. But, in a more limited way, the old Roman dams, reservoirs and aqueducts were still useful to the Byzantines and Arabs, making possible the two fortress-palaces called Qasr al-Heir (meaning walled castle), one 65km southwest of Palmyra as the crow flies and easily accessible, the other 95 feathered kilometres to the northeast and more difficult to reach. Both now stand ruined amid an expanse of desert, though formerly they were surrounded by walled gardens.

Qasr al-Heir al-Gharbi (West)

Qasr al-Heir al-Gharbi was built in 727 by Hisham, the last great Umayyad caliph, who two years later built the much grander and far more intact Qasr al-Heir al-Sharqi (East) (*see* p.288). The tall shattered tower of a 6th-century Byzantine monastery still guides you from a distance to the ruins. Of the luxurious Arab palace that partly incorporated the monastery, nothing survives above the lower masonry of the walls. These enclosed an area 70m square and had round towers at the corners (except for the square Byzantine tower rising three storeys high at the northwest corner) and rounded bastions midway along three of the walls. The east wall was pierced by a gate flanked by a pair of round towers. Inside, the remains of numerous rooms, originally two storeys high, surround a central court formerly adorned with Corinthian colonnades. Like the gardens that once lay outside the palace, perhaps this courtyard too was lushly planted and sang with splashing water, piped here from the Roman dam, still intact today, at Harqaba, 17km to the south.

Though the *qasr* was a means of keeping an eye on the nomadic tribes, its decorations clearly indicate that it was a place of delight, a desert resort (favoured especially in summer!) whose pleasures included not only gardens and hunting but also wine, women and song. In the verse of the last Umayyad caliph, Walid II, a man fond of bathing in a swimming pool of wine:

> *There's no true joy but lending ear to music,*
> *Or wine that leaves one sunk in stupor dense.*
> *Houris in Paradise I do not look for:*
> *Does any man of sense?*

Not that the site announces as much now, and indeed the atmosphere is somewhat spoilt by modern structures, including a power station, near by. In fact the most important find made when the palace was excavated in the 1930s was the fragile fresco and stucco decoration picked up in fragments at the foot of the gate towers. This entire gate complex, complete with its bust of a bare-breasted woman, has been restored and re-erected as the main entrance to the National Museum in Damascus (*see* p.57), whose vestibule is decorated with other elements of the palace, while a contemporary khan that once stood near by is now in the museum's garden.

Palmyra (Tadmor)

> *Palmyra—its slender creamy beauty rising up fantastically in the middle of hot sand. It is lovely and fantastic and unbelievable, with all the theatrical implausibility of a dream.*

> Agatha Christie, *Come, Tell Me How You Live*, 1946

'The work of *jinns*,' declared Said ibn Taimur, sultan of newly oil-rich Oman, when he visited Palmyra in the 1950s, which he meant literally, though his astonishment is shared by less credulous travellers arriving upon so grand a city amid the isolation of the desert. Two hundred years earlier, as the English travellers James Dawkins and Robert Wood approached Palmyra, an opening in the hills 'discovered to us, all at once, the greatest quantity of ruins we had ever seen, all of white marble, and beyond them towards the Euphrates a flat waste, as far as the eye could reach, without any object which shewed either life or motion. It is scarce possible to imagine anything more striking than this view: So great a number of Corinthian pillars, mixed with so little wall or solid building, afforded a most romantic variety of prospect'.

On closer examination the two Englishmen saw and indeed illustrated in marvellous detail not only columns but a great deal of solid and beautifully-carved masonry (mostly limestone rather than marble, however), two years later publishing the results of their 1751 visit in *The Ruins of Palmyra* that became a fountainhead of the Neo-Classical movement in European architecture. Yet the greatest impression remains with those Corinthian colonnades, at once ethereal and monumental, the backbone and limbs of an entire city along whose avenues you can wander to explore sanctuaries, porticoes and public buildings.

A special pleasure of Palmyra, even as visitors unload from tour buses and archaeologists continue at their excavation and restoration work, is all sense of busyness being swallowed up within the extent and complexity of the city. The appeal is enhanced by the almost complete absence of modern buildings in view, and by the natural beauty of the setting. Northwards a backdrop of rocky hills ranges from east to west, almost reaching the verges of Palmyra. With operatic effect, an Arab castle has been placed upon a hilltop to the west where it fills the vista as you walk along the central colonnade. A vast palm oasis sighs against the eastern fringes of the ruins, beyond it the shallows of a salt lake, home to the rare sea-lavender, while southwards the great desert shimmers into infinity. Clambering atop the Temple of Bel to survey the silent stones of Palmyra articulated against the formless sands, you feel that like the early travellers you have come upon the city alone and almost for the first time.

Getting There

For arriving by car, *see* p.263. The road from Damascus, Homs and Hama winds round the Palmyra Cham Palace Hotel and continues round the south of the site, then curves round to the modern town of Tadmor to the northeast of the site before continuing on to Deir ez Zor.

By bus: the Karnak office and station is on the main square, opposite the museum, at the west end of Tadmor town. Private bus and microbus companies also drop off and pick up at this square, or at their offices (mostly east along Al-Quwatli Street) or at the square at the eastern end of Al-Quwatli Street, 500m from the museum. Between Karnak and the private companies there are plenty of services, with several daily buses to Deir ez Zor, Homs and Damascus (some via Homs), each taking 3hrs (except Damascus via Homs, in 4½hrs), and a daily bus to Haseke and Qamishli in 5–6hrs.

By car with driver: hiring a car with driver in Damascus would allow you to visit sites en route and would serve you in Palmyra itself for going round the tombs, to the museum, and to the Arab castle.

Tours: various tour companies in Damascus offer trips to Palmyra.

If it is terribly hot or you are pressed for time or you are lazy or unfit, you can hire a taxi locally to take you round Palmyra. In any case you might need one if visiting the tombs, which are unlocked only at appointed times (*see* p.283). A taxi from Palmyra to Qasr al-Heir al-Sharqi will cost you an arm and possibly a leg. There are no car hire companies at Palmyra.

The Tourist Office, open from 8am to 2pm and from 5 to 7pm, is opposite the museum in Tadmor town.

History

In 1929 the Temple of Bel was cleared of its mud brick houses and the new town to the northeast was built; before that, as Baedeker advised: 'Visitors to the ruins need have no hesitation in entering the houses or climbing on their roofs'. The curious now have Palmyra to themselves, free of domestic encumbrances, and with it the name, meaning 'place of palms', given to the city by the Greeks and Romans in the 1st century AD. The locals, however, have taken with them the more ancient name of Tadmor, a word of pre-Semitic origin, probably meaning guard post. Record of Tadmor has been found in early 2nd millennium Assyrian inscriptions at Mari on the Euphrates and Kültepe in Turkey. The Assyrians were then the dominant power in the East and carried on an adventurous trade between Mesopotamia and Anatolia. The people of Tadmor were Arameans, Bedouin from the south who had settled in northern Syria and came under Neo-Hittite influence. Their guard post settlement protected an oasis fed by a sulphurous spring. It was a living of sorts.

What transformed Palmyrene prospects was the collapse of the Seleucid empire in 64 BC. The Seleucids had been a bridge between East and West, though they ignored Palmyra, their principal trade route from Seleucia, their eastern capital in Mesopotamia, following the Euphrates north until it drew close to Aleppo, bypassing the desert, and then crossing to Antioch, their western capital, and so down the Orontes to the Mediterranean. Now instead, the Romans in Syria and the Parthians beyond the Euphrates faced each other across a no-man's land, the already forbidding desert made insecure by bandit tribes. Palmyra rose to the opportunity, organising a camel corps to police the desert and establishing a secure caravan route between Dura Europos and Emesa (Homs). Though 1st-century BC Palmyra was still hardly more a trading post, its leading inhabitants were amassing enough wealth to build the tower tombs rising from the valley to the west. Around a stinking spring amid a sea of sand, calculation and enterprise were raising this most improbable of cities.

But to the eastward extension of Roman authority, most of all, Palmyra owed its fortune. During the 1st century AD, the city was assimilated into the province of Syria, yet retained both its army and a great measure of independence. It was also provided with the funding and imported skills that went into Palmyra's first monumental civic and religious buildings of stone, among them the Temple of Bel, dedicated in AD 32, which replaced an earlier mud brick structure. Rome's most important contribution, however, was to decisively alter the routes of trade in Palmyra's favour. The Euphrates route via Thapsacus (near Sura) and then overland to Aleppo and Antioch still remained popular, as was the southern route from

Mesopotamia westwards via Petra. After the Emperor Trajan broke the power of the Nabateans in 106, their capital at Petra was eclipsed, the Romans ensuring that the wealth of the orient flowed instead through Palmyra. Nor did the city's merchant families wait to receive; they plunged into finance and far-flung commerce in luxury goods, their strings of camels following the Silk Route to China, their ships on the lower Euphrates meeting the traffic of spices and aromatic oils, of ivory, ebony and pearls from India and the Gulf. They traded also in slaves, and in dried fish from the Sea of Galilee, and in Syrian glass and olive oil from the Mediterranean littoral. Palmyrenes set up shop in Rome itself, where they even built their own temple.

The money was rolling in by the time the Emperor Hadrian was treated to a three-week fête at Palmyra in 129, to which he responded by granting the city free status within the Roman Empire, thus entitling it to set and collect its own taxes. The Palmyrene authorities imposed tariffs on goods by the donkey- or camel-load according to value, a rate was demanded for the use of water, and even prostitutes had to pay a monthly tax equal to the amount they charged per sexual act. These tariffs meant that the city shared in the profits of its merchants, whose success it encouraged and publicly celebrated—on Palmyra's columns you notice consoles on which once stood not statues of mythic heroes or generals, but of businessmen who had literally earned the honour. Palmyra was a trading city through and through; a relief at the Temple of Bel shows that gods as well as goods travelled about on the backs of camels.

Hadrian also gave Palmyra the honorific title Hadriana, and as though in curtsey its citizens took to adding Roman surnames to their Semitic ones. Over half the local names were Arab, however, as in the preceding several hundred years an increasing number of nomads abandoned the harshness of desert life and came to settle among the original Aramaeans. Roman ways, in fact, went only skin deep. Palmyra had a senate and a theatre, and in Zenobia's time it even had an imported philosopher, Longinus, who probably did *not* write *On the Sublime*, the work for which he is celebrated. But in style of dress, in the formulaic nature of their art and the opulence of their architecture, in their religious beliefs and in their tribal organisation, the Palmyrenes remained oriental.

Within 100 years of Hadrian's sojourn almost the entire grandiose city whose ruins now lie before you had been built. Its population was around 200,000, comparable to that of Antioch. Yet at the same moment, Palmyra's fate began to turn. The balance of power between Rome and Parthia on which the stability of the city's mercantile economy depended was upset. Successive power struggles in Rome weakened authority throughout the empire, while a new power, the Sassanians, arose in the East. Seizing the lower reaches of the Tigris and Euphrates rivers, the Sassanians began to strangle Palmyra at the very source of its caravan trade. Then in 260 the Sassanians advanced across Syria and stood at the gates of Antioch, while the Roman army sent out to meet them was defeated at Edessa (Turkish Urfa), the Emperor Valerian taken prisoner and killed. Palmyra's merchant families suffered heavy losses of income, their power weakened, and the dynastic ambitions of an Arab family headed by Septimius Odainat, and with the army behind him, supplanted the former ruling oligarchy. Where Valerian failed, Odainat succeeded, driving the Sassanians out of Syria and chasing them deep into Mesopotamia. The Romans honoured him with the title Corrector of All the East, but Odainat proclaimed himself King of Kings. It may have been no more than a touch of that ostentation Palmyra had long demonstrated in other spheres of life. At any rate, he never put the substance of his claim to the test; in 267 he was murdered in mysterious circumstances, rumour had it by his wife Zenobia.

For a brief impetuous moment, Zenobia touched Palmyra with romance and then brought it to destruction. Taking advantage of Roman troubles with the Germanic tribes, Zenobia declared herself Augusta and laid claim to the eastern half of the Roman Empire. In 269–70 she led her armies to the Nile and into Anatolia, seizing Bosra and Antioch along the way. 'She claimed her descent from the Macedonian kings of Egypt,' crooned Gibbon, 'equalled in beauty her ancestor Cleopatra, and far surpassed that princess in chastity and valour. Zenobia was esteemed the most lovely as well as the most heroic of her sex.'

Zenobia was in fact of Semitic stock, her family originally merchants who, before that, had perhaps been desert nomads. But her husband had declared himself King of Kings, and she certainly meant to make herself Queen of the East. Nothing less than control of the trade from China, India and the Persian Gulf to Europe via the Euphrates, the Red Sea, the Nile and the Bosphorus was her aim. But in AD 272 the Emperor Aurelian, an experienced cavalryman, rode against her, defeating a large Palmyrene force outside Emesa (Homs) and then went on to attack Palmyra. Zenobia fled by camel across the desert but was captured as she tried to cross the Euphrates, presumably to seek Sassanian help. Aurelian brought her back to Rome in triumph, leading her through his city in chains of gold. When the Senate mocked him for his victory over a woman, Aurelian is said to have replied: 'Ah, if they only knew what a woman I have been fighting! And what would history say if I had been defeated?'

Zenobia is said to have ended her days in a villa at Tivoli. The philosopher Longinus, her political advisor, was less lucky; Aurelian took the precaution of separating his head from his body. Palmyra was left to exhaust itself alone, once more rising against the Romans, forcing Aurelian to return. This time he sacked the city and massacred its inhabitants. In the 30 years to the end of the Emperor Diocletian's reign, Palmyra was transformed into an armed and walled strategic camp, a guard post once again, the short straw for the lonely legion standing picket at the dead end of the Roman Empire. As a trading centre, it never recovered, and though in the 6th century the Emperor Justinian strengthened the walls and several churches were built during the Byzantine period, the city was falling to ruin. Though the Umayyads built their fortress-palaces of Qasr al-Heir to the west and east, the Arabs neglected Palmyra, except to fortify the Temple of Bel in the 12th century and perhaps at the same time to build the Arab castle on the hilltop to the northwest. Slowly the sands washed in and Palmyra was forgotten by the outside world.

The Rediscovery of Palmyra

What impressed Benjamin of Tudela when he arrived at Palmyra in 1192 was that it possessed a population of 2000 Jews. These were recent settlers, refugees from the Crusader states. The Jews of Jerusalem had been massacred by the Christian knights when they conquered the city in 1099, and continuing persecution led them to seek safety in lands still held by the Muslims. More Jews lived in Damascus, for example, than throughout the Christian-held Holy Land. Benjamin was a rabbi from Navarre in northern Spain, newly reconquered from the Muslims; it was partly in search of his roots that he travelled through the Mediterranean and the Middle East, though his journeys also carried him as far as the borders of China. As for the remains of ancient Palmyra, he had nothing to say; classical antiquity was not yet in fashion.

Five hundred years later, during the 17th century, the first trickle of curious Italians, Frenchmen and Englishmen reached Palmyra, though the earliest to provide an account was Dr William Halifax, chaplain to the English factory (trade counter) at Aleppo, who in 1691 found the population reduced to 30 or 40 Arab families living in 'little huts made of dirt within the walls of a spacious court, which enclosed a most magnificent heathen temple'—the Temple of Bel. But it was Dawkins' and Wood's *Ruins of Palmyra*, published in 1753 with comprehensive illustrations by their companion Giovanni Borra, that fulfilled their intention to 'rescue from oblivion the magnificence of Palmyra'. The inscriptions they recorded also permitted in that same year the decipherment of Palmyrene script (it runs from right to left), a variation of Aramaic. Learned travellers visited Palmyra throughout the 19th century, though it was the Russians who first undertook archaeological excavations in 1900, followed since by other European missions and by the Syrians themselves.

Lady Hester Stanhope

The most bizarre visit to Palmyra, in 1813, was that of Lady Hester Stanhope, niece and confidante of William Pitt the Younger, prime minister at the age of 25, and granddaughter of William Pitt the Elder, Lord Chatham, who had also been prime minister. At the death of her uncle in 1806, Lady Hester lost her position at the centre of British public life and travelled eastwards in search of a world she could make her own. She lived the rest of her days at Joun (*see* p.331) on the slopes of Mount Lebanon, reading, riding and loving, receiving European visitors and never ceasing to interfere in local tribal and more general Eastern political affairs. Her daring and imperiousness impressed the Arabs, who took her eccentricities for the mysterious ways of a prophetess and treated her as a queen.

'On one of the days of her residence at Palmyra,' wrote one of her visitors, the traveller John Carne (*Letters from the East*, 1826), 'she gave a kind of fete to the Bedouins. . . . It was a lovely day, and the youth of both sexes, dressed in their gayest habiliments, were seated in rows on the fragments of the pillars, friezes and other ruins with which the ground was covered. Her Ladyship, in her Eastern dress, walked among them, addressed them with the utmost affability, and ordered a dollar to be given to each. As she stood, with all that Arab array, amidst the columns of the great Temple of the Sun, the sight was picturesque and imposing; and the Bedouins hailed her, with the utmost enthusiasm, Queen of Palmyra, Queen of the Desert! . . . They speak of her now with the utmost veneration and respect. They also retain another mark of her bounty, one which, out of regard for her countrymen, she might well have spared. The Great Sheikh received from her a paper, in her handwriting, in which she directs him to demand a thousand piastres of every traveller who visits the ruin. The Sheikh never fails to enforce this counsel, and displays the paper, with the addition, that the great lady, the Queen, said that the English travellers were rich, and that they ought to pay well for the privilege of seeing Palmyra. This enormous tax, which it is impossible to escape, causes several travellers to leave Syria without seeing the finest ruin in the world. One indeed, of no small eminence, absolutely refused to pay it, telling the Sheikh, who drew the mandate from his bosom, that the great lady had no right whatever over his purse, and that she showed little wisdom in leaving such a mandate in his hands. He passed four days at Palmyra, and would have left it as wise as he came, if he had not made a compromise with the chief, and consented to pay half the sum. The Arabs, though they would not personally injure him, did not suffer him to leave the hut, and at last placed some wood and fagots round the walls, and, setting them on fire, filled the habitation of the traveller with such clouds of smoke, that he could neither breathe nor see, and was obliged to give way. This injudicious and needless written mandate from the noble visitor to the chief, will, no doubt, be handed down from sheikh to sheikh for many generations; and travellers, for centuries to come, will be doomed to see the ominous scroll produced, and the thousand piastres demanded, with the comment that it was given to their forefathers by the great lady from beyond the sea.'

Exploring the Site

Generally the site is open and can be explored at will. The Sanctuary of Bel is open daily 8–1 and 4–6 in summer, 8–4 in winter; adm. For the tombs, see p.283.

A long colonnade running roughly east–west forms the central axis of Palmyra. The Temple of Bel is at the eastern end of the axis and Diocletian's Camp is near the western end. The site will be explored in that direction. The description then continues with the Palmyra Museum, which is on the near side of Tadmor town to the north. Here you can join a tour for the Valley of the

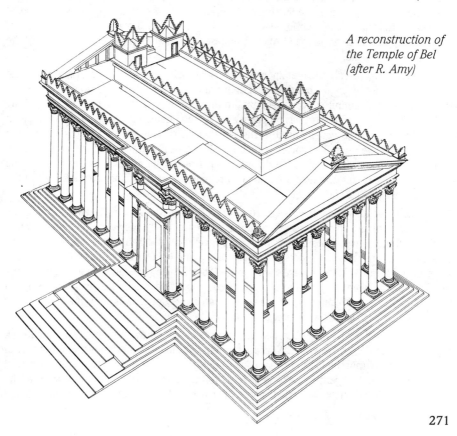

A reconstruction of the Temple of Bel (after R. Amy)

271

Tombs to the southwest of the site. Penultimately, the Efqa spring and the palm oasis to the south of the site are described, and finally Qalaat Ibn Maan, the Arab castle, to the northwest.

At least a full day should be allowed for even a superficial exploration of the site, the tombs and the museum. While everything can be reached on foot, you might welcome the use of a car for reaching the Valley of the Tombs, the museum and most of all the Arab castle, especially during the hotter times of year.

Bear in mind that in summer it becomes fiercely hot after about 11am and the temperature does not become comfortable again until 5 or 6pm. The days are milder from autumn through spring, but then the early mornings and nights are chilly, even cold. The most beautiful moments at Palmyra are at dawn and sunset.

The Sanctuary of Bel

On the edge of the oasis but rising higher than the palms themselves, the great Corinthian columns of the Temple of Bel, the most high god of Palmyra, dominate the city. As so often happens, trade and pilgrimage went hand in hand at Palmyra. Not surprisingly, its principal gods, like almost everything else, were imports—Allat from Arabia, Baalshamin from Phoenicia, Bel from Babylonia. Together they made Palmyra an important religious centre.

Identified with Zeus of the Greeks and Jupiter of the Romans, Bel means Lord or Master and is the masculine form of Belili, the Sumerian Mother Goddess, whom in later Babylonian belief he replaced as creator of the world. Associated with him in a triad were two Palmyrene gods, Yarhibol, representing the sun, and Aglibol, representing the moon, but Bel, as master of the heavens, was supreme.

The sanctuary stands on a slight eminence, a *tell* or artificial mound, marking the original site of the settlement. Potsherds found at a depth of 6m beneath the courtyard go back to at least the early 2nd millennium BC, corresponding to the earliest Assyrian inscriptions mentioning Tadmor. A shrine of some sort has probably always stood here, and fragments of a temple of the Hellenistic period were re-used in the existing walls. It is worth walking around the outside of these walls to fully appreciate their massiveness and the enormous area they encompass. (The remains of two grand 3rd-century AD **houses** lie behind the east side of the sanctuary, their rooms arranged around a central courtyard, their floor mosaics now in the Palmyra and Damascus museums.)

This walled sanctuary consists of two parts, a paved courtyard 205m by 210m surrounded by colonnaded porticoes on all four sides, and near the centre of the courtyard the temple proper. Entry was from the west, through a powerful propylaeum approached by a broad flight of stairs. (The Palmyra Museum has a model of the sanctuary as it originally looked.) The Arabs replaced the propylaeum in 1132 with a solid and severe-looking keep (the date is over the door); the temple had long been converted to use as a mosque, and now the entire sanctuary became a fortified settlement. To the right of the keep, you can see an Arab bastion made of ancient pillars. The keep is blocked; you enter the sanctuary to its left.

Probably the best way to get your bearings is to walk straight across the courtyard to the temple, dedicated on 6 April AD 32 during the reign of Tiberius, making it the oldest part of the sanctuary. Within the cella are chambers to north and south, remarkable for their carved monolithic ceilings. A gentle rise of steps leads to the southern chamber, the smaller of the two, in which it is thought a movable image of Bel was kept, to be trundled down the stairway

Plan of Palmyra

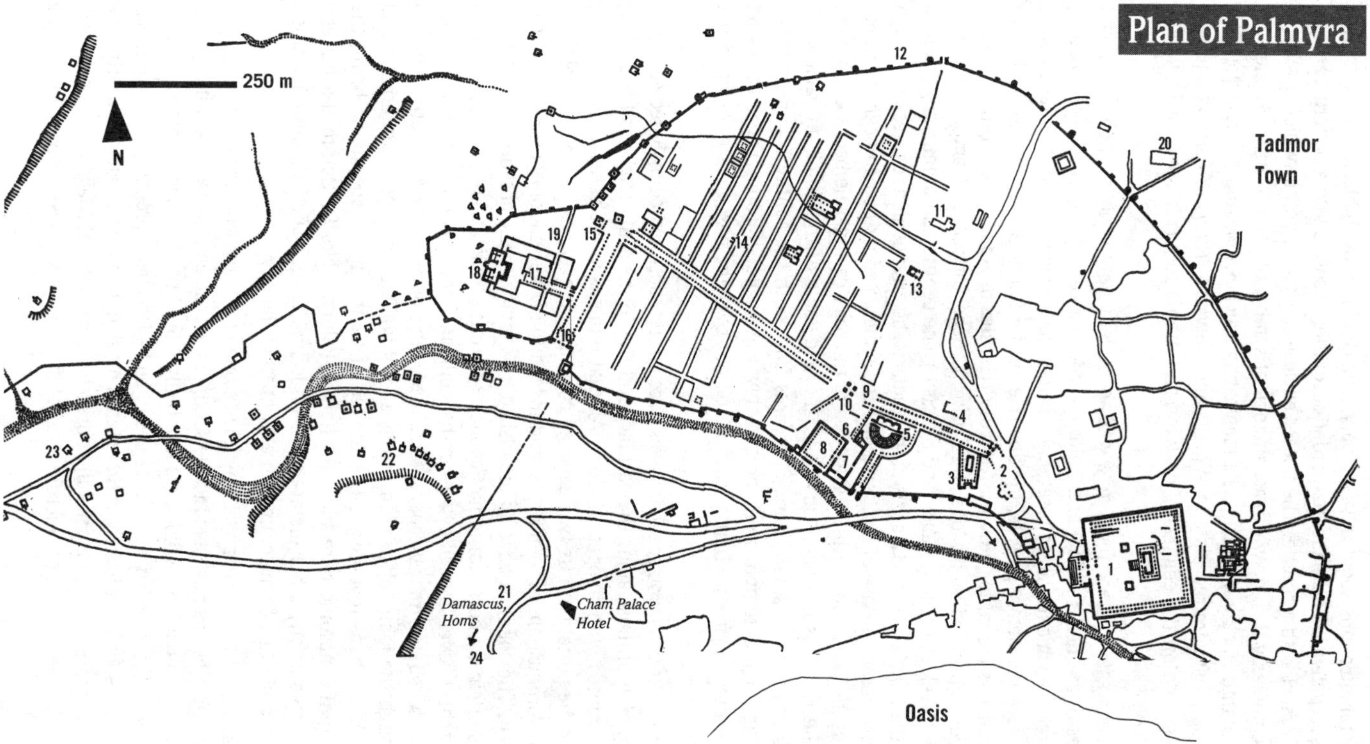

Tadmor Town

Oasis

250 m

N

Cham Palace Hotel

Damascus, Homs

1 *Sanctuary of Bel* 2 *Monumental arch* 3 *Temple of Nabu* 4 *Baths of Diocletian* 5 *Theatre* 6 *Senate* 7 *Tariff Court* 8 *Agora* 9 *Zenobia inscription* 10 *Tetrapylon* 11 *Hotel Zenobia* 12 *City wall* 13 *Temple of Baalshamin* 14 *Residential quarter* 15 *Funerary temple* 16 *Damascus gate* 17 *Camp of Diocletian* 18 *Praetorium* 19 *Temple of Allat* 20 *Palmyra Museum* 21 *Efqa spring* 22 *Tower-tomb of Iamliku* 23 *Elahbel Tower* 24 *Hypogeum of the three brothers*

for ceremonial perambulations about the sanctuary. The ceiling, though blackened by smoke, retains all of its sharp detail. The elaborate border decoration resolves into a pattern of octagonal coffers, each filled with a rosette. The border encloses a square, within which is a circle decorated with complexly linked swastikas, an ancient symbol of good fortune. At the very centre is a huge acanthus, all too much like a man-eating artichoke looking down at you. Yet this was the single most admired plate in Wood's and Dawkins' *Ruins of Palmyra* and was reinterpreted in stucco on the ceilings of drawing and dining rooms in some of England's greatest country houses.

The north chamber was no storage room for a walkabout deity but the holy of holies itself and contained images of the Bel, Yarhibol and Aglibol triad. The ceiling is carved with squares, diamonds and circles, each enclosing a rosette. At the centre is a cupola filled with seven busts representing the seven planetary powers, the Sun (Helios) for illumination, the Moon (Selene) for enchantment, Mars (Ares) for growth, Mercury (Hermes or Apollo) for wisdom, Jupiter (Zeus) for law, Venus (Aphrodite) for love and Saturn (Cronos) for peace. (Compare the Latin to the days of the week in French, Italian and Spanish.) The central and dominating figure is Jupiter. Around the cupola are the 12 signs of the zodiac. The arrangement expresses, though probably not consciously, the rise of Bel, for under the lunar calendar he had been identified only with a day of the week, but with the adoption of the solar calendar he became supreme. Bel as Lord of the Heavens has been carved on the underside of the lintel: an eagle with outstretched wings against a sky of stars. Staircases from both the southern and northern chambers lead up to the temple roof, presumably the scene of some ritual involving communing with the sky, from where you can look out over the oasis, the desert and the whole of Palmyra.

Now emerging from the cella, you see that it was once entirely surrounded by fluted columns, though only a number of those along the east face still rise to their full height and bear their entablature surmounted with stepped merlons. All that remains of the peristyle on the west (entrance) side is the portal with its two engaged columns. In every case, the columns have been badly sand-worn just above their bases, and indeed the lower masonry of the portal has had to be replaced. The columns have an unfinished look owing to the absence of capitals; in fact the columns originally bore Corinthian capitals of bronze which were perhaps plated in gold or silver and must have shone like flares in the sunlight. These were presumably removed by the Arabs and melted down for weapons; certainly for this purpose the Arabs are known to have bored through the joints of column drums and of walls to extract the internal metal clamps used to hold them together, the evidence of their mining operations being the numerous holes in the masonry here and elsewhere in Palmyra. Nor for that matter has any statue of bronze, gold or any other metal ever been found, though such statues once stood upon the consoles projecting from columns in every part of the city.

The peristyle was linked to the cella walls by huge stone beams on which the roofing blocks were laid. Two of these beams now stand to the south of the cella entrance and bear interesting reliefs. One shows the moon god Aglibol, his face badly worn but identified by the lunar crescent on his shoulders. With his left hand he seems to pull a loo chain (probably a staff or spear, but wear and damage encourage licence). He extends his right hand across an altar bearing the fruits of his beneficence; in fact he is reaching out to hold the hand of Malakbel (all but swallowed by a great crack in the beam), a fertility god of the fields and flocks whose altar, on the left, has not only fruits but a kid. Farther to the left, badly damaged, are two robed Parthian worshippers. On the reverse of this beam, two gods, one on horseback, the other in a chariot, are in battle against evil, represented by a creature with a human body and snakes for legs, while an assembly of other gods stands by.

Another beam shows priests burning incense, and on the reverse an intriguing processional scene. Priests and worshippers attend a camel bearing a pavilion, which probably housed the god's image. Following behind are a group of women who, veiled and robed from head to toe, bear themselves in a manner marvellously expressive of humility and religious awe. You may encounter some Muslims who point to this as proof that the veil long antedated Islam, and who use it to justify the complete covering of the face. Certainly at various times both in the East and the West, notions of respectability and social class have persuaded some women to reveal little of themselves. But no general conclusion can be drawn from this relief: the women here are depicted specifically as taking part in a ritual, while other statues of women in the Palmyra Museum do not show them covering their faces, rather at most, and then signifying death, drawing the drapery of their headdresses close to their faces but not across them. In fact neither of the two references to the veiling of women in the Koran (Suras 24:31 and 33:59) refers to veils being worn over the face, and indeed Sura 24:31 is precise in enjoining women simply 'to cover their adornments, except such as are normally displayed; to draw their veils over their bosoms'.

The expressiveness of these veiled women is all the more striking given the crudeness of the carving overall. As these beams had originally been placed 18m above your head, there was little point in executing the reliefs with delicacy. You notice also that the work is generally stiff, with human figures usually presented face-on, a hieratic quality common in Palmyrene and indeed Eastern art, so different to the classical tradition of the Greeks and Romans, though ultimately Byzantine art would be informed by oriental rather than classical tradition. The beams were once painted, a wash of delicious colour still adhering to their friezes of vine leaves and succulent grapes.

Now sweeping your gaze around the courtyard, you see that it was surrounded on its north, east and south sides by double colonnaded porticoes. These porticoes were built some time between AD 80 and AD 120, that is after the temple. Built later still, around the mid-2nd century, was the western portico, which has only a single though taller colonnade. Only some of the numerous Corinthian columns that once supported the flat roofs of the porticoes still stand. South of the steps leading down from the temple are the remains of a sacred basin, while opposite it, to the north, is an altar. Sheep, cattle and camels were brought into the courtyard through a sunken arch near the north corner of the west portico and up a ramp, both still evident, to this altar where they were sacrificed. Between ramp and altar you can trace the remains of a banqueting hall where selected Palmyrenes were invited to partake in ritual meals. You can imagine this being a rather noisy, sticky and smelly business, the animals bellowing before the knife, their blood being poured out over the altar, their carcases washed, burnt and then eaten in a kind of sacred barbecue. 'The priests shall bring the blood, and sprinkle the blood round about upon the altar that is by the door of the tabernacle of the congregation'; then the animal is cut into pieces, its innards washed, 'and the priest shall bring it all, and burn it upon the altar: it is a burnt sacrifice, an offering made by fire, of a sweet savour unto the Lord'; 'and the remainder thereof . . . shall it be eaten in the holy place; in the court of the tabernacle of the congregation they shall eat it'—which is how the Bible, in Leviticus 1:5, 1:13 and 6:16, describes the ancient Jewish ritual of burnt offerings, which was probably not dissimilar to that of the Palmyrenes.

The Museum of Popular Culture

Open daily 8.30–2.30; adm.

This museum of regional ethnography and natural history is housed in the whitewashed building immediately outside the Sanctuary of Bel. It is not to be confused with the Palmyra Museum at the entrance to Tadmor town, which displays antiquities from the site. You are likely to come across similar museums elsewhere in Syria, their collections meagre, poorly presented and repetitive, but this one (housed originally on the upper floor of the Palmyra Museum) is quite well done. Labels are in Arabic and French.

Along with various crafts, tools, jewellery and the like, the displays are most interesting for their recreation of domestic interiors. There is a Palmyrene house, for example, presumably one of those houses that until 1929 filled the Sanctuary of Bel, with its courtyard, reception room, women's quarters, kitchen and pantry, all traditionally furnished. Mannequin men lounge about, as mannequin men will, smoking their *narghilehs*. Elsewhere a Bedouin tent has been set up, its interior divided into several quarters and furnished, its inhabitants costumed. And of course there are camels, fully rigged-out in Bedouin style, one like a quadruped Christmas tree.

There are also geological specimens and stuffed wildlife. Birds of prey, mostly owls but also vultures, are most common in the desert. Gazelles once lived here until exterminated by man, and panthers survived into this century. Nowadays wolves, foxes, hyenas and jackals eke out an existence, hunting down hares and rodents and perhaps the occasional tourist.

Palmyra's East–West Colonnades

A colonnaded processional way once ran from the propylaeum of the Sanctuary of Bel to the monumental arch which marks the entry to the civic centre of the city. The arch and the processional way, both built during the reign of the Emperor Septimius Severus (193–211), were the last additions to the city plan, if plan it was, for it was carried out piecemeal.

Work on Palmyra's main colonnaded street (its decumanus) in fact began at its western end; the segment between the funerary temple and the tetrapylon was built during the first half of the 2nd century. Had it been extended in a straight line eastwards, it would have come up to the propylaeum of the Sanctuary of Bel. But that would have meant the destruction of the pre-existing Temple of Nabu. Therefore that segment of the colonnaded street running eastwards from the tetrapylon and built during the second half of the 2nd century was angled slightly northwards. To finally reach the propylaeum, however, required a rather sharp turn southwards at some point. This was very neatly done at the monumental arch, which was constructed in such a way (*see* below) as to mask the awkward change of angle at that point where the main colonnaded street intersects with the processional way.

Therefore in walking from the Sanctuary of Bel to the funerary temple, a distance of 1.2km, you are encountering the several segments of colonnades in the reverse order to which they were built. You are also slightly changing compass direction as you go along; overall you are heading from southeast to northwest, but for simplicity's sake the route is described as though it runs from east to west.

The Processional Way and the Monumental Arch

Nowadays the asphalt road from Damascus to Tadmor town cuts across the colonnaded **processional way** that once ran westwards from the propylaeum of the Sanctuary of Bel. Excavation shows it to have been as broad as the full width of the monumental arch which served as its climax. Between the modern road and the arch rise four re-erected columns, the **portico of an exedra**, thought to have been part of a nymphaeum, a public fountain, that stood along the south side of the processional way.

The **monumental arch**, over 10m high and comprising a high central arch flanked by a lower arch on either side, functions as the single most important joint along the colonnaded spine of the city. Despite the processional way and the main colonnaded street joining here at a 30° angle, the arch gives the appearance of standing at a right angle to each. It achieves this dramatic effect by having a triangular ground plan, its apex to the south, its base to the north. The two façades of the monumental arch, therefore, are not parallel to one another. The western façade faces the tetrapylon, while the eastern façade has been rotated 30 degrees southwards so that it faces the processional way. The trick only really becomes noticeable when you compare the shorter passage through the southern flanking arch to the longer passage through the flanking arch to the north.

The monumental arch is architecturally cunning in another way too. On the east side it presents all three of its arches to the broad processional way, emphasising the width of that avenue. On the west side its flanking arches give on to the colonnaded pavements of the main street so that only the high central arch, but not the flanking arches, would have been noticeable from the street itself, thereby creating a tunnel effect emphasising the length of the main street. The grandeur of each approach was therefore heightened but in a different way.

The arch is also richly and variously decorated with patterns of acorns and oak leaves, palmettes and rosettes, and geometric patterns, typically Syrian in its exuberance. You see this mostly now on its western façade and on the soffits of the arches. Another Syrian characteristic, noticeable here and elsewhere in Palmyra, is a fondness for niches, surmounted by either a classical pediment or a semi-circular arch. At some point in recent centuries the keystone of central arch had slipped, threatening to bring down the entire structure, but it was secured in place by a wedge of stone when restoration began in the 1930s.

Along the Central Colonnade to the Tetrapylon

Downtown Palmyra lay between the monumental arch and the tetrapylon. Here along the **central colonnaded street**, the best-preserved segment of the decumanus, were a theatre and baths, civic buildings and commercial houses and presumably the city's finest shops. The street is 11m wide and was left unpaved to provide soft and secure footing for camels. Pedestrians passed along the paved and shaded 7m-wide colonnaded porticoes on either side, where the consoles projecting from every column once bore statues of leading merchants and other notables. Today at sundown flocks of sheep amble across this once busy thoroughfare, past rival to Antioch, Alexandria and Rome itself, while at night it is filled with the sound of baying dogs.

Sand-worn columns, like those at the Sanctuary of Bel, are seen here too and everywhere in Palmyra. Winds and breezes lift the sand particles a metre or so and flick them against the stone. Usually the columns are worn away just above their bases, but not always; the wearing is sometimes two-thirds up the column shaft and its effect can also be seen on capitals. Damage higher up indicates that the column, capital, entablature or other piece of masonry once lay on the ground or that the sands had once been heaped up about it. (The central colonnaded street has been excavated and restored by Syrian archaeologists since 1957.) This abrasion has gone on ceaselessly for centuries, but sand alone may not be the only cause of the disfigurement you see at Palmyra, where a strange chemical process has also been suggested. Masonry is not always worn away smoothly; often the process seems to knead and suck, taking from the stone its shape and substance—sometimes more the one than the other. When the substance remains but the shape is gone, the effect is peculiarly grotesque, like elephantiasis.

On the south side of the colonnaded street, immediately after you have passed westwards through the monumental arch, you see the restored though paltry remains of the late 1st-century AD **Temple of Nabu**. It is facing away from you; shops along the colonnaded street backed on to the north side of its enclosure. Two engaged fluted columns mark the propylaeum at its southern end. Porticoes lined the south, east and west sides of the courtyard within; a number of their columns, which unusually for Palmyra are Doric, have been re-erected. The temple proper stood at the centre of the courtyard; all that remains is its podium and the bases of its Corinthian peristyle. Nabu, identified with Apollo, was part of the Babylonian pantheon; his power lay in being the scribe of the gods, for it was he who set down human destinies. For fear of upsetting him, the colonnaded street was angled to the north. The wealthy Elahbel family, who built the best of the tower tombs, made especially sure of keeping on the right side of Nabu by contributing generously to his temple funds.

Across the street, on its north side, stand four monolithic columns of pink granite from Upper Egypt, the portico of the **Baths of Diocletian**. A peristyled sunken pool, possibly the frigidarium, is evident within. The difficulty of channelling ample supplies of water to this site after construction of the colonnaded street suggests that baths had stood here a century before Diocletian's reign (284–305) and that only the portico, which bears an inscription in his name, dates from his time.

Returning again to the south side of the street, you see just to the west that its colonnaded portico has been broken by an arch leading onto a transverse street, also colonnaded, that sweeps round behind the theatre. You should try to resurrect the original scene at this intersection in your mind, imagining the dramatic interplay of sunlight and columns, how one street would have been bathed in sunshine while the other would have been barred with shadows. Sun and shade were as much elements of Palmyrene architecture as was stone. The curving side street brings you to a vaulted passage of the **theatre** and leading to the base of the cavea, nine of the original 12 rows of seating rising in a semicircle around you. The *scaenae frons* or stage building has been reconstructed to the height of its first storey; once it was clad in marble and must have been almost as elaborate as that at Bosra. There is some argument over whether the theatre dates from before or is contemporary with the central colonnaded street which runs immediately behind the stage building, though at least this part of the theatre seems to be contemporary. But it has been so squeezed into the available space that the actors, had they followed the usual practice of retiring behind the stage instead of, as here, having their dressing rooms to the side, would have stepped back into the passing traffic.

You should follow the side street off which you entered the theatre as it now continues in a half-circle round behind it. Two-thirds of the way round, you come, on the south side, to a row of truncated columns, the portico of a small building with a peristyled court leading to an apsidal chamber with tiers of seating, leading some archaeologists to suppose this may have been the **Senate**. This and the so-called Tariff Court south of it and the agora west of that all belong to the early 2nd century. You are here walking around a quarter of 'old Palmyra' that predates the construction of the central colonnaded street. The **Tariff Court** was entered from the south through three high portals, two of which retain their lintels. These were preceded by an imposing portico (partly dismantled to make way for the city wall built during Diocletian's reign). A stele found at the portico late last century and dated AD 137 set out the tariffs due on all goods entering and leaving Palmyra. Caravans would probably have come into this court, which was unpaved, to have their cargoes assessed and to pay their tariff accordingly. The court was connected by gates to the adjacent **agora**, a large open space of 48 by 71m which served as a public meeting place and market. Inscriptions indicate that over 200 statues of senators, officials, soldiers and caravan leaders once stood upon consoles projecting from the columns of the surrounding Corinthian porticoes. At the southwest corner is a small **banqueting chamber**, where ritual feasts would be held in honour of a presiding deity whose image would have been in the niche above the altar, the guests reclining on couches. Perhaps caravan leaders had a bite to eat here before exposing themselves to the dangers of the desert.

You can now return to the street that runs behind the theatre and follow its half-circle clockwise. It takes you past four **shop doorways** (or perhaps ticket booths for theatre performances) on its west side; then, just as you rejoin the central colonnaded street and running parallel with it, you notice a line of blocks at your feet, part of a **conduit** in fact (notice the holes bored through them) built at Justinian's time, which can be traced to a spring 12km west of the city.

You can now head west along the central colonnaded street to the tetrapylon. But pause for a moment as you walk along the **last eight columns** of the southern colonnade. Statues would of course have stood upon the consoles of these columns, and here as elsewhere they are missing. But inscriptions allow us to know who was honoured. The third column from the tetrapylon bore a statue of Odainat, 'King of Kings and Corrector of All the East'. The second column from the tetrapylon has even its console missing, the inscription reading: 'Statue of Septimia Bat-Zabbai (the Palmyrene for Zenobia), most Illustrious and Pious Queen; the excellent Septimii Zabda, general in chief, and Zabbai, military Governor of Palmyra, have raised it to their Lady, in the year 582 (Seleucid reckoning for AD 271) in August'. Exactly a year later, in August 272, Aurelian was in Palmyra and Zenobia was in chains. Her husband had given good service to Rome, and probably his statue was left intact; in Roman eyes Zenobia was a traitor, and it was probably then that her statue and console were obliterated.

The **tetrapylon**, standing in an oval plaza, consists of four pedestals, each supporting four massive columns, each set of columns topped with an entablature. A statue stood amid the columns on each of the four pedestals, one badly worn example surviving today. Until 1963 you would only have seen here the four pedestals; everything else lay shattered on the ground and has had to be reconstructed by the Syrian Antiquities Department. The monolithic columns were of pink Aswan granite (it is staggering to think of 16 such behemoths being shipped and dragged all the way from Upper Egypt to the middle of the Syrian Desert), but the pieces of only one column could be found (this is the northeast column on the southeast pedestal); the other 15 columns are reproductions made of a coloured concrete compound.

There has been some carping about the amount of reproduction that has gone into this restoration effort. But the primary purpose of the tetrapylon was to serve as a visual counterpoint to the monumental arch at the western end of the central colonnaded street and also to act as a joint for the central and western colonnaded streets which meet here at a 10° angle. The recreation of the tetrapylon (the pedestals and entablatures being in any case genuine) restores that visual effect and helps draw the plan of the city into a coherent whole.

North and West from the Tetrapylon

The Temple of Baalshamin requires a northwards detour from your generally westwards direction, but you can reward yourself with some refreshment at the **Hotel Zenobia** near by. The hotel sits amid unexcavated ruins, Corinthian capitals put to use as tables along its terrace. Some distance behind it are the remains of the city's **north wall**, built probably at the time of Diocletian but strengthened during the first half of the 6th century by Justinian. How far Palmyra had by then declined, its past as a great trading city been all but forgotten, is evident from this account by Procopius, historian of Justinian's reign: 'And there is a city, Palmyra by name, built in a neighbourless region by men of former times, but well situated across the track of the hostile Saracens. Indeed it was for this very reason that they had originally built this city, in order, namely, that these barbarians might not unobserved make sudden inroads into the Roman territory. This city, which through lapse of time had come to be almost completely deserted, the Emperor Justinian strengthened with defences which defy description, and he also provided it with abundant water and a garrison of troops, and thus put a stop to the raids of the Saracens' (*Buildings*).

The merchant who picked up the tab for Hadrian's three-week fête in 129, Malé, son of Yarhai, was also a benefactor of the **Temple of Baalshamin**. Malé's name, the Seleucid date 442 (AD 130–31) and mention of the 'divine Hadrian's' visit are inscribed on the most southeast of the six Corinthian columns of the portico. The pediment of the portico is missing, also the cella roof; otherwise the eastwards-facing temple, re-erected from numerous fragments by Swiss archaeologists in the 1950s, is entire and elegantly proportioned, the interior elaborately detailed in an almost baroque manner. The once colonnaded courtyards to the north and south were built in phases, from the early 1st century AD and continuing after completion of the temple. As at the Sanctuary of Bel, a triad was worshipped here, its two local components being Aglibol, the moon god who was also part of Bel's triad, and Malakbel, the fertility god of flocks and fields. But supreme among them was the Phoenician Baalshamin, a sky god of storms, rain and so also fertility, associated with Zeus and corresponding to the Babylonian Bel, but less remote, inscriptions repeatedly referring to Baalshamin as 'the one who hears'.

Little else has been excavated or restored in this entire northern sweep of the city, so that what was the wealthier **residential quarter** of Palmyra, its still traceable grid of streets once lined with houses, now has an air of utter desolation. These houses, often two storeys high, would often have been built of mud brick, though many would have made use of stone as well. All would have presented blank façades to the narrow streets, but inside the better-off decorated their houses with frescoed walls and mosaic floors, while the homes of all classes always enclosed an open courtyard, which in the houses of the wealthy would have been surrounded by a Corinthian peristyle. The quarter is now all the more eerie for the survival of two of these **peristyles**, their houses having crumbled away, but the inner rectangle of columns still stand and bear their entablatures, like Hiroshima memorials to the private shaded courtyards they once enclosed. These are about 400m west of the Temple of Baalshamin; before coming to them you can look out for the foundation remains of two Byzantine basilical **churches**. Christianity is known to have flourished here well before then, however, Palmyra sending a bishop to the Council of Nicaea in 325 and Christ-worship being kindly regarded in this import-export city, alongside the cults of Bel, Baalshamin and numerous others, even in the times of Odainat and Zenobia.

The colonnaded street running west from the tetrapylon has hardly been excavated, its shambles illustrating by comparison how much work has been done along the central colonnaded street to the east. This **western colonnaded street** appears not to have been an address for much public building, the one structure of note, 100m along on the south side, being perhaps another nymphaeum, marked by the usual semi-circular **exedra**.

The street terminates 500m farther west at the façade of the **funerary temple**, in fact a 3rd-century family tomb. Steps rise to a six-columned Corinthian portico with fine vine-leaf decorations running up the pilasters where it joins the chamber behind. The portico and its partly intact pediment survived through the centuries, but the chamber has only recently been rebuilt with the heavy use of concrete. The chamber would have contained numerous *loculi*, compartments for the dead stacked in rows against the walls, and the same in the crypt below, reached by a stairway behind the rear wall. Each *loculus* (you will be able to see this properly in the tower tombs) was faced with a portrait relief of its tenant, a virtual gallery of dead but well-placed relations through whom the living might seek divine favours.

A **transverse street,** also once colonnaded and lined with shops, runs north to south across the face of the funerary temple. It ends 250m to the south in an **oval place** and beyond it is what is called the **Damascus Gate**, another entry point for caravans. But about 100m before reaching the gate, and just to the west, is the **Camp of Diocletian**, where irony more than evidence places the remains of Zenobia's palace. The walled Roman military camp was built within 30 years of Zenobia's downfall when, as a trading centre, the city was in sharp decline and Palmyra had become primarily a legionary outpost against the Sassanians. Past the crossroads within the camp, a broad flight of stairs, worn to a smooth *glacis* that is easier to slide down than creep up, raises you to a once grand structure, the architectural and cultural counterbalance to the Temple of Bel at the opposite end of the city. This was the **praetorium**, seat of the commander of the legion. The steps led into a vast transverse hall, then into a deep central apsidal chamber, the Temple of the Signa, where the legionary standards were kept and where, perhaps, a state-approved military cult was fostered. Administrative rooms were on either side. The lintel over the temple entrance carried a dedicatory inscription: 'Restorers of the World and Patrons of the human race, our lords Diocletian and Maximian, invincible emperors, and Constantius and Galerius, most noble Caesars, have established this camp under happy omens'. In 293 Diocletian had established a tetrarchy of two emperors and two caesars to govern the Roman Empire, each with their own capital, respectively at Nicomedia (Turkish

Izmit), Milan, Treviri (Trier in Germany) and Thessaloniki. The Senate remained in Rome, but neither the Senate nor Rome really mattered any more; the empire was run by generals, and with their armies they kept close to the frontiers. This camp, which served as barracks and administrative centre, is aptly named, for it was very much in Diocletian's sphere of operations.

North of the camp crossroads you see several fluted columns and a doorframe, all that remains of the 2nd-century **Temple of Allat**, properly al-Lat, meaning goddess in Arabic. She was already worshipped on this spot in the late 1st century BC, an inscription of that date describing her as 'Allat who is also Artemis', the Greek protectress of wild animals. This perhaps makes sense of the giant 1st-century AD statue of a lion found here and now in the Palmyra Museum garden. An oryx huddles between its paws, and the inscription asks Allat 'to bless the one who does not spill blood against the temple'. A century later, however, when the temple whose remains you see was built, Allat was being equated with Athena. The statue of Allat-Athena in the museum was also found here: it was copied from the famous version by Phidias, who made the chryselephantine statue of Athena in the Parthenon, another of Zeus at Olympia, both lost, and superintended the carving of the Elgin Marbles. According to pre-Muslim Arab belief, Allat was a sun goddess and daughter of Allah, the centre of her worship being a rich temple at Taif. Though Mohammed conquered Mecca in 630, her worship at Taif survived for a year yet, her overthrow marking the final victory of Islam over paganism, the Koran stating (Sura 53:22) that the old pagan deities 'are but names which you and your fathers have invented: Allah has invested no authority in them'.

From here you can visit the tower tombs in the Valley of the Tombs (*see* p.283), but for keys to the underground tombs of the southern necropolises you will first have to go to the Palmyra Museum, unless you arrange for a guide at the Temple of Bel to get them for you.

The Palmyra Museum

Open 8–1 and 4–6 in summer, 8–1 and 2–4 in winter, closed Tues; adm. Tickets for the locked tombs in the Valley of the Tombs are also sold here (see p.283).

The Palmyra Museum, housing antiquities from the site, is located northeast of the ruins and at the entrance to modern Tadmor town, about 500 metres along the asphalt road from the monumental arch. Exhibits are labelled in Arabic and also either in French or English.

To the museum you come to meet the Palmyrenes, for along with their inscriptions and their religious art, what most fills these rooms is their funerary sculpture, those tomb portraits by which they intended posterity to know them. Not that posterity would wish to. Here you see statues of these middlemen of antiquity lounging at their banquet tables, their women drowned in jewels, setting off their ostentation with a sourness in the downturned corners of their mouths. And though you know how they made their money, they do not look like a people who would go out in the midday sun. Neither energy nor adventure nor spirit nor even beauty disturbs the almost flabby complacency of their gaze. Only on their tombstones is there a hint of feeling, when sometimes they were so far moved as to inscribe, 'Alas!'

Some of this is of course a consequence of deliberate formalism. In their funerary portraits and indeed in all their art, Palmyrenes were less concerned with realistic expression than with timelessness, preferring frontal and static representation. Though their images lack movement, the onlooker's eye is treated to a restless, almost baroque, decoration, the men wearing embroidered Parthian dress, the women encrusted with jewels. This formalism broke down somewhat under Roman influence, so that late funerary sculpture expresses a greater degree of realism and psychological insight. Nevertheless, they are a dull lot, and you might begin to think that their city, wrecked and sandblown, is more romantic without them.

The Valley of the Tombs and the Southern Necropolises

You can wander round this area at any time, but the hypogea are kept locked, as are the Iamliku and Elahbel tower tombs. To visit those, you will need tickets from the Palmyra Museum, which does guided visits at 8.30, 10, 11.30 and 4.30, lasting about an hour. Transport to the tombs is your own responsibility; indeed in winter, when the guide has been unable to latch himself on to a tour group, you might have to transport him out there yourself. Tour groups make visits to the tombs a disagreeable experience; it is best to hang back and follow far in their wake.

At evening, when the sun has slipped from the sky, the stone of Palmyra's ruined temples, arches and colonnades still seems to glow with the stored radiance of the day. It is then that your eyes fasten on the most special thing about Palmyra, eerie and entirely alien—its tower tombs pulsing against the blackening west. Built from the 1st century BC, before the city dressed itself in Roman forms, to the early 2nd century AD, the oldest of these tower tombs are Palmyra's most ancient monuments.

The tallest and best preserved of these sepulchral towers are in the Valley of the Tombs, southwest of the city. Its tower tombs of Iamliku and Elahbel are described below. Rising several storeys high, tower tombs are arranged inside like left-luggage lockers, each body stacked atop the compartment, or *loculus*, of another. As many as 300 family members could be deposited within a single tower, but such an ambitious undertaking also had its risks, and, as you might expect, the merchant families of Palmyra were not above selling off their towers when they suffered a financial reverse.

But though it is the tower tombs that draw your attention to the western horizon, they are not the only type of tomb. In the late 1st century AD they began to be superseded by the underground chamber or hypogeum, again with stacked *loculi*. One of the best of these, the Hypogeum of Yarhai, was in the Valley of the Tombs near the Elahbel Tower but has now been reconstructed in the National Museum at Damascus (*see* p.60). The best still *in situ*, and described below, is the Hypogeum of the Three Brothers in a necropolis south of the Cham Hotel (which is something of a necropolis in its own right).

There is also a transitional tomb type, combining both tower and hypogeum. Additionally there are house or temple tombs, such as the funerary temple, already described, in the western precincts of Palmyra. All these were family tombs, though also some individual tombs have been found. All belonged to the wealthy; no burial ground of Palmyra's less well-off population has been found, nor for that matter of the Byzantine or Arab periods.

All the most important tower tombs and hypogea are identified by signs.

The four-storey **Tower Tomb of Iamliku**, built in AD 83, stands on the slope of a hill on the south side of the eastern entrance to the kilometre-long Valley of the Tombs. The architrave over its doorway once bore a pediment; above this, projecting from an upper storey, are the remains of a niche, the lost columns on either side once supporting an entablature and pediment, within which would have been placed a sculptural group depicting the founding family. The plaque below this reads 'Iamliku, son of Mokimu Akalish, son of Maliku, son of Belakab,

Tower tomb

son of Mike, son of Maththa, Councillor of Palmyra'. A carved cornice runs round the top of the tower. Altogether, the tower has a crisply finished appearance and was in fact the first to be built of well-dressed and regularly shaped stone blocks, earlier towers employing blocks of irregular, polygonal shape. Inside, on the ground floor, Corinthian pilasters rise to a high geometrically coffered ceiling. *Loculi* here and on the upper storeys, reached by a stairway to the rear, accommodated 200 bodies. The **Elahbel Tower**, built in AD 103 and also four storeys high, is the one other wholly intact tower tomb in the valley. Situated 750m west of the Iamliku Tower, it is also the largest, with a capacity for 300 bodies. The family was largely responsible for the construction of the Temple of Nabu, and this tower was erected by Elahbel and three of his brothers, whose names are engraved on its face below the distinctively arched niche containing a representation of a sarcophagus. The ground floor interior is similar to though more lavishly decorated than the Iamliku Tower; a good deal of colouring survives on the coffered ceiling, while the north wall *loculi* retain their reliefs of the dead. You can go right up to the roof for the views. Below the tower is a hypogeum, entered from the north.

Bedouin Among the Tombs

Sometimes a Bedouin family will erect their tent amid the tower tombs, and you see their woolly sheep obsessively hoovering the hillsides in the hope of turning up some green-growing thing. In winter it rains, and once every six or seven years it snows on the mountains. If the winters are wet there will be enough grass for the Bedouin's sheep to eat, and then the price of lamb will be high, for instead of having to sell their sheep, the Bedouin will prefer to keep them for their milk, the traditional staple drink of their nomadic life.

But nomadism is gradually passing as the Bedouin flirt with a more settled way of life in the vicinity of Palmyra. Short of driving out into the desert, and much better than visiting the Museum of Popular Culture, call on one of these tents in the valley, where probably you will be invited in for a refreshing glass of hot sweet tea. Despite the ferocity of the summer sun, the interior of their tents is remarkably cool, their sides rolled up to let the breeze blow through. It is then you may discover that the floor of the tent is made of cement.

You learn that the head of the household has put in some work on the gas or oil pipelines that cross the Syrian Desert or has even spent some time in Saudi Arabia or the Gulf, while he will tell you that his sons have received an education and have become teachers or hotel workers. You sit cross-legged on rugs, with woven bolsters to lean on, while the master of the tent, in his checked *kafiyyeh* and white *galabiyya*, lies like a Roman against his—like an ancient Palmyrene in fact. The women serve tea, several women, a wife and sisters- or daughters-in-law perhaps, brightly dressed in long red embroidered robes, gold rings on their fingers, gold bracelets on their arms, gold flashing at their incisors, unveiled and with none of that purdah of the towns and cities, instead open, amiable, direct and chatty, puffing elaborately on cigarettes.

You think of the neighbouring sepulchral towers, once filled with bodies arranged in left-luggage lockers, dead yet unburied. It is like having a tent with a cement floor; their occupants had come to rest, but they still liked to feel in transit.

The Hypogeum of the Three Brothers

This finest of over 50 excavated underground tombs lies just west off the Damascus road, about 150m south of the Cham Hotel. You descend a brief stairway to the entrance where an inscription gives the names of the brothers whose undertaking this was in the mid-2nd century AD, with the additional information that it was a commercial proposition, several sections being sold off to other families. The right half of the original stone entrance door is in place beyond the modern bars and metal door; the left part of the door lies on the floor within. Ahead of you is a central barrel-ceilinged chamber, with chambers also to the left and right, forming a T-plan. Each chamber in turn has numerous recesses, 65 in all, each recess having six *loculi*, giving a total of 390 *loculi*.

The ceiling of the central chamber is painted with a hexagonal pattern in blue with gilded rosettes and flowers, while depicted within a circular panel is the abduction of Ganymede, a child of Troy whom Zeus, in the form of an eagle, took off to be his cup-bearer. The symbolism is of the soul being carried off to the hereafter, and the theme is repeated at the far end of the chamber by a scene from the *Iliad*. Here Achilles, at the behest of Odysseus, throws off his women's clothes (his mother having hidden him among the daughters of Lycomedes, King of Skyros, to save him from his mortal fate)—the borrowed clothes being the body of this life, exchanged for immortality. The three brothers are themselves portrayed within fresco medallions raised aloft by winged Victories.

In the left chamber is the sarcophagus of Malé, one of the brothers; he is shown in Parthian costume, wearing a knee-length blouse with baggy trousers beneath and embroidered boots. In the right chamber, three sarcophagi show family groups. They recline in long, deeply folded robes and wear embroidered footwear, and are attending a banquet probably representing the fulfillment of the afterlife.

The Efqa Spring and the Oasis

You are led to the spring today by the sound of laughter. From a fissure in the rock it pumps its hot sulphurous waters at the rate of 60 litres per second into a sunken pool by the roadside in front of the Cham Hotel. Peering down, you see local boys splashing one another. Without the Efqa (or Afqa) Spring there would have been no Palmyra. This was the source of empire.

Its steaming waters, a constant 33° Celsius, are led through channels round the oasis of date palms, half a million it is said, though pomegranates grow here too, and figs, apricots and olives. When you are within the oasis you see that olives are the most common but, as they are shorter, you do not notice them from a distance beneath the tall palms.

The oasis is run through with lanes, stone walls on either side packed with mud. The spring is channelled along, never ceasing to smell of sulphur. In the west most of the gardens draw their water off the spring, their right to do so being traditional, though some use pumped water. In the east the gardens are irrigated entirely by pumped water, the wells reaching a depth of 40 to 50m. Increasingly, electric pumps are used; they are cheaper than petrol pumps and quieter.

At night, when the westerly breeze blows through the leaves, it is like the sound of waves lapping against a distant shore. By day it is wonderful to wander here among the shadows and fragrances and the swoops of brilliantly feathered birds. Children surge along the dappled lanes, their laughter bubbling like the channelled water.

The Arab Castle: Qalaat Ibn Maan

On a hillcrest 2km northwest of Palmyra is the Arab castle that forms such a splendid backdrop to the ruins. It is attributed to the early 17th-century Lebanese Emir Fakhr al-Din al-Maani II who under Ottoman suzerainty ruled all the Arab lands from Aleppo to the borders of Egypt and extended his authority clear across the Syrian Desert. He was a diminutive man, whose enemies described him as so short that if an egg dropped from his pocket to the ground it would not break. But his ability, and his tolerant and modernising policies, soon convinced the Ottoman sultan that he was too big for his boots. In 1635 he was defeated, captured and taken in chains to Constantinople where he was strangled.

Possibly an earlier castle, of the 12th and 13th centuries, and therefore contemporary with the Arab fortifications at the Sanctuary of Bel, stood on this site. However that may be, you now climb up the 150m slope (which you can walk to or reach by car along a track from Tadmor) and discover a compact circle of walls with seven towers surrounded by a deep ditch. Crossing a metal bridge at the southeast corner, you enter an inner court from where you can climb to the highest terrace, on the south side, from which there are terrific views, especially at dawn or sunset, along the ridge of the Jebel al-Tadmoria to the north and over the ruins of Palmyra below you to the south. At evening the sky goes a blue pastel, the tracery of the city's colonnades shift through pink to orange to deepening violet, and the brown mountains of afternoon smoulder into charcoal. There is then the sound of wind with the coming darkness and finally a great stillness. But you should take care about being able to find your way back, which is why a dawn visit might be better.

Where to Stay
very expensive

★★★★★**Palmyra Cham Palace**, on the Damascus–Homs road just south of the site and 2km from Tadmor, ✆ (031) 937000, ✉ (031) 921245. Originally a Meridien hotel, they could not make it pay; now it is part of the Cham chain, who presumably cannot make it pay either. Emptiness and characterlessness define the place, and the service is half-witted; if it were not for tour groups, you suspect, it would be entirely vacant. There are two empty restaurants, an empty bar and an empty disco, plus a pool, tennis courts, business centre and shops, all bereft of human life. For activity there are the rooms, where apart from brushing your teeth, having a bath, making love and sleeping you can listen to the air conditioning, watch TV and raid your minibar. The hotel also has access to the sulphurous waters of the Efqa spring.

moderate

★★★**Zenobia Hotel**, smack in the middle of the ruins. ✆ (031) 910156, ✉ (031) 912554. Agatha Christie and her archaeologist husband Max Mallowan stayed here in the 1930s, when she described it as a handsome building, arranged inside with taste and charm. Since when the place went downhill, though for its location it still remained the best place to stay at Palmyra. Now it has been refurbished, so that the beds no longer break your back, while its air-conditioned high-ceilinged rooms still give the sense that they were built for giants. The terrace overlooking the ruins is wonderful. Here you sit, Corinthian capitals serving as tables, watching the cool lemon sunlight slice through the pearly morning atmosphere or at sundown seeing the sky go mauve and black beyond the marching colonnades of the ancient city.

inexpensive

★★**Orient**, ✆ (031) 910131, ✉ (031) 910700, in Tadmor town, just north off the main east–west street (Al-Quwatli Street), 100m east of the museum and the Karnak office. Clean, comfortable, quiet rooms; restaurant.

★**Ishtar**, ✆ (031) 913073, ✉ (031) 913260, in Tadmor town adjacent to the Karnak office and opposite the museum. Rooms with fan, shower, toilet; clean, friendly place but can be noisy.

cheap

There are numerous hotels in Tadmor town that fall into this category. The best thing to do is to inspect them—all are ranged along the main street (Al-Quwatli Street) running past the museum and the Karnak office, or just off it.

camping

There is camping in the garden of the Zenobia Hotel, which includes use of its showers.

There are several cheap restaurants and cafés in Tadmor, including one by the Karnak office. Otherwise for a moderate sum there is the terrace of the Zenobia Hotel, especially agreeable at dawn or night, and a choice of two expensive restaurants at the Palmyra Cham Palace Hotel.

The Desert East of Palmyra

Qasr al-Heir al-Sharqi (East)

At 110km northeast of Palmyra along the desert road to Deir ez Zor a sign in Arabic and English 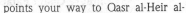 points your way to Qasr al-Heir al-Sharqi. An indistinct track, manageable in dry weather by ordinary car, but requiring four-wheel drive if there has been a recent rain, runs north by north-west for 30km to the qasr. The going is slow and you should allow an hour to get there. After you have visited the site, you return to the Palmyra–Deir ez Zor road by the way you came. The qasr here is far grander and more intact than Qasr al-Heir al-Gharbi (west) (*see* p.264) and also all the more impressive for its isolation in the middle of

nowhere. If you are weighing up whether to come here, however, note that it is not so grand a place as Resafa, which has the same desertic quality and is much easier to reach.

Like the western Qasr al-Heir, this eastern qasr was built by the Umayyad Caliph Hisham, though two years later, in 728–29. His motives were the same, combining both business with pleasure, the business being control over the desert tribes and also to secure the caravan route between the Euphrates and Damascus. The outpost, like Syria generally, declined under the Abbasids and was abandoned after the 13th-century Mongol invasions. The site is vast, for as you approach from the south there are already traces of the outer walls 5km before you reach the qasr. Within this was a walled garden, 3 by 6km, and within this in turn the palace garden and the town, with the two castle buildings finally surrounded by a wall 200m in radius. The smaller eastern building is the best preserved, with massive walls and rounded towers, its function primarily military though probably it also served as a khan for caravans. Its interior is in ruins. The all but adjacent western building, separated by a channel of sand and a lone minaret that may also have served as a watchtower, is six times larger. This was virtually a city in miniature and, though also ruinous, it was once complete with residential areas, administrative quarters, a mosque and olive presses, these last a reminder that whatever the military and commercial functions of the eastern Qasr al-Heir, it was at the centre of a self-sufficient, indeed grandiose, agricultural settlement.

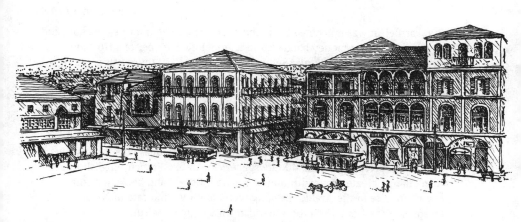

Beirut's Martyrs' Square in the late 19th century

History   291

Getting There   292

Orientation   293

Getting Around   294

Tourist Information   294

Around Martyrs' Square   296

West Beirut   298

Beirut

East Beirut   299

Where to Stay   300

Eating Out   301

This place was called anciently Berytus . . . and afterwards being greatly esteemed by Augustus had many privileges conferred upon it. . . . But at present, it retains nothing of its ancient felicity, except the situation; and in that particular it is indeed very happy. It is seated on the seaside, in a soil fertile and delightful. . . But besides these advantages of its situation, it has at present nothing else to boast of.

Henry Maundrell, *A Journey from Aleppo to Jerusalem at Easter, AD 1697.*

Pre-war Beirut was enlivened by a kind of eczema, its itch for deal-making and its suppurations of money bandaged in a Frenchified veneer of strip shows, smart shops, bars and bikinis. Being in the Middle East, there was something beguiling about this. Here both Arabs and Westerners could meet and breathe easily and sell their guns, butter and bodies to one another. Business was strictly *laissez-faire*, with numerous European, American and Japanese firms based in the city, well over 100 banking companies, a third of them foreign, a stock exchange and free port, and no restrictions on the exchange of gold, silver and currencies. There was a free market also in ideas, albeit derivative, with a free press publishing 40 newspapers in Arabic, French, English and Armenian, a greater concentration of book publishers and bookshops than anywhere else in the Arabic-speaking world and two first-rate universities, St Joseph's of the Jesuits and the American University of Beirut.

While the war's destruction has for the time being diminished Beirut's glitz, the shattered and bullet-pocked buildings that have not yet fallen to the bulldozers make the city if anything more interesting. Hardly picturesque before and possessing next to nothing of historical value, the irony is that in clearing its wreckage Beirut has been discovering, excavating and restoring a number of long-buried vestiges of its past.

It remains to be seen, however, how well the city's communities of Christians, Muslims and Druze can function together again. 'I had decided at the outbreak of the war not to sing to any one Lebanese faction or area,' said Fairouz, the famous Lebanese singer, a Christian as it happens, when she gave a concert in 1994 to an emotional mixed crowd in Martyrs' Square, which had once straddled the Green Line battle zone that divided Beirut into warring Christian and Muslim sectors. And as she sang 'We have broken free, we have broken into the sun', one Muslim onlooker remarked, 'Fairouz is a part of Lebanon's collective memory, and I think it was the political theme of unity and peace which she symbolises that brought all this diversity together.'

But sentiment is one thing, money another, and in Beirut, as in the whole of Lebanon, it is money that sings. In the same year as the concert the Société Libanaise pour le Développement et la Reconstruction du Centre-Ville de Beyrouth (Solidere for short) was formed with the aim of returning Beirut to its former importance as the business capital of the Middle East. The devastated downtown area around Martyrs' Square along with landfill to be reclaimed from the sea is to be developed as a purpose-built modern financial centre, in fact more a city within the city, with attendant shopping, entertainment and cultural facilities, also residential quarters, gardens and two marinas. Solidere, a private company but with powers of appropriation, issued shares worth $1.7 billion to the more than 40,000 people with property rights in the area, binding them to its future. But not only they are involved. As the engine by which Lebanon is to be hauled clear of the abyss, the plan may have derived some inspiration from Riad Solh Street, near the Green Line yet virtually untouched by the fighting, one Beiruti explaining that as it is lined with banks, 'everyone in Lebanon had a common interest here'.

History

Beirut is mentioned in ancient Egyptian texts of the 14th century BC when it was ruled by a vassal king, but it played only a minor role in comparison with that of Byblos to the north. While the records of Alexander's coastal campaign speak of Arwad, Byblos, Sidon and Tyre, on Beirut they are silent. Its period of importance began with the Emperor Augustus, who named it Julia Augusta after his daughter and gave it the rights of a Roman city. The first law school in the Roman Empire was founded here in the mid-3rd century AD and maintained an unrivalled prestige for 300 years. Silk weaving became a major industry, its techniques carried from Beirut during the Byzantine period to Greece and then to Sicily.

But in 551 Beirut was destroyed by earthquakes and tidal waves. With its industry and law school ruined, the city sank into oblivion, the Arabs on their arrival in 635 finding that little had been rebuilt. The place revived somewhat under the Crusaders, who remained in more or less continuous occupation from 1125 to 1291.

In 1516 Beirut became part of the Ottoman Empire, whose interest in Lebanon however was merely to exact what taxes it could from local emirs who otherwise were permitted a measure of autonomy. One of these was Fakhr al-Din al-Maani II, who between 1585 and 1635 took advantage of Turkish laxity to establish Lebanon's independence and promote its prosperity. As at Sidon, where he encouraged mercantile relations with the French, so at Beirut Fakhr al-Din particularly favoured the Venetians, counterposing European influence to the power of the Ottomans. He had visited Florence of the Medicis and introduced examples of European architecture to Beirut, which became his favourite residence and where he laid out his palace gardens in the Italian manner. But Fakhr al-Din's ambitions for Lebanon were intolerable to the Turks, who defeated him and brought him to Constantinople where he was strangled, while Beirut was left to stagnate. Clearly, the city's fortunes depended on the stability of the country and its freedom from the oppressive indolence of the Turks. Its next revival came during the early 19th-century under the Emir Bechir. But his alliance with Ibrahim Pasha, son of Egypt's Mohammed Ali, who had marched into Anatolia and was on the point of overturning the Ottoman dynasty, drew the alarm of Britain which feared that its own interests in the region would be harmed by this new and vigorous power. A British fleet bombarded Beirut in 1840 and Bechir was captured and handed over to the Turks, who kept him prisoner on the Bosphorus for the remaining ten years of his life.

Renewed Turkish misrule contributed to the 1860 massacre of the Maronites by the Druze and brought French intervention. The modern history of Beirut dates from these events, for it quickly received an influx of population from the insecure mountain regions, principally Greek

Orthodox and Maronite, who formed the overwhelming majority of the city's inhabitants and who brought to it their talent for enterprise. Yet up to the First World War, Beirut hardly extended more than 500m to the east and west of Martyrs' Square and was entirely surrounded by gardens and orchards, except towards the western headland where there were sand dunes.

In its subsequent growth, people from the predominantly Christian north travelled down along the Tripoli road and tended to settle where it enters Beirut from the east, while people from the predominantly Muslim south travelled up the Sidon road and for the most part settled where it joins Beirut to the west. Meanwhile the Christian-Muslim balance within the country was upset after the creation of Israel by the large numbers of dispossessed Palestinians, mostly Sunni Muslims, who poured into Lebanon as refugees. Their presence and activities, and the successive Arab-Israeli wars, tore apart Lebanon's attempt to somehow be an Arab nation but with an attachment to the West, and in 1975 a civil war broke out that soon brought massive Israeli and Syrian intervention. In Beirut, the Green Line running south through the Martyrs' Square marked the no-man's land between the Muslim west and Christian east of the city. Fighting continued wholesale until 1989 and the Green Line was dismantled only in 1991.

Getting There

By air: Beirut Airport is 10km south of the city. The only practical means of transport into town is by taxi, $25–30 being the sum they will try to extort from you—and probably succeed. By walking some distance away from the airport and by bargaining hard you ought to be able to get this down to $10–15. If your flight arrives during daytime (most do not) you can take the LCC bus no. 5 from the airport to the port, or ask to be let off at Balbirs near the National Museum where buses and service taxis will take you to West Beirut or elsewhere in the city. Unfortunately, to get the airport bus you will have to walk 1km from the arrivals terminal to the traffic circle at the airport entrance. Getting to the airport is cheaper: take a taxi for about $10–15, or the LCC no. 5 bus from the port or Balbirs.

Before the war there was a take-off or landing each minute. During the fighting the airport was often closed, and when it was open only MEA, the national airline, used it. Now it is served by a growing number of European and Middle Eastern airlines. Several of the airport buildings were badly shot up during the war but the facilities are being repaired or rebuilt.

On departure you discover reasonably well-stocked duty-free shops selling the usual spirits, wines, tobaccos, perfumes and photographic and sound goods. This is also about the only place in Lebanon where you can buy Château Musar wine, available in red, white and rosé, the best the country produces and reserved, it seems, for export. Lebanese currency is not accepted.

Driving in from the airport you see that everyone has put up a poster to greet you: the Maronite president, the Sunni prime minister, the Shia speaker of the assembly and President Assad of Syria. There are even larger-than-life smiling and waving roadside cut-outs of Ayatollah Khomeini.

By long-distance bus and service taxi: there is a depot for long-distance buses and service taxis at **Cola** (named after the cola bottling plant near by) in the south of the city, serving destinations to the south and east of Beirut, and some in the north as

Airline Offices

Middle East Airlines (MEA), the Lebanese airline, has an office at the airport, ✆ (01) 822780, and several offices in town, including at the Gefinor Centre, Clemenceau Street (in the Hamra district), ✆ (01) 368000.

Other airlines have their offices in town.

Air France, Bliss Street, Ras Beirut, ✆ (01) 864492.

Austrian Airlines, Sabbagh Centre, Hamra Street, ✆ (01) 353013.

British Airways, Gefinor Centre, Clemenceau Street, Hamra, ✆ (01) 351499.

Cyprus Airways, Smeha Building, Sursock Street, ✆ (01) 200886.

Egyptair, Gefinor Centre, Clemenceau Street, Hamra, ✆ (01) 361615.

KLM, Gefinor Centre, Clemenceau Street, Hamra, ✆ (01) 371381.

Lufthansa, Hamra Street, ✆ (01) 346595.

Olympic Airways, Hamra Street, ✆ (01) 340285.

Royal Jordanian Airlines, Bliss Street, ✆ (01) 863783.

Swissair, Emile Edde Street, ✆ (01) 370911.

THY Turkish Airlines, Gefinor Centre, Clemenceau Street, Hamra, ✆ (01) 867425.

well. From here you can take a bus to Damascus or Tartus in Syria (about $6) or get a seat in a five-seater service taxi to the same destinations (about $12). For a taxi to Syria taken privately you will have to pay for all five seats (about $60), however many seats you and your party take up. There are also buses from here to Sidon (about $1), but for Tyre, Beit Eddine and Baalbek you will have to take a service or private taxi.

At **Balbirs**, by the Hippodrome and about 500m west of the National Museum, the LCC bus no. 5 makes a stop between the airport and the port. Service taxis and local buses congregate here; there is also an hourly bus service to Tripoli.

There is a depot at **Dora** (pronounced Dauwra), east of the Beirut River. This is for LCC buses to Jounieh and Byblos (*see* Getting Around), though principally for service taxis (which can also be taken privately) and is convenient for the north, e.g. Byblos (about $3) and Tripoli (about $5), though you ought also to be able to get a taxi here for Syria. Note that service taxis north usually drop you off along the motorway from where you will have to take another service taxi or thumb a lift or walk to get to your destination.

Orientation

The best place to begin a visit to the city is Martyrs' Square. From here the Green Line approximately followed Bechara al-Khoury Street south, dividing Beirut into Muslim west and Christian east. Each side defended the Green Line by blocking streets with tyres, stacks of containers and buses—indeed all the city's buses were put to use this way. The shortage of public transport here and throughout the country means heavy traffic jams as cars and taxis are largely relied upon to cover any distance. Or you can walk: from Martyrs' Square it is about 2.5km south to the National Museum and about 3km west to the American University.

Most people get about Beirut in their own car or by taxi or service taxi, though walking is entirely practical over much of the city (e.g. from Martyrs' Square to Hamra Street or the American University is about a 2km walk). There is also a developing bus system.

By bus: Beirut has a new and expanding privately owned bus company, the Lebanese Commuting Company (LCC), operating red and white buses, both small and medium in size, along several routes at a flat fare of LL500. The buses are numbered (in Western numerals) according to route. Routes are to be increased; at the moment they are as follows:

Bus no.	Routes (to and from)
1	Hamra–Achrafieh–Dora–Antelias
2	Hamra–Cola–Mcharafieh
3	Dora–National Museum–Balbirs–Cola–Raouche–Ain el-Mreisse
4	Balbirs–Moukales–Salome–Nahr
5	Airport–Balbirs–Port
6	Dora–Jounieh–Byblos (Jbail)

By taxi: most taxis in Beirut operate as service (shared) taxis. Just hail one if it looks like it's going in your direction and expect to pay no more than LL1500; also expect up to four other passengers to share all or part of the journey. Private taxis cost about five times more. Note that taxis, usually Mercedes, have white on red number plates, while private cars have white or silver on black number plates.

Car hire: to hire a car you will need a valid driving licence and depending on the company will need to be at least 21 to 25. A deposit covering at least the estimated cost of rental is payable unless you have a credit card. Charges are usually daily or weekly regardless of distance travelled; expect to pay about $35 a day, $200 a week. A number of better hotels will have car hire desks. Note that Lebanese drivers are probably the most reckless in the Middle East. Road rules count for nothing; risk-taking is commonplace. Aggression and machismo are all. Before deciding to hire a self-drive car, *see* the comments on p.7. The best car hire companies in Lebanon, combining good prices with good insurance cover, are Europcar, head office ✆ (01) 480480, ⊜ (01) 500788, and Hala, head office ✆ (01) 393904, ⊜ (01) 601331.

Tours: guided tours can be a convenient and inexpensive way of seeing the highlights of Lebanon, especially for those short on time. American Express, ✆ (01) 739793, ⊜ (01) 602200, in the Gefinor Centre, Clemenceau Street, Hamra, can arrange tours of the country; Nakhal, ✆ (01) 389507, ⊜ (01) 389282, Ghorayeb Building, Sami el Sohl Avenue east of the National Museum, is a respected established company offering tours of Lebanon and of Syria too; Tania Travel, ✆ (01) 739679, ⊜ (01) 340473, Sidani Street, Hamra, also runs regular tours in Lebanon and to Syria.

Tourist Information

The Tourist Information office is on the ground floor of the Ministry of Tourism where Hamra/Banque du Liban streets are intersected by Rome Street, ✆ (01) 343073; open

9–1, closed Sun. Offers newly produced brochures to all parts of the country and a good general map of the city.

communications

The central **telephone** office (Centrale) is adjacent to the tourist information office in the Ministry of Tourism (*see* above); open Mon–Sat 7am–10pm, Sun 7–11am. There are also cheaper private exchanges throughout the city from where calls can be made and faxes sent, e.g. Saroulla Services, Hamra Street, open daily 8.30–10.

The **central post office** is on Riad Solh Street, west of Martyrs' Square, and is open Mon–Thurs and Sat 8–noon, Fri 8–11am, closed Sun. It operates a *poste restante* service: recipient's name, Poste Restante, Bureau de Poste, Riad el Sohl Street, Beirut, Lebanon. Parcels can only be posted from the central post office, the contents inspected on the spot before the package can be sealed; 1kg is the maximum weight for parcels to Europe, 500g the maximum for North America. There is a branch office within the grounds of the American University of Beirut on Bliss Street, open 8–4, closed Sat and Sun, but no *poste restante* or parcel service.

Malik's Bookshop on Bliss Street near the American University offers e-mail, phone and fax services. Beirut Express, Chartouni Building, Naccache Street, Hamra, ✆ (01) 341400, are agents for DHL, the courier service, though rates are far higher from Lebanon than from Syria.

embassies

Your embassy can assist you by holding onto your mail, advising on emergency financial and medical problems and effecting emergency communications home.

Australian: Bliss Street, ✆ (01) 868349.
Canadian: same address as UK embassy, ✆ (01) 521163.
Irish: Chile Street, Verdun, ✆ (01) 863040.
UK: Coolrite Building, Autostrada, Jal el-Dib, ✆ (01) 406330, ✉ (01) 402033.
USA: Aoucar, opposite the Municipality, ✆ (01) 417774, ✉ (01) 407112.

maps and publications

There are several excellent bookshops on Bliss Street near the American University and on Hamra Street, for example the **Librairie du Liban** has shops on both streets. Maps, magazines and newspapers are also sold at the bookshops and at major hotels.

money

Cash can be freely exchanged almost anywhere at anytime. Try any bank, hotel or shop. Credit cards are widely accepted but you may have trouble changing travellers cheques except at a bank. Prices are quoted either in Lebanese pounds or American dollars, the one as readily acceptable as the other.

There is an American Express Bank at the Gefinor Centre, Clemenceau Street, ✆ (01) 341879. Though open Mon–Fri 8.30–12.30, Sat 8.30–12, closed Sun, it will not change travellers' cheques after 11, and it will not change cash at all. Thomas Cook, represented by Nahas Travel and Tourism, is also at the Gefinor Centre, ✆ (01) 370771. The British Bank of the Middle East, Omar Ibn Abdul Aziz Street, off Hamra Street, has cash machines where Visa and Mastercard holders can withdraw cash.

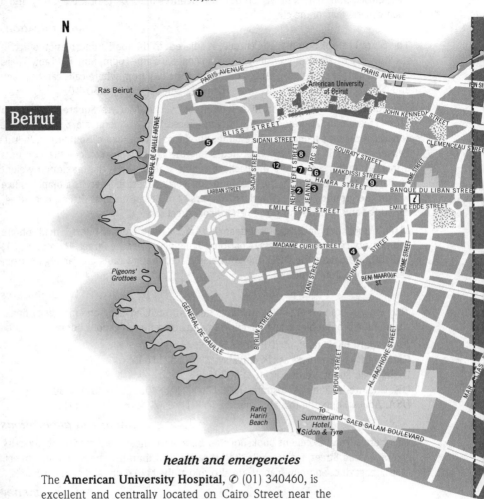

750 metres
750 yards

N

Ras Beirut

PARIS AVENUE

PARIS AVENUE

IBN SI

American University
of Beirut

JOHN KENNEDY STREET

CLEMENCEAU STREE

BLISS STREET

SIDANI STREET

SOURATY STREET

MAKDISSI STREET

ROME STREET

HAMRA STREET

BANQUE DU LIBAN STREET

LABBAN STREET

EMILE EDDE STREET

EMILE EDDE STREET

MADAME CURIE STREET

STREET

DUNANT

BENI MAAROUF
ST.

Pigeons'
Grottoes

TITANI STREET

ROME STREET

GENERAL DE GAULLE

BERLIN STREET

VERDUN STREET

AL-RACHIONE STREET

MAR-ILIAS

Rafiq
Hariri
Beach

To
Summerland
Hotel,
Sidon & Tyre

SAEB SALAM BOULEVARD

health and emergencies

The **American University Hospital**, ✆ (01) 340460, is
excellent and centrally located on Cairo Street near the
University in Hamra. **SOS Doctors**, ✆ (01) 344444, operates a
24hr emergency call-out and ambulance service.

Police: ✆ (01) 425250; **tourist police**: ✆ (01) 350901; **fire**: ✆ (01) 310111.

Around Martyrs' Square (Place des Martyrs)

Between Martyrs' Square and the port was Phoenician Berytus, but nothing of it survives
except in the American University and National museums. There are a few traces *in situ* of the
Roman city, which extended beyond the square in all directions. Until 1975 **Martyrs' Square**
was the hub of the city; now it is a vast building site. Before the war its central gardens waved
with palms and a few of its surrounding buildings even hinted at character, with balconies and
awnings and pitched red-tiled roofs. There were a number of pavement cafés, and through a

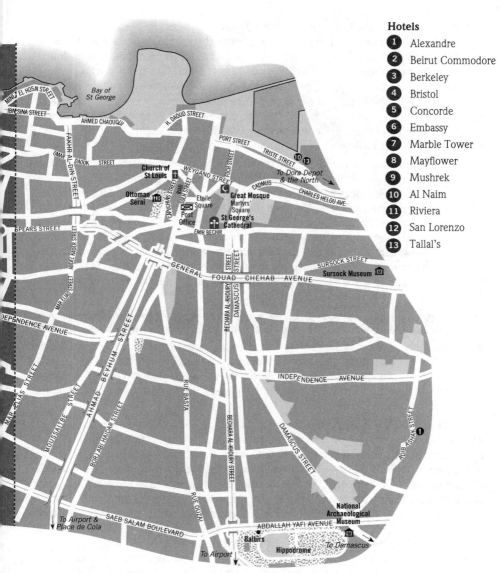

Hotels

1. Alexandre
2. Beirut Commodore
3. Berkeley
4. Bristol
5. Concorde
6. Embassy
7. Marble Tower
8. Mayflower
9. Mushrek
10. Al Naim
11. Riviera
12. San Lorenzo
13. Tallal's

vaulted passage off its west side you came to the goldsmiths' souk and beyond that the picturesque fruit and vegetable market. The war reduced all this to such rubble that everything has had to be bulldozed away. Even the martyrs have gone—though they are due back soon: or rather the bronze statue of the leaders of a rebellion against Ottoman rule who were executed here in 1840, the agony of the figures further embellished with bullet holes during the civil war. Now the holes are being plugged up.

At the north end of the square excavations have brought to light the **remains of a palace** with pointed arcades that had long since been built over (and may be built over again).

Perhaps this was Fakhr al-Din's palace, already ruinous when Maundrell described it as being near the **Great Mosque**, which stands off the northwest corner of the square on the south side of Weygand Street. The mosque, which is domeless, had earlier been the Crusader church of St John the Baptist. Running north off Weygand Street is Foch Street, lined with battered but handsome old buildings and houses, some built in the Turkish style with overhanging upper storeys, which they say will be restored (though sometimes promises are broken and bulldozers are sent in under cover of night). If you continue west along Weygand Street you eventually come into Omar Daouk Street and so on to the American University (*see* below). But before that you can follow a little circular walk.

Off the southwest corner of the square and running westwards is Emir Bechir Street. On the north side is the turn-of-the-century Maronite **cathedral of St George**, gutted and open to the sky. North of here Etoile Square is thought to have been the site of the **Roman forum**. Ruins of the period have been unearthed during recent demolition work. Continuing west along Emir Bechir Street you cross Riad Solh Street, lined with banks and so virtually untouched, and then come into Capuchins Street which curves round to the north. On its west side are the excavated remains of **Roman baths**. Up the embankment to the west is the shot-up **Ottoman barracks and serai,** the governor's residence, to be restored. At the north end of Capuchins Street restoration work is underway at the handsome 19th-century Roman Catholic **church of St Louis**. From here it is a few steps north to Weygand Street.

West Beirut

Beirut did not need a war to destroy its heritage; in the interest of making money its developers had already been destroying almost everything charming about the city. And so it is a rare thing to see some beautiful survivals of Beirut's turn-of-the-century **villas** along Omar Daouk Street. This continues westwards as John Kennedy Street which runs into Bliss Street and so to the American University.

But at Fakhr al-Din Street, where the blown-out shell of the Holiday Inn on its corner has been undergoing restoration, you can turn north past the blown-out shell of the Phoenicia Hotel to the corniche where, overlooking the **Bay of St George**, is the blown-out shell of the St George Hotel, once the finest in the city, not least for attracting the finest women round the finest pool. Along these shores, goes an old legend, St George slew the dragon. The corniche road along here is Ahmed Chaouqi Street, once jumping with bars, whores, bistros and strip joints. There is nothing here at all now but mounds of garbage that accumulated during the war and the shell of the unfinished Hilton Hotel that was due to open in 1975. The reason, incidentally, why so many of these large hotels were shot to bits was not aesthetic, nor even anti-Western, but because they made such good perches for snipers and so were especially targetted by the opposing side. There are now plans to turn the rubbish heaps into a garden.

The buildings of the **American University in Beirut** (AUB) on Bliss Street are scattered round an agreeable expanse of park on the slopes of Ras Beirut promontory. Though during the war some of the staff suffered kidnap and murder, the university itself survived unscathed, and once through the gate there is an immediate sense of sanctuary, where students and lecturers go about their business in veils or blue jeans in a mood of purposeful calm. The Syrian Protestant College, as it was first known, was founded as a non-denominational institute of higher education by Daniel Bliss in 1866. It has a good **Archaeological Museum** (*open Mon–Fri 10–12 and 2–4, Sat 10–12; free*), its collection including the pharaonic dedicatory inscriptions from the temple of Baal-lat Gebal at Byblos.

Bliss Street curls round a black and white banded lighthouse to the sea. The Syrian army patrols the area and has camps along the shore. About 750m south of the lighthouse is the Raoucheh district where the modern glass and concrete skyline stands on cliffs dropping into the sea. Offshore is a pair of sea-hollowed rocks, the **Pigeons' Grottoes** (Grotte aux Pigeons), which formerly (and perhaps again soon) you could visit by boat. There is good swimming from the beach, and from the cliffs at sundown a magnificent view along the Lebanese coast.

Southwest Beirut, towards the airport, is mostly Shia, its streets hung with yellow and green Hezbollah flags of an upraised hand clutching a gun.

Half a kilometre south of Bliss Street and parallel with it is **Hamra Street**, once filled with smart shops and soft porn cinemas, and the fashionable place to sit at a pavement café watching the girls slink by in their tight chemises and the guys spurting up and down in their MGs leaving rubber. The street is tawdry now and what glitz there is has slunk off to Jounieh.

East Beirut

East of Martyrs' Square in Sursock Street is the **Sursock Museum** (*open daily 10–1, during special exhibitions 5–8; adm*) with exhibitions of paintings, sculpture and old manuscripts, as much worth visiting for the house itself, a beautiful Levantine villa built in 1902 and still maintained by the Sursock family. The Sursocks are one of those Levantine families whose fortunes spanned both Lebanon and Egypt. Their palatial villa in Alexandria survives, while in Cairo they married into the Lotfallah family, whose palace on the island of Gezira is now the Marriott Hotel. Along with other foreigners who once gave Egypt and especially Alexandria a cosmopolitan ambience and a dose of entrepreneurial vigour, they departed when Nasser seized their properties, while this branch of the family had remained in Beirut all along.

To reach the reopened **National Archaeological Museum** (*open Mon–Sat 9–6; adm*) from Martyrs' Square you head south along Damascus Street (Rue de Damas); the museum is at the intersection with Abdallah Yafi Avenue. As Bechara al-Khoury Street just to the west more or less marked the Green Line, the museum was badly shot up, though no fundamental damage was caused and restorations to its Egyptian-style façade with its lotus columns and cavetto cornice have been completed. Inside, the museum became something of a bunker, its treasures gathered together and covered for their protection in concrete.

The museum's collection covers the whole of antiquity down to the Romans and there are also some Byzantine and Crusader exhibits. But its greatest strength lies in the treasures excavated at Byblos and illustrating all periods of its history, pride of place given to the **sarcophagus of Ahiram** (*see* p.317), bearing one of the earliest alphabetical inscriptions.

Sports and Activities

The Rafiq Hariri Beach, to the south of West Beirut heading towards the Summerland Hotel, is the only real sand beach in the city and the only beach open to the general public with membership or entrance fee. It is kept fairly clean and has changing rooms, showers and a snack bar. There are also several beach clubs along the coast of West Beirut, the two best that are open on a daily fee basis being the Riviera Beach Club belonging to the Riviera Hotel, ℘ (01) 602273, on Paris Avenue near Ras Beirut, with pool, scuba diving, restaurant and bar; and the St George's Yacht Club, ✆ 365065, at the eastern end of West Beirut, with pool, jet skiing, diving club, bars and restaurant. The Summerland Hotel, at Jnah on the coast towards the airport, ✆ (01)824112, has health and sports clubs for guests and members, including a gym, sauna, heated pool, martial arts, diving and waterskiing centres and squash and tennis courts.

Shopping

The locals go for opium, gold chains (for hairy chests), assault weapons and girlie magazines. Try the Hamra district for carpets and oriental antiques, but everything is expensive and you would do better to shop in Damascus.

Beirut (01)– *Where to Stay*

Before unthinkingly deciding that you must base yourself in Beirut, consider what would be for many people the more pleasant and convenient alternative of Byblos up the coast (*see* p.311). But in Byblos (and elsewhere round the country) hotels are few, while in Beirut they are almost as plentiful as bullet holes.

very expensive

★★★★★**Summerland Hotel**, Jnah, southwest Beirut, ✆ 824112, ✉ 863163. Luxurious fully-equipped rooms overlooking the sea or gardens, with restaurants, bars, nightclub, disco, business centre, shopping centre, beauty parlour, health and sports clubs and private beach. Conveniently situated close to the Iranian Embassy in a popular Hezbollah area.

★★★★★**Bristol Hotel**, Madame Curie Street, ✆ 351400, ✉ 351409. Between Hamra Street and the sea at Pigeons' Grottoes. Very pleasant rooms with air conditioning and TV, oriental lounge, restaurants, bars, hairdressers. Complimentary use of the Heliopolis Health Club (pool, gym, squash, sauna) and courtesy airport transfer.

★★★★★**Riviera Hotel**, Paris Avenue, ✆ 602273, ✉ 602272. Overlooking the sea west of AUB. Air-conditioned rooms with bath and TV. Japanese, Italian and Lebanese restaurants, bar and use of the Riviera Beach Club (*see* above).

expensive

★★★★**Alexandre Hotel**, Adib Ashak Street, ✆ 200242, ✉ 425870. In east Beirut, 750m northeast of the National Archaeological Museum. Health club, business services, restaurants, coffee shop. Rooms with TV and air conditioning.

★★★★**Berkeley**, Jeanne d'Arc Street, Hamra, ✆ 340600, ✉ 602250. Modern and luxurious hotel, rooms fully equipped; restaurant, bar.

★★★★**Beirut Commodore**, Commodore Street, Hamra, ✆ 350400, ✉ 345806. Fully equipped rooms, French, Japanese and Lebanese restaurants, bar, pool, gym and roof terrace. The hotel, and especially its bar, became famous as the haunt of journalists covering the civil war raging outside, though it has been completely made over since then.

moderate

★★★★**Mayflower Hotel**, Nehme Yafet Street, ✆ 340680, ✉ 342038. Between Hamra and Bliss streets. Comfortable hotel, air-conditioned rooms with TV, restaurant, notorious Duke of Wellington Bar (*see* 'Entertainment and Nightlife').

★★★Concorde Hotel, Bliss Street, ✆ 805683, 📧 862267. Very agreeable hotel west of AUB. Air-conditioned rooms with TV. Restaurant and pub.

★★★Marble Tower Hotel, at the west end of Hamra Street, ✆ 354586, 📧 346262. Air-conditioned rooms with TV. Restaurant, coffee shop and on the roof a piano lounge.

inexpensive

★★★Embassy Hotel, Makdissi Street, just north of Hamra Street, ✆ 340814, has rooms with air conditioning, bath, TV and balcony; the ones at the rear are better. The patio garden is an agreeable place to relax.

★★Mushrek Hotel, also in Makdissi Street, ✆ 345773, has clean, simple rooms, some with washbasin, fridge and balcony; shower and toilet is shared.

★★San Lorenzo Hotel, Hamra Street, ✆ 348604, has recently refurbished rooms with fan and shower, and cheaper basic rooms without. Restaurant and bar.

cheap

There are few cheap hotels in Beirut, and usually they accommodate transient Syrian workers rather than Western backpackers. Rooms are shared, you pay by the bed; places with private rooms are rare. Women should not stay alone in hotels in the cheap category. **Al Naim**, ✆ 447297, and **Tallal's New Hotel**, ✆ 446520, are in the same street down by the port; both are clean and friendly, with dorm beds, though Tallal's has one double room.

Beirut (01)–   ***Eating Out***

There are plenty of restaurants, cafés and snackbars to choose from in and around Hamra Street and also Bliss Street near the American University.

Beirut seems a long way to come for Kentucky Fried Chickens, McDonalds, TGI Fridays and local variations, but it is solid with them. For something more interesting, try **Nasr**, ✆ 860113, one of the best and most expensive restaurants in the city, its speciality seafood, overlooking the sea and the Pigeons' Grottoes in the Raoucheh district. **La Grotte aux Pigeons**, ✆ 812895, is next door, has the same view, serves seafood and grills, and is less expensive, though like much else in Beirut it is a shadow of its former self.

Beirut (01)–   ***Entertainment and Nightlife***

During the civil war, Beirut's nightlife upped and went to Jounieh, north along the coast, where most of it still remains. But lately bars and nightclubs have been springing up at such a rate that the best thing to do is to ask what are considered the latest hotspots. They are almost always expensive and usually do not get going until 11pm on Thursday, Friday and Saturday nights. By way of example, in East Beirut on Sursock Street is Le Retro, ✆ 202118, a fashionable nightclub and restaurant, while in West Beirut at the western end of Ibn Sira Street west of St George's Bay is the more lavish of the city's two Hard Rock Cafés. For something quieter and more nostalgic, look in on the Duke of Wellington bar at the Mayflower Hotel (*see* above), a favourite place for journalists to meet and reputed to be the place where many a hostage had his last drink.

Lebanon

40km
25 miles

N

Land over
1000 metres

To Tartus

Qubaiyat

Tripoli
(Trablus)

Al-Mina
Qalamun
**Belmont Abbey
(Deir Balamand)**
Enfeh
Ras al-Shakka

Hermel

Amiun

Bcharré

Batroun

Qadisha

**Cedars of
Lebanon**

Mediterranean

Sea

Yanua
Qartaba
Mashnaqa *Adonis*

Byblos
(Jbail)

Afqa

Jounieh

M o u n t   L e b a n o n

Baalbek
Baalbek

Litani

Dog

BEIRUT

Karak
Nouh
Zahleh
Chtaura
Sajdnayel

Anti Lebanon

Bhamdun

Qabb Elias

Damur

**Beit
Eddine**
**Deir al
Qamar**

Jebel Barouk

Anjar
(Haouch Mousa)

Bekaa Valley

To Damascus

Nebi Yunes
Sidon
(Saida)
Maghdouche

Joun

Jezzine

Rashaya

Sarafand

Litani

Marjayun

Hasbaiya

Mount

Tyre
(Sour)

Litani

**Beaufort
Castle**

302

Tripoli castle

Getting Around	304
The Dog River (Nahr al-Kelb)	304
Jounieh	306
Afqa	308
Byblos (Jbail)	310
From Byblos to Tripoli	318
Tripoli (Trablus)	320
To the Cedars of Lebanon	326

The North

This chapter follows the coast north from Beirut to Tripoli with excursions also up into Mount Lebanon. The mountain range is higher here than in the south and impresses itself more closely on the Mediterranean. At two points the coastal plain is actually transected by mountain spurs that overhang the sea, one south of Jounieh at the Dog River, the other north of Batroun at the headland called the Face of God.

From Jounieh, which the war has transformed from a small town to almost an alternative centre to Beirut, the old two-lane road follows the coastline to Tripoli, passing through all the towns along the way, while just inland from it a divided four-lane motorway runs from Beirut up to Tripoli. The outstanding points of interest are the Crusader, Roman and Phoenician remains at Byblos (Jbail), 40km north of Beirut, which also is one of the loveliest and most convenient places to stay in Lebanon, and the Mameluke and Crusader monuments at Tripoli, 90km north of Beirut. Excursions up the valley of the Adonis River (Nahr Ibrahim) to Afqa and up the especially beautiful Qadisha Valley to the Cedars give you a taste of Lebanon's mountain scenery.

The north is predominantly Christian, mostly Maronite, whose heartland this is, an important exception being Tripoli, which is largely Sunni Muslim. Had Lebanon disintegrated during the recent war, the intention of many here in the north was to establish a separate Christian state, and indeed it does feel a different world to the rest of the country, more Mediterranean in outlook, for the Maronites have long had ties with the West.

Security is good throughout the north. As well as Lebanese and Syrian checkpoints, the United Nations has a camp near the Cedars above Bcharré.

Getting Around

Service taxis ply endlessly between Beirut and Tripoli. Apart from going to the depots at either city you can hail them as they pass through the streets or at any point along the way. Mostly they follow the motorway and will charge extra if they have to divert to let you off at some place lying off it. There are also locally-based service taxis, for example at Byblos. Expect to pay about $3 from Beirut to the roadside drop-off for Byblos (40km) and about $5 for the full distance to Tripoli (90km).

Less frequent service taxis run from Tripoli up to Bcharré and for an extra sum one might take you right up to the Cedars. Otherwise, for the Cedars and for Afqa at the source of the Adonis River, you will have to hire a service taxi for your own use.

Where to Stay

There are numerous hotels along the way, for example at Jounieh (*see* p.307), Byblos (Jbail) (*see* p.318), Tripoli (*see* p.325), Ehden (*see* p.326) and Bcharré (*see* p.328), but there is nowhere to stay at Afqa.

The Dog River (Nahr al-Kelb)

From at least the time of the Pharaoh Ramses II in the 13th century BC, armies marching north or south along this coast have had to negotiate the steep slopes of the Nahr al-Kelb, the Dog

River (called the Lykos by the Greeks, river of the wolf), where it empties into the Mediterranean 15km north of Beirut. During the civil war it was a defended boundary between Christians and Muslims. Along the river's rocky flanks or on the promontory above the sea the Egyptians, Assyrians, Greeks, Romans and Mamelukes all carved reminders of their passage. To these the French added a commemoration of their 1860 expedition, obliterating one of Ramses' reliefs as they did so, while the British and again the French celebrated here their 20th-century exploits in Lebanon and Syria. Complementing this palimpsest of military advertising are nearby roadside hoardings promoting the virtues of the Show Biz Pizza Palace, Big Burger Falafel, Naff Naff and Tapirama ('the world's largest carpet centre').

Seeing the Inscriptions and Reliefs

Pollution from passing traffic probably accounts for the considerable deterioration the reliefs and inscriptions have suffered over the past several decades, and in some cases they will be hardly discernible in a decade or so more. All have been copied, however, which is what most concerns scholars. Each is identified by a Roman numeral, number I being an obscured cuneiform inscription on the north bank of the gorge near the road that records the early 6th-century BC exploits of Nebuchadnezzar in Mesopotamia and Lebanon. The rest are on the south bank or on the steep sides of the promontory and are numbered II to XVII as you go from east to west and then climb up the promontory.

On the South Bank

One way of getting your bearings on the south bank is to look for number IX, the plaque in English reading: 'The Desert Mounted Corps composed of British, Australian, New Zealand and Indian cavalry with a French regiment of Spahis and Chasseurs d'Afrique and the Arab forces of King Hussein captured Damascus, Homs and Aleppo October 1918'. This is above two badly-worn Assyrian reliefs, numbers VI and VII. Numbers II to V are therefore to your left (upriver), numbers VIII and X to XVII to your right (downriver and up the promontory). The various inscriptions and reliefs are here identified in numerical order.

II: On a rock at river level, a large Arabic inscription of the Mameluke Sultan Barquq (AD 1382–99).

III: A little downstream, a Latin inscription of the Roman Emperor Caracalla (AD 211–17).

IV: Farther on, an inscription commemorating the victorious entry into Damascus of French troops under General Gouraud on 25 July 1920. This, in accordance with the San Remo Conference, was the imposition by force of arms of the French Mandate and the overthrow of Syria's elected government and of King Feisal, one of the leaders of the Arab Revolt that had helped the Allies to victory against the Turks and was now betrayed by them.

V: An inscription (obliterating a relief of Ramses II) commemorating the French expedition of 1860, an event occasioned by the Druze massacre of the Maronites.

VI: A badly-worn relief showing an Assyrian king wearing a crown and with his right hand raised.

VII: Another Assyrian figure, badly worn.

VIII: Nearly 20m on, yet another Assyrian relief, this one almost totally indiscernible.

IX: The inscription referred to above, commemorating the Allies' capture of Damascus, Homs and Aleppo in October 1918.

Close to the above there are some more recent and unnumbered commemorations. One, in English, recalls the liberation of Syria and Lebanon from the Vichy French in June and July 1941; another, in the form of an obelisk and carrying the date 20 December 1942, commemorates the Allies' construction of the Tripoli–Beirut–Naqura railway; while a third, in Arabic and dated 30 December 1946, marks the evacuation of Lebanon by French troops.

Following the Ancient Roads Round the Promontory

At about the position of VI, VII and IX is the ancient Egyptian and Roman road, a path in fact, that climbs round the promontory.

X: About 45m along the rising ancient road, an English inscription of October 1918 honouring British and French troops.

XI: A bit higher up, a Greek inscription.

XII: Where the road turns to the southwest, another Greek inscription, very worn.

Near here, to your right, is a white rock cut to the form of a plinth, where legend has it there stood a statue of a dog or wolf (lykos), said to howl at the approach of an enemy.

Beyond this point the Roman road continues horizontally while the older stony path of the Assyrians and Egyptians climbs sharply to the left. Ascending this you come to:

XIII: An Assyrian king in an attitude of worship, next to:

XIV: An older relief of Ramses II sacrificing a prisoner in the presence of Re-Herakhte (an aspect of Horus combined with the sun god).

XV: About 15m onwards, the figure of an Assyrian king.

Now, passing over a mount of rock, go down the steps to the right, overlooking the sea. You are in fact backtracking along the Egyptian and Assyrian road so that you come first to XVII and then, next to it, XVI.

XVI: Relief showing Ramses II (right) holding his enemies by the hair and smiting them in the presence of the Theban god Amun (left), recognisable by his double-plumed headdress.

XVII: To the right of the Ramses relief (XVI) and seen first, the Assyrian King Esarhaddon shown in profile, the cuneiform text recounting his Egyptian campaign of 671 BC. The path is impassable beyond this point and you must return the way you came.

The Jeita Grotto

The road along the south bank of the Dog River leads you eastwards in 6km to the Jeita grotto, the river's sole source in summer and the year-round source of Beirut's water supply. The grotto served as a weapons and munitions store for Christian militias throughout the war but reopened in 1995, so that now as in the past boats float you across its illuminated subterranean lake past beautiful and richly-coloured stalactite formations.

Jounieh

Getting to Jounieh by Sea

There is a passenger ferry service between Larnaca in Cyprus and Jounieh. Sailings are once-weekly, on Fridays, in summer, though the service is expected to increase. There is a booking office on the road to the port, or contact Sonade in Beirut, ℰ (01) 585834, ✉ (01) 448006.

Before the war, Jounieh, 20km north of Beirut, was a small town and fishing port on a magnificent sweep of bay. Now the entire coast from Beirut almost to Byblos is built up with apartment blocks and large retail outlets, the roadsides thick with advertising signs. Many of these hoardings promote popular male entertainers, invariably sporting Groucho Marx moustaches, epitomising the hirsute ideal of Lebanese manhood.

All this clutter began not after the war but during it. Anyone who could afford to got out of Beirut to escape the fighting and bombings, and many were in any case forced out when their homes were blasted to smithereens. For the Maronites, Jounieh became an alternative capital, and also, as Beirut's port and often its airport were closed or too dangerous to get to, Jounieh became the port for Cyprus, which Lebanese can enter without a visa and so from there travel onwards. The wealthy built villas here or moved into smart apartments, while the less wealthy made do with slapped-up blocks, some unfinished but nevertheless inhabited, others already deteriorating. In its amenities, Jounieh is now all but self-sufficient, with schools, a university and numerous hotels, restaurants, nightclubs, cinemas and fashionable shops.

But the real glory of Jounieh, or at least the promise of such, is its **Casino du Liban**, which when it opened in 1958 quickly rivalled Monte Carlo and left Las Vegas in the shade. Here French chic met Middle Eastern wealth in shameless hedonistic exhibitionism; Sinatra and Aznavour entertained; Onassis, Loren and Bardot dropped in for a flutter; dancing girls filled the chandeliers, satellites descended from on high, a real train roared across the stage, waterfalls splashed, elephants pranced and dolphins showed how human they could be in a tank with naked women. The casino kept going till the last year of the war when militiamen shelled the complex, but in 1996 it opened again. There are gambling tables in private rooms where the minimum bet is $2000 and 300 slot machines for the hoi polloi, but no saucy dolphins or choo-choo trains yet.

Nor is it all Mammon: along the motorway at the south end of Jounieh is a statue, the size of a building, of **Christ the King** with a lightning rod sticking out of the top of its head, while at **Harissa**, 600m above Jounieh, is the still more gigantic statue of the **Virgin of Lebanon**, made in France and erected in the late 19th century. The Maronite Church of Our Lady of Harissa and the Roman Catholic Cathedral of St Paul stand near by. You can get there along a switchback road or by taking a cable car (*téléphérique*) from Jounieh (*daily 10am–11pm in summer, 10am–7pm in winter*). Again the buildings climbing the steep wooded slope up to Harissa date only from the war; in a few more years the trees will be entirely gone.

Where to Stay

Jounieh is a sprawling area with a plethora of hotels, restaurants, nightclubs, shops, etc., extending from Zouq Mechael south of the headland through Kaslik, the commercial district, and then the coastal district north of the headland along the bay up to Maameltein. Before the war it was hardly more than a village of a few thousand people along a magnificent sweep of bay; now, whatever its value to the Lebanese, it offers nothing to the traveller that cannot be better satisfied at Beirut or Byblos. A few places to stay in the coastal area of Jounieh are listed below.

expensive

★★★★**Beverly Beach**, recently opened on the coast road just south of the cable car (*téléphérique*) up to the Virgin of Lebanon, ✆ (09) 900255, ✉ (09) 916637. Rooms with air conditioning, bath, TV, minibar. The hotel has a private beach, pool, health club, restaurants and bar.

moderate

★★★**Arcadia Marina**, on the coast road south of the *téléphérique*, ✆ (09) 915546, 🕮 (09) 935956. Comfortable if slightly worn, with private beach and swimming pool, restaurant and bar; room s with air conditioning, shower, TV.

★★★**Bel Azur**, on the coast road at the south end of Jounieh, ✆ (09) 915582. Rooms with air conditioning and bath; the hotel has a restaurant, swimming pool and private beach where a wide variety of watersports is available.

★★**Montemar**, just north of Jounieh at Maameltein on the coast road, ✆ (09) 931996, 🕮 (09) 918134. Rooms have air conditioning, bath, TV, fridge and balcony; swimming pool, nightclub, restaurant and bar. A comfortable place to stay.

inexpensive/cheap

★★**St Joseph**, in the centre of old Jounieh, on the coast road, ✆ (09) 931189. Housed in a well-kept old Ottoman building, the rooms are spacious and come with bath, cheaper rooms without bath. A lovely place to stay but often booked up in summer, so best to reserve.

Afqa

The Nahr Ibrahim, the ancient river of Adonis, flows into the sea 13km north of Jounieh and 7km south of Byblos. Its source is the Afqa grotto, reached in about 40km by following the mountain road along the north side of the valley. In late winter and early spring the river runs red to the sea, swollen by winter rains that leach the uplands of their iron-rich minerals, but stained according to old belief by the blood of Adonis, the beautiful young lover of Aphrodite.

The Myth of Adonis

The myth is best known in that form recounted by the Greeks from the 5th century BC. The nub of the story has Adonis born of the incestuous love between King Cinyras of Byblos and his daughter. Aphrodite hid the infant in a chest, which she placed in the care of Persephone, queen of the underworld. But when Persephone opened the chest and saw the child's beauty, she wanted to keep him for her own. Zeus was called in to mediate in this dispute between death and love and decreed that Adonis must live part of each year in the dismal underworld but during the other part could return to the shining world above. There Adonis and Aphrodite become lovers, exchanging their first kisses at Afqa and also their last, for near the gorge Adonis was gored by a wild boar, perhaps jealous Ares in disguise, and though Aphrodite tried to heal his wounds, Adonis bled to death, bright spring anemones growing where his blood touched the ground.

It is an eternal story, the alternation of seasons expressed in the death and rebirth of men and gods, the theme resonating through the stories of Osiris, Attis and Christ, while at Maalula in Syria, Afqa's pagan tale is reproduced, though in perverted form, in the legend of St Thecla (*see* p.129).

Aphrodite of course is the Roman Venus, and in her earlier Semitic form she was Astarte, and in Babylonia Ishtar, the great mother goddess who was the embodiment of the reproductive energies of nature. Her lover was Tammuz, addressed by his devotees as Adon, that is lord, his title mistakenly taken by the Greeks to be his name. Tammuz was a vegetation god who every year was believed to die, his divine mistress journeying into the underworld in quest of him. In her absence the passion of love ceased to operate in the upper world, and men and animals forgot to procreate, and all life itself was threatened with extinction.

At Byblos, the principal centre of the Adonis cult, these were days of lamentation: 'He is dead, Adonis the beautiful, he is dead!' Women would beat their breasts and shave their heads, or could offer themselves for sacred prostitution. Then on the eighth day the sorrow turned to rejoicing: 'He is risen, Adonis, he is risen!' And today still the old fertility rites are recalled, though not in carnal form. In the days before Christmas and Easter, the mountain villagers place 'Adonis gardens' on their window sills or by their doors, earthenware pots planted with quick-growing seeds that spring to life in commemoration of the birth and resurrection of Christ.

Visiting the Grotto

You have to climb very high up the valley of the Adonis River before getting out of the built-up area. This was the Beirut–Baalbek road of the Romans whose temple remains can be seen en route at **Mashnaqa** and **Yanua**, though what more readily meets the eye are chalets and their swimming pools. The landscape is broken by outcrops of grey rock, calciferous oxidised limestone, worn and fractured, as in the Northern Highlands of Syria, while higher up are winter ski slopes. Most villages are Maronite, clean, bright and alert, with well-tended terraces growing vines, maize and walnut and fruit trees. Tight-fitting blue jeans on the young women are de rigueur. There are also Shia villages round about, no less prosperous, their inhabitants isolated non-combatants during the war and keeping still to their traditional ways. Their houses often have verandas formed of slender pillars and pointed arches, while their women drape themselves down to the ankles and wrap headscarves round their faces.

As you approach the apex of the valley you see the grotto, a great hole in the rock wall ahead. The nearby village of **Khirbet Afqa** is also Shia, some of its children with remarkable creamy green eyes. Placards hang across the street bearing photographs of Nabih Berri, leader of the Amal militia and of the Shia deputies in the assembly, dressed in a Western suit, and of Imam Moussa Sadr, a robed and turbaned mullah kidnapped during the war and not seen since.

An earthquake in 1911 brought down great blocks of stone from the rock face above the **grotto** and they lie in a tumbled mass at its mouth, giving it more the look of an abandoned quarry than a spot once renowned for its beauty. In winter a covering of snow makes the immediate scene more attractive, and in spring the river gushes from the cave with dramatic force while anemones carpet the falling valley below. The grotto is more impressive when you get into it, a great cavern with naturally worn galleries and connecting tunnels running round the back.

In late summer and autumn the flow from the grotto is reduced to a trickle that runs away beneath the **Roman bridge** as a clear, slightly turquoise stream. From the grotto the ancient bridge is obscured by a modern concrete span faced in rough stone that runs above, but steps down from the roadside lead to the Roman construction, a semicircular arc of nicely cut and fitted stone, and to a rocky ledge where there is a pleasant café run by a large woman of the village and her sons. Here, where the water collects into a deep cold turquoise pool, you can watch the local youths dive and swim in summer, and over a beer can enjoy the grandeur of the opening valley beyond.

The remains of a Roman **temple of Venus** lie between the village of Khirbet Afqa and the grotto. Here the love affair between Venus, or Aphrodite, and Adonis was localised, and its importance as a pilgrimage site meant that nothing was spared in its construction. Its granite columns were quarried at Aswan in Upper Egypt, floated down the Nile and shipped along to the Lebanese coast from where they were dragged up the valley. Now they lie broken among wall sections of well-cut blocks that still hang together though they have fallen on their sides like dominoes. Constantine, the first Christian emperor, ordered the temple's destruction because the cult of the goddess was licentious, since when earthquakes have furthered the confusion.

> This was a grove and a sacred enclosure, not situated as most temples are, in the midst of a city and of market places, and of broad streets, but far away from either road or path, on the rocky slopes of Libanus. It was dedicated to a shameful goddess, the goddess Aphrodite. A school of wickedness was this place for all such profligate persons as had ruined their bodies by excessive luxury. The men there were soft and womanish—men no longer; the dignity of their sex they rejected; with impure lust they thought to honour the deity. Criminal intercourse with women, secret pollutions, disgraceful and nameless deeds, were practised in the temple, where there was no restraining law, and no guardian to preserve decency.

Eusebius (AD *c.* 240–340), Bishop of Caesarea and friend of Constantine, from his *Vita Constantini Magni*.

Yet worship has not finished here. A gnarled fig tree grows from the ruins and to its branches local believers tie bits of clothing belonging to the sick whom they pray will be restored to health, while both Christians and Shia speak of the 'lady of the place', and in a vault beneath the temple on the river side light oil lamps in her honour.

Byblos (Jbail)

There is no more pleasant place to stay along the Lebanese coast than Jbail, the ancient port of Byblos, 40km north of Beirut. For a time Byblos was a Crusader stronghold, and its medieval walls enclose a charming town of honeyed stone with a castle and a 12th-century church still doing service for the local Maronite population. As you pass up and down its stepped lanes between walls overflowing with bougainvillaea you notice enormous stone flower boxes. These turn out to be recycled sarcophagi, Roman, Phoenician or older still, for Byblos goes back 7000 years and lays claim to being one of the oldest continuously inhabited settlements in the world. From the high keep of the castle, itself partly built with more ancient fragments, you have a marvellous view over the Crusader town to one side and the Phoenician city, excavated during the 20th century, to the other.

Known originally as Gebal and to the Crusaders as Giblet, it was the Greeks who gave it that familiar and resonant name of Byblos. From Egypt Byblos imported papyrus and re-exported it as scrolls throughout the Mediterranean, so that it is from Byblos that books, *biblia*, and *the* book, the Bible, derive their names. In return for papyrus and gold, Byblos sent Egypt shiploads of cedarwood. Being fragrant and durable, cedar of Lebanon was highly prized, Solomon building his Temple with it and the Egyptians using it in their palaces and to help build the Pyramids, where pieces have been found.

After compassing millennia of history by day, you can sit on the terrace of a restaurant overlooking the tiny circular harbour, a busy and prosperous cosmopolitan port those thousands of years ago, and with a glass of Bacchus' vintage in hand indolently watch the small fishing boats bobbing about on the evening sea and lowering their nets for your dinner.

Getting Around

Byblos is an ideal place to base yourself for trips around Lebanon, given the rebuilding in Beirut and its traffic jams, which delay any excursion out of the city. When you do want to visit Beirut, you can get there from Byblos in well under an hour and reach almost anywhere else including Baalbek within three. Its drawback is the limited accommodation: there are only three hotels.

Service taxis running along the Beirut–Tripoli motorway will either drop you off en route or for an extra sum will take you right into Byblos. Some will be going to Byblos in any case.

In Byblos, taxis and service taxis gather on the main street running through the new part of town near the top of the road running down to the Byblos sur Mer Hotel by the old harbour.

History

Seven thousand years ago Byblos was a small neolithic village on the edge of the promontory, its inhabitants living in circular stone huts whose floors of beaten earth or plaster can still be traced today. Their implements show that they practised fishing, agriculture and animal husbandry, while blades of obsidian indicate that they engaged in trade with Anatolia. From about 3800 BC they were replacing their stone weapons and tools with ones of copper, its sources the mines of Cyprus and the Caucasus, but it was specifically the introduction of the metal axe around 3200 BC that was to transform the destiny of Byblos. The nearby mountain slopes were forested with pine, juniper and cedar, all tall trees valuable in construction, and their large-scale exploitation opened up rich trading opportunities with treeless Egypt. Impressive evidence of this trade survives at Giza from the reign of the Pharaoh Cheops (2549–2526 BC) in the form of his magnificent solar boat, 40m long and built of Lebanese timber, now on display in a special museum alongside his Great Pyramid, which itself was constructed with the aid of cedar beams that have been found within it.

At a time when Sidon and Tyre were probably still no more than fishing villages, Byblos with its small but adequate harbour, at the base of forested mountains plunging down to the sea, became a wealthy trading city encircled by a defensive wall, a section of which survives along with a complex entry gate. The city's temple of Baal-lat, the feminine of Baal and identified by the Egyptians with Hathor, who among other things was the goddess of Egypt's foreign interests, was generously endowed by the Old Kingdom pharaohs, whose offerings of alabaster vases inscribed with their names survive in fragments displayed at the Archaeological Museum of the American University in Beirut.

It is probably no coincidence that the collapse of the Old Kingdom around 2100 BC also saw Byblos overrun by the Amorites, a Semitic people from the deserts to the east. While the Amorites of the Syrian interior looked towards Mesopotamia, those who intermingled with the coastal culture contributed to the amalgam known as Canaanite or Phoenician. Within a couple of centuries, as conditions in Lebanon became settled again and the Middle Kingdom pharaohs re-established a central authority in Egypt, trading relations between the two were resumed, and soon the rulers of Byblos were mimicking Egyptian titles and style and erecting a temple filled with obelisks. With the Asian conquests of the New Kingdom Pharaoh Tuthmosis III (1479–1425 BC), Byblos, like other regions in Syria and Lebanon, was reduced to vassalage and remained under Egyptian control even after the battle of Kadesh (see p.134), when Ramses II (1279–1213 BC) was obliged to pass Tripoli and Ugarit to the north over to Hittite domination.

Shortly after Ramses' reign Byblos was ruled by King Ahiram, whose grave shaft lies exposed at the site, though his sarcophagus, important for its early alphabetical inscriptions, is now at the National Museum in Beirut. Then several decades into the 12th century BC, almost all the eastern Mediterranean was overrun by the Sea Peoples, the Hittite Empire succumbing to their onslaught, while Egypt, though successfully defending itself, lost what last hold it had over Lebanon. Some Sea Peoples settled on the Lebanese coast, contributing the final ingredient to that culture which henceforth becomes definitively Phoenician.

But now Arwad in the north and Tyre in the south became the chief cities of first millennium BC Phoenicia, the decline of Egypt once again mirrored at Byblos. When Solomon wanted cedar for his Temple at Jerusalem, it probably came from Byblos but it was Hiram of Tyre who provided it. Until the late 7th century BC, when the Greeks established their own trade counters in Egypt, at Naucratis, Byblos was the principal transshipment point between Egypt and the Aegean for papyrus, byblos in Greek, the name they consequently gave the port. Little survives from this millennium during which the empires of Assyria, Persia and Alexander the Great imposed themselves on the coastal cities. By the coming of the Romans in the 1st century BC the deforestation of its hinterland had brought Byblos close to economic collapse. Nevertheless the Romans built here, a theatre and the remains of a colonnade surviving, for if Byblos' commercial fortunes had failed, its importance as the centre for the cult of Adonis persisted (see p.309) until the final suppression of paganism.

During the Byzantine period, from which an abandoned Greek Orthodox church survives, it was the seat of a bishop. The Arabs contributed nothing and let deteriorate what they found; in removing their capital eastwards to Baghdad, they turned their backs on the Mediterranean world. Ignored from the east and cut off from the West, Lebanon suffered, its once great ports, Byblos among them, reduced to sleepy fishing villages.

A modest revival accompanied Byblos' capture in 1104 by Raymond de Saint-Gilles, Count of Toulouse, who as leader of the First Crusade was among those who had captured Jerusalem five years before and had meanwhile been laying siege to Tripoli. Soon after his death in 1105, Byblos was passed on to his allies, the Genoese, through whom it again enjoyed a trade with Europe. Though Saladin took Giblet, as the Franks called it, in the year of Hattin, 1187, and recolonised it with Kurds, it was recaptured in 1199 and remained in Western hands till 1266, when the defenders, beset by one of Baybars' lieutenants, escaped under cover of a stormy night to Tripoli, their monuments a castle and a fine church, while the Mamelukes and Ottomans rebuilt their walls.

When Henry Maundrell passed this way during his Easter 1697 pilgrimage to Jerusalem there was little to say: 'In three more hours we came to Gibyle, called by the Greeks Byblos. . . At present it contains but a little extent of ground, but yet more than enough for the small number of its inhabitants . . . though anciently it was a place of no mean extent, as well as beauty, as may appear from the many heaps of ruins and the fine pillars that are scattered up and down in the gardens near the town.'

The French military expedition of 1860 was also the occasion of the first archaeological survey of the site, though excavations began only in 1921.

The Medieval Town

The medieval town was enclosed by **walls** running about 270m from east to west and 200m from north to south. These were rebuilt on Crusader foundations by the Mamelukes after 1266 and by the Ottomans after 1516. The north wall is pretty much intact and is pierced by a gate. The east and south walls are mostly gone, while the west wall that ran along the sea following the line of Phoenician ramparts has completely vanished.

In the southeast quadrant of the medieval town towards the castle there is a small **square** with some shops and, nearby, a mosque. Running east off the square is the souk leading into the new town. Heading west from the square through a vaulted passage you descend past gardens and houses to the port. South of the square is the castle, through which you enter the ancient site, while to the north of the square and set back a bit to the west is the Crusader Church of St John.

The **Church of St John the Baptist**, now in the hands of the Maronites, was built in Romanesque style in about 1115 but was damaged and partly rebuilt after the great earthquake of 1170 that had also shaken Krak des Chevaliers. The incongruous bell tower is modern. Added to the northwest corner of the church in about 1200 is its finest feature, an open-sided baptistry, its dome raised upon four slightly pointed arches variously carved with ribbing, zigzags and rosettes, probably Italian in inspiration and lending a happily crazed touch to the baptistry's otherwise restrained Romanesque. The north doorway through which you enter is 18th-century, but first you should make a clockwise circuit round the outside. At its east end you see a pronounced triple apse, while severe Romanesque doorways are set into the south façade, its stonework incorporating ancient columns and powerfully buttressed. The buttressing probably followed the 1170 earthquake, and in fact you can see at the upper levels of both the south façade and the southernmost apse that there has been considerable rebuilding using smaller blocks of stone.

You can continue reading the history of the church in this way when you go inside, where you are struck by the voluminous nave, its high barrel roof supported along the north aisle by square pillars with engaged columns supporting slightly pointed arches. But the pillars along the south aisle are shorter and thicker and, except for the pillar nearest the altar, are without engaged columns. The arches supported by these south pillars are more pointed and of lesser span than those along the north aisle. The ambitious barrelled nave would have exerted considerable lateral pressure, making the church particularly vulnerable to an earthquake. Most of the damage appears to have been caused along its south side, as already observed from outside where the remedy was buttressing, while inside the south aisle was rebuilt with stouter pillars linked by shorter arches.

Immediately west of St John's a column stands on a level site adorned with geometric and vine **mosaic paving**, all that remains of a Byzantine church. A small Orthodox **church of the Byzantine period** does survive a bit farther along down the hill.

Returning through the square to the southeast corner of the medieval town you climb to the **castle** (*open daily 8–7.30 in summer, 8–5.30 in winter; adm, which includes the ancient site beyond*), begun as soon as the Crusaders had captured Byblos. It consists of a rectangular wall with a deep moat running round it and a considerable central keep built of impressively large blocks of stone, especially at the base and five courses upwards. Apart from the gigantic blocks used at Baalbek and at a few other Roman monuments, these are the largest anywhere in Lebanon and Syria. It seems unlikely that the Crusaders would have quarried blocks on this scale for so modest a fortress. Certainly much of the material used in building the medieval town was recycled from the ruins, these blocks perhaps coming from one of the Roman temples built over ones more ancient. From the top of the keep you have a wonderful view over the medieval town and the ancient ruins, while immediately below you, running off to east and west, are the oldest ramparts of Byblos, 3rd millennium BC. You enter the site by going down through the castle.

Ancient Byblos

Entrance is via the Crusader castle. Open daily 8–7.30 in summer, 8–5.30 in winter; adm includes both the site and the castle.

Excavations began at the site in 1921. At that time there was a small village on the headland and this was cleared away. Also to lay bare the most ancient structures, less ancient ones were transferred and reconstructed elsewhere, rather as you would cut a pack of cards. The Crusaders had also quarried the site, recycling columns and blocks from Roman temples that had been built upon the temple of Baal-lat Gebal and the 3rd millennium temple to the unknown deity on either side of the sacred lake. Emerging from the castle, you should at first go counterclockwise so that you are walking along its southern wall heading east past various fragments of statuary that have been propped up here. The **rampart** beyond and the **gate** cutting through it belong to the 3rd millennium BC. The gate is more elaborate than it first appears. You climb several steps to a passage laid with stone blocks running between stone walls and then descend several steps at the other side. Along the way, notice the transverse grooves in the paving, each representing a point where the gate could be closed by a portcullis, making the city impregnable. Now with an air of ceremony you can return back through the gate and enter ancient Byblos as though newly arrived. There is something pleasing about this, as there is about entering the inner sanctum of a temple, because you know that in the past there would have been somebody officiously blocking your way, but after several thousand years it transpires that the meek, if they do not inherit the earth, can at least traipse where they like among its ruins.

Opposite the gate, 40m south, are the partly reconstructed remains of a **temple to an unknown deity**, destroyed by fire at the end of the 3rd millennium when the Amorites captured the city. Between this temple and that of Baal-lat Gebal to the west are traces of a **sacred lake**. The temple to the unknown deity was then built over by another, and so to excavate the older temple the later temple was removed to the southeast. This is the early 2nd-millennium **obelisk temple**. It was entered up the flight of steps on the east side from where a narrow passage leads to the inner sanctum containing a tall obelisk, though only its base survives. Behind this is a courtyard containing 30-odd smallish obelisks, some no more than 25cm high. Nearly all of these were found upright, placed there by believers to perpetuate their presence in the sight of Reshef, a god of war, and left unmolested by passing generations as they were slowly covered by soil. The notion of obelisks was imported from Egypt where they were solar symbols pointing to the divine sun. But here their function was transmuted to suit local beliefs. Some contain small niches in which the divine image or offerings might have been placed. Instead of pointing they enclosed; they were empowering symbols, houses of the gods.

A depression 100m to the west of the obelisk temple (and just southwest of the sacred lake) marks the site of a large rock fault opening on to a deep **spring** that could be reached by a

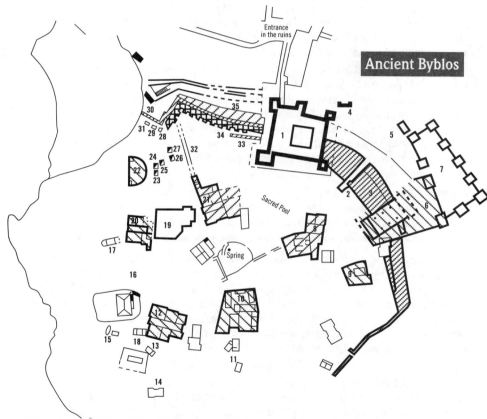

1 Crusader castle 2 Gate 3 Pre-2000 BC ramparts 4 Roman nymphaeum 5 Byzantine oil pres 6 Persian podium 7 Persian fortress 8 Temple of 3rd millennium 9 Obelisk temple 10–11 Houses of the pre-urban settlement 12 Great Residence 13 Early urban settlement 14 House of Amorite conquest 15 House of Chalcolithic period 16 Neolithic houses 17 Early Neolithic (?)sanctuary 18 Late Neolithic sanctuary 19 Quarry of Amorite period 20 Pre-Amorite residence 21 Baal-lat Gebal temple 22 Roman theatre 23–31 2nd-millennium royal tombs 32 Roman colonnade 33 Early 3rd-millennium walls 34 Late 3rd-millennium walls 35 Mid-2nd-millennium walls

flight of steps still partly visible today. From the earliest times until the 1930s, except for a period when the Romans drew water from the mountains by an aqueduct, this spring was the sole source of Byblos' water supply.

The Myth of Isis and Osiris at Byblos

Associated with the spring is Plutarch's 1st-century AD version of the Isis and Osiris myth. Osiris, the brother-husband of Isis, had been murdered by his brother Seth and put into a coffin that was cast into the Nile. Eventually it was washed ashore at Byblos where it was enclosed by a young growing tree. Admiring the tree for its straightness and beauty, but not knowing what it contained, the king had it cut down and made into a column to support the roof of his palace. Learning of this, Isis came to Byblos where she sat by the well and wept. Befriended by the queen, Isis revealed her identity and the cause of her sorrow. The column was removed and the coffin released, and Isis returned with the body of Osiris to Egypt.

In older Egyptian versions, Seth dismembers Osiris, or in the form of a boar castrates him, but Isis makes him whole again and brings him back to life, though as ruler of the underworld. In other words it is a resurrection myth and in Plutarch's late version concerning Byblos has similarities with that of Aphrodite and Adonis who died when gored by a boar at the Afqa spring (*see* p.308). Osiris was originally a vegetation god, and given Byblos' traditional timber trade with Egypt, he was hardly out of place inside a tree. In fact, continues Plutarch, Isis left the tree behind at Byblos where it was placed in the temple and became an object of veneration.

A curious postscript to this tale is that near by is the so-called Great Residence, whose superstructure was supported by a forest of wooden columns, while the women who still drew water from the spring in the 1930s called it the King's Well.

To the southwest of the site, 100m from the spring, is the **Great Residence**, built in about 2500 BC and the best preserved of several monumental domestic structures at the site. There was a large central hall whose roof was supported by 30 wooden columns, and all the bases of 120 columns can be traced throughout the building. Far humbler **4th-millennium dwellings**, built when copper implements had only recently been introduced, can be seen 30m west of the Great Residence, while 30m to its northwest are the outlines of **neolithic huts** marking the first settlement at Byblos.

Immediately south of the Roman colonnade and 100m north of the Great Residence is the **Baal-lat Gebal temple**, now excavated down to its earliest 3rd-millennium level. This most venerable of Byblos' temples continued in use, much restored by each succesive age, for 3000 years down to the Roman period. Dedicated to the Lady of Byblos (Baal-lat is the feminine of Baal and Gebal was Byblos' most ancient name), she was identified by the Egyptians with Hathor whom they worshipped here, as evidenced by the discovery of inscribed offerings sent from the Pyramid-building pharaohs Cheops and Mycerinus.

You can now climb west to where the Roman **theatre** overlooks the sea, a dramatic and natural choice of setting you would think, yet originally it stood at the northeast corner of the site near the obelisk temple and was removed here to make way for excavations. Coins found at the theatre date its construction to AD 218. It seems very small, with only four tiers of seating, but these represent only a third of its former capacity, the stones of the upper tiers having been recycled by the Crusaders. The orchestra was paved with white tesserae within a black border, and facing the audience a mosaic of Bacchus, now in the National Museum at Beirut. The waist-high back of the orchestra is charmingly decorated with five miniature Corinthian temple façades, their pediments alternately triangular and rounded.

Running along the knoll to the east of the theatre is a Roman **colonnade** that once met at a right angle with another that ran eastwards beyond the castle. Five of the six raised monolithic columns are of grey granite, while one to the south is red, this last, and probably all the columns, from Aswan in Upper Egypt. Four carry marble Corinthian capitals and two are spanned by an architrave. Other columns lie near by, also fragments of bases, capitals and architraves.

Just seawards of the colonnade is a 2nd-millennium BC **necropolis** where nine hypogea have been found. The Romans had built baths here and over these lay, ironically, a modern cemetery. That was the situation in 1922 when a landscape revealed one of the ancient tombs. All but three had been looted in ancient times, while one, unaccountably, contained an English newspaper. In one hypogeum, though it had been looted, was found what is now the prize of Beirut's National Museum, the late 2nd-millennium BC limestone sarcophagus of King Ahiram inscribed—in one of the earliest examples of alphabetical writing—with curses against anyone who should violate his tomb.

Between here and the castle are three lines of defences. The innermost, extending only a short distance west from the castle, is part of Byblos' first city walls and dates from the early 3rd millennium BC. This marks the moment when Byblos, no longer a village but instead a booming commercal timber port, was acquiring great wealth and had something worthwhile to defend. The middle dentated wall was built during the second half of the 3rd millennium BC. Outermost is a succession of *glacis* of the late 2nd and early 1st millennium BC.

The Port

North of the walls of ancient Byblos and at the base of the medieval town is the little semicircular **port**, now anchorage for a few fishing boats, but for over 3000 years, from the first large-scale felling of timber on Mount Lebanon in about 3200 BC down to the Christian suppression of the Adonis cult, one of the great international harbours of antiquity. Later the Crusaders defended the port with **towers** on either side of its narrow mouth across which they could suspend a chain. The northern tower is ruinous but you can climb to the top of the southern one. Beneath you passed those ships laden with the cedarwood of which Solomon built his Temple, and 1600 years earlier those 'forty ships filled with cedar logs', recorded by the Pharaoh Snofru, for building

ships and 'making the doors of the royal palace'. Snofru was the father of Cheops, who also shipped cedarwood from Byblos to help build his Great Pyramid. 'Soldiers!' said Napoleon after the Battle of the Pyramids, 'forty centuries of history look down upon us'. From this tower you look down on a good many more.

Where to Stay

expensive

★★★**Byblos sur Mer**, on the sea close to the old port, ✆ (09) 540356, ✉ (09) 944859. Air-conditioned rooms with TV and balconies, the best overlooking the sea. The hotel has a restaurant and bar, as well as a floating seafood restaurant, L'Oursin, and a swimming pool, private beach and marina, with watersports, tennis, squash and health club facilities available.

moderate

★★★**Ahiram**, ✆ (09) 540440, ✉ (09) 944726. Following the road along the north wall of the old town towards the sea, you turn right (north) about halfway along and in about 200m come to the hotel. It is set back from the sea a bit. Rooms are air-conditioned with TV, and there is a restaurant and bar. Watersport facilities are offered on the hotel's stretch of beach.

★★**Byblos Fishing Club**, ✆ (09) 540213, ✉ (09) 217276. Associated with the restaurant of the same name (*see* below), accommodation here is in 12 bungalows on the hillside overlooking the port, with air conditioning, shower and toilet, simple but comfortable and pleasantly secluded, some bungalows set in their own private gardens.

inexpensive

There is **camping** at Amchit, ✆ (09) 540322, 5km north of Byblos.

Eating Out

There are several moderately-priced restaurants along or off the road running parallel to the north wall of the old town down to the sea. For an inexpensive light meal, try the vaulted passage running south off the square in the old town. There are also a couple of places to eat on the old port, including the best place of all to enjoy a drink or a meal at Byblos, the moderate to expensive **Byblos Fishing Club** (also known as Pepe's for its octogenarian owner), ✆ (09) 540213, ✉ (09) 217276. Tables are set among plants and numerous fine ancient architectural and sculptural fragments on a veranda overlooking the harbour. The cellars, where there are also tables, are a virtual antiquities museum.

From Byblos to Tripoli

From Byblos to Tripoli it is about 50km, and for much of the way north the coast is hardly built up. You see bananas growing, though they are less common here than in the warmer south. Between the road and the sea you also notice stretches of the railway line built during the Second World War, a rare sight, as during the recent fighting people would tear up the track and sell it off by the kilo.

In about 16km, near **Batroun**, an ancient dependency of Byblos, the old Tripoli road keeps to the sea, climbing round the precipitous headland of **Ras al-Shakka**, known to the Greeks as

Theouprosopon, the **Face of God**. Round it crept the
army of the First Crusade on their way to Jerusalem.
The promontory is especially impressive from the
north, a great table dropping almost sheer to the
sea, the white-domed chapel of a Greek
Orthodox monastery on the top. Though the road
round the face was in use during the Middle
Ages, it has not always been passable since. The
alternative was to swing inland through the rocky
pass now followed by the motorway, where off to
your right (east) you see **Musaylaha castle**, whose
origins are obscure (the name is the Arabic diminutive of
Maslaha, meaning fortified post). Greek sculptural fragments are
built into its walls, a Crusader habit, though the Crusader chronicles make no mention of the
place and architecturally it looks more Muslim. It might have been a Shia lair, its purpose to
blackmail passers-by, or it might have been built by Fakhr al-Din al-Maani II early in the 17th
century to make the road secure. Certainly it was here late that same century when Maundrell
passed by, saying it was called Temseida. At any rate the castle can serve you as a marker for
something very odd: just past it is a slip road rising to a bridge passing over the motorway—
at least there is no visual doubt that the road does rise—and yet, in apparent defiance of
gravity, vehicles can roll up it with their engines off.

At about 23km from Byblos is **Enfeh**, meaning nose, approached via a cementworks. The
coast along here is again built up, almost all of it concrete, much of it very new. Only rarely do
you see a house or building of any age or traditional character. The population of Enfeh is
mostly Greek Orthodox, as it is at **Qalamun** to the north, a town reputed for its brass, olive oil
and rosewater.

Belmont Abbey (Deir Balamand)

A few kilometres north of Enfeh, on the crest of a hill to the east, is Deir Balamand, a Greek
Orthodox monastery from sometime after the fall of the Crusader state of Tripoli in 1289 but
founded by the Cistercians in 1157, for whom it was Belmont Abbey. The Cistercian order
had been founded in France only 60 years earlier, and its rule was strict, its churches plain, its
monks given to lives of communal seclusion and self-sufficiency based on primitive manual
labour. Before the Crusades there might have been a Byzantine monastery here, but no trace
of it survives. The road to Belmont climbs up through a rugged landscape of rock-strewn
maquis, planted with olive trees but empty of habitations and roamed by flocks of goats. From
the top there is a marvellous view along the coast, the high white modern buildings of Al-
Mina, the harbour suburb of Tripoli, large and shining to the north.

A vaulted gate leads on to a delightful stone-flagged courtyard with arcades of pointed arches
to the east (right), off which is a chapel, and north (ahead), where there is a remodelled 12th-
century **church** and behind it a lime grove on the edge of a drop to the sea. Though now filled
with the impedimenta of Orthodoxy, the church has a severe Cistercian look and is all of one
space, nave and apse without aisles beneath a gently pointed, almost barrelled roof. From the
outside you can climb the 13th-century **bell tower** from where you are struck at how closely
the mountains come down to the sea. Bell towers rarely survived the expulsion of the

Crusaders, and indeed the bell itself has been removed (but *see* below), Maundrell recording that the Orthodox priests here called their congregation together 'by beating a kind of tune with two mallets on a long pendulous piece of plank at the church door, bells being an abomination to the Turks'.

Now walk across to the eastern arcade where there is a gate on the left and to the left of this an old bit of Crusader embellishment built into the wall, a capital bearing the face of a cat. To the right of the gate is the **Chapel of St George**, as it is known now, but originally a chapter room, a meeting place for the Cistercian monks. It is a more complex structure than the church and consists of two cruciform vaults and a half vault at the back, this being the apse and 12th-century, the rest having been remodelled at a later date. An iconostasis has been set part way into the apse.

The 14th-century **kitchen**, at the southwest corner of the court, now houses architectural fragments. If you pass through the gate leading out from the west side of the court and look back and up you can see the **bell** that was removed from the tower and reset here between stone posts atop the wall of the court but invisible from within it. Like the tower it is 13th-century and is perhaps the oldest bell in Lebanon.

Round the upper level of the court are the **monks' cells**.

Tripoli (Trablus)

Until recent decades Tripoli was a city of two distinct parts, suburban Al-Mina with its sea harbour and then 3km or so inland across gardens and orchards Al-Medina (meaning the town) on the banks of the Nahr Abu Ali, the local name for the Nahr Qadisha flowing down from the Cedars of Lebanon above Bcharré. The explosive growth of the city has now joined the two. As elsewhere in Lebanon from Beirut northwards there is a sense of busyness about the place, though here the atmosphere is more conservative, for most of the population is Sunni Muslim.

Originally there was only **Al-Mina**. This was the site of the Phoenician city, first mentioned in 8th-century BC accounts, where Sidon, Tyre and Arwad each had their district, occasioning the Greeks to call the place Tripoli, 'three cities'. But though Al-Mina subsequently passed through the hands of the Seleucids, Romans, Byzantines, Arabs and Crusaders, flourishing under each in turn, nothing except the **Tower of the Lions**, a late 15th-century coastal fortification against a possible Turkish invasion, has survived.

Instead interest lies at **Al-Medina**, where atop Mount Pilgrim the Crusaders built their castle and below which the Mamelukes afterwards founded the medieval town whose mosques, hamams and khans make a visit worthwhile today. The best way to get your bearings is to head for the castle, the Abu Ali River flowing by beneath its eastern ramparts, while from its western ramparts you will be able to look down on the medieval town and pick out the Great Mosque and other monuments to be visited later.

Getting Around

The centre of Al-Medina is Al-Tal Square (Place du Tell), 500m west of the castle and 250m west of the Great Mosque. Service taxis arrive and depart from the square, and from here you can catch a taxi to Al-Mina. Medieval Tripoli between the square and the river is fairly compact and can easily be covered on foot.

The Castle of Saint-Gilles (Qalaat Sanjil)

History of the Castle

Raymond de Saint-Gilles, Count of Toulouse, had left Tripoli unmolested in 1099 when as leader of the First Crusade he marched southwards to Jerusalem. Though Bohemond, his rival, had already made himself Prince of Antioch, Raymond was looking forward to greater things, but intrigues denied him the crown of the Kingdom of Jerusalem.

Between the Crusader states of Antioch and Jerusalem and still in Muslim hands lay Tripoli, and here Raymond now determined to carve out his domain. In 1102 he won a remarkable victory outside Tripoli's walls when his force of 300 knights slaughtered 7000 of the Muslim army. Yet Tripoli did not fall and Raymond had to resort to siege. By the spring of 1104, with Byzantine help, he had built his castle atop Mount Pilgrim and from here controlled the land approaches to the city. Though Tripoli was able to supply itself by sea, the castle was a menace and in summer the Muslims attacked it. The attempt failed, but Raymond was injured and died early the following year.

Nevertheless, the siege continued, aided at sea by the fleets of Byzantium, Genoa and Provence, until in 1109 Tripoli was starved into surrender. The usual massacre and destruction followed, and Tripoli's library, the finest in the Muslim world, was burnt to the ground. The city quickly revived, however, and became a leading intellectual centre, with schools of medicine and philosophy, while 4000 looms for weaving silk ensured its prosperity, and as the seat of the Counts of Tripoli, stretching north to Margat in Syria and south nearly to Beirut, it endured for 180 years.

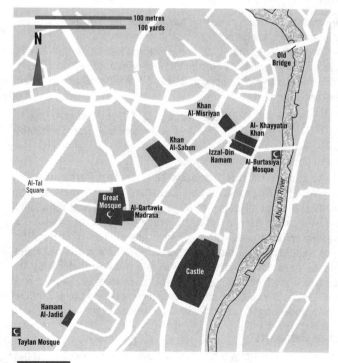

Raymond's fortress was much rebuilt by the Mamelukes and Ottomans, so that barely more than its foundations and here and there the lower courses of its walls and keep are Crusader work. By the time Maundrell gave it a look, the castle had ceased to have any military importance and was used by the Ottomans as a prison.

> There was shut up in it at this time a poor Christian prisoner called Sheikh Eunice, a Maronite. He was one that had formerly renounced his faith and lived for many years in the Mahometan religion: but in his declining age he both retracted his apostasy and died to atone for it, for he was impaled by order of the pasha two days after we left Tripoli.

> This punishment of impaling is commonly executed amongst the Turks for crimes of the highest degree and is certainly one of the greatest indignities and barbarities that can be offered to human nature. The execution is done in this manner. They take a post of about the bigness of a man's leg, and eight- or nine-foot long, and make it very sharp at one end. This they lay upon the back of the criminal and force him to carry it to the place of execution, imitating herein the old Roman custom of compelling malefactors to bear their cross. Being arrived at the fatal place, they thrust in the stake at the fundament of the person who is the miserable subject of this doom, and then taking him by the legs, draw on his body upon it, till the point of the stake appears at his shoulders. After this they erect the stake and fasten it in a hole dug in the ground.

> The criminal sitting in this posture upon it remains not only still alive but also drinks, smokes and talks, as one perfectly sensible; and thus some have continued for 24 hours. But generally after the tortured wretch has remained in this deplorable and ignominious posture an hour or two, some one of the standers-by is permitted to give him a gracious stab to the heart, so putting an end to his inexpressible misery.

> Henry Maundrell, *A Journey from Aleppo to Jerusalem at Easter*, AD 1697.

Visiting the Castle

The 25 square towers of the castle recall the Byzantine help given to Raymond in its construction, for as at Krak des Chevaliers (*see* p.169) the Crusaders favoured round towers, a militarily superior innovation. You see evidence of Mameluke and Ottoman rebuilding work as you look along the western exterior of the castle where except at the base of the talus the wall has been shoddily reconstructed with fairly small stones. You enter from the north through an Ottoman gate and then over the moat where a Mameluke gate of black and white *ablaq* admits you into the castle proper. Immediately within is the Crusader keep, its lower courses of large well-laid stone blocks of bigger and better stonework. Beyond this almost all is ruinous. Down steps to the east are vaulted chambers, open to the sky, while straight ahead (south) are the foundations of a church with an octagonal crypt.

The View from the Castle Ramparts

Climbing up to the top of the eastern ramparts you can trace the course of the Abu Ali that has come down from the mountains, here set back very far from the coast. Upstream the river is called the Qadisha, whose source lies near the Cedars of Lebanon. The castle mount deflects the river northwestwards so that it debouches into the Mediterranean above Al-Mina. From the western ramparts you look down on medieval Tripoli, its older houses with red-tiled roofs and its tenements of three and four storeys hedged between the castle heights and the high modern buildings towards the sea. You see the Great Mosque with its open square court and rectangular minaret below you to the west, and adjoining it the green domes of the Al-Qartawiya Madrasa. Beyond it is Al-Tal Square (Place du Tell), the modern centre of town. Some distance southwest of the Great Mosque is the green-domed Taylan Mosque. Between the two is the Hamam al-Jadid, while sweeping your gaze round to the north of the castle you might be able to pick out the Khan al-Khayyatin close by the river.

The Fall of Crusader Tripoli

In 1289 Sultan Qalaun utterly destroyed the old Tripoli that had been the city of the Crusaders and indeed of all who had come before. For the most part, the earlier city had stood by the sea at Al-Mina, the Franks withdrawing within its walls at the sultan's approach, so that the castle played no part in what followed. Qalaun, at the head of an enormous army, began his siege of the city towards the end of March, and pounded its walls with catapults. For a month Tripoli was gallantly defended, but then the Venetian and Genoese merchants based there decided that defence was impossible and hastily loaded their ships and fled. Their departure spread panic among the population, and the following morning, 26 April, Qalaun ordered a general assault.

In the sultan's army that day was the 16-year-old Abu al-Feda, the future historian and emir of Hama (*see* p.147).

> *The Muslim troops penetrated the city by force. The population fell back to the port where some escaped on ships; of the rest, the men were all put to death and the women and children taken as slaves, and the Muslims amassed an immense booty.*
>
> *Just off the headland there was a small island with a church, and when the city was taken many Franks took refuge there with their families. But the Muslim troops swam across to the island, massacring the men and carrying off the women and children. I myself went out to the island on a boat after the carnage, but I was unable to stay, so strong was the stench of corpses.*

Abu al-Feda, *Annals,* written at Hama, early 14th century.

When the killing and pillage were finished, Qalaun had the city razed to the ground to prevent the Crusaders, with their command of the sea, ever recapturing it. In its place, a safe distance inland at Al-Medina and under the lee of Raymond's castle, he built his new city.

A Walk through Medieval Tripoli

The view of medieval Tripoli described from the western ramparts of the castle is followed from south to north in the following description. The monuments are both Ottoman and Mameluke, the latter often incorporating Crusader stones, and together comprise the greatest concentration of medieval architecture in Lebanon.

The **Taylan Mosque**, with its several green domes and adjacent cemetery, was built by the Mameluke governor of Tripoli in 1336 and incorporates the remains of a 12th-century Carmelite church. An outer court leads to the entrance on the north, and within is a high chamber, its slightly pointed arches supported by four stout columns of Aswan granite with marble Corinthian capitals. This was the nave and aisles of the church. To the rear, in what would have been the apse, is a towering portal, magnificently decorated in black and white *ablaq* inset with lovely geometric panels and bands of finely executed inscriptions. This and the prayer room beyond are 14th-century Mameluke work. Of later date is the wooden gallery for women's prayers, with nicely carved openwork and painted floral decoration.

Leaving the mosque and turning right (east), you jig through to a high street running north, which in about 75m brings you, on your left (west) to the Ottoman **Hamam al-Jadid**, built in about 1740 by Assad Pasha al-Azem, famous for his palaces in Damascus and Hama. The façade is plain and you may need to ask (it bears a plaque reading 'Monument Historique No.30'). You enter a handsome stone-built chamber with arches springing from its corners and supporting a high dome with a skylight, so that everything is softly illuminated within. The floor is paved with variously coloured stone set in geometric patterns, and at the centre is a fountain and pool, which as you walk round it looking into the water brings the reflected image of the dome closer one moment and makes it more distant the next. The baths are off through a doorway to the right, a series of smaller chambers, here the domes pierced with numerous round and star-shaped openings through which pass shifting beams of light creating constellational patterns within.

About 250m farther north but set back to the left (west) is the **Great Mosque**. There is a narrow way through to the east door of the mosque and to the Al-Qartawiya Madrasa standing by it (*see* below). Alternatively you can follow the streets round to the north door of the mosque, its principal entrance. Though the mosque is the largest and oldest in Tripoli, it is not very interesting except perhaps for its historical associations. It was begun by the Mameluke Sultan Qalaun, who incorporated the remains of the early 12th-century Crusader cathedral, St Mary of the Tower, and was completed by his son, Sultan Khalil, in 1294, five years after the city's fall. The arrangement is that of a congregational mosque, a large central court where the faithful can gather, surrounded on four sides by porticoes, that on the south doubly deep and containing the mihrab, indicating the direction of Mecca. The treatment is heavy and without architectural merit throughout, as though the Mamelukes, who were otherwise magnificent builders, could not be bothered to do more than schlep together a place to pray from the rubble at hand. That takes no account, however, of the few remaining Crusader features, among these the high rectangular minaret, originally the **bell tower**, in style reminiscent of Lombardy, from which the cathedral took its name, and the beautiful **north doorway** into the court.

Outside the east door of the Great Mosque is the **Al-Qartawiya Madrasa**, a theological school built about 30 years later, most probably on the site of the cathedral's baptistry, whose columns and Romanesque capitals have been incorporated as decorations into the high doorway.

From here you can return to the northwards-running street, or from the north door of the Great Mosque you can turn right into a street that brings you to the northwards-running street in about 150m. Just west of where the two streets meet is the large **Khan al-Sabun**, built early in the 17th century as an Ottoman barracks but afterwards used as a warehouse for soap, *sabun*. There is nothing remarkable about it except its bulk, which attracts your attention and reminds you that almost everywhere you look there is a khan, souk, madrasa, mosque or hamam of the Mameluke or Ottoman periods which if of minor interest in themselves do contribute to the atmosphere of this quarter and make it a pleasure to wander about.

Continuing northwards you come on your left to an opening leading into the **Khan al-Misriyin**, the Egyptian khan, built between 1309 and 1356 for the use of merchants from Egypt. Now it is given over to workshops and hardly seems a historical monument, but it is agreeable to stand here in the quiet amid trees and potted plants, rubber tyres, corrugated metal shutters and awful gilt Louis XV imitation furniture, where the past is treated with common familiarity.

Across the street is the **Khan al-Khayyatin**, built sometime before 1341, a long handsome souk spanned by arches supporting a partial roofing against the sun. Tailors have worked here since the 14th century, as they do now, though also T-shirt sellers and other tourist hookers have been making the running ever since the place was smartened up. Adjacent to the south is the **Hamam Izz al-Din**, built in about 1295. Vestiges of Crusader Tripoli survive at its doorway, which is decorated with two shells and bears the inscription 'Sanctus Iacobus'.

If you walk through the Khan al-Khayyatin you emerge facing the **Al-Burtasiya Madrasa** standing by the river. This is an elaborately decorated Mameluke building dating from sometime before 1381, with a stalactite portal and a richly inlaid mihrab within the domed prayer hall. From here you can walk south along the river, in 300m returning to the castle; or north to the old bridge where several mosques and khans of the Mameluke and Ottoman periods are clustered near its western approach.

Where to Stay and Eating Out

There are several beach resorts in the moderate category along the coast road south of Tripoli. The best of an indifferent lot is ★★★**Naoura**, 6km south, ✆/✉ (06) 431428; rooms with air conditioning, bath TV; pool, restaurant and health club.

In Al-Mina, on the corniche looking north over the sea, are the moderate ★★★**Qasr al-Sultan**, ✆ (06) 601627, with air conditioning, TV, fridge, shower and toilet, some rooms with balconies, restaurant; but a bit run down and rather overpriced. The inexpensive ★★**Hayek** nearby, ✆ (06) 601311, is a much better deal: clean rooms, sharing shower and toilet, some with sea-view balconies; a pleasant family-run place.

In Al-Medina accommodation and restaurants are on or just off Al-Tal Square (Place du Tell), west of the medieval quarter.

In the inexpensive category are the ★★**Palace Hotel**, Al-Tal Square, ✆ (06) 432257, a grand old building but in need of refurbishment, rooms with shower and toilet; and the ★**Tal Hotel**, on this square, ✆ (06) 628740, clean rooms with shower and toilet, some with TV. Cheap places to stay if you are content with dorm accommodation are **El Ehram** in the square (also double rooms available) and **El Koura** just off the square.

Tripoli is famous for its patisseries, the most renowned of these, established in 1881, being Abdul Rahman Hallab and Sons towards the east end of Riad Sohl Street.

To the Cedars of Lebanon

The cedar is the symbol of Lebanon and adorns the national flag which you see fluttering everywhere and pasted to walls, outnumbering even Hezbollah placards and advertisements for Karl Lagerfeld couture, and so you begin to think you ought to see what is left of those great cedar forests that once covered the mountain slopes. The largest grove is above Bcharré, reached by following the beautiful Qadisha Valley up from Tripoli.

There are several ways up, for example from Batroun, and also from just south of Tripoli, these joining to run along the south side of the Qadisha Valley. But from Tripoli the most direct route to the Cedars (56km) is via **Ehden**, reached in 36km, a mountain resort in a lovely setting north of the valley with pleasant walks and several open-air restaurants amid splashing streams. There are numerous villas here owned by wealthy Maronites; the building workers and fruit harvesters are often Syrians who come over the border and offer themselves as casual labour. Beyond Ehden the road draws closer to the ever deeper **Qadisha Valley**. A church bell rings, for the valley is the spiritual heart of Maronite country where even the Ottomans never held sway.

Ehden   ***Where to Stay***

Being a summer resort, prices are higher and rooms are more difficult to get, so it is best to book ahead. The following moderately priced places are open year-round, rooms with shower and toilet: ★★★**Belmont Hotel**, ✆ (06) 662441, a modern hotel; and ★★**La Mairie**, ✆ (06) 662822, a traditional-style building, pleasant and well-furnished.

The Maronites

The Maronites take their name from St Maro (or Maron), a hermit near Cyrrhus in Syria, who died in 433 and was buried near Hama on the Orontes where a monastery grew up around his tomb. There, 200 years later, so the story goes, the Byzantine Emperor Heraclius paused on his return from his campaign against the Persians and discovered what he hoped would be the solution to the long-running doctrinal dispute that was tearing the Christian world apart. This was the argument over the natures or persons of Christ. Cast in its religious formulation, as almost everything was then, the argument may now seem obscure and irrelevant, but defining the nature of Christ had implications for regarding the nature of man, an evolving argument that continues in the religious and secular spheres to this day.

On one view, Christ had two natures as he was at once both human and divine. This dyophysite (two natures) doctrine is still held by the Greek and Western Churches. The opposing view, favoured most strongly in the East, was that Christ's human nature had been absorbed in the divine. This was the monophysite (single nature) doctrine. At the Council of Chalcedon in 451 the former received the stamp of orthodoxy, while the latter was declared a heresy. As national and ethnic ambitions had identified themselves with the contending arguments, these took on a political quality as well, of the gravest importance for the unity of the Byzantine Empire. Instead of falling in with the decision reached at Chalcedon, the monophysites bitterly denied the Council's authority, creating a split between Rome and Constantinople on the one hand and much of the East on the other.

What Heraclius discovered at the Monastery of St Maro was that the monks were happy with the orthodox dyophysite doctrine but insisted that Christ had only one will, the divine. To the emperor monothelitism, as it was called, looked like a compromise solution on which the opposing parties could unite: two natures but one will.

It was not to be, for after some hesitation the dyophysite Church decided at the Council of Constantinople in 681 that monothelism was, like monophysitism, a heresy. Not that by then it mattered politically anymore, for the damage had been done, the Byzantine Empire had been weakened by discord, and the Arabs had overrun the Christian East. Nevertheless, on the basis of Heraclius' imperial sanction, the monothelites of Syria and Lebanon had established their religious identity, taking their name from the Monastery of St Maro and taking to the mountains to preserve their faith against Islam. As for St Maro himself, whose views on the nature and will of Christ are unknown, he had nothing to do with it, Gibbon observing that the name Maronite was 'insensibly transferred from a hermit to a monastery, and from a monastery to a nation'.

The valley of the Qadisha River (known at Tripoli as the Abu Ali, after a Sunni holy man), described in the 1830s by Lamartine, the French poet, historian and statesman, as a vast nave with the sky for a ceiling, is the heartland of that nation, its precipitous walls cut with hermits' caves, its ledges and pinnacles fixed with churches and chapels, and indeed Qadisha in Syriac, a version of Aramaic, means valley of the saints. Here also, where the road from Ehden comes close to the edge of the gorge on its way up to Bcharré, there is the Monastery of Qannubin down below, founded by the Emperor Theodosius I (reigned 379–395) and the summer residence of the Maronite Patriarch of Antioch and All the East (whose winter residence is in fact near Jounieh).

On the arrival of the Crusaders, the Maronites hesitated but then offered their cooperation, a fact registered in the surnames of some present-day Maronite families such as Franjieh, meaning Frank, and Solibi, meaning Crusader. Presidents of the Lebanese Republic have always been Maronite, and one of them, from Zgharta on the route between Tripoli and Ehden, bore the name Franjieh. After the collapse of the Crusader states, some Maronites departed along with the Franks to Cyprus, while those who remained never surrendered their formal communion with the Roman Catholic Church, which dates from 1182. The Maronites recognise the supremacy of the Pope and have adopted various Roman usages and symbols, but they allow their priests to marry and observe their own calendar of saints and fasts and retain their own Syriac liturgy.

Against the powers representing Sunni orthodoxy, the Maronites had as allies the Druze, a heterodox and some would say heretical offshoot of Islam who inhabited Mount Lebanon farther south. The history of Lebanon from the 16th to 19th centuries was an attempt by the Ottomans to divide and rule, which was successfully opposed by local emirs who managed to maintain the Maronite-Druze alliance and the independence that came with it. But ultimately this cooperation broke down, partly because the Maronites, the most flourishing of Lebanon's inhabitants, were extending southwards into Druze territory, and because they were encouraged by the French, allowing the Ottomans to play on Druze fears. The consequence was the Druze massacre of 10,000 Maronites in 1860, which in turn brought the intervention of French forces. Many Druze fled into Syria, to the Jebel al-Arab (see p.101), while much of northern Lebanon became an auto-nomous Christian enclave, effectively guaranteed by France, though remaining part of the Ottoman Empire.

An industrious and independent people, nurtured by their contacts with the West and instilled with an egalitarian ethos through their ownership of small mountain fields and orchards, Maronite Lebanon has long been a different place, travellers such as Maundrell offering testimony to the freedom and security of movement enjoyed by Europeans there and the kind welcome received.

Continuing beyond Ehden, there are fine views of the Qadisha Valley, the slopes below the stone village of **Bcharré** (13km from Ehden) falling precipitously into the river gorge. The Lebanese poet Khalil Gibran (1883–1931) was born here; his house is in the town's main square. He died an alcoholic in America, but promised 'should my voice fade in your ears, and my love vanish in your memory, then I will come again'—at any rate as a corpse he came back to Bcharré and is entombed alongside his bed in a cave beneath the **Gibran Museum** (*open daily 9–5 July–Sept, closed Mon in winter; adm*), filled with his paintings (he faked a testimonial from the sculptor Rodin calling him the 'William Blake of the 20th century') up the hill to the east of town.

Bcharré　　　　　　　　　　　　　　　　　　　**Where to Stay**

★★★**Chbat Hotel**, ✆ (06) 671270, 📠 (06) 671237, perched on terraces above the town, is a moderately priced resort hotel with a swimming pool and nightclub, two restaurants and a café. The rooms are air-conditioned and have TV. Inexpensive dorm beds are also available. The inexpensive ★★**Palace Hotel**, ✆ (06) 671460, has simple clean rooms with shower and toilet; restaurant. *See* Chbat Hotel (above) for inexpensive dorm beds.

The Cedars (Al-Arz)

Climbing the final 7km above Bcharré you reach the Cedars of Lebanon, not the only grove in the country nor even the largest, but at 1900m the highest, with the best-formed trees, some reputed to be 3000 years old. Alas, the truth is that the journey proves better than the arrival, for the grove is down to about 100 trees and you will see better individual specimens at Kew. On one of them is a plaque commemorating Lamartine's attempted visit in 1832, in the event frustrated by deep snow. The Maronites call this grove the Cedars of the Lord, and on 6 August each year their patriarch celebrates mass among the trees, though some older mountain people half cling to the more ancient belief that the trees themselves are deities.

The Syrian army has a camp up here and the UN a base guarding the road (usually blocked by snow from late October to late May) that continues over the top of the mountain ridge and down into the Bekaa valley to Baalbek.

Where to Stay

In winter there is skiing here; the ski station and several year-round hotels (*see* below) are a couple of kilometres below the cedar grove. Rates are highest in winter.

In the expensive/moderate range are: ★★**Cortina**, ✆ (06) 671533, rooms with shower and toilet, simple and overpriced; ★★**Alpine**, ✆ (06) 671057, at the ski station, cosy rooms with shower and toilet; restaurant; ★★★**St Bernard**, ✆ (06) 671517, rooms with shower and toilet, suites with bath, very comfortable with marvellous views; restaurant and bar. The inexpensive ★**Rancho Grande**, ✆ (06) 671501, has simple rooms with shower and toilet; restaurant.

The Castle of the Sea, Sidon, before the 1840 bombardment

Getting Around   330

From Beirut to Sidon   330

Sidon   333

Sidon to Tyre   336

Tyre (Sour)   337

The South

Given the present situation, this southern Lebanon chapter covers only the coast from Beirut down through Sidon (Saida) and Tyre (Sour). Even when the Israelis cease to occupy their 10 to 30km-deep zone across the south of the country and up along the Litani River into the southern Bekaa valley (which at the time of writing they have said they will do), things may be unsettled for some time. As long as you stick to the coast, however, and barring an Israeli bombing raid, travel is safe. There are both Lebanese and Syrian army check-points along the way (though there are no Syrian forces south of Sidon), and there is a United Nations base on the harbour at Tyre.

The landscape is far less attractive than along the northern coast, the mountains lower and more distant the farther south you go, and to this is added a pervasive torpor and marked lack of development. The coastal population is generally Sunni Muslim. Native Sunnis form the majority of the population in Sidon, augmented by numerous Palestinian refugees. In Tyre, however, the overwhelming majority is Shia Muslim. Both towns are also inhabited by Greek Catholics, few in Tyre, many in Sidon.

Normally, the principal places of interest in the south would include one of the greatest Crusader castles, Beaufort, 65km east of Tyre and 5km southwest of Marjayoun. Unfortunately, is out of bounds. Though it lies just outside the Israeli-occupied zone, it is held by Christian forces and used as a prison.

Apart from satisfying your curiosity at Joun, where Lady Hester Stanhope lived and is buried, that leaves Sidon and Tyre to visit, two of that great tetrarchy of Phoenician trading states that included Byblos in northern Lebanon and Arwad in Syria. Unlike at Byblos, however, traces of the Phoenician past are slight, and at Sidon it is the Crusader presence that you encounter, while at Tyre, its fortified sanctuary island razed and forever joined to the mainland by Alexander the Great during his determined siege, it is the Roman.

For a map of Lebanon, *see* p.302.

Getting Around

Without a car, the only practical way of getting around is by service taxi. (Buses run from Beirut to Sidon, but there are no buses to Tyre.) The distances are not long, about 50km from Beirut to Sidon and another 45km from Sidon to Tyre, so both can be visited as a single daytrip.

Where to Stay

There is accommodation at Sidon and at Tyre and between the two, though there is very little choice compared with northern Lebanon.

From Beirut to Sidon

Immediately south of the airport with the usual cut-out figures of Ayatollah Khomeini along the roadside and Hezbollah pennants and signs (there is also a cut-out figure of Rowan Atkinson as Mr Bean), you pass a large gipsy shanty town and enter the coastal plain filled at first with an enormous banana plantation. The impression is very different to that made along the coast north of Beirut. Here the area is hardly built upon at all. A house is a rarity. Soon cultivation gives way to a landscape broken by rocky outcrops, and stones lie on the land sloping down to the sea. At Damur, a Christian town 24km south of Beirut, a road climbs eastwards into the Druze region of the Chouf to Beit Eddine (*see* p.344).

But continuing along the coast, at 30km you reach **Nebi Yunes**, a mixed Christian and Muslim village of smashed-up houses that suffered, as did much of this stretch, very badly during the war. Though now recovering, it is a listless and squalid place. The Yunes after whom the village is named is Jonah, for here according to Muslim tradition he was disgorged by the whale. Ancient Porphyreon stood somewhere in the region of Nebi Yunes and the village of Jiyye to the north, its name in turn probably owed to the murex fishing that flourished along this coast, which together with vast olive groves on this last southerly escarpment of Mount Lebanon, raised the place to great prosperity as evidenced by its 6th-century AD mosaics, displayed at Emir Bechir's palace at Beit Eddine (*see* p.345).

A few kilometres before reaching Sidon (and 1km before the bridge crossing the Awali River) there is a turning off east for **Joun** (signposted 'Convent St Saviour'), a large village set among olive groves reached in 12km from the main Beirut–Sidon road. If you pass straight through Joun you come in 5km to the Greek Catholic Monastery of St Saviour (Deir el Mukhalles), founded in 1711 and only recently restored after being damaged by an earthquake in 1956 and then abandoned during the civil war. The Israeli occupation zone pushes up close by, this part of it administered by the South Lebanese Army (SLA), a Christian militia allied with the Israelis against Hezbollah, and so there are several army checkpoints as you approach the monastery, which possesses a number of beautiful icons and where the monks seem very happy to show you around. But if after passing through Joun you turn left at 2km and follow the road down to the bottom of the hill, then bear right and right again, you finally climb towards the ruins of a once imposing residence. Here from 1818 to her death in 1839 lived Lady Hester Stanhope, and in the shade of an olive grove 40m to the southwest is her tomb.

The Prophetess of Joun

A woman of intelligence and energy, Hester Lucy Stanhope had been the niece of Prime Minister William Pitt, his confidante, advisor and the distributor of patronage. Together during the early years of the Napoleonic wars they had held the destiny of Britain in their hands. But Pitt's death in office in 1806 cast her from the heart of political life. 'I can scarcely tell why it should be,' wrote A. W. Kinglake, who famously described his visit to Lady Hester in *Eothen*, 'but there is a longing for the East, very commonly felt by proud-hearted people, when goaded by sorrow.'

In addition to suffering Pitt's death, her fiancé, Sir John Moore, was killed at Corunna in Spain in 1809 at the moment of his victory over Napoleon's more numerous army, as was her brother Charles. A witness of those events was the young Michael Bruce, and this connection made him immediately sympathetic to Lady Hester when they met on Malta on her way East. They became lovers, and Bruce accompanied her to Palmyra where she was hailed by the Bedouin as queen (*see* p.270). Within a few years, however, she had tired of Bruce's affections, and while back in Europe he consoled himself in the arms of Lady Caroline Lamb, the cracked wife of Lord Melbourne and brief mistress of Lord Byron, and in the embraces of the widow of Marshal Ney, Napoleon's favourite general. Hester was rumoured to have had an Arab sheikh as a lover, possibly as a husband. Settling at Joun in 1818, she involved herself in Lebanese political affairs, opposing the ambitions of both the Emir Bechir, her neighbour at Beit Eddine (*see* p.344), and Ibrahim Pasha, whose father, Mohammed Ali, ruler of Egypt, said that the Englishwoman had given him more trouble than all the peoples of Palestine, Lebanon and Syria, whom in 1832 he had sent his son to conquer.

Yet when Kinglake came to Joun in 1836, he found the place stripped bare of its finery and derelict, his the only room secure against the rain. By her wealth, her magnificence, her imperious character and her dauntless bravery, Hester had long impressed herself on the Arabs about her. Now through a lifetime's prodigality she was all but destitute, but still she held sway, not least by her devotion to the occult. She was 60 when Kinglake met her, wearing a turban and dressed in trousers, and had the look of 'a good businesslike, practical, Prophetess, long used to the exercise of her sacred calling. . . She never, she said, looked upon a book, nor a newspaper, but trusted alone to the stars for her sublime knowledge; she usually passed the nights in communing with these heavenly teachers', and gave Kinglake to understand she was of heavenly rank.

While Kinglake found Hester merely eccentric, the locals were convinced she was mad, though in this contemporary account by Lieutenant Welsted (*Travels in Arabia*), it was her Englishness that proved the point.

> *A group of Bedouins were disputing, respecting the sanity of Lady Hester Stanhope; one party strenuously maintaining that it was impossible a lady so charitable, so munificent, could be otherwise than in full possession of her faculties; their opponents alleging that her assimilating herself to the Virgin Mary, her anticipated entry with our Saviour into Jerusalem, and other vagaries attributed to her, were proofs to the contrary. An old man with a white beard called for silence (a call from the aged amidst the Arabs seldom made in vain).*

'She is mad,' said he; and lowering his voice to a whisper, as if fearing lest such an outrage against established customs should spread beyond his circle, he added, 'for she puts sugar in her coffee.'

Three years after Kinglake's visit, in rags and alone but for her squalling cats, she died. The British consul came up from Beirut and though it was night decided the funeral must take place at once. By candlelight the vault in the garden was opened and her body laid to rest, her plain deal coffin draped with the Union Jack. Now, in place of the vault constructed in four layers of stone and crowned with a marble plaque inscribed 'Lady Hester Lucy Stanhope, born 12th March 1776, died 23rd June 1839', there is nothing more than a few shattered blocks and a gaping hole in the ground, for it was looted and completely destroyed during the civil war.

Returning to the main Beirut–Sidon road and now crossing the bridge over the Awali River, another turning east (signposted) leads in 1½km to the **temple of Eshmun** in an area known as Bustan el Sheikh, or the Garden of the Sheikh (*no fixed opening times; free*). Eshmun was identified with Adonis (*see* p.308) by the Phoenicians who first built this temple in the late 7th century BC, though much of what remains dates from the Persian period, 6th to 4th centuries BC, while subsidiary temples were built in Hellenistic times, and the Romans added a colonnaded street and processional stairway leading to the temple. The enduring sanctity of the site (the Byzantines built a church here) was owed to the familiar story of love and death and resurrection, for Eshmun, a mortal born in Beirut who took pleasure in hunting in the mountains, founded himself pursued for his beauty by the goddess Astarte. For reasons best known to Eshmun, he decided he would be better off dead, but Astarte was not so easily put off and brought the poor fellow back to life, conferring on him immortality and taming him to her own delights. The Greeks and Romans, uncharacteristically dispensing with the erotic element, in turn identified Eshmun with Aesculapius, the great healer and master of medical skills who was said to be able to revive even the dead, so that the site became a sort of sacred spa, the waters of the Awali River channelled through the complex to numerous ablution basins, the unabating stream of pilgrims drawn to the font of the Christian church long after the passion of Astarte had been forgotten. Foundations, mosaics and standing stones remain in something of a confusing jumble and picnic rubbish is strewn among the trees, but the place does retain a special atmosphere still.

Sidon

Sidon, 50km south from Beirut, is typical of Phoenician cities in being sited on a promontory with an island offshore. In this case the island is minute and is entirely covered by the Crusaders' Castle of the Sea. Island and promontory together formed the Phoenicians' maritime town while the upper town stood inland on a mountain spur. Between the two were gardens, as there are now, where oranges, lemons, bananas, apricots and almonds grow. As you drive in along the coast road, Sidon does not seem an immediately attractive place, but there is a salty atmosphere along its seafront where the castle, a khan and a Crusader church offer interest, and a maze of narrow alleyways behind to explore, amid these another castle.

History

Sidon is one of the oldest towns along the Syro-Lebanese coast and at first was more important than Tyre. By 1700 BC it had established trade depots on the Orontes and Euphrates and its merchant fleets roamed across the Mediterranean. But success invited foreign interest which the coastal cities, divided by commercial rivalry, could never oppose. From about 1450 BC Sidon fell within the sphere of influence of the pharaohs of New Kingdom Egypt, with which it enjoyed a flourishing trade. In Genesis, composed from 9th-century BC sources, Sidon is identified as the northern border of Canaan, while in the *Iliad*, composed in the 8th century BC but referring to the 13th-century BC Trojan war, Homer mentions 'the elaborately wrought robes, the work of Sidonian women', a reference to that much-prized purple dye extracted from the murex shell.

In the 9th century BC, Sidon fell under the heavy-handed domination of the Assyrians, and then in 539 BC passed to Persian control. An uprising against the Assyrians cost Sidon the lives of its leading figures, while its rebellion against the Persians was put down by the sacking of the city and the massacre of 40,000 inhabitants. Twelve years later in 332 BC, the memory of this holocaust still fresh in their minds, the Sidonians welcomed their liberation from Persian rule by Alexander the Great. A new king was appointed by the Macedonians, a man who until then had been simply a gardener. He proved a popular choice, and in return he entertained Alexander's generals to a lion hunt near by. When he died this hunting scene was carved on the king's sarcophagus, the so-called Alexander Sarcophagus now on display in Istanbul's Archaeological Museum.

Sidon subsequently alternated under the control of the Syrian-based Seleucids and the Egyptian-based Ptolemies, passing to the Romans in the 1st century BC. By the time St Paul visited Sidon on his way to Rome, the city was in decline, though still important enough to become the seat of a bishop under the Byzantines. In AD 667 it was captured by the Umayyads and ruled from Damascus, its name changed to Saida.

From 1111 to 1291 Sidon passed several times in and out of Crusader hands, incidents including its capture by Saladin in the same year he took Jerusalem, 1187, and St Louis' sojourn here in the middle of the following century, when he repaired its fortifications. Its links with the West were again revived, this time by the Emir Fakhr al-Din al-Maani II, in the early 17th century, whose power extended as far east as Palmyra where he built the hilltop fortress (see p.286), while here at Sidon he built the Khan of the Franks by way of encouraging trading relations with France. From that time, Sidon became the premier port of Damascus, but when the French were expelled in 1791 the town lost its importance to Beirut. Though today it is called 'the capital of the south' and has a larger population than Tyre, its prosperity and that of the region in general has suffered greatly from the recent war.

The Castle of the Sea

Open daily 9–8 in summer, 9–5 in winter; adm.

Already from some distance as you approach Sidon from the north you see the Castle of the Sea standing out on its islet from the town. The Château de la Mer of the Crusaders, in Arabic the Qalaat al-Bahr, the castle was built in 1228 immediately after Sidon's recapture by the Christians during the Third Crusade, its purpose to defend the North Harbour which was to serve as an outpost for their main stronghold at Acre down the coast in present-day Israel. In ancient times a temple, perhaps to Melkart, had stood here, and many columns can be seen embedded in the castle's stonework, while the castle itself remained fairly intact until it suffered bombardment by a combined British, Turkish and Austrian fleet bent on driving Ibrahim Pasha (see p.344) out of Lebanon and back to Egypt. The castle has recently been partly restored and the causeway to the island is modern, though apparently the castle had been linked by a bridge to the mainland in Crusader times.

The sole entrance to the castle is on the landward side (here south); above the **gate** you can see the carved figures of lions and men, one of the men appearing to hold a stave or lance over his shoulder. As you enter, notice the numerous **columns** of grey and red granite built into the castle's outer and inner walls, the red, and probably the grey also, quarried at Aswan in Upper Egypt and brought here by sea in ancient times. To the east and west are **towers**, the west tower restored by the Arabs, the east tower, originally the keep, largely destroyed, a small mosque set upon it. The castle essentially consisted of these two towers, linked by a wall.

Passing through the outer gate, you walk round to the right to an **inner gate** with pointed arches and vaulted, which is set in what remains of the **east tower**. Behind this (north) is a half-ruined round-arched vaulted **vestibule**, presumably built as a loggia opening onto the sea. Atop this tower where there is now a mosque there may have been a small church. At any rate you can see up here the remains of a finely cut corner pillar of clustered columns from which arches and vaults would have sprung. Also from this vantage point you should look down on the inner face of the landward walls; you can see how the ancient columns pass right through them, serving as strengthening beams for the stonework.

Going across to the **west tower**, a stairway climbs to its upper chamber, high and spacious, with pointed vaulting. From here there are stairs onto the roof with views southwest across the **Northern Harbour**. Round the headland, marked by a pointed minaret rising out of the Crusader church, now the Great Mosque, is the **Egyptian Harbour**. Such double harbours allowed the Phoenicians to sail from either depending on the winds.

Along the Waterfront of Sidon

Returning to the mainland from the Castle of the Sea and walking southwest past the mosque with the yellow minaret and the fruit and vegetable market, you come in 200m to the pictur-esque **Khan of the Franks** (Khan al-Franj), built for French merchants in 1610 by the Emir Fakhr al-Din II. Maundrell stayed here on his way to Jerusalem in 1697, noting that the French trade counter at Sidon was their largest in the Levant. Damaged during the war, it has been undergoing restoration and is sometimes used for exhibitions. Originally there were trees and a fountain in the central court, with shops set around the ground floor arcades as well as stabling on the far side (note the stone tethering rings projecting from the pillars). The arcading with pointed arches in black and white *ablaq* is continued round the upper floor where the traders had their accommodation. The circular shaft rising from the ground floor to upper level is a well with openings at each level through which water could be raised by buckets. From the terrace on the upper level there is a fine view across the Northern Harbour to the Castle of the Sea.

Following the curve of the waterfront southwestwards and then south for another 400m, you come to the **Great Mosque** (Masjid al-Kabir) sprouting a pointed minaret, but preserving the outer walls of the church of the Knights of St John Hospitaller. It is an imposing edifice, all the more so for being raised on a high terrace, a large, handsome basilica with engaged buttresses, powerfully built with the Crusaders' usual eye for defence in case of need. The church dates from the 13th century and was converted to a mosque by the Mamelukes. Behind it, to the east, Fakhr al-Din II began but never finished a palace, which now is entirely gone.

Another 250m south along the waterfront is a mound of debris called **Murex Hill**, 100m long and nearly 50m high, created by the ancient Sidonians who deposited here the refuse left over from the production of purple dye which was extracted by pounding the small spiny murex shell.

Striking inland (east) just before Murex Hill brings you in 200m to the **Castle of St Louis** (Qalaat al-Mezzeh), a ruinous fortress probably built by the Mameluke Sultan Baybars on the site of a 12th-century Crusader castle in which, it is said, St Louis stayed for some time. This was the acropolis of ancient Sidon and has been inhabited since about 1500 BC, while traces of important Graeco-Roman buildings have also been found here. From the Castle of St Louis you can walk almost due north along one of Sidon's main streets to the Castle on the Sea, or you can return to the waterfront at any point along its arc by meandering a bit off to the west and working your way through the maze of little streets.

★★★**Le Frigate Orasse**, ✆ (07) 723562, is on the coast 9km north of Sidon, the better and more expensive rooms with air conditioning and facing the sea, the less expensive ones with fan and facing the road, all with shower, toilet and balcony. Restaurant and swimming pool.

cheap

The **Orient** is the only hotel in Sidon itself. It is on the street running south from the sea castle and has basic dorm accommodation and double rooms with shared facilities.

Eating Out

The **Khan al-Debbagh**, at the landward end of the causeway to the Castle of the Sea, has been beautifully restored and is now an expensive restaurant and café with a very pleasant terrace to seaward.

Sidon to Tyre

At 3km south from Sidon there is a turning southeastwards running in another 3km to the Greek Catholic village of **Maghdouche** with a huge statue of the Virgin. In a grotto a few hundred metres southeast of the village there is an ancient and roughly sculpted figure of a woman. The local belief is that the Virgin came here to await the resurrected Jesus (he had been this way before: *see* Mark 7:24). Another kilometre or so south along the road to Tyre, again off to the east, is a Palestinian refugee camp.

All along the route between Sidon and Tyre the hills show gnarled outcrops of crystalline limestone. The plain is filled with orange and lemon groves, as well as bananas, while the ranks of transparent half-cylinders, miniature greenhouses in effect, produce vegetables throughout the seasons. Agriculture, like everything else in Lebanon, receives no state assistance, not only because the government is broke but because of its long-standing *laissez-faire* policy, making the energy and success of the country's hardpressed farmers all the more remarkable. Also along the roadside, attached to electricity poles, are those familiar Hezbollah signs, a red automatic weapon in a raised fist against a yellow background. These alternate with advertisements for razors: 'Personna, the great American shave'. And then coming towards Sarepta, there is another gipsy camp to the east, its inhabitants imitating the methods of intensive agriculture by living in huts made of frames covered with plastic sheets.

At 16km south of Sidon you pass by the village of **Sarafand** on a hill to the east. This occupies part of the much larger site of Old Testament Zarephath where Elijah performed miracles, in the New Testament called by its Greek name **Sarepta**, both perhaps deriving from the Hebrew *saraph*, to melt, for it owed some of its ancient fame to the making of glass, and indeed glassworks have been found here along with monuments to Tanit, a deity worshipped also in Carthage. It continued to flourish into Crusading times, when it possessed a bishop and was surrounded by walls. Now it lies covered by this village and the surrounding cultivation, while the coastline has shifted westwards, Sarepta's once important harbour now silted up and offering anchorage to groves of bananas.

Farther southwards you look about for mountains and see none, only low hills running down to the coast, their slopes cultivated or patched with trees, elsewhere bare and broken by outcrops of pale rock. At 37km south of Sidon and 8km north of Tyre you cross the Nahr al-Litani, the Litani River, which has risen in the Bekaa Valley just west of Baalbek.

Where to Stay and Eating Out

A few kilometres south of Sarepta and 25km north of Tyre is the village of Khayzaran with an inexpensive and simple but good and friendly restaurant just back from the road to the west with a terrace overlooking the sea. (When they try to delight you with loud recorded music, tell them to turn it off.) About 100m before coming to the restaurant there is a turning towards the sea, indeed leading to a concrete causeway running across the water to the moderate offshore ★★★★**Mounes Hotel**, ✆ (07) 724932, with swimming pool, restaurant, bar and outdoor terrace. It is an utterly sterile place. In a peaceful location overlooking the Litani River, 8km north of Tyre, is the moderately priced ★★★★**Abou Deeb**, ✆ (07) 740808, with comfortable rooms with air conditioning, bath, TV, balcony; there is a restaurant and swimming pool. An agreeable place to stay.

Tyre (Sour)

> *This city, standing in the sea upon a peninsula, promises at a distance something very magnificent. But when you come to it, you find no similitude of that glory for which it was so renowned in ancient times. . . On the north side it has an old Turkish ungarrisoned castle; besides which you see nothing here but a mere Babel of broken walls, pillars, vaults, etc., there being not so much as one entire house left. Its present inhabitants are only a few poor wretches, harbouring themselves in the vaults and subsisting chiefly upon fishing.*

> Henry Maundrell, *A Journey from Aleppo to Jerusalem*
> *at Easter, AD 1697.*

Tyre has been a dump ever since the Crusaders left it, and it should not be surprising to find modern Tyre, 45km south of Sidon, a stagnant and shattered place. As long as the border with Israel is closed, it is at the end of the line rather than being on the way to somewhere. Also, it was badly smashed up during the war, as you can especially see around the harbour where the United Nations has a post.

Considerable excavation and restoration work has been undertaken, however, giving you some idea of Roman if not Phoenician Tyre. And perhaps most fascinating, at any rate for those who like to read history in topography, is to see the evidence of that huge causeway constructed by Alexander in 332 BC, by which he advanced upon the fortified and seemingly impregnable island, that causeway the neck of land upon which most of Tyre is built today.

History

Tyre is a very ancient place and probably goes back to the early centuries of the 3rd millennium BC. From about 1500 BC it came into the sphere of influence of New Kingdom Egypt with which it carried on a lucrative trade, though Sidon at this time was more important.

After the decline of Egyptian power, Tyre's golden age began and was marked by the accession, late in the 11th century BC, of King Hiram I, a contemporary of Kings David and Solomon. He joined together the two islands off the coast and linked these with the mainland, incidentally creating good harbours to north and south. With Solomon he signed a trade treaty, sending cedars obtained from Byblos and skilled workmen to Jerusalem to help build the temple and in return was granted 20 towns in Galilee. Together they sent a fleet to Arabia and East Africa, bringing back gold, myrrh, ivory and baboons, the very stuff with which Solomon wowed the Queen of Sheba. Hiram's formidable merchant marine, its ships built of that same exported wood, its sails of that same linen made from flax by which Tyre established a renowned clothing industry, also ventured clear across the Mediterranean, establishing commercial colonies in Sicily and North Africa.

For some time after Hiram's death, these successes continued, with Tyrian sea captains sailing through the Straits of Gibraltar (the Pillars of Hercules, as they were anciently known, Hercules having started life as the Tyrian god Melkart), turning south down the coast of West Africa for gold and north to Britain for Cornish tin. For a while, Tyre became the commercial centre of the entire world. But in the 9th century BC, in common with the rest of Syria and Lebanon, Tyre fell under Assyrian domination and suffered also from revolutions and conspiracies. Most famous were the events of 814 BC when Dido, sister of the king, failed in an aristocratic plot against his authority and that of the priesthood. Seizing the city's treasure, as well as a fleet that lay at harbour, she set sail for North Africa where she founded the city of Carthage near present-day Tunis. Ultimately outstripping Tyre in power, Carthage in the person of Hannibal in the 3rd century BC would challenge Rome for mastery of the Mediterranean.

The decline of Assyrian power did not relieve the pressure on Phoenicia from the East. Tyre still knew greatness, and it was Phoenician and among them probably Tyrian sailors whom the Pharaoh Necho commissioned in the late 7th century BC to explore the coasts of Africa. Their fleet sailed south through the Red Sea and returned to Egypt three years later via the Pillars of Hercules, the first circumnavigation of the continent, more than 2000 years before Vasco da Gama found his way round the Cape. But in 586 BC the Babylonian Nebuchadnezzar began his 14-year siege of the city, and though he failed to capture it, Tyre's commercial eminence was broken and once again the primacy passed to Sidon. During this siege, the Tyrians destroyed their causeway, abandoning their mainland city and withdrawing onto their fortified island, its walls 50m high. Here too they yet again flourished and, while vassals of the Persians from the 6th century BC, contributed fleets to their masters' designs against Greece.

This was the danger Tyre presented to Alexander the Great when he approached the city in 332 BC. He could not dare to march eastwards against Persia as long as Phoenician ships under Persian control threatened his lines of communication with Greece and Macedonia. But Tyre refused to submit, having every confidence that as it had withstood Nebuchadnezzar, so it could withstand Alexander, while he had no intention of surrendering his ambition for an Asian empire on account of a rock. (Sour, incidentally, Tyre's modern and ancient name, derives from the Arabic for rampart and the Hebrew for rock.) Using the debris from the mainland town abandoned two centuries before, he spent seven months constructing a causeway towards the island. When finally he stormed it, he destroyed half of it and slaughtered or enslaved the whole of its population.

Even after that, Tyre managed to rise from its ruins, prospering under the Greeks and Romans and becoming an archbishopric in Byzantine times. Recently the earliest recorded church, described by Eusebius in about 313, has been unearthed not far from the Roman hippodrome. In AD 636 Tyre fell to the Arabs. In 1124 it was taken by the Crusaders and became part of the Kingdom of Jerusalem. A great cathedral was built where in 1173 William of Tyre, author of the famous chronicle of the kingdom, also of a now lost history of Mohammed's successors, was elected archbishop. In 1187, the year of his victory at Hattin and his conquest of Jerusalem, Saladin was repulsed at the walls of Tyre. But in 1291, after they had lost Acre, the Crusaders were forced to abandon the place. The Muslims destroyed it, using its stones as a quarry, leaving it as Maundrell described it 400 years later.

Stinking Rich

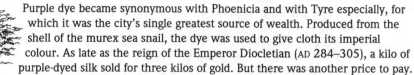

Purple dye became synonymous with Phoenicia and with Tyre especially, for which it was the city's single greatest source of wealth. Produced from the shell of the murex sea snail, the dye was used to give cloth its imperial colour. As late as the reign of the Emperor Diocletian (AD 284–305), a kilo of purple-dyed silk sold for three kilos of gold. But there was another price to pay. One hundred shells were needed to produce one gram of purple dye, and the shores of Tyre, Sidon and other cities were heaped with their stinking debris. Strabo, writing at the beginning of the 1st century AD, described Tyre as the most evil-smelling town he knew. Today, look out for the shop along Tyre's main street called Murex Lingerie.

Exploring Tyre

Driving into Tyre from the north, you sweep along a broad open bay towards the headland. You are sweeping in fact along the neck of land that has silted up around Alexander's causeway, while the headland was the offshore island (originally two islands joined together by King Hiram) where the Tyrians made their last stand. Here you come to a northwards-facing harbour, the ancient **Sidonian Harbour**, as it exactly faces Sidon. Now by heading south across the headland (its diameter is no more than a kilometre), you come to the **excavation site** overlooking the ancient **Egyptian Harbour**.

The 'Island' Site

Open daily 8–7 in summer, 8–4.30 in winter; adm.

The site reveals Roman remains and much restoration work has been done, so that you now see a **Corinthian colonnade** running westwards through it towards the sea. This colonnade was once part of a continuous avenue of columns that you can pick up again towards the east where it passes by a hippodrome, through an arch and into the ancient cemetery. The columns are of variegated marble and they line a broad ancient street still paved in places with marble or geometric mosaics. At the point where this main colonnade intersects with a **north–south colonnade** of monolithic grey granite, there are **baths** overlooking the Egyptian Harbour to the south, while to the north is an unusual rectangular **arena** which, it is thought, could be filled with water from nearby cisterns (the conduits are visible) for nautical games. Farther north and across the road skirting the site are several standing columns marking the remains of a Roman **temple** built over the Phoenician temple of Melkart. Somehow the best thing to do is to turn your back on it all and stare out to sea.

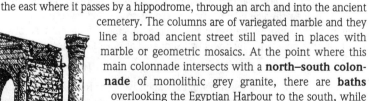

Along the Causeway to the Hippodrome and Necropolis

As you walk straight east back through the town, you are following the line of **Alexander's causeway**. In about a kilometre, having crossed over to the mainland, you come to the second site, the columned avenue resuming and passing through a single **arch** with engaged Corinthian columns and surmounted by a triangular pediment. Off to the south is a huge 2nd-century AD **hippodrome**, on its east side a great section of its grandstand intact (which would be more intact had not many of its stones been taken away in the 18th century to build the Arab fortress at Acre), with variegated marble columns having Corinthian capitals running along the top. Beneath the stand were ticket booths, shops and the like. The horse races took place around the central spina, where much of its patternless mosaic paving is still in place along with an Egyptian obelisk of pink Aswan granite, bearing no discernible inscriptions.

Returning to the arch and passing eastwards through it (the diagonally laid stone paving here is Byzantine), you enter the **necropolis**, strewn with sarcophagi. The earliest sarcophagi are 2nd-century BC, but most belong to the Roman period, especially to the 2nd-century AD when the cemetery, so to speak, flourished, while there are also some Byzantine sarcophagi. Often the sarcophagi were recycled from one century to another, a Roman inhabiting a sarcophagus made for a Phoenician, and in turn turfed out to make way for a Byzantine Christian, with a few adjustments to the external decorations along the way. Notice on the sarcophagi, and also on the burial chapels, the motifs of hearts, garlands and cupids: it was the Graeco-Roman world that invented schlock. The occasional bulls' heads, Medusas and crosses come as a relief, as does the beautifully sung call to prayer from a nearby minaret. Running through this graveyard is the occasionally exposed pipe of the underground conduit that brought water from cisterns on the mainland to the island, allowing it to withstand siege. The system was built originally by Hiram.

Not far from the necropolis and hippodrome, but tucked away in a backstreet among concrete apartment blocks, archaeologists uncovered late in 1995 the **earliest recorded church**, the basilical cathedral built by Paulinus, bishop of Tyre, soon after the Emperor Constantine's Edict of Toleration in 313. In his *History of the Church*, Eusebius, an intimate friend of the emperor, describes 'its dazzling beauty, the incredible vastness, the brilliant appearance of the workmanship, the towering walls that reach for the sky, and the costly Cedars of Lebanon that form the ceiling'. Foundations, an altar, gold crowns, plates and cups engraved with crosses are being unearthed amid an atmosphere of some secrecy until the archaeologists have completed their work. The site is in any case difficult to find, but possibly someone will lead you to it, though eventually it will be trumpeted as one of the most important in Christendom.

Where to Stay and Eating Out

There are two hotels in Tyre, the expensive ★★★★**Rest House**, ✆ (07) 740677, rooms with air conditioning, shower, toilet, TV, fridge; private beach offering water sports, swimming pool, health club, restaurant and bar; and the moderate ★★★**Elissar Beach Club**, ✆ (07) 741267, some rooms with air conditioning, shower and toilet; restaurant.

It is agreable to sit at the cafés and restaurants round the old fishing harbour, though owing perhaps to the presence of the UN soldiers prices are pretty high. The best is the expensive **Petit Phoenician**, once owned by Pepe who still owns the Byblos Fishing Club at Byblos, the speciality seafood though less costly if you stick to the Lebanese mezes. Good and less expensive grills are served at the **Al Mina** and the **Tanit**, also on the harbour, the latter more in the style of a bar and particularly frequented by the UN.

Palace at Anjar

Getting Around	**342**
Into the Chouf	**342**
Beit Eddine	**344**
Into the Bekaa Valley	**347**
Baalbek	**348**
Visiting the Temples	**351**
Anjar (Haouch Mousa)	**356**

The Chouf Mountains and Bekaa Valley

The great Roman temples at Baalbek and the remains of the strange Umayyad town of Anjar are in the Bekaa Valley, an extensive agricultural plain, the country's largest, at an elevation of 900–1100m lying between the parallel ranges of the Lebanon and Anti-Lebanon, its population a mix of Christian and Muslim. To whet your appetite, Baalbek is overlooked by a Hezbollah fortress and is thought to have been one of the places where Western hostages spent some of the best years of their lives chained to radiators. The quickest way into the Bekaa is along the Beirut–Damascus highway, which like Baalbek itself has been made secure by a strong Syrian army presence.

The Syrians have also put an end to the Bekaa as a major producer of hashish, Red Leb as it was known in Europe and North America to where it was exported in huge quantities. Indeed in the 1960s and '70s hashish exports and prostitution were Lebanon's two greatest sources of income.

A roundabout approach (or a separate excursion) is via the Chouf, the beautiful highland region inhabited by Maronites and Druze, the Druze more numerous the farther south you go. Their traditional headquarters was to the southeast near Hasbaiya at the western foot of Mount Hermon, now under Israeli occupation. In the northern Chouf is Beit Eddine, with its palace of Emir Bechir; it is reached from Damur, 24km down the coast from Beirut. From Beit Eddine you can then join the Beirut–Damascus highway just west of the high pass that drops you into the Bekaa.

For a map of Lebanon, *see* p.302.

Getting Around and Where to Stay

As usual, unless you have hired a car, you will have to rely on service taxis, though travelling this way it would be almost impossible to visit Beit Eddine, Anjar and Baalbek in a single day's excursion from Beirut. Distances in the mountains are misleading: from Beirut to Beit Eddine, 49km; from Beirut to Baalbek, 85km; but each journey can take 2hrs in each direction. Instead you would have to make separate journeys to Beit Eddine and into the Bekaa or stay overnight somewhere. There is accommodation in the Bekaa at Chtaura and at Zahle (*see* p.348), which is also a major staging post for taxis, and at Baalbek (*see* p.356), while in the Chouf mountains to the southwest there is accommodation at Beit Eddine (*see* p.346), a convenient (and luxurious) place to lodge yourself between visits to south Lebanon and the Bekaa.

From Damascus the distance to Baalbek via Anjar is 93km.

Into the Chouf

The road soon ascends the sides of Lebanon, and winds along the face of precipitous hills, where the crumbling soil often gives a scanty footing to the horse's hoof, then down into deep valleys and across mountain streams, and away through a wilderness of mingled rock and wood, which at every step grows finer and more striking. At one moment the hills towered high above our heads, with dark grey masses of stone starting from their sides, and shooting up into strange and ragged forms: at another the landscape softened, and we rode through dense woods of fir or thickets of olive trees. But the further that you penetrate into the bosom of the mountains, the more striking are the signs of human industry and cultivation. Man has triumphed where Nature interposes her greatest obstacles, and sometimes where she seems almost to deny access. The scanty soil of the valleys has with infinite care and labour been conveyed in baskets up and along the hillsides, as in the Tyrol and the Maritime Alps, and has been built up into terraces, which rise like the graduated steps of some large and natural amphitheatre. Thus, the parsimony of Nature within these rugged fastnesses is more than compensated by the security which their precipitous sides and defensible defiles have for generations past afforded against the misgovernment and oppression of Turkish rule. . . The mulberry, which nurses the silk trade of the entire district, mingles with the long alleys of grey olive trees, and the vines and melons succeed to the slender patches of corn which manual labour has raised on the occasional strips of level ground; whilst between the intervals of this painful cultivation the mountain streams, clearer than crystal, break from the living rock, and are conducted in numberless channels over and round each declivity, to eke out, by artificial irrigation, the resources of a stony soil.

The Earl of Carnarvon, *Recollections of the Druses of the Lebanon*, 1860.

The fourth Earl of Carnarvon was the father of that Lord Carnarvon who financed Howard Carter's discovery of the tomb of Tutankhamun in 1922. A brilliant classical scholar who served as colonial secretary in the governments of Lord Derby and Disraeli, the fourth earl had just graduated from Oxford when, in 1853, he made his visit to Lebanon. The date of publication of his book—autumn 1860—is significant, for the Druze had earlier that year massacred 10,000 Maronites, which also excited the killing of thousands of Christians in Damascus, and Carnarvon thought it an appropriate moment to dilate on the Druze, their country and 'their singular faith'. (For more on the Druze and also their relations with the Maronites, *see* pp.109 and 343.) Already in 1853 Carnarvon was travelling through these mountains against a background of inter-communal fighting that had first broken out at Deir al-Qamar.

From Damur on the coast you climb in 15km to **Deir al-Qamar**, the monastery of the moon, scene of 'the first affrays between Maronite and Druse, which led to the unfortunate civil war of 1842; and it was in the streets of the town that the son of the Druse chief of the Abou Nekad house was then killed, and by his death provoked so sanguinary a retaliation, that all reconciliation became impossible' (Carnarvon).

At the decision of Fakhr al-Din al-Maani II, who in the course of 50 years, from 1585 to 1635, welded the feudal factions of Lebanon into a united nation, this small and pretty place clinging to the steep slopes of the valley became the capital of the country, though with his eye on developing trading relations with the West while repelling Ottoman attentions, he also established headquarters at the ports of Sidon and Beirut. Fakhr al-Din's earlier capital had been at Baaqline, a Druze village just south of Beit Eddine, an indication of his origins. But much of his success lay in being all things to all people, so that his Druze, Muslim and Christian subjects hardly knew to which confession he belonged, while he himself claimed French descent. Around the square at Deir al-Qamar are several buildings of his dynasty and that of its successors, the Chehab family, including the 17th-century **Fakhr al-Din Mosque** and the 18th-century **palace of the Chehabs**. It was one of this family, Emir Bechir al-Chehabi II (1767–1850), who in the early 19th century transferred the seat of government to Beit Eddine, 5km farther up the valley, and built his magnificent palace there.

Emir Bechir

By balancing the interests of both Maronites and Druze, the Emir Bechir, who himself was Druze by birth but a secret convert to the Maronite faith, succeeded in giving stability and prosperity to Lebanon and, along with Fakhr al-Din al-Maani II, counts as one of its national heroes.

But Ottoman power in the region was weakening. During the 1820s and 1830s, Ibrahim Pasha, on behalf of his father, Mohammed Ali, the Egyptian ruler, conducted a series of brilliant campaigns against the Ottomans, conquering Arabia, Palestine and Syria, even beating the sultan's army at Konya in southern Anatolia, so that by 1839 it seemed that Mohammed Ali might himself be installed as sultan at Constantinople. Ibrahim remarked of the Ottomans that they 'had taken civilisation by the wrong side; it is not by giving epaulettes and tight trousers to a nation that you begin the task of regeneration; instead of beginning with their dress, they should endeavour to enlighten the minds of their people'.

French policy, however, was to seek advantage in Lebanon by encouraging the Maronites against the Druze, while the British became thoroughly alarmed at what they saw as the destabilising ambitions of the French on the one hand and the Egyptians, with whom the Emir Bechir was in alliance, on the other. In the background too was the fear of Russia, against whom the Turks had long served as a buffer. In response, the British chose to prop up the Ottoman Empire, the 'Sick Man of Europe', threatening Egypt into retreat and capturing Bechir, whom in 1840 they handed over to the Turks to spend the remaining 10 years of his life in exile on the Bosphorus.

For Lebanon the consequences were immediate, for with Bechir gone the Maronites and Druze were at each other's throats in 1842 and again in 1860. More broadly, stability in the Middle East was preserved well into the 20th century, though increasingly it was maintained only by European intervention.

Beit Eddine

A couple of kilometres before reaching Beit Eddine you pass on your right **Mousa's castle** (*open daily 7–9 in summer, 7–6 in winter; adm*), looking like something transplanted from Disneyland. The story goes, no doubt put about by Mousa himself, who is still kicking, that he was something of a daydreamer at school, given endlessly to drawing castles, his teacher teasing him by asking if he lived in one. 'No, but I will one day.' And so starting in 1947, Mousa began cutting and laying blocks of stone, each one different, until he had made his dream come true. Between here and the village you also pass on the right a long stone building with a red-tiled pent roof, an old **silk mill**, one of many that helped account for the region's prosperity in the past. A few shops mark the centre of the village and occasionally you see Druze women sweeping by in flowing white headscarves and black dresses down to the ground.

Sprawling immediately below and looking back towards the Mediterranean along the wonderfully terraced valley of vines and fruit trees is Bechir's fantastical oriental **palace** of beautifully cut and inlaid stone amid Italian gardens, a pleasure in itself and now as well a museum of provincial Byzantine mosaics.

Bechir's Palace

Open daily 9–5; adm.

The palace is in three parts. First you enter through a vaulted passage into the great courtyard of the **Dar al-Baranieh**, the exterior lodgings. All were welcome here, the courtyard serving as a place of public ceremonial and festivities, while any traveller, without any questions being asked, was welcome to stay for three days in the guest wing with its double flight of stairs along the long (northeast) side of the court. These rooms now contain exhibits of daily life at the time.

The **Dar al-Wousta** or middle lodgings, also with a double stairway, faces the courtyard on the northwest. The upper level was the administrative heart of the palace, while below were the stables, now the museum displaying—at the order of minister Walid Jumblatt, the sign tells you—the Byzantine mosaics excavated near the coast at Nebi Yunes (*see* p.331). Outside the stables and overlooking the valley is a garden where more mosaics are displayed, set into the ground.

Walid Jumblatt is the present-day Druze leader, and it perhaps gives him some satisfaction to order exhibitions in the palace of his family's great adversary.

> *For many years the supremacy of the Emir Beschir was divided and balanced by the power which was wielded by the chief of the great Druse family of Jumblatt from his rival castle of Moktara. Of Koordish lineage, the Jumblatts*

migrated from the plains of Aleppo into the Lebanon, where, step by step they improved each advantage, and steadily built up an influence that was ultimately converted by the late Sheik into an authority which emulated and imperilled the ascendancy of the Emir. Friends and allies in early life, they became under the influence of ambition and political rivalry estranged from their former intimacy, till opposing interests grew into direct antagonism and it became evident that the security of the one demanded the sacrifice of the other. The contest, though chequered, was not of long duration: the Emir Beschir triumphed, and his rival was overthrown, betrayed and strangled in the dungeons of Acre, whilst his castle at Moktara was plundered and burned to the ground. But with the next revolution of the wheel of Fortune, which had degraded and removed the Emir Beschir, Said Bey, the son of the late chief—with whose name recent events have made us familiar—succeeded to the wasted patrimony and the ruined halls of his family.

The Earl of Carnarvon, *Recollections of the Druses of the Lebanon,* 1860.

Leaving the administrative quarters, you cross the central courtyard with its fountain and enter through a magnificently decorated portal the **Dar al-Harem**, the private apartments of the emir and his family. The Irish novelist and traveller Eliot Warburton was an early guest of the emir's and was privileged to enjoy the baths at the northeast corner of the harem, after which he reclined on silken cushions by an arched window, through which cool breezes and the perfume of orange blossom reached him from the gardens.

The bubbling of fountains, the singing of birds, the whispering of trees, were the only sounds that reached the ear. The slaves glided about silently and somnambulistically; or stood with folded arms watching for a sign. If the languid eye was lifted to the window, it found a prospect of unequalled splendour over the mountains to the sea; and nearer were rich gardens, and basins full of goldfishes, swimming about with such luxurious motion that it rested the eyesight to follow them. There were amber-mouthed pipes of delicious Latakia, and fragrant coffee, and sherbet cooled in the fountain, and black slaves to wipe our hands with gold-embroidered napkins.

Eliot Warburton, *The Crescent and the Cross,* 1844.

In 1948 Bechir's ashes were returned from Turkey to his palace at Beit Eddine where they joined the remains of his first wife, Sitt Chams, whom he had buried in 1818 in the domed **sepulchre** in the gardens north of the harem. She had given Bechir three sons, and for each of them the emir had built a palace, that for his son the Emir Amin now a hotel (the **Mir Amin Palace** on the heights above Beit Eddine), worth a look at and, if you want to treat yourself to something of the sweetness enjoyed by Warburton, worth staying at.

Where to Stay

There is only one hotel at Beit Eddine.

very expensive

★★★★★**Mir Amin Palace**, PO Box 113-5881, ✆/✉ (05) 501315. This palace of Emir Bechir's son Amin stands on a hillside high above the valley. It has three restaurants, a swimming pool, tennis court and 24 fully-equipped voluminous rooms. The palace was gutted during the war and none of the original furnishings remain, and the service is hapless. Nevertheless, its spaciousness, calm and setting make it a wonderful place to indulge your fantasies. There are courtyards with pools and fountains, and terraces to sit and enjoy the morning view down the valley and the stillness and stars at night.

moderate

In **Samqaniyeh**, 2km south of Beit Eddine, there are two hotels: ★★★**SJS Motel**, ✆ (05) 501567, on the main road so somewhat noisy, but clean and comfortable rooms with TV, shower and toilet; and ★★★**Rif**, ✆ (05) 501281, simple but comfortable rooms with TV, fridge and bath.

Into the Bekaa Valley

The Beirut–Damascus highway climbs amid barren peaks and litter to the 1540m pass where there is a Syrian checkpoint. Off to the south a small grove of cedars grows on the shoulder of the Jebel Barouk. Then you see the Bekaa below you, Coele Syria, the Romans called it, hollow Syria, a vast upland suspended between the Lebanon and Anti-Lebanon ranges that wear their winter snows until early summer. This is the most extensive agricultural area in the country, a pattern of wheatfields and vineyards, walnut and apricot, mulberry and silver poplar rooted in the rust-red soil, though it was still more intensively cultivated in classical times. For a moment you feel suspended yourself, as between two worlds, and are overtaken by a sense of isolation.

You descend to **Chtaura**, 44km from Beirut, a substantial town on the western edge of the valley and a popular way station for resting, shopping and changing money between Lebanon, Syria and Jordan. There are supermarkets, restaurants and hotels, and also a taxi depot (the yellow taxis run to and from Syria).

At Chtaura the road forks, straight ahead for Anjar (*see* p.356) and Damascus, left (north) for Baalbek. Taking the Baalbek road you pass through Saidnayel; around here are the vineyards of the Jesuit Fathers that produce Ksara wine. Elsewhere in the valley are the Kefraya and the prize-winning Château Musar vineyards. The grapes for wine are allowed to grow along the ground, while those for eating are raised on trellises. About 8km from Chtaura you see **Zahle** on the slopes of Mount Lebanon to the west, a Christian town, mostly Roman Catholic though Maronite too, with a statue of the Virgin set on a high concrete tower: in one hand she holds the infant Christ, in the other a bunch of grapes. A bit farther on is the Catholic village of **Karak Nouh**, possessing, say the inhabitants, the tomb of Noah (Nouh), in fact a fragment of an ancient aqueduct.

After Karak Nouh the road bends towards Rayak, crossing the upper reaches of the Litani River whose source is just west of Baalbek. In fact Baalbek, at 1170m, is the highest point within the Bekaa and marks a watershed, the Litani flowing southwards to the sea near Tyre, the Orontes, which rises just beyond Baalbek, flowing north through Homs and Hama and only reaching the Mediterranean after curling round through Antioch. You appreciate what an avenue the Bekaa must have been in ancient times, as when Ramses II came this way to Kadesh (*see* p.134), and now you notice the occasional *tell* breaking the flatness of the plain, each *tell* the site of some long-ago settlement whose inhabitants, perhaps, witnessed the march of pharaonic armies. Apart from *tells*, almost the only other perpendicular sights in midplain are the larger than life cut-out figures of Ayatollah Khomeini.

★★★★★**Chtaura Park**, ✆ (08) 540011, ✉ (08) 825122, Chtaura. Coming from Beirut, this very expensive hotel is set back from the road on the left; large, modern, luxurious and dull. It has become something of a high-level meeting place between Syrian and Lebanese officials. ★★**Khater**, ✆/✉ (08) 540659, is a simple, small inexpensive place in Chtaura, on the right just before the fork for Zahle and Baalbek. Clean rooms with shower and toilet.

Zahle is a busy summer resort with several hotels, though in season advance booking is essential. Both the ★★★**Casino Arabi**, ✆/✉ (08) 821214, and the ★★★**Monte Alberto**, ✆ (08) 800342, ✉ (08) 801451, offer comfortable, moderately priced, well-equipped rooms with good views. At the centre of town on Brazil Street are four inexpensive hotels housed in Ottoman buildings, all atmospheric places to stay, rooms with shower and toilet, and clean. The first two are the best: ★**Traboulsi**, ✆ (08) 820534; ★**Aki**, ✆ (08) 820701; ★**America**, ✆ (08) 820536; ★**New Versailles**, ✆ (08) 820955.

Baalbek

> *A row of Corinthian pillars . . . stand alone on an elevated site, and their rich capitals and architrave are still entire. Six only now remain, and their appearance is peculiarly elegant. On them the setting sun lingers the last of all the ruin; and their slender and dark red shafts, beheld at some distance in the purple light, as they stand high and aloof, have a solemn and shadowy appearance—as if they stood on the tomb of former greatness.*
>
> John Carne on the Temple of Jupiter, *Letters from the East,* 1826.

Approaching Baalbek across the plain, the sky can seem to lie very close about you, a sensation expressed in Baalbek's very name, from the Semitic sky god Baal who was lord of Bek, the land. To the Greeks and Romans who blended the old worship with their own it was Heliopolis, City of the Sun. Here during the first three centuries AD the Romans built magnificently, vaunting gods and empire and raising those colossal Corinthian columns seen from afar to match the capacious landscape.

Before the war in Lebanon Baalbek was the site of an annual festival of the performing arts, the biggest in the Middle East, and in 1973, for example, when The Who gave a rock concert at the Temple of Jupiter, the audience was almost entirely composed of Kuwaitis who had specially flown in on chartered jets. It is a different place now. About 2km before reaching Baalbek you see a Palestinian refugee camp off to the east. Then there is a Syrian checkpoint. Baalbek's population is largely Muslim, mostly Shia. On a hill overlooking the town from the south is a Hezbollah fortress, bristling with antennae and discs, and you suspect they are doing more than tuning in to satellite pop videos. Here Hezbollah are thought to have held some of their Western hostages.

Three hundred years ago Maundrell set up camp by a spring below this very hill and then decided to visit the town, at that time walled, and its ruins. 'But we thought fit, before we entered, to get licence of the governor, and to proceed with all caution. Being taught this

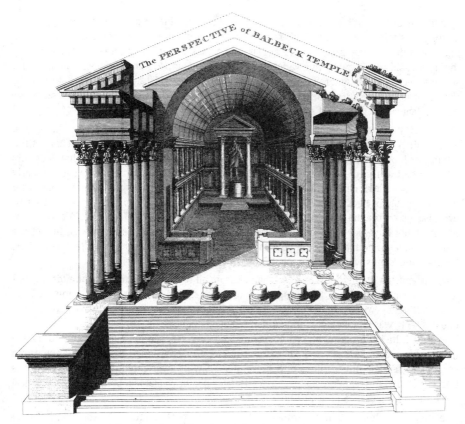

A reconstruction of the Temple of Bacchus (after Maundrell)

necessary care by the example of some worthy English gentlemen of our factory, who visiting this place in the year 1689, in their return from Jerusalem, and suspecting no mischief, were basely intrigued by the people here, and forced to redeem their lives at a great sum of money.' *Plus ça change, plus c'est la même chose.*

Background to Baalbek

The name Baalbek appears in Egyptian and Assyrian inscriptions, proving the site's long association with the worship of Baal, though little is known of it before the Seleucid period when the Greeks who settled in the region chose to identify the Semitic god of thunder, rain and tempest with their own sun god Helios and called the town Heliopolis. Though in classical times it was an important caravan station connecting Tripoli to Damascus and Beirut to Palmyra, Baalbek's rise to grandeur came with the massive Roman temples of the first three centuries AD, the greatest assertion of their imperial presence in the East.

Yet uncertainty surrounds the identification of the temples. The largest of them was dedicated to Jupiter Heliopolitan, the Roman successor to Baal, equivalent to the Aramean Hadad as at

Damascus. But Semitic deities were worshipped in a familial triad in which the principal divinity was joined by its male and female siblings or children. Depending on the era, the region and the cultural cross-currents at play, the names and attributes of the gods composing the triad could be of bewildering variety. In essence, though, you find some enactment of the seasonal cycle of death and rebirth, as in the myth of Astarte and Tammuz at Afqa (*see* p.308), with whom the Greeks identified Aphrodite and Adonis, with perhaps similar roles played at Roman Baalbek by Venus and Mercury.

The remains of a temple thought to be that of Mercury have been located on that hill where Hezbollah is now perched, but that leaves a surplus of temples down below. There is the Temple of Jupiter, and also the small round temple, a delicate feminine affair, that is usually taken to be the Temple of Venus, while the larger one to the south of Jupiter's is popularly called the Temple of Bacchus for its vine and grape decoration. However there are some who say the Temple of Bacchus is really the Temple of Venus, others who say this and not whatever was up on the hill was Mercury's temple, while the little round Temple of Venus might therefore not have been dedicated to Venus but on the other hand maybe was. In fact the scholars have no better idea than you do of what was what and as stylistic epithets Jupiter, Bacchus and Venus will do well enough.

Pilgrims and the mighty journeyed to Baalbek from all round the Roman Empire, drawn not least to consult its oracle at the Temple of Jupiter which had a reputation for laying it on the line. To the Emperor Trajan, who came here in 114 at the outset of his Parthian campaign, the oracle's reply was a broken centurion's staff wrapped in a funerary shroud. Undaunted, he led his army into Mesopotamia and even reached the Persian Gulf: no Roman had penetrated so far east, and for a time the emperor envisioned his destiny as that of a second Alexander. But his lines of communication were over-extended and the Parthians attacked him in the rear, forcing his retreat. Trajan's health weakened, perhaps a psychological response to his failure, and in 117 he was dead.

The empire did though shift its centre of balance eastwards, and under Constantine the Great (324–337) its capital became Constantinople, though its new-found Christian religion, also an Eastern acquisition, demanded the end of the old gods. As at Afqa, Constantine suppressed the cult of Venus at Baalbek, while paganism was outlawed altogether during the reign of Theodosius (379–395), who demolished part of the courtyard and the façade of the Temple of Jupiter, which had already been damaged by earthquake, and built a Christian basilica there instead. But the old gods died hard, one visitor reporting that pagan offerings were being made at Baalbek as late as 559. Even up to 1948 Baalbek, the last town to do so in the Bekaa, was celebrating a curious spring festival that took place on four successive Thursdays: the feast of men, the feast of women, the feast of animals and the feast of the dead. The festival was attended by Christians, Druze and Muslims alike, and perhaps it is no accident that Thursday, as indicated by its name in French and the other Romance languages, is Jupiter's day (*see* the Temple of Bel, Palmyra, p.272).

The town was taken by the Arabs in 634. Forty years later an Arab fleet laid siege to Constantinople itself but was repelled by Greek Fire, a secret combustible liquid that could be propelled by means of siphons against enemy ships and which burst into flames on contact. Its inventor, the man who can be said to have saved the Byzantine Empire for nearly 1000 years more, was a Greek called Kallinikos, a refugee from the Arab conquest of

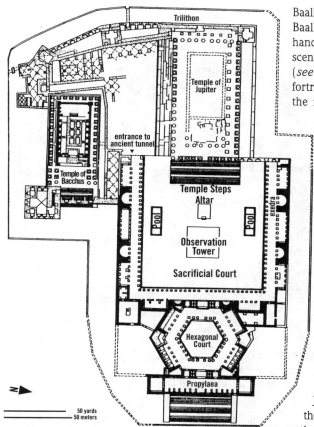

Trilithon

Temple of
Jupiter

entrance to
ancient tunnel

Temple of
Bacchus

Temple Steps

Altar

exedra

Observation
Tower

Sacrificial Court

Hexagonal
Court

Propylaea

N►

50 yards
50 meters

Plan of Baalbek

Baalbek. Throughout the Crusades Baalbek remained in Muslim hands, though in 1139 it was the scene of internecine fighting, Zengi (*see* p.204) laying siege to the fortress that had been built out of the ruins and for several months pummelling it with catapults. When Benjamin of Tudela came to Baalbek a few decades later, he found that all memory of its classical past had vanished, the inhabitants supposing the great monuments to have been the work of Solomon. In 1260 the Mongols and in 1400 Tamerlane contributed to the wreckage.

Though visited by Europeans from the mid-16th century, Baalbek only became widely known again in the West through the travels of Robert Wood and James Dawkins in 1751 when they also visited Palmyra. Serious earthquakes in 1664 and 1750 had caused further damage, and perhaps the most famous image of Baalbek is that of the artist David Roberts, who during his tour of Egypt and the Holy Land in the late 1830s made a drawing of the massive portal of the Temple of Bacchus, its slipped keystone suspended almost anti-gravitationally above the heads of lounging locals. Kaiser Wilhelm II's visit in 1898 was a prelude to important excavation and restoration work begun by German archaeologists in 1900, which was followed up by the French under the Mandate.

Visiting the Temples

The ruins lie adjacent to the town on its west side, and so at first as you enter Baalbek there is only the grubby main street with the old Palmyra Hotel on the right standing on the site of the ancient amphitheatre. Then you curve round to an open excavated site lying before the Baalbek acropolis. There are some small eating places here and opposite them the ticket booth. To your right (north) is the **Great Mosque**, erected probably in Mameluke times with materials taken from the ruins and itself a ruin now.

The Temple of Bacchus, by David Roberts (1839)

The Temple of Venus

Behind you (east) is the small **Temple of Venus,** built after the major temples in a baroque style that in several ways breaks with classical tradition. The circular and once domed cella is raised on a podium with five concave bays, the concavities echoed by the five niches in the cella walls. The attribution to Venus derives from the seashells and doves that decorate the niches, which in turn are framed by free-standing Corinthian columns. The arrangement is not unlike that of the apse at the Qalb Loze church in Syria.

Seeing it in 1689, Maundrell observed that it 'is at present in a very tottering condition, but yet the Greeks use it for a church; and 'twere well if the danger of its falling, which perpetually threatens, would excite those people to use a little more fervour in their prayers than they generally do; the Greeks being seemingly the most undevout and negligent at their divine service, of any sort of people in the Christian world'. From lack of fervour or otherwise, a good part of the temple did come crashing down, Baedeker reporting in 1912 that only one column remained standing, and even now, after some reconstruction, it looks something like a punctured crème caramel. As church or chapel it was apparently dedicated to St Barbara, a young woman of Heliopolis in the early 4th century whose pagan father, outraged that his daughter had converted to Christianity, took her up on a mountain and killed her with his sword. Instantly he was struck by lightning and reduced to a pile of ashes. In consequence, a prayer to St Barbara is a specific against lightning or sudden death.

Entering the Acropolis

Open daily 8.30–7 in summer, 8.30–4.30 in winter; adm.

Opposite the Temple of Venus is the ticket entrance to the two main temples. There is no natural acropolis here, rather everything is raised on enormous man-made substructures. By the 13th century the entire precinct had been fortified by the Muslims. Some of their defensive works have been cleared by the archaeologists, but some remain. The route described here takes you through the propylaea at the east end of the site and straight on through the Temple of Jupiter, its orientation east–west, then down steps at the back of it and across (south) to the parallel Temple of Bacchus, leaving the site by an ancient vaulted tunnel through the substructure, so that you emerge again by the ticket entrance.

First you climb the flight of steps (modern, replacing the full-breadth stairway destroyed in the construction of the Muslim fortress) of the **propylaea,** a monumental gateway preceded by a colonnaded portico, six Corinthian columns on either side of red Aswan granite, not all now standing or complete. Three of the column bases carry Latin inscriptions dedicating statues of gold to the Emperor Caracalla (211–217), the clearest one on the third base along from the left. The Roman towers at either end of the portico became part of the Muslim defence works. That to the left (south) was dilapidated and pulled down by the French, but the Roman features inside the right-hand tower (north) can be examined.

Passing through the propylaea you enter the sacred enclosure across the high threshold of the **hexagonal court,** a form not associated with the classical repertoire and instead derived from Eastern prototypes. It may have been the work of Philip the Arab, who was emperor from 244 to 249 (*see* Shahba, p.103). The arcades of the hexagon were roofed over, the centre open to the sky, though this too was roofed over in Byzantine times. The large lower stones of the hexagon are Roman, while the smaller stones laid upon them are of the Muslim fortress.

Continuing west you come into the great rectangular **sacrificial court** of the Temple of Jupiter, which was arcaded and richly decorated on its north, east and south sides. Exedras, alternately semi-circular and rectangular, were set within the arcades, with niches within them and between them for statues. The best preserved is the semi-circular exedra towards the northwest corner of the court. On the north and south sides of the court are pools, the north pool finely carved with tritons, nereids and medusas, and with cupids riding dragons. All about lie architectural fragments and inscriptions in both Greek and Latin, one to the Emperor Vespasian (AD 69–79).

A large **basilica**, probably built by Theodosius and dedicated to St Peter, was built in the centre of the court, its apse set into the broad stairway to the west leading up to the Temple of Jupiter. Indeed the church was partly built with stones taken from these steps. The substantial columned and arched remains of the basilica were standing here until removed by French archaeologists, leaving a semi-circular gouge in the stairway where the apse used to be. The clearance of the church revealed the base of the court's sacrificial **altar**, in fact a tower with the altar at the top, now largely reconstructed, that would have allowed the priests a clear view into the temple, raised on its platform high above any of the surrounding buildings. Also revealed was the base of a second and larger tower immediately east of the altar. Four storeys high with four sets of interior staircases to each storey as well as a final flight of steps leading to an open terrace at the top, it would seem that this was an **observation tower** capable of granting a large volume of queueing pilgrims glimpses of the sacrifice below and into the recesses of the Temple of Jupiter beyond.

The Temple of Jupiter

The monumental stairway at the west end of the sacrificial court ascends the huge podium, a man-made acropolis, 13m high, on which the peripteral Temple of Jupiter stood, its cella surrounded by a peristyle of 54 Corinthian columns, 10 along the east and west façades and 19 on either side (counting the corner columns twice). The temple was completed in AD 68 in the time of Nero, but little of it stands today. Dawkins and Wood saw only a row of nine gigantic columns in place in 1751 and travellers arriving 30 years later reported that three of these had fallen, perhaps from yet another earthquake in 1759.

Statistics alone fail to convey the enormous size of these surviving **six columns** along the south edge of the platform. The columns, each consisting of three drums, rise 20m into the shining sky and there support a five-metre high entablature. Add to this the 13m-high platform, and the entire assemblage towers to three-quarters the height of Nelson's Column in Trafalgar Square, so that you wonder whether Trafalgar Square itself might not be too small a space to contain the whole of Jupiter's temple. Yet still the columns fail to impress until a human figure comes into view, insect-like in comparison; then you are hit by the overwhelming scale on which the Temple of Jupiter was built.

But there was more to it than size, for its entablature and cornice were marvellously decorated with carved reliefs of lions' and bulls' heads linked by garlands, with acanthus leaves and geometric patterns, and the heads of gaping lions serving as gutters. Going down steps at the rear of the temple you can have a good look at one such **spout-mouthed lion** propped up below the podium to the south on your way to the Temple of Bacchus.

The Temple of Bacchus

Though earthquakes, depredations and the anti-pagan fervour of early Christianity helped topple Jupiter's temple, the Little Temple as this is sometimes called but which in any other surroundings could only be called stupendous, has preserved its cella walls and peristyle and is perhaps the most intact temple to have survived from classical times. It is also one of the most flamboyantly decorated, David Roberts describing it as 'the most elaborate work, as well as the most exquisite in its detail, of anything of its kind in the world'.

You approach the temple from the east up a broad flight of steps, the effect somewhat spoiled by the defence tower built amid them by the Muslims. Once up on the platform, five and a half metres high, you stand before the great entrance **portal** and see that the once dangerously slipped keystone illustrated by David Roberts has been more or less shoved back and cemented into place. Sir Richard Burton came to Baalbek while he was consul at Damascus from 1868 to 1871 and made sufficient noise about the imminence of the portal's collapse that a stone pier was built to secure the keystone. During later archaeological restoration work, the keystone as you see it now was properly fixed and the pier removed. On its lower surface is an eagle holding in its claws a caduceus, the snake-enwrapped rod that was the symbol of Mercury. The interior of the **cella** is given interest and scale by the engaged fluted columns that knit together the two tiers of niches along its walls. On the right wall is a plaque commemorating Kaiser Wilhelm's visit in 1898, and to the right of it a plaque commemorating Sultan Abdul Hamid who never came at all. The broad rising stairway at the rear of the cella led to the image of the god which stood upon a dais, its canopy resting against the four pilasters set into the wall behind and supported at the front by columns rising from projecting bases. The bases are carved with figures, badly mutilated, of Bacchus and Ariadne on the left base and of Bacchus sitting on a panther surrounded by bacchantes on the right base.

Leaving the cella, you can now walk round the outside of it, following the **porticoes** with their smooth Corinthian columns, paying particular attention to the coffered roof bearing reliefs of various deities and mythic figures. Several of the roofing slabs of the south portico have fallen and have been propped up against the cella wall, allowing a close look. From here there is also a clear view of the Hezbollah fortress on the hill to the south.

The Tunnel and the Trilithon

Between the Temples of Bacchus and Jupiter is the entrance to an ancient vaulted **tunnel**, 120m long, that cuts through the substructure supporting the sacrificial courtyard and brings you out by the ticket booth.

After leaving the site you should follow the narrow path that leads westwards round the south side of the Temple of Bacchus. This brings you to the western retaining wall that helped bolster the enormous platform on which the Temple of Jupiter stood. Continue along the outside of this wall, so that you are standing immediately behind (to the west of) the Temple of Jupiter's six columns. The wall's lowest courses consist of 10m-long stone blocks.

Above these is the famous **trilithon**, a row of three still larger blocks, each nearly 20m long, four metres high and three metres thick, among the most gigantic blocks ever cut. (There is an even larger block, 21.3m long, lying in the quarry at the southern entrance to Baalbek town. But the largest hewn stones in history are the 29.5m obelisk of Hatshepsut at Karnak in Upper Egypt and the 32.3m obelisk of Tuthmosis III, also originally at Karnak and now outside the church of St John Lateran in Rome.)

The Baalbek Festival

The annual Baalbek Festival, the biggest in the Middle East, flourished until the civil war (*see* p.348). In July 1997 a modest comeback was attempted and since then it has grown. Performances are at the Temple of Jupiter and the Temple of Bacchus. For information, call ✆ (01) 373151, 🖷 (01) 373153, or alternatively visit their website, *www.baalbeck.org.lb.*

Where to Stay
moderate

★★★**Palmyra Hotel**, ✆ (08) 370230, as you enter the town from the south. Built in the latter part of the 19th century and reminiscent of the Baron in Aleppo, the hotel stands on the site of the Roman amphitheatre. Rooms have bath and are spacious, cool and well furnished; some have balconies overlooking the temples. Also restaurant and bar.

inexpensive

★★**Khawam Hotel**, ✆ (08) 870230. On the east side of town by the Ras al-Ain spring where Maundrell pitched his tent 300 years ago.

cheap

★**Al-Shams Hotel**, a flea pit in the main street; ★**Pension Shuman**, a cesspit.

Eating Out

There are a couple of café-restaurants opposite the ticket office to the site and several towards the far end of Ras al-Ain Boulevard which runs southeast from the temples, also some around Ras al-Ain spring itself. Otherwise for *haute* atmosphere if not *haute cuisine*, the Palmyra Hotel.

Anjar (Haouch Mousa)

An alternative route in or out of the northern Bekaa valley is via Anjar in the lee of the Anti-Lebanon, 40km south of Baalbek and a kilometre north of the highway from Beirut (57km) to Damascus (53km). The **village** with its typically Armenian high-drummed and conically-domed church is inhabited mostly by Armenian refugees from Turkey, survivors of the Turkish genocide which took the lives of up to 2,000,000 Armenians between 1915 and 1918. It was an example that commended itself to Adolf Hitler, who in a speech at Nuremburg in 1939 exhorted his followers to the mass murder of Jews, saying, 'After all, who remembers the murder of Armenians by Turks now?'

Adjacently south of the village, archaeologists have partly excavated and restored a 7th- and 8th-century **Umayyad town** with palaces, baths, mosques, shops and houses. Anjar is a gentle site by a shady pine wood, a place rarely visited and filled with silence, with sweeping views of the Bekaa. There is a strangeness, too, for if you did not know that this had been an Umayyad founding you would think it Byzantine, so much were the invading Arabs at first influenced by Graeco-Roman architecture and planning while plundering temples and churches to build edifices of their own. Anjar is especially worth visiting as it possesses the only significant remains of the period in Lebanon, while even in Syria little Umayyad work has survived apart from the Great Mosque in Damascus and the desert palaces at Qasr al-Heir east and west, the vengeful Mesopotamian-based Abbasids destroying what works they could of the 'heretical' Umayyads and destroying too what might have been a more fruitful cultural conjunction between Islam and the West.

The site can be entered from the village to the south or from the open fields to the north. The town was rectangular in layout, 350m from east to west and 385m from north to south, and enclosed by a wall studded with round towers and a gate on each side. From the east to the west gate ran the decumanus, from the north to the south gate the cardo maximus, each 20m broad, dividing Anjar into quadrants. Where the two main streets meet at the centre there stands, strangely, a Roman-style **tetrapylon**, while the streets themselves are colonnaded, the capitals various but always classical or Byzantine and often showing a crown surmounted by a cross. Both the decumanus and the cardo maximus were lined with over 600 shops from end to end.

The southwest quadrant seems to have been entirely taken up with humdrum residential quarters. The northwest quadrant has been little excavated, though along the cardo maximus are two large enclosures, possibly used as animal pens, perhaps for livestock or for caravan camels.

In the southeast quadrant, just east of the cardo maximus, is an elegant **palace** built round a central court and partly reconstructed to two storeys, its flights of arches springing from Byzantine capitals set upon slender columns. This may have been the residence of the early 8th-century Umayyad Caliph Walid I who built the Great Mosque at Damascus and whose empire stretched from the Atlantic to China. Between the palace and the decumanus are the remains of a **mosque**.

In the northeast quadrant and flanking the north side of the decumanus are the more ruinous remains of a slightly **smaller palace**, also built round a court. But this palace was more intricately decorated than the other, with owls, doves, eagles, lilies, seashells and clusters of grapes in the Graeco-Roman tradition, as well as with nude maidens (all now in the National Museum). Close by the north wall in this same quadrant is a public **baths**, entirely classical in arrangement and with varicoloured geometric mosaic paving.

Archaeological investigation of Anjar was interrupted by the war and there is still much to do, not least to understand its purpose. Like Qasr al-Heir al-Sharqi, east of Palmyra, it may at once have been an imperial residence, a caravan station and a strategic outpost, in this case not controlling Bedouin tribes, but rather keeping a protective eye on the Damascus– Beirut traffic and on the Bekaa.

Eating Out

There is a shaded and pleasant terrace restaurant called **The Sun** on the west side of the village, which you pass getting to or from the Beirut–Damascus highway. Its speciality is freshwater fish, which you select live and have cooked to your taste.

Glossary

Ablaq	The alternating use of red and white or black or white stone, as in an arch, found especially in Mameluke and Ottoman architecture.
Abu	A holy man or saint, whether Muslim or Christian.
Agora	Greek for forum, a meeting place.
Amphora	A tall two-handled jar with a narrow neck.
Apse	A semi-circular domed recess, as at the altar end (usually the east end) of a church.
Architrave	Horizontal supporting beam across columns of a temple, or the frame around a door.
Atrium	The courtyard of a Roman house.
Azan	The Muslim call to prayer.
Bab	A door or gateway.
Baptistry	A place for the baptism of converts, either part of or separate from a church.
Basilica	A building in the form of a long colonnaded hall, for example a church, usually with one or more apses at the east end and a narthex at the west end.
Bastion	A fortified tower or other strongpoint in a fortification.
Beit	A house.
Caliph	Literally 'successor' to Mohammed, the title taken by those claiming the spiritual and temporal leadership of Islam.
Corinthian capital	A leafy motif based on the acanthus plant; in the style known as blown acanthus, as at Qalaat Samaan, the capital imitates a wind-blown acanthus.
Cardo maximus	The principal, usually north–south, thoroughfare of a Roman city, its roadway flanked by colonnaded pavements lined with shops and public buildings, and intersecting with the decumanus maximus.
Cella	The enclosed inner 'house of the god' within a temple.
Decumanus maximus	The major east–west cross street, intersecting with the cardo maximus of a Roman city.
Deir	A monastery.
Exedra	A recessed semi-circular structure.
Frieze	A horizontal band decorated for example with carving or calligraphy.
Glacis	A smooth sloping surface of stone; its function in medieval castles was to make it difficult to scale a wall while at the same time exposing attackers to fire.
Gumruk	A customs house where duties were imposed on goods, the word a corruption of the Greek *emporikós*, meaning commercial, from *emporía*, meaning traffic, trade, commerce or business.
Hajj	The pilgrimage to Mecca; a Muslim is expected to undertake the Hajj at least once in his lifetime.

Hamam	A public bath.
Haremlek	That part of a house reserved for women, the family; the private quarters.
Hegira	Mohammed's flight, or more properly his 'withdrawal of affection', from Mecca in AD 622; the Muslim calendar starts from this date. Mohammed's flight was owed to the Meccans' hostility to his message; he returned subsequently as its conqueror.
Hippodamian grid	The rectangular street plan of Hellenistic urban planning, used by the Seleucids and followed by the Romans; named after Hippodamos of Miletos, 5th century BC.
Hypogeum	An underground tomb chamber.
Iconostasis	The screen carrying icons between the main part of a church and the sanctuary or choir.
Iwan	See liwan.
Kalybe	An open-fronted shrine with niches for the display of statuary.
Keep	The innermost structure of a castle; the last redoubt.
Khan	An inn for travelling merchants built around a courtyard, with stables and warehouses at ground level and living accommodation above.
Kufic	An early style of Arabic calligraphy with angular letters.
Liwan	A vaulted hall opening onto a court; also called an *iwan*.
Loculus	A niche inserted lengthwise into the wall of a chamber or tower, serving to contain the body of the deceased.
Loggia	An arcaded extension to a hall or building, usually overlooking a court.
Machicolation	A projection from the wall of a castle with an opening through which hot liquids, stones, etc., could be dropped on attackers. It could also be used as a latrine, not necessarily defensively.
Madrasa	A theological school, often attached to a mosque.
Maristan	A hospital.
Menorah	An ancient symbol of Judaism: a candleholder of seven branches, three curving upwards on either side of a central shaft. The Hanukah candleholder has nine branches.
Merlon	An architectural embellishment atop the walls of a mosque or along the edge and spine of a temple roof.
Mihrab	The niche in the *qibla* wall of a mosque serving to orient prayer by indicating the direction of Mecca.
Minbar	The pulpit in a mosque from which the Friday prayer is spoken.
Monophysitism	The doctrine of certain Eastern Churches that the two natures of Christ (human and divine) are absorbed into one nature (the divine), condemned as a heresy at the Council of Chalcedon, 451, which affirmed that Christ's two natures are unmixed and unchangeable even though indistinguishable and inseparable.

Monothelitism	The doctrine of certain Eastern Churches, for example the Maronite Church, that while Christ has two natures (human and divine), he has one will (divine).
Moulid	The birthday of a saint or holy man, Christian or Muslim.
Muezzin	A crier who, as from a minaret, calls the faithful to prayer.
Narthex	The entrance vestibule of a church.
Naskhi	A cursive form of Arabic writing, subsequent to Kufic.
Nave	The main body or central aisle of a church.
Necropolis	Greek for cemetery, literally city (polis) of the dead (necros).
Noria	A waterwheel.
Nymphaeum	A structure serving as a public fountain, usually with niches for statues.
Pediment	A triangular area, as below the pent roof of a temple, or atop an arch.
Peristyle	The row of columns round the outside of a temple.
Praetorium	A Roman barracks or governor's residence.
Propylaeum	A monumental entrance to a temenos or sacred precinct.
Qadi	A judge knowledgeable in Islamic law.
Qalaat	A fortress, though the term is often applied to any structure thought to have been a fortress or that might have been turned into one, for example Qalaat Samaan.
Qasr	A palace.
Qibla wall	The wall of a mosque facing Mecca.
Scaenae frons	A façade, often elaborately decorated, behind the stage of a Roman theatre.
Selamlek	The men's quarter of a house, the reception and entertainment area.
Serai	The headquarters of a governor or other high administrator.
Soffit	The underside of a lintel or beam.
Squinch	A small arch across the corner of a square, enabling support of a circular dome.
Talus	The same as *glacis*.
Tekke	A dervish monastery.
Tell	The mound of debris that builds up at a long-occupied site or covers the site after it has been abandoned, or both.
Temenos	A sacred enclosure, for temples, etc.
Tesserae	The small pieces of stone used in mosaics.
Tetrapylon	An arrangement of four columns marking a major intersection in a Roman city.
Transept	A transverse section across a basilica, usually between the nave and the apse, creating a cross-shaped plan.
Wadi	A valley or watercourse, dry except during rain.

*c.*9000 BC	The Agricultural Revolution begins in the Middle East.
*c.*4000 BC	Stone tools and weapons give way to those of copper.
*c.*3000 BC	By now bronze has replaced copper: the Bronze Age begins. Byblos becomes an urbanised settlement and soon begins a close trading relationship with Egypt.
2549–2526 BC	Cheops builds the Great Pyramid at Giza.
*c.*2500 BC	Mari develops as a trading centre.
*c.*2400 BC	Ebla flourishes.
*c.*2340–2150 BC	The Akkadian Empire, based in Mesopotamia.
*c.*2250 BC	Mari and Ebla sacked by the Akkadians.
*c.*2100 BC	The Amorites overrun Syria and Lebanon.
*c.*2000–1760 BC	Byblos, Mari and Ebla revive. Ugarit becomes a prosperous trading city.
*c.*1800 BC	Aleppo dominates trade in northern Syria.
*c.*1759 BC	Mari destroyed by Hammurabi of Babylon.
*c.*1600 BC	Ebla destroyed by the Hittites.
1600–1200 BC	Syria and Lebanon contested by the Egyptians and Hittites.
1479–1425 BC	Tuthmosis III advances to the Euphrates.
*c.*1400 BC	Development of the alphabet at Ugarit.
1275 or 1274 BC	The battle of Kadesh between the Egyptians, led by Ramses II, and the Hittites. Spheres of influence thereafter agreed between the two powers, with the Hittites as far south as Damascus.
*c.*1213 BC	The Exodus: Moses leads the Israelites out of Egypt.
*c.*1200–1150 BC	Iron replaces bronze: the Iron Age begins. The Sea Peoples overrun the Eastern Mediterranean and Middle East; Ugarit is destroyed, the Hittite Empire collapses, but the Sea Peoples' attack on Egypt is repulsed by Ramses III.
*c.*1150 BC	The Arameans arrive in Syria.
*c.*1000 BC	The coastal cities revive; the beginning of Phoenician culture; under King Hiram, Tyre becomes preeminent.
*c.*850 BC	The Arameans establish Neo-Hittite city states in northern Syria.
*c.*850–612 BC	The Assyrian Empire, based in northern Mesopotamia, extends its authority over almost the whole of Syria and Lebanon.
612 BC	The Babylonians overturn the Assyrian Empire.
539 BC	The Persians capture Babylon and soon extend their rule over the Middle East, Egypt and Asia Minor.
490 BC	The Persians invade Greece but are defeated at Marathon.
480–79 BC	A second Persian invasion of Greece meets defeat at Salamis and Plataea.
333 BC	Alexander the Great defeats Darius, the Persian king, at Issus.

Chronology of Syria and Lebanon

323 BC	Death of Alexander at Babylon; he has established an empire extending from Greece to the Nile and the Indus.
312–280 BC	Reign of Seleucus I Nicator, founder of the Seleucid Empire.
85 BC	Damascus under Nabatean rule.
64 BC	Pompey, on behalf of the Roman Republic, creates the province of Syria. The Nabateans continue to enjoy autonomous authority in Damascus and Bosra.
31 BC	Octavian, the future Augustus, defeats Antony and Cleopatra at the battle of Actium.
30 BC	By this date the Romans have brought the entire coast of Lebanon under their control.
27 BC–AD 14	Reign of Augustus, founder of the Roman Empire.
C.AD 37	Paul's conversion on the road to Damascus.
AD 68	The temple of Jupiter at Baalbek is completed during the reign of Nero.
AD 70	Following the Jewish revolt, the Romans destroy Jerusalem.
AD 98–117	Trajan is Roman emperor; campaigns against the Parthians.
AD 106	The Romans create the province of Arabia, its capital at Bosra, absorbing the Nabatean kingdom based on Petra.
AD 117–38	Hadrian establishes the boundary of the Roman Empire along the Euphrates; he visits Palmyra in 119.
AD 193–211	Septimius Severus is Roman emperor.
AD 224	The Parthians are replaced by a new Persian dynasty, the Sassanians.
AD 244–9	Philip the Arab is emperor; he builds at Shahba.
AD 256	Dura Europos falls to the Sassanians.
AD 260	The Sassanians capture the Emperor Valerian. Odainat of Palmyra drives the Sassanians back to the Euphrates.
AD 266	Odainat murdered; the career of his widow Zenobia begins.
AD 272	The Emperor Aurelian captures both Palmyra and Zenobia.
AD 284–305	Diocletian reorganises the Roman Empire.
AD 306–37	Constantine the Great is emperor.
AD 313	Christianity wins legal toleration under the Edict of Milan.
AD 330	Constantine founds Constantinople and makes it his capital.
AD 379–95	Emperor Theodosius I.
AD 389–459	Life of St Simeon the Stylite.
AD 392	Christianity declared the official religion of the Roman Empire.
AD 395	Establishment of the Byzantine Empire, its capital at Constantinople, upon the division of the Roman Empire into East and West, the latter with its capital at Rome.
AD 451	The Council of Chalcedon declares Monophysitism a heresy.
AD 476	Fall of the Roman Empire in the West.

AD 527–65	During the reign of the Emperor Justinian, the Byzantine Empire reaches its greatest extent.
AD 537	Completion of the Haghia Sophia in Constantinople.
AD 610–41	Heraclius is emperor; he reconquers Syria from the Sassanians.
AD 632	Death of Mohammed.
AD 636	The Arabs defeat the Byzantine army at the battle of Yarmuk and recapture Damascus which they had taken once the year before.
AD 644	By this date the whole of the Byzantine Middle East as well as Persia becomes part of the Arab Empire.
AD 661	Muawiya is acclaimed caliph; he founds the Ummayad dynasty and makes Damascus his capital.
AD 705–15	Reign of the Caliph Khalid ibn al-Walid I, who builds the Umayyad Mosque in Damascus.
AD 750	The Abbasids overthrow the Umayyads and make Baghdad the capital of the Arab Empire.
AD 786–809	Harun al-Rashid is caliph in Baghdad.
AD 969	The Fatimids establish a rival caliphate in Cairo; the Byzantines begin reestablishing control over northern Syria.
AD 978	Southern Syria occupied by the Fatimids.
AD 996–1021	Hakim, the Fatimid caliph, inspires the founding of the Druze religion.
AD 1037	The Seljuk Turks take control in Baghdad.
AD 1071	The Byzantines defeated by the Seljuks at the battle of Manzikert.
AD 1095	Pope Urban II preaches the First Crusade.
AD 1098	The Crusaders take Antioch.
AD 1099	Jerusalem falls to the Crusaders.
AD 1128–46	Zengi governs Aleppo as nominal vassal of the Abbasid Caliphate; in 1144 he captures the Crusader state of Edessa, to which the West responds with the Second Crusade.
AD 1146–74	Nur al-Din succeeds Zengi.
AD 1171	Saladin abolishes the Fatimid Caliphate in Cairo; in 1176 he succeeds Nur al-Din and initiates the Ayyubid dynasty.
AD 1187	Saladin defeats the Crusaders at the battle of Hattin and reconquers Jerusalem; in the following year he campaigns along the Lebanese and Syrian coasts, taking Acre, sacking Latakia and capturing Saône.
AD 1191	Richard the Lionheart leads the Third Crusade and recaptures Acre but fails at Jerusalem.
AD 1229–1244	The Crusaders regain Jerusalem by treaty.
AD 1258	The Mongols destroy Baghdad.
AD 1260	The Mamelukes, who have usurped power at Cairo, defeat the Mongols at the battle of Ain Jalud.

AD 1260–77	Baybars, the Mameluke sultan, takes Antioch, Krak des Chevaliers and Safita from the Crusaders.
AD 1280–90	The Mameluke Sultan Qalaun takes Margat, Latakia and Tripoli.
AD 1291	The last Crusaders driven from the mainland.
AD 1400	Tamerlane ravages Syria.
AD 1453	The Ottoman Turks conquer Constantinople, putting an end to the Byzantine Empire.
AD 1468–95	Sultan Qayt Bey, the last of the successful Mameluke sultans, brings a period of stability to Syria.
AD 1516	The Ottoman Sultan Selim I defeats the Mamelukes and occupies Syria; in the following year he takes Cairo and puts an end to Mameluke rule.
AD 1520–66	The reign of Suleiman the Magnificent. The Ottoman Empire extends from Mesopotamia to Hungary and Algeria.
AD 1535–1612	The French, English and Dutch establish trade counters at Aleppo.
AD 1571	The Ottoman fleet is defeated at Lepanto.
AD 1585–1635	Fakhr al-Din II rules in Lebanon.
AD 1683	The Ottoman siege of Vienna fails. Their empire has reached its greatest extent.
AD 1749	Assad Pasha Azem, Ottoman governor at Damascus, builds his palace.
AD 1789–1840	Emir Bechir rules in Lebanon.
AD 1832	Ibrahim Pasha takes Damascus and improves conditions.
AD 1840	Ottoman authority restored in Syria and Lebanon.
AD 1860	The Druze massacre of Maronites in Lebanon, leading to the Muslim massacre of Christians in Damascus; French intervention in Lebanon.
AD 1914–19	The First World War; Damascus the Turkish and German headquarters in the Middle East.
AD 1915	Turkish extermination of the Armenians begins; many Armenians seek refuge in Syria and Lebanon.
AD 1918	British and Arab forces enter Damascus.
AD 1920	The French Mandate over Syria and Lebanon established.
AD 1925	Druze revolt against French rule breaks out in the Hauran and spreads to Damascus.
AD 1939	The French cede Syrian Antioch (Antakya) and Alexandretta (Iskenderun) to Turkey.
AD 1945	Syria and Lebanon become independent.
AD 1948	Declaration of the state of Israel.
AD 1958	Civil war in Lebanon.
AD 1975–89	Second civil war in Lebanon.

The language of both Syria and Lebanon is Arabic, though French and English are widely spoken. Certainly most staff at hotels, restaurants and travel companies catering to foreigners will speak English. Generally, language is unlikely to be a problem. Even so, a phrase book can prove useful, and knowledge of a few Arabic words and phrases is always appreciated. Here are some courtesies and simple questions and remarks to set you off on the right track. Note that the ' (ain) is a guttural vowel sound, achieved by constricting the throat as far back as possible.

Hello/goodbye	*sa'eeda*
Please	*min fadlak* (if addressing a man)
	min fadlik (if addressing a woman)
Thank you	*shukran*
No thank you	*la, shukran*
Yes	*aywa* or sometimes *na'm*
No	*la*
I want	*'aayiz* (if addressing a man)
	'ayza (if addressing a woman)
How much?	*bekaam?*
Good	*kuwayyis*
Bad	*mish kuwayyis*

Also the general greeting when entering a shop, restaurant or home is al-*salaam aleikum*, peace be upon you, to which the reply is *wa aleikum al-salaam*, and upon you be peace.

The word for street is shar'a and that for square is midan, but English or French are so often used on maps, street signs and when speaking with people that the English has been used throughout this guide.

Note that there are several methods of transliterating Arabic into the Latin alphabet. So when looking for places in the index to this book, or on maps or elsewhere, it helps to think phonetically. For example, beit (house) could as well be bayt, while instead of Umayyad you often see Omayyad. Quwatli (a Syrian prime minister, Shukri Al-Quwatli, after whom many streets are named) may appear as Qouwatly, Kouatli, etc, while Deir ez Zor might appear as Dayr az-Zawr, among other variations. Also al- could be el-, and in any case its sound is meant to elide (subject to certain rules) with the sound of the word following it, for example Jebel as-Sariya, not al-Sariya, but this guide, along with other less than pedantic works, settles on al- throughout, unless a place is well-known in some other form, such as Deir ez Zor.

As well as learning to speak (if not read) a few words in Arabic, it would be useful to be able to recognise the Arabic numerals. As in the West, units are at the right, preceded by tens, hundreds, etc, as you move left. Recognition will prove a great help when shopping, examining bills, boarding numbered train carriages and looking for your numbered seat on a bus or train.

١	٢	٣	٤	٥	٦	٧	٨	٩	١٠
1	2	3	4	5	6	7	8	9	10

Language

Further Reading

Many authors and sources are quoted throughout the text of this guide, and you might like to pursue those titles that appeal to you. However, the number of books on Syria and Lebanon is not great, and still fewer titles are in print. The following titles (with their most recent dates of publication) are of general interest.

Browning, Iain, *Palmyra* (London, 1989). A history and description of the city.

Fedden, Robin, *Syria and Lebanon* (London, 1965). The best general account of the two countries, their monuments and history.

Fisk, Robert, *Pity the Nation* (London, 1992). A journalist's experience of the war in Lebanon.

Hourani, Albert, *A History of the Arab Peoples* (London, 1991). The definitive work.

Maalouf, Amin, *The Crusades Through Arab Eyes* (London, 1984). A concise account; there is almost nothing in it that is not found in Runciman.

Mansfield, Peter, *The Arabs* (London, 1992). A readable overview of the region, including a general history and brief analyses of each of the Arab countries since independence.

Runciman, Steven, *A History of the Crusades* (London, 1978). The definitive work, in three volumes.

Stark, Freya, *Rome on the Euphrates* (London, 1966). The story of Roman expansion eastwards.

Thubron, Colin, *The Hills of Adonis* (London, 1987). A personal exploration of Lebanon and its past.

Thubron, Colin, *Mirror to Damascus* (London, 1986). Also interweaving history and personal exploration.

Quotations in this guide from the Bible are from the King James version; those from the Koran are from the translation by N.J. Dawood (London, 1990).

Abana river 125
Abbasids **31–2**, 48, 65, 69, 242, 246, 248, 357
Abd al-Kader 90, 91
Abd al-Rahman 31, 69
Abdel Hamid 63
Abdullah 36
Abel 91, 123, 126
Abraham 214, 216
Abu al-Feda 147, 323
Abu Bakr 30, 243
accommodation 21–2
Acre 33, 34
Adonis 130, **308–9**, 310, 312, 316, 332–3
Aesculapius 333
Afqa 304, **308–10**
Aglibol 272, 274, 280
agriculture 25, 28, 110, 163, 336, 347
Ahiram, King 299, 312, 317
Ain al-Fijeh 125
Ain Dara 209, 227
air travel 2, 3, 5–6, 49, 293
Aisha 73, 243
Akhenaton 26
Akkadians 25, 260
al-Arabi 90–1
al-Ashraf Khalil 187
Alawis 37–8, 161, 171, 174, **189–90**
al-Azrab, Jane Digby 90
Aleppo (Beroia) 13, **201–22**, *208*
  citadel 169, 205, 214–16
  communications 18, 207
  Great Mosque 204, 212–13
  history 25, 28, 31–2, 33, 34, 35, 37, 203–5
  Jdeide Quarter 217–18
  khans 211, 212, 214
  madrasas 205, 213–14, 216, 217
  Museum 209–10
  shopping 19, 20, 218–19
  travel 2, 205–7
  where to stay 219–22
Alexander the Great 27, 47, 242, 248
  Amrit 182–3
  Sidon 333
  Tyre 330, 337, 338, 340

Alexandretta (Iskenderun) 203
al-Hakim, Caliph 101
Ali 189, 243
Allat 282
al-Maamun 250
Al-Medina 320, 323
Al-Mina 320, 323
al-Mundhir 246
alphabet 24–5, 26, 161, 198
al-Salih Ayyub 33, 88, 90
al-Thawra 12, 240, 242
al-Zaher Ghazi 205, 214–16, 217
Amarna letters 26
Amorites 25, 47, 312
amphitheatres 106
Amrit (Marathos) 182–4
Amshit 22
Ananias 86, 87
Anderin 154, 156
Anjar (Haouch Mousa) 30, 342, 356–7
Anti-Lebanon 13, **121–30**, *122*
Antioch (Antakya) 28, 30, 32, 34, 151, 203, 205
Apamea 28, 30, 133, **150–3**, *152*
Aphrodite *see* Astarte
Arab Revolt 36, 62, 305
Arabic language 382
Arabs 30, 158
  Aleppo 204, 210
  Baalbek 350–1
  Byblos 312
  Palmyra 268, 269, 272, 286–7
  see also Abbasids; Hamdanids; Umayyads
arak 107
Aramaic language 27, 127, 129
Arameans 27, 47, 209, 214, 227, 267
Armageddon 136
Armenians 35–6, 253, 356
  Aleppo 202, 205, 217, 220–1
Artemis 130
Arwad (Arados) 34, 161, 176, 177, 178, **181–2**, 312
Assad, President Hafez 37, 143, 189, 242
Assad Pasha al-Azem 35, 80, 147, 324

Assassins 33, 174, **175–6**, 187
Assyrians 27, 47, 137, 267, 305, 306, 333, 338
Astarte 130, 162, 173, 308–9, 310, 316, 333, 350, 353
Atargatis 66, 258
Athena 282
Attis 130
Augustus 28, 291
Aurelian 140, 269, 279
Awaj river 125
Ayyubids 33, 48, 77, 112, 113, 145, 186–7, 215

Baal 123, 140, 173, 200, 348
Baalbek (Heliopolis) 342, 347, **348–56**
Baal-lat 26, 311, 316
Baalshamin 280
Baaqline 343
Baathists 37
Babylonians 27, 209
Bacchus 355
Baedeker 62, 151, 262, 267, 353
Bahira 115
Bahnasi, Dr Afif 158
Bakhaa 129
Baldwin III 112
Baldwin IV 119
Balfour Declaration 36
bananas 318, 331
Baniyas (Valenie) 184
banks 16, 18, 19
Bara 236
Barada river 56–7, 80, 89, 125–7
Barbara, St 353
basilicas *see* cathedrals, churches and chapels
Basofan 228
baths
  Aleppo 212, 216, 222
  Anjar 357
  Basra 114
  Byzantine 236
  Damascus 56, 81, 89
  Roman 114, 153, 278, 298, 339
  Shahba 106
  Tripoli 324, 325

Baybars 33, 34, 48, **78–9**, 187
Alawis 190
Krak des Chevaliers 165, 167,
168, 170, 176
mausoleum 77–8
Sidon 335
bazaars 18–19, 20
Aleppo 210, 212, 218–19
Damascus 63–4, 79, 80, 83, 86,
92–3
Homs 140
Bcharré 328
beaches 299–300
Beaufort Castle 330
Bechir al-Chehabi II, Emir 35, 291,
332, 342, **344**, 345–6
Bedouin 31–2, 63, 262–3, 276,
285
see also Arameans
beehive houses 240–1, 264
Beirut **289–301**, *296–7*
East 299
history 33, 36, 38, 291–2
Martyrs' Square 296–8
National Archaeological Museum
299, 312, 317
shopping 20, 300
sports and activities 299–300
travel 2, 5, 6, 292–4
West 298–9
where to stay 300–1
Beit Eddine 342, **344–7**
Bekaa valley 12, 14, 28, 330, 342,
347–57
Bel 272, 274
Bell, Gertrude 36, 106, 172, 202,
240
Alawis 189
Husn Suleiman 173
Ismaelis 161–2
Qalaat Samaan 233
Benjamin of Tuleda 269, 351
Beroia *see* Aleppo
bicycles 5, 162
Bilal 86
Bludan 125, 126
Bohemond 32, 157
Borra, Giovanni 270
Bosra 28, 100, **110–17**, *111*
British 35, 36
Dura Europos 256
Lebanon 291, 305, 344
Bronze Age 25–6, 134, 135, 158,
197, 209

Bruce, Michael 331–2
Buqeia plain 164
Burckhardt, John Lewis 145
Burqush 127
Burton, Sir Richard 35, 90, 122,
124, 125, 145, 355
buses 2, 4, 6, 50, 51
business facilities 10
Butler, H. C. 225, 228, 236
Byblos 299, 300, 304, 309, **310–18**
ancient 314–17, *315*
history 25, 26, 28, 33, 311–13
medieval town 313–14
port 317–18
Byzantines 29–30, 31
Aleppo 204, 214, 215
Anderin 156
Burqush 127
Byblos 312, 314
Halabiye 240, 251–3
Monastery of St George 171
norias 148
Northern Highlands 225, 232–3,
236
Orontes 150
Palmyra 269
Qasr al-Heir al-Gharbi 264
Qasr Ibn Wardan 154–5
Resafa 240, 244–8
Saône 191, 192
Sidon 334
Tyre 338

Cain 91, 126
camping 22
cannibalism 157
Caracalla 140, 305, 353
caravanserai *see* khans
Carnarvon, Earl of 342–3, 346–7
Carne, John 270–1, 348
cars 4–5, 7, 50–1, 52, 294
castles 162–3
Arwad 181, 182
Beaufort 330
Burzey 153
Byblos 314
Krak des Chevaliers 163–71
Margat 184–6
Masyaf 174, 175
Mousa 344
Musaylaha 319
Qalaat al-Mehelbeh 189
Qalaat Jaber 242

Qalaat Rahba 255
Qalaat Sanjil 321–3
Safita 172–3
Saône 190–3
Sidon 334–5
see also citadels
cathedrals, churches and chapels
Aleppo 204, 212, 213–14, 217
Anderin 156
Apamea 153
Baalbek 354
Beirut 298
Bosra 115
Burqush 127
Byblos 313
Damascus 85–6
Deir Balamund 320
Deir ez Zor 253
Dura Europos 257–8
Ezraa 119–20
Homs 141
Krak des Chevaliers 169
Latakia 196
Maalula 129
Margat 186
Northern Highlands 228, 234–5
Palmyra 281
Qalaat Samaan 231–4
Qanawat 108–9
Qasr Ibn Wardan 155
Resafa 247–8
Tartus 161, 177, 179–80
Tyre 338–9, 340
Yabrud 130
cedar 311, 312, 317–18, 326, 328
Cedars of Lebanon 326, **328**
cemeteries 83, 86, 340
see also mausolea
Central Plain (Syria) **131–58**,
132
Chalcolithic Age 25
chapels *see* cathedrals, churches
and chapels
Cheops, Pharaoh 311, 318
children 10
Chouf **342–7**
Christianity 29, 130
Lebanon 38, 292, 304, 331
Syria 127, 140, 217, 281
see also cathedrals, churches and
chapels; Greek Catholics; Greek
Orthodox; Maronites;
monasteries and convents;
Roman Catholics

Christie, Agatha 40, 138, 200, 220, 221, 248, 260, 265, 287
chronology
Chtaura 347, 348
churches, *see also* cathedrals, churches and chapels
Cistercians 319–20
cisterns 247
citadels
  Aleppo 205, 214–16
  Apamea 152
  Cyrrhus 227
  Damascus 62
  Dura Europos 258
  Ebla 158
  Halabiye 252
  Hama 148
  Homs 141
  Shaizar 150
  Tartus 178–9
  see also castles
climate 10–11, 19, 272
clothing 19–20
Coele Syria *see* Bekaa valley
columns 152–3, 174, 274, 278, 279–80, 317, 354
communications 53
Constantine 29, 127, 310, 350
Constantinople 29, 34
convents *see* monasteries and convents
Cook's Handbook 138
Cosmas, St 153, 227
crime and security 11–12
Crusades 32–4, 76–7, 78
  Aleppo 204, 212, 214
  Arwad 181, 182
  Baalbek 351
  Beirut 291, 298
  Bosra 112
  Byblos 304, 310, 312, 313, 314, 317
  cannibalism 157
  castles 161, 162–3, 175, 330
  cathedral 161, 178, 179–80
  Damascus 48, 65
  Face of God 319
  Krak des Chevaliers 168, 169
  and Maronites 327
  Saône 191–3
  Shaizer 150
  Sidon 330, 333, 334–5
  Tripoli 304, 320, 321–3, 324, 325

Tyre 338–9
currency 3, 7, 15–16
customs and duty 3, 7
Cybele 130
cycling 5, 162
Cyrrhus (Nebi Uri) 203, 204, **227**, 326

Damascus 10, **45–98**, *54–5*
  Azem Palace 79–81
  Barada 56–7
  communications 18, 53
  eating out 74, 95–7
  entertainment and nightlife 98
  history 26, 28, 30–1, 32, 33, 34, 35, 36, 37, 47–8
  Khan of Assad Pasha 81–2
  National Museum 57–60, 148, 197, 256, 265, 283
  needs and services 55–6
  Old City 62–6
  shopping 19, 20, 92–3
  sports and activities 91–2
  Straight Street and City Walls 82–90
  Tekkiye Mosque 34, 60–1
  tourist information 52–3
  travel 2, 48–52
  Umayyad Mosque 30–1, 34, 35, 66–76, 244
  where to stay 93–5
Damian, St 153, 227
Darazi, Mohammed ibn Ismael al-101
Darwish Pasha 82
Dawkins, James 265, 270, 274, 351, 354
Deir al-Qamar 343–4
Deir Balamand 319–20
Deir ez Zor 35, **253–5**, *254*
Deir Mar Girgis 171
Deir Samaan 228–9
Deraa **117–19**
Dido 338
Diocletian 29, 245, 278, 281–2
disabled travellers 12
Dog River 26, 123, **304–6**
driving 4–5, 7, 50, 52, 294
Druze 24, 32, 35, 38, **101–2**
  Chouf 331, 342, 343, 344, 345
  and Maronites 35, 48, 291, 327
  Qalb Loze 234
  revolt 37, 48
  Shahba 104, 105

Dumeir 264
Dura Europos 28, 59–60, 240, **255–8**, *257*

Ebla 25, 133, **158**, 209
Egypt 24, 25, 26, 37, 47
  Byblos 311–12, 316
  Sidon 333
  Tripoli 325
  Tyre 337
Ehden 326
Elagabalus 140
Elahbel family 278, 284
electricity 12
elephants 149
Elijah 336
e-mail 10, 11
embassies 12, 53, 295
emergencies 5, 11, 14–15, 296
Enfeh 319
English 202, **211–12**
entertainment 13
entry formalities 2–3, 6, 56, 122
Eshmun *see* Adonis
Euphrates 12, 24, 132, 203, **237–59**, *238–9*
Eusebius 310, 338, 340
Ezraa **119–20**

Face of God 304, 318–19
Fairouz 290
Fakhr al-Din al-Maani II 35, 286, 291, 334, 335, 343–4
Fatima 83
Fatimids 31, 48, 76, 101, 116
faxes 10, 11
Fedden, Robin 143
Feisal, King 36, 305
Fertile Crescent 132
festivals 356
food and drink 13–14
  see also wines
Franks *see* Crusades
Frazer, J. G. 130
French 35, 102, 107, 202, 344
  Dog River 305, 306
  Sidon 334, 335
French Mandate 36–7, 48, 190, 205, 305, 313, 327

Genoese 312, 323
George, St 298
Geta 140
Gezira 238, *238–9*, 240, **260**

Ghab 149
Ghazi 205, 214–16, 217
Gibbon, Edward 104, 269
Gibran, Khalil 328
glass 336
Golan Heights 37, 38, 56, 122
Graeco-Roman period *see* Greeks;
  Romans
Greek Catholics
  Lebanon 330, 331, 336
  Syria 120, 127, 129, 130, 218
Greek Orthodox
  Aleppo 217
  Beirut 291–2
  Bosra 112
  Byblos 312, 314
  Damascus 85
  Deir Balamund 319–20
  Deir Mar Girgis 171
  Enfeh 319
  Ezraa 119–20
  Latakia 196
  Maalula 129
  Safita 173
  Seidnaya 127
  Suweida 107
Greeks **27–8**
  Aleppo 203
  Baalbek 349
  Byblos 310, 312
  Damascus 75
  Dura Europos 240, 255–8
  Lebanon 306
  Orontes valley 151
  Palmyra 272
  see also Seleucids
Green, John 62, 140, 142, 157,
  202, 203
grottoes 306, 308–10
Gulf War 38

Hadad 47, 67
  see also Jupiter
Hadrian 28, 268, 280
Hakim, Caliph 32
Halab *see* Aleppo
Halabiye 30, 240, **251–3**
Halifax, Dr William 270
Hama (Epiphania) 35, 59, 133,
  142–9, *144*, 209, 326
hamams *see* baths
Hamdanids 31, 204, 214
Hamid, Sultan 76
Hammurabi 25, 259

Haroun al-Rashid 31, 238, 250
Haseke 260
hashish 174, 342
Hassan 243
Hatay 37
Hatti *see* Hittites
Hattusilis III 137
Hauran 28, 29, 37, 59, **99–120**,
  100
health and emergencies 5, 11, 14–
  15, 296
Hebles islands 181
Helena, St 204
Hellenistic Period *see* Greeks
Heraclius 30, 88, 252, 326, 327
Herod the Great 84, 105
Herodotus 24, 27, 146
Hezbollah 11–12, 38, 43–4, 330,
  331, 336, 342, 348
Hippodamus of Miletus 83, 203
hippodromes 340
Hiram I, King 312, 337–8, 339,
  340
Hisham, Caliph 31, 69, 245–6,
  264, 288
history 24–38
hitchhiking 5, 7
Hitti, Philip 91
Hittites 26, 47, 134, 135, 136,
  137–8, 145–6, 203
holidays 17–18
Homer 333
Homs (Emesa) 13, 133, 134, **138–
  42**
Hospitallers 33, 165, **165–6**, 184–
  5, 186, 335
hotels 21–2
Husn al-Akrad *see* Krak des
  Chevaliers
Husn Suleiman (Baetocecea) 173–4
Hussein 71, 243–4

Iamliku family 283–4
Ibn Nosairi, Mohammed 189
Ibn Tulun 48
Ibrahim Pasha 24, 35, 48, 141,
  216, 291, 332, 334, 344
inscriptions 75–6, 305–6
iron 138
Iron Age 26–7, 209
Ishtar 309
Isidorus 155, 251
Isis 316
Iskenderun

Islam 17–18, 30, 72
  see also Druze; Shia Islam; Sunni
  Islam
Ismaelis 156, 161–2, 174, 175–6
Israel
  Golan Heights 37, 38, 122
  Lebanon 38, 292, 330, 331
Isriya 154, 156
ivory 58

Jbail *see* Byblos
Jebel al Sheikh 122, **123–4**, 127,
  342
Jebel al-Ala 234–5
Jebel al-Aqra 200
Jebel al-Arab 13, 37, 59, 100,
  102
Jebel al-Sariya 76, 133, **159–200**,
  160
Jebel Arbaine 189
Jebel Barouk 247
Jebel Riha 235–6
Jebel Samaan 228–34
Jeble (Gabala) 161, **188**
Jeita grotto 306
Jerusalem 32, 33
Jesus 72, 87
Jews 36–7, 47, 85, 157, 205,
  269
Jisr al-Shugur 153, 154
John the Baptist 73, 216
John of Byzantium 251
John Chrysostom 130
Joinville, Geoffrey de 169
Jonah 31
Jordan (river) 122
Joun 270, 330, **331–3**
Jounieh 6, 13, 304, **306–8**
Jubb Adin 129
Julia Domna 139–40
Jumblatt, Walid 345
Jupiter 67–8, 173, 264, 350, 354
Justinian 30, 154, 155
  Cyrrhus 227
  Halabiye 251–2
  Palmyra 269, 280
  Resafa 244, 247
  Seidnaya 127

Kadesh 133, **134–8**
Kallinikos 350–1
Karak Nouh 347
Khalid (Sword of Islam) 141
Khalil, Sultan 34, 324

khans
   Aleppo 205, 211, 212, 214
   Apamea 151
   Damascus 79, 81–2, 84
   Hama 148
   Maarat al-Numan 157
   Resafa 247
   Sidon 335
   Tekkiye Mosque 61
   Tripoli 325
Khayzaran 337
Khirbet Afqa 309
Kinglake, Alexander 46, 331, 332
Knights Hospitallers 33, 165, **165–6**, 184–5, 186, 335
Knights Templars 33, **165–6**, 172–3, 178, 181, 182, **182**
Koran 71, 73, 116, 275, 282
Krak des Chevaliers 22, 33, 34, 78, 134, 161, **163–71**, *165*, 187
Kurds 90, 228, 312

Lake Assad 12, 240, 242
Lamartine, Alphonse 327, 328
language 27, 127, 129, 382
Latakia 2, 28, 33, 34, 76, 151, 161, **193–7**, *195*
Lawrence, T.E. 40–3
   Arab Revolt 36, 62
   Baron Hotel 220, 221
   Crusader castles 43, 162, 163–4, 168, 169, 170, 184, 185, 191
   Damascus 46
   Deraa incident 117–19
Lebanon 122, *302*, **303–40**
   climate 10–11
   Druze 102
   entry formalities 6–7
   getting around 7
   getting there 5–6
   history 24–38
   where to stay 22
Litani river 337, 347
Longinus 268, 269
Louis, St 33, 78, 334, 335

Maalula 27, 127, **129–30**, 308
Maarat al-Numan (Arra) 157
madrasas 116
   Aleppo 205, 211, 213–14, 216, 217
   Damascus 61, 75, 77, 79, 82
   Tripoli 324, 325
Maghdouche 336

Malakbel 274–5, 280
Malé 280, 286
Mallowan, Max 209, 260, 287
Mamelukes 24, **33–4**, 48, 78, 112, **186–8**, 205, 215, 313
   Tripoli 304, 320, 321, 322, 323–4, 325
maps 15
Margat 33, 34, 161, **184–6**, 187
Mari 25, 58, 209, **258–9**
Mark Antony 151
markets *see* bazaars
Maro, St (Maron) 326
Maronites 29, 32, 304, 309, **326–8**, 347
   Aleppo 218
   Beirut 291–2, 298
   Byblos 310, 313
   Chouf 342
   and Druze 35, 102, 343
   Jounieh 307
Martyrs' Day 36
Marwan II 69
Mashnaqa 309
Masyaf 149, 169, **174–5**
Matthiae, Paolo 158, 220
Maundrell, Henry 211, 328
   Baalbek 348–9, 353
   Baniyas 184
   Beirut 290
   Byblos 313
   Damascus 62, 71, 80, 86
   Deir Balamand 320
   Jebel al-Sariya 188, 191–2
   Jisr al-Shugur 154
   Mecca pilgrimage 66–7
   Musaylaha 319
   Seidnaya 127
   Sidon 335
   Tartus 179
   Tripoli 322
   Tyre 337
mausolea 76, 77–8, 90–1, 147
Mazloumian family 220–2
Mecca 35, 48, 66–7
media 15
Mediterranean **159–200**, *160*
Melkart 183
Meskene 242
Mirdasids 31–2, 204
Mitanni 26, 136
Mithras 258
Mohammed 30, 46, 71, 91, 115, 116, 243

Mohammed Ali 332, 344
monasteries and convents
   Deir Balamand 319–20
   Joun 331
   Maalula 129
   Qannubin 327
   Seidnaya 127–8
   St George 171
money 3, 7, 15–16
Mongols 33–4, 62, 78, 112, 186, 214, 238, 246, 351
mosaics 70, 106, 107
mosques
   Aleppo 204, 210, 211, 212–13, 216, 217
   Baalbek 351
   Beirut 298
   Bosra 114, 115–16
   Damascus 82, 84, 86, 90
   Deir al-Qamar 344
   Hama 147, 148
   Homs 140, 141
   Jeble 188
   Latakia 196
   Raqqa 250
   Salihiye 90–1
   Sidon 335
   Sinan Pasha 82–3
   Tekkiye (Damascus) 34, 60–1
   Tripoli 323–4
   Umayyad (Damascus) 30–1, 34, 35, 66–76, 244
Mount Hermon 122, **123–4**, 127, 342
Mount Kassioun 90–1
Mount Lebanon 25, 331
Mousa 344
Muawiya 30, 47–8, 69, 243
Muhammed, Fathi 210
Munqid family 150
murex (purple dye) 333, 335, **339**
Musaylaha 319
museums 18–19, 20
   Aleppo 209–10, 217–18
   Apamea 151–2
   Bcharré 328
   Beirut 298–9, 312, 317
   Beit Eddine 345
   Deir ez Zor 253
   Epigraphy (Damascus) 75–6
   Hama 147
   Latakia 196
   Maarat al-Numan 157

museums cont'd
Maristan of Nur al-Din (Damascus) 64–5
Military (Damascus) 60–1
National Museum (Damascus) 57–60, 148, 197, 256, 265, 283
Palmyra 276, 282–3
Raqqa 250
Shahba 106
Mushabbak 228
Mushennef 106
Muwatallis 135, 137
Mycenaeans 26, 137–8

Nabataeans 28, 47, 111
Nabu 278
Nahr Abu Ali (Abu Ali river) 320, 322
Nahr al-Assi 10, 19, **131–58**, *132*, 347
Nahr al-Furat 12, 24, 132, 203, **237–59**, *238–9*
Nahr al-Kelb 26, 123, **304–6**
Nahr al-Litani 337
Nahr Ibrahim (Adonis river) 308–10
Nahr Qadisha 320, 322
narghilehs 97
Nasser, Gamal Abdel 37
national holidays 17–18
Nebi Uri 203, 204, **227**, 326
Nebi Yunes (Lebanon) 331
Nebi Yunes (Syria) 189
Nebuchadnezzar 47, 338
Neo-Hittites 27, 47, 209, 214, 227, 267
Neolithic 25, 197, 311, 316
Nestorians 115
nightlife 13
Nimrod 122
Noah 347
norias 143, 147–8
Northern Highlands 204, **223–36**, *224*
Nosairis *see* Alawis
Nur al-Din 33
Aleppo 204, 211, 213, 214, 216
Apamea 152
Damascus 48, 65, 90
Hama 147
Qalaat Rahba 255
Raqqa 250
Safita 172
Tartus 178
tomb 79

obelisks 314–15
Odainat 28, 268–9
oil 138, 238, 240, 253
Old Man of the Mountains 174, 175, 176
olives 28, 204, 225, 228, 236, 331
Omar 30, 243
opening times 18–19
Orontes (river) 10, 19, **131–58**, *132*, 347
Osiris 316
Othman 30
Ottomans **34–6**, 291, 327, 344
Alawis 190
Beirut 298
Byblos 313
Damascus 48
Tripoli 321, 322, 325
see also Turks

packing 19–20
palaces
Anjar 357
Beirut 297–8
Beit Eddine 345–6
Damascus 79–81
Deir al-Qamar 344
Dura Europos 258
Hama 147
Mari 259
Qalaat Ibn Maan 286–7
Qanawat 107, 108–9, *109*
Qasr Ibn Wardan 155
Raqqa 250
Tell Brak 260
Palestine 24, 36–7, 292
Palmyra 18, 59, 210, **261–88**, *273*
Efqa Spring 286
history 28, 204, 212, 267–70
Museum of Popular Culture 276
Palmyra Museum 282–3
praetorium 72
Qalaat Ibn Maan 286–7
Sanctuary of Bel 272, 274–6
travel 266–7
Valley of the Tombs 283–6
where to stay 22, 287
Palmyrenes 59, 258, 272, 276, 282–3
Parr, Peter 134
passports 2–3, 6
Paul, St 28, 84, 85–6, **87–8**, 334
Paulinus 340

Persians 27, 47, 183, 251, 252, 333
see also Sassanians
Pharisees 87
Pharpar river 125
Philby, Kim 220, 221
Philip the Arab 28, 104, 353
Phoenicians 26–7, 174
Amrit 183
Arwad 161, 181
Beirut 296
Byblos 304, 310, 312
Jeble 188
Joun 332
Latakia 194
Sidon 330, 333, 335
Tartus 177
Tripoli 320
Tyre 330, 338
Ugarit 161, 197–200
photography 20
Plutarch 316
Poche, Adolphe 212
Pompey 28, 204
Porphyreon 331
Porter, Reverend J.L. 63, 89, 112, 123, 126, 128–9
postal services 11
Procopius 227, 244, 251, 252, 280
Proto-Neolithic Age 25
Ptolemy 27

Qadisha (river) 320, 322
Qadisha Valley 304, 326, 327
Qadmus 174, 176
Qalaat al-Bahr 334–5
Qalaat al-Husn *see* Krak des Chevaliers
Qalaat al-Kahf 176
Qalaat al-Mehelbeh 189
Qalaat Burzey 76, 153–4
Qalaat Ibn Maan 286–7
Qalaat Jaber 30, 242
Qalaat Marqab 33, 34, 161, **184–6**, 187
Qalaat Mudiq 28, 30, 133, **150–3**, *152*
Qalaat Rahba 255
Qalaat Saladin 33, 76, 149, 161, **190–3**, *191*
Qalaat Samaan 29, 225, 229, 231–4
Qalaat Sanjil 321–3
Qalaat Shaizar 150
Qalamun 319

Qalaun, Sultan 34, 185, 187, 196, 323, 324
Qalb Loze (Kulb Lawze) 233, 234–5, 248, 353
Qamishli 260
Qanawat **107–10**
Qariatayn 262
Qasr al-Heir al-Gharbi 31, 57, 263, 264–5
Qasr al-Heir al-Sharqi 31, 263, 264, 288
Qasr Ibn Wardan 154–5
Qayt Bey 34
Qirdaha 189
Qunaitra 56, 122
Qutuz 78

rail travel 2, 3–4, 61–2, 117, 205
Ramadan 17, 18, 19
Ramses II
  Dog River 26, 304, 305, 306
  Kadesh 26, 133, 134–5, 137, 312
Ramses III 47
Raqqa 31, 58, **248–50**, *249*
Ras al-Bassit 200
Ras al-Shakka 304, 318–19
Raymond de Saint-Gilles, Count of Toulouse 32, 157, 164–5, 312, 321
Resafa (Sergiopolis) 30, 240, **244–8**, *247*
Richard I (the Lionheart), King of England 33, 77, 185
Robert of Saône 192
Roberts, David 351, 352, 355
Roman Catholics 298, 307, 327, 347
Romans 28–9
  Aleppo 204, 210
  Apamea 151, 152, 153
  Baalbek 342, 348, 349–50, 353
  Beirut 298
  Bekaa valley 347
  Byblos 304, 312, 316–17
  Damascus 47, 62, 65–6, 68, 73, 83, 85, 86
  Dura Europos 256, 258
  Hauran 100–1, 103, 104–7, 108–10, 111, 112–15, 119
  Homs 139–40
  Husn Suleiman 173–4
  Isriya 156
  Jeble 188
  Joun 332–3
  Latakia 194–5

Lebanon 306, 309–10
  Northern Hoghlands 225, 227
  Palmyra 267–74, 276–82
  Sidon 334
  Suq Wadi Barada 126–7
  Tyre 330, 338, 339–40
  Yabrud 130
Roqaiya, Lady 90
Rozah 161
Russians 270
Rustem Pasha 148

Saffin 30
Safita 34, 172–3
Sahyun *see* Saône
Said ibn Taimur 265
Saladin 33, 62, **76–7**, 186
  Aleppo 204–5
  Assassins 176
  Byblos 312
  Damascus 48
  Jisr al-Shugur 153–4
  Krak des Chevaliers 165
  Latakia 195–6
  madrasas 116
  Margat 184
  Qalaat al-Mehelbeh 189
  Saône 190, 193
  Sidon 334
  Tartus 178
  Tyre 339
Salamiya 156, 176
Salihiye (Graeco-Roman city) *see* Dura Europos
Salihiye (Mount Kassioun) 90–1
Saône 33, 76, 149, 161, **190–3**, *191*
Sarafand (Sarepta) 336
Sargon 260
Sassanians 28, 30, 256, 258, 268
Saul *see* Paul, St
Sayce, A. H. 146
Sea Peoples 26, 138, 198, 203, 312
sea travel 2, 6
Seidnaya **127–9**
Seleucia 15
Seleucids 27–8, 133, 151, 256, 267, 334, 349
Seleucus I Nicator 27, 47, 151, 194, 227, 248
Selim I 34, 35, 48, 91
Selim II 34
Seljuks 32, 33, 113, 204, 212
Septimius Severus 28, 68, 139, 276

Sergius, St 129, 245
Serjilla 236
service taxis 2, 4, 6, 7, 49
Seth 123
Shagarat al-Durr 33, 78
Shahba (Philippopolis) **103–6**
Shaizar (Cesara) 150
Shamash 258
Shia Islam 33, **243–4**
  Lebanon 38, 299, 309, 330, 348
  origins 115
  pilgrimage centres 71, 83, 90, 310
  see also Alawis; Ismaelis
shops *see* bazaars
Sidon (Saida) 26, 33, 330, **333–6**
silk 291, 344–5
Simeon the Stylite 29, 225, 228–9, **229–31**
Sinan 34, 60–1, 216
Slenfeh 153
Snofru, Pharaoh 317–18
Solomon 27, 312, 317, 337–8
souks *see* bazaars
Spindles (Amrit) 183–4
sports and activities 20, 91–2
Stanhope, Lady Hester 270–1, 330, 331–2
Stark, Freya 107, 220
Strabo 339
students 21
Suleiman, Caliph 213
Suleiman the Magnificent 34, 60
Sunni Islam 33, 161, 243
  Lebanon 38, 304, 320, 330
  Syria 143, 171, 187
Suq Wadi Barada 125, 126
Sursock family 299
Suweida (Dionysias) 107
synagogues 59–60, 258
Syria
  climate 10
  entry formalities 2–3
  getting around 3–5
  getting there 2
  history 24–38
  where to stay 21–2
Syrian Catholic Church 217
Syrian Desert 262–3, *262*, 264, 288

Tamerlane (Timir i-Leng) 34, 48, 62, 69
Tammuz *see* Adonis

Tancred of Antioch 152, 165
Tanit 336
Taqla *see* Thecla
Tartus 2, 20, 161, **176–80**, *178*
    history 33, 34, 76, 177–8
taxis *see* service taxis
telephones 11, 53
Tell Ahmar 209
Tell Arslan Tash 209
Tell Brak 209, **260**
Tell Hajib 209
Tell Halaf 209
Tell Hariri 25, 58, 209, **258–9**
Tell Mardikh 25, 133, **158**, 209
Tell Nebi Mend 133, **134–8**
tells 198, 238, 258, 260, 347
Templars 33, **165–6**, 172–3, 178,
    181, 182, **182**
temples
    Afqa 310
    Amrit 183
    Apamea 152
    Baalbek 350, 351, 353–5
    Byblos 311, 314–15, 316
    Dumeir 264
    Dura Europos 258
    Isriya 156
    Joun 332–3
    Latakia 195
    Mari 259
    Mushennef 106
    Palmyra 267, 270, 271, 272,
    278, 280, 282
    Qanawat 110
    Shahba 105–6
    Tell Brak 260
    Tyre 339
    Ugarit 200
theatres
    Apamea 152
    Bosra 112–13
    Byblos 316–17
    Cyrrhus 227
    Damascus 84

Jeble 188
    Palmyra 278–9
    Qanawat 110
    Shahba 106
Thecla, St 129–30, 308
Theodoret of Cyrrhus 225–6, 227,
    228, 230–1
Theodosius I 29, 68, 327, 350, 354
Tigris 132
time 21
tipping 21
tobacco 161
toilets 21
Tortosa *see* Tartus
tour operators 7–8, 52
tourist information 21
Trablus *see* Tripoli
trains 2, 3–4, 61–2, 117, 205
Trajan 28, 111, 153, 350
travel 2–7
Tripoli 6, 19, 26, 34, 35, 304,
    320–5, *321*
    medieval 323–5
    Qalaat Sanjil 321–3
    where to stay and eating out 325
Troy 138
Turks 31, 35–6, 107, 291
    see also Ottomans; Seljuks
Tuthmosis III 26, 47, 111, 133,
    136, 149, 312
Tyre (Sour) 26–7, 28, 312, 330,
    337–40

Ugarit (Ras Shamra) 26, 58, 161,
    197–200, *199*, 209
Umayyads **30–1, 69**, 243
    Aleppo 204, 212–13
    Anjar 342, 356–7
    Bosra 113
    Damascus 47–8, 57
    Palmyra 269
    Qasr al-Heir 263, 264–5, 288
    Sidon 334
United States 38

Valerian 28, 268
Venetians 202, 205, 212, 323
Venus *see* Astarte
Vespasian 354
visas 2–3, 6, 56, 122

Walid I, Caliph 30–1, 68–9, 73,
    212, 357
Warburton, Eliot 346
water 44, 125, 247, 286
waterwheels 143, 147–8
Welsted, Lieutenant 332
where to stay 21–2
Whirling Dervishes 60, 61
Wilhelm II, Kaiser 76, 351, 355
William of Saône 192
William of Tyre 338–9
Winckler, Hugo 146
wines 13, 14, 107, 292, 347
women 22, 161
    Alawis 189–90
    Bedouin 285
    dress 19–20, 133, 143, 275
    narghilehs 97
    shrines 73, 90, 91, 128
Wood, Robert 212, 265, 270, 274,
    351, 354

Yabrud 127, 130
Yanua 309
Yarhai 60
Yarhibol 272, 274
Yarmuk river 122
Yazidis 228

Zabadani 125, 126
Zahleh 347, 348
Zalebiye 251, 252–3
Zengi 32, 33, 351
Zenobia 28–9, 269, 279, 281
Zeus *see* Jupiter